DEPARTMENT OF HEALTH AND SOCIAL SECURITY

REPORT OF THE COMMITTEE ON ONE-PARENT FAMILIES

CHAIRMAN: THE HON SIR MORRIS FINER

VOLUME 1

Presented to Parliament by the Secretary of State for Social Services
by Command of Her Majesty
July 1974

LONDON

HER MAJESTY'S STATIONERY OFFICE

£3·15 net

Cmnd 5629

The estimated cost of this Report (including the expenses of the Committee) is (a) £206,332, of which (b) £25,952 represents the estimated cost of the printing and publishing.

COMMITTEE ON ONE-PARENT FAMILIES

MEMBERS OF THE COMMITTEE

The Hon Sir Morris Finer, Chairman

Mr D C H Abbot CB

Mrs J M Scott-Batey

Mr W B Harbert

Mr S Isaacs

Mrs B J Kahan

Professor O R McGregor

Baroness Macleod of Borve JP*

Mr N Murchison OBE

Mrs C M Patterson OBE

Mrs M Proops OBE

Mr H G Simpson OBE

Professor R M Titmuss CBE†

SECRETARY

Mr D G John (November 1969–February 1970)

Mr G C F Sladden (February 1970–December 1971)

Mrs M L Meadon (from January 1972)

---

* Resigned September, 1972.
† Died April, 1973.

TABLE OF CONTENTS

PART 7. EMPLOYMENT

PART 9. SUMMARY

TABLES

VOLUME 2

APPENDICES

REPORT OF THE COMMITTEE ON ONE-PARENT FAMILIES

To the RIGHT HONOURABLE BARBARA CASTLE MP,
Secretary of State for Social Services

PART 1—PRELIMINARY

SECTION 1—APPOINTMENT OF COMMITTEE ON ONE-PARENT FAMILIES

1.1 We were appointed on 6 November 1969 by the Right Honourable Richard Crossman MP, then Secretary of State for Social Services, with the following terms of reference:

1. To consider in the light of paragraphs 41 and 42 of the White Paper (Cmnd 3883) the problems of one-parent families in our society.

2. To examine the nature of any special difficulties which the parents of the various kinds of one-parent families may encounter; the extent to which they can obtain financial support when they need it; and the ways in which other provisions and facilities are of help to them.

3. To consider in what respects and to what extent it would be appropriate to give one-parent families further assistance, having regard to:

   i. The preservation of the discretion vested in local authorities by Section 1 of the Children Act 1948, Section 1 of the Children and Young Persons Act 1963 and Sections 12 and 15 of the Social Work (Scotland) Act 1968 as to the exercise of their duties under those provisions.

   ii. The need to maintain equity as between one-parent families and other families.

   iii. Practical and economic limitations.

1.2 The relevant paragraphs of the White Paper, *National Superannuation and Social Insurance* (Cmnd 3883), which set out the then Government's plans for the future of social security and is referred to in the terms of reference, are as follows:

40. Besides its pension provisions, the new scheme, like the present one, will include benefits for widows of working age. These benefits will be based on the earnings record of the husband, and will be available to widows with children and to childless widows above a certain age.

41. It is often suggested that the national insurance scheme should go further and cover either all " fatherless families " or at least the children in such households: this would mean an insurance benefit for divorced, separated and unmarried mothers. " Fatherless families " as a whole, however, not only divide into obvious groups but also show wide variations of need and circumstances within each group. There is a great difference between the needs of an unmarried mother who supports her child alone, and those of another girl who has a stable relationship with her child's father; and there are many possible gradations between these two extremes. Similarly, it is often very difficult to distinguish between temporary separations and marriages that have finally broken down. Again, the father of the children is normally liable to contribute towards their maintenance, while he may or may not be liable for the maintenance of the mother. Whatever the extent of his liability, he may or may not be honouring his obligation. The available information about the number, structure and needs of these families is very inadequate.

42. Social security benefits are one obvious method by which fatherless families can be helped by Government action, and many of them are already receiving

supplementary benefit. But they are also affected by the law on family matters and the practices of the courts (on which the Graham Hall Committee[1] have recently made a valuable contribution) and by central and local Government policies, especially policies on housing, education and child care. The Government have therefore decided, first to start a further study[2] of the circumstances of families with children, paying special attention to one-parent families (whether fatherless or motherless); and, secondly, to appoint a committee to consider the general position of one-parent families in our society and whether there are further methods by which they should be helped. The results of the study mentioned above will be available to the Committee,[3] who will meanwhile proceed with other aspects of their work. The appropriate provision for one-parent families will be further considered when the results of the study and the committee's report are available.

SECTION 2—INFORMATION AND RESEARCH

1.3 The lack of information about one-parent families to which the White Paper refers meant that our first concern was to build up a body of knowledge sufficiently comprehensive and reliable for us to be able to make responsible and informed recommendations about the measures of assistance needed. To this end the Committee had its own full-time research officers to initiate and develop various projects and enquiries, and a considerable amount of work was undertaken or commissioned by the Department of Health and Social Security with our needs in mind.[4] In addition, we had access to surveys and research projects undertaken by universities and government departments and by other organisations and individuals. Some of the research projects have since been published, and others appear as Appendices to this Report. The extent to which we refer directly to particular pieces of research in later parts of the Report varies considerably, depending on the subject and the nature of the research; but all have contributed to the detailed picture of the lives and problems of one-parent families which we seek to draw. We are greatly indebted to all those who have helped us in this way, for without the information derived from these studies this Report could not have been written.

SECTION 3—EVIDENCE TO THE COMMITTEE

1.4 Partly in response to a general invitation to the public, which was issued through the national press in November 1969 when the appointment of the Committee was announced, and partly in response to specific requests we have made, we have also received a substantial volume of written and oral evidence. A full list of all those organisations and individuals whose evidence we have received appears in Appendix 1 and we take this opportunity of expressing our sincere gratitude to them all. The considerable help we received from the National Council for One Parent Families (formerly the National Council for the Unmarried Mother and her Child)[5] and Mrs Margaret Wynn in relation

---

[1] *Report of the Committee on Statutory Maintenance Limits*, Cmnd 3587, 1968.
[2] The results of a study made in 1966 were published as *Circumstances of Families*, HMSO, 1967.
[3] Reproduced as Appendix 10.
[4] A list of the research and statistical enquiries undertaken or sponsored by the Department of Health and Social Security, with brief details, is at Appendix 2.
[5] This council changed its name on 1 November 1973 to reflect a widening of its role and interests.

2

to proposals for a special social security benefit for one-parent families was particularly valuable. We discuss the proposals they made to us in Part 5.

SECTION 4—MEETINGS

1.5 We held our first meeting on 11 December 1969. Altogether we have met as a full Committee on seventy-eight occasions including six days in London and two days in Scotland hearing oral evidence. There have also been numerous meetings of sub-committees and groups of members have met to consider particular issues in greater detail. Some of us have visited local offices of the Department of Health and Social Security.

SECTION 5—ACKNOWLEDGMENTS

1.6 An enterprise on the scale reflected in this Report must owe as much to the ability and energy of the Departmental officers who served the Committee as to the Committee themselves. To these officers we are indebted to an extent that we alone can appreciate and for which this general expression of our thanks is nothing like adequate.

1.7 Our first secretary, Mr D G John, died tragically within four months of our appointment. A memorandum on our files which he prepared on the main problems we might have to consider now bears witness in its prescience to the extent of the loss we suffered. He was succeeded by Mr G C F Sladden, who conducted our affairs through what was, in many ways, a most difficult period, during which we were taking evidence, organising research, and collecting materials. Mr Sladden was in turn succeeded by Mrs M L Meadon, who was our secretary during the constructive and drafting period of our deliberations. Mrs Meadon served the Committee with never-failing efficiency, and was as successful in the organisation of complex material as in the despatch of our day-to-day business. In the last few months of our work Miss K E W Blunt took on secretarial in addition to her other duties and performed them in a manner that earned our admiration. We are also grateful to Dr L G Wooder, our officer in charge of research, and to his assistant, Mr R A Balfe.

1.8 The very extensive range of topics covered made it necessary, also, to consult with a number of governmental departments and agencies both in England and in Scotland. We are grateful to all of these for their assistance.

1.9 In addition, on some matters we sought informally for the help of distinguished experts within their fields of special knowledge. It is hardly possible to mention by name everyone who in this way made a contribution to the Report, but we are specially conscious of and grateful to those to whom we are about to refer. Dr Colin Gibson, Mrs Jenny Brock and Mrs Margaret May, all members of the Bedford College Legal Research Unit, gave us indispensable help in connection with Part 4 of the Report and Appendices 5 and 7. Mrs Christine Cockburn was in charge of surveys and research abroad which are summarised in Appendix 3. Miss Della Nevitt stirred up our ideas on housing. All of the following also considerably helped us with the benefit of their comment or advice or other assistance: Mrs Joan Beales, Mr L J Blom-Cooper QC,

3

Professor L Neville Brown, Mr A Chislett, Dr E M Clive, Mr G A Dell, Miss F M Drake, Dr J W B Douglas Mr John Eekelaar, Miss L Faithfull, Professor L C B Gower, Judge Jean Graham Hall, Dr H Heclo, Professor A R Ilersic, Mr Joseph Jackson QC, Professor Margot Jefferys, Mrs Jennifer Levin, Mr A Lynes, Professor Michael Meston, Mr Mervyn Murch, Professor R A Pinker, Mr R Poor, Mr P H Priestley, Mr L M Pugh, Dr Olive Stone, Dr D J West and Mr Richard White.   Needless to say, none of the persons or organisations we have mentioned is responsible for any statement or conclusion which we make.

PART 2—ORIGINS AND THEMES

2.1 This Report on "the problems of one-parent families in our society" is grounded in a socio-legal analysis of lone parenthood which begins by showing how much of the past still survives to darken the present. We think it appropriate, therefore, to open this introduction to our recommendations for changes in social policy and family law in Britain by examining some of the major long-run influences, as distinct from the immediate political considerations, which led to our appointment late in 1969.

2.2 Since the second world war, high and ever increasing expenditures by public authorities on social policies testify to the acceptance of new conceptions of citizenship throughout the western world. The central importance of these policies in the social organisation of all countries with high standards of living underlines the conclusion of Professor R M Titmuss that the " social services (however we define them) can no longer be considered as ' things apart '; as phenomena of marginal interest, like looking out of the window on a train journey. They are part of the journey itself. They are an integral part of industrialization."[1] We here mention Richard Titmuss because his premature death removed from our deliberations a scholar who was a giant in his fields of study and whose writings on social policy shaped the outlook of a whole generation. Conventional platitudes of regret cannot express the extent to which the Committee were impoverished by losing a colleague of his intellectual stature, but we are comforted by the knowledge that he regarded our endeavours as worthy of his time and painfully husbanded strength in his last months when he knew that he was dying.

2.3 We also mention him here as the leader of a small group of social investigators who destroyed the myth, widely believed in the late 1940s and 1950s, that the welfare state had eradicated poverty. That myth did not survive the statistical and other demonstrations by Titmuss and his fellow workers that the promise of welfare through widening social services had been more impressive than its performance. This rediscovery of poverty led to new definitions and investigations of " the poor ", from which it emerged that several millions of British citizens were living in or close to poverty in the affluent society after a long period of full employment and rising real standards for the rest of the population. Among those living in poverty, the fatherless families which Mrs Margaret Wynn[2] studied in the early 1960s came to be seen as a distinctive group. Knowledge of the poverty and like circumstances of all one-parent families stimulated the long established National Council for the Unmarried Mother and her Child to re-define its aims and to become the National Council for One Parent Families,[3] and led to the creation of such new and effective organisations as the Child Poverty Action Group. Lone parents, themselves more consciously aware of their common disadvantages, began to throw up their own self-helpful agencies such as Mothers in Action and Gingerbread, which now has more than one hundred groups functioning throughout the United Kingdom.[4] By 1969, one-parent families had been

[1] *Essays on ' the Welfare State'*, 2nd edition, Allen and Unwin, 1958, pages 8–9.

[2] *Fatherless Families*, Michael Joseph, 1964.

[3] The change actually took place in 1973 but its advisability " has permeated our thinking since 1962." (*Annual Report* 1972–1973, page 1.)

[4] *One Parent Families—A Finer Future?*, Gingerbread, 1973, page 3.

forced upon the attention of politicians and administrators of the social services as a special group having exceptionally low standards of living. Today, one-parent families have achieved the assured status of having an all-party parliamentary group devoted to their interests.

2.4 Economic failure in a society which elevates the pursuit of higher living standards into a major and desired end of private and public effort will be harshly felt by all who have to endure poverty; but lone parents also experience the additional failure of their emotional or family lives. In Part 3, we show how Britain, since the end of the second world war, has entered into a period in which marriage is well nigh universal. At no time in our history has it been so easy to obtain the sexual and other comforts of marriage without troubling to enter the institution; yet, in no earlier period, have so many entered upon marriage so young. To fail in marriage nowadays is to go bankrupt in a business of life in which almost everyone engages and in which the large majority, at least, appear to be successful. So it is likely that a family in which a mother or a father has to bring up children singlehanded will think of itself, and be treated by others, as a little cluster of deviants from the marital norm.

2.5 Parts 3 and 7 also show how demographic events have affected women who work outside their own homes. These women have always played an important part in the country's economy, but the timing of their contribution to the labour market has changed decisively since 1939. Until the eve of the second world war, all but a small proportion of women stopped work when they got married. Today, most married women bear their children within the early years of marriage and then go back or out to work until they retire. Moreover, now that the numbers of men and women in the age groups in which most marriages occur are roughly equal, the reservoir of women who could not marry because there were not enough men to go round has dried up. As one result, society cannot any longer rely, as in the past, upon the inevitable dedication of spinsters to such occupations as nursing, teaching and social work in which low pay used to be excused by describing them as vocations. The representative woman worker on whom the community's standard of living will in no small measure depend in the future will be a mother whose direct maternal role is drawing to a close. Again, lone mothers differ from other mothers in their working lives. In the first place, the lone mother, more often than others, works full time in order to escape dependence upon supplementary benefit, and she has to face the acute difficulties of securing adequate care for her children when they are very young which we describe in Part 8. Secondly, the family has to rely on one woman's wage, and most women workers do unskilled manual jobs at significantly less than men's rates of pay because they are the main source of cheap labour in Britain, as in all other countries. We show in Part 5 how the low earnings of the lone mother put her at a considerable disadvantage even when compared with a lone father. Fatherless families not on supplementary benefit have to depend upon a single wage at a time when men have largely ceased to be the sole breadwinners for their families save for a short period early in the family building cycle. Thus, lone mothers experience multiple disadvantages in the labour market. By the early 1960s, they had emerged as a distinct category, requiring special assistance for themselves and their children.

2.6   The 1950s and 1960s witnessed the cumulative removal of customary and legal restraints upon certain forms of sexual behaviour and upon their public portrayal in print or by the visual arts or for commercial purposes. Legal restrictions on the freedom of married people to escape from the bonds which used to be defended as essential safeguards for the integrity of monogamous marriage have been relaxed, and the sexual freedom of men and women has been enlarged.   Some think of these developments as creating a "permissive society"; for others, they represent no more than tardy social and legislative adaptation to new knowledge and to new notions of desirable relations between men and women within and without marriage.   From whatever angle these changes may be viewed, they cannot be interpreted merely in terms of the more freely visible and often grotesque commercial exploitation of sex which is now making available cheaply to the whole male population the gratifications purchased dearly by the well-off in earlier generations.   One result has been to confer new powers of self-direction upon women, so that the double standard of sexual morality retains little vitality in law or in life.   When Victorian parents told their daughters about to be married that they were making their beds and would have to lie on them, they spoke the precise truth.   Wives were then held in marriage by legal, economic and theological bonds: the bonds of matrimony were bonds indeed.   These have now dissolved into ties of choice, and modern marriages are sustained by affection or by loyalty or by use and wont. The discipline of marriage has become the consent of the partners and derives no longer from external compulsions.   The family has evolved into a democratic institution because, as John Stuart Mill observed, " not a word can be said for despotism in the family which cannot be said for political despotism."   The collapse of a marriage used to be denounced as causing shame, particularly to wives, no matter what the cause might have been.   The public declaration of personal failure embodied in a decree of divorce was held to unfit men and women for civic and political office and even to justify their exclusion from certain public, social events.   However imperfectly it works in practice, the prevailing social attitude requires that the breakdown of marriages should not impose shameful disabilities on the unsuccessful spouses and they should no longer be stigmatised if they marry again.   In this climate of opinion, compassion for the disadvantages suffered by one-parent families has grown quickly.   The old tariff of blame which pitied widows but attached varying degrees of moral delinquency to divorced or separated women or to unmarried mothers is becoming irrelevant in the face of the imperative recognition that what chiefly matters in such situations is to assist and protect dependent children, all of whom ought to be treated alike irrespective of their mothers' circumstances.

2.7.   Most people are brought up to think of marriage as central to their own personal security and to the wellbeing of society.   They are therefore quick to interpret changes in the institution as threatening evidence of moral decay.   During the last hundred years, many proposals to ameliorate the situation of wives or children have been criticised, not as being bad in themselves, but as securing the welfare of individuals by undermining the integrity of monogamous marriage.   One example will serve to illustrate the anxieties that are likely to be aroused when legislation affecting marriage and the family is proposed.   When the Legitimation Act 1926 was being discussed, the Home Office argued in an official memorandum[1] that a concern for children's

---

[1] 1920–1926 Reform of Illegitimacy Laws, Parts I and II, Public Record Office 12259/405558.

welfare ought not to be carried to the point of permitting the legitimation of all children whose parents subsequently married because " to allow children born in adultery to have the benefit . . . may remove a deterrent against adulterous intercourse, and may therefore be prejudicial to family life (which) in the interest of children generally is more important than the interest of a comparatively few illegitimate children." The history of family law which we have put together in Appendix 5 shows that such prophecies have always been falsified. We have no fear that the implementation of our proposals to reduce the " problems of one-parent families in our society " will weaken family life or undermine the institution of marriage. Indeed, we demonstrate in Part 3 of this Report that the transition from marriage in the past, buttressed by external compulsions, to marriage in the present, based on the consent of the parties, has not been accompanied by diminished respect or enthusiasm for the institution. On the contrary, it flourishes today as never before. In this area of life at any rate, freedom works.

2.8 We should also mention the report in 1968 of the (Graham Hall) Committee on Statutory Maintenance Limits as a significant influence in encouraging " those looking at the wider issues to strive for a more rational inter-relation of the roles of the State and the individual in the maintenance of ' fatherless families '."[1] The committee concluded that the " widely deplored financial difficulties of deserted wives under the present procedures leave little doubt that a full study of possible changes should be undertaken as soon as possible."[2] The committee added that " we have been convinced by the evidence assembled for our limited study that further and far-reaching evolution of the maintenance system will be found necessary in the next decade or so."[3]

2.9 We have been alluding to the social and demographic changes which made the situation of one-parent families in our society a subject ripe for consideration at the time of our appointment. But their situation at that time was, despite the flux that we have been describing, still largely determined by public attitudes and institutional arrangements of long standing, which, in their most typical and powerful form, were entrenched in the legal system. The Beveridge Committee was, as we shall see later, only the last of a series which from towards the end of the first world war had given consideration to improving the financial position of the unsupported mother and her child through some form of social insurance. This movement led to the introduction of widows' pensions, but, for the rest, it foundered on the rocks of matrimonial law, and the morality which the law embodied. On the one hand, the law gave an innocent wife a right of maintenance against her husband; and it was asked: how could the sanctity of marriage and the institution of the family be maintained if the State were to permit the husband to escape this liability? On the other hand, the guilty wife was likely, and in very many cases certain, to be condemned in law to forfeit her right of maintenance; and it was asked again: how could the State subsidise a woman whom the courts regarded as guilty of matrimonial crime? No answer was found to these questions, nor could it be found until there was a shift in the law and in the attitudes which the law embodied.

[1]Cmnd 3587, paragraph 234.
[2] *Ibid*, paragraph 237.
[3] *Ibid*, paragraph 240.

8

2.10   That shift took place during the years following the Beveridge Report and resulted in the enactment of a new divorce law in 1969. Part 4 of our Report deals with legal and Part 5 with financial considerations affecting one-parent families. There are, of course, many areas in which neither has any particular relevance for the other. One-parent families are directly concerned with the efficiency of the matrimonial law and its administration in ways other than the provision it makes for financial support; and there are, on the other hand, a host of problems associated with the provision of financial support which are of no special concern to courts or lawyers. The two subjects have, therefore, to be treated separately. We lay very great emphasis, however, on the linkages between the legal and financial aspects of our remit, since it is through them that the answers are provided to the questions which our predecessors found insoluble, or, rather, that the questions themselves have become inapposite.

2.11   The primary means of identifying the relationship between the one-parent family and the rest of the community is through the law. The peculiarity of this relationship in England and Wales (although it was exported to many of the Dominions and other countries of the Commonwealth) is that it is determined not by one, but by no fewer than three systems of law. Two of these are systems of private law, governing the relations between citizen and citizen. These are the law of divorce, and the law which the magistrates administer as between husband and wife, and mother and putative father. The third system is one of public law, governing the relations between citizen and State; this was formerly the poor law, and is now the successor of the poor law, the law of supplementary benefits.

2.12   The earlier history of these three systems, although briefly summarised in Part 4, Section 2, is set out in Appendix 5 to this Report. It is placed there for convenience of exposition, but Appendix 5 should be regarded as integral with the Report, in particular as providing the setting both for Parts 4 and 5.

2.13   Part 4 of the Report is mostly concerned with the interaction of the three systems of law; their disparate philosophies; their divergent rules; their lack of administrative integration; their pursuit of different objectives; their perpetuation, in terms of family law, of a distinct grouping of the very poor; the confusion, anomalies, anachronisms and hardships to which all these features give rise; and our recommendations for curing them.

2.14   It is not possible, especially by way of anticipation, to do more than indicate some of the main strands in a story that is rich in detail and complexity. We trace, to begin with, the process whereby the institution of divorce became secularised and democratised, while there was set up in parallel, as an offshoot of the criminal jurisdiction of the magistrates, a separate and summary procedure intended to deal with the matrimonial troubles of the poor through the provision of remedies short of divorce. This summary jurisdiction, which is now nearly a century old, has demonstrated remarkably persistent characteristics. Not only did it start as a service intended for the poor, but, despite the growth of a most general acceptance of divorce, and the advent of legal aid, it has remained the domain of the poor. We demonstrate the facts in this regard in Part 4, Section 6, and in Appendix 7.

2.15   Like other services fixed in their origins with the obligation to make discriminatory provision for poor people, the summary matrimonial jurisdiction

9

has tended to provide a poor quality service. Our criticisms in this respect are chiefly developed in Part 4, Sections 7, 8 and 9. It is to be emphasised that these criticisms are not directed against the magistrates, but against the system whose inherent defects they do much by their efforts to mitigate; and that in criticising the jurisdiction we are joining a line of distinguished predecessors that may be traced back to the Royal (Gorell) Commission on Divorce and Matrimonial Causes who reported as long ago as 1912.

2.16   In 1969, after much public debate, with the encouragement of a report from the Law Commission, and with the support of the established church, Parliament made irretrievable breakdown of marriage the basis for its dissolution. The new law recognises that the divorce rate does not measure the rate of breakdown in marriage. It enacts a morality which may be summed up in the propositions:

(1) the institution of the family is buttressed, not weakened, by a divorce law which is well understood, respected and free from cant;

(2) such a law has to be based on the existence of irretrievable breakdown rather than proof of an offence by spouses bandying charges against each other's conduct; and

(3) it is a proper object of public policy to dispose of dead marriages in a manner that encourages and affords the spouses the best possible opportunity to make rational and conciliatory arrangements for their own and their children's future.

2.17   But these decisive changes in the law of divorce, which broke with centuries of ecclesiastical and legal tradition, left the jurisdiction of the magistrates unaffected. That jurisdiction stays rooted in proof of the matrimonial offence; it gives no relief from the bond of marriage; every year, so far from dissolving, it embalms thousands of dead marriages brought to the jurisdiction by people acting under the pressure of their own ignorance, fear and poverty, and of encouragement from social agencies with which their troubles bring them into contact. The consequences of this system involve wives who are the victims of permanent desertion, mistresses in a condition of perpetual cohabitation, and children born illegitimate.

2.18   The contrasts between the two jurisdictions are examined in Part 4, Sections 3, 4 and 5. It is, of course, true that not all marriage breakdowns are permanent, and that the legal system must provide facilities which should be cheap, local and expeditious for dealing with the temporary troubles in matrimony; but that is another story, which we take up in Part 4, Sections 13 and 14. We do not agree that, as some would have it, the summary jurisdiction is providing an acceptable service at least at that level.

2.19   We turn next to the multiplication of the frictions and inconsistencies arising as between the two systems of private law through the further impact of the law of social security. This system of public law cuts across both of the others, but particularly across the summary jurisdiction, which services the population who are most likely to gravitate between claims for maintenance and claims for supplementary benefit. In Part 4, Section 10, we examine the nature and consequences of the relationship between the obligation of men to support their wives and children as it arises from the law of husband and

10

wife (or of affiliation) and the obligation of men to reimburse the State for the support which it may provide to those wives and children. This also involves consideration of the relationship between the institutions which respectively enforce those obligations—the courts and the Supplementary Benefits Commission.

2.20 These relationships constitute another major theme of the Report. A range of material points emerge, of which two only are here selected for mention.

2.21 First, although the Supplementary Benefits Commission have gone far, through dedicated and ingenious efforts, to reduce the strains and confusion arising from the collision between the systems, they have far from achieved total success. This would, indeed, be impossible within the framework of the existing law. There is, for example, no way, other than by sheer accident, of equating an assessment which the Commission make on a liable relative, and the assessment which the court may have to make on the same individual, in circumstances where the Commission proceed on one set of statutory principles, elaborated by the exercise of an administrative discretion, while the court works on a different set of statutory principles elaborated by a body of case law.

2.22 The second point that we select for mention is a fundamental one. Our research establishes that even if court maintenance orders made in favour of supplementary benefit claimants were paid regularly and in full (and only about half of them are so paid) the claimant and her children would, almost without exception, still be better off as a recipient of the benefit than as a recipient of the maintenance. Contrary to the view which has informed some of the discussion on the financial problems of one-parent families, and, in particular, a recent parliamentary attempt to ameliorate them, a more rigorous enforcement of maintenance orders would achieve very little. (We discuss in Part 4, Section 9, how far more rigorous measures of enforcement are, in any event, possible or desirable.) Thus, not only is the community already contributing in large measure towards the cost of marriage breakdown and the rearing of children born out of wedlock, but we see no method consistent with the basic tenets of a free society of discharging the community from this responsibility. This finding carries large implications for our financial as well as for our legal proposals.

2.23 In Part 4, Section 12, we move on to consider how—even on the assumption that the two streams of matrimonial jurisdiction were to remain separate, and that no new social security benefit, of the kind we recommend in Part 5, were introduced for one-parent families—the methods of the courts and the Supplementary Benefits Commission, and the relationship between them in their dealings with the maintenance obligation, could be improved. The essence of the scheme we propose is that through a device that we call an " administrative order " a supplementary benefit claimant could be relieved of the court process, and the burden and responsibility of assessing and collecting maintenance could be in large measure shifted away from the courts and more efficiently discharged by the body—the Supplementary Benefits Commission—which already bears much of that responsibility and the brunt of the existing muddle. We have worked out this scheme in sufficient detail to be satisfied that it is administratively viable. Its advantages are listed in Part 4, paragraph 4.277.

2.24   We have been alert to the possibility that it may be argued that the shift from the courts to an administrative authority would entail some loss of liberty or other advantage for the citizen.   This would be in some sense reminiscent of the opposition to the transformation of the litigious system of workmen's compensation to industrial injuries insurance in 1946.   We cannot guard against objections founded on dogma, but are confident that an appraisal of the facts that we have established, and of the details of the administrative order scheme, will show that while the scheme preserves judicial safeguards wherever they are necessary, it for the rest makes over to administration what is in the great majority of cases nothing but an administrative process.   The result would be not only improved efficiency, but less harassment, and a greater measure of justice for everyone—liable relative as well as claimant—who is affected.   It may be added that the studies we commissioned to be made abroad (aspects of which are discussed in Appendix 3) show a marked European trend to make maintenance assessment and enforcement the subject of administrative rather than judicial responsibility.   We do not consider this to be persuasive of its own accord, but there is a consistency between that trend and the direction into which we have been led by our own enquiries.

2.25   In Part 4, Sections 13 and 14, we draw out of our investigations into the two systems of matrimonial law, and our criticisms of the divergences which have arisen between them, a plan for their amalgamation into a single jurisdiction.   This jurisdiction would be vested in the " family court ".   We conceive of the family court as a new judicial institution, although it would be composed of some elements of the existing matrimonial jurisdictions, continuing, in particular, to involve the Family Division of the High Court.   In Section 13 we discuss the major criteria which should govern the shape and purpose of this new institution.   Section 14 is given over to a more detailed discussion of the structure of the family court and the law it will administer.   We envisage that the jurisdiction will be administered both centrally and locally through appropriate tiers, will draw on the services of lay justices as well as professional judges, and administer a unified and rational body of law that will reflect current values, command respect, and advance the social good.   These are all matters of the first importance, but our views and recommendations are readily ascertainable from the text and do not require any preliminary exposition.

2.26   We would underline, however, that our proposals for the family court involve the abolition of the summary jurisdiction of the magistrates in matrimonial and affiliation cases.

2.27   Thus far, we have been concerned only with the law of England and Wales.   The matrimonial law of Scotland is different, although Scotland's law of supplementary benefits is the same.   We have been much assisted by the study of the Scottish matrimonial legal system provided to us by the Scottish Law Commission, which, as it is one of the very few studies of its kind, we have with their permission reproduced in Appendix 6.   This itself emphasises that much basic research is required as a preliminary to consideration of any large scale reform.   In dealing with Scotland in Part 4, Section 15, we have therefore been rather less concerned with legal reform as such than with the question whether the legal system in Scotland would raise any insuperable obstacles to the introduction there of our schemes for an administrative order and for a new one-parent family benefit.   We conclude that it would not.

2.28   We move on, in Part 5 of the Report, to consider the financial circumstances of one-parent families, and to make financial recommendations. Here again, Appendix 5 should be treated as introductory, especially where it deals with the official consideration previously given to the introduction of a special benefit for one-parent families. Work on these lines began in the Ministry of Reconstruction in 1916, and the subject continued to be agitated after that Ministry was wound up in 1919 until, at length, the Anderson Committee advised the government in 1925 to reject as " wholly inappropriate and impractical " the notion of providing mothers' pensions to anyone other than a widow who had suffered the loss by death of the family breadwinner. The Anderson Committee thought it was impossible to bring divorced, deserted and separated wives, or unmarried mothers, into a contributory benefits system; that these classes were already provided for by the poor law, in case of need; and that it was important not to weaken the support obligations which the law put on husbands and fathers.

2.29   The Beveridge Committee, as we have found by examination of its unpublished papers and memoranda, gave considerable thought, but with little outcome, to the same question. We have found this material of very great interest as showing how other minds discovered and debated the doubts and obstacles with which we became familiar through our own discussions. How was a one-parent family, eligible for benefit, to be defined? How much would such a benefit cost? How was it to be administered? What was to be the relationship between the benefit and the husband's obligation to maintain his wife and children? Could the State pay benefit to a wife guilty of a matrimonial offence? If, as it was thought was essential, such a wife had to be excluded from benefit, how could the administrative agencies avoid becoming involved in the determination of matrimonial guilt or innocence? Would not the provision of a benefit encourage immorality and weaken the bonds of marriage?

2.30   The discussions of the Beveridge Committee in effect petered out against two main obstacles. First, Beveridge went on the principle that a wife would be insured through her husband, this being reinforced by his assumption that the massive engagement of married women in paid employment was a phenomenon that would not survive the war. Secondly, since any benefit paid to the married woman had to come through the husband, it was inconceivable to award it to a guilty wife whose husband was himself innocent of matrimonial misconduct. It followed that anything in the nature of a one-parent family benefit would put the administering authority in the impossible position of having to rule on matrimonial conduct. Thus, the Beveridge Committee, no less than the Anderson Committee, were trapped within the iron framework of the fault principle inherited from the canon law, and found themselves unable to reconcile insurance rights with the complications of marriage breakdown.

2.31   By the time we came to consider financial provision for one-parent families, these presuppositions had been exploded. Part 3 of the Report demonstrates how one of the major dimensions of our subject is the willingness and the ability of mothers, over the best span of their years, to engage in outside employment. Part 4 demonstrates how breakdown rather than guilt has become the accepted criterion of the divorce law, how conduct has become of relatively minor importance in determining the financial arrangements which ought in justice to prevail when parents with children dissolve their marriage, and how the existence of a summary jurisdiction which flies in the face of these principles has become an anomaly due for rectification. In approaching the financial question, therefore, we were the beneficiaries of changes which both enabled and obliged us to take up a posture which was entirely different from any that was possible in the past, although many conceptual and practical difficulties associated with the introduction of a one-parent family benefit remained to be solved.

2.32 Our research into the matrimonial orders made by the magistrates (Appendix 7) already demonstrated the comparative poverty of the one-parent family in our society. Part 5, Section 2, deals with an investigation on a broader front that we conducted into the financial circumstances of one-parent families. The statistical material and the research studies overwhelmingly confirm the general impression of financial hardship amongst one-parent families which had been noted at the time when our Committee was set up.

2.33 From this and associated conclusions we move on in Part 5, Section 3, to consider whether there is a need and a justification for the provision of extra financial help for one-parent families. We come to the unhesitating conclusion there is both. A number of schemes to this end that were submitted to us in evidence, or that we have canvassed to ourselves, are analysed in Part 5, Sections 4 and 5, and rejected for the reasons there explained.

2.34 This brings us, in Part 5, Section 6, to our recommendations for the introduction of a new kind of non-contributory benefit payable to one-parent families. We call this benefit " guaranteed maintenance allowance " (GMA). Our proposals for GMA form the central financial recommendation in this Report. A full summary of the proposals will be found in Part 9, and there is no useful purpose to be served in giving yet a further explanation of them at this point. We shall, however, list what we conceive to be the principal advantages of GMA:

(1) GMA provides for all one-parent families, including the motherless, compensation for the loss of support of the other parent in a world where the two-parent family constitutes the norm, but where the provision of compensation has until now been illogically confined to widows;

(2) GMA will enable most one-parent families to avoid entry into the supplementary benefits system. It is a social objective of the tax-credit scheme to remove people from dependence on supplementary benefit, and it would already be the effect of that scheme, if credits were given at the Green Paper level, to secure this objective for about one million people, mostly pensioners;

(3) it is intrinsic in the make-up of GMA that if the tax-credit scheme is implemented, GMA will act as a qualifying source of income for membership of the scheme and the level of GMA will adjust to take account of what is available by way of tax credits. On the other hand, GMA is not dependent on the introduction of tax credits, and its principal advantages could be preserved even if these were not introduced;

14

(4) GMA channels resources towards children; and towards children who have a higher probability than others of being deprived;

(5) GMA is framed so as to give the parent in the one-parent family a high degree of choice in deciding whether or not to go out to work. In particular, as the dependence of the children on the lone parent decreases, GMA will enable him or her to take up employment or extend the hours of work while retaining far more of the remuneration than the supplementary benefits scheme allows;

(6) the arrangements proposed for obtaining contributions from the absent parent simplify and rationalise the hotchpotch now arising from the overlap and collision between the courts and the Supplementary Benefits Commission. The family and the absent parent will alike be able to calculate or be advised about their financial entitlements and obligations with a high degree of certainty. Payments to the one-parent family will come under regular review, and be adjusted in accordance with the changing circumstances of the parties, and to take account of inflation;

(7) the GMA proposals are equitable both as between the better and worse-off one-parent families, and as between one-parent and two-parent families taken as a whole.

2.35 It is to be stressed that in selecting figures for GMA we have aimed as at a given point in time at the minimum which is consistent with attaining the objects of the benefit. So far as rates are concerned, our proposals should therefore be regarded as in the nature of a model. It would be essential that the level of GMA should remain sensitive to the specific purposes it is intended to serve, and not be allowed to erode as time proceeded.

2.36 There is a considerable difference, of which we are conscious, between conceiving a notion for a new social security benefit, broadly designed to fit the contours of a perceived social problem, and making certain that the answer to the mundane question " Will it work? " is in the affirmative. The introduction of GMA will be a major administrative enterprise. To establish and supervise the conditions of eligibility; to control abuse while ensuring—and this we regard as essential—that it will be easy and convenient to apply for and collect the benefit; to set up a new relationship with the legal system; all these, and many other problems, will test the experience of administrators. We have not been content to leave all these problems of administrative viability to future solution. In Part 5, Sections 6 and 7, we have deliberately set ourselves the task of following through in detail a whole range of practical considerations that would arise in connection with the introduction of GMA. Section 6 deals with problems arising as to the terms, eligibility for and administration of GMA. Section 7 is concerned with the problems, some of them difficult, of re-making the relationship between the courts and the authority responsible for administering GMA after its introduction. We look forward, at that stage, to the removal from the courts to the authority of the basic function of the assessment of the amount of maintenance obligations in every case where an assessment needs to be made, but without prejudice to the retention for judicial determination of other issues, such as matrimonial conduct, which may affect the maintenance obligation. Our proposals here are in line with, but of wider application than, those to which we have referred in paragraphs 2.23 and 2.24 above.

2.37 Our terms of reference require that in considering the possibility of giving further assistance to one-parent families, we should have regard to equity. We construe this as amounting to no more—and no less—than an injunction to be fair.

2.38 The need to be watchful over fairness has been present throughout. It arises not only as between one-parent families and other families, but also as between one-parent families themselves. Thus, one of the reasons to which we gave weight in rejecting the thoughtful schemes submitted to us in evidence is that they unduly favoured lone parents who were at work as against the others. Similarly, the proposal which has gained a certain popularity for the State to guarantee maintenance orders would not only, given the average amount of such orders, do little good to the women it is intended to benefit; it would also create considerable inequity as between the few women with very large orders, but recalcitrant husbands, and the much larger number who have no orders at all.

2.39 The risk of being unfair to other people in general arises particularly at the point where the facts concerning one-parent families have been established and the recommendations to be derived from the facts begin to come under consideration. In investigating the facts, we have put the one-parent family under the microscope. After that, if we are to be fair, we have to enlarge the field of vision and consider the case upon a scale which recognises that one-parent families form only one element in a larger community. It is a question of proportion. We believe that the facts show that one-parent families are, as a group, subject to special disadvantages which can to a worthwhile extent be remedied through a benefit which it is in the broad national interest to provide; and that the benefit that we have recommended is a reasonable one both in relation to its purposes and in relation to the national housekeeping.

2.40 There is, perhaps, another concept of equity which would involve us in assigning a place to one-parent families in a league table of disadvantaged groups, the concept being that it is unfair to devote resources to any one group while the wants of any other occupying a higher place in the league remain unattended. We do not regard this as either a useful or a practical exercise. We recognise that there are other groups in the community, in particular families in which a parent is disabled, with special claims for attention. But in making recommendations for one-parent families we are concerned with a group which comprises no fewer than one million children. We find ourselves unable to construct a table of relative disamenities from such components.

2.41 In general concerning this important principle of equity, we have thought it wrong to limit the improvements in financial provision for one-parent families that we find justified by reference to the condition of two-parent families as a whole, by taking account of the position of the small minority of two-parent families who are at or about the supplementary benefit level. Valid comparisons of like with like are very difficult to make in this restricted context. It follows that, outside a means-tested scheme like the supplementary benefits scheme, the relief of poverty by identical means as between one-parent and two-parent families is simply not feasible. The most significant fact is that when the earnings of a two-parent family are interrupted, or have ceased, there is usually a national insurance benefit for that family to fall back on,

16

and the other spouse may sometimes add earnings of her own. But there is no specific national insurance benefit for one-parent families, unless the parent is a widow. Thus the progressive and meaningful step which needs to be taken in the pursuance of equity as between one-parent and two-parent families on supplementary benefit is to give the former the right to a social security benefit based on the particular contingency of lone parenthood.

2.42 Although Part 5 is mostly concerned with GMA, it contains also, in Section 8, a number of proposals for improvements in other benefits, especially supplementary benefits, that we regard as having importance for one-parent families pending the introduction of GMA, or, in some instances, even after it has been introduced. All of these proposals could be implemented outside any major programme of change. They include our recommendations on the much-debated " cohabitation rule ".

2.43 We summarise the cost of our financial recommendations in Part 5, Section 9.

2.44 Part 6 of the Report deals with the subject of housing. No subject, other than the financial circumstances of one-parent families, commanded more attention in the evidence given to the Committee. We have made a particular effort, in a complex and controversial field, to single out all that pertains to the special circumstances and needs of one-parent families, and we find ourselves making a large number of recommendations to which we attach a high priority. It is interesting to note that, like so much else that we have had to consider, housing in relation to one-parent families raises problems which occur at the confluence of public and private law—in this case, the public law of housing as administered by local authorities, the public law of supplementary benefits, the private law of landlord and tenant and of mortgages, and the private law concerning the disposition of the home on the breakdown of marriage. However, underlying Part 6 and our recommendations on the subject of housing is the dominant fact, as to which we are satisfied for reasons that we have stated, that among one-parent families as a whole there are housing conditions which involve a special and distressing incidence of hardship.

2.45 In Part 7 of the Report we deal, as has previously been mentioned, with problems of employment. We show in Part 3 how it has now become commonplace for married women, including those with children, to work. A job outside the home can offer a lone mother much in terms of extra income, social contact and an easier transition to the time when the children have grown up and she has to become self-supporting; but these advantages have to be considered in the light of the double burden of working and caring for the home, and the needs of the children. It is fundamental to our approach that lone parents should have a free and effective choice whether or not to take up paid employment. The decision is one which lone parents must make for themselves, and the outcome will depend on a variety of factors which affect different families in different ways—among them the ages and number of the children, the wage the parent can command, the availablity of relatives or neighbours to help with the children, the risks of social isolation, and so on. Our concern is to see that the choice is a real one and that the selection made is not, as we believe now to be often the case, dictated in either direction by external circumstances: some women, for example, may feel compelled to take full-time work because of the hardship of managing at the existing supplementary benefit level, while others who want to work may feel they cannot do so because they cannot find good day care for the children.

2.46 We have designed GMA very much with this choice in mind. It offers to the woman who decides to stay at home an income generally better than and free from some of the disadvantages of supplementary benefit; and to the woman who takes paid employment it offers a supplement to her earnings which gives her a worthwhile financial gain from working. But this is not enough. It is essential also to look at the wages lone parents can command and the conditions under which they work; and this is the theme of Part 7. The central problem is the low wages generally paid to women, a problem which we see persisting despite equal pay legislation. It is essential that anti-discrimination legislation should accompany it; and even this will not be sufficient unless employers, trade unions, those concerned with the education and training of women, and women themselves, raise their sights and recognise the need for women to acquire the education, training and skill which are essential if they are to be able to support themselves and their families as adequately as can a man. The lone parent, of course, encounters particular difficulties in this respect because of the difficulty of combining employment with looking after home and children. Flexible working conditions can help, but many lone parents may feel that part-time rather than full-time work provides the better solution, particularly for those with younger children. One of the advantages of GMA is that, unlike supplementary benefit, it is particularly suitable for combination with part-time work, and it may be that one result of its introduction will be an increase in the numbers of those wanting to work part time. To meet this demand, more opportunities for part-time work of good quality and with comparable working conditions and status to full-time jobs are likely to be needed.

2.47 Besides employment opportunities and pay, the other big problem confronting the lone parent who desires to work is obtaining suitable care for the children. This is a problem which faces all working mothers, but it is particularly acute for the lone parent both because of the absence of the other parent and because there is usually only one set of relatives upon which to rely. Unless facilities outside the family are available, the choice to work is not a real one, and given the cost and unsatisfactory nature of a good deal of private provision, it is inevitable that it should become a question of public, or at least publicly supervised, provision. The provision of day care especially in relation to children under 5, is considered in Part 8. We regard this as a difficult as well as an important topic. Certainly there is need for a considerable expansion of day-care services. But this bald assertion disguises a host of problems concerning the needs of young children, the availability of resources, the wise use of available resources and the choice among possible patterns of development in the future of day-care services. We discuss these matters in Section 4 of Part 8, and state our preferences.

2.48 The need for more and better day care is only one of the themes of Part 8, though an important one. Most of this Report is concerned with matters that involve technical considerations based on organised knowledge and which lend themselves to structured analysis and argument. In Part 8 we are more concerned with human needs, emotional reaction and personal problems and behaviour, which cannot readily be quantified; yet these are vital components in understanding the needs of the one-parent family. In this Part of the Report we examine ways in which the personal social services can be harnessed to promote the welfare of parents and children by assisting them to take advantage of the other services and helping to make good the loss of the practical and emotional support that might otherwise have been provided by the missing parent.

2.49 The conclusions and recommendations of the whole Report are summarised in Part 9.

2.50 We have excluded from our consideration a number of topics, to which we might otherwise have addressed ourselves in some degree, because they have been or are being dealt with by other committees, or because they involve very specialised knowledge which lies elsewhere. We might, in this connection, mention in particular the Report of the Departmental (Houghton) Committee on the Adoption of Children;[1] the investigation into abortion of the Committee on the Working of the Abortion Act;[2] and the Report of the Naval Welfare (Seebohm) Committee,[3] which looked at the problems of the families of naval servicemen.

2.51 We did give some attention to the situation of the families of long-term prisoners, which is in many vital respects no different from that of other one-parent families. On the other hand, the subject has a special dimension in that it involves penological considerations which we are certain require expert knowledge for their proper evaluation. We decided that, if full consideration is to be given (as we think it should be) to prisoners' families as one-parent families, it would better come from a body that was alive to the penological implications, but which could draw on this Report for other relevant information.

2.52 We are conscious that our Report contains repetitions, as well as omissions. As we have been showing in this introductory tour round the Report, certain themes recur over a spread of topics which on the face of them may not seem to be especially closely connected. Sometimes we have coped with this by cross-referencing, but we have not hesitated where it seemed to be the more convenient course to repeat what is said elsewhere.

2.53 In the course of our work, we acquired a mass of materials on all aspects of the one-parent family in our society, much of which seemed to us to retain an intrinsic value even after we had quarried it for the purposes of the Report. We had, in particular, a collection of intensely researched statistical materials which provides the factual basis for some of the most important generalisations in the Report proper, and we considered that these materials should be made available to experts and students, so that our conclusions might be tested, debate promoted, and the results of breaking into much new ground be preserved. In addition, some materials of broader application and interest seemed important enough to warrant preservation. The result is the volume of Appendices which accompanies this Report.

---

[1] Cmnd 5107, HMSO, 1972.
[2] Publication of the results of this investigation is awaited as we complete our Report.
[3] HMSO, 1974.

2.54   It will be evident by now that we have not found our task a simple one. We have had to investigate and form conclusions about many matters which are the subject of moral, religious and social controversy; to explore the interaction between law, social security and social administration, and the no man's land between their managing institutions; and to concern ourselves with human relationships at personal, sexual and familial levels.   It was not easy to draw the perimeter round our subject.   This often involved a process of judgment rather than discovery.   Some overspill into surrounding areas was inevitable, and we have been more or less strict in preventing it according to how we thought it would assist the main flow of the argument.   And just as the nature of the enquiry was complex so are the conclusions and recommendations which emerge from it.   But we are not seeking to replace practical working arrangements with theoretical constructs.   Familiarity alone disguises and breeds acceptance of the immense complication of the arrangements that we criticise; they work, after a fashion, because until they are reformed they have to be made to work; but the scope and need for reform are very extensive.

2.55   We should acknowledge the value of the professional skills on which through individual members we have been able to draw.   But the interaction of one professional ethos with another can be a demanding process if a true consensus is to emerge, and we have been encouraged to find that made up, as we were, of individuals of diversified training, experience and outlook, we have been able to reach unanimity.   Gibbon describes how, among the Locrians, any man who proposed a new law stood forth in the assembly of the people, with a cord round his neck, and, if the law was rejected, the innovator was instantly strangled.   We all earnestly hope to survive; but, however it goes, we have assured ourselves of the consolation of a common fate.

PART 3—THE MAKING OF ONE-PARENT FAMILIES

SECTION 1—INTRODUCTION

3.1 Over 900,000 people married in Britain in 1972. In the previous decade, the total approached eight and a half million. No one supposes that these husbands and wives will all cleave to their spouses until death parts them. The pursuit of individual happiness through wedded love has gone far to turn marriage into a romantic lottery,[1] and nobody can predict how many of the brides and grooms of 1971 will have drawn losing tickets. Indeed, nobody even knows what proportion of earlier marriage cohorts have experienced breakdown. Some relationships are cemented only by the birth of a child and valid marriages collapse for so many different reasons and with so many different outcomes that, death apart, only those regulated by the courts leave a statistical record. The relationship between *de facto* and *de jure* marriage breakdown in the past or today cannot be measured and it is therefore impossible to know whether the stability of marriage has changed from one generation to another.[2] Nevertheless, the statistics of marriage breakdown are formidable. After interpreting 1971 census data in the light of information derived from national insurance records and other sources, the Department of Health and Social Security estimate that nearly one tenth of all families with dependent children have only one parent by reason of death, divorce, separation or births outside marriage.[3] The absolute numbers are set out in Table 3.1, extracted from the Department's valuable paper, *The Number of One-Parent Families in Great Britain*, which we print in Appendix 4.

---

[1] In 1832, John Stuart Mill wrote to Harriet Taylor that " Marriage is really, what it has been sometimes called, a lottery: and whoever is in a state of mind to calculate chances calmly & value them correctly is not at all likely to purchase a ticket. Those who marry after taking great pains about the matter, generally do but buy their disappointment dearer." (F A von Hayek: *John Stuart Mill and Harriet Taylor*, Routledge and Kegan Paul, 1951, page 69.)

[2] Writing in 1952, Professor R M Titmuss thought, " It is highly probable that the proportion of broken marriages under the age of sixty, marriages broken by death, desertion and divorce, is, in total, smaller today than at any time this century." *Essays on ' The Welfare State.'* 2nd edition, Allen and Unwin, 1963, page 100.

[3] It is to be noted that this estimate refers to the period when the census was taken. As the circumstances which create some one-parent families are temporary and as other one-parent families become two-parent families as a result of the remarriage or cohabitation of one or both of the parents, the proportion of the population who will have experienced the condition at any one time will be greater than one tenth.

21

TABLE 3.1

ESTIMATE OF NUMBER OF ONE-PARENT FAMILIES WITH DEPENDENT CHILDREN[1] RESULTING FROM ILLEGITIMACY, FACTUAL SEPARATION, DEATH AND DIVORCE: GREAT BRITAIN, 1971[2]

Thousands

Parent	Number of families	Number of children
Female:		
Single	90	120
Married	190	360
Widowed	120	200
Divorced	120	240
Sub-total	520	920
Male	100	160
Total	620	1,080

Source: Department of Health and Social Security—1971 census estimate adjusted in the light of supplementary benefit and national insurance statistics and of data derived from the General Household Survey (see Appendix 4).

Nearly two thirds of a million parents are looking after one million children single-handed. Of these, some 400,000 lone mothers are immediately responsible for 720,000 children whose fathers are alive but not living with the family.

3.2 Elsewhere in this Report we demonstrate that Church and State have always permitted disaffected spouses to live apart, although they remained married, if the one had behaved towards the other in a manner held to cut at the root of the marriage. In addition society always provided rich and powerful husbands, whose marriages had failed to ensure the succession to family estates and properties, with a means through annulment or Act of Parliament to obtain a licence to marry again during the lifetime of their wives even though marriage was held to be indissoluble as a matter both of religion and of law. In this, as in many other areas of social life, recent changes have simply generalised to the whole population facilities which used to be restricted to a privileged few. In the past, monogamous and indissoluble marriage was not compatible with private property and freedom of bequest, and so a small number of licences to marry again were issued to a favoured few for whom the familial and economic purposes of marriage had been intolerably frustrated.

[1] The Department's estimate uses a special definition of a one-parent family, that is, a single parent with his or her never-married children usually resident in the same household and either below school leaving age or, if between 15 and 19, undergoing full-time education.
[2] Whenever possible, the statistics in this Part are given for Great Britain. Otherwise we have utilised data which the Registrar General for Scotland has kindly provided for us by indicating the Scottish experience separately. Given the difference in size of population in the two countries (nearly 49 million in England and Wales and some 5¼ million in Scotland), we have put England and Wales in the forefront of our exposition. Most regrettably, the fourth (1973) number of the Central Statistical Office's admirable annual publication, Muriel Nissel (ed): *Social Trends*, HMSO, was published after this Part had been written. Readers are referred to the analyses by the Office of Population Censuses and Surveys which are contained in the introductory ' Social Commentary ' and especially to pages 6–12.

Today, indissoluble marriage is not compatible with prevalent notions of married love and the right to personal happiness, and so a democratic welfare society issues many thousands of licences to marry again without restriction to all citizens who meet minimal legal requirements. It is therefore unhistorical and socially unrealistic to interpret marriage breakdown merely or exclusively as a concern of social pathology. Some degree of breakdown has always been anticipated and provided for, and some means of enabling spouses who have drawn losing tickets in the lottery of marriage to try again has always been recognised as an essential prerequisite of the stability of the institution. The numbers and fate of one-parent families cannot be examined meaningfully save in the context of the radical changes that have occurred in the community's marriage habits in the recent past. Accordingly, Section 2 of this Part sets out some of the social and familial implications of demographic developments as the necessary preliminary to the analysis of the statistics of lone parenthood which are assembled in Section 3. Those readers who are happier with plain prose than with figures can turn forthwith to Section 5 of this Part where our conclusions are summarised without statistical embellishments.

SECTION 2—MARRIAGE

3.3   The ratio of bachelors to spinsters in the population is one determinant of the number of new marriages which will take place in a society which practises monogamy. Also, since most children in Britain are born in wedlock, the sex-ratio determines the number of new families which will be formed.

3.4   The distinctiveness of todays' situation with a surplus of men in all age groups up to 44 may be appreciated by recalling how, in mid-Victorian England, almost one third of the women aged 20–44 had to remain spinsters because differential mortality and large-scale emigration so depleted the reservoir of men that there were not enough to go round.[1] The social implications of this distorted sex-ratio were profound. A society which accorded assured status and social fulfilment, at least in the middle and aspirant ranks, only to women who had become wives and mothers, experienced demographic circumstances which actually denied marriage to a large group. In the contemptuous language of that day these unfortunates came to be dismissed as the old maids to be—the redundant or superfluous women. But many of these female bankrupts who had failed in their business in life had to earn their own living because they had no fathers or brothers to look after them and hence they became the driving force behind the establishment and development of a " women's movement " which, among other objects, sought to break the male monopoly over professional occupations.

3.5   This movement did much to force into politics many of the reforms of family law discussed later in this Report, and it is therefore relevant here to stress the inadequacy of explanations of the movement to improve the status and situation of women in terms exclusively of democratic ideas. This neglects the demographic and occupational changes which, rather than the revival of the ideas promoted by the French Revolution, were the effective sources of Victorian campaigns to secure the emancipation of women.[2]

[1]Alan Deacon and Michael Hill: ' The Problem of " Surplus Women " in the Nineteenth Century: Secular and Religious Alternatives,' in Michael Hill (ed): *A Sociological Yearbook of Religion in Britain*—5, SCM Press, 1972, page 90.
[2]These are examined by O R McGregor: ' The Social Position of Women in England, 1850–1914: A Bibliography ' in *The British Journal of Sociology*, Volume vi, Number 1, 1955.

3.6 As emigration slackened off, the sex-ratio became less distorted in the early twentieth century only to be thrown back to its earlier imbalance by the slaughter of nearly a million young men during the first world war. In 1901, there were 962 bachelors for each 1,000 spinsters in the age group 15–54, in which nearly all first marriages take place; by 1921 there were only 894.[1] Table 3.2 shows the situation in the United Kingdom by the middle of the century with projections until 2001.

TABLE 3.2

TOTAL POPULATION: NUMBER OF MALES FOR EACH
100 FEMALES IN EACH AGE GROUP: UNITED KINGDOM

	Mid-year estimates			1969-based projections			
	1951	1961	1969	1971	1981	1991	2001
Live births in year ...	106	106	106	106	106	106	106
Age groups:							
0–4	105	105	105	105	105	105	106
5–9	105	105	105	105	105	105	105
10–14	103	104	105	105	105	105	105
15–19	102	104	104	104	104	104	104
20–24	101	102	103	102	103	102	103
25–29	100	104	103	103	103	103	103
30–34	98	101	104	104	102	103	103
35–39	97	99	104	105	102	103	103
40–44	97	97	101	102	103	102	103
45–49	95	95	99	99	105	102	102
50–54	88	95	95	96	101	102	101
55–59	81	92	92	91	96	101	99
60–64	78	81	87	87	89	93	95
65–69	75	71	78	79	79	83	88
70–74	72	64	61	64	70	71	74
75–79	68	58	53	52	58	57	60
80–84	60	52	44	44	44	47	47
85 and over	45	44	37	35	31	33	32
All ages	93	94	95	95	96	97	98

Source: Jean Thompson: ' The Growth of Population to the End of the Century ' in Muriel Nissel (ed): *Social Trends*, Number 1, 1970, HMSO, 1971, page 32.

[1] O R McGregor and Griselda Rowntree: ' The Family,' in D V Glass *et al* (eds): *Society: Problems and Methods of Study*, Routledge and Kegan Paul, 1962, page 398.

In her commentary on this Table, Miss Thompson observes that the

effect of the mortality of the first world war can be seen as depleted cohorts of males in relation to females. The age-group 70-74 in 1969 contains the survivors of one of the younger age-groups to have been particularly affected by that war. The sex ratio in 1969, at 61 males *per* 100 females, is very much lower than the corresponding figure of 72 in 1951 for a generation just too old to have been much affected by military service in the first world war, and the figure of 70 projected for 1981 for a generation just too young to have been affected.[1]

3.7 Currently, the fall in male mortality at younger ages since the end of the second world war has further raised the age at which there is a surplus of males over females. Table 3.2 shows that there was a surplus at all ages up to 30 in 1951, up to 35 in 1961, up to 45 in 1969 and the projection for 1991 takes it up to 60. Thus, for the first time since statistics have been kept, there are now more men than women in the age groups in which most marriages occur. Ever since working class "teddy boys" began in the late 1940s to ape the mufti and hair style of Edwardian guards' officers, the cosmetic habits of young men have testified to women's new found equality of opportunity to marry.

3.8 The sex-ratio is not the only determinant of the number of new families which are created, since some of those for whom spouses exist in the national aggregate will choose to remain single. Nevertheless, one of the most significant features of recent times has been the increased popularity of marriage. The annual total of first marriages for both parties has risen with the growth of population from about 253,000 in Great Britain each year at the beginning of this century to some 357,000 in 1971, but some part of this increase reflects also a growing propensity to marry. Among women born in various nineteenth century quinquennia, a steady proportion amounting to 860–880 in each 1,000 had married by the ages of 50–54 years. By contrast, a more sophisticated nuptiality calculation based on the marriage registrations of 1951–1955 showed that as many as 945 women in each 1,000 (that is, some 75 in each 1,000 more than in the Victorian period) would be likely to marry before they were 50.[2] The Registrar General calculated a net nuptiality table for 1960 which showed that, taking the age group 45–49, the proportions ever married would be 95 per cent for males and 96 per cent for females, which Professor Grebenik and Miss Rowntree described as " as near an approach to practically universal marriage as has been achieved in this country."[3]

3.9 Indeed, given what is known about such factors as the distribution of homosexuality and chronic ill-health, psychological as well as physical, among the population at large, it is obvious that the present popularity of marriage must be drawing into the institution large numbers who lack any evident vocation for it. From this point of view, a very high marriage rate will lead to a disproportionately high rate of breakdown. The proportions of men and women marrying, allowing for the age differential at marriage, are shown for the last hundred years in Table 3.3.

---

[1] Muriel Nissel (ed): *Social Trends*, Number 1, 1970, HMSO, 1971, page 27.

[2] O R McGregor and Griselda Rowntree: *op cit*, page 398.

[3] E Grebenik and Griselda Rowntree: 'Factors Associated with the Age at Marriage in Britain ' in *Proceedings of the Royal Society, Series B*, Volume 159, 1964, page 180.

TABLE 3.3

PERCENTAGE EVER MARRIED: ENGLAND AND WALES, 1871–1971

Year	Men Age 25–29	Men Age 50–54	Women Age 20–24	Women Age 45–49	Sex-ratio (*per* 1,000) Males age 20–54 Females age 15–49
1871	60·8	90·4	34·8	87·6	818
1911	50·8	88·6	24·3	83·5	838
1931	52·9	89·3	25·8	83·2	856
1951	65·1	91·4	48·2	84·8	967
1961	70·6	91·1	58·0	89·5	994
1971	74·3	91·3	60·3	92·2	991

Source: D V Glass: 'Components of Natural Increase in England and Wales' in *Population Studies*, Volume 24, 1970, Supplement, page 12; data for 1971 provided by the Registrar General.

3.10   Table 3.3 shows the slow change in marriage habits between 1871 and 1931 followed by what Professor D V Glass describes as the " dramatic swing to higher probabilities of marriage and to consistently falling ages at marriage . . . . In all, the changes in marriage frequency and age since the 1930s have been of a magnitude unequalled in any other period since the beginning of civil vital registration, and probably in the past two or three centuries."[1]   Table 3.4 shows the fall in the mean age at first marriage at different periods since the beginning of this century.   The age in both countries rose slightly in the first thirty years of the century but has fallen since the end of the last world war by two and a half years for men and by two years for women in England and Wales and by three years for men and by two and a half years for women in Scotland.   Table 3.5 shows that, in England and Wales since the end of the war, the proportion of boys marrying in their teens has quadrupled whilst that of girls has doubled, whilst Scotland shows an even higher increase.   The figures for the most recent years are still remarkably high.

---

[1] 'Components of Natural Increase in England and Wales' in *Population Studies*, Volume 24, 1970, Supplement, pages 12–13.

TABLE 3.4
MEAN AGE AT FIRST MARRIAGE: ENGLAND AND WALES AND SCOTLAND

	1901–1905		1931–1935		1946–1950		1961–1965		1966–1970		1971	
	England and Wales	Scotland	England and Wales	Scotland	England and Wales	Scotland	England and Wales	Scotland	England and Wales	Scotland	England and Wales	Scotland
Bachelors[1]	26·9	26·9	27·4	27·5	27·2	27·1	25·4	24·9	24·6	24·1	24·6	24·2
Spinsters[1]	25·4	25·1	25·5	25·4	24·5	24·8	22·9	22·8	22·5	22·3	22·6	22·4

Source: Registrar General's Statistical Review of England and Wales for the Year 1971, Part II, Tables, Population, Table L, page 63; Annual Report of the Registrar General for Scotland, 1971, Part II, Population and Vital Statistics, No 117, Table Q1.5, page 69.

TABLE 3.5
PROPORTIONS OF FIRST MARRIAGES UNDER THE AGE OF 20: ENGLAND AND WALES AND SCOTLAND
Percentage

	1901–1905		1931–1935		1946–1950		1961–1965		1966–1970		1970		1971	
	England and Wales	Scotland	England and Wales	Scotland	England and Wales	Scotland	England and Wales	Scotland	England and Wales	Scotland	England and Wales	Scotland	England and Wales	Scotland
Bachelors[1]	1·6	2·8	1·8	2·7	2·5	2·7	7·9	9·5	9·3	12·4	10·0	12·1	10·2	12·8
Spinsters[1]	8·1	11·3	9·3	13·2	15·5	14·8	30·2	28·5	30·0	30·8	30·7	29·7	31·1	31·6

Source: Registrar General's Statistical Review of England and Wales for the Year 1971, Part II, Tables, Population, Table K, page 60; Annual Reports of the Registrar General for Scotland.

[1] For 1901–1905 and 1931–1935, bachelors include divorced men and spinsters include divorced women.

3.11 The fall in the age of marriage is a demographic development of pervasive social importance yet it has not attracted extensive study and is not fully understood. In their analysis of the factors associated with the age at marriage in Britain, which reported on one part of the Population Investigation Committee's national marriage survey of 1959–1960, Professor Grebenik and Miss Rowntree attempted " to find out whether specific social and economic changes, especially the greater security of jobs and incomes in the post-war period, had affected informants' decisions . . . . We were, however, unable to find any association between such factors and the falling age at marriage. . . . "[1] Further, there is very little knowledge about social class differences in the age at marriage. An analysis of 1961 census data made by the Registrar General

TABLE 3.6

WOMEN OF VARYING AGES MARRYING HUSBANDS BY DIFFERENT OCCUPATIONAL GROUPS IN 1947-1951, 1955-1956 AND 1960-1961

A ENGLAND AND WALES

Husband's socio-economic group	Age at marriage	Percentages of women marrying in:		
		1947–51	1955–56	1960–61
		%	%	%
Unskilled manual	Under 20	20	29	41
	20–24	45	46	42
	25–29	20	13	9
	30–34	8	6	4
	35–44	8	5	4
Skilled manual	Under 20	19	26	32
	20–24	55	56	53
	25–29	18	12	10
	30–34	5	4	3
	35–44	3	3	2
Employers and managers in central and local govern- ment, industry, commerce *etc:* large establishments	Under 20	8	8	9
	20–24	53	57	54
	25–29	27	23	22
	30–34	8	9	7
	35–44	4	4	7
Self-employed professional...	Under 20	4	2	4
	20–24	45	48	49
	25–29	36	35	31
	30–34	8	8	12
	35–44	7	7	4

Source: *Registrar General's Statistical Review of England and Wales for the Year* 1965, *Part III, Commentary*, adapted from Table C17, page 42.

[1] *Op cit*, page 194.

B SCOTLAND

Husband's socio-economic group	Age at marriage	Percentages of women marrying in:		
		1947–51	1955–56	1960–61
		%	%	%
Unskilled manual	Under 20	19	31	39
	20–24	45	46	43
	25–29	19	11	11
	30–34	9	5	4
	35–44	8	7	3
Skilled manual	Under 20	16	21	23
	20–24	51	55	59
	25–29	22	17	13
	30–34	6	4	3
	35–44	4	2	3
Employers and managers in central and local government, industry, commerce etc: large establishments	Under 20	5	11	7
	20–24	47	42	45
	25–29	29	34	18
	30–34	11	11	20
	35–44	8	3	9
Self-employed professional...	Under 20	1	—	—
	20–24	40	30	27
	25–29	42	40	27
	30–34	13	23	9
	35–44	5	7	36

Source: Computed from *Census* 1961, *Scotland, Volume Ten, Fertility*, Table 14.

suggested that " although the trend towards earlier marriage has occurred in all sections of society it has gone very much further amongst manual workers than it has amongst non manual, professional and managerial workers. Indeed the difference between the marriage patterns of different socio-economic groups has widened since the 1930s."[1]   Table 3.6 compares the experience of women marrying husbands in four occupational groups between 1947–1951 and 1960–1961, in England and Wales and in Scotland. The Table shows the influence of occupation, and hence of social class, on the age at marriage of brides. The proportion of women in England and Wales marrying in their teens rose from 20 per cent between 1947–1951 to 41 per cent in 1960–1961 for the brides of unskilled workers. In Scotland, the proportion increased in the same period from 19 per cent to 39 per cent. In the case of brides marrying skilled workers, the increase in the proportion of teenagers was greater in England, where it rose from 19 per cent in 1947–1951 to 32 per cent in 1960–1961, than in Scotland which experienced a change from 16 per cent

[1] *Registrar General's Statistical Review of England and Wales for the Year 1965, Part III, Commentary*, pages 40–41.

to 23 per cent in the same period. In both countries, the proportions of teenagers marrying husbands who were employers and managers or self-employed professionals were low and showed little increase over the period.

3.12 The changes in marriage so far outlined have affected fertility because they result in a higher proportion of women being exposed for longer periods to the risk of pregnancy. Professor D V Glass estimates that " about 30 per cent of the increase in the average number of live births *per* married woman (for women married at under 45 years of age) between the 1931 and 1956 marriage cohorts is accounted for by the fall in the age at marriage. . . . The decline in the age at marriage will in particular have tended to reduce the frequency of childlessness, for this is very strongly linked to marriage age."[1] But these trends must be seen against the background of the transformation which has taken place in family size during the last hundred years. Table 3.7 traces the elimination of the large family of Victorian days.

TABLE 3.7

DISTRIBUTION OF WOMEN (*PER* 1,000) WITH VARIOUS NUMBERS OF LIVE BIRTHS FOR SELECTED MARRIAGE GROUPS: GREAT BRITAIN

Number of women (*per* 1,000) with specified numbers of live births	1870 to 1879	1900 to 1909	1925
0	83	113	161
1 or 2	125	335	506
3 or 4	181	227	221
5 to 9	434	246	106
10 or more	177	29	6
All	1,000	1,000	1,000

Source: D V Glass and E Grebenik: ' The Trend and Pattern of Fertility in Great Britain ' in *Papers of the Royal Commission on Population*, 1954, Volume vi, Part I, page 3.

Of the women married in the 1870s, nearly two thirds had five children or more; of the women married in 1925, two thirds had two children or less. At the extremes, the proportion of childless wives doubled in fifty years whilst the proportion with ten children or more fell from 18 per cent to 0·6 per cent in the same period.

[1] *Op cit*, page 13.

3.13   Changes in family size during this century are set out in Table 3.8.

TABLE 3.8

**DISTRIBUTION OF FAMILY SIZE IN GREAT BRITAIN
(BIRTHS OCCURRING TO FIRST MARRIAGES)**   Percentage

Number of children live-born in marriage	Women married in period		
	1920-24	1935-39	1955-59 (part-estimated)
0	16	15	9
1	24	26	18
2	24	29	34
3	14	15	20
4	8	7	(11)
5 or more	14	8	(8)
	100	100	100
Average number of children	2·38	2·07	(2·38)

Source: Office of Population Censuses and Surveys: *Report of the Population Panel*, Cmnd 5258, 1973, Table II, page 40.

Family size declined to its lowest point in the 1930s, and increased in the post-war period.   Over the first fifty years of the century, the proportion of families with two children almost doubled whilst the proportion of those with five children or more decreased from nearly one third to fewer than one tenth.

3.14   The achievement of the small, consciously-planned family took place about the same time throughout the greater part of western Europe, and it must be reckoned a climacteric in social history.   Although this development has attracted extensive demographic, historical and sociological study, a generally accepted explanation has not yet emerged.   It is clear that neither variations in fecundity nor improvements in the manufacture and efficiency of contraceptives are causal explanations.   Indeed, it is likely that the importance of contraceptives as a means of controlling fertility has been over-estimated. We know, for example, that 27 per cent of the couples who married in Britain in the 1950s used *coitus interruptus,* a technique of birth control familiar to Adam and Eve, as their primary method.[1]   Even today, modern methods continue to play a minor role in many western countries.   The significance of contraception is therefore as much as a means of achieving civilised and unfrustrating sexual relations as of control over fertility.   Whatever the social mechanisms involved, the initiation and spread of family limitation appears to have been the response of married cou꜀ ꜀s to social and economic changes, including the rising cost of preparing children to take their place in the adult world, which threatened an achieved standard of living.

[1]Rachel M Pierce and Griselda Rowntree: 'Birth Control in Britain' in *Population Studies*, Volume 15, Number 2, 1961.

3.15 Accordingly, the rise in marital fertility in recent years is not the result of a return to the large family of a hundred years ago but of the sharp reduction in childlessness and of a shift from the one-child family to families with two or three children. Table 3.9 demonstrates the change in family building habits which has occurred in the last thirty years.

TABLE 3.9

MEAN FAMILY SIZE: WOMEN MARRIED ONCE ONLY AT AGES UNDER 45: ENGLAND AND WALES

Marriage duration (exact years)	Year of marriage						
	1940	1945	1950	1955	1960	1965	1969
3	·61	·86	·85	·84	·94	·95	·84
5	·95	1·24	1·25	1·29	1·45	1·42	
10	1·63	1·79	1·84	1·99	2·13		
15	1·87	2·06	2·12	2·24			
20	1·97	2·16	2·22				
25	2·00	2·19					

Source: *Registrar General's Statistical Review of England and Wales for the Year* 1971, *Part II, Tables, Population*, Table QQ (b), pages 184–189; 1969 information provided for the Committee by the Registrar General.

Table 3.9 shows mean family sizes for all ages at marriage. Women married in 1960 have a higher average than those married in earlier years for each duration of marriage up to ten years. The upward trend now seems to have been checked or even reversed, since marriages of the late 1960s are showing slightly lower figures than those of the early 1960s. Finally, the combination of relatively low family size and shortening of the childbearing period has resulted in a compression of fertility so that more than half of all babies will be born within the first five years of marriage and more than three quarters within eight years.

3.16 Changes in fertility have been associated with the spread of birth control from the upper income groups a hundred years ago to practically the whole population today, despite the opposition during much of the period of many doctors and of the major social institutions. Such past hostility and active obstruction help to explain why a survey, *Family Planning Services in England and Wales*, carried out in 1970 on behalf of the Department of Health and Social Security,[1] found that only 31 per cent of married women at risk of pregnancy[2] were using the services. On the other hand " 93 per cent of those at risk (used some form of contraception) . . . . About a third of the women at risk were either using the least reliable methods (withdrawal and safe period) or none, and about the same proportion were using either the pill or IUDS."[3]

---

[1] By Margaret Bone, HMSO, 1973.

[2] Defined as those who were fecund but were neither pregnant nor planning to become so.

[3] *Ibid*, page 5. This finding may be compared with that of the Population Investigation Committee which reported that, for the 1961–1965 marriage cohort, the proportion stating past or current use of birth control was around 95 per cent. Professor Glass comments that " allowing for infecund and sub-fecund women, and for the small proportion unalterably or at least strongly opposed to any form of birth control, a figure of 95 per cent implies practically total coverage of all married women." D V Glass: *op cit*, page 17.

It is salutary to recall that the welcoming official attitudes and political enthusiasm for extensions of public provision for family planning in the last few years are the product, not the explanation, of birth control. In this, as in other vital areas of morality, it is the sheep who have led and the shepherds who have followed. This brief indication of trends in fertility suggests that, despite all the difficulties of controlling births at a time when there is greater exposure to the risk of pregnancy than ever before, Britain may have reached a stable plateau of relatively small and fairly uniform family size.

3.17 Table 3.10 shows how the expectation of life has changed during this century. Between 1901 and 1971, the expectation of life at birth for males has increased by more than twenty-two years and for females by almost twenty-six years. For those who survived to their fifth birthday, the increases are less striking. The main feature is not that the long-lived live longer than in the past but that a much higher proportion of the population survives to become long-lived. The longer survival of women creates a surplus of widows in the higher age groups.

TABLE 3.10
EXPECTATION OF LIFE: GREAT BRITAIN, 1851-1971

		1851	1901	1911	1921	1931	1951	1961	1971
Expectation of life (in years)									
At birth:	males	40	46	51·4	55·4	58·4	66·2	67·9	68·6
	females	42	49	55·2	59·3	62·5	71·2	73·8	74·9
At age 5:	males	50	55	57·0	58·3	60·0	63·9	65·0	65·2
	females	50	57	59·7	61·1	63·0	68·5	70·5	71·2

Source: Office of Population Censuses and Surveys: *Report of the Population Panel, op cit*, Table 7, page 32.

3.18 Longer life, a sex-ratio near unity, more and younger marriage and small, consciously-planned families, with fertility compressed into a narrow band of years, have resulted in revolutionary alterations in women's lives as wives, as mothers and as workers. Britain has not yet begun fully to assimilate the social meanings of this transformation. First, the duration of marriage has increased. Today's spouses will enjoy or endure the experience of matrimony for much longer periods than in earlier generations.[1] Indeed, it will become commonplace for marriages to last for more than half a century. One consequence will be that, from now onwards, most children will be the fourth living generation in their families. When the eldest children are born, they will normally be seen by all four grandparents and most of their eight great-grandparents.[2] Another consequence is the difficulty and hazard of any attempt to measure or to generalise about changes in the stability of marriage from generation to generation.

[1] A further factor which must be allowed for is the increased observance of the formalities of marriage among the working class. At the beginning of this century cohabitation without marriage was not uncommon.
[2] Jean Thompson: *op cit*, page 30.

3.19 Secondly, the spread of birth control is separating sex from pregnancy for women within the childbearing ages. It seems reasonable to predict success in the near or middle future in the search for an effective, simple, harmless and aesthetically acceptable contraceptive which does not depend upon persistent motivation.[1] Such is the context of present uncertainties and anxieties about sexual morality. Today, as yesterday, the fundamental rule is no sex outside marriage. The secular justification for this rule was that sexual intercourse carried a high risk of pregnancy and few women could provide for, or protect themselves, or their children, outside marriage; it was accepted without demur because it was evidently in accord with the realities of life. Believers justified the rule as part of their religious ethic. Clearly these justifications no longer adequately support the inherited code. The religious justification makes sense only for practising believers but not for the majority of the population. For the young, the deterrent fear of pregnancy has been blunted by birth control, and it is irrelevant to the middle aged. Moreover, sexual morality cannot be persuasively grounded in a theory of inefficient contraception. There is nothing new in the present gap between actual and approved sexual behaviour, between, that is, how we tell our children they ought to behave and how we behave ourselves. What is new is the widespread and articulate questioning of the proper rules of sexual conduct, and what matters is to recognise that contraceptives, by giving women freedom to choose how to exercise their reproductive powers, have brought about what Professor R M Titmuss described as " nothing less than a revolutionary enlargement of freedom."[2] Writing some twenty years ago, he estimated that:

> ... the typical working class mother of the 1890s ... (experienced) ... ten pregnancies, spent about fifteen years in a state of pregnancy and in nursing a child for the first year of its life. She was tied, for this period of time, to the wheel of childbearing. Today, for the typical mother, the time so spent would be about four years. ...The typical working class mother in the industrial towns in 1900 could expect, if she survived to fifty-five, to live not much more than another twelve years by the time she reached the comparative ease, the reproductive grazing ground, of the middle fifties.[3]

However, the situation is now remarkably different:

> Even though we have extended the number of years that a child spends at school and added to the psychological and social responsibilities of motherhood by raising the cultural norms of child upbringing, most mothers have largely concluded their maternal role by the age of forty.[4]

Demographic change in the twentieth century has given women a new life. When Victoria came to the throne, the typical woman would think herself lucky to get a husband; he would father upon her the maximum number of children that she was physiologically capable of bearing given her age at marriage; she would rear them and then die. Today, mothers have more than half their active, adult lives to lead after completing their direct maternal role. Motherhood used to be a woman's whole existence; it has become now the lesser part of the chronology of her life cycle.

---

[1]We have to contemplate that the consequence may be that, whereas today people in their fertile years go to the family planning clinic to avoid pregnancy, tomorrow they will be rendered infertile at puberty and will go to the clinic only when they want to conceive.

[2] *Essays on " The Welfare State,"* 2nd edition, Allen and Unwin, 1963, page 91.

[3] *Ibid*, pages 91–92.

[4] *Ibid*, page 92.

3.20 In the third place, these demographic events have altered decisively the character of the female labour force. It is a common delusion to suppose that world wars brought women into employment on a large scale for the first time. In fact, they have always been an integral part of the labour force in all industrial societies.[1] The historical situation is shown in Table 3.11.

TABLE 3.11

NUMBERS OF GAINFULLY OCCUPIED MEN AND WOMEN AT CENSUS DATES: GREAT BRITAIN, 1851–1971

| Year | Men | Women | Total | Percentages of total | |
		Thousands		Men	Women
1851	6,757	2,989	9,746	69	31
1861	7,439	3,387	10,826	69	31
1871	8,266	3,851	12,117	68	32
1881	8,851	3,887	12,738	70	30
1891	10,104	4,573	14,677	69	31
1901	11,548	4,763	16,311	71	29
1911	12,927	5,424	18,351	70	30
1921	13,656	5,701	19,357	71	29
1931	14,790	6,265	21,055	70	30
1951	15,649	6,961	22,610	69	31
1961*	16,071	7,740	23,811	67	33
1971	15,917	9,186	25,103	63	37

* Corrected for sample bias.

Source: 1851–1881: *Economic Development in the United Kingdom*, Labour Information, ECA Mission to the United Kingdom, 1952, page 18; 1891–1971: Office of Population Censuses and Surveys.

The Table demonstrates the remarkable stability of women's contribution to the country's labour force. It hardly varied between 1851 and 1951 but it has risen since 1961. Their contribution to the national economy has been regulated by the timing of marriage and the progress of family building. In the generations before the second world war, women used to work for several years between leaving school earlier than they do today and getting married later than they do today. They withdrew from the labour market upon marriage. Few ever returned and then only if they had suffered a domestic catastrophe in such form as a broken marriage or a disabled or unemployed husband unable to provide. So, before the last world war, the representative woman worker was young and single. Working women in the older age groups were mostly lifelong spinsters drawn from the large reservoir of unmarriageable women. The custom both among the middle and the working class was

[1] See, for example, Alva Myrdal and Viola Klein: *Women's Two Roles*, 2nd revised edition, Routledge and Kegan Paul, 1968.

for work to cease on marriage and therefore the proportion of married women in paid jobs was less than 10 per cent. If the numbers of women working remain the same or increase during a period in which the proportion of the population marrying is rising and the age at marriage falling, it follows that the composition of the female labour force will change. Accordingly, when the statistics of women at work in Table 3.11 are superimposed upon the demographic changes of the last forty years, one result is an increase in the proportion of married women in the labour force from 10 per cent to almost two thirds today. Moreover, this change results from new marriage patterns and owes little to altered attitudes either to marriage or to work.

3.21 Associated with this development has been a decisive shift in the age structure of the female labour force. Table 3.12 sets out the findings of Mrs Audrey Hunt's *Survey of Women's Employment*, undertaken by the Government Social Survey in 1965, in respect of the proportions of each age group working full time and part time.

TABLE 3.12

PROPORTION OF WOMEN IN DIFFERENT AGE GROUPS WORKING FULL TIME AND PART TIME: GREAT BRITAIN, 1965

	Percentage of each age group		
	Full time	Part time	Total "economically active"[1]
Age group	%	%	%
16–19	71·7	1·1	75·2
20–24	52·1	5·9	60·3
25–29	24·3	11·5	37·3
30–34	20·0	20·3	43·1
35–39	24·3	24·1	50·9
40–44	29·4	26·3	57·6
45–49	37·4	23·0	63·5
50–54	29·9	22·5	54·9
55–59	27·0	20·1	49·4
60–64	15·3	17·4	34·9
All ages	32·4	17·8	52·6

Source: Audrey Hunt: *A Survey of Women's Employment*, HMSO, 1968, Volume 1, page 24.

The level of economic activity rises to two peaks: the first in the age group 16–19, the second in the age group 45–49.[2] The effect of marriage and of family building may be seen as the proportion of women economically active falls by half for those in the age group 25–29. The proportion in the higher age group should be interpreted in the light of Mrs Hunt's comment:

these figures show the position at a given point in time and . . . the rapid post-war changes in women's employment may well be reflected in future employment levels at different ages. The women aged 50 and over at the time of the survey

---

[1] Includes unemployed, temporarily sick and "regular casual".

[2] More recent data show the same picture.

were most of them first married at a time when it was unusual for married women to work and may thus not have the same urge to return to work that younger women have at present or will have in the future.[1]

3.22 The full measure of the transformation of women's working lives that has taken place in little more than one generation is that the representative working woman of today is married, over forty and has a grown-up family. This is why so many occupations traditionally dependent on the reservoir of unmarriageable women now have to attract the indispensable but inelegantly described " married woman returner ".

3.23 Many acute conflicts of values cluster around the altered demographic and occupational situation of women. The movement towards social and legal equality was greatly prompted by demographic circumstances but its very successes have created a society in which it is much harder to be a wife than to be a husband. Husbands can be single-minded about their work and careers. They acquire whatever training or qualifications they need and then they work without a break for forty or fifty years. Women have to live two lives and they must learn to play the different and often conflicting roles of mothers and workers. They are taught the lesson, too, that formal equality is mocked by the practical inequalities of the labour market where women still serve as the main reserve of cheap labour.

3.24 The inescapable conclusion from many recent studies of women's experience in trying to reconcile the claims of marriage, motherhood and work is the existence of a firmly rooted double standard of occupational morality. As a society, we pay lip-service to equality for women whilst practising discrimination. The most recent and substantial study of *Sex, Career and Family* by a Political and Economic Planning group[2] observes that:

> women generally, quite apart from any question of promotion to top jobs, tend not to be offered the same chances of training for skilled work or promotion as men nor to be motivated by their education or work environment to take them; that they tend to be segregated into " women's work ", devalued by unequal pay, treated as lacking in commitment to their work and as unsuitable to be in authority over men, and trained and encouraged not merely to accept these conditions but to think them right; and that husbands, the community (for example as regards nursery schools and shopping hours) and employers have only half-heartedly adapted to the change in the womens' labour market due to the increased share in it taken by married women. If factors like these account for women's poor representation in skilled and supervisory work generally, surely they account still more powerfully for women's underrepresentation in work in the highest ranges".[3]

3.25 Women's work used to be undertaken in the interval between school and motherhood, and the sting of occupational inequality was mild. Today, motherhood is taking place in the interval between school and work and the sting of inequality has become sharp indeed. In recent years the gains of formal equality have been exposed to the brute realities of the labour market, with the result that the emancipation of women has been followed by demands for their liberation. Most women do unskilled jobs in a narrow range of industries and services for rates of pay between one half and two thirds of the earnings of unskilled men. Several surveys have shown that most do not go back to work

[1]*Op cit*, page 24.

M P Fogarty and Robert and Rhona Rapoport. Published by Allen and Unwin in 1971.
Ibid, page 25.

until the children are at school, many fit part-time work in with their household duties and where children have to be looked after during holidays, it is a member of the family who steps in. In part, it seems that wives work in order to retain their independence and a hold upon the outside world, but their chief incentive to return to the labour market is to add to the family income, especially at a time when growing children make their major demands upon the family budget. All the surveys suggest that most mothers who go out to work are motivated by desire to strengthen their families, not to escape from them, and " that it is sometimes the inadequate mother who is also too inadequate to work; her very fecklessness keeps her at home."[1] For such mothers unskilled work offers the advantages that they can move easily in and out of employment in accordance either with their family building cycle or with the exigencies of their households. But two categories of mothers face especial difficulties. First, highly trained women with professional qualifications have only a short period to establish themselves occupationally before starting their families and face many frustrations when they attempt either to work part time or to return full time. When they return they are personally mature but professionally inexperienced, and may often require refresher training, at a time when their male contemporaries are reaching the peak of their careers.[2] The present generation of mothers with professional qualifications probably faces greater obstacles in pursuing a career than did their grandmothers if only as a result of the disappearance of reliable and permanent domestic servants. Secondly, the mothers who are the sole parents to their children are at a special disadvantage. They mostly have more need than their still married contemporaries to seek work and they are significantly less able to adapt their household cares to their jobs.

SECTION 3—MARRIAGE BREAKDOWN

3.26 The third Section of this Part sets out what is known about the numbers of one-parent families against the background of the demographic developments outlined in the first part. For the last quarter of a century, such terms as " marriage breakdown ", " parental deprivation " and " broken home " have been used in the study of situations where children lack the continuous support of two parents. Although many of these investigations have seemed to demonstrate a causal connection between broken homes and disturbed or delinquent behaviour in children,[3] such critics as Lady Wootton have observed that:

> attempts fairly to assess the significance of their findings are . . . thwarted, first, by the absence of precise definition of what constitutes the " breaking " of a home, and, second, by lack of any information as to the frequency of the " broken home " amongst the population in general.[4]

---

[1] Canon Gordon Dunstan: *The Family is not Broken*, SCM Press, 1962, page 56.

[2] There are a large number of studies which include Margot Jefferys and Patricia M Elliott: *Women in Medicine*, Office of Health Economics, 1966; R K Kelsall: *Women and Teaching*, HMSO, 1963; C E Arregger: *Graduate Women at Work*, British Federation of University Women, Oriel Press, Newcastle, 1966; A J Allen, Isobel Allen, Patricia Walters and M Fogarty: *Women in Top Jobs*, Allen and Unwin, 1971; R K Kelsall, Anne Poole and Annette Kuhn: *Six Years After: First Report on a National Follow-up Survey of Ten Thousand Graduates of British Universities in* 1960, Higher Education Research Unit, Department of Sociological Studies, Sheffield University, 1970.

[3] See Appendix 12.

[4] *Social Science and Social Pathology*, Allen and Unwin, 1959, page 118. Research undertaken since this book was published has done little to blunt its criticisms on this score.

3.27 The first difficulty arises from the multiplicity of causes of breakdown. Marriages may collapse as a result of death or of *de facto* or *de jure* separation or of the prolonged absence of a partner for voluntary or involuntary reasons. On the other hand, some relationships may be consummated and result in the birth of children but never be celebrated as marriages. This wide range of possibilities was reflected in the Committee's own suggested framework for written evidence which explained that:

> a one-parent family, for working purposes, shall simply be defined as a family in which there is an adult and dependent child or children, one parent or partner is absent (for whatever reason), there is no reasonable prospect of his or her return within a fairly short period and there is no effective parent substitute. Under this definition the wife and children of a long-term prisoner or long-term hospital in-patient, for example, would therefore be regarded as a one-parent family, but the family of a woman living in a stable union with a man, to whom she was not married, would not.

The paucity of information about some forms of breakdown, together with the many circumstances in which it can occur, makes a formidable obstacle to the systematic assessment of its effects upon those involved.

3.28 Other difficulties result from the need when estimating the consequences of parental deprivation upon children to allow both for their ages at the time of breakdown as well as for the great diversity of upbringings which may follow. It is vital to relate children's ages at the time of breakdown to their subsequent behaviour, and it clearly makes a great difference whether the child is a baby or an adolescent when his parents part; or whether he is subsequently brought up by his mother alone, or by his mother and her next partner, or in an institution. The children of broken homes may experience two or more families and occupy a different ordinal position in each. This is illustrated in an extreme form by one example taken from the admirably designed study by Professor Illsley and Dr Thompson of the incidence of broken homes among a cohort of women having their first pregnancies in Aberdeen in the period 1952 to 1954:

> Mrs J's father, who died when she was nine, had three children by a previous marriage; her mother had two illegitimate children born before her marriage. Mrs J herself was the first of five children born to these two parents. After her father's death her mother remarried and had a further child. At some point in the family history, two " nieces " appeared and were brought up with the other children. According to different definitions of the term " family " which include or exclude step-siblings, half-siblings or foster-siblings, Mrs J might be variously regarded at one extreme as the sixth of twelve children or the first of five, with several intermediate combinations ... Mrs J's experience was unusually varied, but many children of broken homes could claim two families and two ordinal positions.[1]

3.29 Few studies have faced up satisfactorily to the difficulties here noted. But sometimes the concept of breakdown has been extended to include a discordant but continuing relationship between parents. If the findings of Illsley and Thompson that " it is not broken homes, but unstable parental and family relationships which produce traumatic effects "[2] upon children is true generally, then the hope of measuring the significance of broken homes

---

[1] ' Women from Broken Homes ' in *The Sociological Review*, Volume 9, Number 1, 1961, page 45.

[2] *Ibid*, page 51.

becomes indeed a chimera. These considerations reinforce the conclusion of Illsley and Thompson that the general concept of the broken home, however phrased, must be treated with extreme caution:

> Broken homes do not possess a monopoly of marital disharmony and child-hood unhappiness—many children from intact homes suffer from family insecurity and emotional deprivation. Conversely many children from broken homes lead a happy normal life. This is particularly true in post-war Britain where social services and concern for child welfare have softened many of the harsher consequences of parental loss. Whatever its past usefulness this highly generalised concept should be abandoned in favour of a more intensive study of defined categories of family and childhood experience in both broken and intact homes. Such studies would help to determine what kinds of experience produce lasting deleterious effects and concentrate attention and therapy where it is most needed.[1]

3.30 But the abandonment of the general concept of broken homes in favour of such defined categories as death, divorce, voluntary separation and the like will serve only to underline the inadequacies of much of the existing statistical data. Moreover, these do not exist in a form which can resolve Lady Wootton's second difficulty concerning the lack of information about the frequency of breakdown among the population at large.

3.31 We set out first what is known about the amount of different categories of breakdown, and we then turn to consider the implications for our work of other relevant statistical material.

3.32 No matter how stable a marriage has been, death will break it up. In Section 2 we showed how the striking increase in the quantity, and fall in the age, of marriage during the last forty years had extended the married lives experienced by almost the entire population. This development has been reinforced by the declining death rates shown in Table 3.13. As a result, divorce has replaced death as the major factor in disposing of the marriages of couples in the younger age groups.

---

[1] *Ibid*, page 52.

TABLE 3.13
AGE SPECIFIC MORTALITY RATES: AGE-GROUPS 1-54: GREAT BRITAIN, 1901-1971

	Rates *per* 1,000 population in each age group			
	Under 1*	1–4	5–44	45–54
Males:				
1901	162	21	5	18
1911	140	19	5	15
1921	94	11	4	13
1931	78	8	3	11
1951	35	1	2	9
1961	24	1	1	8
1971	22	1	1	7
Females:				
1901	134	21	5	14
1911	115	18	4	11
1921	73	10	3	9
1931	59	7	3	8
1951	26	1	1	5
1961	19	1	1	5
1971	15	1	1	4

* Deaths in the first year of life, *per* 1,000 live births.
   Source: Office of Population Censuses and Surveys: extracted from the *Report of the Population Panel*, *op cit*, Table 8, page 32.

Clearly, no foreseeable further decline in mortality could significantly reduce the influence of death as a cause of one-parent families. It is noteworthy that awards of widowed mother's allowance over the past ten years have declined only very slightly from 106,000 in 1963 to 98,000 in 1972.

3.33   Like deaths, divorces are easy to count and official statistics have been published since 1857. There has been an enormous increase in the number of divorces during this century from a few hundreds in the years before the first world war to some 110,000 in 1972. Table 3.14 shows what has happened since the second world war.

TABLE 3.14
NUMBER OF PETITIONS[1] FOR DISSOLUTION AND NULLITY OF MARRIAGE: ANNUAL AVERAGES, ENGLAND AND WALES, 1946-1972

Period					Number	
1946–1950					38,901	⎫
1951–1955					32,168	⎪
1956–1960					27,478	⎬ Annual averages
1961–1965					37,657	⎪
1966–1970					57,090	⎭
1970					71,661	
1971					110,895	
1972					110,722	

Source: Annual *Civil Judicial Statistics*, HMSO.

[1] Petitions rather than decrees provide a surer indication of the divorce trend because they are less liable to fluctuations resulting from the rate of despatch of court business.

3.34   Since the end of the last world war, the number of divorce petitioners has nearly trebled and there has been an even steeper rise between the late 1950s and today.   There cannot be a simple explanation of these statistics because, as one commentator has observed:

> the increase in divorce since 1900 has resulted from many complex changes. There have been extensions of the grounds for divorce and, of greater significance, a widening access to the High Court for the lower social classes.   Today, full employment and legal aid ensure that poverty is no bar to divorce.   Social and demographic changes have affected the expectation of life, the proportion of the population who marry, and the age at marriage.   The structure and functions of the family, the position of women, and prevailing conceptions of desirable familial, parental, and sexual relationships have all changed.   These—and other— interdependent variables have been operating within a society conditioned by continuously expanding industrialism and intermittent war.   The present situation is the result of the coincidence in point of time of a multiplicity of social changes.   Any attempt to select a *primum mobile*, or to arrange factors in order of importance, is necessarily an essay in futility.[1]

3.35   However, one negative conclusion is well established.   In the 1950s the great increase in the number of divorces was often interpreted as evidence of a collapse both of family life and of moral standards.[2]   This would have been plausible only if the divorce rate had been an index of broken homes. Since then, compelling evidence has been produced to demonstrate that the divorce rate does not measure the number of marriages which actually break down but only the number of factually separated spouses who acquire licences to marry again.[3]   One crucial development since 1900 has therefore been a massive increase in *de jure* dissolutions of marriages already broken *de facto*.[4]

3.36   One result of the co-existence in England of two systems of matrimonial law (a subject upon which we have much to say in Part 4) is that we must look to matrimonial proceedings in magistrates' courts as well as in the divorce courts for a record of marriage breakdowns which must be taken into account when interpreting the divorce statistics.   In the early years of this century, magistrates were hearing more than 15,000 applications for orders, most of which can be reckoned to represent marriage breakdowns.[5]   Indeed, over 90 per cent of all matrimonial proceedings in England and Wales were then heard in magistrates' courts.   The situation since the end of the last world war is shown in Table 3.15.

---

[1] O R McGregor: *Divorce in England*, Heinemann, 1957, page 55.

[2] See, for example, the *Report of the Royal (Morton) Commission on Marriage and Divorce*, Cmd 9678, 1956, especially Chapter 1.

[3] We discuss this at length in Part 4.

[4] See, in particular, the report of the Law Commission, *Reform of the Grounds of Divorce: The Field of Choice*, Cmnd 3123, 1966, paragraphs 5–12.

[5] The data are difficult to interpret: there is a discussion in O R McGregor, Louis Blom-Cooper and Colin Gibson: *Separated Spouses*, Duckworth, 1970, Chapter 2.   The 15,000 odd orders are made up of (*a*) some 11,000 matrimonial applications and (*b*) some 5,000 appliations for poor law orders, that is, attempts by the poor law authorities to secure reimbursement from liable relatives.

TABLE 3.15

MAINTENANCE PROCEEDINGS IN MAGISTRATES' COURTS: ENGLAND AND WALES, 1945-1972[1]

Period	Married women maintenance orders	Guardianship of minors orders
1945–1949	19,138	6,120
1950–1954	26,835	6,960
1955–1959	24,089	7,763
1960–1964	25,653	7,003
1965–1969	27,350	5,199
1970–1972	26,462	5,285

Source: 1945–1959: annual *Criminal Statistics*, HMSO; from 1960: annual *Civil Judicial Statistics* for 1968 and subsequent years, HMSO.

3.37 In Part 4 of this Report we comment on the inadequacies of the official statistics relating to the exercise of matrimonial jurisdiction by the summary courts. All that can be inferred from Table 3.15 is that the jurisdiction, notwithstanding the increase in divorce, has retained its vitality over the last quarter of a century and shows no signs of growth or decline. For our immediate purpose, we have an estimate that half of the wives with magistrates' orders go on to become petitioners or respondents in the divorce court.[2] Thus, it is probable that the number of marriage breakdowns which leave a legal record are the total number of divorces plus half the matrimonial orders made by magistrates' courts. There are no data to show whether the 50 per cent of wives with magistrates' orders who do not end up in the divorce court are involved in temporary or permanent breakdowns of their marriages. In our comments on the Home Office and Law Commission Working Paper, *Matrimonial Proceedings in Magistrates' Courts*,[3] we state our reasons for thinking that a high proportion of matrimonial proceedings in magistrates' courts relate to marriages as finally dead as those which are terminated by law in the divorce court.[4]

3.38 Differences in the legal systems and in the form in which statistical data are published make it impossible to compare directly the divorcing populations in England and Wales and in Scotland. Table 3.16 shows the number of divorces in Scotland since the end of the second world war.

---

[1] The Table shows applications for orders. In the period 1970–1972, 66 per cent of married women applications and 81 per cent of guardianship of minors applications were successful. The latter have been included because they provide in most cases a sure indication of marriage breakdown.

[2] *Separated Spouses, op cit*, page 140.

[3] The Law Commission: *Family Law: Matrimonial Proceedings in Magistrates' Courts*, Working Paper No 53, HMSO, 1973.

[4] See Part 4, Section 14.

TABLE 3.16

DIVORCE ACTIONS IN WHICH FINAL JUDGMENT WAS GIVEN: SCOTLAND, 1946-1972

	Annual averages							Total
1946–1950	...	...	...	...	...	...	...	2,429
1951–1955	...	...	...	...	...	...	...	2,307
1956–1960	...	...	...	...	...	...	...	1,840
1961–1965	...	...	...	...	...	...	...	2,310
1966–1970	...	...	...	...	...	...	...	4,196
1970	...	...	...	...	...	...	...	4,809
1971	...	...	...	...	...	...	...	5,041
1972	...	...	...	...	...	...	...	5,796

Source: Annual *Civil Judicial Statistics for Scotland*, HMSO.

Since the late 1950s, the number of divorces in England has quadrupled; in Scotland, in the same period, it has more than trebled. The pattern of increase has been similar in the two countries but the immediately precipitating influences have been different. The sharp rise in the number of divorces in England and Wales after 1970 is to be explained by the implementation of the Divorce Reform Act 1969.[1] The Succession (Scotland) Act 1964 resulted in a sharp rise in the number of divorces in Scotland: they doubled between 1963 and 1968.[2] Although the sheriff courts in Scotland are competent to deal with such actions relating to marriage as separation and aliment and adherence and aliment, which do not affect the status of spouses, these cannot realistically be compared with the matrimonial proceedings that come summarily before magistrates in England and Wales. Accordingly, we do not here print a table showing the number of such actions,[3] and we reserve our discussion for Part 4, Section 15, of this Report which examines those areas of family law in Scotland which are pertinent to our work. (See also the Memorandum from the Scottish Law Commission which appears at Appendix 6.)

3.39 Even when collapsing marriages leave an easily counted legal record, the statistics are hard to interpret. But many broken marriages never come into a court. The spouses concerned may part without formality, or they may make their own agreement or make one through a solicitor; but nobody knows in how many cases this happens. We may nevertheless guess that the effects of legal aid in widening access to the courts, of the greater acceptance of divorce as a socially respectable method of resolving intolerable marital situations, and of improvements in the status and occupational opportunities of married women, have all increased the likelihood that couples who cannot live together will resolve their difficulties by divorce.

---

[1] See Part 4, Section 3.
[2] See Part 4, Section 15.
[3] See Part 4, Section 15.

3.40 We now turn to consider some of the characteristics of the divorcing population revealed by the Registrar General's regular analyses of data derived from divorce petitions. Table 3.17 shows rates of divorce since 1961 for each 1,000 married women by the age of the wife at marriage and by the duration of the marriage.

TABLE 3.17

DISSOLUTIONS AND ANNULMENTS OF MARRIAGE MADE ABSOLUTE FOR EACH 1,000 MARRIED WOMEN, BY AGE OF WIFE AT MARRIAGE AND BY DURATION OF MARRIAGE: ENGLAND AND WALES, 1961, 1966 AND 1971

Age of wife at marriage	Year of dissolution	Duration of marriage (completed years)				
		3	4	5–9	10–14	15–19
Under 20	1961	3·7	9·9	9·1	6·7	4·4
	1966	5·9	16·0	14·2	9·9	7·5
	1971	11·0	26·3	23·2	17·0	12·1
20–24	1961	1·8	4·1	4·1	3·4	2·5
	1966	3·2	7·1	6·6	5·0	3·6
	1971	7·1	14·2	11·7	8·5	5·9
25–29	1961	1·3	3·7	3·2	2·4	1·9
	1966	2·1	5·1	4·3	3·1	2·4
	1971	4·2	9·7	7·5	5·3	3·8

Source: *Registrar General's Statistical Review of England and Wales for the Year* 1971, *Part II, Tables, Population*, Table P4.

Table 3.17 demonstrates, first, the extent to which young brides are at greater risk of divorce than older brides at all durations of marriage; secondly, that rates reach a peak for all ages of wife at marriage in the fourth year[1] of the marriage; and lastly, that the rates have increased steadily since 1961 for all ages and all durations although the increases have been higher for the younger age groups. Regrettably, similar data are not available for Scotland.

3.41 Table 3.18 shows the percentage of divorces occurring at different durations of marriage.

_____

[1] This is to be interpreted in the light of the fact that, save in exceptional circumstances, divorce is not possible until the marriage has lasted three years.

TABLE 3.18

PROPORTION OF DIVORCE DECREES MADE ABSOLUTE, BY DURATION OF MARRIAGE: ENGLAND AND WALES, 1957–1971

Percentage

Duration of marriage (completed years)	1957	1961	1969	1970	1971
0–4	11	11	13	14	13
5–9	31	31	33	33	30
10–14	21	23	21	21	19
15–19	16	14	13	13	13
20 and over	21	21	20	19	25
All durations	100	100	100	100	100

Source: *Registrar General's Statistical Reviews of England and Wales, Part II, Tables, Population*, Tables P4.

The above Table indicates a slight movement towards earlier divorce since 1957. Until 1961, some 42 per cent of divorces occurred within the first ten years of marriage, by 1970 this percentage had risen to 47 per cent. Conversely 37 per cent took place after fifteen years of marriage in 1957 and 32 per cent in 1970. Allowing for the fact that the divorces of 1971 probably contained an exceptionally high proportion of longer duration marriages as a result of the Divorce Reform Act 1969 (which came into operation at the beginning of 1971), the percentage of divorces in marriages which had lasted more than twenty years has remained remarkably stable at around one fifth. Scottish experience is set out in Table 3.19.

TABLE 3.19

PROPORTION OF DIVORCES IN WHICH FINAL JUDGMENT WAS GIVEN, BY DURATION OF MARRIAGE: SCOTLAND, 1957–1971

Percentage

Duration of marriage (completed years)	1957	1961	1969	1970	1971
0–4	13	18	19	21	20
5–9	29	32	31	31	32
10–14	21	18	21	21	21
15–19	17	13	13	13	12
20 and over	21	18	15	15	15
All durations	100	100	100	100	100

Source: *Annual Reports of the Registrar General for Scotland.*

There has been a slightly more marked movement towards earlier divorce in Scotland than has been the case in England and Wales. In 1957, 42 per cent of divorces in Scotland occurred within the first ten years of marriage; by 1971, this percentage had risen to 52 per cent. Conversely, the proportion of divorces taking place after fifteen years of marriage declined from 38 per cent in 1957 to 27 per cent in 1971.

3.42 The information displayed in Tables 3.17 and 3.18 is conveniently summarised in the Registrar General's computation, set out in Table 3.20 of the proportion of marriages which would be dissolved at different durations in England and Wales if the age at marriage divorce rates for particular years were maintained indefinitely.   A similar calculation is not available for Scotland.

TABLE 3.20

PROBABILITY OF DIVORCE WITHIN CERTAIN DURATIONS OF MARRIAGE FOR EACH 1,000 MARRIAGES: ENGLAND AND WALES, 1957–1971

Age of wife at marriage	Year of divorce	Duration of marriage (completed years)			
		5	10	15	20
Under 20	1957	13	53	82	99
	1961	14	58	89	109
	1966	22	88	131	157
	1971	37	140	210	247
20–24	1957	6	26	42	52
	1961	7	27	43	55
	1966	10	42	66	80
	1971	21	76	114	136
25–29	1957	5	20	32	38
	1961	6	22	33	43
	1966	8	29	43	53
	1971	14	51	76	90
All ages under 45	1957	7	28	45	55
	1961	8	31	49	60
	1966	13	52	78	92
	1971	24	88	130	153

Source: *Registrar General's Statistical Review of England and Wales for the Year* 1967, *Part II, Tables, Population,* Table C16, extended.

The above Table shows both a higher probability of divorce in all age groups and the greatest incidence among marriages contracted by young brides.   The rates of divorce experienced by teenage brides whose decrees were made absolute in 1957 were not reached by women marrying between the ages of 20 and 24 until they divorced after 1966, whilst the brides aged 25 to 29 did not reach similar rates until 1971.

3.43 The calendar year divorce rates which have so far been considered aggregate all divorces occurring in one year whatever the date of the marriage, and may therefore distort trends by reflecting fortuitous circumstances and

47

changes in the population at risk. The method of cohort analysis removes these disadvantages by presenting the experience of a group of people married in the same year or period in such a manner that different cohorts can be compared. Only in this way can the changing incidence of divorce be determined accurately. The first analysis of divorce by marriage cohorts was undertaken for England and Wales by Mr N H Carrier and Miss Griselda Rowntree in 1958.[1] Regrettably, the Registrar General has never provided such computations in his published reviews, but he has kindly prepared Table 3.21 for the Committee partly on the basis of revised unpublished data for which we are indebted to Mr Carrier, and partly by his own additional calculations.[2]

TABLE 3.21

PROPORTION OF COHORTS DIVORCED BY SPECIFIC ANNIVERSARIES OF MARRIAGE *PER* 1,000 COUPLES, BY AGE OF WIFE AND DATE OF MARRIAGE: ENGLAND AND WALES

Age of wife at marriage	Marriage cohort	Duration of marriage (completed years)				
		5	10	15	20	25
Under 20	1950–51	20	62	100	141	
	1955–56	14	70	127		
	1960–61	20	106			
	1965–66	33				
20–24	1950–51	8	28	47	67	
	1955–56	6	33	62		
	1960–61	10	49			
	1965–66	18				
All ages under 45	1935–36	1	10	42	51	69
	1940–41	3	41	63	76	88
	1945–46	10	37	55	72	90
	1950–51	8	30	52	74	
	1955–56	8	38	71		
	1960–61	12	59			
	1965–66	21				

Source: Registrar General, now published in *Social Trends*, Number 4, HMSO, 1973, Tables 6 and 7.

3.44 Table 3.21 shows the proportion of successive cohorts divorced by different durations of marriage. The experience of any one cohort can be examined by reading across the Table from the shorter to the longer durations. Thus, taking the all ages of brides under 45 (the great majority of brides) section of the Table, 6·9 per cent of those in this statistical model who were married

[1] It appeared in their pioneering article, 'The Resort to Divorce in England and Wales' in *Population Studies*, Volume XI, Number 3, 1958, pages 214–218.

[2] He comments that "figures below the . . . line have been computed . . . from published and unpublished statistics. It is well to note here that in order to calculate these figures considerable manipulation of the available statistics was necessary and methods used were not identical to those used by Carrier. Thus, small differences must be treated with extreme caution."

in 1935–1936, 8·8 per cent of those married in 1940–1941 and 9·0 per cent of those married in 1945–1946 had been divorced by the twenty-fifth anniversary of their wedding. The increased incidence of divorce emerges from a comparison between these and earlier cohorts. After twenty-five years, 1·97 per cent of the marriages of 1921–1922 and 4·5 per cent of those of 1929–1930 had ended in divorce.[1] Thus, the marriages which took place at the close of the second world war experienced four times as much divorce as those contracted in the aftermath of the first world war. Comparisons between different marriage cohorts can be made by reading down the columns of the Table. Thus, 2·0 per cent of teenage brides marrying in 1950–1951 and 3·3 per cent marrying in 1965–1966 were divorced within five years. Generally, the Table demonstrates the trend towards more and earlier divorce as well as the higher risks to which younger brides are exposed. It now seems well established that marriages between teenagers are at three times the risk of divorce and a husband over 20 whose wife is under 20 at the time of the marriage is at twice the risk experienced by all marriages.[2]

3.45 The evidence here assembled leaves no doubt that a higher proportion of marriages than in the past now terminates in divorce. We argue elsewhere that divorce is the method of resolving a permanent breakdown of marriage which normally best accords with the requirements of public morality. From this point of view, a rising divorce rate that was an accurate index of marriages which had irretrievably broken down should in itself cause no concern; if there be a misfortune, it is in the breakdown, not the divorce. But, of course, there are at present no reliable means of relating *de facto* and *de jure* breakdowns. The increasing incidence of divorce may merely reflect higher rates of transfer from the former to the latter category. On the other hand it may indicate a greater amount of breakdown. We cannot determine the issue on the basis of present knowledge, although the balance of probability may fall on the side of more breakdown.[3]

3.46 As we have not experienced a stable demographic situation in Britain in this century, it is impossible to predict when or at what level the rate of marriage breakdown will level out. A possible hint may be extracted from the experience of the United States shown in Table 3.22.

---

[1] Rowntree and Carrier: *op cit*, Table 10, page 216.

[2] *Report of the Committee on the Age of Majority*, Cmnd 3342, 1967, Appendix 8, page 198.

[3] There is a discussion by Robert Chester; 'Current incidence and trends in marital breakdown' in the *Postgraduate Medical Journal*, September 1972.

TABLE 3.22

MARRIAGES BY PREVIOUS MARITAL STATUS OF WHITE BRIDES AND GROOMS: UNITED STATES, 1967

Sex and previous marital status	Percentage distribution
Brides:	100
Single	75·9
Widowed	5·8
Divorced	18·2
Grooms:	100
Single	76·3
Widowed	4·7
Divorced	19·0

Source: *Marriages: Trends and Characteristics: United States*, US Department of Health, Education and Welfare, 1971, page 18.

The Table shows that nearly one quarter of the white brides and grooms in the United States in 1967 had been married before. Of these, 18 per cent of the brides and 19 per cent of the grooms had been divorced.

3.47 The Government Actuary has computed for the Committee a projection of the proportions of men who will have been married more than once in England and Wales up to the beginning of the next century.

TABLE 3.23

PROJECTION OF PROPORTIONS OF MARRIED MEN AGED 65 WHO WILL HAVE BEEN MARRIED MORE THAN ONCE: ENGLAND AND WALES, 1976–2001

Year	Percentage
1976	12
1981	13
1986	14
1991	15
1996	17
2001	20

The above proportions combine widowhood and divorce. Any estimate of future rates of breakdown for these reasons must be speculative but they increase, on this estimate, from 12 per cent in 1976 to one fifth at the turn of the century.

3.48 As the worst consequences of divorce are likely to fall upon dependent children, it is especially regrettable that the statistical data are very poor. Table 3.24 shows the proportion of divorces among childless marriages.

TABLE 3.24

DISSOLUTIONS AND ANNULMENTS OF MARRIAGE MADE ABSOLUTE FOR CHILDLESS MARRIAGES AS A PERCENTAGE OF ALL DIVORCES: ENGLAND AND WALES, 1957–1971

Percentage

Age of wife at marriage	1957	1961	1966	1971
Under 20	21	23	20	19
20–24	31	31	30	30
25–29	43	38	34	32
All ages	34	32	28	27

Source: *Registrar General's Statistical Reviews of England and Wales, Part II, Tables, Population*, derived from Tables P5(a).

The proportion of divorces in childless marriages has fallen for all age at marriage groups by substantial amounts over the past fourteen years. For example, in the all ages group the proportion has fallen by about 7 percentage points to a level of 27 per cent. Thus divorces with children have increased by a greater proportion than those without children. Furthermore, excluding childless marriages, more children are involved *per* divorce now than in the past; the average was 2·01 in 1961 and 2·16 in 1971. Although this average is calculated for all existing children in the family, it is likely that it reflects an increase for dependent children as well.

3.49   Data for Scotland are shown below, but they cannot be differentiated by the age of wife at marriage.

TABLE 3.25

DIVORCES FOR CHILDLESS MARRIAGES AS A PERCENTAGE OF ALL DIVORCES: SCOTLAND, 1957–1971

Year	Divorces for childless marriages as a percentage of all divorces
	%
1957	33
1961	31
1966	24
1971	26

Source: Scottish Home and Health Department.

3.50   In Scotland as in England and Wales, no children were involved in more than one quarter of all the divorces in 1971. Until that year children in England and Wales were defined as issue of the marriage and might therefore include adults. In his review for 1971, the Registrar General was able to publish for the first time a table[1] showing the age of children at the time of the

[1] *Registrar General's Statistical Review of England and Wales for the Year* 1971, *Part II, Tables, Population*, Table P5(b).

petition: 53,980 divorcing mothers had a total of 116,726 children of whom 70 per cent were under the age of 16. Of these children under 16 one quarter were under the age of 5, one half between 5 and 10 and one quarter between 11 and 16.

3.51 One important demographic factor associated with divorce in the recent past has been the high incidence of pre-marital conceptions among teenage brides. One commentator notes that in England and Wales " calculations based upon the *Registrar General's Statistical Review . . . for* 1969 show that some 36 per cent of . . . young brides were pregnant at the time of marriage compared with 11 per cent for wives aged 20 to 44."[1] Although the statistics are inadequate, it may be conjectured that in 1969 " half (49 per cent) of all births occurring within eight months of marriage—the total was some 73,000—were to wives aged under twenty at the time of their child's birth. Thus, today, half of all pre-maritally conceived legitimate maternities are to teenage brides."[2]

3.52 We conclude this Section of our demographic exposition by examining the high proportion of divorced persons who marry again and thus reduce the population of one-parent families. The experience of the decade 1962–1971 is set out in Table 3.26.

TABLE 3.26

DIVORCED PERSONS WHO ENTERED A SECOND MARRIAGE IN THE DECADE 1962–1971: ENGLAND AND WALES[3]

	Number	Percentage
		%
Decrees absolute: dissolutions and annulments	445,580	100
Divorced men remarrying	283,397	64
Divorced women remarrying	267,990	60
All divorced persons remarrying	551,387	62

Source: Annual *Abstract of Statistics*, HMSO.

About two thirds of all divorced persons married again but the proportion of women is slightly lower than that of men.

3.53 The falling age at divorce of men and women is shown in Table 3.27. The proportion of men in England and Wales divorcing under the age of 35 increased from 39 per cent to 48 per cent in the 1960s; in the same period, the proportion of women divorcing under the age of 35 increased from one half to 58 per cent. In Scotland, the decline in the age at divorce is more clearly marked. The proportion of men divorcing under the age of 35 increased

---

[1] Dr Colin Gibson. The quotations are taken from an unpublished paper delivered in 1972 to a conference of medical advisers. See also the same author's article, ' Social Trends in Divorce ' in *New Society*, 5 July 1973.

[2] *Ibid.*

[3] The number of divorces doubled between 1968 and 1971 as a result of the Divorce Reform Act 1969. Table 3.26 therefore understates the proportion of divorced persons who will enter a second marriage because a disproportionately large number of divorces (some 110,000) occurred in 1971.

from 49 per cent in 1961 to 57 per cent in 1969; the proportion of women of the same age divorcing increased in the same period from 59 per cent to 66 per cent.

TABLE 3.27

AGE AT TIME OF DIVORCE FOR HUSBANDS AND WIVES DIVORCING IN 1961, 1969 AND 1970: ENGLAND AND WALES AND SCOTLAND

Year	Age at divorce Husband:			Age at divorce Wife:			Total divorces
	under 35	35–44	all under 45	under 35	35–44	all under 45	
			Percentages				
A ENGLAND AND WALES							
1961	39	33	72	50	30	80	25,394
1969	48	29	76	58	24	82	51,310
1970	54	29	83	59	24	83	58,239
B SCOTLAND							
1961	49	30	79	59	25	85	1,624[1]
1969	57	26	83	66	23	88	3,911[1]
1970	58	26	84	67	22	89	4,270[1]

Source: For England and Wales: *Registrar General's Statistical Reviews of England and Wales for the Years 1961 and 1969, Part II, Tables, Population*, Tables P2; for Scotland: *Annual Reports of the Registrar General for Scotland.*

3.54 Age at the time of divorce influences the probability that divorced men and women will marry again, and the chances of another marriage are greater for the young. The Registrar General observes that "the marriage rates of divorced persons . . . demonstrates the pattern of marriage rates declining with increased age."[2] Therefore, such marriages have been taking place at earlier ages. Table 3.28 shows that the age of divorced men and women marrying again fell steadily between the mid-1950s and 1970.

[1] Persons both married and divorced in Scotland. The actual numbers of divorces in Scotland were 1,808 in 1961, 4,217 in 1969 and 4,591 in 1970.

[2] *Registrar General's Statistical Review of England and Wales for the Year 1964, Part III, Commentary*, page 27.

TABLE 3.28

AGE AT SECOND OR SUBSEQUENT MARRIAGE OF DIVORCED PERSONS BY YEAR OF NEW MARRIAGE FOR 1956–1971: ENGLAND AND WALES

Age at second marriage	Date of second marriage							
	1956–60	1961–65	1966	1967	1968	1969	1970	1971
	Cumulative percentages							
Men:								
under 35	33	37	41	41	44	45	46	43
under 45	69	71	73	73	74	75	76	71
under 50	83	82	84	84	85	86	86	81
Mean age (years)	40·6	40·0	39·2	39·2	38·7	38·6	38·2	39·8
	Cumulative percentages							
Women:								
under 35	46	50	52	54	55	58	59	57
under 45	80	80	80	81	81	82	83	80
under 50	90	89	90	90	90	91	91	89
Mean age (years)	37·1	36·8	36·2	36·0	35·7	35·4	35·0	35·7

Source: Calculations based upon the *Registrar General's Statistical Review of England and Wales for* 1971, *Part II, Tables, Population,* Tables K and L, pages 60–63.

71 per cent of the men and 80 per cent of the women who contracted a second marriage in 1971 were under the age of 45. These proportions have decreased slightly. Inevitably, given the changes in marriage age and frequency and the frequency of marriage breakdown, there has been an increase since the mid-1950s in the proportions of men and women under the age of 35 who marry again. The experience of Scotland has been similar.

3.55 One further factor is that the social class of the husband influences age at divorce as a result of its influence on age at marriage. A national random sample of petitioners for divorce in England and Wales, investigated by the Bedford College, University of London, Legal Research Unit, shows that the Registrar General's social classes I and II (professional and intermediate occupations) have a much older age at divorce distribution than that of the other classes. This is set out in Table 3.29.

TABLE 3.29

AGE OF HUSBANDS AND WIVES AT DIVORCE BY SOCIAL CLASS OF HUSBAND AT DIVORCE: ENGLAND AND WALES, 1961

| Age at divorce | Social class of husband | | | | | Total |
	I & II	III NM[1]	III M[1]	IV	V	
	Percentages					
(a) Wife:						
under 35	38	59	56	56	54	53
35 but						
under 45	28	27	25	24	25	26
45 and over	34	14	19	20	21	21
(b) Husband:						
under 35	28	46	42	43	45	41
35 but						
under 45	35	32	32	31	27	32
45 and over	37	22	26	26	28	27
(100%) Total number in (a) and (b)	103	110	219	96	66	593

Source: Bedford College Legal Research Unit.

One third of the divorcing wives in classes I and II were at least 45 years old at the time of divorce compared with one fifth of the same age who were married to manual workers in classes IV and V. There is a very similar age at divorce distribution among both wives and husbands in the three manual classes. Class III non-manual experienced divorce at the youngest ages, with 59 per cent of the wives under 35 and 78 per cent of the husbands under 45. The age at divorce of the white collar class III was much more in line with that of the manual workers than with that of classes I and II. Thus, husbands and wives in the manual classes divorce at earlier ages than those in the higher income groups represented by classes I and II.

---

[1] NM = non-manual and M = manual.

3.56 The rates of second or subsequent marriage for divorced men and women of different ages in England and Wales and in Scotland are set out in Table 3.30.

TABLE 3.30

RATES OF SECOND OR SUBSEQUENT MARRIAGES OF DIVORCED PERSONS IN EACH AGE GROUP FOR EVERY 1,000 DIVORCED MEN AND WOMEN IN THE SAME AGE GROUP

A ENGLAND AND WALES

| Year | Age group at remarriage | | | | | All ages |
	25–29	30–34	35–44	45–54	55 and over	
Men: 1961	474	348	197	112	58	162
1964	511	364	210	110	56	172
1968	552	375	224	118	53	187
1969	529	346	214	115	54	183
1970	507	347	222	117	54	189
Women: 1961	405	249	111	52	17	96
1964	398	253	121	53	16	104
1968	391	230	131	60	16	112
1969	368	216	118	58	15	108
1970	384	218	124	59	15	115

Source: *Registrar General's Statistical Review of England and Wales for the Year* 1970, *Part II, Tables, Population*, Table H 2, page 56.

B SCOTLAND

| Year | Age group at remarriage | | | | | All ages |
	25–29	30–34	35–44	45–54	55 and over	
Men: 1961	587	399	213	103	46	170
1964	334	309	217	103	50	170
1968	470	431	242	125	44	210
1969	444	361	214	111	48	180
1970	435	317	187	106	36	175
1971	446	376	217	99	38	190
1972	353	309	197	87	21	142
Women: 1961	383	183	96	43	10	88
1964	307	235	89	49	9	93
1968	310	240	120	54	12	112
1969	284	230	124	46	13	114
1970	305	197	118	46	14	111
1971	284	190	100	49	12	109
1972	261	193	110	52	13	110

Source: *Annual Reports of the Registrar General for Scotland.*

The Registrar General for England and Wales notes that the rate for men aged 25–29 in 1964 " indicates an average interval between divorce and remarriage of less than a year."[1] He goes on to comment on the 1964 rates shown in Table 3.30: " The rates of 364 *per* 1,000 for men aged 30–34 and 398 *per* 1,000 for women aged 26–29 both imply an average interval between divorce and remarriage of well under 2 years." These high rates point to an average interval between the time of divorce and entering a second marriage of under four years for divorced men under the age of 45 and divorced women under the age of 35.[2] The rates decline rapidly up to the age of 35, and then move more slowly. Thus for some two thirds of all divorcing couples, divorce is a temporary condition between the dissolution of one marriage and the next attempt. This conclusion applies similarly to Scotland. A comparison between the Scottish and English rates would seem to indicate that the average interval between divorce and remarriage is probably slightly longer. A special study of a sample of divorces recorded in Scotland in 1969 suggests that around one quarter of divorced persons (26 per cent of men and 23 per cent of women) married again within twelve months of divorce.[3] Of these, some three quarters had married within six months of divorce.

3.57 As maintenance after divorce in England and Wales now ceases upon remarriage, it must serve many younger divorced women as bridging finance which will see them through until the next husband takes over. Of course, the exchange of partners may not dovetail neatly, and the new husband may find himself still paying maintenance to his divorced wife and her children. If this occurs, it will precipitate a serious situation because most divorced men earn only manual workers' wages. But, by and large, the stringencies, though acute while they last, are likely to be short-lived because between two thirds and three quarters of the men and women who lose partners acquire new ones. In the younger age groups, the waiting phase is short. Middle and upper class women come to divorce at later ages than their lower class sisters and therefore enjoy poorer chances of finding new husbands.

3.58 There are no national data for England and Wales or Scotland which enable the ages of mothers and their dependent children to be related to their chance of marrying again after divorce. But Table 3.31 presents information about the age of divorced wives and the number of their dependent children in 1961 which emerges from a study by the Bedford College Legal Research Unit.

---

[1] *Registrar General's Statistical Review of England and Wales for the Year* 1964, *Part III, Commentary*, page 28.

[2] *Ibid.*

[3] ' Divorce in Scotland—A Special Study of Divorces in 1969 ' in the *Annual Report of the Registrar General for Scotland*, 1971, *Part II, Population and Vital Statistics*, Section X, page 33 and Table H.

TABLE 3.31

AGE OF WIFE AT DIVORCE BY THE NUMBER OF DEPENDENT CHILDREN AS A PERCENTAGE OF ALL DIVORCES IN 1961: ENGLAND AND WALES

Age of wife at divorce	Number of dependent children				Total wives with children under 15	Total wives with no dependent children	All wives
	1	2	3	4 or more			
	Percentages						
Under 40	21·6	12·6	5·0	2·1	41·3	23·9	65·2
40 and over	7·8	2·4	0·7	0·4	11·3	23·5	34·8
All wives	29·4	15·0	5·7	2·5	52·6	47·4	100·0
					Total number of wives		719

Source: Bedford College Legal Research Unit.

Table 3.31 shows that only 8 per cent of all wives had at the time of their divorce three or more dependent children and that almost half had no children at all.

3.59 Table 3.32 presents another aspect of the situation displayed in Table 3.31.

TABLE 3.32

DIVORCED WIVES IN EACH AGE GROUP WITH DEPENDENT CHILDREN AS A PROPORTION OF ALL WIVES IN THAT GROUP: ENGLAND AND WALES

Age of wife at divorce	Number of dependent children				Total wives with children under 15	Total wives with no dependent children	All wives
	1	2	3	4 or more			
	Percentages						
Under 40	33·0	19·4	7·8	3·2	63·3	36·7	100 (469)
40 and over	22·4	6·8	2·0	1·2	32·4	67·6	100 (250)
					Total number of divorced wives		719

Source: Bedford College Legal Research Unit.

Only one in ten of the older wives had two or more dependent children compared with almost one third of those under 40 with the same number of children. Over one third of the wives under 40 had no dependent children, compared with over two thirds of the over-forties with no dependent children.

58

One indication of the effect of dependent children upon a mother's chances of marrying again is provided by Table 3.33 which compares the remarriage rates of widowed mothers with those applying to all widows.

TABLE 3.33

REMARRIAGE RATES OF WIDOWS: GREAT BRITAIN, 1968–1970

Age at remarriage	Widowed mothers	All widows
	(Annual rates expressed as a percentage)	
	%	%
25–29	12	15
30–34	7	10
35–39	5	8
40–44	4	5
45–49	3	4
50–54	1·5	2·0
55–59	0·7	1·0

Source: Government Actuary's Department.

The Table shows that widows with children are less likely to marry again than are other widows. It would be surprising if what is true for widows were not also true for divorced women. An indication of the effect of different numbers of dependent children upon the likelihood that a divorced woman will marry again is provided by the special study of divorces recorded in 1969, undertaken by the Registrar General for Scotland, to which we have already referred.[1] Table 3.34 tabulates the subsequent marriages, within twelve months of divorce, of a sample of men and women divorcing in 1969 in Scotland by the number of dependent children of the marriage. The Table also compares the actual number of subsequent marriages with those which would have been expected on the distribution of the sub-sample by number of children.

TABLE 3.34

REMARRIAGE BY PARTY AND NUMBER OF CHILDREN: SCOTLAND

Number of children	Sample cases*	Man remarrying		Woman remarrying	
		Number	Expected frequencies	Number	Expected frequencies
0	174	46	44·7	48	39·2
1	159	45	40·8	37	35·8
2	99	23	25·4	15	22·3
3	49	13	12·6	11	11·0
4 or more	25	3	6·4	3	5·6
Total	506	130	129·9	114	113·9

* 12½ per cent sample of divorcing population in 1969.
Source: 'Divorce in Scotland—A Special Study of Divorces in 1969,' *op cit*, Table F.

[1] Paragraph 3.56 above.

The Registrar General for Scotland comments on Table 3.34 that:

it will be seen that the distribution of men remarrying follows the expected fairly closely indicating that the number of children in his previous marriage has little effect upon remarriage. Whilst the female distribution differs only a little from the expected, the figures do seem to indicate that the woman's chance of remarriage is greater, the fewer children she has, and considerably greater when she has no children at all.[1]

SECTION 4—ILLEGITIMACY

3.60 In this Section we deal separately with illegitimacy as a source of one-parent families because it is more convenient to distinguish between actual marriages which collapse and those which never take place. Moreover, statistics of illegitimacy are extremely difficult to interpret. Very puzzling differences have existed between the rates experienced by different countries in the same periods and those experienced within the same country at different times. No convincing explanation has yet been offered for the change in England since the middle of the nineteen-thirties from 5·5 illegitimate births for each 1,000 unmarried women aged 15 to 44 to 19·1 for each 1,000 in the years 1961–1965, and none is likely to be forthcoming. Accordingly we make no attempt to provide a social or moral commentary upon the statistics.

3.61 In 1950 the number of illegitimate births in England and Wales was rather more than 35,000; in 1960 it was nearly 43,000; and it approached 66,000 in 1971 after a peak of almost 70,000 in 1967. Table 3.35 shows illegitimate births as a proportion of all births.

TABLE 3.35

ILLEGITIMATE BIRTHS AS A PROPORTION OF ALL LIVE BIRTHS: ENGLAND AND WALES AND SCOTLAND, 1950–1972

Percentage

Year	England and Wales	Scotland
1950	5·1	5·2
1955	4·7	4·3
1960	5·4	4·4
1965	7·7	5·8
1970	8·3	7·7
1971	8·4	8·1
1972	8·6	8·5

Source: *Registrar General's Statistical Review of England and Wales for 1971, Part II, Tables, Population*, Table D1; *Annual Report of the Registrar General for Scotland for 1972, Part 2, Population and Vital Statistics*, Table P 1.2.

3.62 Teenage promiscuity has often been blamed for the rise in the number of illegitimate births since the end of the second world war. Young women

1 *Op cit*, page 34.

undoubtedly contribute substantially to the absolute number of illegitimate births; but then they constitute most of the unmarried women of reproductive age in the population. The Registrar General observes that:

> it remains clear that extra-marital conception is not specifically a teenage problem; the probability that an unmarried woman will conceive in the course of a year is one in thirty-four if she is under 20, rises to a peak of one in fifteen if she is 20–24, falls to one in twenty if she is 25–29 and to one in forty-five if she is 30–39.[1]

Many of the babies born illegitimate do not become members of one-parent families. In the first place, an investigation of 1961 census data by the Registrar General has shown that " nearly one illegitimate child in three may be born to a married woman, or, at least, to a woman who would describe herself as married in a census."[2] Some of these births will be to unmarried parents living in a stable union.[3] Secondly, some women with an illegitimate child or children will marry, but this possibility cannot be measured directly. Thirdly, some illegitimate children will be adopted. There are no statistics showing the number of children placed for adoption by their mothers, but Table 3.36 gives the figures for illegitimate children adopted into two-parent families.

TABLE 3.36
ADOPTION OF ILLEGITIMATE CHILDREN INTO TWO-PARENT FAMILIES: ENGLAND AND WALES AND SCOTLAND

Period	Average number of adoptions each year	
	England and Wales	Scotland[4]
1951–55	10,244	
1956–60	10,925	
1961–65	14,742	
1966	17,713	1,809
1967	18,107	1,885
1968	19,120	1,889
1969	17,696	1,939
1970	15,765	1,701
1971	14,777	1,595

Source: *Registrar General's Statistical Reviews of England and Wales, Part II, Tables, Population,* Tables T5; *Annual Reports of the Registrar General for Scotland.*

The number of adoptions has fluctuated considerably during the last two decades. A steady quantity of adoptions in the 1950s was followed by a sharp rise in the 1960s to a peak in 1968 from which there has been a decline. But the figures suggest that 1 illegitimate child in every 3 in England and Wales

[1] *Registrar General's Statistical Review of England and Wales for the Year* 1964, *Part III, Commentary,* page 67.

[2] *Ibid,* page 64.

[3] Independent studies provide some confirmation. For example, Barbara Thompson: ' Social Study of Illegitimate Maternity ' in the *British Journal of Preventive and Social Medicine,* Volume 10, 1956, found in a study of illegitimate births in Aberdeen that only 49 per cent were first births to single women. Of the remainder, at least one third were to women living in a stable illicit union with the father.

[4] Statistics of the adoption of illegitimate children into two-parent families were not kept in Scotland before 1962.

was adopted in the 1950s, about 1 in 3·7 in the late 1960s and 1 in 4·4 in 1971. In Scotland, 1 illegitimate child in 3·5 was adopted in the late 1960s and 1 in 4·4 in 1971.

3.63 Finally, the number of children born illegitimate is subsequently reduced by the procedure of legitimation. The annual total of births re-registered as legitimate almost doubled between 1960 and 1966. Since that date, it has fluctuated around 12,000 a year. We conclude that a significant proportion of the 66,000 or so children born illegitimate in 1971 in fact became members of two-parent families. The number of children who remain dependent upon their unmarried mothers is a small proportion of the total. Nevertheless, the absolute numbers of children in this position at any one time will be very large. The census estimates of 1971, revised by the Department of Health and Social Security and printed in Appendix 4, suggest that some 90,000 unmarried lone mothers in Britain had the responsibility for 120,000 children under the age of 16.

SECTION 5—SUMMARY

3.64 An analysis of official sources of information by the Department of Health and Social Security suggests that, at any given time, nearly one tenth of all families with dependent children have only one parent by reason of death, divorce, separation or births outside marriage. In round numbers, our terms of reference required us to examine problems peculiar to nearly two thirds of a million mothers and fathers, though mostly to mothers, who are looking after one million children single-handed. The largest group of mothers and children consists of married women living apart from their husbands. They are followed by the divorced and widowed who make up groups of similar size, whilst unmarried mothers and their offspring are by far the smallest contingent.

3.65 Marriage breakdown is as inescapable a fact of life today as it was in the later middle ages. The stability of the family as the institution which regulates sexual relations, provides for the rearing and socialisation of the young, and secures the transmission of property, depends in part upon a machinery which enables spouses whose marriages have failed to establish new unions. One-parent families are therefore not things apart: they are an integral product of the normal working of the institution of marriage. Accordingly, the quantitative definition of our terms of reference must begin with marriage and not with breakdown.

3.66 There has been a silent revolution in marriage habits in Britain in the last two generations. In the past, a significant proportion of women could never marry because the large-scale emigration or wartime slaughter of men reduced the number of potential husbands. Since the end of the second world war, the long persistent surplus of women in the marriageable age groups has disappeared; there are now more bachelors than spinsters; and women have acquired equality of opportunity to marry. The proportion of the population which marries has increased to the point at which marriage has become a universal institution which working class boys and girls enter at very young ages and will therefore experience for long durations. More and earlier marriage has not resulted in a return to the large family of Victorian days. There has been a sharp reduction in childlessness; there are fewer only children; and there has been a shift to families with two and three children. Fertility has been compressed so that three quarters of all children are born within eight years of their mother's wedding. This control over the exercise of reproductive power was not in origin dependent upon the use of contraceptives, although changes in fertility have been associated with the spread of birth control which is now practised by almost all married women, many of whom still use primitive or unreliable methods.

3.67 These changes have given women a new life. In the past, motherhood was the whole life of most women. Today, mothers have more than half their active adult lives to lead after their youngest child has reached school leaving age. One result has been a transformation in the character and age structure of the female labour force upon which the economy has been dependent for cheap labour ever since industrialisation. On the eve of the second world war, the representative woman worker was young and single, doing a job between leaving school and getting married. Now, she is married, over 35 and with a grown up family.

3.68 The pattern of marriage breakdown reflects both demographic developments and wider social changes. In the earlier part of this century, death broke more marriages in the younger age groups than divorce. The decline in mortality and the growth of equality before the law have reversed the position. The fourfold increase in divorce, from some 27,000 petitions annually in the late 1950s to 110,000 odd in 1972, is hard to interpret because there are no means of judging what proportion represents a transfer from the category of de facto to de jure marriage breakdown and what proportion an increased propensity to divorce. The only other form of marriage breakdown which leaves a legal record consists of matrimonial proceedings before magistrates. This jurisdiction has retained its vitality unimpaired during the last twenty years. It is thought that in half of the 30,000 or so cases before the magistrates every year, petitions for divorce are later presented whilst many of the remainder represent permanently broken marriages.

3.69 The evidence shows that a higher proportion of marriages than in the past now terminate in divorce, and it is well established that young brides are at much higher risk than their older sisters. This is associated with the high incidence of pre-marital conceptions among young brides. There is very little information about the children of divorcing parents.

3.70 More and younger marriage results in more and younger one-parent families with larger numbers of young children. Any estimate of future rates of marriage breakdown from all causes must be highly speculative but they are likely to lie between a minimum of 15 per cent and a maximum of one quarter.

3.71 A large number of one-parent families resulting from divorce survive as such for relatively short periods because they are reconstituted as two-parent families by second marriages. Between two thirds and three quarters of divorced persons marry again. The younger the spouse at the time of divorce the greater the speed and likelihood of another marriage.

3.72 The 66,000 or so children born illegitimate in 1971 will not all become members of one-parent families. Some are born to women living in stable unions, and the mothers of others will marry. Finally, some illegitimate children will be legitimated, and some will be adopted. Thus, the number who remain dependent upon their lone, unmarried mothers is a small proportion of the total.

PART 4—FAMILY LAW, SOCIAL SECURITY AND ONE-PARENT FAMILIES

SECTION 1—THE FUNCTION, METHOD AND CONTENTS OF PART 4

4.1 The family is the basic institution which prescribes the conditions for sexual relationships, childbearing and child rearing, and ensures, in the course of socialising the young, the transmission of ethical and cultural values across the generations. It is the unit within which most men and women find themselves best able to satisfy not only their sexual needs, but also the psychic needs for sympathy, mutual aid and intimacy. The family is not the product of the law, which is powerless to insist that the members of a family shall display towards each other the sentiments which the creation and preservation of their group require. But the law can, and everywhere does, fix the secondary—that is to say, all other than the natural or sentient—terms upon which a family, whether in or outside marriage, comes into being, functions and dissolves. It is the law which determines who may marry and how they shall marry; prescribes and enforces the web of rights and obligations, both as to person and property, deriving from the status and relationships of spouses, parents and children; fixes or controls their claims for physical and economic protection; and deals with the failure to meet such claims. In all this, the first and dominant purpose of the law is to uphold the family. The essential background to most of what our terms of reference require us to consider is family law, regarded not merely as a set of rules for dealing with broken marital earthenware, but as the law which fortifies and regulates an institution central to society, which still in most cases is dissolved only by death.

4.2 It is, however, inevitable that some part of an investigation into the condition of one-parent families should concern itself with the law of family breakdown. We refer here to the rules and agencies which exist to deal with the fact and the consequences of the overt collapse of a marriage or the assumption of parenthood outside marriage. This is the pathology of family law, which affects all one-parent families coming into being otherwise than through the death of a parent. The subject includes the description of the categories of marital and sexual behaviour which may attract legal intervention; the nature and ambit of the obligation of spouses and parents to maintain each other and their children; the structure and jurisdiction of matrimonial courts; their practice; the kinds of orders which they make; and the methods of enforcing their orders. The spirit, structure and fitness to the times of these branches of the law and its administration, their quality and their shortcomings, are all matters of the first importance to one-parent families. This Part of our Report is directed to these matters.

4.3 The provision made for family breakdown affects, of course, single spouses who have no responsibility for a child (for example, a divorced or separated wife who is childless, or whose children have grown up) as well as one-parent families. It is not possible to examine the situation of one-parent families within the law without at the same time reaching conclusions that are relevant to the situation of dependent women on their own. It follows that our discussion and recommendations will often cover both situations, not as the result of an excursion beyond our terms of reference, but because there are areas of automatic coincidence in the effect of the law upon the two categories, and in the benefits they would gain from reform.

4.4 We have had to grapple with difficult problems of presentation. Some account of these is desirable, since it will help to explain points of substance as well as of organisation.

4.5 The main conclusions and recommendations of this Part derive essentially from the circumstance that one-parent families are the subject not of a single system, but of no fewer than three systems, of family law. The lack of integration, both substantive and procedural, of these systems is one major cause of the hardships from which many one-parent families suffer. The three systems are administered respectively by the divorce courts, the magistrates' courts and the supplementary benefits authorities. The first system stems from the matrimonial jurisdiction formerly exercised by the ecclesiastical courts, and the parliamentary procedure of granting divorce by private Act. These facilities in combination disposed, more or less satisfactorily, of the marital problems of the wealthy and powerful. The second system originated in a statutory extension of the summary procedure for trying petty crime, intended deliberately to create a special jurisdiction for the protection of working class wives. The third system stretches back to the provision which the poor law made for the dependent poor: it is a system which survived intact until quite recently, and survives in part to this day. The lack of co-ordination between the three systems produces, as we intend to demonstrate, some most undesirable consequences both for the individuals directly affected and for society as a whole. The remedies which we propose include a revision of the matrimonial jurisdiction now exercised in magistrates' courts, and of the arrangements governing financial provision for the victims of family breakdown. This will involve an exploration in detail of the relation between the obligation upon members of a family to support each other and the rights of citizens without resources to support by the State.

4.6 This brief preview will convey a notion of the complexity of the materials it has been necessary to study and evaluate for the purposes of this Part, and of the resulting problems of exposition. In the first place, no proper understanding of the subject can be achieved except through a long historical perspective. Partly this is because in dealing with family responsibilities and family law we quickly arrive at the roots of institutions and attitudes. More particularly, it is because the present situation is a resultant of the uneven rate and mode of response of what we have called " the three systems " to profound changes in the areas of life which they are intended to regulate. As no secondary account of this history or its dynamics existed, two of our members wrote one. The problem then was whether to set out the whole of the history in the Report. We decided to divide the material between the two periods before and after 1945, and to put the account of the earlier period in an Appendix (Appendix 5), while summarising it in the Report (Section 2 below). This division, however, is more arbitrary than logical, and reference to the earlier period remains necessary not only as an introduction to this present Part, but also for a perspective on Part 5, which contains our recommendations for a new one-parent family social security benefit.

4.7 We have had to include in our discussion a good deal of purely expository or descriptive material such as may be found in legal textbooks or law reports. Its inclusion was necessary to give sense and continuity to the explanation of the matters in hand. On the other hand, no textbook contained the information we required to enable us to make an assessment, based so far as possible on fact and measurement, of the numbers and characteristics of the population which resorts to the magistrates' jurisdiction and of the social consequences of the exercise of that jurisdiction, particularly in its connection with the supplementary benefits administration. We were able to make use of a few existing studies in these areas, but we also commissioned further research which was carried out by the Legal Research Unit, Department of Sociology, at Bedford College, University of London. The results of this special research are of great importance for our conclusions, and again gave rise to a problem of presentation. We decided to summarise the findings at an appropriate place in the Report (Section 6, paragraphs 4.91–4.101), but to reproduce the full version of the study as Appendix 7. To this extent, the Report generalises, but the Appendix contains the facts in justification.

4.8 Scotland is included in our terms of reference. Scots family law and the structure and procedure of the courts which administer it are different from the English system, and there are consequential effects on the relation in Scotland between the courts and the supplementary benefits authorities. These differences have not attracted comparative studies. The Scottish Law Commission specially wrote for us a paper outlining some relevant aspects of Scots law, which we found most valuable.[1] For the rest, however, we were compelled to make our own investigations in Scotland based—since the time and resources at our disposal did not permit research—on the very limited secondary sources that are available and on discussions with interested individuals and representatives of organisations. Our account of this part of the Committee's work and our conclusions regarding Scotland appear in Section 15 below.

SECTION 2—THE THREE SYSTEMS OF FAMILY LAW: HISTORICAL SUMMARY

4.9 This Section consists essentially of an abstract of the story which is told in detail in Appendix 5. It sets out the three systems of family law which have emerged from the ecclesiastical courts, from the criminal jurisdiction of the magistrates and from the poor law.

4.10 Although there is some evidence that divorce was permissible in early English law, by the twelfth century the ecclesiastical courts had gained control over this branch of the law. The Church held marriage to be a sacrament and to be indissoluble. In the case of a validly contracted and consummated marriage, the ecclesiastical courts might grant a decree of divorce *a mensa et thoro*, but this was only in the nature of a separation. The parties remained married. The problems thus created for men of property in attending to their dynastic needs were eased by the proliferation of the grounds upon which these same courts were prepared to find that there had been no valid marriage contracted in the first instance, and so to pronounce a decree of nullity. Following the Reformation, the ecclesiastical courts, which retained sole jurisdiction in matrimonial causes, cut down the excesses of the canon law of nullity. At the same time, they continued to insist on the indissolubility of a

---

[1] The Scottish Law Commission have permitted us to publish this paper as Appendix 6, where it provides a source of information which is otherwise surprisingly difficult to obtain. We stress, however, that the Scottish Law Commission has not been concerned with any other material or conclusions regarding Scotland contained in this Report.

true marriage, in regard to which they were prepared, in appropriate circumstances, to grant the spouses a legal separation, but no more. Men of property who had need of a full divorce accordingly had to look to other methods. They found one by resorting to the sovereign power of Parliament. Thus in, say, 1850, the legal scene concerning matrimonial relief presented the following appearance. The ordinary civil courts had no jurisdiction at all. The ecclesiastical courts, at an expense which put the jurisdiction out of the reach of nearly everyone, granted separations, nullities, and certain other sophisticated reliefs such as decrees for the restitution of conjugal rights (enforceable until 1813 by excommunication and thereafter until 1844 by imprisonment), but never dissolution of marriage. An undefended separation would ordinarily cost £300 to £500 in money of those times. Dissolution of a valid marriage was obtainable only by private Act of Parliament. The costs of a private Act were enormous—not less than £700, but rising to many times that amount if it was disputed. Only 317 such Acts were passed down to 1857, about one quarter of them in the immediately preceding twenty years.

4.11 Looking again at the scene in 1850, this time to observe the legal effect of marriage on rights of property and maintenance, one finds that in common law the husband took ownership or possession of virtually the whole of his wife's property, whether she brought it into the marriage or acquired it afterwards. In theory, he was bound to support his wife, but the courts provided no remedy she could enforce against her husband for breach of that obligation. At best, she might pledge his credit to purchase necessaries for herself and their children. This was the legal regime which governed the condition of the vast majority of all married women in England, created, oddly enough, when the bridegroom said, " With all my worldly goods I thee endow." It was mitigated only among the propertied classes, for whom their lawyers invented, and the courts of Chancery enforced, modes of settling property on a married woman for her separate use in such a manner that no one, herself included, could alienate the capital or future income, and so that it reverted to the wife's kin if her marriage proved childless. In pronouncing a decree of separation, the ecclesiastical courts might order the husband to pay alimony to an innocent wife, calculated as a proportion of his income, or if the wife had separate estate, the joint incomes. But there were no ready means of enforcing such an order if it were disobeyed. Of greater importance, not for the numbers of people it affected, but as setting a precedent for later developments, was the parliamentary practice, when granting a private Act of divorce, always to insist upon at least some financial provision being made for the wife. This provision differed from alimony, firstly, in that Parliament insisted upon it irrespective of the matrimonial misconduct of the wife; and, secondly, in that it could always be enforced against security which the husband had to make available for that purpose.

4.12 In 1850, the first Royal Commission on Divorce (the Campbell Commission) was appointed to enquire into the state of the law which, as was widely recognised at the time, denied matrimonial relief to all but the wealthiest. The report of the commission led to the Matrimonial Causes Act 1857, which transferred to a newly established civil court of law, the Court for Divorce and Matrimonial Causes, the jurisdiction already being respectively exercised by the ecclesiastical courts and by Parliament. The Act of 1857 did not aim to change

67

the existing law, but rather to secularise and democratise its administration. Divorce, legal separation and nullity thus became the subject of ordinary legal process. The new court, after an initial period of uncertainty, adopted the principles of its predecessors in awarding maintenance, so that a guilty wife, as under the former parliamentary practice, would still be granted some maintenance, while an innocent wife, as under the former ecclesiastical practice, would be granted a proportion, generally one third of the joint incomes, and an additional amount in respect of any children of whom she was given the custody. But the new civil jurisdiction remained entirely based in London. It was still very expensive. It continued to discriminate, as had its predecessors, between the sexes by making divorces available to husbands on grounds that were insufficient to entitle their wives to a decree. Up until 1900, there was no year in which more than 583 divorces (in 1897) and 57 judicial separations (in 1880) were granted.

4.13 Thus, the reforms of 1857 did nothing for the matrimonial ills of the poor. When their turn came, in 1878, the provision made was by way of an extension of the criminal law, aimed at wife-beating. The Matrimonial Causes Act 1878 provided that, when the magistrates convicted a husband of aggravated assault on his wife, they could grant her a separation order, with maintenance and the custody of the children under the age of 10. Subsequently, by a long series of statutes (ending only with the Matrimonial Proceedings (Magistrates' Courts) Act 1960) the jurisdiction was progressively enlarged and adjusted. The grounds upon which a wife could obtain an order were extended to cover a whole variety of misconduct in addition to assault; for example, desertion, habitual drunkenness and wilful neglect to maintain. The husband became entitled to apply for an order against his wife on grounds which have now become nearly reciprocal under the Act of 1960. Certain maxima were fixed on the amounts of the maintenance which magistrates could order, either in favour of a spouse or a child. These limits were not abolished until the Maintenance Orders Act 1968.

4.14 Meantime, over most of this period, no fundamental change took place in the divorce jurisdiction. The jurisdiction of the Court for Divorce and Matrimonial Causes was transferred to the Probate, Divorce and Admiralty Division of the High Court in 1873, but this did not affect the substantive law. Proof of a matrimonial offence remained essential, and the principal grounds remained discriminatory as between the sexes. It was not until the Matrimonial Causes Act 1923 (Lord Buckmaster's Act) that a wife, like her husband, became entitled to a divorce on proof of simple adultery.

4.15 Thus, for nearly a century, two different systems of matrimonial law have been administered by courts in England. Long acquaintance with this duality may blunt the power to recognise its peculiarities. We repeat here a passage from Appendix 5:

First, two separate jurisdictions, High Court and summary, existing side by side, but administering different and overlapping rules and remedies, came into being for the purpose of dealing with the same human predicament. Secondly, while the reforms of 1857 were designed to remove matrimonial disputes to the arbitrament of a superior and civil court of record, the jurisdiction created in 1878 was vested in inferior tribunals, given over to the criminal process, and universally known, because of their close association with the police, as "police courts." Thirdly, whereas the 1857 reformers regarded legal intervention into matrimony, maintenance and the custody of children as so delicate and important that the jurisdiction had to be entrusted to professional judges of the highest rank, the 1878 jurisdiction was to be exercised by a magistracy overwhelmingly lay in its composition. Finally, the concern for extending to a larger population the benefits which the 1857 reforms had afforded to the wealthy bore fruit in the creation of a secondary system designed for what were considered to be the special and cruder requirements of the poor.[1]

4.16 These peculiarities did not go unnoticed. When the second Royal Commission on Divorce and Matrimonial Causes (the Gorell Commission) was appointed in 1909 to enquire into the state of the matrimonial law, their terms of reference specifically added " especially with regard to the poorer classes in relation thereto ". By this time, while the High Court was dealing with about 800 petitions a year for divorce and judicial separation, the magistrates (who had made more than 87,000 separation orders between 1897 and 1906) were dealing with some 15,000 applications a year for matrimonial orders. The report of the Gorell Commission made an assault on practically every aspect of the magistrates' jurisdiction. It objected to a court whose main duties lay in crime dealing with the domestic relations of men and women and their children. It found the practical details of administration by the lay magistrates to be unsatisfactory. Above all, it deplored the encouragement which the jurisdiction gave to spouses to live in a state of permanent separation, promoting as this did adulterous connections and illegitimate children. The Gorell Commission would have abolished the matrimonial jurisdiction of the magistrates altogether, but felt inhibited from so recommending because it provided " the only remedy within the reach of the very poor", and a remedy for Roman Catholics and persons disapproving of divorce. Their recommendation therefore took the following form:

> We consider that the power of courts of summary jurisdiction to make orders which have the permanent effect of a decree or judicial separation should be abolished . . . . The proper principle to apply to such courts is that their orders should only be granted where they are necessary for the reasonable immediate protection of the wife or husband, or the support of the wife and the children with her, and that if it is or becomes necessary for the parties to be permanently separated, application for that purpose should be made to the superior court . . . . For the reasons we have given, we are of opinion that no separation order of such (summary) courts should be continued for a period of more than two years from the date of the original order separating the parties, at the expiration of which time the order . . . should determine, unless, before such expiration, the party obtaining the original order apply to the High Court to deal further with the matter.[2]

4.17 The Gorell Commission made a number of recommendations relating to the divorce jurisdiction as such which were ultimately, if belatedly, implemented. These were that the two sexes should be placed on an equal footing as regards the grounds on which divorce might be obtained (implemented, as noted above, in 1923); that the grounds for divorce should be extended to include, *inter alia*, desertion for three years and upwards, cruelty, and incurable insanity (implemented by the Matrimonial Causes Act 1937—Herbert's Act); and that the administration of the divorce jurisdiction be centralised, so that the High Court could sit locally in divorce, for the benefit, in particular, of people of small means (effectively implemented after the Reports of the Com-

---

[1] Appendix 5, paragraph 36.
[2] Quoted more fully in Appendix 5, paragraph 46.

mittee on Procedure in Matrimonial Causes in 1946). But there has been no legislative response to the criticisms which the Gorell Report, more than sixty years ago, made of the summary matrimonial jurisdiction. After that lapse of time, we found ourselves traversing the same ground and we have concluded, as will appear, that the passage of the years, so far from weakening the criticisms which Gorell made of that jurisdiction, has reinforced their essential validity.

4.18   We have described the emergence and consolidation of two concurrent systems of family law, one for the use of the rich and powerful, the other for the rest of the community. But English society made another distinction between the independent poor and the destitute, who, for whatever reason, did not earn their own subsistence. It was the function of the poor law to enforce this distinction. In doing so, the poor law became a third system of family law. In assuming public responsibility for the support of the destitute, and seeking to minimise the cost of maintaining them, it took control or exercised supervision over private and domestic relationships between spouses, parents and children, which are of the essence of family life.

4.19   The proper exposition of poor law as family law requires an investigation into fertile and complex areas of English legal and social history which defies *précis*. We must, here, refer to the account given in Appendix 5. It may be said, however, that the essence of the poor law system was that it was the means through which the public supported those who were unable to support themselves, but sought reimbursement by imposing a legal liability upon their relatives in accordance with early seventeenth century notions of kinship. The operation of the system in its later developed forms is best observed in its mid-Victorian application to unmarried mothers and their illegitimate children. Relief was provided to the mother in the workhouse. After childbirth and a period of nursing she was separated from her child, and she usually left the workhouse. The child remained there. Girls, in due course, were put out to domestic service and often ended on the streets. Boys were put out to the merchant service or other harsh trades. The mother could bring proceedings for an affiliation order against the putative father, but these could only take the form of a complaint to the magistrate. The maximum amount payable until the end of the first world war was five shillings a week. (It thereafter rose in stages until it reached fifty shillings in 1960; and the limit was altogether removed in 1968.) The poor law authorities could themselves lay complaint against the putative father—the " liable relative "—to recover the cost of the maintenance of his illegitimate child.

4.20   The treatment within the poor law of widows and deserted wives and their children followed a more diverse pattern, according to the policy of the particular poor law union. The husbands of the deserted women who were assisted were liable to reimburse the authorities, but the latter appear to have had a very limited success in making recovery. Up until 1914, in half the cases in which the poor law authorities obtained an order against a liable relative, the only result was that he went to prison for failure to pay.

4.21   By the turn of the century, the Victorian poor law system was under assault. Its treatment of the illegitimate child, in particular, outraged a

70

nascent public conscience that was fed from many sources, ranging from concern for the physical quality of the population as exposed in recruiting offices for the Boer war to a new kind of philosophical and emotional regard for the child as an individual. This conscience was reflected in legislation dealing with the care and protection of children and their welfare and education. The Adoption of Children Act 1926 enabled adopters to step into the shoes of natural parents, and the Legitimacy Act 1926 began a process of reform which, although still not complete, has come close to abolishing the legal status and consequences of illegitimacy. However, while shorn of its worse stringencies, the poor law continued to be the chief resource of the unmarried mother and her child.

4.22 There were other groups who had survived only under the poor law who began to be relieved, or partly relieved, of such dependence. Thus, non-contributory old age pensions were introduced in 1908. The movement towards what has been called " the breakdown of the poor law " sought to extend itself to unsupported mothers of all categories through the introduction of a " mother's pension ". This topic was considered by the Ministry of Reconstruction between 1916 ahd 1919, and again by the Anderson Committee in 1925. It was further considered by Sir William Beveridge in the drafting stages of his famous Report, in 1942, on *Social Insurance and Allied Services*.

4.23 We refer in Part 2 to the doubts and obstacles encountered in previous attempts to construct a social security benefit for one-parent families (difficulties from which our deliberations were by no means immune, as Part 5 shows). In the event they were considered to be insuperable, except in the case of widows, to whom they were mostly inapplicable. In 1925, widows were given pension entitlement with additional allowances for their children. They thus became, as they remain, the only species of one-parent family for whom specific provision outside the poor law, or the systems replacing it, has been made.

4.24 The National Assistance Act 1948 repealed the poor law and its administration by local authorities, and substituted a system of national assistance, administered by the National Assistance Board, and financed from central funds. " National assistance " in turn became " supplementary benefits " when the Ministry of Social Security Act 1966 created the Ministry of Social Security, now merged into the Department of Health and Social Security, to administer all social security benefits including supplementary benefits. The Supplementary Benefits Commission was established as an independent statutory body responsible for the administration of the supplementary benefits scheme, including decisions on entitlement to benefit and proceedings against liable relatives. Involved in these changes was the determination to abolish the stigma attaching to the old poor law, and to emphasise that the financial assistance which the system affords to the poor is theirs as of right. The principle of recovery from the liable relative remains, however, unaffected.[2]

---

[1] The papers and memoranda concerning these deliberations are discussed in Appendix 5, Section 5.

[2] For the current " liable relative " provision see the opening paragraph of Section 10 below.

SECTION 3—THE NEW DIVORCE LAW

THE INCREASE IN DIVORCE

4.25 Since the second world war there has been considerable change both in divorce law and in the number of divorces. Certain institutional changes may first be briefly mentioned. The divorce jurisdiction transferred to the Probate, Divorce and Admiralty Division of the High Court in 1873 continued to be solely exerciseable there until 1967, in which year the jurisdiction to try undefended divorces was extended to county courts. There are now about one hundred county courts which are designated for that purpose. In matters other than divorce the Probate, Divorce and Admiralty Division shares a family jurisdiction, notably in disputes relating to custody and access, with the other two Divisions of the High Court—Chancery and Queen's Bench. The overlap in disputes affecting children was productive of much inconvenience. This was remedied by the Administration of Justice Act 1970, which re-named the Probate, Divorce and Admiralty Division " the Family Division ", and re-organised the business of the High Court so that the Family Division now deals exclusively with " family " matters, including appeals from the decisions of magistrates in their matrimonial jurisdiction.

4.26 Procedural reform has, however, been overshadowed by the massive post-war increase in the divorce rate itself. We have discussed in Part 3 the statistics of divorce and what is known of the causes of the increase in divorce. The many factors to be studied range from the changing situation and status of women to the weakening authority of religion. In any case, it is certain that two world wars provided circumstances peculiarly favourable to change. It could not be otherwise, because the conduct of modern wars compels a massive break-up of family life. In their aftermath, divorce inevitably assumed significance as a major " social problem ". This coincided with a twentieth century disposition to promote the welfare and happiness of individuals as distinct from the Victorian concern to protect the integrity of marriage. One consequence of this disposition, which in turn had profound consequences for the divorce rate, was the establishment of the legal aid scheme.

THE INFLUENCE OF LEGAL AID UPON DIVORCE

4.27 Facilities to help the poor bring and defend litigation in the civil, including the matrimonial, courts existed long before the introduction of the legal aid scheme in 1949. The Poor Persons' Procedure, as it was called, relied essentially on the charitable contribution of their services by the legal profession. As the value of money fell, more people fell outside the limits of the procedure, which for very many years before 1949 had proved inadequate to the demand for assisted legal services. Nevertheless, there was a steady increase between the two world wars in the number of assisted petitioners in matrimonial cases. Between 1921 and 1925, they constituted almost one quarter of all petitioners; on the eve of the second world war the proportion was well over one third. The details are set out in Table 4.1.[1]

---

[1] This table is extracted from Dr Colin Gibson's valuable analysis ' The Effect of Legal Aid on Divorce in England and Wales, Part 1: Before 1950 ', in *Family Law*, Volume 1, Number 3, May/June 1971.

TABLE 4.1

THE PROPORTIONS OF PETITIONS FILED WITH LEGAL AID: 1921–1968

Period	All matrimonial petitions filed (yearly average)				Total: All petitioners (100%)	Percentage of husband/wife petitioners with legal aid		
	Husband		Wife					
	Number	Percentage	Number	Percentage		Husband	Wife	All
		%		%		%	%	%
1921–25	1,367	43	1,840	57	3,207	32	19	24
1926–30	1,715	41	2,495	59	4,210	34	35	34
1931–35	2,181	44	2,766	56	4,947	40	37	38
1936–40	3,583	47	4,082	53	7,665	32	41	37
1941–45	8,938	55	7,257	45	16,195	36	19	23
1946–50	21,374	55	17,750	45	39,124	Not available		22
1951–55	14,311	44	18,026	56	32,337	46	67	58
1956–60	12,423	45	15,276	55	27,699	23	58	42
1961–65	15,706	41	22,219	59	37,925	53	78	68
1968	20,614	37	34,642	63	55,256	43	75	63

Source: Calculations based upon the annual *Civil Judicial Statistics*.

4.28   During the last world war, the morale of the citizen soldier was early recognised by the military authorities as a crucial factor in the organisation of victory.   For this reason, the provision of speedy solutions for the matrimonial difficulties of members of the armed services became a public duty. By the end of the war, a Services' Divorce Department administered by the Law Society and financed by the Treasury had underlined the deficiencies of the Poor Persons' Procedure and created an appetite for post-war improvements. These were achieved in the Legal Aid and Advice Act 1949, which set up the present legal aid scheme.   It is significant that more than three quarters of the expenditure on civil legal aid since 1950 has been devoted to matrimonial cases. Until 1961, it was available only for the High Court, but was then extended to the magistrates' courts.

4.29   Table 4.2 shows the social class distribution of assisted petitioners in 1961, and also the relative significance of legal aid for husbands and wives.

TABLE 4.2

PROPORTION OF PETITIONERS IN EACH SOCIAL CLASS WHO RECEIVED LEGAL AID IN 1961

Party petitioning	Husband's social class by present occupation						In prison, retired, disabled, servicemen, students	Occupation not known or inadequately described	All classes
	I and II Professional and intermediate	III Skilled non-manual	III Skilled manual	IV Semi-skilled	V Un-skilled	Total I-V			
Percentage legally aided:									
Husband	20	32	47	52	81	44	62	71	46
Wife	48	64	78	82	80	71	81	89	74
Total	36	50	63	67	80	58	74	87	62

Source: Reproduced from C Gibson and Miss A Beer: 'The Effect of Legal Aid on Divorce in England and Wales, Part II: Since 1950', in *Family Law*, Volume 1, Number 4, July/August 1971.

Dr Gibson and Miss Beer comment that:

> . . . the availability of legal aid is very important in helping those with low incomes to seek a divorce upon the breakdown of marriage. Some two-thirds of all manual petitioners proceed to the divorce courts with the assistance of legal aid. The similarity in the resort to legal aid of the husbands (81 per cent) and wives (80 per cent) petitions in social class V shows that the very low wage earning husbands in this social class are no more able than their wives to pay for divorce. In the other social classes there is roughly a 30 per cent difference between the proportion of husbands and wives who are legally aided in each social class. In all but social class V, therefore, wives are more dependent than husbands upon financial assistance when seeking divorce.[1]

Lord Buckmaster's Act in 1923 had put husbands and wives on a footing of formal equality in respect of the grounds of divorce, by making it possible for each to petition against the other on the grounds of simple adultery. But it was not until the legal aid scheme of 1949 compensated wives for their lack of income or low earnings that they won practical equality of access to the court.

THE THIRD ROYAL (MORTON) COMMISSION ON MARRIAGE AND DIVORCE

4.30 In 1951, Mrs Eirene White proposed, in a private member's bill, to permit divorce to spouses who had lived apart for seven years: that is to say, divorce which depended on the fact of separation over this period, and did not involve the proof, by one spouse against the other, of the commission of a matrimonial offence. Coming as it did, at the time when legal aid regarded as a social service was replacing help for the poor as a form of professional charity dispensed by lawyers, and the financial bar to the divorce courts was being lifted, Mrs White's bill was seen by its opponents as a measure to open the floodgates. Nevertheless, to the alarm of its opponents, and to the surprise of many of the supporters of the bill, it appeared as though the House might respond favourably. At this juncture, the government offered Mrs White a Greek gift in the shape of a Royal Commission. Mrs White accepted.

4.31 The Report of the Morton Commission[2] in 1956, though divided, was decidedly against change. Reformers had urged that the doctrine of the matrimonial offence was out of step with people's actual behaviour and expectations in marriage, that the law was brought into contempt by the perjury thereby encouraged, and that the result was illicit unions and the birth of illegitimate children. The Church of England was the most influential opponent of change in the matrimonial law. It explained to the Royal Commission that the doctrine of the matrimonial offence was "entirely in accord with the New Testament",[3] asserted that divorce was "a very dangerous threat to the family and to the conception of marriage as a lifelong obligation",[4] and upheld its traditional view that, although much individual suffering and hardship might be relieved by making divorce easier to obtain, the damage to the social order must outweigh such benefits.[5]

---

[1] *Ibid*, page 126.

[2] *Report of the Royal Commission on Marriage and Divorce*, Cmd 9678, 1956.

[3] *Royal Commission on Marriage and Divorce, Minutes of Evidence, Sixth Day*, HMSO, 1952, page 160.

[4] *Ibid*, page 142.

[5] *Ibid*.

4.32 In 1956, it must have seemed that the Morton Commission and the Church of England had between them put the quietus on divorce law reform for many years to come. But the appearances were deceptive. The report proved to be little more than a ripple on the surface of a tide that was moving strongly in the other direction.

4.33 In the Commonwealth countries closest to Britain in their laws and culture, there had long been legislation in force which admitted the possibility, in certain circumstances, of divorce at the option of either party after a period of separation. The situation in New Zealand from 1920 onwards is described by a judge of its Supreme Court as one in which three years' separation by agreement gave a virtual right to divorce in the vast majority of cases.[1] The policy of the law in New Zealand was that:

> It is not conducive to the public interest that men and women should remain bound together in permanence by the bonds of marriage the duties of which have irremediably failed. Such a condition of marriage in law which is no marriage in fact leads only to immorality and unhappiness.[2]

In 1945, Western Australia allowed divorce after five years' separation, whatever the cause or origin of the separation.[3]

4.34 At home, the practice of the courts was putting a strain on the theory that divorce was a reward for the (more or less) innocent and a punishment for the guilty. The law was that if the petitioner had himself or herself committed adultery, that was a discretionary bar—that is to say, an impediment which the court could enforce or forgive—to divorce or judicial separation. In such a case, the petitioner had to make a written " discretion statement ",[4] and the divorce judge might then be faced with the question whether he should, in the exercise of his discretion, pronounce a decree against a guilty respondent at the suit of a guilty petitioner. Until the first world war this discretion was exercised within narrow limits. Thereafter, it was exercised with increasing freedom. An unpublished investigation disclosed that about one third of all petitioners in the mid-1960's asked for discretion to be exercised in their favour. In 1943, the House of Lords enunciated five considerations which the court should have in mind when exercising its discretion:

> .... the court should have regard to (a) the position and interest of the children of the marriage; (b) the interest of the party with whom the petitioner has committed adultery, with special regard to their future marriage; (c) the question whether, if the marriage be not dissolved, there is a prospect of reconciliation

---

1 Sir George McGregor: ' The Development of Divorce Law in New Zealand ', in *Family Law Centenary Essays*, Victoria University of Wellington, Law Faculty, 1967.

2 *Mason v Mason* (1921) NZLR 955, *per* Salmond J at 961. See also *Lodder v Lodder*, *ibid*, 876 at 877.

3 A valuable discussion of these developments is to be found in A C Holden: ' Divorce in the Commonwealth, A Comparative Study ', in *International and Comparative Law Quarterly*, Volume 20, 1971, pages 58–74.

4 This took the form of a sexual autobiography in the nature of an inventory of the occasions, with dates, names and places, on which the petitioner had illicitly succumbed to his or her frailties, together with such explanations and excuses, or even expressions of remorse, as the talents of counsel who settled the document might devise. If the variety of illicit experience had been so rich as to defeat itemised recollection, the discretion statement would traditionally begin, " On divers occasions your petitioner has committed adultery at times and places so numerous that your petitioner can no longer give any particulars of the same, save and except that . . . ." The " discretion statement " was a judicial invention, not a statutory requirement.

between the spouses; (*d*) the interests of the petitioner, particularly as regards allowing him to remarry and live respectably; (*e*) the interests of the community at large, judged by maintaining a true balance between respect for the binding sanctity of marriage and the social considerations which make it contrary to public policy to insist on the maintenance of a union which has utterly broken down.[1]

4.35 These criteria were essentially incompatible with a divorce law whose central tenet was punishment and reward. Thus, the seal of highest authority was placed on what by this time was the practice of the courts in attaching great importance to the fact of breakdown. There was nothing to be found about breakdown in the grounds of divorce as enacted by Parliament. But the reality was that thousands passing through the divorce courts were obtaining consensual decrees under a system in which they were theoretically prohibited. Over 90 per cent of petitions were undefended. Legal aid assisted this process, not only by permitting so many more to gain access to the courts, but also by promoting a certain reluctance among the judiciary to preside over the expenditure of large sums of public money in heavily contested cases in which three parties or even more—depending on the number of co-respondents or parties cited—might all be legally aided although the outcome might be plain almost from the start. In all these circumstances, many responsibly-minded people, whether conservationist or reformist in their attitudes to what the divorce law ought to be, shared a common anxiety over the factitiousness of the law they saw in operation.[2]

4.36 Most important of all, the solidity of the attitude which the Church itself had adopted in its evidence to the Morton Commission was more apparent than real. The Anglican position was in fact in a state of flux. This was revealed when the Archbishop of Canterbury set up a group to examine the circumstances and implications of population growth in parts of the world of special concern to the Church overseas, in particular so as to enable the Lambeth Conference of 1958 to make a clear statement of attitude to contraception. The report, under the title *The Family in Contemporary Society*, was skilfully contrived to make the spectre of Malthus haunt the conference hall in order to secure an approbation of contraception from the bishops. It made an effort " to ensure that the theological principles brought to bear are not contaminated with out-of-date sociological assumptions "; in the course of which it reached the conclusion that, in Britain, " far from disintegrating, the modern family is in some ways in a stronger position than it has been at any period in our history of which we have knowledge ".[3] The notable inconsistencies between this statement and the evidence of the Church to the Morton Commission required the latter to be discarded, and with it went the Church's special attachment to the matrimonial offence. Accordingly, when Mr Leo Abse made a further private member's attempt in 1962 to add a *de facto* period of seven years' separation to the other grounds for divorce, the Archbishop of Canterbury announced that he wished to consider " a principle at law of breakdown of marriage " and to " work at this idea, sociologically as well as

---

[1] *Blunt v Blunt* (1943) AC 517.

[2] Memorable expressions of this anxiety are to be found in the evidence given by Professor L C B Gower to the Morton Commission, *op cit* (*Minutes of Evidence, First Day*, pages 16–26), and in the article by the late C P Harvey, QC: ' On the State of the Divorce Market ', in the *Modern Law Review*, Volume 16, 1953, page 129.

[3] Moral Welfare Council of the Church of England: *The Family in Contemporary Society*, SPCK, 1958, page 109.

doctrinally, to discover if anything can be produced ".[1] He convened a group of churchmen, lawyers and laity " to try to discover whether it would be possible to frame a law of marriage not based upon the matrimonial offence but based upon a law of breakdown ".[2] They succeeded. The group's report, published in 1966 as *Putting Asunder*, implicity rejected the Church's previous pronouncements because:

> We are far from being convinced that the present provisions of the law witness to the sanctity of marriage, or uphold its public repute, in any observable way, or that they are irreplaceable as buttresses of morality, either in the narrower field of matrimonial and sexual relationships, or in the wider field which includes considerations of truth, the sacredness of oaths, and the integrity of professional practice. As a piece of social mechanism the present system has not only cut loose from its moral and juridical foundations: it is, quite simply, inept.[3]

The group recommended that the notion of breakdown of marriage should be substituted for the matrimonial offence as the basis of divorce law. This abrupt reversal of the Church's historic and recently stated position was one major factor in releasing the log jam obstructing reform.

4.37 Meantime, although Mr Abse's attempt to make a period of long separation in itself a ground for divorce had failed, he had succeeded, in a manner that was better understood by the lawyers than by the reformers, in pushing the law to the verge of a consensual divorce. Collusion had always been an absolute bar to divorce. The Matrimonial Causes Act 1963 made it a discretionary bar. This change in the law has been described by a former President of the Divorce Division as " revolutionary ".[4] It enabled the court to take into consideration any agreement or arrangement made or proposed to be made between the parties. The effect was:

> to allow the implementation of agreements or arrangements which can dispose without acrimony of such matters as maintenance, damages, custody of and access to children, and property disputes; and to obviate long and damaging contests on issues which were really otherwise being fought only because their outcome was believed to be likely to affect such matters.[5]

4.38 In 1966, the Law Commission were established " to take and keep under review all the law . . . with a view to its systematic development and reform ".[6] The Law Commission's first programme included a survey of matrimonial law " having regard to the variety of views expressed in and following the Report of the last Royal Commission on Marriage and Divorce ", and they quickly published a commentary[7] on *Putting Asunder* which focused attention on the range of choice and practical possibilities for reform. The Law Commission provided as complete a social perspective for their purposes as the then available material permitted and, in particular, demonstrated that

---

1 House of Lords Official Report, 21 June 1963, column 1547.

2 *Ibid*, 23 November 1966, column 270.

3 *Putting Asunder: Divorce Law for Contemporary Society*, SPCK, 1966, page 32.

4 Sir Jocelyn (now Lord) Simon: *Recent Developments in the Matrimonial Law*, Riddell Lecture, 1970. The substance of this lecture is conveniently printed in Rayden on *Divorce*, 11th edition, Appendix VII, pages 3227–3240.

5 *Ibid*, page 3231.

6 The establishment and functions of the Law Commission are discussed in the article of Lord Chorley and Gerald Dworkin, ' The Law Commissions Act, 1965 ', in the *Modern Law Review*, Volume 28, November 1965, pages 675–688.

7 Law Commission: *Reform of the Grounds of Divorce: The Field of Choice*, Cmnd 3123, 1966.

the divorce rate cannot be used as a measure of the number of families which collapse. They concluded that "there is no real evidence that the proportion of marriages which break down has increased during the century ".[1]

4.39 Of particular importance to our present purpose is the Law Commission's statement that:

a good divorce law should seek to achieve the following objectives;

(1) to buttress, rather than to undermine the stability of marriage; and

(2) when, regrettably, a marriage has irretrievably broken down, to enable the empty legal shell to be destroyed with the maximum fairness, and the minimum bitterness, distress and humiliation.[2]

The Commission went on to explain that:

The second objective has two facets. First, the law should make it possible to dissolve the legal tie once that has become irretrievably broken in fact. If the marriage is dead, the object of the law should be to afford it a decent burial. . . . It should not merely bury the marriage, but do so with decency and dignity and in a way which will encourage harmonious relationships between the parties and their children in the future.[3]

4.40 Finally, the Commission emphasised as another important requirement of a good divorce law that it:

should be understandable and respected. It is pre-eminently a branch of the law that is liable to affect everyone, if not directly at any rate indirectly. Unless its principles are such as can be understood and respected it cannot achieve its main objectives. If it is thought to be hypocritical or otherwise unworthy of respect, it will not only fail to achieve those objectives but may bring the whole of the administration of justice into disrespect.[4]

4.41 Characteristic of the great significance which the Commission attached to the social importance of viewing divorce as a means of providing decent burials for dead marriages was their estimate that a change of law to admit breakdown of marriage or separation as a ground of divorce would result in the legitimation of about 180,000 illegitimate children and that " in each future year 19,000 children who would be otherwise condemned to permanent illegitimacy might be born in wedlock or subsequently legitimated".[5] The Law Commission's definition of a good divorce law provided both the basis of its approach to reform and a solution of what its Chairman described as " the perennial dilemma of a law reform agency". The Commission's approach, he wrote:

managed to focus attention on what was legally possible, without committing itself to any but the most obvious social judgements. Indeed the whole report

---

[1] *Ibid*, page 7.

[2] *Ibid*, page 10.

[3] *Ibid*, pages 10–11. *Putting Asunder* puts the same point in the following way: ". . . we should learn to think in terms, not of ' innocent ' and ' guilty ' parties, but of the condition of the matrimonial relationship . . . . If, after hearing the evidence, the court then decided that the relationship was ' dead ', . . . it would not be giving a decree ' in favour ' of the petitioner or endorsing his or her conduct, but simply giving effect to a finding of fact . . . the only answer to the allegation that a marriage relationship is ' dead ' is evidence that it is not: rebuttal cannot be achieved by referring to the relative deserts of the parties. In this respect proceedings on the basis of breakdown of marriage resemble nullity proceedings." *Op cit*, page 50.

[4] *Reform of the Grounds of Divorce, op cit*, page 11.

[5] *Ibid*, page 19. This estimate was made for the Law Commission by the Registrar General.

79

is based upon two social judgements[1] which are really beyond the reach of controversy . . . . It avoided any commitment to any social view of marriage that could be considered in the slightest degree controversial.[2]

THE DIVORCE REFORM ACT 1969

4.42 The result of all these developments in the single decade following the rejection by the Morton Commission of any radical divorce reform was the most radical measure in the history of our divorce law. The Divorce Reform Act 1969 provided[3] that henceforth " the sole ground on which a petition for divorce may be presented to the court by either party to a marriage shall be that the marriage has broken down irretrievably ".[4] Proof of breakdown consists of establishing any of a number of specified " facts ". These facts include cases of matrimonial misconduct, but also the fact of consent by the respondent to a decree after the parties have lived apart for a continuous period of two years, and the fact, even if there is no consent, that the parties have lived apart for a continuous period of five years.[5] The law thus recognises both consensual divorce, and, if total breakdown has been established by a sufficient period of separation, divorce of an unwilling and blameless spouse at the option of the other. Similarly, although " irretrievable breakdown " would obviously not be suitable as, and is not made, the legal basis for a decree of judicial separation, the Act makes each one of the " facts " in itself a ground for such a decree.[6] Thus the grant of a decree either of divorce or of judicial separation no longer has any necessary connection with the establishment of fault. The speed and extent of the acceptance, within the present decade, of divorce as a " mechanism "[7] to deal with breakdown may be gauged from the most recent innovation in divorce procedure. In cases based on two years' separation and consent to a decree, the parties, if there are no children of the family, can now get divorced merely after filing the appropriate documents without either of them appearing in court.[8] We estimate that at least 5,000 cases would have qualified for the procedure had it been available in 1972.

---

[1] Sir Leslie Scarman is referring to the statement by the Law Commission, quoted in paragraph 4.39 above, on the objectives of a good divorce law.

[2] Leslie Scarman: *Law Reform: The New Pattern*, 1968, pages 33–34.

[3] Section 1.

[4] The Act of 1969 has now been consolidated with other family law legislation in the Matrimonial Causes Act 1973, which came into effect on 1 January 1974. It remains more convenient in this Report to continue to refer to the Act of 1969 rather than to the corresponding provisions in the Act of 1973.

[5] The " facts " are specified in section 2(1), which provides:

" The court hearing a petition for divorce shall not hold the marriage to have broken down irretrievably unless the petitioner satisfies the court of one or more of the following facts, that is to say—

    (a) that the repondent has committed adultery and the petitioner finds it intolerable to live with the respondent;

    (b) that the respondent has behaved in such a way that the petitioner cannot reasonably be expected to live with the respondent;

    (c) that the respondent has deserted the petitioner for a continuous period of at least two years immediately preceding the presentation of the petition;

    (d) that the parties to the marriage have lived apart for a continuous period of at least two years immediately preceding the presentation of the petition and the respondent consents to a decree being granted;

    (e) that the parties to the marriage have lived apart for a continuous period of at least five years immediately preceding the presentation of the petition."

[6] Section 8.

[7] See paragraph 4.36 above.

[8] *Practice Direction*, Disposal of Matrimonial Causes: Divorce Reform Act 1969, Section 2(1)(d), 1 November 1973.

4.43   It is doubtful whether any reform in the law as large as that effected by the Divorce Reform Act 1969 has won so rapid and easy an acceptance. Long though the tradition has been of a law founded on proof of guilt, the judiciary proceeded without pause to implement the spirit as well as the letter of the law founded on breakdown, adopting, in doing so, the language of the reformers:

> All three of the parties would, in the ordinary course of events, have many years to live; and in my view, unless there were strong reasons to the contrary, it would be ridiculous to keep alive this shell of a marriage and prevent perhaps all three of the parties settling down to a happier life in happier circumstances.[1]

All this goes to demonstrate that the Act was one of those measures which commended itself to the general conscience long before it succeeded in gaining the statute book.

SECTION 4—THE NEW LAW OF MAINTENANCE

PRINCIPLES OF MAINTENANCE BEFORE 1970

4.44   At the opening in 1945 of the period which is the subject of this Section, the powers of the divorce court to make financial provision for spouses and children were governed by statutory formulae of the most general character whose ancestry went back to the beginning of the jurisdiction in 1857. A husband might be ordered to secure payment to his wife of such sum as " having regard to her fortune, if any, to the ability of her husband and to the conduct of the parties, the court may deem to be reasonable "; and to pay her unsecured maintenance " as the court may think reasonable ".[2]   The court was further empowered to " make such provision as appears just with respect to the custody, maintenance and education " of the children.[3]   There were no circumstances in which maintanance could be ordered against the wife in favour of the husband other than in the case where she had obtained a decree against him on the ground of insanity.[4]   There were certain limited powers in the court to order or to adjust settlements of property when granting other matrimonial relief. In 1963, the divorce court obtained a new power to order payment of a lump sum in addition or alternatively to maintenance.[5]   Thus the situation stood at the time of the passing of the Divorce Reform Act 1969.

4.45   Over the century in which they had exercised the jurisdiction, the judges had to some extent filled out these general formulae by their decisions, so that reference could be made to reported cases for guidance on the amount of maintenance that was to be regarded in the normal case as " reasonable " or "just ", and on what adjustments should be made to reflect special circumstances —in particular, how far a wife entitled to maintenance should have it scaled down to reflect her own misconduct or the part she had played in causing the breakdown of the marriage.

---

[1] *Mathias v Mathias* (1972) Fam 287, *per* Davies LJ at 301.

[2] Judicature (Consolidation) Act 1925, section 190.

[3] *Ibid*, section 193.

[4] Matrimonial Causes Act 1937, section 10(2).

[5] Matrimonial Causes Act 1963, section 5(1).

4.46   As regards the innocent wife, the ecclesiastical practice had in general been to award her upon the grant of a decree of divorce *a mensa et thoro* one third of the husband's income (or of the joint incomes, if she had separate estate), with additional amounts for the support of any children left in her custody.[1]   This practice was, after a period of uncertainty, adopted in the divorce court when it succeeded to the matrimonial jurisdiction.[2]   The "one third rule " was, however, always flexible in its application, yielding to special circumstances.   In the decade preceding the Act of 1969 it was being described as " discredited "; the correct general concept being stated to be that an innocent wife was entitled, following the loss of cohabitation, to be maintained at a standard of living no less than her husband's:

> If any general principles are to govern the approach to a wife's maintenance, I think they are as follows: In cohabitation a wife shares with her husband a standard of living appropriate to his income or, if she is also earning, their joint incomes.   If cohabitation is destroyed by the wrongful conduct of the husband, the wife's maintenance should be so assessed that her standard of living does not suffer more than is inherent in the circumstances of separation.   Her standard of living may well have to be lower after the breach of cohabitation than it was before, since there may now be two households to be maintained in place of the former one, in which household expenses were shared.   Although the standard of living of both parties may therefore have to be lower than it was before there was the breach of cohabitation, in general the wife should not be relegated to a lower standard of living than that which her husband enjoys.   In saying that I am not advocating a " one-half rule " or a " one-half approach " in place of the discredited " one-third rule " or " one-third approach ".   In the first place, there may be many other circumstances which have to be taken into account; for example, inescapable expenses of one or other party, or an obligation to support, or to contribute towards the support of, a child at its appropriate standard . . . . [3]

4.47   This statement of the law touched on the fundamental problem, but did little to solve it.   The question was how to resolve a conflict of responsibility which the court had pointed out a few years earlier was:

> one of very great difficulty.   It is a situation with which the courts nowadays are trying to deal very frequently.   Divorce and the right to remarry have been with us for a very long time, but it is only in comparatively recent times that it has been a common thing for people to remarry who have not the means to keep more than one wife; and the odd situation has now come on us in which a man of large means who pays surtax is able to have several wives and deduct the maintenance from his income and be very little worse off than he was; whereas a man in the position of a working man who pays neither surtax nor any considerable amount of income tax, finds it quite impossible to comply with the law which still in this country enables divorced wives or wives who have obtained divorces to obtain maintenance from their husbands who have to provide for a number of wives in excess of one . . . .   The law being as it is, it is quite impossible for the courts to ignore the just claims of the first wife because the man has taken on himsef other obligations, although the courts have to take into account those

---

[1] The theory underlying the " one third rule " is said to be that " in a typical case the court was concerned with three groups of needs . . . those of the wife, those of the husband and those of the children for whose support the husband was liable; again, after divorce, a respondent husband will sometimes have remarried and thus have undertaken obligations to another woman and possibly to their children . . .": *Sansom v Sansom* (1966) P 52, *per* Sir Jocelyn Simon P at 55.

[2] The ecclesiastical practice and its adoption by the divorce court are discussed in more detail in Appendix 5, paragraphs 26 and 33.

[3] *Kershaw v Kershaw* (1966) P 13, *per* Sir Jocelyn Simon P at 17.

obligations as involving a reduction in the capacity of the man to pay for the upkeep of his first wife (and child).[1]

4.48　In a case reported in 1970,[2] this problem was further considered.　The court asked itself:

> (i) whether the fact that a husband is providing financial support for a mistress and for children whom he is not legally bound to support is one of the relevant circumstances of the case which may be taken into account; and (ii) if it is, whether there are any principles which govern the extent to or manner in which account should be taken of these facts, and in particular whether any priority should in general be observed in relation to, on the one hand, legal obligation to support a wife and a child of the marriage, and, on the other, " moral " obligations to support a mistress and her children.[3]

To the first question the court replied:

> . . . no hard and fast line can be drawn between " legal " and " moral " obligations.　Such obligations frequently involve the support and maintenance of children, and in this context nice distinctions between whether or not they are enforceable in law at any relevant time are often impracticable of application and in any event undesirable . . . .　Our conclusion, therefore, based on principle, authority and practice, is that, when fixing the amount of maintenance . . . a court is entitled (indeed is bound) to have regard to all the relevant circumstances of each particular case, including obligations and advantages which may not be legally enforceable.[4]

On the second question, the conclusions of the court can be summarised:

(1) neither the husband nor his mistress can claim to be in a better position than they would have been had he married her upon divorce from his first wife;

(2) the general rule is that one spouse takes the other subject to that other's obligation to support the wife or child of a dissolved marriage, so that a mistress could not be better placed;

(3) nevertheless, when the court is dealing with people of small means, it has to take this " into account " not by making a mathematical deduction for the expenses of the mistress's keep, but by giving some weight to the realities:

> It is little use ordering a man to pay what is beyond his capacity, or on which he will in every probability default.[5]

---

[1] *Cockburn v Cockburn* (1957) 1 WLR 1020, *per* Hodson LJ at 1024–1025.　Lord Justice (later Lord) Hodson, a divorce judge of the greatest experience, had made some similar observations in his Memorandum to the Morton Commission:
"There is one practical difficulty which is already assuming prominence now that divorce is comparatively rife among couples who are dependent on the weekly wages of the husband.　According to our law a man has to maintain his wife and if she divorces him by reason of his fault the wife still in theory retains this right.　I say in theory because it is practically impossible for her to enforce her rights in a large number of cases.　The wage-earner . . . if he is divorced . . . is free to marry again and his wife, that is, the particular woman to whom he is at the time married, has herself a right to be maintained by him . . . .　If she has a child or children and his wage is in the neighbourhood of £6 or £7 a week . . . the financial prospects of any earlier wives or their children by this man are not very good.　There simply is not enough money to go round.　This problem is not noticeable among well-to-do people.　A super-tax payer may and quite frequently nowadays does have a number of wives living at the same time and since after divorce his ex-wives are not treated as one with him for tax purposes he can manage quite nicely . . . ."
Minutes of Evidence, Thirtieth Day, page 772.
[2] *Roberts v Roberts* (1970) P 1.
[3] *Ibid*, at 6.
[4] *Ibid*, at 7–8.
[5] *Ibid*, at 10.

4.49 In all of these citations from recently decided cases the court is to be observed engaged in a struggle to extract fair and practical rules from a set of assumptions which, when they are applied to the poor, are hardly capable of producing a fair and practical result. Once it is conceded that the law cannot any longer impose a stricter standard of familial conduct and sexual morality upon the poor than it demands from others, it follows inexorably that part of the cost of breakdown of marriage, in terms of the increase of households and dependencies, must fall on public funds. We later demonstrate this point in detail. It is therefore not surprising—indeed, we regard it as inevitable—that a legal system which abandons the double standard but continues to approach the maintenance question in terms of the re-allocation of a working wage is apt to encounter difficulties.[1]

4.50 It is to be noted that the cases cited apply both to the assessment of maintenance after divorce and to its assessment in the magistrates' courts. Thus the difficulties which have been mentioned are endemic to both jurisdictions, although they are more apparent in the magistrates' courts, because the clients of the summary matrimonial jurisdiction are nearly all poor, whereas the clients of the divorce court include not only the poor but others whose resources will stretch, whether easily or painfully, to their legal responsibilities.

4.51 The difficulties to which we have referred were further exemplified by the preparedness of the court, despite its attempt to spell out principles, to retreat, if need be, behind the veil of discretion inherent in a power to make an award " as the court thinks reasonable " or " as appears just ". It was pointed out to be of the essence of this discretion that:

> on the same evidence two different minds might reach widely different conclusions without either being appealable.[2]

It was put in another case:

> The discretion given to the court is complete and unfettered by anything in any statute or other instrument.[3]

And again:

> How much she ought to get is, I suppose, very much a jury question, and I can only make my own assessment, for what it is worth.[4]

4.52 These are classical expressions of the type of approach which courts make to problems of assessment and quantification when they are the subject of a discretion. The court may assist itself to decide such questions by setting up guidelines, like the " one third rule ", but these are voluntary aids, such as might be suggested to a jury, which can always be dispensed with. Such an approach to the determination of maintenance is as likely to produce a fair conclusion as any other provided that the resources being considered are ample. Indeed, the law is by historical derivation adapted to deal with this

---

[1] The rules more specifically laid down by the court for the situation where maintenance and supplementary benefit are both in payment will be considered later (see Section 10, paragraphs 4.203–4.205 below) and—as will then appear—solve none of these difficulties.

[2] *Bellenden (formerly Satterthwaite) v Satterthwaite* (1948) 1 All ER 343, *per* Asquith LJ at 345.

[3] *Porter v Porter* (1969) 1 WLR 1155, *per* Sachs LJ at 1159.

[4] *Bradley v Bradley* (1956) P 326, *per* Willmer J at 334.

situation, being in its origins directed to the re-allocation of resources which became necessary on the breakdown of the marriages of the well-to-do. It is, however, far from evident that this large approach is suitable to the division of a small income when, in proportion to the amount available for distribution, a difference of a few shillings may have an important effect on the living standards of payer and recipient.[1] It stands in remarkable contrast to the rules of another institution—the Supplementary Benefits Commission—responsible under law for the assessment of means and needs, and which, so far from treating its cases as raising a " jury question ", applies detailed standards and calculations. We here touch upon a theme that will assume major importance in this Report.

4.53   So far, we have been referring to the law of maintenance as it affected the innocent wife. Whether, and to what extent, misbehaviour on her part reduced her entitlement to maintenance depended on the view the court took of the gravity of the misbehaviour and its influence in causing the breakdown of the marriage. At the time of the Divorce Reform Act 1969, the law on this subject was adequately summarised in the following two citations:

> In practice a wife's adultery may or may not disqualify her from succeeding in her application for maintenance and may or may not reduce the amount allotted. At one end of the scale her adultery may indeed disqualify her altogether. It may do so, for example, where her adultery has broken up the marriage, where it is continuing and where she is being supported by her paramour. At the other end of the scale, her adultery will not disqualify her and may have little, if any influence on the amount.[2]

> The application of those principles (ie governing the exercise of the discretion as to maintenance) and the practice of the Divorce Division has varied from decade to decade. The court takes into account the human outlook of the period in which they make their decisions . . . (it) is a living thing moving with the times and not a creature of dead or moribund ways of thought . . . a decree based on a matrimonial offence, whilst of course establishing the factum of that offence, is often of little and sometimes of no importance in reaching conclusions as to whose conduct actually broke up the marriage . . . the adultery of the wife against whom a decree has been granted may be of great or it may be of little significance according to the background . . . .[3]

Here again, it will be seen, there was wide scope for discretion.

THE MATRIMONIAL PROCEEDINGS AND PROPERTY ACT 1970

4.54   Closely connected in point both of substance and time with the reform of the divorce law came the reform of the law we have been describing governing the making of financial provision on divorce. In the same year as saw the passing of the Divorce Reform Act 1969 the Law Commission published proposals for the reform of the law on financial provision.[4] These proposals were substantially adopted in the Matrimonial Proceedings and Property Act 1970,[5] which enacts a new code of financial provision in the divorce court.[6]

---

[1] There were one or two cases in which the Court of Appeal showed some awareness of this point: see especially *Irvine v Irvine* (1963) 107 Sol J 213.

[2] *Iverson v Iverson* (1967) P 134, *per* Latey J at 138–139. (See also the reference to this decision in Appendix 5, paragraph 38.)

[3] *Porter v Porter, op cit, per* Sachs LJ at 1159–1160.

[4] *Report on Financial Provision in Matrimonial Cases*, Law Com No 25, HMSO, 1969.

[5] Many of the provisions of the Act of 1970 are now consolidated in the Matrimonial Causes Act 1973, but it is convenient to continue to refer to the Act of 1970: see paragraph 4.42, footnote 2, above.

[6] The court's powers under the Act of 1970 to order financial provision are the same whether exercised on granting a decree of divorce, judicial separation or nullity. We refer exclusively to the case of divorce only for simplicity in exposition.

The Act does not in any respect now material affect the maintenance jurisdiction of the magistrates.

4.55 The Act of 1970 preserves the power of the court to order secured or unsecured maintenance (now called " periodical payments ") and lump sums to or for the benefit of spouses and children, and much enlarges such powers as previously existed to order transfers, settlement or variation of settlements of property. As between spouses, however, these rights are made wholly reciprocal. The order may be made against either party to the marriage in favour of the other. Next, the purpose of the exercise of these powers is stated to be:

> to place the parties, so far as it is practicable and, having regard to their conduct, just to do so, in the financial position in which they would have been if the marriage had not broken down and each had properly discharged his or her financial obligations and responsibilities towards the other.[1]

In order to promote this purpose, the Act abandons the old formula which left it to the discretion of the court to do what was " reasonable," and sets out a specific list of considerations to be taken into account along with all the other circumstances. Among these is:

> the contributions made by each of the parties to the welfare of the family, including any contribution made by looking after the home or caring for the family.[2]

THE DECISION IN WACHTEL V WACHTEL

4.56 The importance of this provision, especially in conjunction with the court's new powers to transfer property, emerges from the first case in which the Court of Appeal gave thorough interpretation to the Act of 1970. It means, says the Court of Appeal:

> that Parliament recognised that the wife who looks after the home and family contributes as much to family assets as the wife who goes out to work. The one contributes in kind. The other in money or money's worth. If the court comes to the conclusion that the home has been acquired and maintained by the joint efforts of both, then, when the marriage breaks down, it should be regarded as the joint property of both of them, no matter in whose name it stands. Just as the wife who makes substantial money contributions usually gets a share, so should the wife who looks after the home and cares for the family. . . .[3]

4.57 The court, in the same case, gave a new lease of life to the " one third " approach to the award of maintenance, adding:

> We would emphasise that this proposal is not a rule. It is only a starting point. It will serve where the marriage has lasted for many years and the wife has been in the home bringing up the children. It may not be applicable when the marriage has lasted only a short time, or where there are no children and she can go out to work.[4]

4.58 Finally, Lord Denning, in giving judgment for the whole court, made the following observations on the meaning to be placed on the requirement in the Act of 1970 to have regard for the conduct of the parties. He said:

> It has been suggested that there should be a " discount " or " reduction " in what the wife is to receive because of her supposed misconduct, guilt or blame

---

[1] Section 5(1).
[2] Section 5(1)(f).
[3] *Wachtel v Wachtel* (1973) Fam 72, *per* Lord Denning MR at 93–94.
[4] *Ibid*, at 95.

(whatever word is used). We cannot accept this argument. In the vast majority of cases it is repugnant to the principles underlying the new legislation, and in particular the Act of 1969 . . . There will no doubt be a residue of cases where the conduct of one of the parties is in the Judge's words " both obvious and gross," so much so that to order one party to support another whose conduct falls into this category is repugnant to anyone's sense of justice. In such a case the court remains free to decline to afford financial support or to reduce the support which it would otherwise have ordered. But, short of cases falling into this category, the court should not reduce its order for financial provision merely because of what was formerly regarded as guilt or blame. To do so would be to impose a fine for supposed misbehaviour in the course of an unhappy married life . . . Criminal justice often requires the imposition of financial and indeed custodial penalties. But in the financial adjustments consequent upon the dissolution of a marriage which has irretrievably broken down, the imposition of financial penalties ought seldom to find a place.[1]

THE CURRENT SITUATION

4.59 The effect, for presently material purposes, of the Act of 1970, as so far interpreted by the courts,[2] may be said to be as follows. The tendency that was already discernible in the cases of the 1960s to attach less importance to misconduct of the claimant as negating or diminishing her right to maintenance has been crystallised, and the area of discretion in taking her behaviour into account has been correspondingly reduced. Henceforth, misconduct is not to affect a claim to maintenance unless it has been so obvious and gross as to make it offensive to justice to require the victim spouse to contribute to the support of the other. This development widens the gap between the law of maintenance in divorce and the law of maintenance in the magistrates' courts. Next, as against the diminishing sphere of influence of misconduct as affecting maintenance in the divorce court, there has been an enlargement of the importance attached to such factors as the age and working capacity of the parties and the duration of the marriage. The courts have been stating that in the case of a divorcing or separating young couple, married only for a short time, without children, and each engaged in or capable of gainful occupation, the marriage certificate is not to be regarded as a passport to a substantial maintenance order. In such cases, only a nominal order should be made in favour of the wife. This principle, which owes as much to the court's taking as serious an attitude towards the equality of the sexes as it does to the Act of 1970, applies equally in the divorce and magistrates' jurisdiction. But, finally, the Act of 1970 has not made any contribution to the solution of the problem, in assessing maintenance as between people of small means, of how to effect an adequate distribution of inadequate resources. Indeed, to the extent that it requires effect to be given, in substitution for the " reasonable " formula, to a considerable number of specific and sophisticated considerations the Act may almost be considered to be irrelevant to cases of this kind. In particular, it will rarely, if ever, be " practicable " to place the parties in such cases " in the financial position in which they would have been if the marriage had not broken down." Neither in the divorce court, nor in the magistrates' courts (to which the principles of assessment of maintenance elaborated in the pre-1970 cases continue to apply), has the law found the method of extracting more than a pint from a pint pot.

[1] *Ibid*, at 90.
[2] The decision of *Wachtel v Wachtel*, *op cit*, was in the Court of Appeal, and was the first in what has now become a line of authority. See, for example, *Trippas v Trippas* (1973) Fam 134 and *Harnett v Harnett* (1973) Fam 156, affirmed *The Times*, 23 November 1973.

4.60   We have traced post-war developments in the law governing economic relations between husband and wife to their present state.   But that is by no means the terminus of the changes which are likely to follow upon the new divorce law.   The financial and property provisions of the Act of 1970 refer to what the court may order when granting a decree.   They enable re-allocations of economic resources to be effected at the point of time when the court recognises that the marriage has broken down irretrievably.   In the great majority of cases, the re-allocation will be in favour of the wife, to provide her with resources which her obligations to the family prevented her from accumulating during the marriage.   But this raises the question: why should she be bound to wait upon the contingency of a breakdown of her marriage to acquire the possibility of sharing in the resources accumulated during marriage?   In other words, should not still married wives, as distinct from divorced wives, become entitled to a share in property in the nature of family assets acquired during the course of the marriage, even though they have made no direct financial contribution to its acquisition?

4.61   These considerations have recently led to the Law Commission's recommending that the matrimonial home, which in the great majority of marriages is the principal family asset, or the only one of any substantial value, should always be treated as shared equally between husband and wife unless they have agreed to the contrary.   We discuss this recommendation at greater length elsewhere.[1]

SECTION 5—THE DIVORCE AND MAGISTERIAL JURISDICTIONS COMPARED

4.62   We have described the origins and growth of the summary matrimonial jurisdiction.[2]   This jurisdiction now stems from the Matrimonial Proceedings (Magistrates' Courts) Act 1960 which brought together the various grounds of complaint created since the foundation of the jurisdiction in 1878 and added some additional grounds.[3]   The magistrates have power to make non-cohabita-

---

1 Part 6, Section 4.   See also Appendix 5, Section 4.
2 Appendix 5, Section 3, and paragraphs 4.13–4.17 above.
3 The grounds as defined in section 1(1) of the Act of 1960 are summarised below, the dates in brackets showing when they were first introduced.   (The list may be compared with the " facts ", quoted in paragraph 4.42 above (footnote 2) which have to be established for a decree of divorce or judicial separation in the divorce jurisdiction.)

  (a) Desertion of the complainant (1895);
  (b) persistent cruelty to the complainant (1895), an infant child of the complainant (1925) or an infant child of the defendant who, at the time of the cruelty, was a child of the family (1960);
  (c) certain convictions for assault on the complainant (1878) or for sexual offences or indecency against an infant child of the complainant or an infant child of the defendant who was at the time a child of the family (1960);
  (d) adultery by the defendant (1937);
  (e) while knowingly suffering from a venereal disease insisting on sexual intercourse or permitting it when the complainant was unaware of the presence of the desease (1925);
  (f) habitual drunkenness (1902) or drug addiction (1925);
  (g) if the defendant is the husband, compelling the wife to submit herself to prostitution or being guilty of conduct which was likely to result in her doing so and has had that effect (1925);
  (h) if the defendant is the husband, wilfully neglecting to provide reasonable maintenance for the wife or any dependent child of the family (1886);
  (i) if the defendant is the wife, wilfully neglecting to provide reasonable maintenance for the husband or any dependent child of the family, but only where the husband's earning capacity is impaired by age, illness, or disability of mind or body, and having regard to the respective resources it is reasonable to expect the wife to make such provision (1960).

tion orders (which the Act declares to have the effect in all respects of a decree of judicial separation while they are in force), maintenance orders, and orders regulating the custody, care and supervision of and access to children. No order, except an order relating to children, can be made unless the complainant proves that the defendant is guilty of one of the specified offences.

4.63 The developments following the second world war culminated, as we have seen in Section 3, in profound changes to the law of divorce in 1969. But the matrimonial jurisdiction of the magistrates has changed very little in detail, and not at all in fundamentals. The result has been to produce two sets of laws dealing with matrimonial breakdown, operating concurrently, but in different courts, and standing, both in the spirit and the letter, in the most remarkable contrast to each other. The fact that the one jurisdiction gives a remedy by way of dissolution of marriage, and the other does not, in no way invalidates the comparison. Both jurisdictions also provide the same remedy—a decree of judicial separation, and a non-cohabitation order which has, by statute, exactly the same effect. Yet a decree of judicial separation may be obtained from the divorce court by establishing any of the " facts " set out in the Act of 1969, while the magistrates cannot make a non-cohabitation order except on proof of one of the offences set out in the Act of 1960.

4.64 The contrast may be further demonstrated by the law in the two juris-dictions regarding bars to relief. Before 1969 the divorce court was in some cases bound and in other cases entitled to refuse a decree of divorce or judicial separation by what were known as " absolute " or " discretionary " bars. The absolute bars were connivance, collusion and condonation. The discretionary bars included conduct by the petitioner conducing to the offence charged against the respondent, or the commission of a matrimonial offence by the petitioner. All of these bars have been abolished in the divorce jurisdiction. This was the corollary of the principle embodied in the Act of 1969 that a decree of divorce or judicial separation no longer marks the guilt or innocence of the parties, but that their marriage has turned out to be not viable. On the other hand, since the jurisdiction of the magistrates to make matrimonial orders remains grounded on proof of an offence, all of the traditional bars (other than collusion) operate in the magistrates' courts. Where the complaint is based on the defendant's adultery, the magistrates cannot make an order (other than one relating to children) unless they are satisfied that the complainant has not condoned or connived at, or by wilful neglect or misconduct conduced to, that act of adultery. On whatever ground the complaint is made, the magistrates cannot make an order in favour of the complainant personally if she (assuming it is a wife's complaint) is proved to have committed an act of adultery during the subsistence of the marriage (unless, again, they are satisfied that the complainant's adultery was condoned, connived at or conduced to by the defendant). Moreover, if an order has been made in favour of the complainant, the magistrates must revoke it if it is later proved that she has committed adultery, whether before or after the making of the order.[1]

4.65 One thus arrives at the following situation. When a petitioner applies in the divorce jurisdiction for a decree of divorce or judicial separation it is

[1] The law on these matters is to be found in the Matrimonial Proceedings (Magistrates' Courts) Act 1960, sections 2(3) and 8(2).

completely irrelevant to the entitlement to that decree that he or she has committed adultery. Again, when the petitioner comes to apply for financial relief, the entitlement to that relief, and the amount of it, will be unaffected by the petitioner's own matrimonial misconduct unless this is both " obvious and gross "; for, as the Court of Appeal has said, to hold otherwise would be to " impose a fine for supposed misbehaviour in the course of an unhappy married life ".[1] But if a woman seeks a separation or maintenance order from the magistrates against a husband who makes a habit of beating her to within an inch of her life, they must reject her application if it is shown that at any time, even years previously, she committed a single act of adultery; just as they would have to revoke such an order if they had already made it. Such a state of the law seems to us to be indefensible.

4.66 One lesser, but still striking, effect of the abolition of the bars in the superior jurisdiction and their retention in the summary jursidiction is that a body of intricate learning, in the form of judicial analysis and exposition, connected with them has ceased to be relevant in the divorce court, but requires to be understood and applied by the magistrates. Similarly, the tendency of the Divorce Reform Act 1969 has been to reduce the jurisprudence of the matrimonial offence for the purposes of the divorce court, while masses of case law continue to surround the offences which give the magistrates much of their matrimonial jurisdiction. In these respects, the law has become simpler for the professional judges than for the lay ones.[2]

4.67 However, the most important feature of the contrast between the two systems is that they expose and give encouragement and effect to inconsistent public policies. The public policy of the latter part of the twentieth century is to promote the welfare of individuals and enhance respect for the law by disposing of dead marriages with decency and dignity, and a minimum of bitterness, distress and humiliation, and to do so in a manner that will encourage harmonious relations between the parties and their children in the future.[3] This policy has been accepted by Church and State, has been legislated into the divorce law, and is implemented in the superior system of courts of law. The public policy of the latter part of the nineteenth century was to provide police court protection for the lower orders in their matrimonial troubles, and this, as we shall be proceeding to demonstrate further, remains at the heart and sets the tone of the summary jurisdiction. There is evidence to suggest that one half of the complainants who obtain matrimonial orders in the summary courts never proceed to a divorce, but remain in a matrimonial limbo in which they are single in reality but married in law.[4] In the five years 1968–1972 the number of matrimonial orders made by the magistrates averaged some 22,000 a year.[5] On this footing, the summary jurisdiction embalms 11,000 dead marriages every year. But it could reasonably be held that the number of applications to the magistrates provides a more realistic measure of the number of collapsed marriages in this category than does the number of orders. Many women are

---

[1] See paragraph 4.58 above.
[2] It is worth remarking, in this connection, that affiliation proceedings remain a matter for the magistrates. This reflects the historical association between the bastardy and poor laws: Appendix 5, Section 5.
[3] See paragraph 4.39 above.
[4] See Section 6 below, and Appendix 7.
[5] *Civil Judicial Statistics* 1972, Cmnd 5333, 1973, Table M.

refused orders because they have committed a matrimonial offence, even though their husbands have deserted them and no longer give them financial support (and, besides, may well themselves be guilty of a matrimonial offence at least as serious). On this view, the 11,000 cases above mentioned will be nearer 16,000 a year. It is notorious that a high proportion of the husbands and a lower proportion of the wives in this situation set up illicit unions and have illegitimate children.

4.68 We conclude that not merely do the two matrimonial jurisdictions co-exist as formerly, but one of them is founded on principles which have been rejected by the other. Even in the act of reforming itself, English matrimonial law has so far failed to escape from its habit of dispensing two brands of matrimonial justice, whose antinomy is now stronger than ever before.[1]

SECTION 6—THE USE MADE OF THE MAGISTRATES' JURISDICTION

THE PAUCITY OF OFFICIAL STATISTICS

4.69 We have set out in Part 3 of this Report, in dealing with the demography of one-parent families, what is known of the social characteristics of the population which has resort to the divorce courts. It was possible to deal with the subject in that way because the bulk of the relevant material may be collected from official and scientifically-based sources. We found a very different situation when we sought to obtain similar information about the magistrates' matrimonial jurisdiction. The only official statistics relating to the exercise of this jurisdiction are contained in one table in the annual *Criminal Statistics* and this is restricted to the number of applications for orders and the number granted.[2]

4.70 We deplore this paucity of information which has hindered our work as it hindered the work of the Graham Hall Committee.[3] Accordingly, we have made detailed recommendations in Part 4, Section 14, for the improvement of the official statistics.

4.71 Table 3.15[4] sets out the information drawn from official statistics of the number of applications for matrimonial orders made in the magistrates' courts during the period 1950–1972. It shows that (notwithstanding the increase in the proportion of spouses taking their marital disputes to the court who petition for divorce)[5] the absolute numbers of applications to the magis-

---

[1] In framing this paragraph we have not directly adverted to the suggestion recently made by the Law Commission that the contrast under discussion reflects a division of function between the two jurisdictions, the divorce court catering for permanent breakdowns, the magistrates providing a clearing station service for matrimonial casualties, and distinguishing permanent breakdowns from temporary separations. We deal specifically with this argument in Section 14.

[2] Since 1968, the annual *Civil Judicial Statistics* have contained a table showing the number of attachment of earnings orders.

[3] See the *Report of the Committee on Civil Judicial Statistics*, Cmnd 3684, 1968, page 60.

[4] See Part 3, Section 3.

[5] In 1935 there were 480 complaints for matrimonial orders to the magistrates' courts for every 100 petitions for divorce by wives. (As the complainants are almost always wives, the proper comparison is with wife petitioners.) In 1970 the ratio was 66 complaints to every 100 petitions. (The year 1970 has been taken to avoid the exceptional situation created in 1971 by the implementation of the Divorce Reform Act 1969.)

trates for matrimonial orders has remained remarkably stable, the yearly average of such applications ranging round 32,000 to 33,000 over the entire period.[1]   This, together with the proportion of applications which are successful, is virtually the limit of what may be ascertained from the official data.

Data from Existing Studies

4.72   As we could not rely upon regularly published official data, we had to start our work by utilising the findings of the only two studies which have been made of this field.   One was the study of maintenance proceedings undertaken by the Home Office for the Graham Hall Committee.[2]   This shows the amounts of maintenance awarded by magistrates' courts throughout the country during September and October 1966.   These data were obtained from returns which all courts are required to make to the Inland Revenue under the provisions of the Finance Acts which apply to small maintenance payments. The other was a national survey of all maintenance orders " live " on 1 January 1966 undertaken by the Department of Sociology at Bedford College, University of London.[3]

4.73   We now summarise sufficient of the leading findings of these two studies to enable us both to draw a social profile of the population which seeks a cure for its marital ills from the magistrates' courts and to test the conclusions which we reached from our own study of the history of family law. At the outset, we knew that the social composition of the divorcing and still married populations were very similar in 1951 and 1961.[4]   There is no reason to think that there has been any change in the last decade.   On the other hand, both the Home Office and the Bedford College investigations demonstrate that complainants and defendants before magistrates are drawn chiefly from the poorer section of the working class.   The authors of *Separated Spouses* record that:

> Even allowing for the strong incentive of defendants to understate their earnings and the inadequate means of checking in many courts, we can record that 70% of the defendants against whom orders were made in 1965 had incomes of less than £16 a week.   This may be compared with the average earnings of men in manufacturing industry of £18 a week in 1965. . . .   These data relating to the occupations and incomes of defendants are crude but they demonstrate clearly that the matrimonial jurisdiction of magistrates is used almost entirely by the working class and very largely by the lowest paid among them.[5]

The Graham Hall Committee reached the same conclusion:

> All the evidence available suggests that the parties in the great majority of broken marriages have very limited financial resources and that those who become defendants to proceedings for maintenance in magistrates' courts have earnings or salaries well below the national average.   This is a factor which cannot be too strongly emphasised.[6]

[1] There is no measure of changes in the population at risk over this period.
[2] The design of the study is explained in the report of the committee, *op cit*, Appendix I.
[3] The design of the study is explained in the report on its findings published as *Separated Spouses*, Duckworth, 1970.
[4] *Ibid*, pages 135–136, and Norman Carrier and Griselda Rowntree: ' The Resort to Divorce in England and Wales, 1858–1957,' in *Population Studies*, Volume XI, No 3, 1958, pages 221–224.
[5] *Op cit*, page 70.
[6] *Op cit*, paragraph 103.

4.74   The low income of defendants is reflected in the amount of maintenance ordered by the courts for wives and children.   Table 4.3 shows the amounts awarded for wives in the Bedford College and Home Office surveys.   As the Bedford College sample contains orders made over a long period of time[1] but " live " on 1 January 1966 whilst the Home Office sample consists only of orders made in September and October 1966, it is to be expected that the amounts payable under orders in the Bedford College survey will be smaller than those in the Home Office survey.   Allowing for this, the results of the two surveys are very similar and show how far the average amounts payable fell short of the statutory limit which then existed[2] of £7·50 a week for wives.

TABLE 4.3

AVERAGE   AMOUNTS*   PAYABLE   TO   WIVES   UNDER MATRIMONIAL   ORDERS: BEDFORD   COLLEGE   SAMPLE   OF ORDERS LIVE ON 1 JANUARY 1966, COMPARED WITH THE HOME OFFICE SAMPLE OF ORDERS MADE DURING SEPTEMBER AND OCTOBER 1966; ORIGINAL ORDERS ONLY

Sample	Number of children on order					Total
	0	1	2	3	4 or more	
Bedford College:						
Number of orders	519	174	120	40	23	876
Average amount payable to wife	£1 18s	£2 1s	£1 19s	£1 18s	£1 8s	£1 18s
Home Office:						
Number of orders	635	755	649	328	256	2,623
Average amount payable to wife	£2 19s	£3 2s	£2 19s	£2 14s	£2 7s	£2 18s

* Amounts rounded to nearest shilling.

Source: *Report of the Committee on Statutory Maintenance Limits, op cit*, Table 9, paragraph 127; *Separated Spouses, op cit*, page 79.

4.75   No wife in the Bedford College sample had been awarded the maximum amount and only 1 per cent had orders for £5·50 or more; in the Home Office sample, 1·9 per cent of wives had orders for £7.50 and 6 per cent had more than £5.50.   The amounts ordered for children are shown in Table 4.4.

---

1 There were ninety orders in the sample older than twenty years.   The earliest order was made in 1920.

2 In 1949 the limits of the amounts that the magistrates could order were £2 a week for a wife and 10s for a child.   This was increased to £5 and 30s in that year, and to £7 10s and 50s in 1960.   The limits were abolished by the Maintenance Orders Act 1968.   See Table in the report of the Graham Hall Committee, *op cit*, page 88.

TABLE 4.4

AVERAGE AMOUNTS* PAYABLE FOR CHILDREN UNDER GUARDIANSHIP ORDERS AND MATRIMONIAL ORDERS WITH PROVISION ONLY FOR CHILDREN: BEDFORD COLLEGE SAMPLE OF ORDERS LIVE ON 1 JANUARY 1966, COMPARED WITH HOME OFFICE SAMPLE OF ORDERS MADE DURING SEPTEMBER AND OCTOBER 1966; ORIGINAL ORDERS ONLY

Sample	Number of children on order				Total
	1	2	3	4 or more	
Bedford College:					
Number of orders ...	166	79	29	15	289
Average amount payable	£1 10s	£2 13s	£3 12s	£4 8s	£2 3s
Average amount payable for each child	£1 10s	£1 6s	£1 4s	£1 0s	£1 6s
Home Office:					
Number of orders ...	417	275	114	53	859
Average amount payable	£2 0s	£3 17s	£4 18s	£5 7s	£3 0s
Average amount payable for each child	£2 0s	£1 18s	£1 12s	£1 7s	£1 14s

* Amounts rounded to nearest shilling.

Source: *Report of the Committee on Statutory Maintenance Limits, op cit*, Table 10, paragraph 128; *Separated Spouses op cit*, page 81.

Maximum amounts were more often ordered for children than for wives; nevertheless, only one fifth of the children in the Home Office sample were given the maximum of £2.50 a week. Both samples show a steady decline in the amount awarded for each child as family size increases and both demonstrate that average amounts fell far short of the statutory maxima.

4.76 The amounts payable under court orders may be contrasted with rates of benefit payable by the National Assistance Board in October 1966. For example, in the Home Office sample of orders, two thirds of the wives with two children were awarded less than £3 5s; on national assistance (assuming that both children were under 5 years old) they would have been entitled to £6 1s with a rent allowance in addition.[1] The report of the Graham Hall Committee commented on this situation:

> One incidental result of the recent development of social security has been to set new standards for maintenance. As it is most often families with the least resources that are involved in maintenance proceedings, it is inevitable that unfavourable comparisons are drawn between uncertain, irregular and meagre payments obtained through a court and the assured support of supplementary benefit provided as of right by the Ministry of Social Security. However hard magistrates and court officials try to operate the present system sensitively and effectively, they cannot provide more than defendants produce.[2]

[1] The annual *Report of the National Assistance Board* for 1965 (Cmnd 3042, page 15) estimated that the average housing costs of householders on national assistance, who had housing costs at all, was 29s 10d.

[2] *Op cit*, paragraph 232.

4.77 Both studies showed that there is a large gap between the amounts the court orders defendants to pay and what the orders actually produce for the wives and children. 39 per cent of all the orders in the Bedford College sample were found to be in arrears. Moreover Table 4.5 shows that the larger the order the more likely it is to be in arrears.

TABLE 4.5

PROPORTION OF MATRIMONIAL ORDERS, INCLUDING ORDERS FOR DEPENDENT CHILDREN, FOR VARYING WEEKLY AMOUNTS LIVE ON 1 JANUARY 1966 IN ARREARS FOR MORE THAN £20

Amount of order	Percentage in arrears
	%
£6 10s and over	57
£5 10s but under £6 10s	52
£4 10s but under £5 10s	49
£3 5s but under £4 10s	47
£2 15s but under £3 5s	40
£2 5s but under £2 15s	31
£1 15s but under £2 5s	42
£1 5s but under £1 15s	27
15s but under £1 5s	22
5s but under 15s	28

Source: *Separated Spouses, op cit*, page 87.

4.78 When the arrears history of orders in the Bedford College sample was examined in terms of the number of weekly payments, 38 per cent of all orders live on 1 January 1966 had been in arrears for more than six weeks and one quarter of them for more than six months.

4.79 Maintenance orders do not respond quickly or proportionately to changes in the cost of living. By the Money Payments (Justices' Procedure) Act 1935, magistrates' courts were empowered to vary maintenance orders without the submission of " fresh evidence ".[1] Accordingly, it might have been expected that the rapid inflation of recent years would have produced a high rate of complaints for variation. This has by no means been the case. The Bedford College sample showed that 6 per cent of orders were varied within one year of being made, 20 per cent were varied within three years, 32 per cent within five years and 39 per cent within nine years.[2] In three quarters of the complaints the amount was reduced and in only one quarter was it raised. Similarly, the Graham Hall Committee found that the:

> power to vary orders is resorted to in respect of only a minority of orders and, when it is, it has the effect of reducing the amount payable more frequently than of increasing it.[3]

[1] This enabled courts to vary orders in accordance with changes in the circumstances of the parties or in the level of prices.

[2] *Separated Spouses, op cit*, page 83.

[3] *Op cit*, paragraph 145.

Thus, the amounts awarded to wives by magistrates' courts are largely insensitive either to changes in the circumstances of the parties or to increases in the cost of living.

4.80   It was possible to use the Bedford College data to compare the duration of marriage at the time when the wife obtained an order from a magistrates' court with the duration of marriage at the time when petitioners for divorce obtained their decree absolute.

TABLE 4.6

DURATION OF MARRIAGE (i) AT DATE OF MAKING A MAGISTRATES' MATRIMONIAL ORDER, ALL ORDERS LIVE ON 1 JANUARY 1966, AND (ii) BEFORE DECREE ABSOLUTE IN 1966

Duration of marriage	Orders made by magistrates' courts		Decrees absolute	
	%	%	%	%
Under 3 months	0·1			
3 months but under 6 months	0·3			
6 months but under 1 year	2·6	16		1
1 year but under 2 years	7			
2 years but under 3 years	6			
3 years but under 5 years	12		12	
5 years but under 7 years	12	34	14	38
7 years but under 9 years	10		12	
9 years but under 12 years	13		15	
12 years but under 15 years	10	36	11	41
15 years but under 20 years	13		15	
Over 20 years	14		20	

Source: *Separated Spouses, op cit*, Table 25, page 73; *Registrar General's Statistical Review of England and Wales for the Year* 1966, *Part II, Tables*, Table P4.

When allowance is made for the number of magistrates' court orders which are obtained within the first three years of marriage when divorce, other than in exceptional circumstances, is not possible, the durations of the marriages of complainants before magistrates and of petitioners to the High Court are remarkably similar.

4.81   The Bedford College study also provides an estimate of the proportion of wives who followed their complaint before the magistrates by subsequently appearing as a petitioner or respondent in the divorce court.   It shows that a:

significantly higher proportion of divorce petitions filed in registries in the Midlands, the North, and Wales, were preceded by hearings before magistrates' courts than was the case with those filed in either London or in the Eastern and Southern counties of England.   The marked regional differences clearly reflect the familiar higher socio-economic level of the population in the South-east. . . .[1]

---

[1] *Separated Spouses, op cit*, page 140.

The authors conclude that:

> The best estimate which we can make suggests that about one half of all wives in receipt of magistrates' maintenance order find themselves in the divorce court . . . .[1]

In other words, for one half of the population which carries its matrimonial problems to the magistrates' courts, the exercise of a jurisdiction that cannot grant a licence to marry again is the terminus of marriage. They calculated that there were some 165,000 matrimonial orders and some 41,000 affiliation orders live in January 1966.[2] The live matrimonial orders represent a vary large number of empty shells of dead marriages.

4.82   Finally, these studies showed that:

> The convenience and feelings of litigants have hardly ever been considered in the administration of this branch of summary justice.[3]

Section 57 (1) of the Magistrates' Court Act 1952 provides that:

> The business of magistrates' courts shall, so far as is consistent with the due dispatch of business, be arranged in such manner as may be requisite for separating the hearing and determination of domestic proceedings from other business.

The Graham Hall Committee reported that:

> Many courts arrange for domestic proceedings to be held in a building separate from the ordinary criminal court and for the collecting office to be located in the same place. In many others, however, arrangements of this kind will not become practicable until out-of-date premises can be replaced. The fault is not always attributable solely to the inadequate accommodation available. We understand that some magistrates are reluctant to organise their sittings in such a way as to enable domestic proceedings to be held on a separate day. This may on occasion be because they are reluctant to sit in the afternoons as well as the morning, or because they are unwilling or unable to sit on more than one day a week.[4]

This experience helps in part to explain why the Bedford College survey reported that :

> . . . some of the most disturbing findings . . . come from the opinions of wives and husbands who have been through the courts . . . we have found compelling the weight of evidence that the working class couples who go to the magistrates with their matrimonial troubles feel that they are treated like criminals in a court which is predominantly concerned with petty crime.[5]

Further, there was convincing evidence that the administrative organisation of the court collecting offices—their hours of opening and their procedures—were often ill-adapted to the needs of those who use them.[6]

---

[1] *Ibid*. The Magistrates' Association does not disclose the evidence for its statement that " for some years something like two thirds of the matrimonial cases before the magistrates have later come before the High Court for divorce, and now if undefended they will come before the county courts." (' Domestic Courts: Memorandum submitted to the Law Commission,' printed as Appendix VI to the *Annual Report of the Magistrates' Association* 1968–69, page 51.)

[2] *Ibid*, pages 41–42.

[3] *Ibid*, page 122.

[4] *Op cit*, paragraph 112.

[5] *Op cit*, pages 207–208.

[6] These matters are further considered in Section 8 below.

4.83   Given the low incomes of the families who take their matrimonial troubles to the summary courts, the small amounts of maintenance there awarded, the high proportion of orders in arrears and the failure of the variation procedure to adjust the amount payable to changes in the cost of living, it is inevitable that a large number of wives and mothers with court orders will have to resort to the Supplementary Benefits Commission.   It is therefore regrettable that there has been no empirical study which follows the same families on their journeys from the one institution to the other.   Such has been the past gap between legal and social research that the complainants and defendants who pass through the courts have belonged to family lawyers, and the clients and liable relatives who meet the officers of the Supplementary Benefits Commission have been the property of the students of social administration.   But to a large extent these two groups are the same folk—a stage army wearing the insignia of legal orders on one shoulder and the epaulets of supplementary benefit on the other.   How they are regarded and classified depends simply on the observer's angle of vision.

4.84   The Commission are the only source of information about this army viewed from the supplementary benefit angle.   The Commission's predecessor, the National Assistance Board, supplied the Graham Hall Committee with tables showing the number of separated wives, divorced women and mothers of illegitimate children receiving national assistance in 1963, 1964 and 1965. These tables also showed the total amount of assistance paid to each category of women, together with the amounts recovered from liable relatives.   A further table showed the proportion of women in each category with court orders, out-of-court arrangements or without either, and the regularity with which orders and arrangements were complied with.   Some of these data are summarised in Table 4.7.

TABLE 4.7

SEPARATED WIVES RECEIVING ASSISTANCE DURING THE YEARS 1963-1965

	Year		
Total number of wives on assistance	1963	1964	1965
	102,000	103,000	104,000
	Percentages		
Proportion of wives with:			
(a) court order	39	42	41
(b) out-of-court arrangement	11	11	11
(c) neither (a) nor (b)	50	47	48
	Percentages		
Payment from husband			
Court order or out-of-court arrangement:			
complied with regularly	28	27	28
complied with irregularly	8	8	8
No payment made ...	64	65	64

Source: Adapted from the report of the Graham Hall Committee, *op cit*, Appendix D.

Table 4.7 shows that half the wives receiving national assistance in the years 1963–1965 had either a court order or had made a voluntary agreement with their husbands for maintenance. Yet almost two thirds of the husbands paid nothing and only between one quarter and one third of them paid regularly.

THE LIABLE RELATIVE ENQUIRY

4.85 The Supplementary Benefits Commission have made available to us the results of an unpublished enquiry (the " liable relative enquiry ") carried out in June 1970 into the number and types of claimants receiving supplementary benefits who ought to have been maintained by a liable relative: in other words, cases in which husbands and wives should have been maintaining each other and in which parents should have been supporting their children.

4.86 The liable relative enquiry shows that the number of divorced and separated wives receiving national assistance or supplementary benefit increased from 104,000 in 1965 to 141,000 in 1971. Table 4.8 sets out the amounts of maintenance awarded under court orders to separated wives, divorced women and their children who were in receipt of supplementary benefit in 1970.

TABLE 4.8

AMOUNT OF MAINTENANCE PAYABLE UNDER THE ORDERS OF THE HIGH COURT AND OF MAGISTRATES' COURTS TO DIVORCED WOMEN AND SEPARATED WIVES IN RECEIPT OF SUPPLEMENTARY BENEFIT IN JUNE 1970 AND TO THEIR LEGITIMATE, DEPENDENT CHILDREN

Amount payable to divorced women and to separated wives	Number of children			
	0	1	2	3 or more
	Percentages			
Up to and including £1	33	21	8	5
Over £1 up to and including £3 ...	47	74	43	25
Over £3 up to and including £5 ...	15	5	43	35
Over £5	5	—	6	35
Total number of orders	30,000	28,500	25,500	18,500

Source: Calculated from the 1970 liable relative enquiry (see paragraph 4.85 above).

Table 4.8 demonstrates at a glance why the beneficiaries of the 102,500 orders which it summarises would have been forced to apply for supplementary benefit even if their maintenance had been paid regularly. More than three quarters of the women without dependent children had maintenance orders for £3 or less and only 5 per cent of them had orders for more than £5 a week. In the case of mothers with three children or more, two thirds had orders for amounts up to £5 and about one third were entitled to more than £5 a week. The findings of the Supplementary Benefits Commission's liable relative enquiry in respect of the amounts of maintenance awarded by the courts are entirely in line with those of the other investigations to which we have referred in paragraphs 4.74 and 4.75 above.

99

4.87   Table 4.9 provides a rough measure of the degree of compliance with court orders. It shows that 45 per cent of the orders were complied with regularly (on the measure of 75 per cent or more), 40 per cent were irregularly complied with (on the measure of 10 per cent or less) and the remaining 15 per cent fell between an 11 per cent and a 74 per cent degree of compliance. Moreover the Supplementary Benefits Commission point out that 91 per cent of the orders falling below the 10 per cent degree of compliance were not paid at all. These data accord well with the findings of the other empirical studies concerning arrears on maintenance orders which we have cited in paragraphs 4.76 and 4.77 above.

TABLE 4.9

DEGREE OF COMPLIANCE WITH MAINTENANCE ORDERS OF THE HIGH COURT AND OF MAGISTRATES' COURTS; ORDERS LIVE IN JUNE 1970

Beneficiary of order	Percentage of orders complied with to the extent of			Total number of orders
	75% or more	11%–74%	up to 10%	
	%	%	%	
Divorced women and wives living apart from their husbands	55	8	37	30,000
Divorced women, wives living apart from their husbands and their dependent legitimate children	35	19	46	48,000
Dependent legitimate children	51	14	35	24,500
Total orders	46,000	15,000	41,500	102,500

Source: Calculated from the liable relative enquiry, *op cit.*

4.88   The liable relative enquiry breaks down into specific reasons why payment on 40 per cent of the maintenance orders fell into the category of less than a 10 per cent degree of regularity. Reasons were known in respect of 53 per cent of the instances. In 29 per cent the liable relative was unable to pay the full amount,[1] and in 24 per cent he could not be traced.

4.89   Finally, it is possible to consider the total liability which falls upon the taxpayer in supporting these casualties of broken homes. The information supplied to the Graham Hall Committee by the National Assistance Board disclosed that in 1965 16 per cent of the maintenance provided for lone mothers on national assistance, where there was a liability to maintain, came from the liable relative, and the remainder was contributed by the Board. The liable relative enquiry shows that the proportions were almost exactly the same in 1970. In that year, the Supplementary Benefits Commission paid out some

---

[1] In practice, this meant that he could not pay anything.

£93·25 million to divorced women, separated wives, and mothers responsible for illegitimate children who received a further £8 million from the men liable to support them. The Commission recovered about £8·40 million from the liable relatives.[1] On any showing, the amount which maintenance orders contribute to the subsistence of their beneficiaries is very small. Moreover, calculations made on the basis of the information available to the Graham Hall Committee suggest that the liability of the taxpayer would be reduced by no more than one quarter even if every maintenance order made were paid regularly and in full.[2]

4.90 Thus the findings of the Supplementary Benefits Commission's liable relative enquiry reinforce those of the studies based on court records. All point irresistibly to the conclusion that the real problem of maintenance is not the unwillingness but the inability of men to pay. There is not enough money to go round.

DATA FROM STUDIES INITIATED BY THE COMMITTEE

4.91 At this point in our enquiries, both our study of the history of the law and the factual information which we had been able to collect from various sources and to analyse brought us to the point of persuasion that much of the Victorian inheritance of one matrimonial law for the better off and another for the poor—an inheritance repeatedly remarked on and condemned in the past— has survived unchanged into the present, those two systems being institutionalised respectively in the divorce courts and the summary courts. Nevertheless, we decided that the confirmation or falsification of this preliminary conclusion would require an up-to-date study designed to test it. Accordingly we arranged for those responsible for the Bedford College study to engage in a further research project.

4.92 The report on this further research is reproduced in full as Appendix 7.[3] It falls into two parts. The original Bedford College study was based on a national, random sample of 1,230 matrimonial orders of the magistrates' courts " live ", that is, being enforced, on 1 January 1966. This study therefore related to orders which had been made before that date. The " follow-up " study Section of the report in Appendix 7 deals with the results of a further investigation of that same sample of 1,230 orders as at 1 July 1971. In addition, a national, random sample was taken of some 500 new matrimonial orders made by magistrates' courts in the months of April, May and June 1971, and the second part of the report in Appendix 7 deals with the results disclosed by a study of those orders.

4.93 The results of this further research impressively corroborate the conclusions to which the rest of the evidence tended. We have abstained from burdening the text by repeating the findings in the detail which gives them their importance, but from the mass of information contained in Appendix 7, we draw particular attention to the following points.

The "follow-up" study

4.94 About two thirds of the orders live on 1 January 1966 were still being enforced on 1 July 1971. Nearly half of the remainder which terminated

---

1 See Table 4.14, Section 10.
2 See *Separated Spouses, op cit*, page 162.
3 It was written by Professor O R McGregor and Dr Colin Gibson.

during this period had been ten years old or more, and the bulk of these had terminated in consequence of an event such as the death of a spouse, the divorce and subsequent remarriage of a wife, or the attainment of the age of 16 by a child, which automatically determines an order, in contrast to a complaint for variation. More than half of the orders still live on 1 July 1971 were ten years old, or older. This would indicate that on that date there were some 58,000 orders in force in England and Wales which were ten years old, or older. We conclude that the summary jurisdiction is not, as is sometimes suggested, restricted to intervention into the petty and evanescent dispute, although, of course, it often does deal with such cases. If a breakdown that lasts ten years or more is to be regarded as permanent, then the marriages of one third of all the spouses who take their cases to the magistrates are no less permanently broken than those of petitioners to the divorce court. The Divorce Reform Act 1969 makes five years of actual separation a fact from which irretrievable breakdown may be deduced. On that footing, the proportion of permanent breakdown among those who resort to the summary jurisdiction must be far larger than one third.

4.95   Despite the inflation which took place between 1966 and 1971, the amounts of maintenance which the magistrates awarded when making orders in the two months of September and October 1966 were significantly higher than the amounts payable in July 1971 on orders made before 1966. The case of orders made in favour of a wife with one child may be taken as an example. Of such orders made in the autumn of 1966, 44 per cent were for weekly amounts in excess of £5, but five years later, in the summer of 1971, only 7 per cent of the orders made before 1966, and still in force, were for more than £5 a week. The pattern holds good for orders in favour of a wife with two or more children, and " for children " only orders. The variations of orders that did occur were much more frequently due to the occurrence of some " automatic " event than to a complaint made by either party relating to a change in financial circumstances. Most variations resulted in a reduction, not an increase, of the amount previously payable under the order. In short, the procedure for variation, one of the main purposes of which should be to keep orders in step with the cost of living, is demonstrated to be virtually useless for that purpose.

4.96   Half of the orders live at the beginning of 1966 and still being enforced in July 1971 were in arrears at the latter date. Of these orders in arrears, half showed arrears of more than £200 and one quarter of more than £500. Three quarters of all the orders live at both dates were more than six weeks in arrears and two fifths of them were more than two years in arrears.[1] There is a direct relationship between the incidence of arrears and the amount of the order: generally speaking, the higher the amount of the order, the greater the chance that there will be arrears. Irrespective of the amount of the order, the likelihood is that a woman who does not go out to work will have to draw upon supplementary benefits.

---

[1] Normally, arrears should not be enforced when more than a year old. This had long been the High Court practice before it was made a statutory requirement in the divorce jurisdiction by the Matrimonial Proceedings and Property Act 1970, section 10. There is no corresponding statutory provision applying to arrears of maintenance in the summary jurisdiction, but the practice was enjoined on magistrates by Lord Merriman P in *Pilcher v Pilcher* (No 2) (1956) 1 WLR 298.

The orders made in April, May and June 1971

4.97 Before their abolition by the Maintenance Orders Act 1968, there were statutory limits of £7·50 and £2·50 a week upon the amounts which the magistrates could order to be paid for a wife and a child. The limits were abolished after an era of rising prices, which thereafter continued to rise. But the new orders made during the three months of 1971 awarded only one mother in ten with one child, one mother in sixteen with two children, and one in ten with three children, a sum in excess of the limits which had been abolished three years previously. Nearly one quarter of all these orders were for £3 or less, and two thirds of them were for £8 or less.

4.98 Most of the husbands against whom the orders were made were in manual jobs. Nearly one third of the court records examined gave no information concerning the husband's income. (We do not pause at this stage to examine the implications of this lack of record when, it may be, years later and before a differently constituted bench of magistrates, a wife applies for a variation.) The information that is recorded puts it beyond doubt, however, that in 1971, just as in 1966 (and, it may be added, just as throughout its history since its inception in 1878), the jurisdiction was used almost exclusively by the working classes, and very largely by the poorest among them.

4.99 The court records were extremely deficient in information relating to the financial situation of the wives. But half of the wives in three quarters of the sample were in receipt of supplementary benefit at the time of the hearing, and of these, half again were receiving £8 a week or more from that source.

4.100 A comparison can be made between the level of maintenance orders in force in 1966, adjusted for changes in the cost of living until June 1971, and the actual amounts awarded by the magistrates in the orders they made in the spring of 1971. For almost every size of family, the wife with an adjusted 1966 order would have been better off than under the order actually made in 1971; this feature is particularly noticeable in the case of the larger families.

4.101 Finally, a comparison can be made between the amounts awarded by the magistrates to fatherless families of different sizes in the spring of 1971 with the amounts which would have been payable to the same families had they been on supplementary benefit. We consider the results of this comparison to be so illuminating that in this one case we reproduce the relevant Table from Appendix 7, together with the comment there made on it.

TABLE 4.10

AMOUNTS OF MAINTENANCE AWARDED BY MAGISTRATES' COURTS TO FAMILIES OF DIFFERENT SIZE IN APRIL, MAY AND JUNE 1971 COMPARED WITH THE ENTITLEMENT OF THE SAME FAMILIES TO SUPPLEMENTARY BENEFIT

Type of order	Number of children	Amounts of maintenance ordered by the courts:[1] Legal Research Unit survey April-June 1971	Supplementary benefit scale rates[2]
		£	£
Wife only	Nil	3·89	8·20
Wife and children	1	6·06	9·70
	2	9·33	11·20
	3	10·72	12·70
	4 or more	12·75	15·70
Children only	1	3·05	9·70
	2	5·45	11·20
	3	7·87	12·70
	4 or more[3]	8·98	15·70

Source: See Table 50, Appendix 7.

Table 4.10 demonstrates beyond any possibility of dispute the extent to which amounts of entitlement under supplementary benefit exceed the amounts of maintenance ordered by the courts, even on the assumption that court orders would be paid regularly and in full.

[1] A mother with a maintenance order keeps her family allowances at the rate of 90p for the second child and £1 for the third and subsequent children. Family allowances are deducted from supplementary benefit payments. Accordingly, family allowances have been added to the amounts of maintenance ordered by the courts.

[2] Supplementary benefit was at the rate of £5·20 for a lone mother who was a householder and £1·50 for each child under 5. The allowance payable increases with the age of the child. It has been assumed that all children were under 5 thus giving minimum amounts of benefit. In addition, rent or mortgage interest payments are met by the Supplementary Benefits Commission. The £3 average for rent used in this calculation has been taken from the study undertaken in 1969 for the Department of Health and Social Security by Rosalind Marshall, *Families Receiving Supplementary Benefit*, HMSO, 1972, page 375, Table 46. In the sample on which this report was based, there were 61 separated wives whose rent allowance averaged £3 a week, taking mid-point of " under £2 " as £1 and of " £4 or more " as £5. A further 3 separated wives were owner-occupiers with mortgage payments outstanding. £3 has been added to the supplementary benefit scale rates to allow for rent allowance. As this average derives from a study undertaken in 1969 and Table 4.10 relates to the spring of 1971, the Table will under-estimate the amounts by which maintenance orders fall short of benefit.

[3] Taken as an average of 5 children.

SECTION 7—THE ASSESSMENT OF MAINTENANCE ORDERS[1]

PROCEDURES IN THE DIVORCE JURISDICTION

4.102   We have seen how the Matrimonial Proceedings and Property Act 1970, as it is being interpreted and applied by the courts, has created a new point of departure in the jurisdiction of the divorce court to make orders for financial provision.   The Act does not provide any automatic solution for the individual case, but, as interpreted, it does establish the landmarks of a modern regime for the adjustment of family property and finances upon the breakdown of marriage.   The salient feature of this regime is that it has taken a step towards the notion of financial partnership in marriage, albeit this becomes effective only upon the termination of marriage.   In the re-allocation of resources at that stage, the partnership notion is particularly reflected through two new rules.   First, the court is bound to take specifically into account the contribution which a spouse—who will in nearly all cases be the wife—has made by looking after the home or caring for the family.   Secondly, complaints by husband or wife about the other's conduct will rarely affect financial orders. For this purpose the rough and the smooth of marriage will not be meticulously weighed.   Misconduct has to be of an obvious and gross character before it will make any difference.

4.103   These reforms should lessen the burden on the divorce court by making it plainer to divorcing spouses that a settlement of their financial differences along broad and equitable lines is likely to produce much the same result as a rancorous litigation.   Where the divorce court does have to adjudicate on financial provision, it has available all of the usual apparatus of civil litigation through which to ascertain the facts it needs to know to make an assessment.   It may order both sides to give evidence of their resources on affidavit, and to disclose all relevant documents such as bank accounts, tax returns, share certificates and company records.   Each side and its witnesses may be cross-examined.   The decision will be given by a professional tribunal —judge or registrar.

4.104   These procedures are probably as efficient as any that can be devised when considerable property is involved or parties with elusive sources of income are reluctant to disclose them.   They are not, however, particularly well adapted to solve the difficulties which face any court in dividing a small income, when accuracy in the details and the clearest possible guidelines for effecting the division assume a critical importance.   The nature of these difficulties is well described in a recent decision in the Family Division in which Payne J, from a long experience, compared the relative capacities of judicial and administrative action in this context:

> The Department's[2] attitude in the present case, which is quite understandable, in the light of their policy, is that the wife has solicitors and counsel under the Legal Aid and Advice Act, that she has agreed on the advice and encouragement

---

[1] In the divorce jurisdiction the term " order for periodical payments " has replaced the term " maintenance order "; and in that jurisdiction financial provision can also take the form of secured periodical payments, lump sum payments, and transfers of property.   The magistrates continue to make " maintenance orders " and, in bastardy cases, " affiliation orders ".   In this and the next two succeeding Sections we shall be mostly concerned with the magistrates' jurisdiction and will continue to use the term " maintenance order " as a generic term unless the context shows otherwise.

[2] This is the Department of Health and Social Security.

of the Department to pursue her own remedies and that the Department therefore relies upon the Court to investigate the facts and make an appropriate order. This system in practice breaks down and plays into the hands of a recalcitrant husband because, whereas the Department has officers skilled in making enquiries and facilities for obtaining relevant information, the wife and her solicitors, even backed by the available procedures of the Court, cannot ascertain reliable facts about the husband's activities without the assistance of an accountant or enquiry agent, and, even if an application for authority were made by the wife's solicitors the Legal Aid Committee would be unlikely to approve of such expense being incurred for the purpose of recovering contributions which would not go to the wife but to the State. In the result the court is left with far less than the evidence which it requires for the purpose of making a proper assessment of the husband's means.[1]

PROCEDURES IN THE MAGISTRATES' JURISDICTION

Discrepancies between the two jurisdictions

4.105 None of the changes we have been describing affects the jurisdiction of the magistrates. They continue to be bound by the Matrimonial Proceedings (Magistrates' Courts) Act 1960, which provides that the magistrates may order maintenance to be paid by the husband to the wife (or, in the case where there is jurisdiction to make the order against the wife,[2] by the wife to the husband) by way of " such weekly sum as the court considers reasonable in all the circumstances of the case "; and either parent to make weekly payments " for the maintenance of any child of the family ".[3] These broad formulations are very like those which before the Act of 1970 applied in the divorce jurisdiction. We have already discussed the case law which applied to these formulations, the effect of which was that the law governing the assessment of maintenance was the same in both of the jurisdictions. The result of the Act of 1970 was therefore to open a gap between the old law which continued to apply in the magistrates' courts and the new law which applied in the divorce court. The abolition of the " bars " by the Divorce Reform Act 1969 had already highlighted the oddity that thenceforward it was only in the summary jurisdiction that the claimant's adultery was fatal to her obtaining any relief at all. But after 1970 the contrast became even more pronounced, for whereas the " obvious and gross " test applies in the divorce court, the magistrates, even when the complainant's adultery does not require them to put her out of court altogether, remain free to reflect their disapproval of any other matrimonial blemish they may detect in her by reference to the vague standards which previously applied in both jurisdictions. It remains true, in the summary jurisdiction, that:

> The magistrates are entitled among all the other circumstances of the case to take into account the conduct of both parties when fixing the amount of the weekly sum to be awarded. In the great majority of cases no doubt, the effect of any reprehensible conduct on the part of the wife will not have great effect on the amount of their award when that conduct is weighed against the conduct of the husband who has been guilty of the matrimonial offence alleged against

1 *Winter v Winter* (unreported; 9 November 1972). We deal elsewhere (Section 10, paragraph 202, below) with the important issue which the learned judge raises concerning the policy of the Supplementary Benefits Commission in encouraging their clients to apply for court orders.

2 See paragraph 4.62, footnote 2 (i) above.

3 Act of 1960, section 2.

him. But the discretion of the justices as to the effect to be given to the conduct of the parties on the amount of the weekly sum is not fettered save that the amount must be reasonable in all the circumstances of the case.[1]

Problems of assessment

4.106 Yet, as the Graham Hall Committee commented, in a passage that remains true only of the magistrates' jurisdiction:

> Neither statute nor case law gives courts guidance about how to compute the appropriate amount of maintenance in relation to the complainant's needs, the defendant's resources and their respective responsibility for the family breakdown. In matrimonial proceedings before magistrates proof of the commission of the matrimonial offence complained of establishes the fault of the defendant out of which the maintenance obligation arises. In many cases the complainant herself will not be free from blame. We understand that it is the practice of the courts to take this factor into account when fixing maintenance but there is no way of assessing the weight attached to this factor by different courts in different circumstances. Nor have we been able to discover whether particularly reprehensible conduct on the part of a defendant ever leads the court to fix a sum of maintenance larger than the complainant's needs would otherwise have required.[2]

4.107 The Graham Hall Report remarked further on the difficulty of reconciling the principle that the conduct of the wife may be taken into account when assessing the amount of her maintenance with the principle, also established in the decided cases, that the needs of the child may require that its mother, despite her own conduct, be fully maintained.[3] The assessment of separate amounts for the wife and each individual child must in any case involve a certain arbitrary element, since the cost of some of the basic needs of the household, such as rent, rates and heating, are only marginally affected by its size.[4]

4.108 The burden which all these complexities impose on the magistrates is aggravated by the circumstances that they are dealing nearly all the time with people of small means. This makes an accurate assessment of the resources and requirements all the more essential. The smaller the loaf, the more meticulous the division needs to be. "It is of the utmost importance that the decisions reached by magistrates about maintenance should be based on adequate and reliable information about the needs of the parties and their resources and liabilities."[5]

Weaknesses in the procedures of assessment

4.109 Yet there is no obligation placed on magistrates, and hardly any means available to them, to obtain information about the needs and means of persons affected by their orders other than what they manage to elicit from the witnesses who appear before them. The magistrates do have power[6] to require a probation officer to investigate and report, but the High Court has

---

1 *Courtney v Courtney* (1966) P 523, *per* Rees J at 537.
2 *Op cit*, paragraph 94.
3 *Ibid*, paragraph 95.
4 *Ibid*, paragraph 96.
5 *Ibid*, paragraph 213.
6 Magistrates' Courts Act 1952, section 60.

ruled that they are not bound to resort to this procedure, and that they should be slow do to so.[1] The power is rarely exercised, and its more frequent employment would embarrass an already over-stretched probation service. Understandably also, magistrates are often loth to adjourn for further investigation, particularly as there may be difficulties in reconstituting the same bench for the next hearing. It is to be emphasised here, as in many other aspects of the summary jurisdiction, that there are great variations in the practice of different courts.[2] Some courts require answers to a questionnaire which, if carefully completed before the trial, with the assistance of the justices' clerk or one of his staff, may well provide the court with sufficient and trustworthy information. Elsewhere, and commonly, the magistrates base their decision on little more than the production of a pay slip, which may easily be untypical of the husband's earnings. It may, for example, give a false impression of his normal overtime. The evidence may be supplemented by information as to the husband's means supplied by the complainant herself, but she is often ignorant of what he earns. Representatives of the magistrates and their clerks have stressed in their evidence to us that a local bench generally has a good knowledge of the going wage rates in its area, the amount of overtime available, the level of rent and other basic outgoings, and is able to bring all this knowledge to bear in assessing the probabilities. We agree that local knowledge is valuable, but as a check, not as a substitute, for ascertainment of the facts in the particular case.

4.110 Reference is made elsewhere to the unsatisfactory method of keeping records in many magistrates' courts. This deficiency is at its most deplorable when the bench which has to deal with the case on a second or subsequent occasion discovers that it has no access, or no ready access, to the materials and findings on which the original order was founded. Such information may be essential if justice is to be done on an application to vary maintenance, or suspend an order committing a man to prison for failure to comply with a maintenance order. In this connection, it is to be remembered that the magistrates are not compelled to give any reasons showing how they made their assessment, and are unlikely to have done so; and that the bench which deals with the same case subsequently may be composed of different magistrates.

The record of criticism

4.111 We are by no means the first to criticise the deficiencies of the summary jurisdiction in assessing financial means and responsibilities. The *Report of the Departmental Committee on Imprisonment by Courts of Summary Jurisdiction in Default of Payment of Fines and Other Sums of Money* (the Fischer Williams Committee) in 1934 recorded its conclusion that the procedure of the summary jurisdiction was inadequate to ascertain the financial circumstances of the parties, and that the court should be given an investigating arm of its own:

> . . . it seems to us that in cases where the decision to be taken by a Court of Summary Jurisdiction must turn on an estimate of the means and circumstances of at any rate one of the parties . . . the mere application of a rule as to the burden of proof often does not give a satisfactory result. . . . In such cases it

---

[1] *Kershaw v Kershaw* (1966) P 13.

[2] This is a very important point, since many magistrates and clerks will rightly fail to recognise deficiencies on which we comment in the practice of their own courts. It is, however, clear from our own and other studies that there is, regrettably, a great diversity of standards.

is necessary, if justice is to be done, that the Court should have its own means of inquiry into the truth and should not be compelled to give a decision based only on what can be gathered from the statements, often confused and imperfect, of the parties. We are therefore of opinion that every Court of Summary Jurisdiction should have the services of an officer to undertake inquiries, whenever the Court thinks such an inquiry necessary or desirable, for the purpose of ascertaining as closely as possible the means and circumstances of a defendant and also (in maintenance and affiliation cases) of the other party, and to present a report for the Court's guidance. . . . The need for the services of an Investigating Officer is felt mainly in maintenance and affiliation cases, where the Court often has difficulty in ascertaining the means and circumstances of the parties for the purpose either of fixing the weekly sum which the man should be ordered to pay, or for the purpose of determining how far a default is due to circumstances beyond the defendant's own control. . . . We recognise that the appointment of Investigating Officers will entail additional expenditure, but our justification for proposing such expenditure is that we think it necessary for the purpose of justice. So as far as such expenditure results in more efficient administration of the law, we believe that it will reduce the number of imprisonments and thereby effect a saving of public money as a set off.[1]

4.112 The *Report of the Committee on the Enforcement of Judgment Debts* (the Payne Committee) in 1969 recommended:

. . . the use universally throughout magistrates' courts in England and Wales of a prescribed form of questionnaire to ensure consistent and thorough examination of means in all magistrates' courts whenever it is necessary to enquire into a defaulter's resources, whatever the nature of the debt.[2]

4.113 The Graham Hall Committee reported:

There is very little general published guidance about the procedures which ought to be followed by magistrates in assessing the means of the parties. Our enquiries made it clear that some courts have worked out elaborate and satisfactory machinery for this purpose. We found no uniformity and we were led to think that some magistrates fail to obtain adequate information about the range of considerations that are relevant to the determination of this issue.[3]

4.114 The Graham Hall Committee went on to consider ways of improving this situation:

An excellent arrangement would be for every court to have a means assessment officer who could undertake the necessary enquiries and provide the court with the information needed. This would require a new service and for all practical purposes must be rejected for the immediate future.[4]

4.115 Reference was made to the possibility that the local offices of the Ministry of Social Security (now the Department of Health and Social Security) should take over the role of means enquiries in respect of all parties to domestic proceedings in magistrates' courts. "However, as the decision of this issue did not fall within our terms of reference we make no recommendation."[5]

---

1 Cmd 4649, 1934, paragraphs 256 and 258–259.

2 Cmnd 3909, 1969, paragraph 1273.

3 *Op cit*, paragraph 214. Mention may also be made of the *Report of the Home Office Advisory Council on the Penal System*, 1970, which as regards fine defaulters states (paragraph 26), " We are not satisfied that magistrates' courts are adequately equipped to carry out the thorough investigation of means which the law requires before a fine defaulter is committed to prison. Too often the evidence available does not amount to much more than reported failure to comply with the demands for payment."

4 *Op cit*, paragraph 217.

5 *Ibid*, paragraph 219.

4.116 A positive recommendation was, however, made to the effect that the parties should be required to complete a questionnaire before any problem of default arose, so that the court might be assisted from the outset to fix the proper amount of maintenance to be ordered:

> The defect of the existing system is that the parties are not put sufficiently on notice before the hearing as to the matters about which the court will need to be informed. This could readily be remedied by sending each party, when the summons is issued, a questionnaire about their resources and liabilities. This might be either in a form which could be completed by them and handed to the court, or it could require them to have available evidence of the matters specified insofar as they were applicable. In either case the information on which the court bases its decision would be much more reliable than that provided at present. Much of the evidence we received from individual women suggested that defendants did not disclose all their earnings or sources of income. We were also informed that the courts were often forced to rely on their knowledge of the average wages of a particular trade in the locality. When evidence was produced it might relate to only one week's earnings which would often not be a typical amount. The defendant might have transferred property to a mistress or be being helped by her separate earnings. . . . We are of the opinion that a standard questionnaire could readily be devised . . . and we accordingly recommend that such a questionnaire should be prepared and that its issue to both parties in domestic proceedings should be prescribed. . . . We are . . . satisfied that in very many cases a procedure of this kind will result in the submission to the court of much more satisfactory information.[1]

4.117 Nothing has been done to give effect to this recommendation, which has now been repeated by the Law Commission.[2] The general picture is that departmental enquiries over a period which now covers some forty years have expressed anxieties over the adequacy of the methods used and the reliability of the results achieved in many magistrates' courts when fixing the amount of maintenance. Our own enquiries show that there is continuing good cause for these anxieties. The improvements which others have recommended have our support; but, as will emerge, the arrangements we consider to be necessary to give efficient administrative effect to the real character of the relationship between " the three systems " would remove much of the work of assessment in the usual run of cases out of the courts altogether.

SECTION 8—THE COLLECTION OF MAINTENANCE ORDERS

THE COLLECTING OFFICE AND FUNCTIONS OF THE JUSTICES' CLERK

4.118 A distinctive and valuable feature of the summary matrimonial jurisdiction is the system through which the magistrates' court itself collects and distributes the payments made in obedience to its own maintenance orders. There is no such provision made in the divorce jurisdiction. It is, however, possible for orders made in the divorce jurisdiction to be registered and enforced in a magistrates' court, and *vice versa*. The great bulk of the traffic is in the direction of the magistrates' court, so that by these means a wife who has been

---

[1] *Ibid*, paragraph 222.

[2] *Family Law, Matrimonial Proceedings in Magistrates' Courts*, Working Paper No 53, paragraphs 87–90 and 101. Meantime, the divorce jurisdiction has improved its own procedure by introducing a suggested form of affidavit of means, including a questionnaire designed to provide the information which seems likely to be required on the hearing of most applications for ancillary relief: Practice Note (Family Division: Affidavit of Means), 22 December 1972 (1973) 1 WLR 72.

awarded maintenance in divorce or other proceedings in the divorce jurisdiction can obtain the advantage of having the money collected for her, in the normal course, through the procedure available in the magistrates' court.

4.119   Until 1914, the responsibility for taking steps to collect and enforce the money due to a woman or her child under a maintenance or affiliation order rested entirely upon the woman herself.   Once the court had made the order, it had no further part to play unless and until the woman came back for a warrant of distress against her husband's goods or an order committing him to prison for his failure to pay.   Legislation in 1914 gave most magistrates' courts a discretionary power to direct that payments of maintenance be made through a third party, and to appoint an officer to act for this purpose.[1]   It became the practice, where these powers were exercised, to appoint the clerk to the justices as the collecting officer: he was remunerated by a commission of up to 5 per cent of the amount collected, payable from local funds.   In 1934 the Fischer Williams Committee recommended the revision and extension of these arrangements.[2]   These recommendations were substantially adopted,[3] and form the foundation of the modern law.[4]

4.120   The justices' clerk is now *ex officio* the collecting officer of any court of summary jurisdiction of which he is the clerk.   He is not separately remunerated for the discharge of his duties as collecting officer.   When the magistrates make a maintenance or affiliation order they must, unless they are satisfied upon the express representation of the applicant that they ought not to do so, require that the payments shall be made to a justices' clerk.   The statute further enacts that where:

> any sums payable under the order are in arrears, the clerk shall, if the person for whose benefit the payment should have been made so requests in writing, and unless it appears to the clerk that it is unreasonable in the circumstances so to do, proceed in his own name for the recovery of those sums . . . .[5]

4.121   The provision that the clerk need not proceed if he thinks it would be unreasonable to do so acknowledges that the existence of a maintenance order and the amount of debt which has been accumulated under it may not be conclusive of the just requirements of the situation at any particular time. The author of a leading text comments on this provision:

> The practice as to the clerk proceeding varies considerably in different areas. Some clerks are less disposed than others to take proceedings in their own name . . . . There would seem to be no authority as to what may properly be considered to be unreasonable, nor as to whether the facts to be considered are only those in relation to the defendant in arrear or those both in relation to the defendant and the person entitled to the payments.   When the clerk knows the defendant is out of employment through no fault of his own he may decline to proceed.   Some clerks . . . decline where the person entitled to the payment is abroad and the defendant's means have changed.   Some decline where there is strong evidence of adultery, and some where they consider the person entitled to

---

1 Affiliation Orders Act 1914; Criminal Justice Administration Act 1914 (the title of which is yet another example of the offensive labelling of the matrimonial disputes of the working classes).

2 *Op cit*, paragraphs 129–137.

3 Money Payments (Justices' Procedure) Act 1935.

4 Justices of the Peace Act 1949; Magistrates' Courts Act 1952, section 52.

5 Magistrates' Courts Act 1952, section 52(3).

the payments is quite capable of taking the proceedings. Is the clerk entitled to decline because the person entitled to the payments is working? The clerk is the person to advise the justices who have to enforce the order. The fact that he is complainant before his own court places him in a difficult and embarrassing position which can be easily misunderstood by the defendant brought before the court. This fact, many clerks feel, justifies their reluctance to proceed in their own name.[1]

4.122 Provision is also made requiring the clerk (unless he thinks that special circumstances make it " unnecessary or inexpedient " for him to do so) to notify the beneficiary whenever an amount equal to four times the weekly sum payable falls into arrears.[2]

4.123 The system of collection and distribution of maintenance through the court office can do much to ensure that a woman will receive what is due to her with a minimum of trouble. There are many courts in which this system is efficiently operated. Unfortunately, this is another area in which, certainly until very recently, the diversity of practice that we have noted was marked; and it operated with particular ill-effect.

DIVERSITY OF PRACTICE AND ITS EFFECTS

4.124 For the purposes of the study reported in *Separated Spouses*, 52 different magistrates' courts, located in all parts of the country, were visited by trained personnel. Court officials were interviewed wherever possible. Notes of interviews were taken, as well as details relating to the court premises, use of staff, type and quality of record keeping, and methods of collection and payment. The courts studied ranged from Leeds, where there were 3,000 live orders, to Longtown (in Cumberland), where there were 8. We quote from the findings:

> Many courts complained of shortage of staff. Only a minority of the fifty-two courts had a separate office for the collection and payment of maintenance. For the rest, maintenance payments are dealt with as part of the general work of a collecting office which handled all court fines and payments. Even where new courts had been built, only one possessed a separate office. Two courts had plans to provide a separate office. For the rest, husbands and wives waited in the queue with those paying fines for criminal offences, and the like. Collecting offices are generally housed within the court building, but in a number of cases the offices are separate from the court, sometimes adjoining the office of a local solicitor if he is part-time clerk of the court. They are usually centrally situated in the town and reasonably accessible to the public. Most court collecting offices are open daily during normal office hours 9.0 or 9.30 to 5.0 or 5.30 for paying in by defendants. Only three of fifty-two courts visited stayed open late enough on one night of the week to enable men to pay in after work.[3] Seven of the

---

[1] L M Pugh: *Matrimonial Proceedings Before Magistrates*, 2nd edition, Butterworths, 1966, page 12. Mr Pugh is Stipendiary Magistrate for Liverpool and formerly himself a clerk to justices.

[2] Magistrates' Courts Rules 1968, Rule 33. Here, again, there is some potentiality for embarrassment. Suppose the staff in the collecting office know or strongly suspect that the wife beneficiary of an order is living in adultery. Does this make it " unnecessary or inexpedient " to inform her of the arrears? Is it permissible to inform the husband of the wife's adultery?

[3] Forty years have elapsed since the Fischer Williams Committee reported: " The collection of moneys due under maintenance and affiliation orders would in our opinion be facilitated considerably and the risk of imprisonment in default of payment correspondingly diminished if the office of the collecting officer were open for the receipt of payments on one evening a week—preferably the evening of the day upon which wages were paid in the particular locality —and we recommend that justices should be required to consider whether such facilities should not be afforded." *Op cit*, paragraph 137.

fifty-two courts open their collecting offices for one or two hours on Saturday mornings. Some collecting offices open for paying in for shorter periods. The hours during which a wife may collect her maintenance are generally shorter than those for husbands paying in. Of the fifty-two court collecting offices, sixteen open daily; the rest range from four days a week to eleven which open for seven hours or less a week. These last include one court with 820 live orders, open on Monday, Wednesday and Friday afternoons, and another with 365 live orders, open from 2.0 pm until 4.0 pm on Tuesdays and Fridays. Only three of the fifty-two court offices stay open for one evening a week for collection. Twelve courts, mainly in rural areas, send most of their payments to the wives by post, but some, including four very large courts, do not allow a woman to receive her money by post unless she lives outside. The majority of courts allow telephone enquiries to find out if money has arrived, but seven, including two large courts, refuse to accept or strongly discourage, telephone calls.[1]

4.125 The authors continue:

> It is certain that the convenience and feelings of litigants have hardly ever been considered in the administration of this branch of summary justice. Such details as the opening hours of collecting offices or the willingness of court staff to save a woman the loss of half a day's earnings by giving her information over the telephone seem too trivial to be considered in legal discussion of the jurisdiction. But these are the sort of trivia that means for the mostly very poor and unhappy citizens who meet family law in the magistrates' courts, the difference between dignity and humiliation, between decency and squalor.[2]

4.126 The evidence given to us supports the findings of this investigation. We have received many complaints to the effect that the collection procedures can be unreliable, time-consuming, expensive and humiliating for the unsupported mother. She has had to go to court each week, or at least each month, to collect her maintenance, perhaps travelling a considerable distance with several small children, and having taken time off from work. If, as is often the case, the maintenance has not been paid, she may[3] have to make a further journey to seek a social security payment.

REFORMS IN THE PRACTICE

4.127 Very recently, the Rules have been amended, so that instead of the clerk having a discretion to pay maintenance by post at the request of the payee, he is required to transmit the money in this way unless the payee indicates that she prefers to collect it personally from the court office.[4] Recommendations have also been made to the clerks with a view to overcoming problems which can arise when the payee has no bank account into which to pay cheques.[5] These improvements in procedure should reduce the inconvenience and distress to which we have alluded, although they came into operation too late for us to test their effect. At the same time, it is disappointing that the Home Office have not as yet sought to meet a major criticism, and a theme of the evidence given to us (as it was in the evidence to the Fischer Williams Committee, so long ago) that the times of opening of collecting offices pay little regard to the working day of the people who have to use them.

---

[1] *Separated Spouses, op cit*, pages 121–122.

[2] *Ibid*, page 122.

[3] This will depend on whether the " diversion " procedure (see, for a description of this procedure, Section 10 below) has been implemented.

[4] The Magistrates' Courts (Amendment) Rules 1973, Schedule, paragraph 16, 1973, No 790, (L 11).

[5] Home Office Circular No 77/1973 (CS 8/1973), 9 May 1973, paragraphs 21–23.

SECTION 9—THE ENFORCEMENT OF MAINTENANCE ORDERS

INTRODUCTION

4.128   We received many complaints over the hardship inflicted on women who, having obtained a maintenance order, find themselves delayed, harassed or entirely frustrated in their efforts to enforce it against a recalcitrant or absconding debtor.   The sense of grievance and injustice which this understandably engenders, not only among the women themselves, but also among the spokesmen for their interests, has led to proposals that the State should guarantee the payment of maintenance orders, and itself take measures of the greatest stringency to ensure recovery of the money from the man who was liable to pay it.   We discuss proposals for State guarantees of maintenance payments, and our reasons for rejecting them as providing anything in the nature of a solution for the financial difficulties of one-parent families, in another Part of this Report.[1]   It is sufficient to remind oneself here that nearly all the maintenance orders made by the magistrates (and it is certain that this would also be true of very large numbers of orders made in the divorce court) are for less than the sum which the woman and children concerned would receive from supplementary benefits—this sum representing the guarantee which the State does in fact provide for the standard of living below which no citizen not in full-time work should fall.

4.129   At the same time, we regard it as most important that men should not be allowed to escape their financial obligations to their families to the extent that these have been fairly assessed and fall within a genuine capacity to pay. This raises the entire subject of enforcement procedures and the possibility of extending or improving on them.   We have given much thought to this subject, and our conclusions are that we recommend no change in existing procedures save that committal to prison as a means of enforcement of maintenance debts ought to be abolished.   Negative conclusions might justify short treatment of the facts and arguments which led us to them; but the expectations held in many quarters of the benefits to be derived from more rigorous enforcement measures, and the intensity of feeling which often goes with that view, have persuaded us that we should deal with the subject in some detail.

4.130   The term " enforcement " refers to something other than the machinery for collection discussed in Section 8.   That machinery is provided in the summary jurisdiction only, to afford the parties a convenient method of payment and receipt.   It has the important incidental advantage of establishing an independent and accurate record in the court's books of the maintenance account between the parties.   The processes of enforcement to be discussed here, however, are those which the law gives to creditors to enable them to compel their debtors to pay what they owe.   They operate by a seizure or charging of the debtor's property, or by pressure, through imprisonment or the threat of it, on his person.   The debtor could be a wife, but for ease of discussion we shall assume throughout that she is the creditor, seeking to recover from the husband what is due to her or to the children on a maintenance order.

---

[1] Part 5, Section 4.

114

Problems in the enforcement of maintenance

4.131 The types of order which can now be made within the divorce jurisdiction for financial provision are provided for in the Matrimonial Proceedings and Property Act 1970. It is sufficient for the present purpose to group the possibilities under three heads. The divorce court may order:

(1) maintenance[1] payments, either secured on property, or unsecured;

(2) lump sum payments; and

(3) the transfer or settlement of property.

There is no difficulty about enforcing an order for secured provision. Property, such as land, shares or a fund or money, will have been set aside specifically to guarantee the payments ordered to be made, and in case of default one or more of the ordinary processes of execution, suitable to the nature of the property, will be available to bring it in. Lump sum orders are also unlikely to give rise to any enforcement problems, since they require a once-and-for-all payment which the court will not order without knowledge of resources from which it can be made. Nor should there be any special difficulty in enforcing an order for transfer or settlement of existing property.

4.132 The enforcement of maintenance orders, however, has always raised problems and anomalies. When a maintenance order is made in favour of the wife, or her children, all that they acquire is a series of claims for each payment as and when it falls due. A payment which is only prospectively due is not a debt, so that there can never be prospective enforcement, or any cumulative enforcement except to the extent that arrears have accrued. No asset is set aside to guarantee the payment. On the other hand, in most cases the only source out of which payment can be made is the husband's earnings, which he personally receives and can usually spend before the law is able to prevent him.

4.133 Further, although arrears of maintenance do constitute a debt, it is a debt of an anomalous character in law. It cannot be assigned.[2] If the husband goes bankrupt, the wife cannot prove as a creditor in his bankruptcy, either for the value of future payments, or even for arrears accrued due before the commencement of the bankruptcy.[3] The reason underlying these rules was that the divorce court kept such a discretionary control over arrears of maintenance, by retaining a power to remit them, wholly or in part, or by requiring that leave of the court should be obtained before execution could issue for the arrears, that the debt lacked certainty.[4] This retention of control by the court was desirable in the interests of justice. It not infrequently happens that a husband who learns of a change in the wife's circumstances such as would justify a reduction or revocation of the maintenance order, merely discontinues payment without applying to the court. When this happens, it may be unfair to permit the wife to let arrears accumulate and then, in her own good time,

---

[1] As has previously been mentioned, the proper term in the divorce jurisdiction is now " periodical payments ", but it remains convenient to use the older nomenclature.

[2] *Re Robinson* (1884) 27 Ch D 160.

[3] *Re Linton* (1885) 15 QBD 239; *Kerr v Kerr* (1897) 1 QB 439.

[4] *Watkins v Watkins* (1896) P 222; *James v James* (1964) P 303.

issue execution for the arrears. In the result, a practice grew up in the divorce jurisdiction of refusing to enforce payment of more than one year's arrears except in special circumstances. This practice has recently acquired statutory force.[1]

The Debtors Act 1869

4.134 For all these reasons, the ordinary methods of execution were of limited assistance to the victim of default on a maintenance order made in the divorce court. The only other remedy available was the process open to all judgment creditors under the Debtors Act 1869. This Act gave the court power to commit to prison for a term not exceeding six weeks, or until payment of the sum due, any person who made default in payment of any debt due in pursuance of any order or judgment of that or any other competent court. Execution of the committal order could be suspended on terms that the debtor paid what was due, by a specified time, or by instalments, as well as what continued to accrue due. It was provided that the jurisdiction " shall only be exercised where it is proved to the satisfaction of the court that the person making default either has or has had since the date of the order . . . the means to pay the sum in respect of which he has made default, and has refused or neglected, or refuses or neglects, to pay the same ".[2]

ENFORCEMENT OF MAGISTRATES' ORDERS

Committal to prison

4.135 There were from the beginning only two means of enforcing maintenance orders made by the magistrates: distress or committal to prison. Distress, which involved execution by the police on the goods of the husband, has become as unpopular with the police as it was unproductive for the wives, and the remedy has consequently fallen into desuetude, and we recommend that it should now be abolished. Thus, from the early days, committal to prison was the sovereign remedy for failure to obey a maintenance order made by the magistrates. The magistrates' power to commit did not derive from the Debtors Act 1869. Committals in the divorce court under the Act of 1869 merely exemplified the use in the matrimonial jurisdiction of a remedy provided by the civil law for the enforcement of debt in general. By contrast, and consistently with the aura of criminality which invested the magistrates' matrimonial jursidiction, the Act which created that jurisdiction in 1878 provided specific penal sanctions for defaulters. It did this by drawing on the bastardy laws. For the previous three centuries, putative fathers who defaulted in their payments had been subject to distraint on their goods and imprisonment. The Act of 1878 provided that this same enforcement procedure should apply in case of default in the payment of maintenance awarded by the magistrates in the exercise of the matrimonial jurisdiction which the Act newly conferred on them; and this remains the law.[3]

---

[1] By virtue of the Matrimonial Proceedings and Property Act 1970, section 10.

[2] Debtors Act 1869, section 5(2).

[3] The 1878 formula was carried through all the intervening legislation and now appears in the Matrimonial Proceedings (Magistrates' Courts) Act 1960, section 13 (1): " The payment of any sum of money directed to be paid by an order made by virtue of this Act may be enforced in the same manner as the payment of money is enforced under an affiliation order."

4.136 The power of the magistrates to commit for breach of a maintenance order was harsher and less subject to control than the power of the divorce judge. The maximum term of imprisonment permissible under the Debtors Act, under which the orders of the divorce court were enforced, was six weeks; whereas the application of the bastardy law as providing the sanction for the magistrates' order involved a maximum term of three months. This difference persisted until 1952. Further, the Debtors Act, as we have seen, prohibited the court from imprisoning the debtor unless satisfied that he had been guilty of refusing or neglecting to pay although he could have done so. But the bastardy law provided merely that " in case such putative father neglect or refuse to make payment of the sums due from him under such order . . . such two justices . . . may, if they see fit . . . cause such putative father to be committed to the common gaol."[1]   The courts held that under this last provision a committal order could be made without proof that the defaulter had ever been able to pay, and that there was no effective appeal from an exercise by the magistrates of their discretion in this regard.[2]   Since the maintenance order was enforceable as an order in bastardy, this ruling applied also to committals for maintenance arrears. Thus, the magistrates were at considerably greater liberty than were the divorce judges to send the delinquent husbands to prison.

The Fischer Williams Committee

4.137 By the 1930s, while the number of committal orders against maintenance defaulters made in the divorce court was negligible, the prisons were silting up with maintenance defaulters sent there by the magistrates. Over the period 1900–1930, the number of maintenance orders (apart from affiliation orders) made annually by the magistrates roughly doubled; from 6,583 in the first year to 11,296 in the last. Over the same period, the numbers of men whom the magistrates annually imprisoned as defaulters increased by three and a half times; from 1,288 in 1900 to 4,274 in 1930.[3]   It was estimated that there were some seven imprisonments for every hundred orders in force.[4]   There were similar disproportionate increases in the number of men the magistrates sent to prison for default on affiliation orders.[5]

4.138 The population of maintenance defaulters in prisons was augmented by growing numbers of people committed by the magistrates for default in the payment of rates and fines. We have already referred[6] to the setting up in 1933 of a departmental Committee on Imprisonment by Court of Summary Jurisdiction in Default of Payment of Fines and Other Sums of Money (the Fischer Williams Committee). The terms of reference were "to consider whether by changes in the law or in the methods of administration it is possible to reduce the number of imprisonments in default of payment, due regard being given to the importance of securing compliance with orders made by the courts."

---

1 Bastardy Laws Amendment Act 1872, section 4.
2 *Richardson v Richardson* (1909) 2 KB 851; *Grocock v Grocock* (1920) 1 KB 1.
3 *Separated Spouses*, op cit, page 22.
4 Report of the Fischer Williams Committee, *op cit*, paragraph 112.
5 *Ibid*, paragraphs 170–173.
6 Part 4, Section 7.

4.139 The Fischer Williams Committee made a number of important recommendations which, so far as they related to the matrimonial jurisdiction of the magistrates, fell into three categories. First, it was proposed that in making a committal order the magistrates should be subject to the same restraints as the judges in the exercise of their jurisdiction under the Debtors Act, namely, that the magistrates should have a positive duty to enquire whether non-payment of the maintenance order resulted from wilful refusal or culpable neglect, and that, if it was due to neither, they should make no order. This recommendation became law in 1935, and a substantial identity was thus established of the grounds upon which the two matrimonial jurisdictions, while continuing to derive their powers from different sources, could make committal orders.[1] Next, the committee, considering that the effect would be to make a considerable reduction in the numbers imprisoned, recommended the institution of a new method of enforcement—attachment of earnings. This recommendation was not, at that time, carried into law. Finally, the committee made suggestions aimed at improving the machinery for the assessment of the amounts of maintenance orders made by the magistrates, and the arrangements which already existed for the collection of the proceeds of such orders through an official of the court.[2]

ATTACHMENT OF EARNINGS

History of attachment

4.140 We have already indicated that the nature of the maintenance order and of the resources which are likely to be available for its satisfaction makes it inherently difficult to devise an efficient method for enforcing it. Committal to prison itself ranks as a method of enforcement only in a figurative manner of speaking. It does not, like execution for debt properly so called, reduce any money or valuable thing into possession. It operates on the person of the debtor, to coerce him physically into paying what he owes, and at the same time to punish him for his disobedience to the court's order.[3] A genuine civil procedure for the enforcement of maintenance has to be one which fastens on the source out of which payment can be made as and when each payment falls due, and deducts from source, for transmission to or for the benefit of the wife, the amount that is due to her. Where, as is the standard case, the source consists of the husband's wages, this amounts to a very difficult prescription. It involves not only considerable administrative problems, but also intervention between the wage earner and his employer, and, above all, decisions on where to draw the line in permitting the machinery of the system to invade the privacy and freedom of movement of the individual.

---

[1] But even now the difference may persist that while the Debtors Act 1869 seems to require the creditor to prove that the debtor could have paid, but wilfully refrained from doing so, the corresponding provision under which magistrates can commit seems to put the burden of disproving wilful refusal or culpable neglect on the debtor: compare the Magistrates' Courts Act 1952, section 74(6). The provision was so construed in *James v James* (1964) P 303.

[2] These suggestions are discussed respectively in Section 7, paragraph 4.111 and Section 8, paragraph 4.119, above.

[3] *James v James, op cit, per* Sir Jocelyn Simon P at 308: " There are two purposes, . . . The first is to punish debtors who have failed to comply with their liabilities through wilful refusal or culpable neglect, and thereby to deter other debtors who may be tempted to take the same attitude. But the second is to bring pressure to bear on debtors to make good their own defaults."

4.141 Before 1958 there had been a few examples, mostly in poor law contexts, of a power to attach earnings, but these were of little importance. In any event, the Wages Attachment (Abolition) Act 1870 protected the wages of " servants, labourers or workmen " from any form of attachment. This Act, together with the Truck Acts, embodied the results of a successful campaign by organised labour to preserve the integrity of the pay packet. The attack on the sanctity of wages, when it first came, was in fact in connection with enforcing maintenance orders.

4.142 In 1912, the Gorell Commission recommended[1] that the courts should be given a discretionary power to make an order authorising, but not compelling, an employer to make a deduction from a husband's earnings in discharge of a maintenance liability. The matter next came under consideration by the Fischer Williams Committee in 1934. The committee listed the objections to attachment of earnings. It had been represented that an employer would dispense with a man's services rather than be put to the trouble of making and accounting for the necessary deductions; that the system would apply to the regular wage earner, but would not catch the casual labourer or the self-employed; that the usual cause of failure to pay was unemployment, yet it was exactly in that situation that there would be no wages to attach. The committee found that there was hostility towards anything which savoured of an attack on wages. As against these considerations, however, the committee concluded that there was no valid objection of principle against a measure which " does nothing more than ensure that a man discharges out of his earnings a liability which ranks very high in the scale of his social obligations and which will have been fixed, if the law has been observed, with special reference to those earnings ".[2] The committee recommended the introduction of a compulsory system of attachment of earnings for arrears under a maintenance or affiliation order. If there were arrears for four weeks or longer and the court was satisfied that the default was due to wilful refusal or culpable neglect to pay, it should have power to make an order, binding on the employer, to pay to the appropriate officer, by way of deduction from salary or wages, such sum as the court should specify in discharge of the liability under the order.[3] The committee considered that these proposals would help to effect a very considerable reduction in the number of committals to prison.

4.143 No action was taken on these recommendations. The matter was next considered by the Royal (Morton) Commission on Marriage and Divorce in 1956. The British Employers' Federation and the Trades Union Congress both, in their evidence, opposed attachment of earnings, and the report recommended against it.[4] In the following year the Advisory Council on the Treatment of Offenders recommended attachment of earnings as a substitute for imprisonment of maintenance defaulters.[5] Meantime, more than one attempt had been made by private members to introduce bills to this effect; and finally the Government proposed the measure which became the Maintenance Orders Act 1958.

---

[1] Op cit, paragraph 174.
[2] Op cit, paragraph 186.
[3] Ibid, paragraphs 179–199. There was one dissentient from the recommendations. Miss (later Dame) Annie Loughlin, the trade unionist, argued that attachment would be " a dangerous innovation " which might be " extended in future to debts in general ": Reservation by Miss A Loughlin, ibid, page 92.
[4] Op cit, paragraph 1105.
[5] Alternatives to Short Terms of Imprisonment, 1957, paragraphs 40–50.

The Maintenance Orders Act 1958

4.144   In the debate leading up to the 1958 Maintenance Orders Act the Home Secretary, Mr R A Butler, put at the forefront of his argument the need to find an alternative to imprisonment:

> Looking first at the public consideration I was immediately struck by the fact that something approaching 5,000 men are sent to prison every year for failure to keep up payments under maintenance orders.   That seems to me to be not only a futile operation, but positively harmful.   It gets no money for the woman, because the man ceases to earn while in prison.   It loses the man his job, and the country his productive capacity.   It exposes a defaulter to what I must say, with emphasis, is the contamination of prison—but not to any of its reformative influences.   It occupies time and space in prison . . . space which ought to be devoted to more constructive purposes.   It also takes up a considerable amount of public money. . . .   There are 5,000 committals a year, for an average of about six weeks each, and it is precisely that six weeks which does the harm to the man going into prison. . . .   I do not take the view that prison is at all a suitable punishment for a period of that duration.[1]

Next, the Home Secretary gave a pledge, for the reassurance of employers' organisations and trade unions who had expressed the anxiety that the future might see the extension of the new remedy from maintenance debts to debts in general.   He said:

> It is an important departure and it is for a specific purpose; and all I can do in commending it to the House is to say with the greatest possible emphasis that it is not our intention to extend attachment beyond . . . what is contained in the Bill before the House today.[2]

This statement seems to have appeased most of the critics of the bill, which went through its second reading unopposed.   The debate itself displayed little insight into the problems of extracting a livelihood for two households out of one pay packet.

4.145   The Act of 1958 extended both to maintenance orders made in the divorce jurisdiction and to maintenance orders (including affiliation orders) made by the magistrates.   It was a complex measure, but the essence of it is that the employer of a defendant who is subject to such an order, but is four weeks in arrears with weekly payments (or, in any other case, in arrears with two payments), may be ordered to pay part of the defendant's earnings directly to the appropriate officer of the court.   The order may issue only if the failure to pay has been due to the defendant's wilful refusal or culpable neglect.   The order specifies " the normal deduction rate " and " the protected earnings rate ", and there is provision for the adjustment of the deduction whenever that is necessary so as to leave intact the defendant's " protected " earnings, that is to say, the amount below which the court considers, in the light of his needs, resources and responsibilities, the defendant's income should not be reduced. The Act also specified that magistrates were not to impose imprisonment for maintenance arrears in any case where they can make an attachment of earnings order, unless they are of the opinion that the circumstances make an attachment of earnings order inappropriate.

---

1 House of Commons Official Report, 12 December 1957, column 1542.

2 *Op cit*, column 1545.   (The words omitted from the passage quoted were merely a slip, which Mr Butler corrected.)

4.146 The immediate effect of the Act of 1958 was encouraging since it appeared to be fulfilling one of its principal and avowed objects in providing, through attachment of earnings, an alternative to imprisonment. The numbers of attachment orders made since 1959 and of maintenance defaulters sent to prison since the mid-1950s are set out in Table 4.11.

TABLE 4.11

ATTACHMENT OF EARNINGS ORDERS,[1] 1959–1972, AS A PERCENTAGE OF ALL MAINTENANCE ORDERS MADE BY MAGISTRATES' COURTS, AND RECEPTIONS IN PRISON OF MAINTENANCE DEFAULTERS COMMITTED BY MAGISTRATES' COURTS,[2] 1955–1972

Year	Number of attachment of earnings orders	Attachment of earnings orders as a percentage of all maintenance orders	Number of maintenance defaulters received in prison	Maintenance defaulters as a percentage of non-criminal prisoners
1955			4,333	72
1956			4,314	68
1957			4,597	62
1958			4,910	52
1959	1,757	7	2,358	29
1960	4,872	17	2,379	28
1961	4,929	18	2,867	30
1962	4,406	15	3,194	27
1963	3,745	13	3,013	26
1964	4,033	13	3,304	34
1965	4,609		3,465	43
1966	4,538	15	3,664	47
1967	3,785	12	3,511	45
1968	3,776	12	3,438	49
1969	3,920	13	3,470	46
1970	3,541	11	3,867	47
1971	3,188	11	3,625	56
1972	3,166	11	3,263	57

Source: Annual *Civil Judicial Statistics* and annual *Reports on the Work of the Prison Department, Statistical Tables.*

Table 4.11 shows that the early promise of attachment of earnings orders was not sustained, and that they have not become established as a major mode of enforcing maintenance orders in magistrates' courts. The number of orders made quickly reached a peak in 1961 and has declined slowly but steadily since then. The number of prison receptions presents the reverse image of a sharp fall immediately after the Act and a slow but steady climb back towards the

[1] Attachment orders made in respect of (*a*) affiliation, (*b*) married women maintenance, (*c*) guardianship of minors, (*d*) social security, and (*e*) children and young persons orders.

[2] In a footnote to paragraph 4.171 we refer to the fact that the High Court rarely imprisons a maintenance defaulter.

level of committals in the period before 1959. At the same time, it is to be borne in mind that the decline in the number of attachment orders and increase in the number of maintenance defaulters committed to prison took place over a period during which, although the numbers are not known, there was almost certainly also an increase in the total of live maintenance orders.

The Payne Committee

4.147 The Committee on the Enforcement of Judgment Debts (the Payne Committee) was appointed in 1965 with terms of reference which (as subsequently extended) required them to consider:

> whether any changes are desirable in the law and practice in the High Court and the county courts and (in relation to their civil jurisdiction) the magistrates' courts relating to the recovery of debts and the enforcement of orders for payment of money. . . .

The situation which existed at that time regarding imprisonment for debt and attachment of earnings appears from the preceding discussion. In summary, there was power in the civil courts, including the divorce court, to commit a debtor to prison under the Debtors Act 1869 for culpable failure to pay a judgment or order for a sum of money. There was a separate power of the magistrates, deriving from different historical and legal sources, to commit for culpable failure to pay maintenance orders which they had made within their own jurisdiction, or which, if made in the divorce jurisdiction, had been registered in the magistrates' court for enforcement. The process of attachment of earnings was available under the Act of 1958 in both jurisdictions for the purpose only of enforcing maintenance orders.

4.148 The Payne Committee commissioned a special study of the results of the attachment of earnings procedure introduced by the Act of 1958.[1] This study demonstrated the following conclusions. When the investigation commenced in 1966, nearly three quarters of all the attachment of earnings orders made between February 1959 and January 1966 had been discharged. Of the discharged orders, more than a third had lasted for less than four months, and three quarters had been discharged in less than one year. In only about one case in every hundred had the order been revoked on an application made by the respondent on the ground that the arrears of maintenance had been cleared. The overwhelming majority of the discharges arose from the fact that the man had changed his job, and the employer, upon whom the order was originally made, had then applied for discharge. The amount of the arrears for which most attachment orders were made was between £40 and £60. Less than one quarter of the orders made had produced a reduction in the outstanding arrears, or even the regular payment of maintenance continuing to accrue due weekly. The orders were being made against men with low incomes, below the average weekly level of earnings of male manual workers. The court records were seriously deficient in recording the other financial responsibilities of respondents to attachment orders, but they did show that at least one fifth of them were supporting paramours and their children, and

---

1 *Report of the Committee on the Enforcement of Judgment Debts*, Cmnd 3909, 1969, Appendix 2, pages 409–431. *Study of Attachment of Earnings Orders made by the Department of Sociology, Bedford College, University of London, for the Committee on the Enforcement of Judgment Debts.* We summarise only some principal findings, and the study needs to be consulted for the methodology of the investigation, and its full results.

at least one third were supporting relatives, paramours or new wives. There was evidence to suggest that some magistrates and their clerks were sceptical of the utility of the attachment of earnings procedure. This may in turn account for the propensity that was noted[1] for magistrates to breach the intention of the Act of 1958 by making a committal order first, and an attachment order subsequently, after the committal failed to produce payment.

4.149 The Payne Committee considered the improvements which experience since 1958 showed could be made to the system of attachment of earnings for maintenance. Beyond that, they recommended that the system as improved ought to be extended to apply not only to the enforcement of maintenance orders, but also to every case where a judgment or order for the payment of money is being enforced against a debtor who has available earnings to be attached. These recommendations were adopted in the Administration of Justice Act 1970, and the law of attachment was then consolidated in the Attachment of Earnings Act 1971. The principal changes in the procedure are:

(1) a debtor under a maintenance order can now himself apply for an attachment of earnings order to be made against him;

(2) change of employment does not discharge an attachment order, but only suspends it;

(3) the debtor has to notify the court whenever he changes his employment, and at the same time give particulars of his earnings, actual or potential; and

(4) a person who becomes the employer of the debtor, knowing that an attachment order has been made, and by what court, must notify the court that he is the employer, stating the debtors' actual and potential earnings.

Thus, the century which began with the Wages Attachment (Abolition) Act 1870 ended with wages becoming liable for attachment for practically every form of civil debt.[2] At the same time, the Payne Committee unanimously recommended the abolition of committal to prison as a process for the recovery of any form of private debt other than maintenance. This recommendation was also adopted in the Administration of Justice Act 1970, so that since then the committal procedure has been available only for taxes, social security contributions, and maintenance payments (both in the divorce and the magistrates' jurisdiction) and (in criminal cases) for fines, costs and legal aid contributions.

Tracing Defaulters

4.150 Sufficient time has not elapsed since the improvements in the attachment procedure to measure their effect in achieving a better rate of recovery on maintenance orders. This consideration, however, has not deterred several of the organisations which submitted evidence to us from urging the need to stiffen still further the procedures for tracing maintenance defaulters and ensuring that deductions to meet their obligations are made from their wages. We have to consider these proposals both in their technical aspects and in point of principle.

---

[1] *Ibid*, pages 422–423.

[2] And Dame Annie Loughlin's prophetic powers were demonstrated to be of longer range and greater accuracy than Lord Butler's.

Technical limitations

4.151 A court cannot make a maintenance or affiliation order unless the man can be traced. In cases where supplementary benefit is in payment to the wife or mother, the Supplementary Benefits Commission will have used their resources to try and trace the man, and the social security records of the Department of Health and Social Security are made available for this purpose. The woman will then be able to take maintenance proceedings if need be. In other cases she may receive unofficial help from the Salvation Army, which operates a special service for tracing purposes, but this is limited to cases where reconciliation is hoped for, and the Salvation Army's facilities are always overburdened. The police can act only in cases where a criminal charge is involved, and when there is a liable relative prosecution.

4.152 The wife or mother may also be helped in another way where the man has absconded. In 1957, the government gave authority[1] for the first time for the disclosure to courts, on request, of addresses from official records to facilitate the initiation of maintenance and affiliation proceedings, and the enforcement of orders. The principal records are the central social security records of the Department of Health and Social Security, and the National Health Service Register, Passport Office and Ministry of Defence records are also available for this purpose. As recently as 1971 clerks to justices were advised[2] to make the fullest use of these facilities wherever they think this would serve a useful purpose, or a complainant asks them to do so. Indeed, the Home Office went so far as to suggest that in order to facilitate the identification of the man's record they should consider the:

> possibility of asking defendants to provide their National Insurance number at the time a maintenance order is made (though there is of course no statutory power for a court to require this information to be supplied at that time).[3]

As the evidence given to us suggests there is still a good deal of confusion about the scope of this procedure, we set out the present position in some detail:

> Arrangements for access to be given to departmental records apply to any proceedings, either initial or for enforcement, which include a claim for the payment of maintenance, brought under the Maintenance Orders (Facilities for Enforcement) Act 1920, the Maintenance Orders Act 1950, the Magistrates' Courts Act 1952, the Affiliation Proceedings Act 1957, the Maintenance Orders Act 1958, the Matrimonial Proceedings and Property Act 1970, the Guardianship of Minors Act 1971, and . . . the Attachment of Earnings Act 1971. The records available are those of the Department of Health and Social Security, the Ministry of Defence, and the Passport Office.[4]

An address is not supplied by the department directly to solicitors, but will be given to clerks to justices:

> only on the understanding that it will be used solely for the purposes of proceedings and will not be made known to the complainant or to anyone else except in the normal course of proceedings.[5]

4.153 Parallel arrangements have been made[6] in the divorce jurisdiction for obtaining the address of a husband for the asistance of a wife seeking to

---

[1] Home Office Circular No 113/1957.
[2] Home Office Circular No 140/1971.
[3] Home Office Circular No 140/1971, paragraph 9.
[4] *Ibid*, paragraph 3.
[5] *Ibid*, paragraph 4.
[6] Practice Note (Disclosure of Addresses), 28 November 1972 (1973) 1 WLR 60.

obtain or enforce an order for maintenance for herself or the children. The request to the department is made by the Divorce Registrar, and the address is passed on by him to the wife's solicitor (or, in proper cases, where she is acting in person to the wife herself) on an undertaking to use it only for the purpose of the proceedings. Although the Direction sets out the arrangements as having been made, like those for the magistrates, with the Ministry of Defence, and the Passport Office, as well as with the Department of Health and Social Security, it adds the note:

> Records held by other departments are less likely to be of use, either because of their limited scope or because individual records cannot readily be identified. If, however, circumstances suggest that the address may be known to another department, application may be made to it by the Registrar, all relevant particulars available being given.

4.154 Some submissions to us wish to carry disclosure from official records much further, and have urged that a government department, such as the Inland Revenue or the Department of Health and Social Security, should be given a specific and positive responsibility for tracing missing husbands and fathers.

4.155 It has been further urged in the evidence submitted to us that in addition to providing assistance in tracing defaulters, the records and machinery of government should be used to improve the efficacy of attachment of earnings orders. These suggestions do not differ from those which were examined in detail by the Payne Committee.[1] All, in the end, amount to two main schemes both of which involve formidable technical and administrative difficulties. Under the first, the attachment of earnings order would be notified to the man's employer and to the local tax office, and the maintenance would then be collected through the PAYE system. The second proposal is that national insurance cards should be used as a means of keeping track of defaulters. For this purpose, the court would inform the employer that an attachment of earnings order had been made in respect of one of his employees, and the employer would mark the insurance card (perhaps by affixing a gummed slip) in such a way that the existence of the order would be disclosed if the employee changed his job. The Payne Committee examined both proposals in detail and discussed them with the Board of Inland Revenue and the Ministry of Social Security. They concluded that the Board of Inland Revenue had " made an overwhelming case " that " it would be impracticable to use the PAYE system for collecting civil debts."[2] They showed little enthusiasm for the national insurance card scheme and thought that " the actual cost . . . might be considerable," but that such a scheme might be feasible.[3] The committee recommended further study of a suggestion that the existence of an attachment of earnings order might be endorsed on the Inland Revenue form P45, recording the holder's PAYE situation, which is given by an employer to a leaving employee for presentation to the new employer. There is no legal obligation upon an employee to hand over the P45 to a new employer and many of the forms are " lost ". We do not

---

[1] See *op cit*, paragraphs 611–627 and Appendix 3.
[2] *Op cit*, paragraph 618.
[3] *Ibid*, paragraph 620. But national insurance cards will no longer be required for employed persons under the reconstructed insurance scheme which is due to take effect in April 1975, when contribution deductions from these persons will be marked on PAYE documents.

examine further the technical difficulties which would arise in seeking to implement these proposals. We believe that their administrative cost would be out of all proportion to their effectiveness. But we turn to other than the technical objections.

The permissible limits of disclosure

4.156 We think it fundamental for efficient public administration in a free society that citizens should have absolute trust in the integrity of departments of state. We hold, therefore, that it is of over-riding importance to maintain the principle that departments do not inform upon citizens by disclosing for extraneous purposes (save in the most exceptional circumstances) information which the individual is compelled by law to provide for determinate purposes such as direct taxation or national insurance. Once citizens know that information about themselves or their affairs will be passed on by the Board of Inland Revenue to persons and for purposes different from those for which it was supplied in the first instance, temptations to dishonesty and deception will multiply. The functions of the Board of Inland Revenue are to administer taxation, and to impose other unrelated duties upon them will impair their capacity for their main task. It is more important for the community that earnings should be honestly declared and taxes on them efficiently collected than that the enforcement of maintenance orders should be marginally improved. Similar considerations would apply to the scheme for using national insurance records even if, contrary to present intentions, insurance cards continued to be issued to employed persons after April 1975. The community is better served by effective administration of national insurance than by the promotion of an illegal market for uninsured labour that would be the consequence of using insurance cards for the collateral purpose of enforcing court orders.

4.157 We do not favour any of the suggestions which have been made to us, nor do we have any proposals of our own, for turning the administrative screw tighter in the supposed interests of the more effective enforcement of maintenance orders. We consider that the arrangements now in force under which government records compiled for other purposes may be made available for maintenance enforcement have gone to the limit of what is tolerable in principle. It was only in 1970 that the law governing the attachment of earnings was made considerably more stringent, and it would, in our view, in any case be premature to consider further changes in the methods of enforcement before the consequences of the 1970 reforms had had time to show themselves and had been evaluated. Finally, we once more stress—this time in the words of the Payne Committee Report—the fact that our research has put beyond a peradventure and which is central, namely, that the problem in dealing with men of modest means is:

> not a problem of enforcement but of economics, and we cannot too strongly or too often invite attention to the simple fact that no improvement which we can suggest in the machinery of the courts will put more money into pockets of husbands and debtors or enable them to meet commitments beyond their capacity to pay.[1]

ADVICE AND ASSISTANCE FOR MAINTENANCE DEBTORS

4.158 It is material to note that when the Payne Committee recommended the extension of attachment of earnings to all kinds of judgment debts, they

---

[1] *Op cit*, paragraph 1306.

made recommendations at the same time for the establishment of a new institution, to be called the enforcement office. There was to be an enforcement office in each district corresponding to the existing county court districts. Most judgments and orders for the payment of money would be automatically transferred to the enforcement office for enforcement. Maintenance orders could be so transferred in certain circumstances. The committee envisage that:

> Into that office will pass for enforcement all money judgments against a debtor. . . . In that way the Enforcement Office will from the start of enforcement be in a position to endure the ordered control of the debtor's affairs which is fundamental to a proper system of enforcement.[1]

4.159   One reason for wishing to ensure ordered control of debtors' affairs within a single enforcement office was the discovery by the Payne Committee that:

> The governors of the prisons which receive debtors . . . present an almost unanimous view that the majority of civil debtors in prison are social inadequates, people incapable of managing their affairs and overwhelmed by a burden of debt. Investigators say that they are left with an overriding impression of the low mental calibre of these debtors who are people unable to understand how and why they were found in prison. The governors describe them as physically, mentally and socially inadequate, unreceptive and unresponsive. Some of them report that imprisonment had no deterrent effect . . . . The general view is that imprisonment for debt is uneconomic and futile.[2]

4.160   This diagnosis of the social and personal characteristics of the debtors who land in gaol led the Payne Committee to the recommendation, which the Government subsequently accepted, to abolish imprisonment for most civil debtors and to extend attachment earnings procedure (which, as has been seen, had hitherto under the Act of 1958 extended only to maintenance debt) to the whole range of civil debt. But the committee did not conceive of attachment as a blunt instrument which could belabour money out of debtors whose problems " are primarily social and which require social rather than legal machinery for their solution."[3] On the contrary, they recommended that professional and specially trained social workers should become part of the enforcement office where they would be servants of the court, carrying out their duties independently because they would be accountable neither to the creditor nor to the debtor. They would have three main duties. First, they would assist debtors by giving information about relevant social agencies and services, including legal aid, and pay special attention to:

> debtors heavily in debt (helping them) to adjust their weekly budget . . . . This elementary form of balancing a light domestic budget might often save a whole family from getting deeper into debt and so into greater misery. We think there is great need for social workers to perform, for financially incompetent or inadequate or irresponsible debtors, the functions which are discharged for more successful members of the community by bank managers, accountants and solicitors.[4]

---

[1] *Op cit*, paragraph 318.
[2] *Ibid*, paragraph 981.
[3] *Ibid*, paragraph 1210.
[4] *Ibid*, paragraph 1216.

Secondly, such social workers would undertake independent means enquiries on behalf of the court. They:

> would present a total picture of that debtor's assets, income, debts, family background and work situation. Then, the court would know how the debtor should be ordered to satisfy the debts being enforced through the Enforcement Office.[1]

The third duty of the social worker in the enforcement office:

> would be to report to the court and to assist it in the kind of order which should be made, particularly as to the amount of any order for attachment of earnings.[2]

4.161 However, when Parliament in 1970 extended the process of attachment of earnings from maintenance debts to civil debts in general, it did so without making provision for an enforcement office, or for social workers to be trained for appointment to any such institution as might be created in the future. In taking this course, Parliament appears to have shorn off the attachment process from an institutional reform that was intended both to civilise that process and to make it more successful.

IMPRISONMENT OF MAINTENANCE DEBTORS

4.162 As we have already noted, following upon the report of the Payne Committee, there was legislation which on the one hand generalised the attachment of earnings process so as to make it applicable to all forms of debt, and on the other hand restricted the older remedy of committal to prison, so far as concerns debts arising between subjects, to arrears accruing under matrimonial orders for maintenance. In no circumstances can a citizen now be sent to prison for failing, however deliberately, to pay a hotel bill or a store account or a hire purchase debt; but he can be for neglect or refusal to pay maintenance.

4.163 We regret the retention of imprisonment as a sanction for the maintenance obligation, and we recommend that it should be abolished.

4.164 The Payne Committee were themselves split on this question. Half of the twelve members concluded that " imprisonment of maintenance defaulters ... is morally capricious, economically wasteful, socially harmful, administratively burdensome and juridically wrong. We wish it abolished forthwith."[3] Three members " did not shrink from the thought of imprisoning a defaulter who is guilty of culpable neglect of his family or defiance of the court."[4] Two others agreed substantially with the abolitionist view, but considered it premature to put it into effect.[5] The twelfth member appeared to agree with the last two.[6] The majority were, accordingly, in favour of abolition, either immediately or at some future date. The conflicting arguments which led to these various conclusions are to be found in the report.[7] We can add little to them.

---

[1] *Ibid*, paragraph 1217.
[2] *Ibid*, paragraph 1218.
[3] *Op cit*, paragraph 1099.
[4] *Ibid*, paragraph 1039.
[5] *Ibid*, paragraph 1104.
[6] *Ibid*, paragraph 1108.
[7] *Ibid*, paragraphs 1008–1108; they are also summarised in *Separated Spouses, op cit*, pages 200–207.

4.165   The evidence given to ourselves on this subject also pointed in different directions.   The Magistrates' Association informed us that:

> We feel it essential to retain the sanction of imprisonment for non-payment of maintenance, since in our experience many husbands only pay when faced with imprisonment as an alternative, and without this sanction the present large number of orders in arrears would undoubtedly increase still more.

These were, in essence, the views also of the Justices' Clerks' Society, although they spoke of " the small number of wilful and persistent defaulters (for whom) this sanction is necessary if they are to be made to comply."   On the other hand, the London Magistrates' Clerks' Association told us of:

> our experience that the sanctions available to a magistrates' court to enforce orders payable . . . are inadequate to secure payment.   All too often it is a case of too many commitments chasing too little money.   When this is so, the imposition of imprisonment, whether immediate or suspended, is pointless, and a realistic attachment of earnings order is impossible.   Imprisonment will very occasionally bring the deliberate non-payer to his senses, but it is appropriate in a minute proportion of cases.

4.166   Submissions we received from the lay organisations demonstrated, with one or two exceptions, a considerable lack of enthusiasm for committal as a sanction.   This was in contrast with their attitudes towards attachment of earnings.   Thus, the Women's National Advisory Committee of the National Union of Conservative and Unionist Associations stated in oral evidence that " wives resented (imprisonment for non-payment of maintenance) because it did nothing to get them the money from their husbands which was what they really wanted."   The National Council for the Unmarried Mother and her Child disliked the anomaly of a criminal punishment for a civil offence, and thought that prison was a useless punishment which did not help the beneficiary of a maintenance order and damaged both the defendant and the taxpayer. Thus, our witnesses exhibited among themselves as wide a range of opinions as is to be found in the pages of the report of the Payne Committee.

4.167   We do not think it would be helpful to rake over arguments exhaustively debated by the Payne Committee.   We recognise that the retention or abolition of imprisonment as a method of enforcing maintenance involves a moral issue which, like all arguments on corporal punishments, cannot be determined finally by an appeal to empirical considerations.   On the other hand, we feel that the importance of the question demands a short statement of our principal reasons for recommending abolition.

4.168   The Payne Committee unanimously rejected the theory of general deterrence in the sense that:

> the imprisonment of civil debtors helps to inculcate or to maintain among the community the social and moral obligation to repay debts freely contracted.[1]

They declared that:

> In the light of the evidence the Committee has received it is unable to accept that the vast structure of credit trading can depend on the threat of imprisonment . . . which results in a few thousand people being sent to prison, even if it were abundantly clear that those in prison were all deliberate defaulters or dishonest or in some other way determined not to pay.[2]

---

[1] *Op cit*, paragraph 1091.
[2] *Ibid*, paragraph 960.

If this be accepted, we are sure that those members who wished to abolish the imprisonment of maintenance defaulters were right to insist that:

> the family is a universal institution and remains, in a variety of forms of which monogamy is the commonest the world over, the basic social unit in all societies. It would, indeed, be astonishing if the existence of this institution in England depended on the maintenance of one particular method of enforcing a municipal legal rule.[1]

4.169 Everyone agrees that sending maintenance defaulters to prison is an essay in economic and social futility as far as the taxpayer is concerned. The defaulter has to be kept in prison where his future earning power is reduced, the wife and family upon whose maintenance he has defaulted fall upon the Supplementary Benefits Commission as do his second wife or mistress and her children if, as he may well have done, he has acquired another family. This might be a justifiable social cost if the result were to inculcate or to strengthen among the population at large a disposition to maintain their dependants. Not only is this proposition manifestly unsustainable in the light of a vast body of sociological knowledge about the family, but what little empirical knowledge we possess suggests that imprisonment hardly serves to deter even those who are imprisoned. The maintenance defaulters in prison are the same type of " social inadequates " as used to make up the bulk of all the civil debtors in prison.[2] Dr Pauline Morris reported in her study, *Prisoners and their Families*, that maintenance defaulters:

> often claimed that their default was a matter of principle, although most of them rationalised the situation and said it was because their wives were living with other men, or the children they were being asked to support were not theirs. In fact they simply hated their wives and were stubbornly prepared to undergo an infinite number of prison sentences rather than pay a penny.[3]

Thus, there is no evidence that imprisonment for maintenance default promotes either general or specific deterrence yet, at the same time, it is an expensive burden upon the community.

4.170 The observation we have made regarding specific deterrence should be qualified by reference to the conviction which many who are concerned with the administration of justice undoubtedly hold that the value of the committal procedure is not in what it permits the court to do so much as in what it permits the court to threaten. (This is similar to the case made for the cane in the headmaster's drawer in the debate over corporal punishment in schools.) It is said that by making a suspended committal order, not to take effect over a period of grace, the court can frequently extract maintenance from men who are unwilling to pay it, but not ready to go to prison for their disinclination. It is difficult to test or quantify the argument, which rests on the experience of those who make suspended committal orders, or see them made, and find that payment is frequently forthcoming before the suspension elapses. It is difficult, also, not to be impressed by the fact that the opinion of the vast majority of the county court judges (which, in this case, was not accepted by the Payne

---

1 *Ibid*, paragraph 1091.

2 *Ibid*, paragraph 1092; and see paragraph 4.159 above.

3 Published by Allen and Unwin, 1965, pages 234–235. The results of this survey were published in 1965. There is immediate need for a further detailed study of the characteristics of defaulters imprisoned by magistrates' courts. It would also be desirable to study the sentencing policy in this respect of courts throughout the country.

Committee) was that the threat of committal was indispensable to the system of recovery of ordinary judgment debts; but there is no sign since the threat ceased to be available in 1970 that the recovery rate has been adversely affected. However we regard the empirical demonstration of the effectiveness or otherwise of the threat as irrelevant to the point of principle. This is that if imprisonment is, as we believe it to be, inadmissible as a sanction to enforce family obligations, so equally must be the threat of imprisonment.

4.171 When the Payne Committee examined the judgment summons procedure in the county court they observed:

> the time does not allow for a full or proper enquiry to be made into the circumstances of each debtor and, even if time permitted, the available evidence is frequently scanty. There is rarely evidence about the general background and home circumstances of the debtor and still less about his need for help and guidance in his affairs . . . . This unhappy picture is not the fault of the county court judges, the registrars or their staffs, who contrive in the most difficult circumstances to reduce hardship to a minimum; but the fault rests with the system itself.[1]

For such reasons, the committee concluded:

> The present judgment summons procedure is not compatible with the administration of justice, especially in circumstances involving the liberty of the subject. The wide variation in the practice of county court judges and the sheer volume and pressure of work in these days make it impossible to distinguish in all cases between the recalcitrant and the inadequate debtor.[2]

When the passage was written, the county court judges were sending 3,329 debtors to prison; in the same year, magistrates sent 3,511 maintenance defaulters to prison. All the more, particularly in view of our own investigation into the assessment procedures in magistrates' courts, we think that magistrates today face exactly the same difficulties in committing maintenance defaulters as the county court judges used to face when making committal orders against debtors. Our view is that the magistrates are victims of the system as were the county court judges who had to do justice in impossible circumstances. We are very impressed by the fact that the High Court rarely, if ever,[3] sends a maintenance defaulter to prison, and we emphatically agree with the members of the Payne Committee who concluded:

> there are grounds for thinking that the liberty of the subject, if he be a maintenance defaulter, is no better protected in the magistrates' courts than if he be a civil debtor appearing in the county court.[4]

4.172 We do not know, finally, of any argument which satisfies us that a system of such harmful futility as was described by the then Home Secretary in 1957 carries compensations sufficient to justify its preservation. But the abolition of imprisonment for maintenance debt would by itself amount to an insufficient, although necessary, reform. Unlike the ordinary civil debt, which can usually be cleared once and for all, within a foreseeable period,

---

[1] *Op cit*, paragraphs 989–990.

[2] *Ibid*, paragraph 961.

[3] The *Civil Judicial Statistics* do not show separately the number of maintenance defaulters imprisoned by the High Court: they are lumped in a general category which itself does not exceed single figures. The Payne Committee obtained figures for 1968 from the Divorce Division in London. These showed that one defaulter was detained in prison for twenty-six days. (*Op cit*, paragraph 1063.)

[4] *Ibid*, paragraph 1093.

the maintenance obligation is a continuing one, lasting sometimes over very many years. It has often been contracted in the form of a court order under circumstances of emotional stress. It is connected with an intimate personal relationship. Its payment by a man who may be in any case hard put to it to make ends meet may give rise to further stress in the form of divided loyalties and sense of responsibility. The man's mind may be affected by anger and unreason. These are precisely the circumstances in which it seems to us the law should avoid punitive remedies, but—in combination with the normal civil processes for extracting money where it is available to be extracted—should be providing as a service of the court access to the advice, guidance and persuasion of an officer who can help such a man to resolve his problem.

SECTION 10—MAINTENANCE AND SUPPLEMENTARY BENEFITS

THE THIRD SYSTEM OF FAMILY LAW: SUPPLEMENTARY BENEFITS

4.173   We have examined the nature of the two jurisdictions through which the courts make provision for family breakdown.   The superior jurisdiction has, by and large, responded, or is in process of responding, to the demands which social and demographic changes have imposed upon family law.   The inferior jurisdiction has made hardly any response whatever.   The result is that the double standards which from the start permeated the philosophy and organisation of the two systems have, in course of time, so far from weakening, become more blatant.   However, the picture is still incomplete.   We now have to take into account the third system of family law, administered by the Supplementary Benefits Commission, and describe and evaluate the relationship between this system and the other two.   Some knowledge of the earlier phases of this relationship is indispensable for an understanding of the current situation, but as these have been fully considered elsewhere,[1] we may begin by setting out the relevant provisions of the statute which now controls the payment of supplementary benefits and the power to recover from liable relatives.

The statutory family

4.174   The Ministry of Social Security Act 1966 provides by Schedule 2, paragraph 3, that:

> Where a husband and wife are members of the same household their requirements and resources shall be aggregated and shall be treated as the husband's, and similarly, unless there are exceptional circumstances, as regards two persons cohabiting as man and wife

and that the requirements and resources of dependants in the same household may, and if the dependant is a child under the age of 16 shall, also be aggregated with those of the person who has to provide for the dependant.   By section 4(2) the Act provides that:

> Where . . . the requirements and resources of any person fall to be aggregated with and to be treated as those of another person that other person only shall be entitled to benefit.

By section 8(1) the Act provides that, save in exceptional cases:

> A person shall not be entitled to benefit for any period during which he is engaged in remunerative full-time work.

---

1 Section 2 and Appendix 5.

4.175   The effect of these provisions is that for the purpose of supplementary benefits a family in being, whether grounded in a marriage or not, is treated as a unit.   The family may consist of a single adult with dependent children, or of a couple, with or without dependent children.   If two persons who are not married cohabit as man and wife, only the man can normally become entitled to benefit.   The woman, in such a case, cannot claim benefit in her own right any more than if she were married, unless the Supplementary Benefits Commission find that there are exceptional circumstances to justify non-aggregation.   The man may claim benefit when he is not in full-time work, and the benefit, as in the case of a married man, will then be assessed by reference not only to his own requirements and resources, but also to those of the woman with whom he is cohabiting and the children of the household for whom he has to provide.   The provisions which equate an unmarried cohabiting couple with a married household have become known as " the cohabitation rule ".[1]

The " liable relative "

4.176   The Act of 1966 also contains the " liable relative " rules. Section 22 (1) provides:

> For the purposes of this Act—
>> (a) a man shall be liable to maintain his wife and his children, and
>> (b) a woman shall be liable to maintain her husband and her children.

" Children " are defined as persons under the age of 16.   For the purposes of these obligations, the children of whom a man has been adjudged to be the putative father are to be treated as his children, and a woman's illegitimate children as her children.

4.177   Under section 23, the Supplementary Benefits Commission may proceed before the magistrates to recover from any person liable to maintain another under section 22 (the " liable relative ") the cost of benefit paid in respect of that other; the court may also make an order under this section payable to the person claiming benefit or to someone else on that person's behalf.   The section 23 procedure does not apply to the case of the putative father, which is covered by section 24.   Under that section, if an affiliation order is already in existence, the Commission may apply for it to be varied, so that the amounts payable thereunder become payable directly to the Secretary of State for Social Services; if there is no affiliation order, the Commission may, within three years of paying benefit in respect of an illegitimate child, themselves apply for such an order which may be made payable to the Secretary of State, the mother of the child or such other person as the court may direct.

4.178   Section 30 attaches a criminal sanction to the liable relative provisions by enacting penalties against a person who persistently refuses or neglects to maintain himself, or someone he is liable for the purposes of the Act to maintain, with the result that benefit has to be awarded or free board and lodging provided in a reception centre.

The dilemma of liable relatives

4.179   At this stage, it will be helpful to create the characters in an everyday drama.   John, let it be supposed, contracted a marriage by which there are

---
[1] The cohabitation rule and its administration are the subject of much controversy.   We consider it in Part 5, Section 8.

children of school age, or younger. He earns an average wage in a semi-skilled occupation. His marriage has broken down, and he has left home. He may or may not be divorced. Mary is John's former or deserted wife. Her lack of training, or the demands of the children, or both, prevent her from taking employment, or, at any rate, from earning more than a small amount in part-time work, insufficient for the needs of herself and the children. John is living with his second wife, or with his mistress. She and John have children of their own, or, it may be, she has children by a former marriage or association whom John looks after as his own. This woman also earns little or nothing.

4.180   In the postulated circumstances, there are two families in being for the purposes of supplementary benefits: Mary's family, consisting of herself and her children; and John's family, consisting of himself, his second wife or his mistress, and the children of their household. Mary, being unemployed or in part-time work only, is eligible for supplementary benefit, the amount of which will depend upon the calculation of the requirements and resources of her family. If John falls out of work, he will be entitled to benefit, the amount of which will depend upon the calculation of the requirements and resources of his family; but if he is in full-time work, then no member of his family is eligible for benefit. The only allowable departure from these rules arises in the case where John is cohabiting with a mistress, in which case, under the " exceptional circumstances " provision in paragraph 3 of Schedule 2 to the Act, the law permits non-aggregation. The Supplementary Benefits Commission confine the exercise of this discretion mainly to cases where there are children not of the current cohabitation and, in addition, the total family income is insufficient for its requirements by supplementary benefit standards. In these circumstances benefit will sometimes be paid to the woman for the requirements of her own children.

4.181   If John is still married to Mary he has a statutory obligation to support Mary's family under section 22 of the Act; that is to say, he is a "liable relative". Further, whether still married to Mary or not, John may be under an obligation to maintain Mary's family under a maintenance order made by the magistrates or in the divorce jurisdiction. Given John's earning capacity, however, it is clear that he cannot, when in work, earn enough money to maintain both the families. If he elects to do his duty by Mary's family, he will to that extent relieve the Supplementary Benefits Commission from paying money to Mary, but the inevitable effect will be to deprive the family of which he is a current member of the means of subsistence in circumstances where, since he is in work, they will not themselves be eligible for benefit. If, on the other hand, he elects to maintain the latter family, then, with equal inevitability, he has to break his obligations towards Mary's family. But she, in that case, can claim supplementary benefit; in such circumstances neither family starves.

4.182   When a man is put in such a dilemma the solution he will lean towards is tolerably clear. He will feed, clothe and house those with whom he is living, knowing that the State will provide for the others. It is the almost inescapable consequence of the principles on which the supplementary benefits scheme is founded that wherever there is not enough money for the husband to support two women, it is the one with whom he is not living who has to resort to the

Supplementary Benefits Commission. This was recognised, with blunt realism, by the Commission's predecessor, the National Assistance Board, in their annual report for 1953:[1]

> If (the husband's earnings) or other resources are not enough to maintain, besides himself, both his wife (with her children, if any) and the paramour (with her children, if any) the defect has got to be met at one point or other by assistance. The Board are then faced with the delicate problem of deciding whether the assistance is to be given to the wife or to the paramour. Respect for the marriage tie suggests that it is the legal wife whose maintenance should be the prior charge on the husband's income . . . but important practical considerations, not least the avoidance of unnecessary expenditure of public monies, lead inescapably to the other view . . . . Extracting money from husbands to maintain wives from whom they are separated is at best an uncertain business; it is easier to enforce the maintenance of those with whom the man is living than of those from whom he is parted.

4.183   Moreover, the Supplementary Benefits Commission's defence of the cohabitation rule[2] suggests, at least implicitly, that this solution of the dilemma is right as well as inevitable. The Commission argue:

> A man who is entitled to supplementary benefit living with a woman not his wife is entitled to benefit for her, and for their children, when he is sick or unemployed; it would be manifestly unreasonable if, while he is at work, his partner could claim supplementary benefit . . . in her own right[3] . . . . (This would be) to treat the women who have the support of a partner both as if they had not such support and better than if they were married. It would not be right, and we believe that public opinion would not accept, that the unmarried "wife" should be able to claim benefit denied to a married woman because her husband was in full-time work.[4]

> It has been suggested that it is morally wrong to infer that because a man and woman are living together as man and wife, the man is in fact supporting the woman and her children especially where these are from a former union. But to leave the choice to pay or not to pay to the man, and to make no effort to get him to maintain the woman would be inconsistent with the Act and *repugnant to the general view of family responsibility*.[5]

POLICIES OF THE SUPPLEMENTARY BENEFITS COMMISSION

Formula for settlement with the liable relative

4.184   We must now consider what happens when Mary applies to the Supplementary Benefits Commission for payment of benefit. The Commission's policy and practice within the very wide discretion they are allowed by the law is set out in the *Supplementary Benefits Handbook*[6] from which the quotations which follow are taken. In the first place, the Commission will meet Mary's needs in accordance with her entitlement. They then try:

> to contact the husband as soon as possible so as to find out why he is failing to maintain his dependants.[7]

---

[1] Cmd 9210, pages 18–19.

[2] *Cohabitation*, report by the Supplementary Benefits Commission to the Secretary of State for Social Services, HMSO, 1971.

[3] *Ibid*, paragraph 5.

[4] *Ibid*, paragraph 7.

[5] *Ibid*, paragraph 30 (italics supplied).

[6] Supplementary Benefits Administration Papers 2, HMSO, revised November 1972.

[7] *Ibid*, paragraph 170.

An attempt is made to obtain an offer of contribution from the husband:

> A husband's offer to contribute . . . is invariably accepted if it equals or exceeds the amount of the supplementary benefit in payment. If the offer is less than the amount of supplementary benefit it is also accepted if it is reasonable having regard to the man's statement of his circumstances which he will be expected to substantiate.[1]

> If legal proceedings are necessary to secure payment from a liable relative the Commission assists and encourages a woman to obtain her own Court order wherever it is practicable for her to do so . . . . Where the evidence is sufficiently cogent proceedings will be taken by the Commission when the woman is unable or unwilling to do so. In either case the Commission's object is to ensure that the liable relative contributes enough to remove the need to pay supplementary benefit to the person or persons for whom he is liable or, if his circumstances do not enable him to do this, to ensure that he pays as much as he reasonably can.[2]

4.185   These procedures apply to cases where the difficulty of spreading one income to cover the needs of two families is not as acute as in our example. But the normal condition of the people involved in this field of administration has already been fully demonstrated. They come from the poorest sections of the community. A very large proportion of them are permanently separated and do contract other alliances, licit or illicit. Half the maintenance orders live at any given time are in arrears, as often as not for amounts in excess of £200. The variation procedure does not succeed in keeping maintenance orders in step with the rising cost of living. Even without taking into account the rent allowance granted by the Supplementary Benefits Commission, the overwhelming majority of one-parent families on supplementary benefits are better off with the scale rates of benefit which they receive than they would be on maintenance orders paid regularly and in full.

4.186   The question thus arises how the policy of the Supplementary Benefits Commission to come to an agreed arrangement with the liable relative, and, failing such agreement, to encourage the wife to obtain a court order against him, fits with the circumstance that the women are nearly always better off on supplementary benefits.

4.187   Although no directly relevant statistics are available, it is known that a significant number of the women who apply for benefit have already, at the time of their application, obtained maintenance orders against their husbands, or are in process of doing so.[3]   In such circumstances, there is no need to implement the policy of encouraging the woman to obtain her own court order. If the woman has not already obtained a maintenance order, or taken action to get one, the Commission's officer will contact the husband to ascertain if it is possible to obtain a voluntary undertaking of maintenance from him. If he makes an offer which is less than the amount of the supplementary benefit it will be accepted if he provides evidence to show that his offer is reasonable.

4.188   We understand that, subject always to the discretion to make any adjustments considered appropriate in the individual case, the Supplementary

---

1 *Ibid*, paragraph 171.

2 *Ibid*, paragraph 168.

3 A study of separated wives on supplementary benefit in 1970 showed that of 311 married claimants 102 (30 per cent) had taken some steps before claiming benefit.

Benefits Commission have established guidelines to help their officers decide whether an offer is reasonable. The requirements of the liable relative are normally taken to be the supplementary benefit scale rates for himself and any dependents with whom he is living, plus an allowance to meet the rent in full (or, in the case of boarders, the appropriate supplementary benefit rate) plus the sum of £5, or a quarter of his net earnings (his take-home pay after deduction of national insurance contributions and income tax), whichever is the higher. Any income in excess of this will be regarded as being available to meet the liable relative's obligation under section 22 of the Act of 1966. An offer by the liable relative to pay an amount approximate to that arrived at under the formula will normally be regarded as reasonable, and will be accepted by the Commission.

4.189 A practical example of the application of the formula would be as follows. Suppose that John earns £38 gross. His family consists of himself, his second wife or his mistress, and two children, so that there are also family allowances of 90p a week. After income tax and insurance contributions his family's net income would be £31.35. His net housing costs, after rent allowance or rebate, are £5.25 a week. The Supplementary Benefits Commission would ordinarily consider an offer of approximately £2.75 a week for the maintenance of Mary's family as reasonable, that sum being calculated as follows:

	£
Requirements of John's family (as from October 1973):	
Supplementary benefit scale rates—	
—for self and second wife	11.65
—for two children (under 5)	4.10
actual housing costs	5.25
one quarter of net earnings	7.60
Total	28.60
Balance of net income available to meet liability under section 22	2.75
Total net income of John's family	31.35

The three different formulae

4.190 It will be noted that the Commission's working formula for enabling their officers to judge whether an offer made by a liable relative is a reasonable one gives him a margin over supplementary benefit levels which he may retain for himself and his second family, while satisfying the claims of the Commission arising from the payment of supplementary benefit to the first family. It was represented to us that our disclosure of this formula might lead to " unnecessary discussion, and even adverse reaction in judicial circles", about a matter within the Commission's discretion. We have already considered in detail the criteria used by the courts to fix the extent of the maintenance obligation, and have observed that different criteria apply in the divorce jurisdiction from those used in the magistrates' jurisdiction. We shall later in this Section consider how the courts, in ignorance of the normal formula of the Supplementary Benefits Commission, try to adjust their own criteria to the cases where giving effect to them would reduce one party or the other to below supplementary benefit levels.[1] Nothing could exceed the confusion created by three modes of assessment of a liability, all different from each other, and two of them employed in courts of law acting in ignorance of the third mode which the Supplementary Benefits Commission use in making decisions which affect the very same group of people. Disclosure of the Commission's formula exposes yet another and most significant feature of the disorderly and anomalous tangle of relationship between the three systems of family law; its publication is essential to a proper consideration of reform.

The policy of encouraging women to obtain maintenance orders

4.191 The liable relative enquiry disclosed that in 1970 there were 59,500 cases in which supplementary benefit was being paid, and where liability for a wife or for legitimate children existed, but where the liable relative was paying no maintenance, and no court order had been made. In about 18,000 of these cases the Supplementary Benefits Commission had accepted that there was no practical possibility of making recovery, because the liable relative was retired or incapacitated and had resources that were sufficient only for his own requirements. There were another 8,500 cases in which it was found that the liable relative was for some other reason unable to make any contribution, and another 15,000 in which he had disappeared or gone abroad.

4.192 These figures suggest that, depending on the point of time when the Supplementary Benefits Commission conclude that there is no practical purpose to be served in pursuing the liable relative, many women will not be advised by the Commission to sue for their own maintenance orders. On the other hand, although there are no means of quantifying the numbers, it is clear from the whole of the available evidence that the Commission do, in accordance with their declared general policy, encourage large numbers of women to whom they pay supplementary benefit to proceed against their husbands or the fathers of their children for maintenance orders. Since, as has been demonstrated, the supplementary benefit in payment will almost invariably exceed the amount of any maintenance which the court will order, and there is in any case only an even chance that the order, once granted, will be regularly and fully paid, it is not surprising that (as the evidence given to us suggests) much of the encouragement to take proceedings is addressed to women who have little heart for doing so. Moreover, from the point of view of the claimant, there may be no immediate advantage of any kind in obtaining an order which, if complied with, results merely in a reduction of her supplementary benefit, leaving her income unchanged. We are satisfied that for all these reasons the Commission frequently urge proceedings on women who have no desire to engage in them.

The allegations of pressure

4.193 Several of the organisations which gave evidence showed concern that women who are reluctant to institute legal proceedings for maintenance against liable relatives are, or at least feel themselves to be, subjected to pressure from officials to do so. We quote from some of the representations we have received:

> . . . health visitors have noted with concern the distress of some deserted or unmarried mothers when social security officers insist that legal proceedings be

---

[1] See paragraphs 4.203–4.205 below.

instituted . . . undue pressure is sometimes brought to bear at a time when the mother is already under considerable stress.[1]

While the Department of Health and Social Security deny that pressure is ever brought on women to apply for court orders against liable relatives, we have knowledge of many cases in which the woman had been given the definite impression that her supplementary benefits would cease if she omitted to take such action. Women in this situation frequently sue their husbands for a matrimonial offence when in fact they have no case and as a result have a very humiliating and embarrassing experience in court. We have known cases of women who have left their husbands by mutual agreement but have, as a result of this misunderstanding, sued them for desertion . . . .[2]

Pressure by the Department of Health and Social Security is often the cause of such (maintenance) proceedings where it might not otherwise be taken.[3]

Mothers of illegitimate children are currently sometimes required to agree to take out an affiliation order against their child's putative father when they apply to receive supplementary benefit.[4]

4.194 Commenting on these representations, the Supplementary Benefits Commission point out that no firm evidence is provided as to pressure actually being applied on any extensive scale. The representations are based on what certain women have said, and the same accounts are no doubt common to many of the representations. This is not to say that the accounts given may not be correct, and the Commission do not doubt that some of them may well be, although they expect that instances will have decreased in view of their determination to see that instructions are followed. But there is no means of telling in how many cases this is so, since such complaints were not reported to the Commission, so that they could be taken up with the officers concerned to ascertain to what extent they were justified. Much, of course, depends on what is regarded as pressure, as no doubt women under severe emotional stress may well misconstrue advice on the question of maintenance as being pressure. The policy of the Commission has always been against such pressure, and instructions to staff clearly state so. Nevertheless, in an organisation as large as the Commission there must inevitably be isolated cases of improper administrative action due to one of a number of factors, such as inexperienced staff, inadequate training and guidance, or the employment of staff whose temperaments make them unsuitable for this kind of work. Finally, comment the Commission, specific allegations of this nature are always fully investigated, and, although no statistics are kept, it is doubtful if the number of complaints substantiated reaches double figures in a year—as compared to an estimated total of about 264,400 women receiving benefit in November 1972.

---

[1] Health Visitors' Association.

[2] Women's National Commission.

[3] National Society for the Prevention of Cruelty to Children.

[4] National Executive Committee of the Labour Party. Similar evidence was supplied by many other organisations, including the National Citizens' Advice Bureaux Council, the Inner London Education Authority, the Board for Social Responsibility and the Family Welfare Association. It is supported, also, by three published studies: *Prisoners and Their Families, op cit,* page 242: " Many wives complained that they had been forced to take proceedings against their husbands, having been told by officials of the NAB that unless they did so they would cease to receive benefit. The head office of the Board vigorously denies that this is ever the case, but it was a practice reported to us so frequently that we feel there is good reason to believe that at a local level it is undesirably widespread "; see also *ibid,* page 269; Dennis Marsden: *Mothers Alone,* Allen Lane, 1969, page 152; *Separated Spouses, op cit,* pages 154–155. It should be borne in mind, however, that the first two of these studies are based exclusively on material drawn from a period before the establishment of the Supplementary Benefits Commission in August 1966.

4.195   In this same area, we have been assisted by Miss Olive Stevenson's recent valuable study of the working of the Supplementary Benefits Commission.[1] Miss Stevenson makes the general point regarding the strains inherent in the work of the liable relative officer:

> Fatherless families are peculiarly " at risk " as far as their handling by officials is concerned since their financial need is often inseparable from their personal problems and their domestic complications . . . it is exceedingly difficult for the interviewing officer to find an appropriate emotional position or stance in dealing with claimants at times of distress. . . .   They will meet with some women whose personal relationships are difficult, disturbed and sometimes destructive; they will sometimes encounter them at times of stress and crisis when claimants' feelings are unusually intense and when the presenting need for money is bound up with the alleged desertion by a husband or cohabitee. Supplementary Benefits officers are no more exempt from reactions to those intense situations than anyone else.   Thus, in an area in which judgment has to be exercised in a variety of ways that directly affect the welfare of claimants—above all in relation to the situation in which allowances may be refused, restricted or withdrawn—the existence of strong currents of feelings and the interaction of these feelings between officers and claimants must be taken into account in considering the administration of the scheme.[2]

4.196   Miss Stevenson then considers the policy of encouragement to women to obtain maintenance orders, and points out that:

> . . . a number of women, especially unmarried mothers, are reluctant to start proceedings and it is easy to see that, in such cases, there may be resentment if pressure is brought by officials to do so.   Thus a situation of potential conflict exists, which may be exacerbated by the fact that the SBC, regardless of the wishes of the mother, may later initiate proceedings against a husband or father to recover benefit paid to those whom he is liable to maintain or they may apply for an affiliation order.   It needs little imagination to see the difficulties this may create, for example in cases in which the father of an illegitimate child is a married man and both he and the mother of his child wish it to. be kept from the wife. However . . . it is remarkably rare for allegations to be made of tactless or ininsensitive handling of these situations.   Closer scrutiny would probably reveal that the Liable Relative Officer can avoid awkward confrontations by accepting, without too much probing, statements declaring that the whereabouts of the man concerned is unknown or that the father of an illegitimate child is not known.   It is, however, regrettable if a woman is pushed to the lengths of accusing herself of promiscuity or of lying about a man's whereabouts in order to avoid legal action or unwelcome contact being made with him.[3]

Conclusions regarding the allegations of pressure

4.197   We see no reason to dispute the view that the cases in which pressure is applied form a very small proportion of the whole, although we think that there may well be more cases than those which result in a complaint, and regard it as a matter of concern that any should occur at all. Equally, the Commission do not dispute that the excercise of their liable relative duties results in some women believing that they are under pressure, and therefore suffering just as much as if the officer has really applied it. So long as people undergo emotional turmoil in the breakdown situation, and the law as to maintenance and supplementary benefits remains as it is, it seems impossible to avoid a situation in which women will think they are being pressed to take action which they would

---

1 Olive Stevenson: *Claimant or Client?*, George Allen and Unwin, 1973.

2 *Ibid*, pages 131–132.

3 *Ibid*, pages 137–138.

prefer not to take. It is, moreover, clear from all of the circumstances we have discussed and the representations we have received that the policy of encouraging proceedings lends itself to much legitimate doubt apart from misunderstanding.

The Commission's grounds for the policy of encouragement

4.198 The Supplementary Benefits Commission justify the policy of "encouragement" in the following ways:

It is the Commission's policy to encourage and assist a wife to take her own proceedings wherever possible, because:

(1) the possibility of reconciliation will receive proper consideration when she is brought into direct contact with Court officials;

(2) if she takes proceedings and the Court makes an order it may be for a sum greater than the current rate of supplementary benefit;

(3) any order made in her favour by the Court will not lapse if she no longer needs supplementary benefit, if for example she goes out to work.[1]

The Commission similarly encourages a mother of an illegitimate child to seek her own affiliation order within the time-limits which apply.[2]

If the liable relative does not comply with the terms of an order it can be enforced on the instructions of the person in whose favour it was granted. The Commission advises and encourages women to approach the Clerk of the Court in appropriate cases to arrange for the enforcement of their own orders.[3]

Criticism of the grounds

4.199 The first of the advantages claimed is that contact with court officials will promote the possibility of reconciliation. It is true that if the Supplementary Benefits Commission themselves take proceedings directly against the liable relative for recovery of the benefit it is much less likely that such facilities as may exist at the magistrates' court for the promotion of reconciliation will be brought into play than if the woman herself lays complaint for a maintenance order. But it is necessary to consider whether the initiation of proceedings by the woman is likely to prejudice rather than foster the prospects of reconciliation. We deal elsewhere[4] with the general question of the utility of reconciliation procedures conducted in the context of hostile matrimonial litigation; but at this point observe only that we have had much evidence from organisations experienced in this field to the effect that the attendance at court, particularly if it occurs only shortly after the separation, when the relationship perhaps still could be mended by a different kind of intervention, is as likely to precipitate a permanent break as to promote a reconciliation. It is not, of course, the function of the Commission's staff to deal with questions of reconciliation, although they must be alive to the possibility not only because of the implications for public funds but also from a proper concern for the welfare of the clients with whom they are dealing. They cannot, therefore, base their advice to women to take proceedings on any expert opinion as to whether such a course will promote reconciliation or not. We find it impossible to quantify on any demonstrable

---

[1] *Supplementary Benefits Handbook, op cit*, paragraph 174.

[2] *Ibid*, paragraph 177.

[3] *Ibid*, paragraph 178.

[4] Section 13 below.

basis, but our considered judgment is that we doubt whether many reconciliations actually occur as a result of the advice given by the Commission's officers. Accordingly, we cannot attach much weight to the first justification claimed for the policy we are now reviewing.

4.200 The second of the advantages claimed is that the court may award maintenance at a higher rate than the benefit paid by the Supplementary Benefits Commission. But the evidence is that it hardly ever does. Applicants have to explain the relevant financial circumstances to the Commission's officer, who will probably be as good a judge as anyone whether an application to the court might produce an order in excess of the supplementary benefits entitlement. In such a particular case, he may be doing a service to the applicant by encouraging her to lay a complaint and there is no reason why he should not do so. But the rarity with which this possibility occurs disqualifies it, in our view, as the foundation for a general policy.

4.201 The third advantage claimed is that an order made in the woman's favour will not lapse, as would an order made in favour of the Secretary of State for Social Services, should she no longer need supplementary benefit, or cease to be eligible for it. Thus, if she obtains full-time employment she will cease to be entitled to benefit, but her entitlement under an existing maintenance order would not (unless and until it was varied) abate by reference to her wages. So again, a maintenance order might be a useful adjunct to a woman's retirement pension. This argument does have force, especially in those cases where, if the woman did not herself take proceedings, the Commission would do so, and seek her attendance in court as a witness. In such circumstances it may be that it is just as well that she should attend on her own behalf and take an order directly in her own favour.

Conclusions on the policy of encouragement

4.202 However, we regard this last point as one that goes towards mitigation rather than vindication of the policy of encouraging women to seek maintenance orders from the magistrates. On balance, we consider that this policy causes pain and anxiety, for no tangible advantage, to far more claimants than those upon whom it may confer some advantage. We recognise that the court order establishes that the claim is honest and not based on a fictitious desertion, and that the liable relative is bound in law to maintain the claimant in an amount which the magistrates have quantified. As the court said in *Winter v Winter:*[1]

> The Department's attitude . . . in the light of their policy, is that the wife . . . has agreed on the advice and encouragement of the Department to pursue her own remedies and that the Department therefore relies on the court to investigate the facts and make an appropriate order.

But, as appears from the rest of this passage as earlier cited, the court immediately went on to say that this system in practice breaks down and plays into the hands of a recalcitrant husband because the Supplementary Benefits Commission have much better means for making a proper assessment of the liable relative's resources than has the court. Objectively, also, though it is not of course designed for that purpose, the policy of the Commission helps to

---

[1] *Op cit.* The full quotation is given in Section 7, paragraph 4.104, above. It should be noted that in describing the official attitude the court was relying on the submissions of counsel who appeared for the Department of Health and Social Security.

perpetuate the historical propensity of the poor to resort to the jurisdiction which embalms the state of breakdown of marriage. Where a woman is divorcing her husband the Commission, if she is on supplementary benefits, will still, if necessary, encourage her to obtain a maintenance order in the divorce proceedings. We understand from our enquiries that consent orders for maintenance for small amounts in the divorce jurisdiction often reflect a desire to satisfy the Commission by producing an order to them. Mainly, however, the policy of the Commission is a factor which helps to steer women towards the magistrates' jurisdiction. This is a form of intervention in the matrimonial situation which, in our view, does much more harm than good.

THE COURTS' APPROACH TO SUPPLEMENTARY BENEFITS

4.203 We have already described[1] the principles which the divorce court and the magistrates respectively apply to the assessment of maintenance. We refrained at that stage, however, from enquiring into how the courts apply these principles in the situation where the applicant for maintenance is in receipt of supplementary benefit. That question now becomes relevant. In other words, reverting to our two hypothetical families, let it be assumed that either of her own volition, or in response to the encouragement of the Supplementary Benefits Commission, Mary seeks a maintenance order against John. The question then is how is the case affected by the fact that Mary is getting income from the Commission?

4.204 The cases in which this problem have been considered relate mostly to orders of the magistrates, but it is clear that the approach is to be the same in whichever jurisdiction the problem arises.[2] The first rule is that the liable relative is not permitted to shift his responsibility to the Supplementary Benefits Commission. He is not permitteed to argue that since the payment of maintenance will benefit the Commission, rather than his wife, in the sense that it will reduce the burden on the Commission without increasing her income, this relieves him of liability:

> ... the fact that the result of an order of the court in favour of a wife is likely to be that the National Assistance Board will ultimately receive the benefit and not the wife at all is wholly irrelevant to the question of what amount the justices should order the husband to pay.[3]

But, secondly, the maintenance order should not be pitched at a level which would reduce the liable relative to below subsistence:

> The matrimonial court . . . should not, at the conclusion of the adjudication, allow the husband to enjoy a substantially higher standard of living than the wife, or shift his responsibilities for his wife and children on to the community generally through the National Assistance Board. On the other hand, the matrimonial court must remember that the National Assistance Board does not supplement wages. They must therefore not make such an order as would bring the husband below subsistence level. If the order so limited leaves the wife and children still below subsistence level, the National Assistance Board may properly be looked to, to supplement their income. Both parties and the children will then unhappily be at no better than subsistence level; but the result will be just as

---

[1] See Sections 4 and 7 above.

[2] *Barnes v Barnes* (1972) 1 WLR 1381.

[3] *Ashley v Ashley* (1968) P 582, *per* Cumming Bruce J at 587.

between the husband and his wife and children on the one hand, and between the husband and the general community as symbolised by the National Assistance Board on the other.[1]

4.205 One thus finds demonstrated the point made earlier that not merely do the basic principles of assessment of maintenance now differ as between the two legal jurisdictions, but also that their common approach to the problem of taking the supplementary benefits factor into account is different from the policy which the Supplementary Benefits Commission apply when dealing on their own with the same people in the same circumstances. If there is insufficient income to go round, the courts aim at producing equality at supplementary benefit levels; the Commission (although this has never been disclosed to the courts) will divide whatever is available so as normally to leave the liable relative somewhat above that level and bring up the claimant's income to her supplementary benefit entitlement. It is hardly to be wondered at that our evidence shows that the law is not always fully understood, even by those who are concerned with its administration.

THE " DIVERSION " PROCEDURE

4.206 It used to be the case that where a woman both had a maintenance order and was also in receipt of national assistance she would frequently find herself on a see-saw between the court collecting office and the National Assistance Board. She would have to attend the collecting office to receive the maintenance payments, accommodating herself to the opening hours and to the company of people awaiting trial on criminal charges, or paying fines. But if, as so often was the case, the maintenance had not been remitted for her to collect, the national assistance assessed on the basis that maintenance was in payment would be insufficient. Such women could be seen, often with children accompanying them, taking themselves back and forth between the two offices, as like as not at a considerable distance from each other, in harassed pursuit of the subsistence which each expected the other to produce.

4.207 This evil has been much mitigated by the arrangements for payment of maintenance by post, which we have already described, and also by the system which has for some years been in force whereby a maintenance order may be " diverted " to the Department of Health and Social Security. The diversion procedure works in this fashion. When a maintenance order is made in favour of a wife who is eligible for supplementary benefit, and the amount of the order is less than the full rate of her benefit entitlement, she is invited to authorise the clerk of the court, subject to his consent, to divert payments received under the maintenance order to the Department of Health and Social Security. When such a transfer is effected, the wife receives an order book entitling her to supplementary benefit (calculated on the basis that there is no maintenance order) which she can cash at the post office; and the clerk of the court transmits to the Department whatever is paid in to the collecting office under the maintenance order. (The procedure is also available in the much

[1] *Ibid, per* Sir Jocelyn Simon P at 590–591. The case was concerned with national assistance payments but applies equally to the succeeding system of supplementary benefits. See also *Attwood v Attwood* (1968) P 591. In *Billington v Billington*, 8 November 1973 (as yet unreported) a similar concept was applied to attachment of earnings, it being held that normally the protected earnings rate should not be fixed below subsistence level by supplementary benefit standards, although there was no fixed rule to prohibit this in all circumstances.

rarer case where the amount of the maintenance order exceeds the supplementary benefit entitlement; but here no invitation to transfer the maintenance order is made until the circumstances, such as repeated failure to pay on the order, show this to be desirable.) The effect is that the wife receives her full entitlement regularly, whether the maintenance order is paid in full, intermittently or not at all. She is relieved of the anxiety of irregular payments and the harassment and indignity of commuting between different officials and different procedures. We show in Table 4.12 the number of orders diverted to the Department of Health and Social Security in 1967 and 1970, the latest date for which we have information.

TABLE 4.12

MATRIMONIAL AND AFFILIATION ORDERS DIVERTED TO THE DEPARTMENT OF HEALTH AND SOCIAL SECURITY IN 1967 AND 1970

Year	Total number of court orders	Number of orders where payment was diverted	Percentage of orders diverted
1967	87,500	56,000	64
1970	129,000	96,000	74

Source: Supplementary Benefits Commission.

It will be observed that the proportion of orders diverted increased between 1967 and 1970 from almost two thirds to almost three quarters.

4.208 The advantages of the diversion procedure are not, however, available to a woman who is not regularly on supplementary benefit. For example, a woman may have an income deriving partly from part-time wages and partly from payments under a maintenance order which normally is sufficient to lift her off supplementary benefits. If she has a period of unemployment, or is forced to take time off to look after her children during an illness, or payment under the maintenance order becomes erratic, such a woman can find herself at least for a time in the situation that was general before the introduction of the diversion procedure.

4.209 Within the confines in which it operates, which are determined by the overlap of entitlements to maintenance and supplementary benefit, the diversion procedure represents a victory of realism over bureaucracy. It is apparent, however, that the success of the procedure can be reliably evaluated only at the local level where the clerk of the court and the responsible officer of the Supplementary Benefits Commission have to co-operate to apply the system to individual cases, keep accounts, and iron out the snags. The Commission issue detailed instructions to their officers, but little information is generally available of how the system functions on the ground. It will be recalled that the consent of the clerk of the court is necessary before the maintenance order may be diverted to the Commission, and it has been suggested that obtaining this consent is no mere formality.[1]   On the other hand, our own more recent enquiries indicated no lack of co-operation between clerks of courts and officers of the Commission in working the diversion procedure.

ENFORCEMENT AGAINST THE LIABLE RELATIVE BY THE COMMISSION

4.210   Whether or not a maintenance order has been made, and whether or not, if made, it has been diverted to the Department of Health and Social Security, the statutory liability of the liable relative under section 22 of the Act of 1966 is unaffected, and the Commission may themselves proceed to enforce this liability by application to the magistrates (section 23) or to prosecute the liable relative if he persistently fails to discharge it (section 30).[2]

Criminal prosecutions

4.211   Table 4.13 shows the number of criminal prosecutions in liable relative cases undertaken by the Supplementary Benefits Commission in 1972, the last year for which we have information.   During the year 1972 criminal proceedings were taken against 604 men for failure to maintain persons for whom they were liable under the Ministry of Social Security Act.   585 convictions were obtained:

TABLE 4.13
PROCEEDINGS UNDER SECTION 30 OF THE MINISTRY OF SOCIAL SECURITY ACT 1966 DURING THE YEAR 1972*

Nature of sentence	Number
Imprisonment	99
Fine and imprisonment	15
Fine or imprisonment	16
Fine	292
Suspended sentence	69
Conditional discharge	19
Probation	29
Admonished	42
Absolute discharge	4
Total	585

*Not including cases where proceedings were taken against unemployed persons because of voluntary unemployment.
Source: Supplementary Benefits Commission.

Table 4.13 shows that quite a small number of cases were prosecuted, but with a remarkable success rate of 97 per cent convictions.   We have no means of telling whether success of this order represents supreme caution in selecting

[1] Marsden, *op cit*, reports (page 156) that at one of the courts he investigated 37 out of 53 mothers had been allowed to direct their orders to the National Assistance Board; at other courts, only 7 out of 42 mothers had been permitted to divert their orders despite requests from the local National Assistance Board manager.   But these results come out of research conducted in 1965.   We believe that the diversion procedure works far better now than it did then.
[2] The statutory provisions are mentioned in more detail in the opening pages of this Section.

cases for prosecution or abnormal incompetence on the part of those prosecuted in defending themselves. A conviction under section 30 is different in character from a committal to prison as a mode of enforcing a maintenance order. The former involves proof of a specifically defined criminal offence, in a criminal court, in which a burden of proof to the criminal standard rests on the prosecutor. Despite this difference, however, we consider that just as committal for neglect to pay maintenance should be abolished, so should the criminal offence under section 30 of the Act of 1966. The reasons we have given in support of our view on the one apply equally to the other. We do not regard the prison officer as an appropriate agent for the regulation of family breakdown.

Civil proceedings

4.212 It would remain open to the Supplementary Benefits Commission to bring civil proceedings under sections 23 or 24 and to enforce any order obtained by attachment of earnings. The liability of the husband or father (or, it might be wife or mother, for this is one area in which the law has resolutely maintained since 1601 a strict equality between the sexes) is expressed in section 22 in absolute terms. But in making an order to pay on the complaint of the Commission the magistrates must " have regard to all the circumstances ". If the complaint by the Commission is in respect of the husband's failure to maintain his wife, proof of her adultery or desertion is so strong a circumstance to be taken into account that it will afford a defence to the Commission's claim.[1] Misconduct short of adultery or desertion on the part of the wife can also be taken into account by the court:

> . . . the justices might think that in all the circumstances of the case it would not be right to make the husband pay a proportion of his income to his wife because they might think that the wife was a good deal more to blame for the state of affairs than the husband.[2]

The wife's misconduct will not affect the right of the Commission to recover from the husband in respect of payments made for the children. Nor will the financial arrangements which the parties may make on a consensual separation affect the husband's liability to the Commission as a liable relative under the Act. Merely by agreeing with his wife that he will pay her no maintenance, the husband cannot escape that liability. He also remains liable to the Commission if, despite payment of agreed maintenance, she becomes a burden on them; although, if the Commission lay a complaint, the agreed amount may be some evidence to the magistrates of the amount which the husband can afford to pay—this being one of the circumstances which the magistrates must take into account in making their order.[3]

Conclusions

4.213 We have attempted in this Section to unravel the tangled connections between the obligation of the individual to maintain his dependants, as it is reflected in the law and practice of the matrimonial jurisdiction of magistrates' courts, the obligation of the community to maintain the needy, which had its origin in the poor law and is currently incorporated in the supplementary benefits system established under the Ministry of Social Security Act 1966, and the policies and practice of the Supplementary Benefits Commission which is charged with the administration of supplementary benefits.

---

[1] *National Assistance Board v Wilkinson* (1952) 2 QB 648, as explained in *National Assistance Board v Parkes* (1955) 2 QB 506.

[2] *Staphir v National Assistance Board* (1955) 1 QB 486, *per* Lord Goddard CJ at 498.

[3] See, in addition to the cases previously cited, *National Assistance Board v Prisk* (1954) 1 All ER 400.

4.214 The dominant features to emerge from this attempt may perhaps be summarised as follows. In the first place, the system we have been examining is one of enormous complexity. History and habit may assist to conceal the extent of this complexity; less so for those who become involved with it than for those who are fortunate enough not to need to become involved. It is true that the legal regulation of family breakdown and its consequences can never be a simple matter. But no one who seeks to improve the system need fear that measures cannot be devised to bring more order, logic and simplicity into it. Secondly, unless and until a new source of income is produced for one-parent families (a subject considered in Part 5 of this Report) the boundaries of possible improvement are set by the size of liable relatives' incomes in the context of the responsibilities which in a free society they must remain at liberty, wisely or foolishly, to contract. Little is to be expected from a tightening of enforcement procedures. This is demonstrated by the results of research, of which our own is the most recent. It can be further demonstrated from the experience of the Supplementary Benefits Commission.

4.215 We have shown how the Commission are under a duty both to assist wives and mothers who cannot live or rely on their court maintenance orders and to seek reimbursement on behalf of the taxpayer from liable husbands and fathers. The Commission have an administrative machine, functioning nationwide, to assess means and estimate the extent to which men can be expected to meet their legal obligations. They have their own statutory powers, including powers of criminal prosecution, to compel men to meet these obligations. They can and do encourage women to enforce their own maintenance orders through the magistrates' courts. Yet the results of all this activity are to produce only a small proportion of the supplementary benefits paid to one-parent family wives and mothers. Figures supplied by the Commission show that in 1965, 1970 and 1972 liable relatives contributed only about 17 per cent of the net benefits paid to such wives and mothers, and that only half of this contribution resulted from direct collection by the Commission (or their predecessors) from the liable relative.

TABLE 4.14

ESTIMATES OF THE AMOUNTS PAID OUT IN LIABLE RELATIVE CASES AND SUMS RECOVERED FROM THE LIABLE RELATIVES

Year	Estimated total yearly rate of national assistance/ supplementary benefit expenditure	Estimated yearly rate of payments received direct from liable relatives by applicants/claimants	Yearly value* of payments received from liable relatives by the National Assistance Board/ Department of Health and Social Security
	£	£	£
1965	42,721,000	4,415,000	3,024,000
1970	93,269,000	8,028,000	8,375,000
1972	144,553,000	12,078,000	12,525,000

*Actual receipts.
Source: The liable relative enquiry in 1970 and the Supplementary Benefits Commission.

The figures in Table 4.14 allow nothing for the cost to the public of collections from the liable relatives, and of legal services deployed in obtaining thousands of abortive or near abortive maintenance orders. There may be some unquantifiable amount saved through the action of the Commission resulting in some cases—there could hardly be many of these—in the liable relative's maintaining his dependants at a level which takes them off supplementary benefits altogether, and so outside Table 4.14. But it is at least clear that objections to the present system cannot be over-ridden by any appeal to the savings which it achieves in public expenditure.

SECTION 11—THE SCOPE FOR REFORM

4.216 We have now completed our examination of the three systems of law operating in England and Wales which have a particular and pervasive importance for one-parent families. We have made many criticisms, for all of which we have given reasons based on the observation, studies and experience of members of the Committee and of those who gave us evidence, and on research findings. Some of these findings became available shortly before our appointment, but they were extended and corroborated by research that we sponsored.

4.217 One of the most important results of the work on the legal side of our investigations is that it has helped to establish the foundations for the financial recommendations made in Part 5. The justification for these recommendations is that, with few individual exceptions, fatherless families suffer from special financial hardship and deprivation in our society. That fact is established from many different sources discussed in Part 5, but one shaft of illumination proceeds from the enquiry we have conducted into the decisions of the courts and the Supplementary Benefits Commission. This has established beyond a doubt that most one-parent families could not subsist on the proceeds of the maintenance orders, or on any amount to which it would be possible to increase them while permitting the liable relative himself to subsist without assistance. In this significant sense, Part 4 may be regarded as introductory to Part 5.

4.218 However, apart from lending support to our propsal for a new social security benefit (" guaranteed maintenance allowance ") for one-parent families, the material so far considered in this Part leads directly to a case for reforms which tend to fall into two categories. These categories, in their briefest possible description, are, first, reforms of the matrimonial law and of the courts which administer it; and, secondly, reforms to achieve a more satisfactory relationship between the decisions of the courts and the social security authorities when both are operating within the area of family breakdown.

4.219 There are several different ways in which and levels at which we might approach the task of making proposals for such reforms. One way of dealing with the first category would be to assume that the dual matrimonial jurisdiction will continue, and to make recommendations within that assumption, and, so far as it allowed, for improving as many as possible of the defects to which we have drawn attention. Quite a considerable amount might be achieved even within these narrow limits. To take a few illustrations: we could discuss ways and means for improving procedures for the assessment of maintenance orders, particularly in the magistrates' courts; how further to reduce the obnoxious association between the matrimonial jurisdiction of those courts and the administration of the criminal law; the rationalisation of the various grounds for relief which, over the years, have become deposited like so many archaeological layers in the summary jurisdiction;[1] the adjustment of the grounds of relief in the summary jurisdiction to take account of the shift in law and morality away from the concept of the offence and towards the concept of breakdown; the abolition of the rule that the complainant's adultery is an absolute bar to her obtaining relief from the magistrates; and so on.

4.220   On the other hand, we are convinced that the reform within the first category which is above all else needed is the abolition of the dual jurisdiction as such.   In terms of the machinery of justice, this has become necessary to remedy inefficiencies which have now become too extravagant to tolerate.   In terms of social purpose, it has become necessary—indeed, it is long overdue— as a measure for democratising justice in the administration of family law.   Taking this approach would require us to deal with the nature of the unified jurisdiction that we envisage as replacing the present dual system, and to discuss specific problems on the footing that they have to be solved within the context of such a jurisdiction.

4.221   Similarly, there is more than one method of dealing with the discussion of reforms within the second category.   We could make the assumption that the basic factors will remain unchanged—that is to say, that courts of summary and superior jurisdictions will continue to make financial orders and the Supplementary Benefits Commission will continue to pay benefit and seek recovery from liable relatives in large numbers of the same cases.   The enquiry would then be into what re-arrangements are possible, within this framework, to achieve better results than at present.   If, on the other hand, we project ourselves into the period when our new one parent family benefit has been introduced and is being administered (as we envisage that it will be) separately from supplementary benefits, the problems take on another dimension. The need would then be to devise the best possible form of relationship between the courts and the new administration, and court orders and the new benefit. Further, it would, at any rate in theory, be possible to consider these prospective relations either on the assumption that the court system remains the dual one or on the assumption that it will by then have been replaced by a unified jurisdiction.

4.222   It is evident that it would be both tedious and profitless to attempt to draw up a list of reforms appropriate for each possible situation arising from the permutation of all the possible alternatives.   In deciding on the course that we shall adopt, we have been influenced by the following considerations.   We are not a committee of technical experts, and (although we of course recognise that the practicality of law reform depends on whether the detail of it can be clearly expressed) consider that it would not be appropriate for us to involve ourselves in the minutiae to be expected of a law reform committee.   The cure for some of the defects that we have criticised seems to us to be relatively simple and obvious once the criticism is accepted.   In other instances, the correction of the defect, however plainly established, calls for specialised skill.   We have been

[1]See footnote 2 to paragraph 4.62 above.

aware that the Law Commission are engaged in considering some aspects of the subjects to which we have addressed ourselves in this Part of our Report. Indeed, as our deliberations neared their conclusion, the Law Commission published a Working Paper[1] on the changes that may be desirable in the matrimonial law of the magistrates' courts as a result of the recent reforms in the divorce law. In the areas where our own responsibilities and those of the Law Commission overlap we naturally hope for at least a broad coincidence of results. But our approach is different, in that we concentrate on legal institutions primarily from the standpoint of social policy. Moreover, the Law Commission do not have under review matters which occupy a central place in our own investigation, namely, the results of the inter-dependence of the maintenance obligation and social security and of the agencies which respectivly administer them.

4.223 Bearing all of these considerations in mind, we adopt the following scheme. In Section 12 we shall set out our proposals for re-organising the existing methods of support for one-parent families, that is to say, on the assumptions that the two legal jurisdictions continue, the guaranteed maintenance allowance has not yet been introduced, and people in need resort to the Supplementary Benefits Commission as they now do. Even within these assumptions it is possible, as we hope to demonstrate, to achieve a transformation for the better of the relationship between the decisions of the courts and the decisions of the Supplementary Benefits Commission and of the contribution they make to the welfare of one-parent families. After the introduction of guaranteed maintenance allowance, the question will arise of fixing the proper pattern of relationship between the new benefit and the new agency which administers it and the courts and their orders. There is a close parallelism between this subject and the subject matter of Section 12, although there are also important differences. In Part 5 we have set ourselves the task not only of examining the circumstances which produce a need for guaranteed maintenance allowance but also of dealing with the administrative problems associated with the introduction of such a benefit in sufficient detail to show that it is workable. We consider that the relationship between the new benefit and maintenance and the new agency and the courts is a topic which falls under this head. We therefore consider it in Part 5, Section 7. Here, as generally in Part 5, the legal background at the time when the guaranteed maintenance allowance is introduced is assumed to be one in which a unified system has replaced the dual one, but none of the recommendations in Part 5 is dependent upon this having taken place. Thus, our proposals which deal with the relationship between the administration of social security benefits for one-parent families and the courts will be found in Section 12 of this Part and Section 7 of Part 5. So far as concerns proposals for reform of the legal system as it affects one-parent families, we have decided that it would not be helpful to take more than one bite at the cherry. Our primary aim is unification of the matrimonial legal system, and the remedies for the defects we have noticed in the present organisation, so far as they are not obvious, or would not be cured by the very process of creating a single jurisdiction, can as well be considered in the context of that proposed jurisdiction as in any other way. Thus, this category of reforms is the subject of Sections 13 and 14 of this Part.

---

[1] *Family Law, Matrimonial Proceedings in Magistrates' Courts,* Working Paper No 53, 7 September 1973, HMSO. We comment on the Working Paper in Section 14 below.

SECTION 12—THE MACHINERY OF SUPPORT: A NEW MODEL

INTRODUCTION

4.224 It would be natural to think that if a women has insufficient earnings or resources to maintain herself and her children, and lacks support from the man who is liable to maintain them, her surest remedy is to go to law. But, as we have shown, for vast numbers of women in this situation proceedings to to enforce the private obligation to maintain produce only an inadequate and uncertain remedy. Their mainstay is the aid which the State, in discharge of a public obligation, provides through the supplementary benefits system. One might say of these women that their rights as citizens are much more valuable to them than their rights as dependants. Yet, as we have also shown, the institutional arrangements for giving effect to these various rights and obligations reflect almost as much of the illusion as of the reality. The fact has to be faced that in a democratic society, which cannot legislate (even if it could enforce) different rules of familial and sexual behaviour depending on the ability to pay for the consequences, the community has to bear much of the cost of broken homes and unmarried motherhood. The question which then becomes plain is how, in the interests both of efficiency and humanity, is such a community to bring about the necessary correspondence between legal and administrative procedures and the social and economic circumstances they are intended to regulate.

4.225 In the present Section we approach that question by way of proposals for reforms within the framework of the existing system of maintenance and public support. We take no account at this stage of the new one-parent family benefit proposed in Part 5. Over the main part of the discussion we shall be dealing with that type of one-parent family which consists of a separated, but still married, wife and her child or children. We refer to her as the " lone mother ". Our proposals would apply equally to the rare case of the " lone father " who has a claim for maintenance on his wife. We assume throughout that the lone mother has a claim both upon the Supplementary Benefits Commission for supplementary benefit and upon her husband for maintenance. Correspondingly, the husband may be under a double obligation, both directly to the lone mother under the general law, and as a " liable relative " in the technical sense of being under an obligation to reimburse the Commission in respect of what they have paid to the lone mother.

CLAIM BY THE LONE MOTHER ON THE SUPPLEMENTARY BENEFITS COMMISSION

4.226 The lone mother who is unsupported or inadequately supported will, as we envisage the reformed system, go to the Supplementary Benefits Commission and make her claim for supplementary benefit as she now does. At the date when the new system came into operation many of these women would already have obtained maintenance orders from the court. We deal later with the method by which these maintenance orders would be absorbed into the new system, but at this stage we assume that the lone mother, at the time when she applies for supplementary benefit, has no maintenance order, although she may be in a position to take proceedings for one. The applicant's entitlement to supplementary benefit will then be assessed, just as in similar circumstances it now is, without reference to her claim for maintenance.

4.227 It will also be necessary, as it now is, for the Commission to make enquiry of the applicant regarding the circumstances of her marriage and its breakdown and generally of her family situation, for this information affects entitlement to benefit and its amount. Such enquiry is relevant also to a decision on whether the applicant should be issued immediately with a book of weekly orders for supplementary benefit (order books are issued for thirteen or twenty-six weekly payments), since if it appears that there is a prospect of the man's return home in the near future it might be inappropriate then and there to make provision for so far ahead. Again, since the Commission will remain responsible for recovery from the liable relative, the applicant will continue to be requested, as she now is, to disclose what she knows of his whereabouts and circumstances.

4.228 Subject to factors of this kind, the lone mother applying for supplementary benefit will be treated as though she were a single person, such as a widow, with no legal entitlement to maintenance against any other person. This means that in contrast with existing procedures of the Commission[1] no encouragement will be offered by the Commission to the lone mother to bring legal proceedings of her own against the liable relative. Once she has established her entitlement to supplementary benefit, the amount of which will be calculated without reference to any claim she may have for maintenance, the lone mother will normally have no financial interest, and be under no inducement, to pursue the liable relative for maintenance, nor will she be concerned with the assessment or enforcement by the Commission of the amount which they require the liable relative to pay to them by way of reimbursement of the supplementary benefit they are paying her. Assessment and enforcement of the liable relative's contribution will be regarded as processes which take place entirely between the Commission and the liable relative, and which do not involve the lone mother.

THE ADMINISTRATIVE ORDER: THE BASIC PROPOSAL

4.229 The Commission will now have a claim against the liable relative. Our basic proposals are:

(1) the Commission will assess the means of the liable relative and determine what it is proper for him to pay to the Commission in or towards satisfaction of the money they have paid out;

(2) the Commission will be entitled to order the liable relative to pay to the Commission the amount so assessed. For the purposes of exposition we shall call such an order made by the Commission an " administrative order ";

(3) subject to rights of review and appeal, the administrative order will be legally binding on the liable relative and enforceable against him by the Commission through normal court processes;

(4) the amount of the administrative order will in no case exceed the amount of the lone mother's entitlement to supplementary benefit.

[1] We have explained and criticised these procedures in Section 10, paragraphs 4.191–4.202, above.

153

Within this limit, the amount will be within the Commission's discretion. In exercising this discretion, the Commission will act in accordance with published criteria for assessment, framed so as to produce a fair result in the normal run of cases; but the discretion will always be available to allow for individual circumstances;

(5) the Commission will never be in a position of having to pass judgment on matrimonial conduct.

4.230 The proposals set out in this short form require elaboration, but it will be seen immediately that they involve a considerable reorganisation of existing procedures, one outstanding effect of which should be that large numbers of the cases in which separated wives now seek financial relief for themselves and their children from the magistrates would not need to come before the courts at all.[1]

THE PROPOSAL IN MORE DETAIL

The means enquiry

4.231 We have elsewhere, particularly in Section 6 above, examined the long-standing deficiencies in the procedures used by the magistrates to establish the means of the parties in matrimonial cases. These deficiencies are partly capable of remedy through improvements in the procedures such as have been suggested for upwards of forty years.[2] But the Commission, with their " officers skilled in making enquiries and facilities for obtaining relevant information ",[3] are intrinsically better placed than the courts for conducting means enquiries. The adversary procedures of the courts are ill-adapted to such enquiries. Standardisation is very difficult to achieve through judicial as distinct from administrative procedures, in addition to which the court has no power or machinery to take the initiative in verifying evidence. On the other hand, the Commission have the experience, techniques and machinery for conducting means enquiries by standardised methods all over the country. They can cross-check information supplied to them and conduct independent investigations whenever that seems to be appropriate. We have no doubt that assessments of means in the general run of cases are more efficiently conducted by the Commission than by the magistrates.

The amount of the administrative order

4.232 Having assessed means, the Commission will go on to assess the amount which they consider it is proper for the liable relative to pay to them at convenient intervals. This amount will not exceed the amount of the lone mother's entitlement to supplementary benefit. In the scheme we are now envisaging, a woman who considered that she had a claim for maintenance at a rate higher than her supplementary benefit entitlement would have to apply to the court for a maintenance order. If she obtained such an order, but then fell back on supplementary benefit because the order was not fulfilled, she could make use, as now, of the " diversion " procedure[4] but the administrative order procedure would not be available.

---

[1] The courts would, of course, remain exclusively responsible for the determination of any dispute involving custody or other arrangements regarding children.

[2] See Section 6 above.

[3] See *Winter v Winter* (1972) quoted in Section 7, paragraph 4.104, above.

[4] The " diversion " procedure is discussed in Section 10, paragraphs 4.206–4.209.

4.233 The Commission will have a discretion as to the amount which they assess the liable relative to pay. Within this discretion, however, and subject to the basic limitation mentioned in the last paragraph, the Commission will make its assessment by reference to standards adapted to produce a fair result in normal cases.[1] These standards will be formulated and issued not only as guidance to officers, but also by way of information to the public, so that everyone concerned will know where he stands, and exactly how the sum he is required to pay has been calculated.

4.234 We attach great importance to these points on formulation and publication of standards of assessment. These are the very points on which it might be expected that the judicial process would do well, and yet the performance, especially in the magistrates' jurisdiction, is poor.[2] The situation is particularly difficult and anomalous since, as we have seen, there is nothing to ensure that the consequences of the court's applying the vague formulation of what is " reasonable " will match up with the calculations which the Commission may be applying to the very same people in exactly the same circumstances. Indeed, it would be quite possible at present for the courts to commit a man to prison for failure to pay an amount which is more than the Commission would find entirely acceptable.[3]

4.235 The standard rules of assessment should be such as to leave the liable relative an amount out of his own income which usually exceeds by a fairly generous margin the amount to which he would himself be entitled in all of his own relevant circumstances if he were on supplementary benefit. This means that his responsibilities to his other dependants—a second wife, or a mistress, and their children—must be taken into the calculation, and that he should not be required to pay an amount to the Commission that will reduce him and those dependants to subsistence at supplementary benefit levels and no higher. The formula currently in use by the Commission for liable relative purposes, which we have mentioned earlier on,[4] seems to produce a satisfactory margin, although it would need to be kept under review in the light of changing circumstances. Such a formula, or some version of it suitable to give effect to the principle we have recommended, should, therefore, be incorporated in the scheme we are now proposing.

4.236 Having regard to all that we have discovered regarding the low income levels of most of the men who find themselves in the liable relative situation, it is apparent that the result of applying such a formula will in a large number of cases mean that the amount which the Commission ask to be paid will be quite small, or even, where a man of modest income is maintaining a second family, the liability may be eliminated altogether. A further effect will be that the minimum standard of living of the liable relative with his new family, being, where possible, pitched in accordance with the formula at

---

[1] There is nothing to prevent an authority vested with a general discretion from formulating rules or policies as to how it will apply its discretion, provided that it does not refuse to listen to a request for a different application of the discretion in the particular case: see *British Oxygen Co Ltd v Minister of Technology* (1971) AC 610.

[2] See Section 7 above, *passim.*

[3] See Section 10, paragraphs 4.184–4.190 and 4.203–4.205.

[4] *Ibid*, especially paragraph 4.189.

something higher than supplementary benefit level, will be better than his first family's standard of living. However, a remedy for this state of affairs is the provision of the special benefit for one-parent families that we recommend in Part 5. Within the framework of the discussion at this stage, in which the assumption is that the sources of support for one-parent families remain unchanged, we are convinced, for reasons that by now require no repetition, that it is futile for the State to try to enforce a division of one income so as to produce an equality of poverty between the family with whom the earner lives and the family with whom he does not.

4.237 Although the rate of recovery achieved by the Commission will, therefore, remain small, we see no reason why it should be smaller than it is at present,[1] and there is reason to think that it may be rather larger. One of the results of legal aid for matrimonial cases in the magistrates' courts is that a considerable period, perhaps three months, may elapse between the time when a woman thinks of going to law for her maintenance and the date when the magistrates finally make a maintenance order. Although there is at present nothing to prevent the Commission from approaching the liable relative during this period, we think that the simplification of procedures arising from the elimination of the maintenance order in many of these cases would shorten the interval between the breakdown and the official demand for money made on the liable relative. The shorter this interval, the less chance for the man to get out of the habit of supporting his dependants, and the greater the likelihood of troublefree recovery of what the Commission think he should pay.

Housing costs

4.238 In calculating requirements for supplementary benefits purposes the individual's housing costs are normally taken fully into account. Consequently the formula to be used to arrive at the minimum level to which a liable relative's income would be reduced by the Commission's administrative order must be such as to bring his housing costs into the calculation.[2]

4.239 The provisions for rate rebates and for rent rebates and allowances mean that, depending on the level of rent and rates and the composition of his household, a man may qualify for a rebate or allowance, even with earnings at roughly the average. Entitlement depends primarily on gross income, although certain items of income may be disregarded.[3] The rules do not, however, allow for any disregard for payments in the nature of maintenance made to another household. The result is that, when such a payment passes from one household to another, it is counted in the gross income of both households and, for both, reduces entitlement to a rebate or allowance. This double counting has been seen as being both awkward and unfair and we understand that representations have been made for measures to eliminate it in relation to the rent rebate and allowance scheme. Consequently, consideration is, we understand, being given to enabling the amount of maintenance payments to be deducted from the gross income of the payer in calculating entitlement under the scheme.

---

[1] Figures on the recovery rate are given in Table 4.14, Section 10, above.

[2] This is the Commission's present procedure: see the discussion in Section 10.

[3] Appendix 8, paragraphs 27 to 28, contain a brief outline of the schemes.

4.240   If this proposal were adopted the situation could arise that the Commission would assess the amount of an administrative order taking account of the liable relative's housing costs; he would then claim a rebate or allowance, or an increase in the rebate or allowance he is already receiving, on the ground that the amount of the payments he was making under the administrative order should be disregarded in assessing his income. If his housing costs were reduced because he was successful in this claim, there would be ground for review of the administrative order and an increase in its amount. This, in turn, would affect the amount of rebate or allowance. In theory one could, therefore, become involved in a vicious circle, with the amount of the order and the amount of the rebate or allowance being interdependent, each responding to a change in the other, and neither, therefore, reaching an ultimate level.

4.241   With the availability of rate rebates and rent rebates and allowances it is now possible for people to receive help with housing costs which are high in relation to their income. We think that the effect of the rebate schemes should in principle be to ensure that no one has housing costs which leave him little by way of resources to meet other normal expenses. For this reason, and also because of the double counting involved in the present system, we agree with proposals that the calculation of income for these schemes should exclude maintenance payments made by the householder under an administrative order or under a court order.

4.242   If the main provision for housing costs is dealt with in this way by the rebate schemes—and for owner-occupiers with mortgages there is help available by way of tax relief—there is, in our view, no reason for making a specific allowance for housing costs in the formula for arriving at the level to which a liable relative's income could be reduced by an administrative order. Although most people will still have housing costs of some kind, even after any rebate or allowance due has been made, these will not be so high as to leave them little money for other expenses. The proper way to take account of the residual housing costs in making the administrative order would then be, we suggest, not to attempt to allow for them specifically (so re-creating the vicious circle) but by ensuring that the liable relative retains a significant margin of his income above the scale rates for himself and the dependent members of his household. This may mean, in terms of the formula at present used by the Supplementary Benefits Commission,[1] revising the " £5 or a quarter of net earnings " allowance to something like " £7.50 or one third of net earnings " in order to achieve a similar effect.

4.243   There will be liable relatives who are too well off to qualify for a rebate or allowance, but who may have relatively high housing costs which, if a court maintenance order were being considered, they would claim should be taken taken into account. The formula approach of the administrative order system with no specific allowance for housing costs, might be said to be withdrawing from them advantages they could reasonably hope for at present in a court order. Such an argument could, however, be largely met by reference to the " £7·50 or one third of net earnings " part of the formula, which means that the extent by which minimum income would exceed the scale rates would increase according to net earnings. The better off liable relative would consequently

---

[1] See paragraph 4.188.

be left with more income available for his own purposes, including, if this were the case, more expensive housing. We would expect, however, that in the usual case where the lone mother is claiming supplementary benefit, the liable relative's financial position is such that his housing costs, after any rebate or allowance, are modest, so that the question of a possible disadvantage in comparison with current court assessment methods is remote. In the context of an administrative order by the Supplementary Benefits Commission, therefore, we take the view that there would be no real problem.[1]

Applicant's earnings

4.244 There will be many cases where the lone mother is in receipt of some income from part-time work as well as supplementary benefit. This gives rise to no particular difficulty. The income, except for that part of it which is disregarded,[2] will have been taken into account by the Supplementary Benefits Commission in assessing the amount of the lone mother's benefit payment, causing it to be reduced. This will correspondingly reduce the maximum amount which the Commission can, by administrative order, require the liable relative to pay. In that sense, the liable relative gains an advantage from the lone mother being in work. But if the lone mother in the same circumstances applies to the magistrates for a maintenance order, the magistrates would have to take her income into account, so tending to reduce the liability of the husband on the maintenance order. There are no means of telling what the size of these alternative reductions, assessed on different principles, might be in any given case: but this merely reinforces the argument for producing as much certainty as possible through the use of the administrative order.

Exercise of the discretion

4.245 Either on the application of the liable relative, or on their own volition whenever the circumstances seem to make it desirable, the Commission (always within the limits of not recovering more from the liable relative than they pay out in benefit) will be entitled to depart from the standard assessment arrived at by means of the formula or waive an asesssment upon the liable relative altogether. Since the purpose of the discretion is to enable the Commission to deal fairly with every case, there is no point in attempting to list the circumstances in which departures from the norm might be made.

Making the administrative order

4.246 Having determined the amount which the liable relative ought to pay, the Commission will seek his agreement to pay that amount before making the administrative order upon him. A point for future consideration is whether, if agreement is forthcoming, and for so long as it is kept, the Commission should refrain from making the order, or whether an order should be made in every case. We think it probable that the latter would prove to be the better course. Some men might consent to attachment orders being made at the same time as the administrative order. There could be a system of registration of all administrative orders in court, and if consent were given for an attachment

---

[1] We return to the question again in Part 5, Section 7, when we discuss orders made by the authority administering the special one-parent family benefit we propose.

[2] In Part 5, Section 8, below we refer to the desirability of increasing the disregard for earnings in the supplementary benefits scheme.

order to be made, that could be transmitted from the Commission to the court which would make the attachment order without further process. If, on the other hand, the liable relative was willing to pay the Commission the amount assessed, and objected to an attachment order being made (the effect of which is to reveal the situation to the employer) there should be no attachment unless and until there has been a default. We consider that the tendency of the system would be to keep better track of the men and to improve still further the rate of recovery.

Binding effect of the administrative order

4.247   A liable relative will always have a right of appeal from an administrative order, and the order will in no case take effect pending a court decision if it is disputed on grounds which raise an issue of conduct. We consider these points later. Subject to them, however, the administrative order will be binding on the liable relative and enforceable by the Supplementary Benefits Commission against him. It will be recalled that at present the Commission are entitled to apply to the court for a court order to enforce the liable relative's obligation to maintain,[1] and to institute criminal proceedings against him for persistent refusal or neglect to do so.[2] But the Commission do not at present have any power to make an order on the liable relative for the payment of money which in itself has binding effect without the intervention of the court, whose intervention would be required only for purposes of enforcement. We are, in making our recommendations, well aware of this situation, which causes us no hesitation. It is important that men who have an objection to payment, based on whatever ground, should have rights of appeal; that objections which involve an investigation of matrimonial conduct or of paternity should be tried by a court of law; and, indeed, from the Commission's own point of view, that they should never be put into the position of having to try such an objection. However, subject to all necessary safeguards, the dominant need is to bring into effect a single and systematic procedure, based on readily ascertainable principles, which will deal promptly, accurately and cheaply with the majority of cases which do not on any rational view of the matter call for the intervention of any court. In all these cases, fair assessment and efficient collection are essentially administrative processes which should be carried out by an administrative authority. Neither the lone mother, nor the husband who is content to meet his obligations, will complain of such a system. She will not be concerned; he will be dealt with by a single authority acting in accordance with an intelligible rule. Only the defaulter stands to lose.

4.248   Cases will no doubt occur in which the liable relative refuses to co-operate with the Commission in providing the information they need to establish his means and make their assessment upon him. This need not be allowed to frustrate the procedure, any more than the failure of a taxpayer to make his return enables him to escape a tax assessment. The Commission should be entitled in such cases to make the best assessment it can on the basis of the available information, and to make an administrative order (which will be open to appeal) for the amount assessed.

---

[1] Ministry of Social Security Act 1966, section 23.

[2] *Ibid*, section 30. On these provisions, see Section 10, paragraphs 4.177–4.178 and 4.210–4.212, above.

Review

4.249   The amount payable under an administrative order will be reviewable on an application made at any time to the Commission by the liable relative based on any material change of circumstances. The refusal of a review, and the results of a review, would both be appealable. In addition to reviews made on application, the Commission themselves should automatically bring up administrative orders for review at fixed intervals following the date when the amount of an order was last considered. As appears from our discussion of the inadequacy of variation procedure in the magistrates' courts,[1] we attach much importance to the opportunities which the scheme under discussion would create for the introduction of efficient review procedures.

Accounts and arrears

4.250   Since the amount paid to the lone mother in supplementary benefit may fluctuate during a period when the administrative orders remain fixed, it will be necessary for the Commission to maintain an account as between themselves and the liable relative. An account is in any case needed to keep track of the situation when a man falls behind when making payments, as he may do for unavoidable as well as other reasons, as when he falls sick. The operation of the " diversion " procedure already involves the Commission in keeping accounts of this description, but we have not found it easy to follow the accounting methods employed. These are not disclosed to the general public. We think it advisable that the accounting methods used in operating the system of administrative orders should be clearly defined and made public. The Commission should be empowered generally to remit any arrears accrued under administrative orders.

Enforcement of the administrative order

4.251   If the liable relative fails to comply with an administrative order, the Commission should be empowered to apply to the court for the enforcement of the order by any of the means of execution available for the recovery of a civil debt. We have mentioned elsewhere that the procedure of distress upon goods, which is still available in the magistrates' jurisdiction for the recovery of maintenance, is a dead letter, which ought to be abolished. It will follow that the remedy by distraint will not be available to the Commission for enforcing administrative orders. No doubt the principal remedy which the Commission would use in practice is attachment of earnings.

Appeals and remittals

4.252   Where the liable relative disputes the amount for which he has been assessed, or the refusal to review the amount, on grounds which do not involve any reliance upon matrimonial conduct, the appeal should go to the appeal tribunal.[2] Thus, the administrative order scheme will in the normal case involve an assessment of means and a determination of the amount of the liability in accordance with clearly defined and published principles, with a right of appeal to an independent tribunal of specialised experience which will re-consider the case in the light of the same principles. This contrasts with

---

[1] See, for example, Section 6, paragraphs 4.79 and 4.95, and Appendix 7, paragraphs 11–17.

[2] The appeal tribunals already deal with appeals concerning the amount of supplementary benefit awards or the refusal to review an award of supplementary benefit.

the current situation in which assessments and determinations of the amount of liability are duplicated between the courts and the Commission, each operating on different principles and maintaining its own appeal structure.

4.253 Cases will occur in which the assessment for the purposes of the administrative order will raise special problems. The Commission may exceptionally have to deal with a liable relative of large means of different descriptions and located in various places; or, more commonly, they may have to assess a self-employed liable relative engaged in the type of business in which it is easy to misrepresent income, and whom it is suspected is bent on misrepresenting it to the extent that he professes an inability to repay all or any of the benefit which the Commission have paid to the lone mother. The ascertainment of the truth or of an approximation to it, may be by no means easy in cases of this description; but the Commission may already have to deal with them under their existing procedures, and while it is arguable that once an assessment of the Commission is to have direct legal effect (as it will do, when embodied in an administrative order) the means enquiry in such cases, or others which involve need for investigative accountancy, or cross-examination, or are otherwise of unusual complexity, should go elsewhere, we are not satisfied that the case for this is made out. Not only is there a problem—until the family courts to which we look forward are introduced—in selecting the body to deal with these more complex cases, but there would also be difficulties in devising machinery for identifying the appropriate cases. Then there would have to be provision for appeals against a refusal to remit cases from the Commission to the other authority, and from assessments made on remission. Some undesirable confusion of authority is likely to result as well as damage to the Commission's status in making administrative assessments, since they might be regarded as second-class adjudicators. Insofar as the Commission's staff may need additional expertise and further powers, we see no reason why they should not be able to acquire whatever is necessary.

4.254 Disputes which involve a finding on matrimonial conduct will not be dealt with by the Commission. Such cases could arise in a variety of ways. The liable relative may dispute the right of the Commission to make an administrative order, or ask for the termination of an existing order, on the ground that his wife has been guilty of behaviour of a kind which entirley releases him from the obligation of making any contribution to her maintenance. Or he might be contending that her conduct has been such that it diminishes, even if it does not extinguish, his obligation to maintain her, and that this ought to be reflected in the amount of the administrative order. It would be necessary in these cases to distinguish between the part of the administrative order attributable to the adult element in the supplementary benefit payment, and the part attributable to the child's element.

4.255 We have previously noticed the situation in the magistrates' jurisdiction in which proof of a single act of adultery will bar a wife's claim to maintenance. We regard the abolition of this outmoded and unjust rule as urgent.[2] But as long as it remains the law it would seem that a liable relative who was separated,

---

[1] See Section 4, paragraphs 4.64–4.65, above.

[2] We recommend that it should cease to be the law in Section 14, paragraph 4.379 below. This recommendation is made in the context of the discussion of our proposals for a family court, but (like several others of those proposals) we would regard it as a necessary reform within the summary matrimonial jurisdiction, were that to continue as a separate jurisdiction.

but not divorced, would be entitled to have the court set an administrative order aside simply by showing that there had been a relevant act of adultery that would have barred the wife's claim had she proceeded against him for maintenance. In these circumstances, we think that if the allegation of adultery is made to the Commission there would be no harm in them asking the wife whether she agreed with the allegation. If she did (and if the Commission were satisfied that the liable relative had a *bona fide* defence) the assessment could be waived. This forms no exception to the rule that the Commission will make no finding on conduct. It is rather a finding on the basis of agreed fact that the husband does not have the status, in the law as it stands, of being a liable relative.

4.256 If before the Commission made any administrative order, the liable relative raised a point requiring a determination on conduct, the convenient course would seem to be for the Commission nevertheless to conduct the means enquiry and make a provisional assessment. This assessment would then be suspended pending the determination by the appropriate court of the point on conduct. If this absolved the relative from all liability, the provisional assessment would never take effect. If it resulted in a finding that the liable relative's obligation should be reduced, the court would have the figure in front of it from which to make the appropriate discount. This discounting would be for the court, not the Commission, to perform, as it would reflect the court's view of the effect of the conduct in question. In the case where the liable relative asked the Commission to terminate or reduce an administrative order already on foot because of a complaint about conduct, rules would have to be established to deal with the situation while the court enquired into the complaint—that is to say, rules on whether the payments under the existing administrative order should in the meantime continue or be suspended, with provision for whatever adjustment of the account became necessary when the court's decision become known. Appeals from any findings of the court with regard to conduct would be determined within the court system.

4.257 In the whole of the preceding discussion on appeals we have been concerned only to indicate the general nature of the problems that would arise and of the arrangements that would be required. Details would require close and expert consideration, but we are satisfied that a just and viable system could quite easily be evolved.

Maintenance orders already in existence

4.258 At the date when the system we are describing came into effect, many thousands of maintenance orders, some recent, many ancient, would be in existence. It would be inconsistent with the purposes of the new system if many of these orders that were capable of being brought into the scheme were to linger on outside it. We therefore now have to consider the case of the lone mother who applies for supplementary benefit after the new system comes into force, but who at that time already has a maintenance order.

4.259 This maintenance order might be for an amount in excess of her supplementary benefit entitlement and in the normal course of events regularly paid, the lone mother's need for benefit having arisen from some temporary misfortune, such as the illness of the liable relative. Since the ceiling of the administrative order is to be at supplementary benefit level, a claimant with an existing maintenance order of this kind would have a clear interest in retaining it. We consider, however, that any claimant with an existing maintenance order who wishes, even without good reason, to retain it, must be permitted to do so. It follows that, after the introduction of the scheme, there will be a continuing need for the "diversion" procedure in its present form to accommodate the cases in which claimants upon the Commission hold maintenance orders.

4.260 Provided, however, they have the consent of the claimant, we consider that the Commission should have the power to terminate an existing maintenance order, and substitute an administrative order on the liable relative. This would not be done by automatically transferring the amount of the maintenance to the administrative order. At the time when the question arose, the Commission would conduct a means enquiry and make a current assessment. Broadly speaking, we would expect the effect to be a very great reduction in the number of maintenance orders, and the achievement, in the bulk of liable relative cases, of a clean start on the basis of a contemporaneous administrative order that was kept up to date by regular review. We think this would go far to remedy accumulated deficiencies from the past, and prevent their recurrence.

4.261 We bear in mind that the proposal in the last paragraph involves the termination of a court order by an administrative authority. We see no intrinsic objection to such a course in the special case under consideration. It would be part of the transitional process in a reform which—putting the practical advantages momentarily aside—finds its main theoretical justification precisely in the proposition that there has to be a re-allocation of responsibilities following a true appraisal of the roles of private and public law in this area.

Scope of the administrative order system

4.262 Thus far in the discussion we have taken the lone mother to be a separated but not divorced wife, with a child or children in her care. But— still without going outside the assumptions stated at the outset of this Section— the administrative order system that we have described would be applicable to several other categories. These are:

(1) separated wives without dependent children. Such a woman is not in a one-parent family situation, but the administrative order system would be just as applicable and helpful to her as to a one-parent family, and it is obvious that she should be included;

(2) separated husbands, with or without dependent children, in the rare case where the husband or child has a claim for maintenance on the wife;

(3) unmarried mothers entitled to maintenance for their children;

(4) wives, whether separated or divorced, who are not for whatever reason entitled to maintenance, but who have dependent children who are so entitled in their care;

(5) wives, with or without dependent children, who have commenced proceedings for divorce but have not as yet obtained a decree absolute. We need say no more concerning the first two of these categories, but some further discussion on the remainder is desirable.

163

TABLE 4.15

RELATIONSHIP BETWEEN AMOUNTS AWARDED ON AFFILIATION ORDERS MADE IN 1964 AND 1965 AND THE INCOME OF THE DEFENDANTS (see paragraph 4.264 opposite)

Income of father per week	Amount awarded on making of order							Total	Cumulative total	Cumulative total percentage
	Under 5s	5s to 14s	15s to 24s	25s to 34s	35s to 44s	45s to 49s	50s			
Under £5	—	—	—	—	—	—	—	—	—	—
£5 but under £8	1	1	3	5	2	—	—	12	12	13
£8 but under £10	—	2	8	4	3	—	—	16	28	30
£10 but under £12	—	—	4	9	12	1	—	26	54	57
£12 but under £14	—	—	4	5	6	2	3	18	72	80
£14 but under £16	—	—	2	3	4	1	1	11	83	88
£16 but under £18	—	—	1	—	—	—	—	1	84	89
£18 but under £20	—	—	—	—	2	—	1	3	87	93
£20 but under £25	—	—	—	1	1	2	3	7	94	100
Total	1	3	22	25	30	6	7	94		
Cumulative total percentage	1	4	28	54	86	93	100			

Source: *Separated Spouses, op cit*, page 180.

4.263   Women in our third and fourth categories have no claim for maintenance for themselves, so that the amount of the administrative order which the Supplementary Benefits Commission could make on the liable relative would be limited to a maximum consisting of that portion of the benefit which was attributable to the child.   It was represented to us when we took soundings in expert quarters on our proposals for the administrative order that these women would be better off if they obtained affiliation orders or maintenance orders for the children.   This objection overlooks the established facts. Table 4.4 shows that in the Bedford College survey of children only orders, live on 1 January 1966, the average amount payable for each child was £1 6s. The Home Office sample of children only orders made during September and October 1966 yielded an average amount of £1 14s payable for each child.[1] The averaging of the figures conceals a decline in the rate of the award *per* child as family size increased.   In October 1966, the scale rates of national assistance ranged from £1 2s 6d a week for a child under 5 to £1 13s 6d for a child aged between 11 and 15.   Table 9, Appendix 7, shows that, in July 1971, 87 per cent of the orders made before 1 January 1966 and still then being enforced were for £2 a week or less for each child.   Table 39, Appendix 7, shows that in the sample of orders made in April, May and June 1971 which provided for children only, 80 per cent of the orders providing for a single child were for amounts not exceeding £3, 54 per cent of the orders covering two children were for £5 or less, 65 per cent of the orders covering three children were for £6 or less, and 85 per cent of the orders covering four children or more were for £8 or less.   This was three years after the Maintenance Orders Act 1968 had removed the limit of £2 10s a week which previously had been the maximum which the magistrates could award for a child.   In June 1971, the scale rates of supplementary benefit ranged from £1·50 for a child under 5 to £2·40 for a child aged between 13 and 16.   There is, therefore, no basis for supposing that amounts awarded for children on court maintenance orders are generally higher than the appropriate supplementary benefit scale rates for children: the evidence suggests a considerable similarity.

4.264   As for affiliation orders, we have information set out in Table 4.15 opposite from the Bedford College sample relating to the years 1964 and 1965. Table 4.15 shows that 7 per cent of the affiliation orders were for the then operative maximum amount of £2 10s but more than half of them were for sums less than 34s a week and were payable by men earning less than £12 a week, which was only two thirds of the average earnings of manual workers in 1965.   It can further be established[2] that the variation procedure was in the mid-sixties as little used to adjust the amounts of affiliation as of matrimonial orders, and that affiliation orders, like maintenance orders, are highly likely to fall into arrears.   Data of this description underly the finding of the Graham Hall Committee that:

> The figures throw some light on the contention that defendants are readier to pay for their children than for their wives.   It may be that they so express

---

[1] The orders in the Home Office sample are for a larger average amount than those in the Bedford College survey because the Bedford College survey was of orders live in January 1966, whenever made, and a substantial proportion were ten years old or more (see Appendix 7, paragraph 7).

[2] See *Separated Spouses, op cit*, pages 180–183.

themselves at the time of the hearing and comply better with the order initially. But the figures show no better standard of compliance overall with orders in respect of children than with any other orders.[1]

4.265 We have no information which enables us to make a comparison between the mid-sixties and the present time regarding the amounts awarded in affiliation proceedings and the rate of compliance with affiliation orders. But there is not the slightest reason to suppose that the trends would be other than can be established for children only orders obtained by wives.

4.266 There are, of course, cases in which the maintenance to be obtained through a court order in respect of a child will exceed the scale rate for that child under supplementary benefits; and the same will be true in a smaller number of cases for affiliation. In such circumstances, the mother responsible for the child, if she thinks that there is a reasonable chance of securing compliance with the court order, will be well advised to seek a maintenance or affiliation order for the child even when she is not entitled, for any reason, to maintenance for herself. But this in no way detracts from the advantages of the administrative order procedure in all those cases which the evidence establishes to be typical of the two categories now under consideration.

4.267 Turning now to the fifth category: after a wife has instituted proceedings for divorce (or for judicial separation or nullity) and while the proceedings are pending, she can apply in those proceedings for maintenance pending suit for herself, and financial provision for the children. An order for maintenance pending suit terminates with the suit, that is to say, in the case of divorce, when the marriage is disolved by decree absolute; although at that time, of course, an order for more permanent provision may be made. During the pendency of the proceedings, the parties still being married to each other, the husband will have, apart from any liability to maintain his wife arising under the general law (this being the liability reflected in the pending suit order of the court) also a liability to maintain her under and for the purposes of the Ministry of Social Security Act 1966, which provides that for such purposes " a man shall be liable to maintain his wife and children ". Accordingly, if the wife comes into receipt of supplementary benefit while the divorce proceedings are pending, this will make the husband a " liable relative " in the statutory sense, from whom the Supplementary Benefits Commission may seek to recover what they pay to the wife in benefit. Once the decree absolute is pronounced, however, any " liable relative " obligation in respect of the wife must cease, and cannot thereafter arise, because although a man always remains liable for the purposes of the Act of 1966 to maintain his children under the age of 16, he is not liable for the purposes of that Act to maintain a former wife.[2] The upshot amounts to this: after divorce, the double obligation to maintain can arise only in respect of a child, and this is one of the cases that we have already considered; but while divorce proceedings are pending, the double obligation can arise in respect of a wife also. Thus, the administrative order system would be entirely applicable to her case over that period.

4.268 If the divorce court is asked to make an order for maintenance pending suit, its approach, in the normal case, is fairly rough and ready. Cases do occur

---

[1] Report of the Committee, *op cit*, paragraph 139.

[2] The relevant provisions of the Act of 1966 are set out and discussed in the opening paragraphs of Section 10 above.

involving difficult or extensive enquiries into accounts and property, but, in general, the court is concerned to make an order tiding the wife over the limited period between the institution of proceedings and their termination, and avoids refinements. For the same reasons, the court has never been inclined to go into disputed questions of conduct when making pending suit orders. In the result, there is comparatively little need in the ordinary case for spouses who are competently advised to apply for pending suit orders, since if the relevant financial facts are known, even in broad outline, this is sufficient to enable the lawyers to strike a bargain for their clients; and this is particularly the situation with people of small means.

4.269 Nevertheless, although figures are not available, we are satisfied from our enquiries that the divorce registrars are being asked to make considerable numbers of pending suit orders for no better purpose than to enable wives on supplementary benefit to produce an order to the Supplementary Benefits Commission. This is only a different aspect of the situation that we have extensively considered in the context of magistrates' orders, and we can see no greater justification for it in the one case than in the other. Under the administrative order system, the need for a wife on supplementary benefit to obtain a pending suit order while waiting for her divorce should very rarely arise. If there were a disputed issue of conduct it would go to the divorce court and be dealt with there in the manner described in paragraph 4.256 above. Such references should be very few indeed, because, as we have just mentioned, the court has never paid much attention to defences based on conduct when making provision pending suit. Given all the circumstances we have described, we think that the administrative order system would in time result in the near-total relief of the divorce court from the business of making orders pending suit in favour of wives on supplementary benefit.

POSSIBLE EXTENSIONS OF THE ADMINISTRATIVE ORDER SYSTEM

4.270 The five categories of cases considered under the last sub-heading all refer to persons to whom the administrative order system could be applied as fully and directly as it could be to the separated lone mother whom we took as the standard case round which to explain the system. One can visualise further categories being included, but only by breaking through the framework of the assumptions that have so far confined the discussion.

4.271 Thus, under the current law, as has been seen, a former husband is not in the statutory sense a liable relative, responsible as such to the Supplementary Benefits Commission in respect of benefit paid to his divorced wife for her own requirements. It would not, however, be difficult to enact that if a divorced wife is entitled to be maintained by her former husband under an order of the divorce court, the Commission would be subrogated to her rights under the order, to the extent that was necessary to reimburse themselves. The Commission could then make an administrative order on the former husband for that amount, not because he was a liable relative (the definition of which would remain the same) but because they had, in effect, paid his debt to his former wife. Once such a right of subrogation had been conferred on the Commission, it would be only a small step forward to extend it beyond strict subrogation, and enable the Commission to recover the whole of a divorced woman's maintenance from her former husband, even when this exceeded the benefit in payment, and to account to her for the balance. But if this were done, then there would seem to be no valid reason why the Commission should not make administrative orders for the whole amount in all the other cases we have considered, which include the separated and unmarried as well as the divorced. Finally, in this series of extensions, one might envisage the Commission being empowered to make an administrative order for an amount in excess of benefit in payment even in cases where there was no court order in existence, but where the process of assessment showed a plain case for making an order at that level.

4.272 All of these notions would bear closer examination. However, for the reasons we have fully explained in Section 11, we have decided to consider the revision of the relationship between the decisions of the courts and the social security authorities in the plane of two cross-sections only, the first of which we have already surveyed, and the second of which, allowing for the introduction of guaranteed maintenance allowance, will be surveyed in Part 5, Section 7. Accordingly, we do no more than draw attention to the scope for extension of the administrative order system.

FORESEEABLE OBJECTIONS

4.273 We summarise the advantages, as we see them, of the proposals made in this Section in its concluding paragraph, but, before doing so, interpose some observations on foreseeable objections. We recognise that legal and administrative procedures, evolved over a long period of time, embodying a large investment of thought and endeavour, crystallised into masses of rules and forms, and regulating sensitive human relationships, cannot be changed without a considerable administrative upheaval. This is a factor which we have carefully weighed, and which we recognise could well affect the timing of the implementation of our proposals if accepted. We remain convinced however that the proposals in this Section (like our proposals for the family court) are not based on some theoretical scheme for improvement, but are a direct response to facts that we have established which call for a prescription that is far removed from leaving well alone, and which must operate sooner rather than later.

4.274 It may be said that our proposals are themselves complicated and fail to provide a neat solution for every problem. Some measure of complexity is inevitable when the subject matter is so intricate; and no scheme will automatically round off every awkward corner. But no one who has learned his way round the labyrinth of the three systems of family law could, except through initial surprise, stumble over the simplicities of the administrative order.

4.275 Then again it might be said that our proposals only cover some one-parent families, namely those on supplementary benefit, and do not eliminate in all cases the need for recourse between the courts and the Supplementary Benefits Commission. The first point is accurately stated, but is not cogent. Elsewhere in the Report we make proposals of which one of the main purposes is to take the bulk of all one-parent families off supplementary benefit; but our purpose at this stage precisely is to deal with those who are in receipt of it. As to the continuing need for recourse between the courts and the Commission: while it is true that many lone mothers spend a short period on supplementary benefit, or claim it only from time to time, it does not follow that a woman in this situation needs a court order. At the beginning of paragraph 4.259 above we have given an example of a case in which a court order would plainly be of value; and there is nothing in the administrative order system to prevent a court order from being obtained by any woman who is entitled to and desires one. The case for the administrative order is that it will regulate the situation in all those scores of thousands of instances when the single procedure is all that is required, and that, as this becomes evident, women who have no need of a court order will cease to ask for one. This will apply not only to all those women who, as we have shown, spend year after year continuously on supplementary benefit, but also to very many of those whose sporadic claims on the Commission, so far from evidencing that they live on the proceeds of a maintenance order between times, demonstrate merely that they change jobs frequently or live with their husbands and men friends intermittently. There will always be cases which do not slot easily into the system, but our proposals are intended for and would cover the case of the overwhelming majority of lone mothers on supplementary benefit who could not survive on any maintenance order which they had, or might obtain, even if it were faithfully discharged.

4.276 Finally, it might be objected that the proposals do not eliminate the conflict between standards of assessment on the liable relative applied by the Supplementary Benefits Commission and standards applied by the courts in ordering maintenance. This is correct; but the number of cases in which a conflict of standards might arise would be very much reduced; and we have very little doubt that publication of the Commission's general formula would strongly influence the courts when dealing with men of similar resources to those upon whom the Commission makes administrative orders. Indeed, we can see no particular reason why the courts should not if necessary be bound, like the Commission, to apply the same formula in the general run of cases, subject to an over-riding discretion.

SUMMARY OF ADVANTAGES

4.277 We conclude with a list of the advantages which are claimed for the scheme proposed in this Section:

(1) very many women who have to claim supplementary benefit for themselves and their children will be relieved of the distress, frustrations and anxiety which attend upon the pursuit of impecunious, unwilling or elusive husbands;

(2) this result will be achieved without weakening the moral and legal principles which put an obligation on men to maintain the women and children towards whom they have assumed responsibilities. There are grounds for thinking that the efficiencies of the scheme might produce a better response to that obligation when marriages break down than exists at present;

(3) the scheme is based fundamentally on recognising the true nature of the relationship between the public obligation to maintain (the law of supplementary benefits) and the private obligation to maintain (the law of maintenance) and giving logical and practical effect to the consequences which flow from that recognition;

(4) from such recognition, procedures emerge for the more efficient handling of the needs of the relevant population;

(5) these procedures do not involve any change in the existing sources of support for one-parent families, or any revision in the law of supplementary benefits;

(6) under the scheme, no disputed issue of matrimonial conduct will ever be decided by an administrative authority, but all such issues will be reserved to the courts;

(7) means enquiries and assessments upon liable relatives will be more uniform, thorough and expert than the machinery available in the magistrates' courts generally allows. There will be contraction in the area of conflict between different authorities applying different criteria, and a large increase in the number of cases in which the only relevant assessment will be made by the application of a set of published and readily understandable rules;

(8) an appeals and review system will safeguard the rights of all those concerned, and ensure a much more prompt and flexible adjustment of rights and liabilities to changing circumstances than now exists;

(9) magistrates will be relieved of much of their present case-load in matrimonial cases and become more free to perform other duties, including their duties in the proposed family court;

(10) the prospects for reconciliation and conciliation[1] may be improved to the extent that confrontation between husband and wife in court will be reduced, and the Commission acting in their own name and through the administrative order will, in effect, be enforcing the maintenance obligation at a level which gives full weight to the difficulty of supporting two homes from a single income;

(11) the scheme operates in a field which is already shared between justice administered in the courts and administrative justice, but, by rationalising the balance between the two systems, should produce much more understanding and co-operation between them than at present exists. This can only bring benefit to the citizens whose needs both systems exist to serve.

SECTION 13—THE FAMILY COURT: PRINCIPLES

INTRODUCTION

4.278 In the last Section we made proposals for the adjustment of the respective roles played by the courts and the Supplementary Benefits Commission in dealing with financial provision for one-parent families. In this Section, and in Section 14, we are concerned with the proposals which our investigations lead us to make for the reform of the matrimonial courts as such, and the law which they administer. As we explained in Section 11, we had a choice of method in dealing with these latter proposals. In the short term, given the co-existence of a superior and summary jurisdiction, there are a whole series of changes which ought to be made, and which are, indeed, long overdue in the summary jurisdiction. The nature of the changes required for

---

[1] See Section 13 for the meaning we attach to these terms.

the most part appear clearly enough from our criticisms of that jurisdiction. In the longer term, there is—we have come to the firm conclusion—a need not merely to revise the summary jurisdiction by abolishing its inefficiencies and anachronisms, but to create a thoroughly unified system of matrimonial law applied through an institutional structure which reflects that unity. The choice before us was whether to deal separately with the short-term and longer-term programmes, or to proceed immediately to the consideration of the longer-term. We have decided, for the reasons given in Section 11, on the second of these two possible courses. In doing so, we are conscious of having sacrificed the opportunity of making a series of specific proposals for the reform of the summary jurisdiction in favour of what must inevitably be a more general approach towards a broader subject. By doing so we hope to emphasise that our proposals for law reform not only proceed from technical considerations, which we think are soundly based, but also are underwritten by the results of historical, demographic and social enquiry. However, much of what we say in adopting this broader approach has an application to the reform of the summary jurisdiction, and by taking this Part of the Report as a whole the reader will have little difficulty in extracting what would have been our short-term programme for himself.

ORIGINS OF THE NOTION OF A " FAMILY COURT "

4.279 The first official use of the term " family court " in this country was in the White Paper of 1965[1] which proposed a scheme to set up special magistrates' courts to assume the jurisdiction of the juvenile courts. When dealing with children under 16 years of age, they were to be called " family courts ". They were also to take over the magistrates' jurisdiction in adoption matters, the granting of consent to marry without parental permission, and, possibly, in affiliation, when the respondent was under 21. The White Paper further proposed the appointment of local " family councils " consisting of social workers of the children's service and others of like experience which would share jurisdiction over juveniles with the family courts. These proposals, which would have vested considerable powers over juveniles in a non-judicial body, and would have involved in many instances the shunting of individuals backwards and forwards between the family court and family council, met with widespread opposition, and they did not re-appear in the next policy statement, *Children in Trouble*,[2] which was the precursor of the changes in law relating to children and young persons made by the Children and Young Persons Act 1969.

4.280 The notion of a " family court " thus came to be canvassed among social workers and family lawyers. Yet it remains difficult to extract from the discussion precisely what are the attributes and advantages of the institution which those who praise it have in mind. With the notable exception of Judge Jean Graham Hall's *Proposal for a Family Court*[3] and some few but valuable

---

[1] *The Child, The Family, and the Young Offender*, Cmnd 2742, 1965, paragraph 28.

[2] Cmnd 3601, 1968.

[3] 1970 (obtainable from the National Council for One Parent Families but Judge Graham Hall is alone responsible for the pamphlet.) We are also grateful to Judge Graham Hall for allowing us to see her paper, *The Case for Unified Family Courts*, which she read to the third Commonwealth Magistrates' Conference in Nairobi in August 1973. Reference may also be made to the short, but useful article by Alec Samuels, ' Family Courts—The Future ', in *The New Law Journal*, Volume 122, 1972, pages 133-134.

paragraphs in the Report of the Adoption Committee[1] very little of substance has, in fact, been written on the subject in this country.[2]   The dearth of material helps to explain why the numerous submissions made to our Committee in favour of the introduction of a family court system for the most part offer more by way of enthusiasm than elucidation.   With this in mind, we went so far as to consider inventing some new term of description for an institution embodying the arrangements and reflecting the values we later expound; but concluded that " family court " is too convenient and well established a description to abandon. This makes it all the more necessary to consider briefly the origins of the family court concept, mainly in order to distinguish it from the proposals we ourselves favour.

4.281   The notion of a " family court " derives principally from more than half a century's thinking and practice in the United States of America.[3]   Its earliest establishment was in Ohio, where from 1914 onwards legislation fused juvenile, divorce, bastardy and family-based criminal cases into a single jurisdiction exercised by a special division of the common pleas court, which was called the " family court " or " domestic relations court ".   These courts (of which the one at Toledo, established in 1925, has attracted particular attention):

> have built up techniques for humane disposition of problems arising out of domestic relations litigation so as to offer a substantially complete battery of jurisdiction, of specially qualified personnel, and of administrative techniques for handling family litigation.[4]

Professor Neville Brown explains:

> In its " classical " form . . . a family court indicates an integrated and unified jurisdiction in a single court with competence over all aspects of family stress . . . it includes therefore: juvenile delinquency (hence family court absorbs juvenile court); divorce nullity, and separation (hence family court absorbs divorce court); guardianship and custody disputes; maintenance; matrimonial property disputes; domestic assaults; child neglect and cruelty; adoption; affiliation.   Instead of jurisdiction over such matters being fragmented between several courts, it is consolidated in a single court, although there may need to be specialised divisions or sections within that one court.[5]

---

[1] *Report of the Departmental Committee on the Adoption of Children*, Cmnd 5107, 1972, paragraphs 276–279.

[2] The Administration of Justice Act 1970 established the Family Division in the High Court and rationalised parts of the family jurisdiction.   This was first suggested by Mr J E S Simon (later President of the Probate, Divorce and Admiralty Division and now Lord Simon of Glaisdale) in his evidence to the Morton Commission (*Minutes of Evidence, Seventh Day, 29 May 1952*, pages 202–203.   See also Section 3, paragraph 4.25 above.)   This useful reform cleared some of the ground, but left the summary jurisdiction untouched, and falls far short of establishing a family court in the meaning we shall be attaching to the term.

[3] There is a voluminous American literature on the subject.   A small but useful selection from this literature is noted in the list of references appended to L Neville Brown: ' The Legal Background to the Family Court ', in *British Journal of Criminology*, 1966, pages 139–151. The article is in itself extremely helpful.   See also the references to the family courts in the same author's ' Matrimonial Maintenance in the United States ', in J Unger (ed): *Parental Custody and Matrimonial Maintenance: A Symposium*, British Institute of International and Comparative Law, 1966, pages 167–188.   Professor Brown points out (page 180) that: " Freed from the English division of matrimonial jurisdiction between two sets of Courts at different levels in the judicial hierarchy, the United States has found it less difficult to create family courts."

[4] Maxine Boord Virtue: *Family Cases in Court*, Duke University Press, 1956, page 180.

[5] ' The Legal Background to the Family Court', *op cit*, pages 140–141.

It appears that most family courts in America incorporate a criminal jurisdiction. This may include a jurisdiction over crimes, even of a serious nature, committed by adults which are regarded as connected with familial situations. It will almost always, but not invariably, include jurisdiction over juvenile crime or delinquency. There is, in fact a bewildering variety of jurisdictions exercised, and objectives pursued, by the courts in different parts of the United States calling themselves " family courts ". In general, and including some manifestations that might be regarded as verging on the bizarre, it may be said that most American family courts are committed to a social work philosophy which regards family breakdown as a phenomenon to be dealt with primarily by diagnosis and treatment. Hence the American family court will see itself to be as much a therapeutic agency as a judicial institution.

CRITERIA

4.282   Our approach owes little to American experience or writings, or to any preconceived attachment to the notions of a " family court ". We have been guided pragmatically by specific considerations emerging from our study of the matrimonial law and courts in this country, which has established for us the need for and the character of the institution we have in mind. We have, in the first place, traced the personal and social mischiefs to which the dual system of matrimonial jurisdiction gives rise. We have also shown how this system offers financial provision to wives, mothers and their children by means of orders which in many cases are not honoured by those whose obligation to maintain their dependants has been affirmed by the courts. To ensure that these women and children survive, the social security authorities provide the susbistence which the law promises. The contribution of the private obligation to maintain is interstitial; that of social security is fundamental. We therefore conclude that only an institution which is shaped by the recognition of these facts can adequately serve the needs of broken families. The second major point is that members of families which have collapsed come to court at a stage when critical decisions will have to be taken about issues, other than those directly affecting matrimonial relief or finance, around which conflicts are likely to develop. There may be disputes over the custody of the children, or the ownership or occupation of the matrimonial home. Such practical matters have to be settled or determined at some time, and the presence of the parties in court provides the best opportunity that may ever occur for discussion and decision. Thus, we have come to think of the family court as an institution which will improve on our inherited system by eliminating the overlap, the contradictions and the other weaknesses and defects of the legal jurisdictions we have exposed earlier in this Part of the Report, and which at the same time will also improve the machinery and services which are available to deal realistically with the practical problems resulting from marriage breakdown.

4.283   In the light of the foregoing considerations, we set out the six major criteria which a family court must in principle satisfy:

(1) the family court must be an impartial judicial institution, regulating the rights of citizens and settling their disputes according to law;

(2) the family court will be a unified institution in a system of family law which applies a uniform set of legal rules, derived from a single moral standard and applicable to all citizens;

(3) the family court will organise its work in such a way as to provide the best possible facilities for conciliation between parties in matrimonial disputes;

(4) the family court will have professionally trained staff to assist both the court and the parties appearing before it in all matters requiring social work services and advice;

(5) the family court will work in close relationship with the social security authorities in the assessment both of need and of liability in cases involving financial provision;

(6) the family court will organise its procedure, sittings and administrative services and arrangements with a view to gaining the confidence and maximising the convenience of the citizens who appear before it.

4.284 In the remainder of this Section we shall deal in turn with each of the above criteria as principles for shaping the establishment and operation of the family court. Under some of the heads the discussion will be short, in that the subject will previously have been explored in earlier Sections in this Part and little more needs to be said. Under other heads, where we have not previously examined the background sufficiently, in particular, in regard to the provisions of the law on reconciliation and in regard to the court welfare service, we shall need to demonstrate the principle from a longer discussion. It is to be stressed, however, that we regard each one of the six criteria, which are to a considerable extent interdependent, as embodying an important point of principle. Then, in Section 14 of this Part, we shall examine some points of practice and detail which stem from the broader considerations, or which it otherwise seems useful to consider in the context of the family court.

THE FAMILY COURT AS A JUDICIAL INSTITUTION

4.285 The fundamental principle which must govern the family court is that it shall be a judicial institution which, in dealing with family matters, does justice according to law. This may seem to be so obvious a point as hardly to be worth mentioning; but the need to emphasise it arises from the nature of a jurisdiction which aims to do good as well as to do right. To promote welfare is an unusual function for a court of law. To some extent, the courts which deal with matrimonial disputes and with children are already familiar with that function through references in the statutes to reconciliation in husband and wife disputes, and through the statutory obligation in many forms of proceedings which involve children to have first and paramount regard, in any decision the court may reach, to their welfare. But the deliberate attempt to expand and systematise the welfare function, which is an essential part of the family court concept, carries risks, as well as potential advantages, which can be eliminated only by clear thinking and firm practice regarding boundaries and priorities. The court must remain, and must be seen to remain, impartial. This is of particular importance now that local authorities and governmental agencies of various kinds have powers and duties imposed on them which bring them into the proceedings, either as interested parties or as advisers to the court. The object of achieving welfare must not be permitted to weaken or short cut the normal safeguards of the judicial process—the dispassionate examination of evidence properly adduced to the court, regular procedures

174

which promote an orderly and fair hearing, and the allowance of legal representation. The court must not see the men, women and children with whom it is concerned as "clients", and still less as "patients" for whom the court process is one form of, or a preliminary to, "treatment". Professional staff serving the court, including any who are responsible for assisting the court to reach sound conclusions on welfare issues, must be answerable to the court for what they do and how they do it. The aim must be to make adjudication and welfare march hand in hand, but there should be no blurring of the edges, either in principle or in administration. Through the family court it should be possible to make a new and highly beneficial synthesis between law and social welfare, and the respective skills, experience and efforts of lawyers and social workers; but the individual in the family court must in the last resort remain the subject of rights, not the object of assistance.

THE FAMILY COURT IN A UNIFORM SYSTEM OF LAW

4.286 The poor are not denied access to the divorce court today as they were in the past. But the magistrates' court remains the resort almost exclusively of the poor. Social and cultural habits originally established among poor people in the days when poverty did bar their access to the High Court have proved remarkably persistent among the poorest stratum of the population. Associated with this is the fact that the social agencies which deal with the poor habitually steer them in their matrimonial troubles to the magistrates' jurisdiction. The Supplementary Benefits Commission are the principal influence in this respect, as we have already demonstrated.[1] But there are several other influences which work to the same effect. In our view, the training and professional practice of most social workers predispose them to encourage their clients in the same direction. Further, many of the women who go to a lawyer of their own accord, and most of those who are directed to one by agencies such as the probation officer or a Citizens' Advice Bureau, will find themselves instructing a solicitor who has a regular practice in the magistrates' court. Often, the solicitor's office will be in the immediate vicinity of the court. It is natural for the solicitor to advise these women of their remedies seen in the context of the jurisdiction with which he is himself familiar and in which he practises. Thus, the availability of legal aid, which enables the poor to get professional advice and assistance, has helped to sustain rather than to erode the summary jurisdiction. Yet again, as appears from our discussion of the housing difficulties of one-parent families,[2] local authorities habitually insist upon a court order being produced as proof of the breakdown of the marriage before they will consider transfer of a tenancy to the deserted wife; and this, in the many cases where she will be on supplementary benefit, reinforces the official pressures on the poor to take themselves to the summary jurisdiction.

4.287 Much of this is tantamount to saying that the two matrimonial jurisdictions continue to exist and to be used because they are there.[3] This would do no harm were it merely to reflect a historical inheritance, anomalous

---

[1] In Section 10 above.

[2] In Part 6, Section 6.

[3] We shall advert in Section 14 to the thesis that the summary jurisdiction as now organised is necessary to provide a casualty service for short-lived matrimonial indispositions.

in modern conditions, but still serving the needs of broken families with reasonable efficiency and productive of no public injury. But we are satisfied, for reasons whose demonstration has been a major theme in this Part of the Report, that the double jurisdiction fails on both these counts. We need not repeat the criticisms we have already made in detail, but in Section 14 we discuss the theme of unification of structure and law in the family court, the achievement of which is in our view important both in the private and public interest.

CONCILIATION AND RECONCILIATION IN THE FAMILY COURT

4.288 In the discussion which follows we shall be using the terms "reconciliation" and "conciliation" to denote two different concepts. By "reconciliation" we mean the reuniting of the spouses. By "conciliation" we mean assisting the parties to deal with the consequences of the established breakdown of their marriage, whether resulting in a divorce or a separation, by reaching agreements or giving consents or reducing the area of conflict upon custody, support, access to and education of the children, financial provision, the disposition of the matrimonial home, lawyers' fees, and every other matter arising from the breakdown which calls for a decision on future arrangements.[1]

4.289 The distinction between reconciliation and conciliation,[2] and the influence which the family court may bring to bear in promoting either of them, is of cardinal importance in the consideration of any proposal for a family court. We have therefore in the first instance to examine the development and current status within the two branches of the matrimonial jurisdiction of these aspects of the court's work. We shall find that the law concentrates almost exclusively on reconciliation.

Reconciliation in the divorce jurisdiction

4.290 In 1946, the Lord Chancellor, Viscount Jowitt, appointed a committee under the chairmanship of Lord Denning (then Mr Justice Denning):

> to examine the present system governing the administration of the law of divorce and nullity of marriage in England and Wales; and, on the assumption that the grounds upon which marriages may now be dissolved remain unchanged, to consider and report upon which procedural reforms ought to be introduced . . . in particular whether any (and if so, what) machinery should be made available for the purpose of attempting a reconciliation between the parties, either before or after proceedings have been commenced.

The report[3] laid great stress on the importance of preserving the marriage tie and attempting reconciliation in every case where there was a prospect of success.[4] It examined the role of the Service Departments during the then recently ended war in effecting reconciliation between serving men and their

---

[1] It may be noted here that in the summary jurisdiction the statute (see paragraph 4.295 below) speaks of attempting " to effect a conciliation between the parties ". This must refer primarily to a reconciliation in our sense.

[2] See also, for a different approach to the terminology, E J Griew: ' Marital Reconciliation —Contexts and Meanings', in *30 Cambridge Law Journal*, 1972, pages 294–315.

[3] *Final Report of the Committee on Procedure in Matrimonial Causes*, Cmd 7024, 1947.

[4] *Ibid*, paragraph 4.

wives, and the part played by voluntary organisations such as the Marriage Guidance Council.[1] The principal conclusion in this area was:

> There should be a Marriage Welfare Service to afford help and guidance both in preparation for marriage and also in difficulties after marriage. It should be sponsored by the State but should not be a State institution. It should evolve gradually from the existing services and societies just as the probation system evolved from the Court Missionaries and the Child Guidance Service from the children's clinics. It should not be combined with the judicial procedure for divorce but should function quite separately from it.[2]

It was also recommended that welfare officers should be appointed to give guidance to parties who resorted to the divorce court or contemplated doing so, and that where there were dependent children the court should at any time after the petition had been filed be entitled to refer the case to the court welfare officer for enquiry and report.[3] The recommendation for a marriage welfare service fell by the wayside, but the report did foreshadow arrangements under which welfare officers (the first of whom was appointed in 1950) became attached to the divorce jurisdiction to investigate and report, when requested, on matters arising in matrimonial proceedings which concern the welfare of a child.

4.291 In 1976, Mr Leo Abse introduced his Matrimonial Causes and Reconciliation Bill. He sought to make separation for seven years a ground, subject to certain qualifications, for a decree of divorce. The Bill, as its name shows, also contained provisions to promote reconciliation. So far as these were intended to propitiate the opposition, they achieved a kind of success in that the extension of the grounds of divorce was rejected, but the reconciliation provision, which had become known as the " kiss and make up " clause, became the law.[4] This provision was to the effect that temporary cohabitation between the spouses, for one period not exceeding three months, should, if it took place "with a view to effecting a reconciliation", not be treated as condonation so as to bar a decree if the attempt at reconciliation failed. The wife was thus exposed in the course of an unsuccessful attempt at reconciliation to the risk both of pregnancy and of divorce. Subsequently, and perhaps fortunately, the courts more or less defeated the purpose of the section by holding that, as the provision referred only to cohabitation " with a view to effecting a reconciliation ", it did not apply at all where the final parting occurred after a cohabitation which was a consequence of reconciliation.[5]

4.292 These problems no longer arise, since, as has been noted,[6] the Divorce Reform Act 1969 abolished the bar of condonation along with all other bars. Section 3 of the Act of 1969, however, contained new provisions designed to encourage reconciliation. These include empowering the court to adjourn proceedings for divorce for such periods as it thinks fit to enable attempts to be

---

1 *Ibid*, paragraphs 10–20.

2 *Ibid*, paragraph 28 (iii).

3 *Ibid*, paragraph 29 (viii).

4 Matrimonial Causes Act 1963.

5 *Brown v Brown* (1967) P 105.

6 Section 5 above.

made to effect a reconciliation if the court considers there is a reasonable possibility of achieving one. It is further enacted that rules shall be made:

> for requiring the solicitor acting for a petitioner for divorce to certify whether he has discussed with the petitioner the possibility of a reconciliation and given him the names and addresses of persons qualified to help effect a reconciliation between parties to a marriage who have become estranged.[1]

4.293 This provision is drawn from Australian law. In commending its adoption into our law, the Law Commission gave as their reasons not that the Commission had any expectation that it would bring about reconciliations between people wanting divorces, but that it might ensure that " all solicitors have ready to hand a list of marriage guidance organisations, so that this can be given to those clients who consult them at an earlier stage ".[2] As to the working in Australia of the corresponding provision, an Australian practitioner has written:

> In my experience, I have never known a case where a client seeking a divorce has shown any interest when the usual procedures as to reconciliation are followed, that is, discussing the possibility of reconciliation and giving him a list of the organisations he may consult. Reconciliation procedures as a preliminary to commencing divorce proceedings do seem to be futile and a waste of time.[3]

4.294 Our divorce law makes one other reference to reconciliation. No petition for divorce can be presented within the first three years of the marriage unless with leave of the court granted on the ground that the case is one of exceptional hardship suffered by the petitioner or exceptional depravity on the part of the respondent. The Act of 1937 which introduced this rule provided (and it still is the law) that the court, in considering whether to grant leave, must have regard to the question whether there is reasonable probability of a reconciliation between the parties before the expiration of the three years.[4] In *S v S*[5] Sir Jocelyn Simon P pointed out that the court could not, in general, realistically perform its duty to consider the possibility of reconciliation unless at least an attempt had been made to ascertain whether reconciliation could be effected. He therefore proposed the setting up of experimental machinery, to operate in the first instance in the Greater London area, whereby with the assistance of its senior welfare officer the prospects of reconciliation might be explored and the court informed of the results. Little or nothing seems, in practice, to have emerged from this proposal.

Reconciliation in the summary jurisdiction

4.295 The Magistrates' Courts Act 1952 provides:[6]

> Where in any domestic proceedings . . . a magistrates' court has requested a probation officer or any other person to attempt to effect a conciliation[7] between the parties, the probation officer or that other person may, if the attempt has proved unsuccessful and he thinks fit in the circumstances of the case to do so, furnish to the court a report . . . .

---

[1] Divorce Reform Act 1969, section 3(1); now Matrimonial Causes Act 1973, section 6(1).

[2] *Reform of the Grounds of Divorce—The Field of Choice*, Cmnd 3123, 1966.

[3] T A Pearce: ' The Broken Marriage—Is Modern Divorce the Answer?', in H A Finlay (ed): *Divorce, Society and the Law*, 1969, pages 53–68, at page 59. We have found this collection of Australian essays most instructive and stimulating.

[4] Matrimonial Causes Act 1937, section 1, now Matrimonial Causes Act 1965, section 2.

[5] (1968) P 185.

[6] Section 59.

[7] It is evident that the word " conciliation " is here employed, at least primarily, in the sense we are giving to " reconciliation ".

The section goes on to provide that copies of the report must be sent also to the parties, and the court may then, if it thinks fit, use the report, not as evidence, but for the purpose of putting questions to any witness.

4.296 Strictly speaking, this provision probably authorises the court to refer a case for a reconciliation attempt only after the summons has been issued by the complainant. Most magistrates, however, in practice operate a system under which such efforts as are made take place before any proceedings are launched. Procedures vary from court to court, but the general pattern will be as follows. A woman will call at the justices' clerk's office to make a complaint, that is to say, to apply, on stated grounds, for a summons to issue against her husband. Or she may call there or upon the probation officer not for such formal purpose, but to seek advice in some matrimonial predicament. Very often she will have been referred by the police or some social agency. It may amount to no more than her saying that her husband has gone missing for a few days, and being advised to wait until the weekend for him to return. In other situations, the probation officer may take an active role, including seeking an interview with the husband. As appears from Table 4.16 the bulk of the work originates in this way, and many of the cases go no further. An applicant, however, is always entitled to have her complaint go forward, and if it does, it comes before a magistrate for him to issue the summons. The probation officer, in many courts, attends with the complainant before the magistrate on this occasion. The magistrate is given no jurisdiction himself to attempt a reconciliation, nor is there any provision under which he is entitled to delay issuing the summons with a view to affording time for the probation officer to attempt it. It seems clear, however, from the third column of Table 4.16, that this sometimes does happen. Once the summons has been issued, the proceedings are in being, and the magistrates then do have legal power to refer the case to the probation officer and, as appears from the fourth column of Table 4.16, sometimes do so.

4.297 There can be no doubt that the probation service performs valuable work in the course of the processes we have described. An analysis of 544 cases in which orders had been made in the magistrates' courts showed the number of husbands and wives in the sample who had sought advice when their spouse left them. Nearly all of the wives, and three quarters of the husbands had done so. Of these, nearly half had consulted a solicitor; just over one third had seen a probation officer; one quarter, their doctor; and 16 per cent, a clergyman. Just over 10 per cent had consulted a marriage guidance agency.[1] It is however, impossible to make any reliable estimate of how much reconciliation is achieved by the efforts of the probation service. There is no machinery for following up cases and no means of determining the extent, if at all, to which the intervention has been causative of a result. The figures in Table 4.16 indicate that there has been a fairly substantial drop in the matrimonial work of the probation service in comparison with the last published figures for the period 1965-1968. The report from which Table 4.16 is taken also contains the following passages:

Marriage conciliation work was one of the functions of the probation and after-care service to which the Expenditure Committee of the House of Commons,

[1] *Separated Spouses, op cit,* pages 124–125.

TABLE 4.16
MATRIMONIAL CONCILIATION WORK BY PROBATION OFFICERS: 1969 TO 1971*

Year		Referred by courts			Dealt with on direct application to probation officers	Referred by social agencies, police, etc	Referred by divorce court	Cases completed		
		Before issue of summons	After issue of summons	Referred by clerks to justices				Total cases seen	Parties known, or thought, to be living together as husband and wife	Other cases
1969	(a)	863	684	519	10,941	2,542	65	15,614	13,213	10,397
	(b)	741	3,603	653	7,804	2,131	71	15,003		
1970	(a)	708	665	419	10,691	2,450	39	14,972	10,932	9,020
	(b)	695	2,467	494	6,479	1,747	44	11,926		
1971	(a)	603	621	387	10,406	2,318	72	14,407	10,051	8,697
	(b)	553	2,065	440	6,536	1,802	193	11,589		

(a) One party was seen.

(b) Two parties were seen.

* Statistics for the Inner London Probation and After-Care Service were unavailable for 1971. Inner London figures for 1970 were considered to be the best estimate and these were inserted in the 1971 figures.

Source: *Report on the Work of the Probation and After-care Department, 1969–1971*, Cmnd 5158, 1972, Appendix E.

in its enquiry into the service, devoted particular attention. In paragraph 13 of its Report[1] the Committee stated that " a considerable amount of work of matrimonial conciliation is carried out by the Probation Service. In any attempt to reduce the burden on the Service this matrimonial work would seem a natural candidate for removal." It went on to say that " the Service seemed keen to keep the duties in order to help maintain a broad humane image "; but it concluded that " the pressure on the Service must be relieved " and recommended that " where an offence is not involved, consideration should be given to removing matrimonial conciliation work to another agency ".

The Government's observations on the Committee's Report as a whole were published in a White Paper in May 1972,[2] and on this particular recommendation were as follows:

" The Home Secretary is not clear that the balance of advantage is at present in favour of restricting the functions of the probation service in the field of matrimonial conciliation. But he will seek the opinions of the national organisations representing the probation service, and of other relevant agencies."[3]

The English experience of reconciliation through the courts

4.298 It may, indeed, be said to be the virtually unanimous opinion of those who have the relevant experience that there is little room for optimism when the court to which the parties have presented themselves to formalise or regulate the breakdown of the marriage seeks to use that occasion for mending it. The Denning Report concluded on the evidence it received:

The prospects of reconciliation are much more favourable in the early stages of marital disharmony than in the later stages. At that stage both parties are likely to be willing to co-operate in an effort to save the marriage; but if the conflict has become so chronic that one or both of the parties has lost the power or desire to co-operate further, the prospects sharply diminish. By the time the conflict reaches a hearing in the divorce court, the prospects are as a rule very small. It is important therefore that the general public should be brought to realise the importance of seeking competent advice, without delay, when tensions occur in marriage.[4]

4.299 The Morton Commission, which took a good deal of evidence on this subject, recorded:

If matters are allowed to develop into a condition of chronic disharmony one or perhaps both of the spouses will probably have lost the ability or desire to make any attempt to restore the marriage, and by the time steps have been taken to institute divorce proceedings the prospects of bringing husband and wife together again are greatly reduced. This view won a wide measure of support from our witnesses.[5]

4.300 The Law Commission considered that reconciliation procedures started after the filing of the petition achieve little success and " have tended to become pointless and troublesome formalities".[6]

---

[1] *First Report from the Expenditure Committee, Session 1971–1972, Probation and After-Care*, HMSO, 1971, page ix.

[2] *Probation and After-Care: Observations by the Government on the First Report from the Expenditure Committee, Session 1971–1972*, Cmnd 4968, 1972.

[3] Cmnd 5158, *op cit*, paragraphs 77–78.

[4] Cmnd 7024, *op cit*, paragraph 22.

[5] Cmnd 9678, *op cit*, paragraph 340.

[6] Cmnd 3123, *op cit*, paragraph 30.

The overseas experience of reconciliation through the courts

4.301 Precisely the same experience is reported from abroad. Australian divorce law requires the judge to consider the possibility of reconciliation, and gives him power, to this end, to adjourn proceedings, interview the parties in his chambers, and nominate an approved marriage guidance organisation or a suitable person to endeavour to effect a reconciliation. We have already quoted[1] one practitioner's view of the efficacy of these provisions. Mr Justice Selby, a Judge in Divorce of the Supreme Court of New South Wales, writes of them:

> . . . experience suggests that the (reconciliation) provisions remain in the realm of pious hope. By the time a matrimonial cause reaches a hearing the parties are too far apart, one of them, at least, is too anxious for a final determination of the suit and too much bitterness has been engendered to allow any reasonable prospects of reconciliation. It is only on the rarest occasions that attempts are made . . . to effect a reconciliation after the hearing has begun, and it is doubtful if any such attempt has been successful.[2]

4.302 New Zealand has recently under the Domestic Proceedings Act 1968, which governs domestic proceedings before magistrates' courts, introduced compulsory reconciliation procedures.[3] In New Zealand, these courts are presided over by professional lawyers. The Act requires the court and the professional advisers of husbands and wives seeking its intervention to take all proper steps to effect a reconciliation. Section 14 provides that:

> On application *ex parte* by any married person stating that unhappy differences have arisen between the applicant and his wife or her husband and that the applicant desires to effect a reconciliation, the Court may order that the matter be referred to a conciliator appointed by the Court or to be nominated by an approved marriage guidance organisation to endeavour to effect a reconciliation.

Section 15 provides that:

> On an application for a separation order, the court shall refer the case to a conciliator . . . .

But when the parties are applying for maintenance only the court has a discretion to refer them to a conciliator if it thinks such a move expedient. The Act defines a conciliator as:

> some person with experience or training in marriage counselling or conciliation, or in special circumstances some other person.[4]

If necessary, the conciliator can ask the magistrate to issue a summons requiring a party to attend before him for conciliation. The conciliator then reports within twenty-eight days to the court whether his efforts have been successful or unsuccessful.[5]

---

[1] Paragraph 4.293 above.

[2] D M Selby: 'The Development of Divorce Law in Australia', in *29 Modern Law Review*, 1966, pages 473–491, at page 487. See also J Neville Turner: 'Divorce: Australian and German Breakdown Provisions Compared', in *18 International and Comparative Law Quarterly*, 1969, pages 869–930.

[3] Two of us were fortunate to be able to discuss the working of the Domestic Proceedings Act 1968 with Mrs Eileen Saunders, the Director of the Christchurch Marriage Guidance Council. Although Mrs Saunders gave us much information and answered many questions, nothing which we have written here is to be taken as representing her views.

[4] Section 16(2).

[5] Section 16(6).

4.303 It is to be noted that this New Zealand scheme for a compulsory attempt at reconciliation applies only in the summary jurisdiction. Couples who take their broken marriages directly to the superior court for divorce are under no legal compulsion to attend before a conciliator.

4.304 We do not know of any published material which permits of an assessment of the efficiency of the compulsory procedure in New Zealand, and it would appear, in any case, to be too early to make a reliable judgment. In its annual report for 1970–1971, however, the National Marriage Guidance Council of New Zealand (the voluntary organisation upon which, rather oddly, the whole legal pyramid of compulsory reconciliation rests) makes some significant observations. It is stated that the short experience of serving the courts under the Act of 1968 has made its counsellors:

> better able to identify their role in this work. (They) felt that while they should accept the client's decision to separate as a sign of real distress, they also had a duty to the courts to make sure that both clients had taken account of all the consequences of a separation—both for themselves and their family. This involves using every means to ensure that both clients are interviewed, no matter how unlikely it is that a reconciliation will result. In many cases where the clients proceed to a separation, after conciliation they may be able to come to certain agreements without the intervention of the court. If this be so it is the duty of the counsellor to encourage them to take further advice from their solicitors to this end. In other cases separated partners may be helped to understand and accept some of the reasons for the breakdown of their marriage, and supported during the subsequent weeks when they may feel loneliness, failure and guilt.[1]

4.305 This perceptive passage may be interpreted as indicating the emergence in New Zealand of a pragmatic, working distinction between reconciliation and conciliation—terms which are used synonomously in the Domestic Proceedings Act. Reconciliation is being restricted to its proper meaning, that is, the action of re-uniting persons who are estranged; whilst conciliation is coming to denote, as it should, the process of engendering common sense, reasonableness and agreement in dealing with the consequences of estrangement.

4.306 Very much the same trend is to be observed in the State of New York.[2] Since 1966, New York State has established " conciliation bureaus " to which any plaintiff seeking a divorce must give notice. The law requires all parties to attend at least one conciliation conference at the bureau unless the commissioner, for good cause, decides that conciliation proceedings would serve no purpose. " Conciliation " is used both in the sense that we have attributed to the term " reconciliation " and in the sense we have attributed to the term " conciliation ". In form, therefore, the procedure is compulsory, but in practice the provision for dispensation makes it almost voluntary. In the

---

[1] Page 5.

[2] The State of New York is chosen from the United States because recent and reliable information is available regarding the law and the practice there applied regarding reconciliation and conciliation procedures. It is impossible to generalise about these programmes in the United States. In 1970, statutes in twenty-four of the States provided for court connected programmes with related marriage counselling; and three States (Massachusetts, New Jersey and Oklahoma) had discontinued such programmes which had been previously established. For a description of some of these systems see Maxine Boord Virtue: *op cit*; B D Inglish: ' The Hearing of Matrimonial and Custody Cases ', in *Family Law Centenary Essays*, Victoria University of Wellington, 1967, pages 35–53; and chapter 4 of the publication next cited. But the literature is far more extensive.

year 1969–1970 the bureaux received notice of 37,430 proceedings, and dispensed with the procedure in 32,518 of these cases (87 per cent). Dispensation is granted after the examination of a questionnaire which the bureau sends to each spouse when the proceedings are notified. In the remaining 4,912 cases which went through some form of conciliation procedure, reconciliations (defined as " cases in which a husband and wife relationship has been resumed ") are reported to have been effected in 1,924 cases (5 per cent of the total reported proceedings) and consensual agreements (defined as " cases, excluding reconciliations, in which an adjustment or settlement of issues, such as property settlement support, custody and visitation, was effected ") to have been made in 1,886 cases (5 per cent of the total reported proceedings).[1]

4.307   However, the official report describing the system comments:

In any evaluation of the program there is the difficulty of determining the extent to which the conciliation process is responsible in effecting reported reconciliations. Some individuals maintain that in certain instances reconciliations are brought about merely through the act of filing the petition or sending appointment letters for conferences. The letters act as a catalytic agent that enables the couple to sit down together and discuss their problems.[2]

Another consideration in determining the effect of the bureaus is the duration of effected reconciliations. This information is not available State-wide since there is no formal follow-up on reconciled cases. The only statistics available are contained in a 1971 study conducted in the eighth district which indicated that 72 per cent of the reconciliations reported from September 1967 until August 1968 were still in effect after a lapse of about three years.[3]

4.308   The Legislative Commission also consulted the opinion of the lawyers, on which it reported as follows:

An overwhelming majority of matrimonial lawyers feel that the Conciliation Bureau is unsuccessful in reconciling married couples. The principle reason given for this failure is that a conciliation process which does not begin until a divorce action has been filed is too late to save the marriage . . . . (But) although most matrimonial lawyers believe that the Conciliation Bureau has been unsuccessful in reconciling married couples, a majority believe that the bureau has been successful in a significant number of cases in effecting consensual agreements on custody of children, visitation rights, and the amount of support. A substantial number of lawyers favor retention of the bureau mainly because the Conciliation Commissioners often have facilitated settlement of collateral issues. Supports of the bureau indicate that such settlements save the judge's time, save trial and other costs, and promote family harmony, despite the divorce.[4]

4.309   As regards the Continent, an expert observer writes:

The real value of the court's conciliatory proceedings has become a matter of skeptical conjecture under those legal systems which have introduced it. This has been the case in France, Germany, Switzerland, Austria and various other countries.[5]

---

[1] The facts are taken from the Program Audit Report of the Legislative Commission on Expenditure Review of the State of New York, *Marital Conciliation in New York State Supreme Court*, 1971. The Commission is a permanent legislative agency established to enquire into the efficient and effective expenditure of funds appropriated by the Legislature of the State for specific programmes. We understand, at the time of writing, that the programme, which the Commission concluded was " experiencing only marginal success in accomplishing the purposes of the legislation ", may be withdrawn.

[2] *Ibid*, page 10.

[3] *Ibid*, page 12.

[4] *Ibid*, page 13. Similar views have been privately expressed to one of us by experienced New York practitioners.

[5] J Gorecki: *Divorce in Poland*, Mouton and Co, The Hague and Paris, 1970, page 77.

This passage occurs in a detailed study of divorce in Poland whose author, while of the view that " a divorce trial is not the best moment to use therapy; it should be applied by marriage counselling centres at an earlier stage of marital conflict ",[1] still regards the prospects of reconciliation effected through the courts rather less pessimistically than does the general consensus.   In support, he cites figures of divorce cases in Poland to the effect that between 3 per cent and 4 per cent of cases coming before the Polish court in the period 1959–1963 ended in a " discontinuation of proceedings caused by reconciliation ".[2]   No explanation is vouchsafed of how the causal nexus was established, and it is conceded that there is a strong body of legal opinion in Poland that " the conciliatory session . . . has given hardly perceptible results."[3]   The same author reports that some of the lawyers and judges who hold this opinion nevertheless wish to retain the session for its beneficial effect in producing agreement or easing the court's task in deciding on ancillary matters.[4]

Conclusions on conciliation and reconciliation

4.310   We have devoted some effort to bringing together materials on conciliation and reconciliation procedures in court because the subject is one of central importance to the family court concept.   It should, in reaching conclusions on the discussion, be borne in mind that the results of all these procedures are difficult to measure.   A recognised authority observes:

> There have been no large-scale detailed studies on the subject of marital therapy, so that there is little evidence on which to answer such fundamental questions as who seeks it, from whom, and what is the long term outcome.[5]

4.311   None the less, wherever one looks for the evidence, two propositions command general assent.   First, that reconciliation procedures conducted through the court at the stage where parties are presenting themselves for decrees that will formalise their marriage breakdown have small success. Secondly, that conciliation procedures conducted through the court at this same stage have substantial success in civilising the consequences of the break-down.   These conclusions are in themselves neutral upon the value and importance of reconciliation procedures conducted by other agencies and at a different time.

4.312   In his valuable paper on marriage counselling,[6] Mr L V Harvey has this to say under the heading of " Some Differences Between Marriage Counselling and Legal Approaches to Marital Disorganisation ":

> It has been suggested by some, most clearly by the Archbishop of Canterbury's divorce law reform committee, that breakdown in marriage be a ground for

---

[1] *Ibid*, page 76.

[2] *Ibid*, page 78.

[3] *Ibid*, page 77.

[4] *Ibid*, page 95.

[5] J Dominian: *Marital Breakdown*, Pelican Press, 1968, page 140.   The only statistically elaborated attempt that has, so far as we know, been made to measure the effect of reconciliation work is in J H Wallis and H S Booker: *Marriage Counselling*, National Marriage Guidance Council, 1958.   The book is sub-titled, *A Description and Analysis of the Remedial Work of the Marriage Guidance Council*, but the presentation of the statistical results does little to clarify their meaning.   The most important conclusion seems to be that " in about one-third of the cases the Counsellors thought they had done good, in about one-third they saw no evidence of improvement, whilst in the other third of cases they did not know what the result had been ": page 141.

[6] L V Harvey: ' Marriage Counselling: A Therapeutic Approach to Marital Disorganisation ', in *Divorce, Society and the Law, op cit*, pages 35–52.   Mr Harvey is adviser to the Commonwealth Attorney General on marriage guidance matters.

divorce, and that a marriage counsellor should be employed to assess the marriage and give the court the benefit of an opinion about whether it had broken down irretrievably or not. Obviously, those who suggest this have it in mind to utilize the growing knowledge of the social and behavioural sciences of which I have spoken. However, I think if we bear in mind what I have said here about the nature of the marriage counsellor's work, then it is clear that there are considerable and important differences between a counsellor who is therapeutically involved with a client and the person who uses the same interviewing methods in order to assess the client's marriage. The relationship between counsellor and client is most important and in the counselling situation this relationship will have characteristics which differ significantly from those which will apply when the main function of the interviewer is to assess and report on the marriage. In the first case, the counsellor is helping the client to make decisions for himself, the discussion is in complete confidence and an important ingredient of the relationship between himself and the counsellor is the feeling the client has that the counsellor is not judging him. In the second case, the interviewer is making judgments and assessments about the client, he will communicate these to others who will make decisions about the client. I feel quite strongly that our experience with marriage counselling services in Australia points clearly to the fact that a therapeutic approach to marriage breakdown is more effective when carried out by local community based organisations rather than centralized agencies attached to courts and perceived by the public as forming part of the judicial process.[1]

4.313 Again this emphasises, this time from the standpoint of marriage guidance, the limitations of a court of law as a vehicle for the promotion of reconciliation. It is, in our view, of fundamental importance that the advantages, in the area under discussion, to be derived from the family court should be seen primarily in terms of its capacity to help families to make the best decisions and reach the best solutions over the whole range of problems which the fact of breakdown produces in the circumstances of each particular case. The welfare service associated with the family court will remain—as will, indeed, the judge—alive to any sign that a reconciliation is possible, and will in such a case take the steps—usually involving referral to an outside agency—which seem most likely to procure it. But it will remain alive, also, to the policy of the law that dead marriages should be decently buried. Decency in this connection involves diagnosing the practical needs of the family at the time when the court assumes control over the relationship between its members and their affairs, invoking the help of other appropriate agencies to minister to those needs, and encouraging the victims of the family breakdown to wind up[2] their failure with the least possible recrimination, and to make the most rational and efficient arrangements possible for their own and their children's future.

4.314 We have now explained our purpose in stating as one of the six major criteria that a family court must satisfy that it will organise its work in such a way as to provide the best possible facilities for conciliation between parties in matrimonial dispute. We see this proposition as intrinsically valid for the reasons we have discussed. It is consistent with our first principle, that the family court must be an impartial judicial institution, regulating the rights of citizens and settling their disputes according to law. It has a close bearing, also, upon the next of our six fundamental points to be discussed, which concerns the relationship between the family court and social work personnel.

---

[1] Page 50.

[2] An interesting exposition of the " winding up " concept as applying to matrimonial as well as financial failure is included in Roscoe Pound's article, ' The Place of the Family Court in the Judicial System ', in 10 *Crime and Delinquency*, 1964, pages 533–545.

4.315   The work involved in reconciliation and conciliation procedures will form one part only of the responsibilities of the family court in offering advice and services to the public which comes before it.   The family court will have a continuing, perhaps an extended, need for investigative, reporting and supervisory services such as are at present available to the matrimonial courts in both jurisdictions through their own welfare officers and the local authorities. The employment of services of this kind does not depend on the consent of the parties, but on the need of the court to inform itself when it is called upon to make orders affecting children, including those occasions when there seem to be grounds for making a supervision order.   However this entire complex of activity in the welfare field is organised, it will involve a division of labour. Some parts of the work will be carried out by personnel serving the court directly, and other parts by outside agencies whose help they have invoked.   This must involve establishing a network of relationships between the court and outside agencies, such as the social services, education and housing departments of local authorities, the national health service, specialised organisations such as those offering marriage guidance or charitable resources, or, it may be, the police.

4.316   The problem we have here to consider is not directly connected with the division of labour to which we have referred.   It relates to the nature of the service through which the family court will act in obtaining the information it requires to make orders concerning children, in ensuring the availability of the supportive services needed to deal with the family problems which come to its notice, and in organising the two-year conference for which we make proposals in Section 14.   We are here concerned, in other words, with the provision of an arm to the court itself, forming part of its structure.

4.317   There are three different ways in which it would be practicable to provide the family court with a social welfare service of this kind.   It could be done through the probation service, through the local authority social services departments, or through setting up a new welfare service to be attached to the court.   We proceed to consider these alternatives.

The probation service

4.318   We have already noted[1] that the burden of promoting reconciliations in the magistrates' courts falls upon the probation service.   It should also be mentioned that the probation officer has the duty, if called upon by the magistrates, to report upon relevant circumstances when they are dealing with children.[2]   Further, in the divorce jurisdiction welfare officers, upon whom the court has powers to call for reports and assistance, are available in London and in every divorce town; and in the divorce towns it is the probation officers who are appointed to act as welfare officers of the court, and who are required to discharge onerous and essential duties in that capacity.[3]

---

[1] See paragraphs 4.296–4.297.

[2] Matrimonial Proceedings (Magistrates' Courts) Act 1960, section 4.

[3] The Matrimonial Causes Rules 1973, rule 95; the Probation Rules 1965, rule 18.

4.319   The probation service thus has considerable experience with the type of activity which the family court would require of a social work service, and has through its efforts in this sphere gained the confidence of the judiciary and magistracy.

4.320   The probation service is, however, currently under extreme pressure. The view has already been expressed that " in any attempt to reduce the burden on the service . . . matrimonial work would seem a natural candidate for removal."[1]   Moreover, historically,[2] currently, and in the minds of the public the probation service is dominantly associated with the work of the criminal courts and with dealings with criminal offenders.   Despite the responsibilities it discharges in the matrimonial jurisdiction, this relationship between the probation service and criminal business has, if anything, been strengthened in recent years.   As a result of the Children and Young Persons Act 1969 the probation service is likely to continue to lose much of the responsibility it formerly had for children and young persons, and this has taken place during a period when it has taken on substantial new responsibilities for prison welfare and under the parole system.

4.321   In our view it is imperative that the family court should be free from the association between the administration of family and criminal law which now characterises the summary jurisdiction.   Some 97 per cent of the entire criminal law business of the country is dealt with by the magistrates, and the probation service is liable to be concerned with all of it.   We have no doubt— indeed, on a balance of national priorities it must be right for it to be so—that magistrates and probation officers will continue to be principally devoted to this business.   But it would be indefensible, in our view, to set up a family court and then to provide it with a welfare arm whose main energies must be concentrated to purposes which would fix the new court with the ancient criminal taint.   We consider the structure and direction of the probation service to be such that there would be too great a risk that the same consequence would follow even if the attempt were made to set up a civil division of the probation service for attachment to the family court.

4.322   We therefore decide against the probation service as the provider of the family court's welfare service.

Local authority social services departments

4.323   Local authority services of one kind or another will be constantly invoked in the interests of the people with whom the family court will deal. Some people coming to court will have already sought the assistance of the local authority social services department about any of the wide range of problems with which they deal, and will already be known to the local authority social workers.   For others, the fact of coming to court may present them with problems—perhaps legal or financial—on which they will need advice and

---

[1] *First Report from the Expenditure Committee, op cit*, page ix; see paragraph 4.297 above.

[2] The Church of England Temperance Society set up its first police court missions in 1876 with the object of reclaiming drunkards who appeared in the police courts.   This was just two years before the Matrimonial Causes Act 1878 gave a matrimonial remedy in the police court to wives upon whom their husbands had committed aggravated assault.   The magistrates began to release offenders on bail to the missioners, and this practice received statutory recognition.   This was the origin of the probation service, which took statutory form with the Probation of Offenders Act 1907.

guidance. And in other cases there will be problems—perhaps in the field of housing, or child care or supervision—which will come to light during the court proceedings and on which the court may seek the assistance of social workers.

4.324 To avoid fragmentation of services, and to ensure that social workers involved have the maximum knowledge of facilities available and of the extent to which the local authority can help, there would be advantages for both the court and the families if the social work help available through the courts were in very close liaison with the local authority social services department. This would mean that, where appropriate, the court welfare officer should be able to have immediate and full access to information about a family's background and any earlier need for help; the officer should, if necessary, be able easily to consult with a social worker who has already been involved; and he should be well known to, well respected by, and very familiar with the various local authority services on which he may need to rely. All this argues strongly for having the court served by a specialised group of welfare officers drawn from among the local authority social workers, and maintaining their attachment to the local authority. In this way overlapping services, administratively uneconomical and confusing for the public, would be kept to a minimum.[1]

4.325 Special steps would be desirable to ensure that the court welfare service measured up to the same high standards we are concerned that the family court should itself achieve. It must demonstrate a commensurate degree of professional integrity and expertise. In particular, it would be necessary for social work posts of this kind to have senior status and to be held by persons of relatively mature age and experience. Such persons could then fulfil the liaison role which would be necessary to ensure that other social service personnel with knowledge needed by the court could be enabled to help the court and the people using it to the full.

4.326 Training arrangements would also fit in with using the local authority social services staff. Training for all forms of social work is now unified under the auspices of the Central Council for Education and Training in Social Work and potential applicants for the local authority social services and the probation service train together. Comprehensive training in all areas of social work, together with the wide range of experience which can be gained by officers in local authority departments from the beginning of a working career, would make local authority personnel well equipped to undertake the role needed in the family courts.

4.327 Social services departments are well able to offer the career opportunities needed to attract persons of suitable calibre, knowledge and experience to service in the courts. In recent years they have been able to provide a unified and rewarding career structure which compares favourably with all other professional groups in local government and with similar employment in the civil service and elsewhere. This is due largely to the range of family and

---

[1] In situations which may arise when local authority services such as housing and education, or other welfare functions such as adoption and child care, are involved in cases before the family court, or where the local authority itself may even be acting as a prosecuting authority, or be an interested party, the court could draw upon either the services of another local authority or the probation service. (This happens now, for example, in some adoption cases where the local authority which would normally fulfil the guardian *ad litem* function has arranged the placing.)

welfare services with which they are involved. If the court welfare service were provided by a specialised section within local authority social services departments, the service would have expert personnel, and the staff themselves would have the advantages by way of training and career structure which a large complex could offer.

4.328 There are also arguments for having a social welfare service which could be seen to be clearly independent of the court. The court and the social welfare service each in their different ways will provide assistance for people with marital problems, and the relationship between the two would therefore not be quite comparable with that which prevails between magistrates and the probation service. A welfare service provided by the local authority would mean that there would be a clear distinction between the court and the service.

4.329 A somewhat similar distinction exists between the health responsibilities of a national health service hospital and the functions of social workers in hospitals. In that case it has been agreed that the national health service will no longer employ its own social workers, and these will be provided by local authorities.[1] The way in which these arrangements operate, their advantages and their drawbacks, may prove a useful guide in due course as to how a local authority provided welfare service might work in the family court system we propose.

A new family court welfare service

4.330 While many advantages can be argued for the provision of the court welfare service by local authorities, there are, in line with our objective in proposing a family court system, strong attractions in equipping the new court with a new welfare service. The family court requires a service specifically adapted and responsive to its own needs. These include knowledge and understanding of family law and of legal procedure, as well as of the local services and of the effect of marital breakdown on spouses and their children. The family court has a particular need for lawyers and welfare workers who are sympathetic to each other's professional outlook and modes of work. We have been impressed by the many examples of collaboration between young lawyers and social workers which is a feature of the proliferation of community law centres and similar institutions throughout the country. It may well be a family court service would attract many of these young men and women whose aspirations will not be satisfied by a career spent exclusively in the practice either of private law or conventional social work. It is likely, too, that the attractions of the work (which would have to conform with standard conditions of pay and service) would produce a good response from faculties of law and social administration, who would begin to educate students especially for this field.

4.331 Moreover, criticisms are at present sometimes levelled against the local authority social services departments on the ground of the relative inexperience of some of their personnel who appear before courts, and because of the frequent changes of staff which it is understood take place. We are currently going through a period of considerable upheaval in the social services and in local government generally. A period of consolidation may well bring

---

[1] Section 12(2) of the National Health Service Reorganisation Act 1973 lays a duty on local authorities to provide social work to the health service.

improvements of services, so that shortcomings which may now exist in local authority services may be overcome by the time a family court system could be introduced. But if they were not, it would be an additional reason for setting up a distinct organisation.

4.332 A new service would also avoid the problems which can arise when the local authority employing the social worker is itself an interested party in the very matters upon which the court has to adjudicate or conciliate. These matters may even involve the consideration by the court of breaches of the law when the local authority is itself acting as a prosecuting authority. These factors can make it very difficult for the local authority to provide the impartial and independent standards which the family court service must not only possess, but be manifestly seen to possess, if it is to achieve its purposes.

4.333 As things stand at present, there would be difficulties in offering satisfactory career opportunities within a specialised court service. There is little doubt, however, that welfare workers who did well in this field would be able to move without difficulty to senior posts in other areas of social work if they wished to, and if opportunities within the service were inadequate.

4.334 Members of the new service would be attached to the family court, and like other workers in the civil courts would be engaged and paid by the Lord Chancellor's Department.

Conclusions on the social work service

4.335 Our main concern is that the welfare service provided for the family courts should be of high quality, with expert staff. There should be no conflicting demands on the time of the welfare workers or on the way in which they carry out their functions; they should be entirely available to serve the court's needs. Their approach and attitude of mind would be as important as their background and experience. Part-time workers, for example, could be useful recruits. There are many married women trained in the law or in social work, whose children have reached school age, who would be attracted to and capable of giving valuable assistance to the service. Their experience with children, as well as their training, would be an advantage.

4.336 The quality of personnel is more important than the formal structure of the service, and the arguments for a local authority provided service and for a special new service are well balanced. By the time a family court system on the lines we propose could be introduced the present reorganisation of local authority services should have settled down, and the choice between the two alternatives now in the field may have become more clear-cut. Whichever is to be preferred, however, we believe that considerable attention needs to be given to underlining the new role of court social workers and giving the service an attractive image.

RELATIONS BETWEEN THE FAMILY COURT AND SOCIAL SECURITY AUTHORITIES

4.337 Throughout this Report we stress that for the bulk of the casualties of broken homes, family law and the law of social security are different sides of the same coin. Nevertheless, the separate institutional structures—the courts and the social security authorities—which are concerned with these casualties are ill-acquainted with each other. Indeed, each has taken pains to define and maintain an isolated identity. Realism and reason alike require that the courts and the social security authorities be brought, not into any sort of merger, but into an intimate working relationship. At this point we do no more than state the principle of co-operation, which we regard as one of the most powerful of all of the keys that are needed to unlock the problems of one-parent families. The precise form of the relationship we desire is a matter for detailed discussion. In Section 12 of this Part of the Report we have entered upon such a discussion on the basis that the new relationship we are recommending would be formed between the existing courts and the Supplementary Benefits Commission. In Section 7 of Part 5 we consider the parallel question as it would arise between the family court and the authority which is given responsibility for administering the new one-parent family benefit which we call " guaranteed maintenance allowance ". Fundamentally, the need for closer relationships and the problems in forming them are the same in both cases; but we consider that the family court, by its structure, possession of its own welfare arm, and other attributes, would find the solution easier.

CONFIDENCE IN THE COURT

4.338   We have stated as the last of our principles for a family court that it will organise its procedures with a view to gaining the confidence and maximising the convenience of the citizens who appear before it. The attitudes of parties who appear before civil courts to the processes of those courts has never been systematically or officially studied. None the less, features of the procedure and administrative arrangements in the magistrates' courts when exercising their matrimonial jurisdiction have been criticised for the last half-century on the grounds of their insensitivities to the needs and feelings of those who use them. These matters have been discussed in Sections 7, 8 and 9 of this Part. In Section 14 we shall take up further aspects of this theme, relating, for example, to the place of ritual in the court process and the buildings in which that process takes place. In the ultimate sense, however, the end product that we seek through all of the recommendations, whether they deal with procedural matters of this kind, or with the reform of the law itself, is to win the respect of the citizen for the system.

SECTION 14—THE FAMILY COURT IN OPERATION

INTRODUCTION

4.339   In this Section, we turn to some of the practical consequences of implementing the principles discussed in Section 13. The fusion of splintered jurisdictions into a comprehensive family court system will be a large-scale enterprise in legal administration. Two committees of experts are already working in this area. In December 1970 the Home Secretary invited the Law Commission to consider " what changes in the matrimonial law administered by magistrates' courts may be desirable as a result of the coming into operation of the Divorce Reform Act 1969 and the Matrimonial Proceedings and Property Act 1970, and any other changes that may appear to be called for in related legislation in order to avoid the creation of anomalies." The Law Commission have not as yet reported on these questions, but a working party of Law Commission and Home Office representatives have recently published a working paper containing provisional conclusions.[1] In addition, in August 1971 the Law Commission set up a working party " to consider what kind of court, below the level of High Court, should deal with family matters." This enquiry is still in progress. We have also referred earlier[2] to Judge Jean Graham Hall's important *Proposal for a Family Court*, the only contribution to the discussion in England, which contains a detailed plan of a scheme for a unified family court at the local level.

4.340 Our own concern is not to produce a blueprint or working model for a family court, but rather to stress those features of it which it will, in our view, be essential to incorporate in the design. These essential features derive from the principles we discussed in Section 13, and, through them, are closely related to the defects in the existing system which we have earlier exposed, and which we wish to correct in the family court. The recommendations in this Section may therefore be seen, in general, as stating the body of minimum requirements needed to give practical expression to our concept of the family court, the purposes it will serve, and the advantages it can bring.

4.341 We have dealt at length with the origins and social consequences of the dual matrimonial jurisdictions, which involve both a separation and an overlap of function between the summary and superior courts, and the creation of a double standard as between the two systems of law which they respectively administer. This accounts for the stress that we have laid, in stating the criteria for a family court, on the theme of unity. That theme will inform a good deal of the discussion in the present Section, since it gives rise to many issues of practical organisation. Unity implies the need to rationalise the structure and manpower arrangements of the courts which grant matrimonial remedies, to abolish the double standard through the reform of the substantive matrimonial law, and to establish uniformity of procedures. It is not possible to keep the discussion of these subjects in watertight compartments, but the division we have made will, broadly speaking, set the pattern of the discussion. We therefore begin with questions of structure and manpower.

RATIONALISATION OF STRUCTURE

The present confusion

4.342 It is desirable, in the first instance, to underline how great is the disorder caused by the patchwork nature of the present arrangements.

4.343 In recent years the divorce jurisdiction has been heavily decentralised. Until the Matrimonial Causes Act 1967 all jurisdiction in divorce (including judicial separation and nullity) was vested entirely in the High Court, whether a case was defended or not. In practice, a considerable measure of decentralisation was achieved even before 1967 by appointing county court judges to sit as commissioners exercising the High Court powers in divorce. However, the Act of 1967 conferred a direct divorce jurisdiction on county courts designated to be divorce county courts. There are now about one hundred of these throughout the country. Every petition for divorce has to be filed either in a divorce county court or in the divorce registry in London. Any case which is defended

---

[1] *Family Law, Matrimonial Proceedings in Magistrates' Courts*, Law Commission Working Paper No 53, 7 September 1973.

[2] Section 13, paragraph 4.280.

is transferred to the Family Division of the High Court. Otherwise, it will be tried in a divorce county court. Since nearly all divorce cases go undefended, the result is that the administration of the law of divorce has become, for the most part, the subject of a local county court jurisdiction.

4.344 In taking over the bulk of the divorce work, the county courts have also taken over the powers of the High Court to make orders for financial provision. The divorce county court judge, in dealing with an undefended divorce, can therefore make ancillary financial orders. Moreover, the divorce county courts now share with the High Court the power to make financial orders on an application based on wilful neglect to maintain even when no other matrimonial relief is claimed. This is parallel with the jurisdiction of magistrates to make maintenance orders on the ground of wilful neglect to maintain.[1] The effect of the decentralisation of the formerly exclusive High Court jurisdiction has therefore been to complicate still further the problems arising from the split between summary and superior jurisdictions, because the latter being divided again between the High Court and the divorce county courts has resulted in the co-existence of two jurisdictions—that of the magistrates and of the county courts—both of which are local, operating in overlapping districts throughout the country, and both of which can make financial orders on the breakdown of marriage. But whereas the magistrates can order only periodic payments, the county court, like the High Court, can order lump sum payments or secured provision. In many parts of the country, the magistrates, the divorce county court judge, and, when he appears in the area, the High Court judge, are all accommodated in the same building; and it is possible for three women claiming financial support from their respective husbands to have their cases tried at the same time, under one roof, in three different types of court, each with its separate procedures, and two of them providing more extensive remedies than the third.

4.345 This is only a segment of the confusion to which we have referred. Adoption procedures provide another example. An adoption order can be made in the High Court, a county court or (except where the parties are not normally resident in Great Britain) in the magistrates' court.[2] The magistrates hear all domestic proceedings, that is to say, matrimonial, guardianship and affiliation cases, sitting as a domestic court. But they hear adoption proceedings in the juvenile court, whose main business is dealing with children in need of care and control and prosecuting children under 17 for criminal offences.[3] Only the magistrates have jurisdiction to make an affiliation order, but, although they do this sitting as a domestic court, a woman who wishes to

---

[1] The divorce court jurisdiction, which was originally introduced because there were financial limits on the orders that magistrates could make, is now contained in the Matrimonial Causes Act 1973, section 27. The parallel jurisdiction of the magistrates is conferred by the Matrimonial Proceedings (Magistrates' Courts) Act 1960 (see Section 5, paragraph 4.62 above). Since the magistrates were relieved of the financial limits in 1968, the two jurisdictions have entirely overlapped.

[2] In 1971, 21,495 adoption orders were made in England and Wales, 40 of them in the High Court, 13,619 in the county courts, and 7,836 by the magistrates. In the same year, 1,904 orders were made in Scotland, all, other than a few made in the Court of Session, in the sheriff courts: *Report of the Departmental Committee on the Adoption of Children*, Cmnd 5107, 1972, Appendix B, page 122.

[3] *Ibid*, paragraph 263, where it is recommended that this practice should cease, and also that " ushers in courts dealing with family matters should be civilians and not police officers."

enforce such an order has to apply to the magistrates in their ordinary sittings. Appeals from the magistrates on a maintenance order go to the Family Division of the High Court; appeals from them on affiliation orders go to the Crown Court, unless they are on a point of law only, when they go to the Family Division. The High Court and the county court can grant a wife an injunction to protect her from molestation; the magistrates cannot do so. The magistrates cannot deal with disputes affecting the matrimonial home or other property; the county court can deal with some of these disputes; the High Court can deal with all of them.

4.346 So might the instances be multiplied. We cannot improve on the comment of one family lawyer:

> The distribution of family law business in the present court structure is chaotic. The demarcation which is most difficult to defend is that between magistrates' courts and the county courts. The overlap of jurisdiction is undesirable in so far as it means that the same provisions can be implemented by tribunals of a very different nature. But a more serious criticism is of the division of powers between them. A family crisis is seldom simple and it is highly desirable that the court dealing with it has a wide range of powers at its disposal. In a given situation orders relating to cash support, occupation of the home, ownership of family assets and the custody of children might be necessary in order to deal with the situation as a whole. The orders relate to and supplement each other. It is quite wrong that a spouse for whom all those orders may be appropriate must seek them from different courts, differently constituted, using their own characteristic procedures and sitting according to their own individual time schedules.[1]

The construction of the family court

Materials

4.347 In seeking to bring structural order out of this confusion there can be no question of starting afresh with brand new materials. There has to be a new model court, but it can only be established by use of the components that are, or are likely to come, to hand. On the manpower side, these components consist of the professional judges who are now engaged for part of their time in matrimonial work—the High Court judges of the Family Division,[2] county court judges and stipendiary magistrates—and the lay justices who sit in domestic proceedings in the magistrates' courts; the High Court and county court registrars, who combine some judicial with administrative functions; and the justices' clerks. The resources in bricks and mortar are a given number of court buildings, with no foreseeable prospect of the rapid construction of new buildings specially adapted and given over to the work of the family court. All of the business of the family court will have to be discharged through a machine which, for the most part at any rate, is constructed from these parts.

The role of the magistrate

4.348 We desire to emphasise that the inclusion of the magistrates in the family court would for us be a matter of choice even if it were not a matter of necessity. The criticisms we have made of the matrimonial jurisdiction of the

---

[1] J Eekelaar: *Family Security and Family Breakdown, op cit*, pages 278–279. See also the report of the Graham Hall Committee, *op cit*, chapter 2.

[2] The judges of the Family Division are not engaged full time in family business, since they share with the Queen's Bench judges in the disposal of the civil and criminal business of the High Court in the provinces.

magistrates are not intended to spill over to the magistracy, whose fate it has been to try to make that jurisdiction work. It is probable, indeed, that only the care which so many magistrates have devoted to this task has saved the jurisdiction from foundering long ago under the weight of its inherent defects. We are encouraged, in this connection, to find that the opinion of the lay bench, as reflected in the annual reports of the Magistrates' Association, and in the evidence given by the Association to the Law Commission, has been moving in recent years towards support for the introduction of a family court. The family court will have a continuing need for the services of the lay magistracy, not only as a source of manpower, but as an equally indispensable source of lay experience and outlook which is a traditional feature in the administration of family law in England and Wales. In our view, it should be a continuing and expanding feature. One of the advantages of the family court is that it will allow greater flexibility in the association of professional and lay judges in the work of the court, and through such association give the magistrates the possibility of sharing in the disposal of more interesting and difficult cases than are apt to come their way at present.

Local jurisdiction

4.349 It will be essential, also, for the family court to provide, as the county courts and the magistrates now do, facilities for the local determination of cases as quickly and as cheaply as the nature of the case permits. It should, however, be mentioned in this connection that it ought not to be assumed that speed of decision characterises matrimonial proceedings before the magistrates in contrast with proceedings before the High Court or county court judges. There is no systematic information on this point, but there is certainly a conflict between the need for speed and the desire to have the parties represented when this involves obtaining a legal aid certificate. Since the introduction of legal aid for family matters in magistrates' courts, there has been an undoubted loss of speed in determining issues; and it is difficult to see how this can be avoided. However, the local determination of cases in itself promotes speed and economy by saving parties and their witnesses the time and expense of travelling, and the family court must continue to provide for it whenever appropriate.

Connection with the High Court

4.350 We can see no argument for disassociating the family court from the rest of the judicial system by severing it from a connection with the High Court. Just as it is essential to localise the family jurisdiction, so, reciprocally, is it essential to have that local jurisdiction supervised by professional judges of the highest rank, to guard against error and promote uniformity in decision. Theoretically, it would be possible to move some judges out of the High Court (no doubt they would be taken from the Family Division) to become the superior judges in a family court that would be structurally independent of the rest of the High Court. The stream of jurisdiction passing through the family court would then join with the other two mainstreams of the law—the rest of the civil jurisdiction, and the criminal jurisdiction—only at the level of the Court of Appeal or, perhaps, of the House of Lords. But we cannot see the slightest advantage in adopting such a procedure, and there would be very many disadvantages. We are therefore of the view that the Family Division of the High Court should remain in being as the top tier of the family court, and as its link with the rest of the higher judicial system.

The shape of the family court

4.351 The local branches of the court, comprising the first tier, will be drawn from the county court judges, stipendiary magistrates and lay magistrates. We shall be expanding on this concept, and referring to the question whether there may be need for an intermediate tier. But already from the discussion so far we can draw in very broad outline the shape of the family court.

4.352 The family court will be an institution to which the whole of the business of family law now dealt with in the Family Division of the High Court, the county courts and the magistrates' courts, will be assigned. It will be a civil court, conducting its business in accordance with the procedures, terminology and spirit of the civil law. It will be linked to the High Court and to the system of second or final appeals through the Family Division, but, subject to that link, the family court will be a unitary structure, operating to a large extent at the local level, and providing internally for the first appeal. It will make full use of existing resources of judicial manpower, professional and lay, and of court staff. It will be provided with its own welfare service, in whichever of the two alternative forms discussed in Section 13 should, when the time comes, appear to be the better. Through that service, and in general, it will lay great emphasis on the promotion of conciliation procedures, intended to promote to the maximum extent possible the orderly settlement of disputes arising from the breakdown of marriage, and assisting the parties with information, advice, introductions, and otherwise as the case may require, to re-organise their lives to adapt to the circumstances following breakdown. The court will have a special relationship with the public authorities responsible for making financial provision for one-parent families, the nature of which is discussed in detail elsewhere. Within the unified structure, the anomalies and confusion caused by overlapping and competing jurisdictions will be eliminated.

One remedy, one court

4.353 It follows from this last point, and we emphasise its importance, that the structure of the family court will not allow for the options which exist within the present system for litigants to select the court from which to ask for a remedy that more than one court provides. Any legal system has the need to service problems of different orders of complexity at different levels. The family court will, like any other, have to devise rules for the efficient distribution of business, and this may well involve cases which fall within the same general category of description being dealt with in different tiers because of the presence of some special factor, such as length or difficulty of the investigation. But this does not breach the principle of eliminating options. There will be no duplication of remedies in the family court, and no possibility of choosing between tiers otherwise than as may be determined by rules which the court itself has established for the proper allocation of its business. The effect will be not only to terminate a state of disorder which does no credit to a judicial system, but, more particularly, to terminate arrangements which, whatever the theory may be, now ostentatiously cater on a second-class basis for poor people seeking matrimonial relief short of divorce.

The county court judge in the family court

4.354 We turn now to elaborate (so far as this is not done elsewhere) the institutional features of the family court which we have outlined in the preceding paragraphs.

4.355 The focus of the family court at the local level should be the county court judge, and the work of the court should be carried on at the county court building. We shall discuss use of buildings later. In selecting the county court judge as the central judicial figure in the first or local tier of the court we have in mind that much matrimonial work is already done in the county court, and that it is desirable that responsibility for local organisation and administration be placed upon a professional judge, although, no doubt, he will be working with local committees upon which the lay bench will be represented. Principally, however, we wish to mould the first tier of the family court so far as possible round a core taken from the county court because of the importance of eliminating from the new jurisdiction all those elements in the summary matrimonial jurisdiction that we have found to be inefficient or unsuitable for the conduct of a matrimonial court. The first tier of the family court, even although it ought and will have to make use of existing resources, must not be permitted to become a second version, under another title, of the existing magisterial jurisdiction. For this reason, although it may be necessary for reasons of manpower economy to include the stipendiary magistrate in the court's muster, we would prefer it if this could in the longer run be avoided, save in the case of the stipendiary who was prepared to specialise in matrimonial work.

The number of tiers

4.356 We do not intend to enter deeply into the detailed and technical field of considerations affecting the solution to the problem of how the business of the family court should be divided between its different tiers, or, indeed, of how many tiers there should be. The main issue in this latter connection is whether there should be interposed between the local and the top tier an intermediate tier, principally for the purpose of dealing with appeals on questions of fact as distinct from appeals on questions of law, which would be dealt with by the judges of the High Court in the top tier. Dealing with this question in a different context Lord Simon, when President of the Probate, Divorce and Admiralty Division, observed:

> Turning to our system of matrimonial judicature, in my opinion its greatest defect is the want of a satisfactory avenue of appeal from the matrimonial decisions of magistrates. Magistrates deal with roughly 30,000 applications in matrimonial domestic proceedings (separation, maintenance and attachment of earnings) in a year, of which, say 60 *per cent* are successful: and on the whole they do the work well. But all courts are manned by human beings, and therefore liable to error. Appeal lies from the matrimonial decisions of magistrates to a Divisional Court of the Probate, Divorce and Admiralty Division—in future it will be the Family Division. But, speaking generally a Divisional Court can only correct errors of law; and most matrimonial litigation turns on matters of fact. The decision of the magistrates is of great importance to the parties: it often leads to a divorce: and a matrimonial maintenance order of only £7 a week will amount to no less than £1,820 in only five years. I would myself like to see an appeal lie on matters of fact or quantum of maintenance to a county court judge sitting with two magistrates of different sex. No doubt, some control would be necessary to prevent an appeal in every case.[1]

Thus, Lord Simon envisaged the interposition of a tier between the magistrates and the Family Division. Similar provision could be made for an intermediate tier in the family court structure; the alternative (which we do not

---

[1] *Recent Developments in the Matrimonial Law*, The Riddell Lecture, 1970.

favour) being for all appeals both of fact and of law to go directly from the first tier to the top tier, which would almost certainly involve all of them having to be dealt with (as are appeals from magistrates at the present time) in London.

Division of business

4.357 We do not wish to canvass any particular scheme for the division of first instance business between the tiers. Presumably, contested divorces would continue to be dealt with by the High Court judge, as would disputes involving protracted investigations of fact or difficult questions of law. In the first tier, the county court judge and the lay magistrates would be associated in the discharge of the responsibilities of the jurisdiction. The unification of the system would, however, allow of a great degree of flexibility in the allocation of work. The first tier jurisdiction might, for example, be divided between that which required a full bench, consisting of the county court judge sitting with two magistrates (being so constituted that at least one man and one woman was present) and that which could be dealt with by a single judge, or by two magistrates sitting on their own. It might well prove possible to associate the lay element even with some of the business transacted in the top tier, in particular in matters concerning custody of and access to children. In general, since a major objective of the family court will be to promote opportunities for dealing comprehensively, in one set of proceedings, with the problems arising from the breakdown, we feel sure that there will be opportunities, of which we recommend that advantage should be taken, of associating the lay magistrates in the family court with a broader and more interesting range of work than tends at present to fall their way.

Selection and training of magistrates for the family court

4.358 Magistrates serving in the family court should be drawn from a panel of volunteers in much the same way as the rules now provide for a juvenile court panel. There are, however, limits to the degrees of specialisation which should be required of lay magistrates. A panel for matrimonial cases may be expected to attract those with special experience or qualifications, but our purpose in proposing it is less to accommodate experts than to ensure that the magistrates who sit in the family court should have a real interest in its work and a desire to participate. We assume that the Lord Chancellor's Department, perhaps in conjunction, in the future, with the Family Division of the High Court, will extend and adapt the training it presently provides for magistrates to meet the needs of the family court. We do not pursue this matter further, bearing in mind that the question of how much training is consistent with a lay status poses difficulties which are not confined to the training of magistrates in a family court.

Gains and losses in judicial time

4.359 In making these proposals we are fully alive to the increasingly heavy demands being made on the judiciary, which create a close limit to the weight of any extra burden which can be placed upon them. An enlargement of the area calling for mixed professional and lay adjudication does increase the burden. On the other hand, we are convinced that the effect of some of our other proposals will more than compensate for this increase. Our recommendations in Section 12 for shifting some of the responsibility for matrimonial orders away from the magistracy to the Supplementary Benefits Commission, and, still more, our recommendations in Part 5 both for a guaranteed maintenance allowance and in relation to the role of the courts in making financial provision after the introduction of guaranteed maintenance allowance must considerably reduce the volume of matrimonial work now coming before the court. This reduction, moreover, will take effect in a particularly time-consuming department of the work which involves investigation of income and expenditure and assets. It will have the further consequence of reducing the demand which, most inappropriately in our opinion, is now made on the police in connection with the matrimonial work of the magistrates' courts. It is not possible to quantify the calculation, but we have no doubt that the sum total of our recommendations having a relevant effect will be to produce a gain rather than a loss in the battle for judges' and magistrates' time.

CRIME AND THE FAMILY COURT

4.360 To deal with people in matrimonial dispute and distress through a court which is almost entirely given over to the trial of criminal offences is to show a manifest disrespect for their needs and feelings. This is a reason which ranks high among the many we have given for wishing to see the magistrates relieved of their matrimonial jurisdiction. One might objectify the principle by saying that family law is far too important a subject for it to be administered otherwise than through an institution which is wholly adapted and sensitive to its requirements. Speaking of the magistrates' courts at a conference in 1972, Mr Mark Carlisle, then Minister of State at the Home Office, praised the situation:

> whereby 97 per cent of our criminal cases are tried in the magistrates' courts, almost entirely disposed of by lay justices . . . I believe that we are for many years going to have a system in this country whereby magistrates' courts, based mainly on lay justices with a legally qualified clerk to assist, will form the broad base of our system of criminal adjudication.[1]

4.361 This, we have no doubt, is as it should be. But it creates no confidence that the present or future demands of such a jurisdiction will bear more than an accidental or marginal relationship to the demands of a family jurisdiction. For this reason alone, it seems to us that the constitution of a separate family court, institutionally responsive to its own purposes, is both desirable and urgent.

4.362 Within the family court, once it has been established, we should prefer to see the exercise of nothing but a civil jurisdiction. We have spoken of family courts elsewhere which deal with crime, especially juvenile crime, whenever that seems to bear some prescribed relationship to the family situation, but we consider that the arguments of principle for an undiluted civil jurisdiction outweigh the advantages (such as they may be) of permitting it to spill over into penal law.

---

[1] *The Future of Magistrates' Courts*, page 14, edited transcript of the proceedings of a conference held at the University of Birmingham in April 1972.

4.363 However, one difficulty arises in connection with care proceedings under the Children and Young Persons Act 1969. These are at present dealt with in the juvenile court. The conditions which the court has to find present before it can make any order[1] frequently arise in connection with matrimonial troubles and family breakdown. It would thus far seem at least logical for a family court to take over this jurisdiction. On the other hand, one of the alternatives in the conditions is that the child or young person should have been guilty of an offence, so that the transfer of care proceedings to the family court would, at least in such cases, involve it in investigation and findings of criminal or delinquent behaviour. We can find no neat solution for this problem, which will merit careful attention at the time when the details of the family court's jurisdiction are being considered. We are certain, however, that no proceedings other than care proceedings which may involve investigation into criminal conduct should be considered for inclusion in the family court jurisdiction.

RATIONALISATION OF THE LAW

The abolition of the summary jurisdiction

4.364 We have dealt with the requirements as regards structure of the family court which emerge from the principle of uniformity. We now have to examine what this same principle yields as regards the substance of the law which the family court will apply.

Law Commission proposals for reform

4.365 Throughout this Part of the Report we have emphasised that the co-existence of the superior and summary jurisdictions now means that we have a matrimonial law which embodies conflicting principles. Since the Divorce Reform Act 1969 and the Matrimonial Proceedings and Property Act 1970 the High Court and the divorce county courts have been making orders affecting the status of spouses and re-allocating their incomes and property on the assumption that the collapse of a marriage generally results from behaviour which is " six of one and half a dozen of the other ". The law of divorce and judicial separation is no longer bound to the proof of a matrimonial offence. There is a minority of cases in which the conduct of one of the parties has been so bad that it would be manifestly unjust to require continued support from the other, but otherwise the court does not, in making financial provision,

---

[1] The conditions, laid down by section 1(2) of the Children and Young Persons Act 1969, are that the court is of the opinion regarding the child or young person that:

" (a) his proper development is being avoidably prevented or neglected or his health is being avoidably impaired or neglected or he is being ill-treated; or

(b) it is probable that the condition set out in the preceding paragraph will be satisfied in his case, having regard to the fact that the court or another court has found that that condition is or was satisfied in the case of another child or young person who is or was a member of the household to which he belongs; or

(c) he is exposed to moral danger; or

(d) he is beyond the control of his parent or guardian; or

(e) he is of compulsory school age . . . and is not receiving efficient full-time education suitable to his age, ability and aptitude; or

(f) he is guilty of an offence, excluding homicide,

and also that he is in need of care or control which he is unlikely to receive unless the court makes and order . . . ."

balance blame or reduce the provision as though imposing a fine for supposed misbehaviour in the course of an unhappy life. But we have also seen that none of this new law has been extended to the magistrates' matrimonial jurisdiction, in which orders continue to be made only on proof of a commission of a matrimonial offence by the defendant, and maintenance continues to be refused or revoked on proof of a single act of adultery on the part of the complainant.

4.366 As will be seen from the terms of reference,[1] these anomalies have led to an enquiry by the Law Commission into the subject of matrimonial proceedings in the magistrates' courts and the publication of a working paper.[2] The working paper became available after we had put our own conclusions in draft, but we were gratified to find that the expert body responsible for it had on the fundamental points reached conclusions similar to our own. Two investigations proceeding from different starting points and informed by different concerns have thus independently arrived at the same terminus. The working paper, it should be noted, is dealing with the reform of the magisterial law on the basis that the two jurisdictions will continue to exist side by side, and not in the context of a proposal for a family court. But, in dealing with the reform of the substantive law, one set of recommendations is to a considerable extent applicable to the two situations, and we are therefore content in the first instance to state the working party's salient recommendations.

4.367 The working party recommend that husbands and wives should be put on the same footing in respect of the obligation to maintain and that:

> the distinction between the formulation of the obligation to maintain in the divorce and social security law and that in the magistrates' court law . . . can no longer be maintained. The time has come, we suggest, when the law should recognise the duty of each spouse to support the other. . . .[3]

4.368 On the basis of a fully reciprocal obligation to maintain, the working party (dealing always with the summary jurisdiction) next recommend that:

> the principal ground upon which a court should have power to order maintenance should be failure by one of the parties to the marriage to provide such maintenance for the other party or for any children as is reasonable in all the circumstances.[4]

4.369 In addition to this principal ground, the working party recommend two other circumstances in which the magistrates' courts should be able to make a maintenance order: that the respondent has behaved in such a way that the applicant cannot reasonably be expected to live with the respondent; or that the respondent is in desertion.[5]

---

1 Quoted in paragraph 4.339 above.

2 Working Paper No 53, *op cit.*

3 *Ibid*, paragraph 34.

4 *Ibid*, paragraph 35.

5 *Ibid*, paragraph 44. The proposal is also made (paragraph 70) that the magistrates should be given power to make a non-molestation order for the protection of a wife who fears violence from her husband. We commented on the absence of such a power in paragraph 4.345 above.

4.370   One thus arrives at the position that in a reformed magistrates' jurisdiction the three simple grounds for an order proposed by the working party would replace the dozen or so (the number depends on the method of counting)[1] offence-oriented grounds, accumulated over the last century, which are now operative in that jurisdiction.

4.371   The working paper then goes on to consider what factors, given proof by an applicant of one or other of the three grounds for an order, the magistrates ought to be required or allowed to take into account in determining whether or not to make an order, and, if making one, for what amount. They divide this topic into the consideration of factors connected with conduct and factors other than conduct.

4.372   We have ourselves traced in detail[2] the discrepancies which have arisen as between the divorce and the magisterial jurisdictions in the law governing the assessment of maintenance. The divorce court now operates under the Matrimonial Causes Act 1973 which sets out a detailed code of considerations (repeated from the Act of 1970, which first made them law) which the court has to take into account when fixing provision, whereas the magistrates operate under the formula of awarding what is " reasonable " in the circumstances, as amplified by a voluminous body of case law evolved over the period when the principles for awarding maintenance were much the same in both jurisdictions. Adverting to this situation, the working paper, in dealing with the factors other than conduct which the magistrates should take into account, suggests that, following the pattern set by the Act of 1970, these should be specified. It states:

> The principles contained in the 1970 Act, because they deal with the termination of marriage, are not wholly appropriate; but we suggest that the court should have regard to the following:
>
> (a) the income, earning capacity, property and other financial resources of each of the parties; and
>
> (b) the financial needs, obligations and responsibilities of each of the parties.[3]

4.373   In considering how the conduct of the applicant should be permitted to affect the determination, the working paper first proposes the abolition of the rule which at present, in the magistrates' court, bars relief to a wife who has committed adultery:[4]

> We can see no justification nowadays for a court's being bound to refuse to make a maintenance order in favour of an otherwise deserving wife because she has committed a single act of adultery; the more so since adultery is not a bar to an award of maintenance in divorce proceedings.[5]

---

[1] They are set out in the second footnote to Section 5, paragraph 4.62 above.

[2] See Sections 4 and 7 above, *passim*.

[3] Working Paper, *op cit*, paragraph 56.

[4] This bar is discussed in Section 5 above.

[5] Working Paper, *op cit*, paragraph 45.

4.374 In dealing, however, with the wider aspects of the effect of conduct, the working paper is (while leaving the questions open) equivocal in its discussion of whether, and if so how, the principle in *Wachtel v Wachtel*[1] can be made to operate in the magistrates' jurisdiction.[2] For ourselves, we would regard this as both possible and entirely desirable; so that were we concerned in this Section with the reform of the magistrates' jurisdiction rather than with its disappearance, we should have felt obliged to analyse the discussion in the working paper with a view to resolving it in favour of that conclusion. As it is, however, we think that it is beyond argument that in a family court the effect of conduct on financial orders, at whatever level these are made, must be the subject of a uniform policy; and, for reasons that have been sufficiently discussed elsewhere, we think that this policy should be the one that is embodied in Wachtel's case.

4.375 The working paper is concerned entirely with the reform of the summary jurisdiction. If its discussion on the effect of conduct is taken as being resolved in favour of the Wachtel principle, then we would agree that the working paper sets out the essential terms of the law required by a jurisdiction to which spouses refer for a remedy short of one that will terminate their marriage, and which is consistent with the pattern and spirit of the law which the superior jurisdiction now applies when terminating a marriage and making consequential financial provision.

4.376 But in the family court there will still be a need for both kinds of remedy. The family court will continue to provide for cases in which the applicant needs relief short of divorce, either because he or she cannot establish irretrievable breakdown, or does not, for whatever reason it may be, seek a divorce even although irretrievable breakdown could be established. The proposals so far discussed would be perfectly suitable[3] to govern this part of the jurisdiction of the family court. They would operate to enable applicants for such relief to obtain it in the appropriate tier pursuant to laws and procedures which gave rise to none of the anomalies and options to which we have previously referred, and which were consistent with the policies inherent in the new law of divorce which the family court would be applying in another part of its jurisdiction.

4.377 The working paper further discusses what kind of financial orders the magistrates in a reformed jurisdiction should be entitled to make. At present, the magistrates can order maintenance only by way of periodical payments, whereas the divorce court can order transfer or settlement of property, lump sums, and secured periodical payments as well as periodical payments.[4] Transfer and settlement of property are inappropriate except upon the termination of a marriage. The working paper does suggest that it would be useful for the magistrates to have the power to order lump sum payments. It takes the contrary view, however, as regards secured periodical payments, for the reason:

> There is no suitable organisation in the magistrates' courts for seeing that security is provided, as there is in the divorce court . . . . This consideration

---

[1] The case is discussed in Section 4 above.
[2] Working Paper, *op cit*, paragraphs 46–55.
[3] Subject to the reservation regarding the formula for assessment to which we advert in paragraph 4.379, item 7, below.
[4] See Section 9 above.

has weighed with us more than the argument that most people who use the magistrates' courts have not sufficient means to provide security; we wish to make it possible for a more general use of the magistrates' courts by all classes of the community.[1]

4.378   In the family court, where all the necessary organisation would be available, this objection would not apply.   We consider, therefore, that the full range of orders should, in the family court, be available when financial relief is granted either within or upon the termination of marriage, or in affiliation proceedings, subject only to the suitability of the particular type of order to the circumstances of the case.[2]

Our proposals

4.379   We can now very shortly summarise our conclusions on how the defects of the matrimonial law as applied in the magistrates' courts, and the tensions which exist between it and the modern law of divorce and financial provision, would be resolved in the family court:

(1) the whole of the matrimonial jurisdiction of the magistrates should be abolished;

(2) the family court, in which the magistrates would play a vital role, should provide financial relief for spouses and their children otherwise than in connection with the termination of marriage, and also in affiliation proceedings;

(3) the grounds for such relief in the matrimonial cases should be failure to maintain, desertion, and behaviour by the respondent such that the applicant cannot reasonably be expected to live with the respondent;

(4) there should be no absolute bars to relief sought on any of these grounds;

(5) the court should be entitled to take conduct into account, but only on the same basis as it does in divorce, namely, only in circumstances where the applicant's own behaviour has been so obviously and grossly blameworthy that it would offend justice to ignore it;

(6) in making financial provision as between parties who remain married, or for their children, the court should be empowered to order lump sum payments and secured maintenance, as well as unsecured maintenance; the same choice of remedy should be available in affiliation cases;

(7) the court should be given specific guidance as to the factors to be taken into account when assessing the amount of financial orders of the above description.

However, these recommendations are insufficient to deal with the question of the assessment of financial orders in the family court, either within marriage, upon its termination or in connection with affiliation proceedings.   Either under the scheme for administrative orders proposed in Section 12 above, or

---

[1] Working Paper, *op cit.* paragraph 58.

[2] See Part 5, Section 7, for the way in which we recommend that responsibility for financial questions should be divided between the court and the authority administering the guaranteed maintenance allowance we propose.

after the introduction of guaranteed maintenance allowance pursuant to our recommendations in Part 5, special problems will arise as to the relationship between the public provision of benefit and the assessment of court orders. We deal with these problems in their appropriate place.

Further comment on the working paper

The analogy of the " casualty clearing stations "

4.380 In the light of our general agreement with the conclusions and recommendations of the working paper, we now turn to comment upon a significant difference between us in our analysis of the matrimonial jurisdiction of the magistrates' courts. We discuss this difference because it is fundamental to our approach to the reconstruction of the jurisdiction and to our concept of a family court. The working paper accepts that, in origin and in operation, the divorce and magistrates' jurisdictions serve different social classes,[1] but it immediately blurs the implications of this conclusion by creating a further distinction to the effect that the superior jurisdiction deals with irretrievable breakdowns, whereas the summary jurisdiction handles breakdowns which are not irretrievable. The working paper asserts that the Act of 1895[2] constituted:

> a code of matrimonial relief designed to deal with the situation where matrimonial breakdown had occurred but was not irretrievable, and to provide relief before it became irretrievable.[3]

4.381 We think that this is a seriously mistaken interpretation of the history which we have set out in Appendix 5. The working paper quotes the results of the research[4] which estimates that resort to the magistrates is followed by divorce in about half the cases and observes that:

> even in those cases the possibility of a subsequent divorce may well not be in the applicant's mind when relief is first applied for from the magistrates.[5]

The working paper maintains that:

> there is a clear contrast between the magistrates' jurisdiction and that exercised by the divorce court under the 1969 and 1970 Acts. The magistrates' jurisdiction is *normally* exercised at a stage earlier than irretrievable breakdown . . . Indeed, the marriage may only temporarily have run into difficulties,[6]

and concludes that:

> the divorce court exercises its powers to make a maintenance order in respect of a party to a marriage principally on the basis that it has terminated the marriage either by divorce or by judicial separation or by a decree of nullity. But when a matrimonial case comes before the magistrates, *the marriage may not yet have irretrievably broken down and may never do so; and even if it has, this is usually incapable of proof at such an early stage.*[7]

---

[1] Working Paper, *op cit*, paragraphs 18–20.

[2] Referred to in Appendix 5, Section 3.

[3] Working Paper, *op cit*, paragraph 10.

[4] See Section 6, paragraph 4.81, above.

[5] Working Paper, *op cit*, paragraph 19.

[6] *Ibid*, paragraph 24 (our italics).

[7] *Ibid*, paragraph 29 (our italics).

4.382   These arguments that magistrates' courts deal with marriage break-downs that have not yet become irretrievable lead the working party to conclude that their function today is to provide first aid in a marital casualty clearing station:

> The role of the magistrates' court in dealing with those involved in matrimonial breakdown may perhaps be illustrated by comparing it with a casualty clearing station.   All the casualties of marriage can be brought to the magistrates' court.[1]   Some are clearly mortal; they should go on to be laid to rest by proceedings in the divorce court; some are serious, being more likely than not to end in final breakdown; some however will respond to local treatment and may well recover completely; others are trivial, requiring no more than sympathetic handling and encouragement.[2]

The analogy refuted

4.383   We think the working party has allowed itself to be misled concerning the actual role of magistrates' courts in matrimonial breakdown by the attractions of a medico-military analogy.   We have assembled compelling evidence to demonstrate that the very existence and persistence of the dual jurisdiction, and of the attitudes and institutions stemming from it, account for the presence in magistrates' courts of many very poor folk who possess neither knowledge nor expectation of any other legal cure for their marital ills.   Nor is the analogy compelling when we find that two thirds of the casualties on the books in January 1966 were to be found there in July 1971, that nearly half of the discharges during this period had been patients for ten years or more at the time of their discharge, and that on 1 July 1971 there were some 58,000 magistrates' orders in force which were ten years old, or older.[3]   We doubt whether many clearing stations would find this a satisfactory work record.

4.384   Happily, our disagreement with the working party over the present role of magistrates' courts does not extend to the future of the jurisdiction. The working party thought it:

> prudent to bear in mind the possibility that in the not too distant future there may be introduced a " family court " which deals with all matters . . . (and we therefore attempted) . . . to formulate proposals for a reformed family law which, while it could be applied within the context of the present jurisdictional framework, would also be suited to a unified system of family courts to which all family problems requiring adjudication would be brought.[4]

4.385   We are pleased that the working party has in mind a unified family court, such as we recommend, as a possibility in the not too distant future. We also agree, as we have already said, on the need in any family court system for a jurisdiction to provide remedies for evanescent marital troubles as speedily as possible.   Thus, it follows that such facilities must be available within the structure of the family court where, for many purposes, they will no doubt be located in the first tier.   The difference between this and the present structure is that these facilities will be part of a coherent design which ensures that a

---

1 This statement is true but unrealistic.   Only the casualties of marriage suffered by working class people are in fact brought to this court.

2 Working Paper, *op cit*, paragraph 24.

3 See Section 6 above.

4 Working Paper, *op cit*, paragraph 6.

uniform set of legal rules will apply to all citizens in accordance with the principle we have stated. The working party, as we have already noted, express their

> wish to make it possible for a more general use of the magistrates' courts by all classes of the community.[1]

But it is in the family court, shaped by our criteria, that the values and objectives towards which the working party are here reaching will be realised.

DURATION OF ORDERS

The problem

4.386 We now have to turn to the problem of the duration of support orders[2] when the parties remain married to each other. We have stressed the criticism of the present jurisdiction of the magistrates that it serves as a permanent encouragement to one section of the population to substitute a continuous and unresolved state of breakdown, which has many evil consequences, for the advantages which obtaining freedom to marry again would in most cases confer on themselves, their children and the community at large.

4.387 We refer again at this stage in our discussion to the Gorell Commission, which reported strongly in 1912 against orders unlimited in time:

> We feel, after the voluminous evidence which we have taken from all parts of the country, that it is not right to leave the administration of powers which may produce the practical though not the legal dissolution of the tie of marriage, to courts whose duties and experience are mainly confined to dealing with petty offences . . . . We consider that the powers of the courts of summary jurisdiction to make orders, which have the permanent effect of a decree of judicial separation, should be abolished.[3]

The Commission went on to recommend that:

> no separation order of such courts should be continued for a period of more than two years from the date of the original order separating the parties, at the expiration of which time the order and continuing orders, if any, should determine, unless, before such expiration, the party obtaining the original order apply to the High Court . . . .[4]

4.388 The shadow of the Gorell Commission falls across the pages of the evidence which the Magistrates' Association gave to the Law Commission in 1969 in a memorandum on domestic courts. The association observed that " unlike a decree granted after a petition for divorce . . . there is an absence of finality " in proceedings before magistrates:

> To hold open the possibility of reconciliation there would be some advantage in providing that matrimonial orders should have a limited validity of, say, one year. After this the complainant (husband or wife) would have to apply for it to be continued either indefinitely or for a fixed period, say, for example, until the children have reached 16 years of age or finished full-time education. The details of this " temporary " and " final " order procedure would have to be worked out.[5]

---

[1] Working Paper, *op cit*, paragraph 58.
[2] The same principles apply in relation to administrative orders such as we propose in Section 12 and in Part 5, Section 7, as to court orders.
[3] *Op cit*, paragraphs 141 and 143. See also Appendix 5, Section 3.
[4] *Ibid*, paragraph 162.
[5] The Magistrates' Association: *Annual Report 1968–1969*, page 51, paragraph 19.

4.389 We agree with the intention behind the Magistrates' Association's proposal to limit the currency of summary maintenance orders. Indeed, we at one stage ourselves considered the notion of fixing a maximum duration beyond which the beneficiary of the order would be required to petition for divorce or judicial separation as the condition of a continuing entitlement to maintenance. Upon reflection, however, we have concluded that this would be an unacceptably draconian method of persuading a spouse to give proper consideration after a period of separation to the relative merits of divorce as against permanent separation within marriage. Many of the circumstances have altered since the Gorell Commission reported. At that time, the commission would have preferred to recommend the complete abolition of the magistrates' jurisdiction, but drew back because it provided " the only remedy within reach of the very poor ".[1] Today, the legal aid scheme ensures that the legal remedies of all courts with a family jurisdiction are within the reach of the very poor, so that it is less because of the inability to pay legal fees than by reason of such correlates of poverty as ignorance of the law, or fear of its process and its agents, that so many of the poor fail to take advantage of their rights.[2]

Objectives of the family court conference

4.390 We have therefore aimed at devising a procedure which will promote our policy objectives by creating proper opportunities for the parties to a long-term separation to give deliberate consideration to their whole situation in the light of sympathetic and informed advice, while they remain entirely free, in the event, to choose their own course.

4.391 Two sorts of cases will arise: those where a spouse (almost always a wife) has a maintenance order from the court, and those where she is receiving supplementary benefit, or, under our later proposals, guaranteed maintenance allowance, and there is a liable person against whom the relevant authority has made an administrative order. We would expect court maintenance orders to become fewer once the guaranteed maintenance allowance authority is operating, but in both sorts of case, one of four courses becomes open after the parties have been separated for two years, at which time they can under the present divorce law proceed for a consensual divorce and by when in many cases they are in a position to give mature consideration to their marital future in the light of all the circumstances which have led up to and succeed the separation. The parties could simply remain apart without any maintenance, supplementary benefit or guaranteed maintenance allowance being paid. Secondly, they could get divorced, obtaining such ancillary orders for financial provision as might be agreed or made by the court or the administrative authority. Thirdly, they could petition for judicial separation, again obtaining ancillary relief. Finally, they could remain informally separated under a maintenance or administrative order.

---

[1] *Op cit*, paragraphs 143 and 144.

[2] See, on this subject, the materials cited in the footnote to paragraph 4.24, also Section 8, paragraphs 4.124–4.126, above, and *Separated Spouses, op cit*, chapter 8 (" How wives and husbands perceive the courts ").

4.392 It would be an unacceptable invasion of privacy and freedom to bring pressure to bear on any spouse to choose any one of these courses in preference to another. At the same time, we are anxious that spouses living in permanent separation from each other should be aware of the different courses which are open to them, and be given help, if they want it, to make up their minds in a considered fashion as to which to choose, rather than to drift on indefinitely in passivity and ignorance, perpetuating undesirable conditions and creating a bleak future as often as not for the adults and children in two families.

Holding the family court conference

4.393 Accordingly we recommend that two years after a maintenance order or (in connection with payments of supplementary benefit or guaranteed maintenance allowance) an administrative order has been made in a subsisting marriage, the circumstances of the parties should be examined at a conference to be held at the family court. One purpose of the conference will be to consider whether, in the case of a court order, it remains appropriate in the light of current needs and means of the parties.[1] In this way life might be breathed into the variation procedure which, as we have demonstrated, at present fails to achieve its object. All interested parties will be invited to the conference, which will be organised and conducted by the court welfare service, but it will be made clear that no one is under any obligation to attend or will be penalised if they do not. This conference will be treated as a formal occasion, but will be conducted informally, with the chief purpose of encouraging the parties to a marriage which has remained broken for two years to consider their matrimonial future.[2] The resources of the court will be deployed in order to ensure that people have all the legal, social and financial information and assistance necessary to make rational choices. The conference, which might run to several sessions, will seek to place poor and ill-informed people in as good a position to make reasoned judgment as are those who can afford to pay for the professional advice of solicitors, bank managers and accountants. In addition, those who wished would be directed to agencies where they could explore the further possibility of reconciliation or receive other help from social work agencies. We think that this would be the best way to overcome the present disadvantages suffered by many of those who now turn to the family jurisdiction of the magistrates' courts. In the case of those who chose to take no further action, provision would be made for further conferences at regular intervals to ensure that the amounts of orders were properly examined and varied if necessary.

4.394 An indication of the results which might flow from the use of the conference procedure can be obtained from the numbers who sought different types of matrimonial remedies in the divorce jurisdiction in 1970. In that year there were 71,939 petitions for divorce, 231 petitions for judicial separation, and 143 originating summonses under section 22 of the Matrimonial Causes

---

[1] Administrative orders will be subject to automatic review at fixed intervals: see, for example, paragraph 4.249.

[2] In appropriate cases, mothers with affiliation orders would be invited to the conference but we should expect that most of them will have received the court's advice and help at a much earlier stage.

Act 1965 alleging wilful neglect to maintain.[1] We can see no reason why women who now go to the magistrates for maintenance orders, or are compelled to become clients of the Supplementary Benefits Commission, should not, *if they were as well advised as those who go to the divorce jurisdiction*, at least show a strong tendency to distribute themselves among the choices for legal action in roughly the same proportions.

FURTHER RECOMMENDATIONS OF LAW
Powers as regards children

4.395 The law regarding the definition of " child " under different family law statutes and regarding the orders that can be made in different circumstances regarding children is badly confused. We welcome the anlaysis of this branch of the law made in the Law Commission's working paper.[2] The working party propose the rationalisation of these provisions, with the ultimate view of a uniform child custody and maintenance statute. We agree with all of the proposals made in the working paper on this topic, and think that no useful purpose would be served in these circumstances in printing here the commentary we had ourselves written upon the legislation affecting children before we had the benefit of the working paper.

Taxation anomalies

4.396 Some twenty years ago, a practice grew up among High Court registrars of assisting the payers and recipients of maintenance after divorce to avoid taxation by spreading the total amount between separate orders for the wife and each of her children. The order for payment direct to a child made him an ordinary taxable individual, entitled to a single person's tax relief. The Finance Act 1969 put a temporary end to the practice by requiring the aggregation of the incomes of parents and children for tax purposes, but the former situation has now been restored by the Finance Act 1971. Even if she were in a financial position to benefit, a woman in receipt of maintenance under the order of a magistrates' court (of potentially unlimited amount since 1968) cannot advantage herself of the facility because the magistrates' courts cannot make an order payable directly to a child. Whatever arguments may be deployed for or against this method of tax avoidance, there can be none in favour of excluding men and women paying and receiving maintenance under the orders of magistrates' courts from the facility. It should be established as a principle that all payers and recipients of maintenance under administrative orders or the orders of the family court are put on the same footing in respect of their tax liabilities.

THE SITTINGS OF THE FAMILY COURT, BUILDINGS AND OFFICES

4.397 The Magistrates' Court Act 1952 provides that:
> the business of magistrates' courts shall, so far as is consistent with the due dispatch of business, be arranged in such a manner as may be requisite for separating the hearing and determination of domestic proceedings from other business.[3]

---

[1] *Civil Judicial Statistics*, 1970, Cmnd 4271, 1971, Table 10. We have taken the year 1970 in order to avoid comparison with the exceptional situation resulting from the first year's operation in 1971 of the Divorce Reform Act 1969. (It may be noted also that the section 22 procedure in the Act of 1965 has now been replaced by the Matrimonial Causes Act 1973, section 27.)

[2] Paragraphs 117–166.

[3] Section 57(1).

4.398 The Royal (Morton) Commission on Marriage and Divorce reported in 1956 that:

> taking the country as a whole, the present arrangements for hearing matrimonial cases are not satisfactory. In our view it is essential that there should be a complete separation of matrimonial business from the other business of the courts.[1]

4.399 Twelve years later the position had not improved. The Graham Hall Committee reported that:

> Many courts arrange for domestic proceedings to be held in a building separate from the ordinary criminal court and for the collecting office to be located in the same place. In many others, however, arrangements of this kind will not become practicable until out-of-date premises can be replaced. The fault is not always attributable to the inadequate accommodation available. We understand that some magistrates are reluctant to organise their sittings in such a way as to enable domestic proceedings to be heard on a separate day. This may on occasion be because they are reluctant to sit in the afternoon as well as the morning, or because they are unwilling or unable to sit on more than one day a week. The evidence we received made it clear how unwilling women often are for their matrimonial breakdowns or the determination of the paternity of their children to be a subject of judicial proceedings at all, and how this unwillingness is increased when courts have a criminal atmosphere. One large court with an inadequate and out-of-date court building was vividly described to us in which the parties to both criminal and domestic proceedings had to assemble in a large, crowded and cheerless waiting room which was the only place available for them to arrange last minute consultations with their legal advisers. We were told that similar conditions prevail in other courts. There is little doubt of the adverse effect conditions like these have on parties to domestic proceedings in many parts of the country.[2]

4.400 The evidence which we have received indicates that many husbands and wives and unmarried mothers and their witnesses go on having to mix to their distaste and embarrassment hugger-mugger with criminals and delinquent motorists. Everyone agrees that this is wrong, but it can only be altered by building new courts or by transferring family law matters to the buildings of other courts exercising a civil jurisdiction. There is little hope of a solution through the immediate provision of new buildings. Moreover, an examination of published materials concerning new court buildings suggests that no thought whatever has been given to the physical environment in which family matters should be dealt with. We see no alternative for the present to housing the family court at its local level in the county court buildings. In some centres, it might also be possible to designate particular magistrates' courts' buildings for the exclusive use of the family court. (An example in London would be the Wells Street court.) We recognise that buildings for the family court will be very difficult to arrange and will depend upon how important improvements in this branch of justice are rated by government.

4.401 One possibility for making scarce space go further would be to hold sittings of the family court in the evenings or at weekends. We have elsewhere discussed the hardship which may be caused to those who use the summary jurisdiction by the court and its offices being closed at times when they themselves are free to attend. We appreciate that to open a matrimonial court out of ordinary hours is likely to present severe staffing problems and to be

---

[1] *Op cit*, paragraph 1079.
[2] *Op cit*, paragraph 112.

inconvenient to the professional advisers. However, we think it is important to make some progress in this direction. This would do more than serve the interests of the litigants. It would have a healthy effect on recruitment to the lay bench. We believe that if the family court could find ways and means of opening on, say, Saturday mornings, this would attract a new and most desirable kind of magistrate to the bench from among young wives and family men who have the appropriate talent and interest, but whose commitments bar them under the present arrangements from making their contribution to the public service.

PROCEDURES IN THE FAMILY COURT

Formality

4.402 There has been a movement in recent times towards making the courts seem less formidable to the citizens who have to use them. The most recently established court, the National Industrial Relations Court, provides an instructive example of present attitudes. At the first sitting in December 1971, its President made a statement about his court's method of working. He said that the use of the word " court " was:

> entirely accurate but at the same time might carry a misleading impression . . . in that in the context of industrial relations traditional court attitudes and procedures are inappropriate.

He commented that uncertainty about proper modes of address often caused litigants and witnesses considerable anxiety in the ordinary courts, and said that his court would not insist upon the adoption of a particular usage because its " interest lies in the substance and not in the form ". The President wished his court to combine sympathetic informality with a defined and orderly procedure but to be:

> completely flexible and to devise special procedures in any case in which the interests of the parties or the public would be better served thereby.

Hearings would not take place:

> in surroundings which in any way resemble a traditional courtroom. The members of the court would wear no robes and there was no bench or witness box. The members' chairs are on a portion of the room which has been raised by about nine inches solely in order that they can see and be seen. The parties and their advisers would sit at tables and would probably address the court seated . . . . Similarly witnesses could sit or, as they wished, stand . . . . The court would not hesitate in appropriate cases to modify or completely depart from that normal procedure, if the interests of the parties or the public so required.[1]

4.403 The form of procedure thus devised to handle legal disputes about industrial relations is very similar to that which has been urged during recent years by some commentators upon the law regulating family relations. They

---

[1] These extracts from Sir John Donaldson's statement have been taken from *The New Law Journal*, 9 December 1971, pages 1101–1102. In the same issue the editor comments (pages 1085–1086), " On almost every feature of the Industrial Court's practice and procedure, the question inescapably arises: if the new court's *modus operandi* is specially advantageous in terms of doing justice more effectively and surely, how can so different and in many respects totally contradictory a life-style be resolutely maintained in the doing of justice in the ordinary courts? ".

have urged the benefits of informality in the form of discarding robes and wigs and of seeking to achieve a cosy atmosphere through the adoption of new furniture and seating arrangements in the court.

4.404 We are impressed by the unanimity of the commentators in favour of greater informality in proceedings in family matters. But we are impressed, too, by the lack of studies of the effect of legal ritual upon citizens who use the courts. We do not know how representative a figure is the trade union leader who observed of the Industrial Relations Court that, if his members are to be sent to prison for contempt of court, he desires it to be done by a judge properly robed in scarlet and ermine. On these aspects of court procedure, we think that decisions should be delayed until they can be based on knowledge of what will best satisfy the citizen user's desire for fairness and dignity in the determination of matrimonial cases.

Inquisitorial—accusatorial

4.405 Another much canvassed procedural question is how far the hearings in the family court should be inquisitorial rather than adversary in nature. In the accusatorial or adversary form of procedure, as it characterises our civil litigation, the parties not only choose the issues which form the subject matter of the dispute, but also determine what evidence shall be brought before the court. The court has no right and no means to act as its own fact-gatherer. In the inquisitorial form of procedure, the court is not confined to acting as a referee, but may, so far as it has the means, take steps of its own to inform itself of the facts and circumstances it considers it ought to know in order to make a just determination. But the two forms of procedure are not, in truth, mutually exclusive. In the divorce jurisdiction, the court has always been charged with the duty of being " satisfied " that it can grant relief, which must involve, in appropriate cases, a duty to enquire into matters as to which the parties themselves may not be in dispute. So again, in matters affecting custody of and access to children the court has to have regard to the child's paramount interests, which is a matter which the views of the parties, even to the extent that they coincide, do not determine. The proper balance of the two forms of procedure in the family court should, in our view, be determined by the following considerations. It is desirable that the court itself should not come into the arena. To the extent that the court requires assistance by way of investigation or expert assessment of circumstances which it considers material, this function should be discharged by ancillary services which are attached to or can be called upon by the court, but whose personnel are not themselves members of the court. The bench of the family court is to consist only of judges, professional or lay, and experts or assessors should not be constituents. On the other hand, the bench as so constituted should, in every aspect of its jurisdiction, be able to call upon the aid of a competent person to make social and welfare enquiries and reports.

Welfare reports

4.406 Since 1958, the law has given special protection to children whose parents are involved in certain matrimonial proceedings. Section 41 of the Matrimonial Causes Act 1973 now provides that the court shall not make absolute a decree of divorce or nullity, or make a decree of judicial separation unless it declares itself satisfied, by order, that there are no children of the family or that such children are all named in the order and that, unless it is impracticable for the parties, arrangements for the welfare of every child so named " have been made and are satisfactory or are the best that can be devised in the circumstances ". The children protected by this section are those under 16 or undergoing full-time education who are either the children of the parties or have been treated as children of the family by the parties. The importance attached to this protection is underlined by the fact that it is expressly enacted that a decree made absolute where this order has not been made will be void. Judges are therefore under a duty to enquire about arrangements proposed for children. In most cases, they will satisfy themselves by reading the petition and questioning the parties in court. If they are not satisfied or if they feel uneasy, they can obtain a report from welfare officers who are attached to all divorce courts.

4.407 A study undertaken by Mr J C Hall on behalf of the Law Commission in 1968 contains the only published empirical information about the working of this system. Mr Hall questioned a sample of judges, registrars, divorce court welfare officers and local authority childrens' officers. He found that:

> among welfare officers in the provinces, there is a fairly widely held view that courts should order enquiries in a higher proportion of cases than at present before approving the arrangements.[1]

Nevertheless, Mr Hall's final conclusion was that:

> in general there does not seem to be any need, as far as the majority of courts are concerned, for reports to be ordered in a greater proportion of cases than occur at present.[2]

Given the high importance which we attach to provisions for securing the welfare of children, we recommend that courts should examine their existing procedures in order to ensure that the statutory provisions are fully implemented and that the courts have all the information they need in reaching their judicial decision. This recommendation will apply to, but need not wait upon, the introduction of the family court.

Publicity

4.408 Similar provisions apply to restrict publicity for matrimonial hearings in all the courts. The general public, but not the press, is excluded. The press (which, in fact, hardly ever attends magistrates' hearings) is restricted in what it may publish to names, addresses and occupations of the parties and witnesses; the grounds of the application, and a concise statement of the charges, defences and counter-charges; submissions of law; the decision of the court; and any observations made by the court in giving its decision.[3] However, this seeming

---

[1] Law Commission Working Paper No 15, *Family Law: Arrangements for the Care and Upbringing of Children* (*Section 33 of the Matrimonial Causes Act 1965*), Report by Mr John Hall of St John's College, Cambridge, 6 February 1968, page 25.

[2] *Ibid*, page 40.

[3] Domestic proceedings before the magistrates, including the regulation of publicity for such proceedings, are the subject of the Magistrates' Courts Act 1952, sections 56–62. The corresponding provisions covering publicity for proceedings in the divorce jurisdiction are to be found in the Judicial Proceedings (Regulation of Reports) Act 1926, and the Domestic and Appellate Proceedings (Restriction of Publicity) Act 1968.

equality established between the two jurisdictions is illusory, because a substantial number of matters which are dealt with by the magistrates in open court are heard in chambers in the High Court and county court jurisdictions, that is to say, in complete privacy and behind closed doors. In particular, all of the various sorts of application which can be made for financial provision, or which concern custody of children or related matters, are dealt with in the divorce jurisdictions by the judge or by the registrar sitting in privacy; and this is so even when an issue arises concerning the conduct of the parties. This does more than provide a guarantee against publicity which is lacking in corresponding cases in the summary jurisdiction; the known fact that the proceedings are " in chambers " helps to quieten the mind of the parties and to produce a more relaxed atmosphere of trial in the superior courts than often exists in domestic proceedings before the magistrates. In the family court, both the rules of procedure and the practice of the court will ensure that there is consistency and uniformity in the provision for publicity or privacy for the proceedings of the court. In general, we would recommend an extension of the chambers practice now operative in the High Court to all hearings in the family court which the public interest did not decisively demand should be conducted in open court.

Registrar and clerk

4.409   Much of the business in chambers to which we have just referred is conducted in the High Court by the divorce registrars in London or the district registrars in the provinces, and by the registrars of the divorce county courts. These officers of the court therefore combine important judicial duties with the administration of their registry. A High Court registrar will deal at first instance with disputes over matrimonial property involving very large sums and complicated matters of accountancy and law.[1] The clerk to magistrates has no judicial powers at all.[2] In the family court structure there would be need of officials discharging a combination of duties of the kind now discharged by the High Court registrar and the magistrates' clerk. We would look to the evolution of a career structure within the family court for officials carrying this large burden of responsibilities. Within such a career structure, it would be desirable, and might be possible, to provide training in the welfare as well as the strictly legal aspects of the work of the family court.

---

[1] But the registrar has no jurisdiction to grant a decree of divorce even in an undefended case, a task which has been described as " an easy open and shut operation, hardly deserving judicial attention ": A Samuels: ' Family Courts;—the Future ', in *New Law Journal*, 1972, page 135. The late Lord Asquith of Bishopstone made the same point even more unkindly when he remarked that the trial of an undefended divorce was a job which Caligula would have entrusted to his horse.

[2] This can be the cause of much inconvenience in cases where parties have to incur the trouble and expense of taking even an agreed order to the bench for its approval. Elsewhere, we have described the procedure in the magistrates' courts for variation of maintenance orders as virtually a dead letter. It might be infused with some degree of vitality if the clerk himself had the power to vary a maintenance order with the consent of the parties. Occasions also arise in the magistrates' jurisdiction when the parties need a consent order to record their matrimonial situation for the purposes of the revenue or housing authorities, and we can see no good reason why the magistrates' clerk should not himself be put on the commission so as to facilitate the cheap and expeditious satisfaction of needs of this kind.

COURT RECORDS

4.410　Good records are essential for the proper administration of justice, and particularly so in family matters when the parties may resort to the court on several occasions.　Unofficial and official enquiries have concluded that the quality of records of proceedings in magistrates' courts is uneven.　The authors of *Separated Spouses* found that:

> in a few courts the records were excellent; but in many, they were defective. Court records vary in type and quality from court to court in a manner not compatible with the proper administration of justice.[1]

The Graham Hall Committee observed that:

> . . . the records of proceedings in magistrates' courts vary considerably from court to court.　The notes of evidence taken in some courts include information (about the means of the parties) but not in others.　Even when it is included, the notes themselves may be untranscribed shorthand and difficult of access . . . we recommend that, at the very least, it should be mandatory that the information obtained about the resources and liabilities of the parties should be clearly recorded in a standard form and kept with the order . . . .[2]

The Payne Committee recommended:

> the use universally throughout magistrates' courts in England and Wales of a prescribed form of questionnaire to ensure consistent and thorough examination of means in all magistrates' courts . . . .[3]

4.411　We recommend that special attention be paid to keeping full and standardised records of all summary proceedings in the first tier of the family court.　We regard the improvement of such records as not the least of the advantages which will flow from the establishment of the family court.

RECOMMENDED IMPROVEMENTS IN THE OFFICIAL STATISTICS

4.412　Court records serve purposes beyond the day-to-day administration of justice.　They are also the main source from which statistical information about the working of the legal system can be compiled.　Between 1894 and 1914, Sir John Macdonell put English legal statistics on to a firm basis and provided them with an illuminating commentary.　After his death in 1921, they deteriorated to their present level.　Fortunately, demographic interests ensured that much data concerning the operation and social results of family law were made available by the Registrar General in his annual publications and thus made good, in some measure, the deficiencies of the *Civil Judicial Statistics*.　These data were derived from the records of the High Court and, after the Matrimonial Causes Act 1967, from the records of the county courts hearing undefended matrimonial causes.　Thus, in matters relating to divorce adequate information has been published regularly for a long time.　Unhappily, the statistics of the matrimonial work of magistrates are very unsatisfactory.

4.413　The first defect of these statistics arises because they still retain in their compilation and presentation all the marks of the criminal associations of that jurisdiction: they are published by the Home Office in the annual

---

[1] *Op cit*, page 189.
[2] *Op cit*, paragraph 223.
[3] *Op cit*, paragraph 1273 and Appendix 6.

Criminal Statistics.[1]   They are presented in a bizarre table, bearing the laconic title " Magistrates' Courts: Certain other proceedings ", in which statistics of the number of applications and orders made in affiliation and matrimonial proceedings are followed by, *inter alia*, the number of applications and orders for the destruction of unsound meat, for the removal of dead bodies and for the forfeiture of indecent photographs.   This table bears annual and eloquent witness to the low official esteem accorded to a jurisdiction which, as we have repeatedly emphasised in our Report, deals almost exclusively with working class marriages.   The recommendation of the Committees on the Age of Majority,[2] on the Criminal Statistics[3] and on Civil Judicial Statistics[4] that information about family proceedings in magistrates' courts should be published in the *Civil Judicial Statistics* was implemented in 1968.   Notwithstanding this, the Home Office continues to publish them in an unchanged Table VI in the *Criminal Statistics*.   We recommend that this objectionable practice cease forthwith.   This would have the further advantage of removing misleading statistics from the *Criminal Statistics*.   A statistical appendix to the report of the Graham Hall Committee revealed that:

> Since 1959 the figures for each category of order published in these volumes (ie in the Table titled " Magistrates' Courts—certain other proceedings ") have included the number of attachment of earnings orders made during the year to enforce substantive orders in that category.[5]

Despite this, the *Criminal Statistics* go on printing the table which contains information about family proceedings in magistrates' courts without warning the reader of the distortion which arises from the inclusion of attachment of earnings orders with the substantive orders in each category.   This carelessness becomes all the more puzzling in the light of the publication since 1968 of tables in the *Civil Judicial Statistics* which distinguish substantive from attachment of earnings orders.[6]

4.414   Furthermore, the present statistics of summary matrimonial proceedings are unreliable and inadequate.   They are compiled today in the same way as in late-Victorian days when an examination of the *Criminal Judicial Statistics*, published with the volume for 1893, pointed to the unreliability of tables compiled from returns made by 191 independent police forces which had not been given adequate instructions to ensure their preparation on a uniform basis.[7]   More than seventy years later, Miss (now Judge) Graham Hall, Chairman of the Committee on Statutory Maintenance Limits, wrote to Chief

---

1 From 1893–1921 they appeared as Table XVI, from 1922–1923 as Table IX, from 1924–1931 as Table XI, from 1932–1934 as Table II, from 1935–1937 as Table XI and in 1938 as Table XXI. They were not published during the war.   They appeared again as Table X from 1946–1948, became Table XII from 1949–1963, and have been Table VI since 1964.

2 Cmnd 3342, 1966, paragraph 185.

3 Cmnd 3448, 1967, paragraph 34.

4 Cmnd 3684, 1968, paragraph 38.

5 *Op cit*, Appendix G, page 102.

6 They appeared as Tables K and L in 1968, as Tables L and M from 1969 to 1971 and as Tables M and N in 1972.   The *Civil Judicial Statistics* are compiled by the Lord Chancellor's Department which must have obtained the data about proceedings in magistrates' courts from the Home Office.

7 C 7725, 1895, page 18.

Master Adams, Chairman of the Committee on Civil Judicial Statistics, to explain how the work of her committee was being hindered by unreliable official statistics:

> The only information published about maintenance orders made by Magistrates' Courts is contained in Table VI of the annual volume of the criminal statistics. This information is confined to the number of applications made and the number of orders resulting from these. Even this information, limited as it is, must be regarded as unreliable. There are approximately 1,000 Magistrates' Courts and this information is returned by police forces whose Statistical Departments have to collect the figures from the individual courts in their area. There appear to be no instructions about the definition of an application and it would seem that the variations between the information provided in respect of different courts are very considerable. The number of applications may in some areas relate to separate summonses (where there are several grounds for complaint in one case, a separate summons may be issued in respect of each ground) and in other areas applications for variation orders may be included as well as those for original orders. You will appreciate, therefore, that such published figures as there are provide no reliable guide for any further studies.

> The existence of 1,000 separate courts, each using local forms for their orders, made the task of seeking information from them almost insuperable; moreover the absence of figures relating to separate courts (as opposed to police districts) made it difficult to find any basis for selecting a representative sample of courts from which to make more limited inquiries.[1]

Unpublished information supplied by the Home Office showed that, in 1966, the success rate of applications in matrimonial proceedings to magistrates' courts varied widely from police district to police district. It was 97 per cent in Liverpool City, 50 per cent in Leeds City and 34 per cent in Birmingham City.[2] Clearly, the national data contained in Table VI of the *Criminal Statistics*, which conceal local variations of this order, must be viewed with suspicion.

4.415 Even if the Home Office statistics were reliable, they would not be useful because they give only the number of applications for orders and the number of orders made. The special study which we commissioned from the Legal Research Unit of the Department of Sociology, Bedford College, University of London, provides an indication of the range of information which could be derived from systematic and uniform record keeping.[3] But we do not here set out the content of an adequate statistical compilation; partly because the Committee on Civil Judicial Statistics has already made detailed recommendations to this end,[4] and partly because we are primarily concerned with demonstrating the importance of ensuring that the new family court is equipped to provide a statistical intelligence service relating to its local tier which will match the range and quality of that already issuing from the courts exercising a divorce jurisdiction. We therefore recommend that a statistical system be devised which will provide annual and integrated data about the work both of the local and of the top tier or tiers of the family court.

4.416 We are gratified by the marked change in opinion about the need for legal statistics which has occurred in the last twenty years. The deficiency in the statistics relating to the exercise of the matrimonial jurisdiction of

---

[1] *Report of the Committee on Civil Judicial Statistics, op cit*, Appendix M, page 60.
[2] *Separated Spouses, op cit*, footnote 3, page 38 and Table 7, page 42.
[3] We print this study as Appendix 7.
[4] *Op cit*, paragraph 103.

magistrates was brought to the notice of the Royal (Morton) Commission on Marriage and Divorce which reported in 1956. The commission thought that:

> There would be some advantages in having fuller statistical information about matrimonial proceedings . . . if this could be readily provided. But we were informed that to collect and tabulate this ir *ormation would involve a good deal of extra work, additional clerical help in many courts and considerable expense. Our conclusion is that, in present circumstances, the value of the additional information would not be sufficient to justify the work and expense involved in obtaining it.[1]

Twelve years later, however, the Committee on Civil Judicial Statistics concluded that the statistics should be improved despite the " restricting factors of limited manpower and limited finance."[2] In a very different field, the Royal (Beeching) Commission on Assizes and Quarter Sessions were so hampered by the lack of statistical information about the caseload of the courts that they were compelled to carry out a special statistical survey,[3] the findings of which were published in a separate report. One result was the establishment of " a comprehensive system for recording and collecting statistics relating to the administration of the courts "[4] which had been re-structured in the light of the recommendations of the Royal Commission. Accordingly, there appeared for the first time in 1973 what will become the annual *Statistics on Judicial Administration*, issued by the Lord Chancellor's Department. Another welcome result is that:

> A Working Party of Civil Judicial Statistics is . . . currently examining the existing publication *Civil Judicial Statistics* in the light both of the Adams Report and of the later recommendations of the Beeching Commission.[5]

4.417 Good court records are essential both for the proper administration of justice and for the compilation of figures relating to the work of the courts in order to provide a measure of their efficiency. But far more important, the doing of justice requires knowledge of the results of its own procedures. Legislators, judges, administrators, critics and citizens must have the knowledge of the social consequences of legal actions without which a democratic society cannot keep its institutions under constant and open scrutiny. Court records and legal statistics cost money; but it is money well spent, for they are an indispensable though humble part of the processes of government in a democracy. Our emphasis on the importance of statistics for the law is not a novel notion spawned in the age of computers. In 1857, a report of the Society for Promoting the Amendment of the Law commented on the paucity of judicial statistics and asserted:

> Such statistics afford the best, if not the only means of noting the practical working of laws and tribunals, of testing the principles of legal reforms, and of estimating the utility of any system of jurisprudence by the testimony of actual fact.[6]

---

1 *Op cit*, paragraph 1153.

2 *Op cit*, paragraph 100.

3 Cmnd 4153, 1969, Foreword, page 17, and Appendix 2, pages 154–155.

4 Julia Whitburn: ' Crown Court Statistics: developments in 1972 ', *Statistical News*, Number 21, May 1973, page 21.9.

5 *Ibid*, page 21.11.

6 Quoted by the Committee on Civil Judicial Statistics, *op cit*, paragraph 9.

We are satisfied that ignorance of the social results of the exercise of matrimonial jurisdiction by magistrates has been a major contributor to the survival of procedures which we have criticised. Nobody knew what happened, and therefore nobody cared.

4.418 We lack the information to make detailed comment on Scottish legal statistics with assurance, although we think that they could be considerably improved. We recommend that the Scottish civil judicial statistics too should be examined when the family court is established, and that the Scottish and English statistics relating to its work be standardised to the maximum extent possible.

4.419 Readers of this Report will recognise the difficulty of separating legal statistics from demographic and social statistics in relation to one-parent families. We therefore go on to consider briefly certain other deficiencies in statistical information on one-parent families which our work has revealed.

4.420 There is no more striking illustration of the gaps in official statistics than the fact that we publish, as Appendix 4, the first official calculation of the total number of one-parent families in Great Britain. It shows how they are distributed among different categories of family breakdown and by the sex of the lone parent and the number of dependent children. This important paper was prepared for us by the Statistics and Research Division of the Department of Health and Social Security, and it sets out in some detail the sources and method of the computation. Before our appointment, the only comparable statistical estimate available to the general public was contained in Mrs Margaret Wynn's pioneering study of *Fatherless Families*.[1] We recommend that such estimates as are provided for 1971 in Appendix 4 be published regularly.

4.421 The Department of Health and Social Security and their predecessors cannot escape criticism for the inadequate and unsystematic statistical data provided in their annual reports (and now in the publication of the Government Statistical Service, *Social Security Statistics*) about recipients of supplementary benefit and the extent of reimbursement of public funds by liable relatives. The extent to which Part 5 of our Report provides new and specially compiled information about the incomes of fatherless families is a measure of the need to improve and standardise the statistics published annually. We recommend that the Department of Health and Social Security should examine their policy in this respect, with the object of providing better and regular series of statistics about the work of the Supplementary Benefits Commission and about the Commission's beneficiaries.

4.422 Our enquiries have made us conscious of the great inconvenience which arises from the frequent difficulty of obtaining comparable statistics for England and Wales and for Scotland. Part 3 of our Report shows that some statistics are available on a Great Britain basis, some exist only for England and Wales whilst separate tables had sometimes to be prepared for us for

---

[1] Michael Joseph, 1964, Chapter 2 and Appendix 1.

Scotland. It would be of benefit, especially to the users of demographic statistics, if all data were provided on a Great Britain basis, with breakdown by country or by region where relevant.

4.423   Finally, we note the wide range of official sources from which information about family matters in Britain must be sought.   At present, these include the annual reviews of the Registrars General for England and Wales and for Scotland, the English and Scottish *Civil Judicial Statistics*, the annual *Social Security Statistics*, the Family Expenditure Survey and several other publications.   We think that great advantage would accrue if one annual publication brought together all the main legal, demographic and social data concerning the family.   Indeed, the Committee on Civil Judicial Statistics expressed " considerable sympathy " for a similar proposal, but felt unable to go beyond the recommendation that the *Civil Judicial Statistics* should contain " a special section devoted to the family ".[1]   We have already drawn attention[2] to the new publication, *Statistics on Judicial Administration*, and we have utilised[3] statistics from the regular annual *Supplement on Abortion* which the Registrar General now prepares.   If judicial administration and abortion are sufficiently important subjects to merit their own publications, we think that the case for an annual volume of family statistics is very strong.   We recommend that the Central Statistical Office should consider the proposal.   It might well be that a special section could be added to the admirable and path-breaking production of the Government Statistical Service, *Social Trends*.[4]

RESPECT FOR THE FAMILY COURT

4.424   The aim of all our recommendations in this Section and the last is to establish a family court and a family law which will command the confidence and respect of the whole community.   We have been compelled to the conclusion that the summary jurisdiction in its present form does not achieve this object.   This failure cannot be explained merely in terms of its inherent weaknesses.   Those who mostly resort to the jurisdiction are drawn from the sections of the community who have the least confidence in any part of the legal administration and who need the most help in learning how to use it for their advantage.[5]   But there is a recent lesson to demonstrate in this very field how the law can rapidly win confidence for itself by remedying its own deficiencies.   The post-war history of the divorce courts until 1969 shows widespread and increasing mistrust and disapprobation for a jurisdiction that was being driven into what was often a virtual disregard of the law it was supposed to apply in order to serve personal and social needs which most of those who used it regarded as legitimate.   Yet the reforms of 1969–1970

---

[1] *Op cit*, paragraph 34.

[2] Paragraph 4.416, above.

[3] Part 8, Section 8, Table 8.1 below.

[4] In this context, we refer the reader to our recommendations in Part 7, Section 5, paragraph 7.27, that statistics on all aspects of women's employment should be regularly available in one publication.

[5] On this subject see *Justice for All*, Society of Labour Lawyers Report, Fabian Research Series 273, 1968, and *Rough Justice*, Conservative Political Centre, 1968; also the *Report of the Advisory Committee on the better provision of Legal Advice and Assistance*, Cmnd 4249, 1970, paragraph 8.

produced on almost instantaneous reversal of public attitudes. We know of no serious criticism which is now directed to the divorce jurisdiction other than in such matters as the costs of litigation, which affect the administration of the law as a whole. There is no branch of legal administration for which the respect of the community is more important than the administration of family law, and in the ultimate resort, the case for a family court is that it is the institution through which respect for the law can be fully achieved.

SECTION 15—THE SYSTEM IN SCOTLAND

INTRODUCTION

4.425 We have explained how our terms of reference required us to consider those areas of family law which regulate personal and economic relations between spouses and between parents and children in the event of the breakdown or termination of marriage, or of unmarried parenthood. In particular, we have had to consider the results of the confluence in these areas between private law and the law of social security. We have so far dealt with these subjects by reference to the law which applies in England and Wales. In Scotland, the law of social security is the same as in the other two countries. But it bites upon a different system of private family law. In Appendix 6 we reproduce the whole of a memorandum prepared by the Scottish Law Commission on the history and present content of Scottish family law and procedure in relation to the one-parent family. This Appendix may be consulted for an expert account of the details of the law; but the Commission are not responsible for any statements made or opinions expressed in our Report. Although we had neither the expertness nor the resources to conduct an investigation into the relevant operations of the Scottish legal system, we did make fairly extensive enquiry in Scotland into those aspects of the legal and supplementary benefits administration which were of most direct concern to us, and we took evidence from and engaged in discussions with a good many organisations and individuals in Scotland who have professional experience in these matters. We are satisfied that we learned enough to draw some broad, but valid, conclusions. It is to be borne in mind that as a Committee we are less concerned with the technicalities than with the efficiency of the law, and we do not believe that there is any difference between one-parent families in, say, Cumberland and one-parent families in Dumfries in the services they require from the law.

4.426 We may say at this stage that our conclusions as regards the system in Scotland fall into three categories. First, we find that there is nothing in that system which makes it less important or less possible to extend to Scotland the " administrative order " proposals set out in Section 12 of this Part. Indeed, it should, as will appear, be easier in Scotland to transfer the weight of the maintenance obligation to orders made by an administrative authority. Secondly, we can find no obstacle to the introduction of our proposals for a new one-parent family benefit—guaranteed maintenance allowance—in Scotland. These are two conclusions of central importance. We do not doubt that dovetailing the proposals into the Scottish law would involve detailed technical work by persons of the necessary skill, but this is a matter of machinery. Thirdly, in the course of our enquiries we have come to suspect that in Scotland, as in England, the general law as it affects one-parent families is capable of much improvement. We were glad to discover that the law of diligence and the law of aliment and financial provision in Scotland are both in the early stages of fundamental review by the Scottish Law Commission.[1]

SOME DIFFERENCES BETWEEN THE ENGLISH AND SCOTTISH SYSTEMS

4.427 One major historical difference between the two countries arises from the early and unambiguous reception in Scotland of Protestant ideas about marriage and divorce. In accordance with the general canon law of the West, Scotland before the Reformation recognised only divorce *a mensa et thoro*. By the 1560s divorce for adultery was recognised by the common law in Scotland, and this was followed in 1573 by the statutory introduction of desertion persisted in for four years as an additional ground. Both grounds were available equally to wives and husbands. The remedy of divorce for desertion in Scotland was governed principally by the Act of 1573 until its repeal by the Divorce (Scotland) Act 1938, whilst divorce for adultery is still entirely dependent upon the common law. Thus Scotland achieved divorce *a vinculo* by actions in a civil court almost three hundred years before it was available in England, and Scots wives enjoyed equality with their husbands in respect of the grounds of divorce for three and a half centuries before their English sisters were trusted with the like facility.

4.428 A second main difference between the two countries lay in the relative ease with which a poor person in Scotland could obtain access to the court in pursuit of a matrimonial remedy. An Act of 1424 provided:

> Gif there be onie pure creature, for faulte of cunning, or expenses, that cannot, nor may not follow his cause, the King for the love of God sall ordaine the judge before quhom the cause suld be determined, to purwey and get a leill and wise advocate to follow sik pure creatures causes: and gif sik causes be obtained, the wranger sal assyith baith the partie skaithed and the advocatis coastes and travel.[2]

Applicants were admitted to the poor's roll on the grounds both of qualification by certified poverty and of demònstrating a *probabilis causa litigandi*.[3] Admission to the poor's roll conferred the right to litigate without payment of court dues and to obtain the gratuitous services of a solicitor and counsel. This was no empty right. The Scottish Record Society has published[4] a list of all consistorial processes and decreets between 1658 and 1800 which shows the occupations of those involved in actions for divorce. The contrast with England is striking. There, in the eighteenth century, only the very wealthy could obtain divorce by private Act of Parliament: in Scotland, humble folk formed the largest contingent among those seeking divorce. Industrialisation did not alter this lower social class predominance in the divorcing population. In 1901, at least 59 per cent of pursuers in actions for divorce and separation

---

[1] See Appendix 6, paragraph 2.

[2] Quoted in *Encyclopaedia of the Laws of Scotland*, W Green and Son Ltd, 1931, Volume XI, page 495.

[3] *Ibid.*

[4] Francis J Grant (ed): *The Commissariot of Edinburgh, Consitorial Processes and Decreets, 1658–1800*, Scottish Record Society, Part XLVII, December 1909.

were engaged in working class occupations: in the same period in England, the percentage was 29.[1] Thus in Scotland the modern legal aid scheme was superimposed on the tradition of centuries.

4.429 Thirdly, the two countries have differed in the policy and organisation of their poor laws. We have argued[2] that the poor law in England also developed as a discriminatory family law applying to the dependent poor. Scots legislation of the sixteenth and seventeenth centuries had given permissive powers to levy a poor's rate and to provide " correction houses " for the employment of idle vagabonds. By 1800 only 92 parishes (one in 10) had assessments for the poor and very few workhouses existed. In Scotland, the poor law was a voluntary system distributing private charity organised chiefly by the church.[3] Even after the English poor law had been reformed in 1834, the Scots system remained administratively less elaborate and much cheaper. In 1840, England spent about £4·5 million on the relief of paupers who constituted nearly 8 per cent of a population of around 15,500,000: in the same year, Scotland spent some £115,000 on the relief of just over 3 per cent of a population of about 2,500,000.[4] With the growth of industry came the growth of towns and an increase in the numbers of dissenters who were disqualified from relief from the State church collections. This forced a revision of the poor law in 1845 and brought it more into line with the English arrangements.[5] Nevertheless, there never was in Scotland an association as in England between the poor law and a family code enforced by summary courts.[6]

4.430 Fourthly, there is no summary matrimonial jurisdiction in Scotland corresponding to that which is exercised by magistrates' courts in England. Jurisdiction is shared between the Court of Session and the sheriff court, but it is a sharing in the administration of a single system of law, and not, as in England, a distribution of two systems of law, one to a superior and the other to an inferior jurisdiction. The Court of Session, sitting in Edinburgh, has exclusive jurisdiction in actions of divorce, declarator of marriage, nullity of marriage, declarator of legitimacy and of bastardy and putting to silence. All such cases must accordingly be tried in Edinburgh, where the parties

---

[1] The figure for Scotland was calculated from Table VII, *Report on the Judicial Statistics of Scotland 1901*, Cd 1317, 1902. It is a minimum figure because no allowance has been made for those of no occupation or whose occupation was unknown. These constituted almost 10 per cent of the total. The figure for England relates to 1907 and was provided for the Gorell Commission by Sir John Macdonell, Table XVA, Appendix III, *Appendices to the Minutes of Evidence and Report of the Royal Commission on Divorce and Matrimonial Causes*, Cd 6482, 1912.

[2] Appendix 5.

[3] George S Pryde: *Scotland: From 1603 to the Present Day*, Nelson, 1962, pages 148–149.

[4] Laurance J Saunders: *Scottish Democracy 1815–1840*, Oliver and Boyd Ltd, Edinburgh, 1950, pages 198–199.

[5] James MacKinnon: *The Social and Industrial History of Scotland from the Union to the Present Time*, Longmans Green, 1921, page 141.

[6] We emphasise that this conclusion is tentative. The poor law in Scotland does not appear to have attracted the extensive scholarly attention lavished on its English counterpart and there are no comparative studies. In particular, there is a dearth of secondary studies of illegitimacy. Nevertheless, such monographs as Alexander A Cormack: *Poor Relief in Scotland*, Aberdeen, D Wyllie and Son, 1924, and Thomas Ferguson: *The Dawn of Scottish Social Welfare*, Nelson, 1948, do not suggest similarities between the two countries in respect of the relationship between the histories of the poor law and of family law.

and their witnesses must attend. The sheriff court is a local court, presided over by a legally qualified judge, and possessing an extensive civil and criminal jurisdiction.[1] The Court of Session and the sheriff court both have jurisdiction in actions of separation and aliment, adherence and aliment, interim aliment, and affiliation and aliment, but nearly all such claims, when they are not associated with any change of status, are in practice brought in the sheriff court.

4.431 Fifthly, the courts in Scotland are not responsible for, and take no part in, the actual collection and enforcement of debts due under decrees. Thus, the enforcement in Scotland of alimentary decrees is a private enterprise procedure. There is no court collecting office such as exists in English county and magistrates' courts.

4.432 Finally, although the law of supplementary benefits and the policies informing its administration are the same in both countries, the scheme in Scotland bites upon different systems of family law and enforcement of financial orders. The practice of the Supplementary Benefits Commission in Scotland has to adjust to this difference, and it does so with particular significance in respect of procedures for obtaining payments from liable relatives. We continue with the elaboration of relevant features of the Scots system.

DIVORCE

Introductory

4.433 The history and present substantive law of divorce in Scotland are set out in Appendix 6, and it is not necessary to elaborate on them here. Although there are differences between the law of divorce now current in Scotland, and the English law of divorce as it existed before the Divorce Reform Act 1969, the Scottish law on the grounds for divorce essentially parallels the former law in England, expecially in its requirement of proof of a matrimonial offence as the condition for divorce. There has been a movement in Scotland similar to that which took place in England to turn the divorce law into an instrument for the disposal of marriages which have terminated in truth and in fact. As in England, the established church has been closely associated with the call for reform. In December 1967 the Social and Moral Welfare Board of the Church of Scotland issued a statement on Divorce Law Reform, called *Whom God Hath Joined . . .* , which recommended that divorce should be granted on the ground of breakdown of marriage as evidenced by separation for a continuous period of at least two years. Attempts by private members to introduce irretrievable breakdown of marriage as the sole ground of divorce in Scotland have been made, so far without success. The last attempt was Mr W Hamilton's Divorce Law Reform (Scotland) Bill which failed to get a second reading and was dropped in July 1973.

Financial provision on divorce

4.434 Prior to the Succession (Scotland) Act 1964, on divorce on any ground other than incurable insanity, an innocent spouse became entitled to the same share of the estate of the guilty spouse as he or she would have obtained

---

[1] The history, jurisdiction, organisation and staffing of the sheriff court are conveniently set out in the *Report of the Departmental Committee on the Sheriff Court* (the Grant Report), Cmnd 3248, 1967.

if the marriage had been terminated by the death of the guilty spouse. These shares, called " legal rights ", still (to a more limited extent than before 1964) exist for the purposes of succession on death, but the Act of 1964 abolished the claim to them which had previously arisen on divorce, and substituted a system more nearly like the English one, whereby financial provision on dissolution of the marriage is made at the discretion of the court. The Act provides that the court, on granting decree of divorce, may order the defender or his executors, on the application of the pursuer, to pay to the pursuer a capital sum or a periodical allowance or both. But the defender cannot apply.[1] Application may be made at a later date by the pursuer if there is a material change in circumstances. The court has a discretion as to the amount of the capital sum or periodical allowance. The only statutory guidelines are that the court must have regard to the means of the parties and the whole circumstances of the case, including any settlement or other arrangements made for financial provision for any children of the marriage. The guidelines which have evolved must be gathered from the case law.[2] The court has held that each case will depend on its own circumstances; but capital awards of about one third of the net assets are not uncommon. The court may vary a marriage settlement. It may also prevent the defender from gratuitously disposing of any property to third parties where it is satisfied that the disposal is made to defeat the pursuer's claim in whole or in part. Although there is no fixed tariff for determining the amount of periodical payments, the proportion normally varies from one third to one quarter of the husband's income, less one half of the wife's own income.

4.435   In his commentary on the Succession (Scotland) Act 1964 Professor M C Meston remarks that the result of the Act:

> Will undoubtedly be to permit a fairer disposal of the marital property than is at present possible. One long standing problem has been the case of the husband who has little capital, but a reasonably large income. Under the previous law, if his wife divorced him, her financial rights were limited to the appropriate portions of his capital, his income being irrelevant, with the result that a highly unrealistic provision was made for the wife. The discretion now vested in the court to make such order as it thinks fit, taking the circumstances into account, and the powers to order capital or periodical payments or both, will deal with this and other problems arising out of divorce. One effect of the new system would seem to have been an increase in the number of divorces because more wives can now face the financial consequences of divorcing their husbands. A number of those who in the past would have chosen separation now seek divorce, and indeed a number of existing separation decrees were converted into divorces shortly after the Succession Act came into force. This increase in the numbers would not, however, seem to amount to an increase in the numbers of *de facto* broken marriages.[3]

Professor Meston's expectations have been amply fulfilled. Even though there has been no change in the grounds for divorce in Scotland, the number of divorces increased from 2,416 in 1964 to 5,501 in 1972; and the great bulk of this increase lay in decrees granted to wives.[4]

---

[1] In the case of divorce for incurable insanity there is express authority (the Divorce (Scotland) Act 1938, section 2, as amended by the Divorce (Scotland) Act 1964, section 7) for the court to award a capital sum or a periodical allowance to either party of the marriage.

[2] See M C Meston: *The Succession (Scotland) Act 1964*, W Green and Son Ltd, 2nd edition, 1969, page 101.

[3] M C Meston, *op cit*, page 99.

[4] To avoid unnecessary duplication with Appendix 6 we have eliminated tables and graphs from this Section. See Appendix 6, Tables 2–3.

Decentralisation of divorce jurisdiction

4.436 There has been much discussion in Scotland on the desirability of decentralising the divorce jurisdiction, now entirely discharged by the Court of Session in Edinburgh, by conferring a concurrent jurisdiction, either in all divorce actions, or in undefended actions, on the sheriff court, or by appointing sheriffs-principal and sheriffs to sit locally to hear divorces as Court of Session Commissioners. The debate on this question is extensively considered in Appendix 6.[1] We do not feel qualified to trespass upon a subject of such apparent complexity, but cannot refrain from remarking that some of the arguments against devolution are very like those which were strenuously put forward to justify the retention of a centralised jurisdiction in England, including the convenience of the Bar and the ceremonial claims of divorce. The Denning Committee in 1946 argued that the divorce jurisdiction in England should be retained in the High Court because:

> In our opinion the attitude of the community towards the status of marriage is much influenced by the way in which divorce is effected. If there is a careful and dignified proceeding such as obtains in the High Court for the undoing of a marriage, then quite unconsciously the people will have a more respectful view of the marriage tie and of the marriage status than they would if divorce were effected informally in an inferior court.[2]

But in England, the Matrimonial Causes Act 1967 conferred a divorce jurisdiction in undefended cases upon the county court. Further, under a division of business which in current practice is often determined by the length of the case, it is not uncommon for judges of the county court, sitting temporarily as High Court judges, to dispose of defended causes. It would now be difficult, if not impossible, to find any professional opinion in England which favoured the view of the Denning Committee.

SEPARATION

4.437 In addition to divorce, other remedies are available on the breakdown of marriage. Both the Court of Session and the sheriff court can grant decrees of separation on the grounds of adultery, cruelty, and, by statute, habitual drunkenness, defined to mean drunkenness such as renders the defender " at times dangerous to himself or herself or others, or incapable of managing himself or herself and his or her affairs ". In order to found a decree of judicial separation based on cruelty it must be shown that separation is required for the protection of the pursuer, so that the question is whether the pursuer would be in danger if cohabitation were resumed. This is not necessary for divorce based on cruelty. But a decree of judicial separation may be treated as sufficient proof of cruelty to found a decree of divorce.

4.438 The parties may voluntarily enter into such agreements and as in England there will normally be an agreement to live apart, provision for aliment of the wife, custody and aliment for the children and property. But, unlike England, in Scotland a separation agreement is revocable at pleasure by either spouse and is not enforceable by the court except as regards arrears of aliment. (The rationale is said to be the old idea, once common to both countries, that contracts of separation are void as being contrary to public policy.) The rule suffers an

---

[1] Appendix 6, paragraphs 67–80.

[2] *Second Interim Report of the Committee on Procedure in Matrimonial Causes*, Cmd 6945, 1946, page 7.

exception in cases (which are probably rare) where the agreement contains an admission of conduct amounting to a ground of separation. The offending spouse is then barred from revoking the agreement until it is judicially established that decree of separation is not warranted.

4.439 Only one action for judicial separation was decided in the Court of Session in 1972.[1] During the five-year period 1968-1972, actions relating to marriage in the sheriff courts averaged some 643 annually.[2]

ALIMENT

In general

4.440 The obligation of aliment derives from the common law of Scotland, although there has been a degree of statutory intervention. The husband has an obligation to provide the wife with the means of subsistence, but the court will not award a cash sum in respect of aliment for a period prior to the action being raised if the wife had in fact been able to maintain herself. The obligation can be performed by supporting the wife while she lives with him. Accordingly, if the wife lives apart from the husband without reasonable cause, he is not bound to aliment her by money payments, for he can discharge his obligation by offering a suitable home in the normal way. There is, further, no way of compelling the husband to make money payments while the parties live together. It is important to note that even if the wife has committed a matrimonial offence, and even after a decree of separation, the obligation to aliment endures for so long as the marriage. Only termination of the marriage cuts off the right to aliment in one form or another. At the point of divorce, as has earlier been noted, the Court of Session has power to make financial provision by ordering payment of a capital sum or a periodical allowance or both under the terms of the Succession (Scotland) Act 1964. Short of that point, however, what we have spoken of in the English context as the husband's obligation to maintain his wife is paralleled in Scotland only by the obligation to aliment as above described. By statute, an obligation is imposed also on the wife to aliment her husband, but only if she has separate estate or income which is more than reasonably sufficient for her own maintenance and he is unable to maintain himself. There are no upper limits to the amounts of aliment which may be awarded, but we are informed that the standard is in practice a low one, and that alimentary decrees rarely provide a sufficient subsistence level. To that extent, there is no difference between the situations in England and Scotland.

4.441 There are three types of action for aliment between spouses: separation and aliment;[3] adherence and aliment;[4] and interim aliment. A decree of separation and aliment can be granted on any of the grounds mentioned in paragraph 4.437 above. A decree of adherence and aliment is granted where a spouse (normally the husband) is in desertion, and the other spouse seeks aliment. The term "interim aliment" has acquired, through a somewhat

---

1 Appendix 6, Table 4.
2 *Ibid*, Table 9.
3 See Appendix 6, paragraphs 85–87.
4 *Ibid*, paragraph 101.

complicated history, more than one meaning.[1] However, the important practical point is that actions for permanent aliment must proceed in the Court of Session in Edinburgh, whereas actions for interim aliment are competent in the sheriff court, locally. Thus, there has been a strong incentive to frame the action, where possible, as being one for interim aliment.

Financial provision for children

4.442 The common law obligation in Scotland to aliment legitimate children devolves in the first instance on the father, but if he is dead, or unable to afford the aliment, upon the mother, and thereafter, in order of priority, upon the father's father, the father's mother, paternal ascendants in their order, and maternal ascendants in their order. The obligation persists after the majority of the child, so that the court may grant a decree against the person liable in favour of a child of any age if he is indigent through physical or mental incapacity, or inability to get suitable employment. The obligation to aliment may be discharged in the least onerous way, as, for example, by taking the child into the home. The standard is to support the child beyond " want ", interpreted by reference to the social position of the parties.

4.443 The courts have power to make awards of aliment for legitimate or adopted children in matrimonial actions, that is, for divorce, nullity and separation in the Court of Session, and for separation in the sheriff court, and also a statutory jurisdiction, which applies both in the Court of Session and the sheriff court, to deal with questions of custody, maintenance or education of children of the marriage on the application of one or other spouse in separate proceedings.

4.444 In Scots law, both parents are liable to aliment their illegitimate child, and the child's claim is transmitted on the death of the parents against their representatives. It is provided by statute that this obligation shall endure until the child is 16 years of age; but this is without prejudice to the common law obligation under which the child is entitled to be alimented until he is able to earn subsistence. Thus, if he is mentally or physically incapable of doing so, the duty of alimenting him will continue during his lifetime. The power of the court to award aliment for legitimate or adopted children in actions of divorce, nullity or separation extends also to the illegitimate children of one spouse received by the other spouse into the family. If paternity is disputed, the claim of the mother who has supported the child for recovery from the father of his share of the joint debt may be enforced by an action of affiliation and aliment either in the Court of Session or the sheriff court. In certain circumstances, the mother may raise an action of affiliation and aliment against the alleged father at any time during the three months before the expected date of birth of the child. There is no statutory limit on the amount of aliment that can be awarded.

4.445 In 1972 final judgment was given in the sheriff court in 237 actions of affiliation and aliment.[2] In Scotland, as in England, only a small proportion of unmarried mothers resort to the law for enforcement of the putative father's obligations.[3]

---

[1] *Ibid*, paragraphs 34–38 and 104.

[2] Appendix 6, Table 6.

[3] For England, see *Separated Spouses*, *op cit*, chapter 11, especially pages 177 and 186–187.

4.446 The bulk of the proceedings that we have been considering, other than those over which the Court of Session has the exclusive jurisdiction, are tried in the sheriff court. They are usually brought by wives whose real purpose is to obtain financial relief for themselves and their children by way of aliment. The summary jurisdiction of the magistrates in England over matrimonial disputes is largely directed to the same purpose, although in that jurisdiction the product is called maintenance. Whatever the differences of law, procedure and nomenclature may be, these two jurisdictions are concerned with the same human predicament in societies which share the same predominant values. We have extensively investigated and criticised the summary jurisdiction in England from the point of view of its suitability and efficiency in serving the needs of the people who resort to it, and the interest of the community in seeing those needs satisfied. We were therefore particularly interested in the practical operation in matrimonial matters of the sheriff court in Scotland.

4.447 To that end, we made this last mentioned subject one of those to which we gave special attention in our work in Scotland. So far as concerns the procedure of the sheriff court in alimentary actions, however, we now have the advantage of the detailed exposition of the Scottish Law Commission, on which we naturally prefer to rely, and to which we would direct the attention of the reader.[1] He will then discover the basis upon which we feel bound to record our strong disagreement with the note of moderate satisfaction which appears to inform the Commission's comment on the system they describe.[2] We ourselves found in Scotland a substantial recognition of the desirability of adopting a simpler and cheaper procedure in alimentary actions in the sheriff court, both among lawyers and social workers and among organisations. It can hardly be denied that of all possible types of proceedings, these are such as should make it possible for the litigant, especially a lone mother with children on her hands, to obtain relief as speedily and inexpensively as is consistent with justice. We fully appreciate that the system in operation is deeply rooted in the history and traditions of Scots law. But we do not believe that its complexity is justifiable or necessary, or that it can be right for it to cost about £150 to determine a defended dispute in which the evidence lasts for not more than one day, and which will not often result in an order for weekly payments in a sum exceeding the scale rates of the Supplementary Benefits Commission.[3]

---

[1] Appendix 6, Section 4, *passim*. We might draw attention to one of the very few points left uncovered, namely a point arising on the assessment of the defender's means. It frequently happens that a wife who requires to take an alimentary action against her husband has no information as to his income or capital. In circumstances where the husband does not contest the amount of aliment claimed such a wife can only either seek an exorbitant amount, so as to force her husband to oppose the claim, or obtain an order of court upon the husband's employers, if she knows them, to disclose the information. The Law Society of Scotland have expressed dissatisfaction with this situation and recommended that it be made mandatory upon a husband to supply his wife with details of his capital and income whether he seeks to oppose the conclusions of an alimentary action or not. The Law Society have further advocated a review of the procedure for enabling a husband to give details of his financial position in an alimentary action by his wife. A husband who wishes to contest only on the amount of aliment craved now has to go through all the procedures of lodging a defence—including obtaining the services of a solicitor and applying for legal aid. The information about his means could be given simply by affidavit.

[2] *Ibid*, paragraphs 120 *et seq*.

[3] There is nothing to prevent a litigant from acting in his or her own behalf, but the technicalities are so daunting that a solicitor is, in practice, nearly always retained.

We have severely criticised the summary matrimonial jurisdiction in England, in which the liability to pay maintenance is at present no less inextricably entwined with the doctrine of the matrimonial offence than it is in the sheriff courts in Scotland; but the English procedure is at least far simpler and significantly cheaper. We think that there can be no justification for saddling the legal aid scheme in Scotland with costs in simple matrimonial disputes which result from a procedure which might be appropriate for settling financial disputes between large commercial organisations. We recommend that consideration be given to the means for remedying the defects we have described.

4.448 We should mention that there is one form of summary procedure available for the resolution of matrimonial disputes. Actions for interim aliment between spouses may be brought in the sheriff's small debt court if the claim does not exceed £5 a week for the pursuer and £1·50 for each child of the marriage. Many of the ordinary procedural steps are dispensed with in the small debt procedure, and the cost of the proceedings may not be more than about £5. Since, as has been previously explained, an award of interim aliment is by way of an order which continues indefinitely, the total sum involved in the order made in the small debt court may be considerable. In fact the jurisdiction appears to be little used. The Grant Report[1] estimated that there were probably not more than 100 cases a year of this kind in the whole of Scotland. This is perhaps not surprising when it is appreciated that the amounts of aliment that may be awarded in the jurisdiction are well below the supplementary benefit scale rates to which the pursuer will normally be entitled for herself and her children.

4.449 The Sheriff Courts (Scotland) Act 1971 provides for the abolition of the small debt process, and we understand that Rules still to be promulgated will provide for actions for interim aliment for small sums to be dealt with under an extended form of summary procedure in the sheriff court. Presumably, this procedure will be made available for the recovery of sums in excess of the inadequate limits of the small debt procedure which it is replacing.

4.450 We have already noted that the sheriff court deals with an average of less than 650 actions relating to marriage in each year, which is a number that is not only minute in comparison with the volume of corresponding business in the summary jurisdiction in England, but is also proportionately to populations still very small. We have little doubt that one reason for this is the weaknesses to which we have already referred; and another, as will appear later, relates to the difficulty of enforcing a decree even after it has been granted. But there is one important and positive consequence which flows from the relatively small involvement of the courts in Scotland with alimentary decrees. It makes it the easier to extend to Scotland some of the major proposals of this Report. The transition to the system of administrative orders discussed in Section 12 of this Part, and the introduction of the guaranteed maintenance allowance proposed in Part 5, both reduce the role of the courts in making financial provision for one-parent families. In Scotland, as compared with England, the role of the court is already small.

[1] *Op cit*, paragraph 201.

232

The Enforcement of Alimentary Decrees[1]

A private enterprise system

4.451   Under Scots law the responsibility for enforcing a court decree for aliment rests with the person in whose favour the decree has been granted; there are no officers of court equivalent to the English collecting officer.   If a husband defaults in making payments under an order for aliment, it is open to the wife to proceed to have his wages arrested, to attach his moveable effects or to apply for him to be sent to prison.   Although she may in theory arrange for these steps to be taken herself, it is difficult to proceed without professional assistance since in practice the sheriff officers who carry out the diligence prefer to have instructions from a solicitor in order to give them some security for their expenses in the event of these not being recovered from the defender.   The form of Scottish alimentary proceedings in general places both the pursuer and defender in a position of far greater dependence on professional help than is found in England.[2]   We have been informed that many solicitors dislike dealing with cases beyond initial consistorial action and may even fail to advise a successful pursuer of the possibility of further proceedings.   Thus, if aliment fails, the unsupported wife may be unaware of her rights and may only be referred back to a solicitor after appealing for help to the Supplementary Benefits Commission, the sheriff court, or some social work agency.

4.452   In the absence of an organised collecting service, it is difficult, unless payments of aliment are diverted to the Department of Health and Social Security, to verify the accuracy of a claim for alimentary debt.   Where the woman receives her aliment direct from the man a record of payments is rarely kept by either party and disputes are difficult to resolve.   Even where a solicitor acts as collecting agent, it is often found that the husband makes some payments direct to the wife, thus invalidating the solicitor's records.   This work is, in any case, an unwelcome burden for the solicitor; it is not of sufficient volume to require the establishment of routine procedures which would make it economically viable.   Most solicitors have only a handful of cases in which they are endeavouring to collect relatively small sums of money.   Efficient and economical collection of aliment should be done in bulk by staff who follow standard procedures for record keeping, issue of reminders and handling of cash.

4.453   Where a woman has received legal aid in alimentary proceedings, her solicitor may act for her under the original legal aid certificate in having diligence done to enforce compliance with the terms of the decree.   The legal aid certificate does not, however, cover work done by a solicitor in informal collection of aliment on behalf of his client, nor the warning letters he is obliged to send before taking action against a defaulting husband.   According to

---

[1] The standard work on the enforcement of judgment debts in Scotland is J G Stewart: *A Treatise on the Law of Diligence*, W Green and Son Ltd, 1898; the modern law is set out in *The Encyclopaedia of the Laws of Scotland*, *op cit*, Volume V, and in the *Report of the (McKechnie) Committee on the Law of Diligence*, Cmnd 456, 1958.   There is a short paper on ' Aliment of Spouses in Scots Law ' by J Aikman Smith and T B Smith in J Unger (ed): *Parental Custody and Matrimonial Maintenance*, the British Institute of International and Comparative Law, 1966.   See also Appendix 6, Section 6.

[2] The ratio of solicitors to the general population is higher in Scotland than in England.

the McKechnie Report,[1] a solicitor will often make no charge to a deserted wife for his attempts to secure regular payment of aliment without recourse to diligence. If he does ask for a fee related to the time value of his correspondence, book-keeping and transmission of money undertaken in his office, it represents a significant charge on the money collected.

Arrestment of wages

4.454 Arrestment of wages is the usual form of diligence used to obtain arrears of aliment. Unlike the English system of attachment of earnings, arrestment is purely retrospective; it is designed to recover a fixed debt and not to ensure future income. Hence, the process can be effective against a persistent defaulter only if repeated arrestments are made. Like attachment of earnings, arrestment is useless against a man who constantly changes his place of employment. Thus, such success as arrestment achieves is likely to be in the nature of a self-fulfilling prophecy because it is worth proceeding only against a defaulter known to have money.

4.455 The order to arrest wages is served on the defender's employer by a sheriff officer. The employer may deduct the debt but should not pay it to the pursuer's solicitors without a mandate from the defender or a court order. If a husband refuses his consent, an action of furthcoming must be taken to release the money. But proceedings for furthcoming are rarely necessary, since most employers will in practice hand over arrested wages without question.

4.456 It is also difficult to do diligence in the more remote parts of Scotland because of the scarcity of sheriff officers and the expense of sending them out from urban centres. The McKechnie Committee concluded that "in the outer Islands, particularly Barra, North Uist and South Uist, a stubborn debtor can get away with anything."[2]

4.457 Despite the report of the McKechnie Committee in 1958, there has been no major legislation on diligence in recent times. The Scottish Law Commission set up a working party on diligence in 1970 under the chairmanship of Mr A M Johnston QC (now Lord Dunpark), but we have been informed that no change in the present system may be expected before 1975. However, we note that the Law Society of Scotland, impressed by the reports of the Anderson[3] and Payne[4] Committees on the enforcement of judgment debts in Northern Ireland and in England, opted in evidence to the Law Commission working party for the transfer of diligence to an enforcement office set up "within the sheriff courts and borrowing from the Sheriff Clerk's staff (augmented probably) for its personnel".[5]

---

[1] *Op cit*, paragraph 273.

[2] *Ibid*, paragraph 235.

[3] *Report of the Joint Working Party on the Enforcement of Judgments, Orders and Decrees of the Courts of Northern Ireland*, HMSO, Belfast, 1965.

[4] *Report of the Committee on the Enforcement of Judgment Debts*, Cmnd 3909, 1969.

[5] Of course, the Law Society was not influenced in reaching this decision by considerations specially affecting maintenance defaulters. Like the Payne Committee in England, they pointed to the general paradox of execution for debt, both under the English and Scots systems, that so long as the debtor is solvent, and may be supposed to possess some assets which might benefit his creditors at large, any one of them is free to make off with the lot; but once he is notour bankrupt (by which time as often as not, the pool has been scooped) the law intervenes to ensure a just and equitable distribution of what is left, if anything : ' The Execution of Diligence in Scotland ', Memorandum by the Council of the Law Society, in *Journal of the Law Society of Scotland*, September 1972, paragraphs 8–9.

Enforcement of maintenance orders and decrees in the United Kingdom

4.458   Part II of the Maintenance Orders Act 1950 provides that maintenance orders (which term includes decrees for aliment) made in one part of the United Kingdom may be registered for the purpose of enforcement in any other part of the United Kingdom.   An order can be registered for enforcement in one court only at any one time.

4.459   The report of the Grant Committee pointed out a defect in this system:

> It was put to us that arrangements for enforcing Scottish alimentary decrees in England should be made more effective.   We are informed that difficulty arises in the case of the husband who moves from one place to another in England. A Scottish decree against him can, under the Maintenance Orders Act 1950, be registered in a magistrates' court for the area in which he lives in England but a fresh registration is necessary every time he moves to a new area.   We should like to see an arrangement whereby one registration in England would be valid, no matter where the man resides, but we recognise that there could still be practical problems, and that such a proposal raises questions of reciprocal arrangements which are not within our terms of reference.   We therefore make no firm recommendation.[1]

Sheriff Aikman Smith and Professor T B Smith concluded that:

> The Maintenance Orders Act 1950 has undoubtedly made it more difficult than formerly for husbands to escape their obligations.   It is still, however, often much more easy to obtain a decree for aliment than to ensure that it becomes effective.   There are many husbands who are prepared to accept the kind of unskilled employment which can be picked up anywhere.   By moving from job to job and place to place, by making at best irregular payments of aliment, and by disappearing for periods, a determined man can create great difficulties for his wife and her solicitors.[2]

We have been told that a street in Corby, Northamptonshire, where many defaulting husbands from Scotland seek work, is known locally as Diligence Row.

Civil imprisonment for alimentary debt

4.460   In England a committal order may be made against a man who has " wilfully refused or culpably neglected " to obey a maintenance order, and magistrates' courts have committed some 3,000 defaulters to prison each year.   In Scotland, civil imprisonment for alimentary debt is comparatively rare.   Between 1948 and 1957 the annual number of imprisonments varied from a minimum of 10 to a maximum of 34.[3]   In recent years, even at a generous estimate, the number is unlikely to have been more than 45 a year. The majority of these actions take place within the sheriffdom of Lanarkshire; in 1971 85 warrants were applied for and 35 granted; a high percentage of these were eventually executed.[4]   The sheriff courts of Edinburgh and Dunfermline, on the other hand, receive annually about half a dozen applications and only one or two of these result in actual imprisonment.   In the smaller sheriff courts, these actions are even more infrequent.

---

[1] *Op cit*, paragraph 649.

[2] *Op cit*, page 193.

[3] McKechnie Report, *op cit*, paragraph 127.

[4] This information was kindly provided by the Sheriff Clerk of Lanarkshire.

4.461 The small amount of imprisonment in Scotland results partly from the reluctance of unsupported wives and their solicitors to take this extreme step. As imprisonment for alimentary debt is not part of the ordinary form of diligence, a pursuer who wishes to use this sanction must raise a fresh action under section 4 of the Civil Imprisonment (Scotland) Act 1882[1] and make a separate application for legal aid where this is needed. The warrant granted to a successful pursuer can be used at any time to imprison the defender for a period of up to six weeks. In some cases it is never implemented, the threat of imprisonment being sufficient in itself to ensure payment of aliment. We consider that an additional reason for the difference between the two countries in the use of imprisonment against defaulters is the stricter application of the law by professional judges in the sheriff courts than by some of the lay magistracy in England, there being no material difference between the provisions of the law in either case.

VOLUNTARY MAINTENANCE AGREEMENTS

4.462 Our investigations show that in Scotland separated spouses and unmarried parents make more use of voluntary maintenance agreements than do their English counterparts. The precise extent of this practice in either country is clearly impossible to ascertain but some statistical evidence may be adduced.

4.463 The report of the National Assistance Board for 1953[2] gives details of a 4 per cent sample enquiry based on the papers relating to 57,700 separated wives who had been receiving national assistance in September 1950. Such wives had described themselves as " married but living apart", and some had dependent children. Of these, 19,000 held a court order (or in Scotland a decree) requiring the husband to make some payment to them but only 500 were Scottish. On the other hand, of 5,500 voluntary agreements for such payments, rather more had been made on behalf of wives in Scotland than in England and Wales so that the proportion of cases where there was either a court order (or decree) or a voluntary agreement " was not widely different in the two countries; for the two countries together it was about 43 per cent".[3] A further enquiry[4] in 1970 showed that the heavier reliance on voluntary agreements in Scotland still persists. Of all wives, ex-wives and unmarried mothers on supplementary benefit in England and Wales, some 46 per cent held maintenance orders and 17 per cent had voluntary agreements; in Scotland only 26 per cent held decrees for aliment but a further 27 per cent had out-of-court arrangements. (The total proportion of women on supplementary benefit with either a court order (or decree) or a voluntary agreement was thus 63 per cent in England and 54 per cent in Scotland.)

4.464 The high proportion of women in Scotland who have entered into voluntary agreements can perhaps be regarded as the reciprocal of the low

---

[1] When the bill was introduced in 1882 its mover, Dr Charles Cameron, MP for Glasgow, proposed that the power to imprison for alimentary debt should be abolished; the select committee to whom the bill was remitted wrote back this power: McKechnie Report, *op cit*, paragraph 123.

[2] Cmd 9210, 1954.

[3] *Ibid*, Appendix XI.

[4] The liable relative enquiry in 1970. See also Section 6, paragraphs 4.85–4.90, and Section 10, paragraph 4.215.

numbers who, as we have already noticed, obtain orders for aliment in the sheriff court. The difficulties and expense of the legal procedure, coupled with the problems attendant on the enforcement of a decree when it is obtained, must persuade many women and their advisers that if an out-of-court agreement can be made, albeit for a smaller amount than the court might order, it will still produce more money.

4.465 This assessment of the situation appears to be shared by the Supplementary Benefits Commission in Scotland. In the early stages of our enquiries we found it hard to reconcile the tendency to make voluntary arrangements for aliment, which such figures as are available disclose, with evidence that the number of such agreements drawn by Scottish solicitors is small, and declining. The solution to this apparent contradiction is that a large proportion of the voluntary agreements are arranged by the officers of the Commission. Once the liable relative officer of the Commission has ascertained liability to his own satisfaction, he will attempt to persuade a deserting husband or a putative father to make some contribution towards the aliment of his wife and children. The object is, if it is possible, to remove the need for payment of supplementary benefit, but the Commission will ask the man to pay only what they consider to be a reasonable sum, taking into consideration his income, work and living expenses, hire-purchase commitments and obligations to support any second family.[1]   Sometimes, the liable relative will agree to meet his obligation without resort to court but still refuse to sign a written agreement. A number of women, who apply to the Commission for assistance, are already receiving some payment, often inadequate, from the liable relative; these count as claimants with voluntary agreements in the Commission's statistics.

ALIMENT AND THE SUPPLEMENTARY BENEFITS COMMISSION

Comparison with England

4.466 The law of supplementary benefits, including its provisions for enforcement of liable relative obligations, is the same in England and Scotland.[2]   But the Commission in Scotland have to operate in the context of a legal system which lacks an effective summary procedure for obtaining aliment and any system for the collection and enforcement of alimentary debt by officers of the court. We have elsewhere[3] set out and criticised, in the English context, the policy of the Commission, stated in the *Supplementary Benefits Handbook*, to " encourage and assist a wife to take her own proceedings wherever possible", and the reasons, which are also stated in the handbook, in justification of that policy. This policy, and the justification for it, officially extend to Scotland, but, in the circumstances we have described, its relevance in Scotland seems to us to be minimal. The Commission in Scotland are fully aware of the deficiencies of alimentary proceedings, and they appreciate that a woman has little incentive to engage in such proceedings when the result of what may be a burdensome litigation will be a decree for a sum which usually leaves her in need of supplementary benefit, and will in any case be extremely difficult to enforce. In the result—and in our view rightly so—the statement of policy is more honoured in the breach than in the observance in Scotland.

---

[1] The guidelines adopted by the Commission are discussed in Section 10, paragraphs 4.184–4.190.

[2] The relevant parts of the law are summarised in Section 10, *passim*.

[3] *Ibid*, paragraphs 4.191–4.202.

4.467   The same points are reflected in the fact that the Commission in Scotland make little use of the civil process against liable relatives. On the other hand, they are responsible for over half the criminal actions for failure to maintain:

TABLE 4.17

PROCEEDINGS AGAINST THE LIABLE RELATIVE UNDER THE MINISTRY OF SOCIAL SECURITY ACT 1966

Year		Criminal proceedings	Civil proceedings
1968	Scotland	352	7
	England and Wales	245	189
1969	Scotland	398	8
	England and Wales	200	198
1970	Scotland	352	14
	England and Wales	323	323

Source: Supplementary Benefits Commission.

The Scottish officers of the Commission emphasised that these figures should not be interpreted to indicate that they are in any way prosecution-oriented. The policy determining which cases should be referred for prosecution under section 30 of the Ministry of Social Security Act is exactly the same north and south of the border, but more cases in Scotland arrive at this point because there is no other effective course of action.

4.468   In Scotland, criminal proceedings for failure to maintain are conducted by the procurator fiscal.[1]   Action is taken in 99 per cent of all the cases referred by the Commission but, once a case is in the hands of the procurator fiscal, the Commission have no further control over it.   The majority[2] of criminal proceedings against liable relatives in Scotland are taken in cases where neither the wife nor the Commission have been able to obtain a satisfactory response from the man; most plead guilty and deferred sentence is quite common. Conviction may result in imprisonment or a fine, but the courts frequently take the view that the interests of justice will be best served by deferring sentence and giving the accused another opportunity to fulfil his obligations.

---

[1] The procurators fiscal are the public prosecutors in the sheriff courts and with the assistance of the police they confidentially investigate criminal offences within their districts. All summary proceedings in the public interest are taken at their instance and they investigate and report more serious crimes to the Crown Office for the consideration and instruction of Crown counsel.

[2] About 90 per cent.

Diversion of aliment payments to the Department of Health and Social Security

4.469 Since 1965 it has been possible for a separated or divorced wife (or unmarried mother) who is likely to require regular supplementary benefit to authorise the clerk to the court in England to divert payments due under a maintenance order to the Department of Health and Social Security; payments under a voluntary agreement may similarly be made direct to the Department.[1] In both cases supplementary benefit entitlement is calculated as though there were no maintenance order or agreement and the wife receives an order book which she can cash at the post office. The advantage of this arrangement is that the wife receives her full entitlement regularly, regardless of whether maintenance is paid in full or intermittently or never, and is thus relieved of the anxiety of an uncertain income. But since in Scotland there is no court collecting office, and orders are not registered with the court for enforcement, the diversion arrangements cannot operate in the same way.[2] It is usual in Scotland for the husband to pay aliment direct to his wife or her solicitor, and the diversion of payments to the Department therefore requires the husband's co-operation and has to be restricted to cases in which this co-operation has been obtained. Such a request may disturb what is already a finely balanced situation, and we can well understand that the Commission are reluctant to intervene if a husband or father is remitting regularly an acceptable amount of aliment, even if it is below supplementary benefit entitlement, direct to the woman recipient. Thus, it is the policy of the Commission in Scotland to seek the diversion of aliment to the Department only if the payments are irregular. In practice, no more than a third of the women who possess a decree for aliment and receive supplementary benefit have payment of that decree diverted to the department, whereas in England about 75 per cent of claimants with court orders arrange for payment to be made direct to the Department. On the other hand, the Commission's special role in arranging out-of-court agreements with liable relatives in Scotland is reflected in the larger proportion of voluntary payments which are made direct to the Department. There is no evidence to support the view, expressed to us in oral evidence by representatives of the Law Society of Scotland, that the Commission are reluctant to accept diversion. The situation is set out in Tables 4.18 and 4.19.

TABLES 4.18 AND 4.19

MAINTENANCE PAYMENTS MADE DIRECT TO THE DEPARTMENT OF HEALTH AND SOCIAL SECURITY : 1970

TABLE 4.18

COURT ORDERS DIVERTED TO THE DEPARTMENT

Scotland		England and Wales	
Total number of orders	Payment diverted to the Department	Total number of orders	Payment diverted to the Department
6,500	2,100 (32%)	122,500	93,900 (77%)

Source: Supplementary Benefits Commission.

[1] The procedure is described in Section 10, paragraphs 4.206–4.209.
[2] See *Supplementary Benefits Handbook*, op cit, paragraph 184.

TABLE 4.19

OUT-OF-COURT ARRANGEMENTS PAYABLE TO THE DEPARTMENT

Scotland		England and Wales	
Total out-of-court arrangements	Arrangements payable to the Department	Total out-of-court arrangements	Arrangements payable to the Department
6,300	3,000 (48%)	36,700	7,500 (20%)

Source: Supplementary Benefits Commission.

Opinion of the Scottish Law Agents' Society

4.470 We have, since forming our own conclusions on the relationship between some of our legal and financial proposals for England and the conditions to which they would have to adjust in Scotland, had the opportunity to read the report by the Council of the Scottish Law Agents' Society made by the Society to the Diligence Working Party of the Scottish Law Commission. The society stresses that the recovery of aliment is now closely linked with the payment of supplementary benefit to women unable to recover periodical payments or aliment from their husbands or former husbands, and it recommends that the Department of Health and Social Security should be given in Scotland the task of collecting alimentary debts and enforcing alimentary claims. Bearing in mind the expert source of these recommendations, their similarity to our own conclusions over the field which they cover has much fortified us. We are particularly impressed by the support they afford for our view that it is both necessary and suitable that the system of " administrative orders " which we have proposed for England should be instituted also in Scotland.

CONCLUSIONS

4.471 We are satisfied that all our recommendations for improving the financial situation of one-parent families can be as readily implemented in Scotland as in England. This conclusion extends to the system of " administrative orders " to be made by an administering authority which we discuss in the context of supplementary benefits in Section 12, and in the context of the guaranteed maintenance allowance in Part 5, Section 7. Indeed, the introduction of such a system in Scotland will be no more than a logical extension of the practice there already established by the Supplementary Benefits Commission.

4.472 In this Part and in Appendix 5 we have demonstrated the gross disadvantages stemming from the dual system of matrimonial jurisdictions in England. If, as we hope, irretrievable breakdown of marriage becomes the sole ground for dissolution of marriage in Scotland, the effect, if the matrimonial offence remains the foundation of the sheriff court jurisdiction, would be to introduce for the first time such a dual jurisdiction to Scotland. We believe that steps should be taken to ensure that reform of the sheriff court jurisdiction should march in step with divorce law reform in Scotland.

4.473   In Sections 13 and 14 of this Part we explain why we advocate a family court system in England.   In our view, the considerations of principle set out in Section 13 which lead to that recommendation apply equally to Scotland.

4.474   We recognise, however, that the application in detail of these principles in the context of Scots law and procedure must raise issues of great complexity on which we are not competent to advise.   We hope they will be investigated by the competent authorities.

4.475   We are satisfied that the procedures of the sheriff court in dealing with alimentary actions need to be simplified and made cheaper for the litigant, and we recommend that this matter, too, be pursued by the competent authorities.

4.476   We have learned in the course of our study in Scotland that the relevant published statistics are no better than they are in England.   We have therefore included Scotland in our recommendation in Section 14 for greatly improved statistics relating to family matters.

4.477   The differences between the private family law system of England and Wales and of Scotland are considerable.   But the social security system which, as we have demonstrated, is for one-parent families also a branch of family law, is common to both countries.   Given that the problems of one-parent families are the same in Scotland as in England and Wales, the considerable differences between the two private law systems should not be permitted to obscure the identity in practical terms of the solutions which are required.

PART 5—INCOME

SECTION 1—THE PROBLEM

5.1 One of the main factors influencing the Secretary of State for Social Services in November 1969 to appoint a Committee to look into the problems of one-parent families was the widespread general impression that, despite improving standards among the population in general, a large proportion of one-parent families were suffering hardship because of a severely restricted income. The idea that unsupported single parents might need special help was not new; as long ago as 1942 Sir William Beveridge considered and made tentative proposals for "separation insurance".[1] Since that time the climate of public opinion has undergone a profound change, due in no small part to the efforts of informed individuals and various voluntary organisations who have highlighted the problems of many one-parent families and brought them to the attention of the public. By 1969 concern for the financial situation of many one-parent families had grown, but the extent of the help that they needed and in what way this could be given was unclear. No comprehensive information existed about one-parent families, their income, their needs or their way of life. Whilst the numbers of such families receiving supplementary benefit were known, and moreover known to be increasing, there was little information about any other one-parent families living near or below supplementary benefit levels, or about the extent of their hardships.

5.2 Our terms of reference required us to examine the extent to which one-parent families could obtain financial support when they needed it, and to consider in what manner, and to what extent, it would be appropriate to give them further assistance, having regard to the need to maintain equity as between one-parent families and other families, and to practical and economic limitations. We found the comparisons between one-parent families and other families difficult to draw, because we were never comparing like with like. The most closely comparable situation might be thought to be that of a family with one parent severely disabled. But even this comparison is not particularly helpful. In many such families, the disability of the one parent places added restrictions on the second parent, over and above those imposed by the need to care for the children, and is a severe drain on the family's physical, financial and emotional resources. Other families may be far less seriously affected by the disability of one of the parents. But detailed comparisons of one disadvantaged group with another present formidable problems yielding solutions which are formal rather than helpful. We have therefore restricted ourselves to such comparisons with the generality of two-parent families as the evidence available to us permitted, but these are of limited utility and not determinative of the right solutions for the problems of one-parent families.

5.3 There is at present no special State benefit for one-parent families as such. Widowed mothers are the only group whose special status is recognised in the national insurance scheme: they receive a benefit for themselves

---

[1] *Social Insurance and Allied Services:* Report by Sir William Beveridge KCB, Cmd 6404, 1942, paragraphs 261 and 347. Appendix 5 examines the reasons for the non-implementation of Beveridge's proposals.

(£7·75 a week from October 1973) and for each of their children (which, with family allowances, makes the total for each child £3·80 a week). (There are also special provisions for widows and children under the war pensions and industrial injuries schemes.) Widowed mothers receive their benefit without any restriction on the amount they can earn.

5.4 There are, however, a number of ways in which one-parent families, including widows, receive special financial help: those families well enough off to pay tax receive an additional personal allowance in recognition of their one-parent family status, and a lone parent is treated in exactly the same way as a married couple in the rent rebate and allowance schemes and for family income supplements. But there is no special support benefit for one-parent families, and in Part 4 we show that maintenance is in the ordinary way hopelessly inadequate for their needs. Those who cannot support themselves by working (or, if sick or unemployed, by the appropriate national insurance benefits) are entitled to receive supplementary benefit; and they get the same family support as is available to other families with dependent children—that is family allowances and child tax allowances. (A list of the main benefits and allowances available to one-parent families is at Appendix 8.)

5.5 We set out to discover how one-parent families supported themselves, how they differed in their material circumstances from two-parent families, and how their levels of income compared. A good deal of information has been analysed for us, notably from the Family Expenditure Survey[1] and from supplementary benefit statistics,[2] and original research (which is acknowledged elsewhere) has been undertaken. Much helpful evidence was also submitted to us about the financial problems of one-parent families. The enormous variety of the situations in which one-parent families find themselves, and the considerable fluctuations which are apt to occur in these situations, require generalisations to be treated with reserve; and the results from the various projects are not totally in accordance with each other either in the groups included or in the point in time to which they relate. But we believe we have been able to piece together a reliable general picture of the financial circumstances of one-parent families. This picture we set out to draw in the Section which follows.

SECTION 2—THE FINANCIAL CIRCUMSTANCES OF ONE-PARENT FAMILIES

5.6 One-parent families have four main sources of income: earnings, maintenance, widows' benefits and supplementary benefit. The general picture is set out in the following Table. This shows fatherless families other than widows' families, widows' families and motherless families separately because their main sources of income are so different.

---

[1] See Appendix 10.
[2] See Appendix 9.

243

TABLE 5.1

MAIN SOURCES OF INCOME* OF ONE-PARENT FAMILIES AT THE END OF 1971

Main source of income	Number of families (thousands)
Fatherless families other than widows' families:	
Earnings	140
Maintenance	50
Supplementary benefits	200
Other	10
All	400
Widows' families:	
Earnings	50
Widows' benefits	60
Other	10
All	120
Motherless families:	
Earnings	90
Supplementary benefits	10
All	100
Total number of one-parent families	620

* By " main source " is meant the largest single source.

Note: Figures rounded to nearest 10,000.

Source: Family Expenditure Survey pooled data, 1969–1971; Department of Health and Social Security supplementary benefit statistics.

This Table shows the importance of supplementary benefit as the main source of income of one half of fatherless families other than widows' families and of one third of all one-parent families. We discuss the situation of fatherless families (including widows' families) on supplementary benefit first, then that of fatherless families (including widows' families) who are not on supplementary benefit, and finally the rather different problems of motherless families.

FATHERLESS FAMILIES ON SUPPLEMENTARY BENEFIT

Numbers

5.7 In November 1971 there were 238,000 fatherless families, out of a total of 520,000, receiving supplementary benefit, and for 200,000 of these, as shown in Table 5.1, supplementary benefit was their main source of income. The number of fatherless families drawing supplementary benefit has risen markedly in recent years. Figure 5.1 below shows the increase in numbers since 1955 in the major group receiving supplementary benefit, that is, those with no national insurance benefit, such as widow's benefit.

FIGURE 5.1

NUMBER OF LONE WOMEN WITH DEPENDENT CHILDREN*
RECEIVING NATIONAL ASSISTANCE/SUPPLEMENTARY BENEFIT
(AND NO NATIONAL INSURANCE BENEFIT) 1955/1972

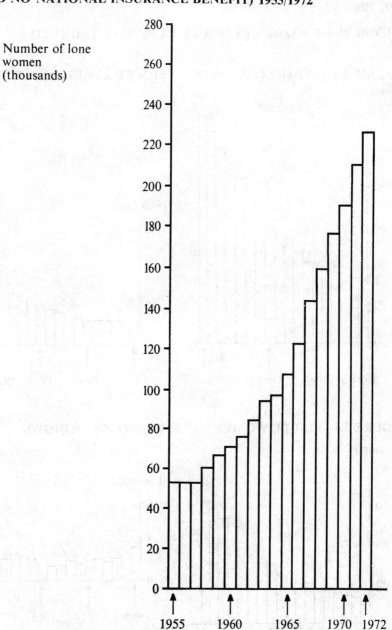

Number of lone
women
(thousands)

* Children under 16 only.

Source: Department of Health and Social Security supplementary benefit statistics.

245

The increase has varied with marital status and the following figures break down the information in Figure 5.1 to show the movement in numbers of fatherless families on supplementary benefit according to whether the mother was a separated wife, divorced, unmarried or widowed.

FIGURES 5.2, 5.3, 5.4 AND 5.5

NUMBERS OF WOMEN IN FIGURE 5.1 BY MARITAL STATUS

FIGURE 5.2—SEPARATED WIVES

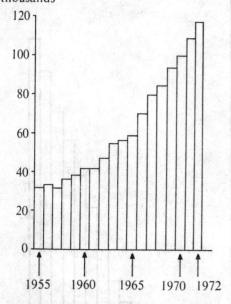

FIGURE 5.3—DIVORCED WOMEN

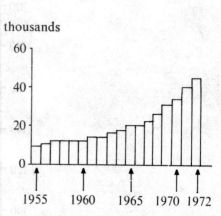

FIGURE 5.4—SINGLE WOMEN

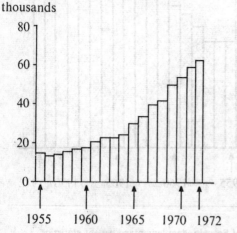

FIGURE 5.5—WIDOWS

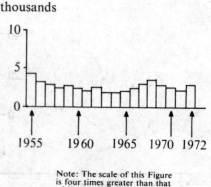

Note: The scale of this Figure is four times greater than that of Figures 5.2, 5.3 and 5.4.

5.8   Excluding changes clearly associated with high levels of unemployment, the numbers of other types of family on supplementary benefit have not increased anything like as dramatically as have the numbers of one-parent families.   What, then, has led to the very steep rise in the numbers of divorced women, separated wives and single women receiving supplementary benefit?   Part of the increase may be explained in terms of an increase in the number of lone women with dependent children in the population at any time.   In recent years, as the demographic information we include in Part 3 shows, there has been a growth not only in the number of young women in the general population but also in the proportion married; in addition there has been a fall in the average age at marriage.   In so far, therefore, as marriages of young women are more likely to break down and result in separation and divorce than are marriages of older women there has been a growth in the number of marriages with a higher than average rate of breaking down, possibly leading the wife to claim national assistance or supplementary benefit.   Between 1956 and 1971 the number of married women under 30 in the population increased by about 600,000 (about 25 per cent).   During this period the number of divorces made absolute increased from 28,000 to 79,000 a year, and the illegitimate birth rate increased to over 8 per cent compared with the level of 5 per cent that had been maintained for the greater part of this century.   All these factors have probably contributed to an increase in the number of lone women with dependent children.

5.9   The data available indicate however that the overall increase in numbers has not been anything like as great as the increase in numbers on supplementary benefit.   Census data from 1951 to 1971 have been examined and do not indicate any dramatic increase in the total number of lone women with dependent children; and the increases referred to in paragraph 5.8 in the number of young married women and the number of divorces have been much lower than the increase over this period in the number of lone women with children receiving supplementary benefit.   Nor have illegitimacy rates increased as rapidly as the number of unmarried mothers receiving supplementary benefit.   It therefore seems that demographic changes are no more than a minor element in accounting for the growth in the number of fatherless families receiving supplementary benefit.

5.10   An important factor may have been the improved real value of the supplementary benefit scale rates.   In 1955 the national assistance scale rate, together with an allowance for average rent for a woman with two dependent children, was about £4.   At the same time the net income of a woman with two dependent children (both between 5 and 11 years old) and receiving average earnings (that is, average gross earnings for a female manual worker in full-time employment plus family allowances less tax and national insurance contributions) was £5·90 (or £6·16 if she was married and paying the married woman's lower insurance contribution).   Thus in 1955 such a woman with two dependent children could increase her disposable income by approximately 45 per cent by working full-time.   By 1965 this percentage had dropped to about 6 per cent. The introduction of family income supplements (available to families with the head in full-time work—see Appendix 8) altered the picture in 1971 so that with family income supplements as well as average earnings and family allowances the lone woman with two dependent children could increase her disposable income by about 30 per cent by working full-time.   The way the relationship between supplementary benefit rates and income from working has changed over the years is shown in Figure 5.6.

FIGURE 5.6

PERCENTAGE INCREASE IN NET INCOME OVER NATIONAL ASSISTANCE/SUPPLEMENTARY BENEFIT RATES WHICH COULD BE GAINED BY A LONE WOMAN WITH TWO CHILDREN, AGED BETWEEN 5 AND 11 YEARS, BY WORKING FULL TIME FOR AN AVERAGE WAGE

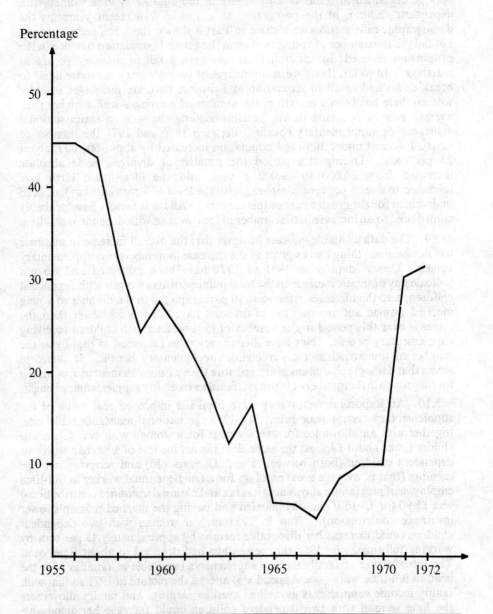

Note: The family income supplements scheme was introduced in August 1971.

Sources: Department of Health and Social Security supplementary benefit statistics; Department of Employment statistics.

5.11 While a whole range of assumptions have been made in reaching these conclusions and the position of individual families would vary widely, there is nevertheless a clear trend showing that from 1955 until 1971 it became progressively less worthwhile for a lone woman with children to take up full-time employment, and cease to claim supplementary benefit, unless she could earn well above the average wage for women in full-time work. It is not known to what extent women have perceived this and have been influenced by it into relying on supplementary benefit.

5.12 A further factor which may help to explain the increase is the greater publicity which has been given to the benefit in recent years, both by the emphasis in the supplementary benefits scheme on " benefit as of right " and by the activities of pressure groups with special interests in low-income families. The result has probably been improved general awareness and acceptability of the scheme.

5.13 The Department of Health and Social Security have also investigated whether the introduction in 1965 of revised arrangements for the diversion to the Supplementary Benefits Commission of payments under court orders in respect of lone women with children receiving supplementary benefit affected the number of such women claiming.[1] There is no clear evidence, however, to show that it did so. It is more likely that it is a combination of the various other factors referred to above which is responsible for the increased numbers revealed in Figure 5.1.

5.14 The most recent figures suggest that the rate of increase has been falling: the figures for May 1972 show a 4·5 per cent increase over those for November 1971, whereas those for May 1973 are only 1·2 per cent higher than those for November 1972. The increase in absolute numbers in the latter period was 2,748 compared with 10,055 in the earlier period. While the numbers may be levelling out—and the introduction of the family income supplements scheme in August 1971 may be partly responsible for this—there is no evidence to suggest that a dramatic reduction may be about to take place.

5.15 At the levels that have now been reached, the proportion of fatherless families drawing supplementary benefit is striking. The supplementary benefits scheme is intended to act as a safety net for those in the population who have fallen on hard times, cannot support themselves by working and are unable to manage on national insurance benefits and any other resources they may have. The high proportion of all fatherless families (40 per cent) whose main source of income is supplementary benefit is an indication of how few of them have significant income from other sources, and, in particular, of the small number with national insurance benefits (such as widow's benefit).

5.16 The proportion of fatherless families drawing supplementary benefit is put into perspective by comparing it with the proportions of motherless and two-parent families doing so. At the end of 1971, out of about 100,000 motherless families, some 7,000 with children under 16 were receiving regular payments of supplementary benefit, and of over 6 million two-parent families (over 400,000 of them with the breadwinner at least temporarily sick or unemployed) the number receiving supplementary benefit with children under 16 was about 175,000. Despite the fact that there are more than ten times as

---

[1] We discuss this diversion procedure in Part 4.

many two-parent families in the population as fatherless families, the number receiving supplementary benefit was quite appreciably lower. The reason for this is, of course, that a male head of a family will normally be in full-time work, and even if he is sick or loses his job he is generally able to claim an insurance benefit for either sickness or unemployment. While the flat-rate benefit itself is not generally sufficient to remove the need for supplementary benefit, those with an earnings-related supplement or a small amount of some other income may well be above the supplementary benefit level. The difference receipt of a national insurance benefit can make is shown by the position of widows with children, who quite often have some private provision such as an occupational pension or insurance payment, as well as a widow's benefit, and rely on supplementary benefit much less than other fatherless families. Of some 120,000 widowed mothers with a widow's benefit about 26,000 claim supplementary benefit and the average payment to them is much lower than that for other fatherless families.

Level of resources

5.17 The families receiving supplementary benefit will normally have financial resources which, including supplementary benefit, will be at or slightly above the basic supplementary benefit level. The extent to which they may be above that level depends on whether there is income which is disregarded to some extent in the calculation of benefit, such as the first £2 of net earnings from part-time employment. Very exceptionally, a family receiving supplementary benefit may have total resources which are less than their normal supplementary benefit requirements because the Supplementary Benefits Commission have decided that their rent is unreasonably high and cannot therefore be met in full for supplementary benefit purposes. The introduction of the national rent rebate and allowance scheme, however, was accompanied by some modification of the Commission's discretionary powers in regard to rent, and there are now likely to be few families in this position.[1]

5.18 In 1972 only about 15 per cent of lone women with children who were on supplementary benefit declared any earnings at all (for single mothers the figure is 10 per cent, for divorced mothers 24 per cent, and for separated wives 14 per cent), and their declared weekly earnings averaged only about £3·60. The majority had no capital assets, but of the 33,000 (13 per cent) who did, only 2 per cent had sufficient to be taken into account in calculating their supplementary benefit entitlement. The average amount of capital held by the 33,000 families was about £155. (The value of an owner-occupied house is disregarded.)

Length of time on supplementary benefit

5.19 The seriousness with which one views the numbers of fatherless families on supplementary benefit must be related to the length of time for which individual families are in this position. If most families rely on the benefit for a period of a few weeks only at a time, while they overcome a temporary setback in their financial situation, this would be no great cause for concern. If, on the other hand, large numbers of one-parent families find themselves drawing supplementary benefit month after month, or even year after year, then careful consideration is needed of alternative forms of help.

[1] We also refer to this in Part 6.

5.20   The length of time during which a beneficiary has been continuously receiving supplementary benefit has been measured in the annual enquiries by the Department of Health and Social Security since 1964.   Average duration has varied comparatively little over the years.   The following information relating to November 1972 shows the length of time for which fatherless families, excluding those families, such as widows', with an insurance benefit, had been drawing supplementary benefit:

less than 3 months	...	...	...	27,300
3 to 6 months	...	...	...	20,300
6 to 12 months	...	...	...	33,400
1 to 2 years	...	...	...	45,900
2 to 3 years	...	...	...	28,400
3 to 4 years	...	...	...	17,300
4 to 5 years	...	...	...	15,100
5 to 10 years	...	...	...	30,700
10 years or more	...	...	...	8,400

About 100,000, nearly one half, had been in receipt of supplementary benefit for over two years.   This represented at that point in time about 25 per cent of all fatherless families, excluding the families of widows.

5.21   This evidence suggests that supplementary benefit is the main support or a significant number of fatherless families for lengthy periods of time. It demonstrates that the problem is not one of a short-term nature and that it would be a mistake to view it as such.   On the contrary, considerable numbers of children are spending their formative years at the basic level of resources provided by the supplementary benefits scheme.

Characteristics of fatherless families on supplementary benefit

5.22   Whether the head of a fatherless family is unable to work full time and therefore relies on supplementary benefit appears to depend on the number of children, the presence of a pre-school child and the type of household, that is, whether only the mother and her dependent children comprise the household (a single-unit household), or whether there are other adults or family units in the same household (multi-unit household).   The following Figures are drawn from the Department of Health and Social Security analysis of the Family Expenditure Survey data,[1] from 1969 to 1971, and they relate to all fatherless families other than widows' families.

---

[1] See Appendix 10.

FIGURES 5.7, 5.8 AND 5.9

ANALYSIS OF FATHERLESS FAMILIES (OTHER THAN THOSE OF WIDOWS) BY FAMILY SIZE, BY AGE OF YOUNGEST CHILD AND BY HOUSEHOLD TYPE, SHOWING THE PROPORTION OF EACH CATEGORY RECEIVING SUPPLEMENTARY BENEFIT, AT THE END OF 1971

FIGURE 5.7—BY FAMILY SIZE

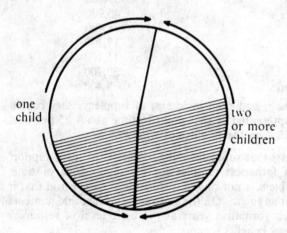

Number with one child	: 210,000
Number of these receiving supplementary benefit	: 80,000 (39%)
Number with two or more children	: 190,000
Number of these receiving supplementary benefit	: 120,000 (63%)

FIGURE 5.8—BY AGE OF YOUNGEST CHILD

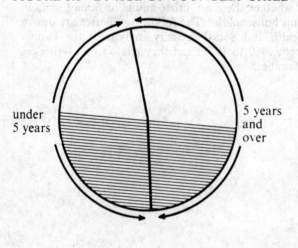

Number with youngest child under 5	: 190,000
Number of these receiving supplementary benefit	: 110,000 (57%)
Number with youngest child age 5 or over	: 210,000
Number of these receiving supplementary benefit	: 90,000 (44%)

252

FIGURE 5.9—BY HOUSEHOLD TYPE

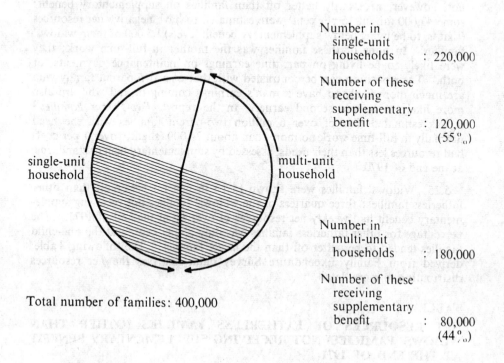

Number in
single-unit
households   : 220,000

Number of these
receiving
supplementary
benefit   : 120,000
                   (55 %)

single-unit
household

multi-unit
household

Number in
multi-unit
households   : 180,000

Number of these
receiving
supplementary
benefit   : 80,000
                   (44 %)

Total number of families: 400,000

Proportion of families receiving supplementary
benefit in each category.

Source: Family Expenditure Survey pooled data, 1969–1971; Department of Health and
Social Security supplementary benefit statistics.

FATHERLESS FAMILIES NOT RECEIVING SUPPLEMENTARY BENEFIT

5.23   Data from the Family Expenditure Surveys for 1969 to 1971 have
been analysed by the Department of Health and Social Security to obtain
information about the financial circumstances of fatherless families not receiving
supplementary benefit.   The full report, from which the data set out in this
Section have been drawn, is at Appendix 10, where there is also an explanation
of the methodology which was employed and the qualifications relating to
the analyses.

Numbers and resources

5.24　On the basis of the Family Expenditure Survey data it can be said that about 300,000 fatherless families were not drawing supplementary benefit at the end of 1971 (100,000 widows' families and 200,000 others). They were not, however, necessarily better off than families on supplementary benefit: some 43,000 (about 15 per cent) were estimated to have negative net resources (that is, to be living below supplementary benefit levels),[1] 5,000 of them widows' families. In none of these families was the mother in full-time work; they were likely to be living on part-time earnings or maintenance payments, or both. Their position can be contrasted with that of a two-parent family who are much more likely to have a man's earnings coming in and who are also more likely to have a second earner. In the report, *Two-Parent Families*,[2] it was estimated that of over 6 million two-parent families with the head normally in full-time work no more than about 74,000 (slightly over 1 per cent) had resources less than their needs, assessed by supplementary benefit standards, at the end of 1970.

5.25　Widows' families were shown to be in general better off than other fatherless families: three quarters of the widows' families not receiving supplementary benefit had weekly net resources of over £5 at the end of 1971. The percentage for other fatherless families was only 55 per cent, and the one-child families tended to be better off than the larger families. The following Table, derived from Family Expenditure Survey data, analyses the net resources distribution in more detail.

TABLE 5.2

NET RESOURCES OF FATHERLESS FAMILIES (OTHER THAN WIDOWS' FAMILIES) NOT RECEIVING SUPPLEMENTARY BENEFIT AT THE END OF 1971

Size of family	Weekly net resources:				
	Less than £0	£0–£1·99	£2–£4·99	£5 or more	All
	Thousands				
Families with 1 child	18	12	23	77	130
2 or more children	20	4	12	33	69
All families	38	16	35	110	199
	Percentage				
Families with 1 child	14	9	18	59	100
2 or more children	29	6	17	48	100
All families	19	8	18	55	100

Source: Family Expenditure Survey pooled data, 1969–1971.

[1] An explanation of the concept of net resources, which is used frequently in this Section, is in Appendix 10.

[2] J R Howe: *Two Parent Families: A Study of their Resources and Needs in 1968, 1969 and 1970*, DHSS Statistical Report Series No 14, HMSO, 1971.

5.26   In relation to two-parent families with the head in full-time work the *Two-Parent Families* report[1] showed that 735,000 (about 11 per cent) had weekly net resources of less than £5 at the end of 1970, and 204,000 (about 3 per cent) had weekly net resources of less than £2.   Comparison with the 45 per cent and 27 per cent for fatherless families (see Table 5.2) confirms once again the relative financial disadvantage suffered by the generality of fatherless families in relation to the generality of two-parent families.

Low earnings

5.27   The low level of net resources among fatherless families not on supplementary benefit is partly explained by the fact that the one-parent family is less likely than the two-parent family to have a second earner.   A highly important factor also is the low earnings of lone mothers.   In addition to 119,000 lone mothers (other than widows) in full-time employment, analysis of the Family Expenditure Survey data suggests that there were 34,000 in part-time employment and not on supplementary benefit at the end of 1971. Figure 10 shows the earnings of all the 153,000 mothers in employment, and not on supplementary benefit, analysed by whether or not there is a pre-school child in the family.   In total 110,000 (over 70 per cent of those in work) had earnings of less than £20 a week.   It can be seen that women with no pre-school child had higher earnings than other mothers: 37 per cent of the former against 13 per cent of the latter earned £20 or more a week while 62 per cent against 43 per cent earned £15 or more.   This trend in the level of earnings was the same for mothers in both single-unit and multi-unit households,[2] although from the very high proportion of working mothers with a child under 5 in multi-unit households (90 per cent) it can be inferred that the presence of others in the household is a key factor in determining whether the mother can work at all.   Amongst all lone women with children (other than widows) not on supplementary benefit 132,000 had earnings of less than £25, 110,000 had earnings of less than £20 and 68,000 had earnings of less than £15.   Two-parent families generally have the full-time wage of a man, and average earnings of men in full-time manual work in manufacturing and some of the principal non-manufacturing industries were £30·93 in October 1971.

---

[1] *Op cit.*

[2] For explanation of these terms see paragraph 5.22.

FIGURE 5.10

EARNINGS OF FATHERLESS FAMILIES (OTHER THAN WIDOWS' FAMILIES) NOT RECEIVING SUPPLEMENTARY BENEFIT AT THE END OF 1971: LEVEL OF GROSS EARNINGS FROM FULL-TIME AND PART-TIME EMPLOYMENT

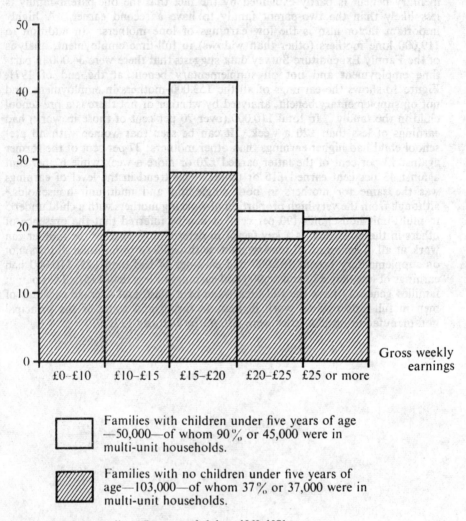

Number of families (thousands)

Gross weekly earnings

£0–£10 £10–£15 £15–£20 £20–£25 £25 or more

Families with children under five years of age —50,000—of whom 90% or 45,000 were in multi-unit households.

Families with no children under five years of age—103,000—of whom 37% or 37,000 were in multi-unit households.

Source: Family Expenditure Survey pooled data, 1969–1971.

256

5.28 A similar analysis of the Family Expenditure Survey data in relation to two-parent families points this contrast between the earning capacity of a two-parent family and of a lone mother. Table 5.3 shows the earnings of two-parent families where the father is in full-time work, and is therefore not comparable with Figure 5.10 which includes lone mothers in part-time work, but the lesson is clear: where for over 70 per cent of fatherless families in work gross earnings were less than £20 a week at the end of 1971, this applied to about 5 per cent of two-parent families with the head in full-time work. Looking at those families with gross earnings less than £25 a week, the data show that over 85 per cent of the fatherless families were in that position at the end of 1971 and about 18 per cent of the two-parent families.

TABLE 5.3

GROSS EARNINGS OF TWO-PARENT FAMILIES WITH HEAD IN FULL-TIME WORK AT THE END OF 1971

Gross weekly earnings	Number of families (thousands)	Percentage of all two-parent families in full-time work
All earnings	6,204	100
Less than £25	1,068	17
Less than £20	320	5
Less than £15	21	*
Less than £10	—	0

* Less than 0·5 per cent.
Source: Family Expenditure Survey pooled data, 1969–1971.

Numbers receiving family income supplements

5.29 A further indication of the relatively low earnings of fatherless families compared with those of two-parent families is given by the pattern of awards of family income supplements. (This benefit is only payable to people in full-time work—see Appendix 8.) The higher awards for fatherless families become more significant when one takes into account the fact that two-parent families claiming family income supplements have, on average, more children than one-parent families.

TABLE 5.4

NUMBER AND AMOUNT OF AWARDS OF FAMILY INCOME SUPPLEMENTS

	Fatherless families		Motherless families		Two-parent families		Total awards	
	Number	Average weekly amount	Number	Average weekly amount	Number	Average weekly amount	Number	Average weekly amount
October 1971 ...	18,000	£2·20	1,000	£1·47	38,000	£1·51	57,000	£1·73
October 1972 ...	33,000	£2·58	1,000	£1·75	51,000	£1·79	85,000	£2·09
April 1973 ...	36,000	£2·90	1,000	£2·23	47,000	£2·38	84,000	£2·59

Source: Department of Health and Social Security family income supplements statistics (20 per cent sample). April 1973 figures are provisional.

Other factors in low income

5.30   The extent to which fatherless families not on supplementary benefit have other income to call on apart from earnings or widows' benefits is limited. Typically such income, apart from family allowances and family income supplements, would be maintenance payments.[1]   Table 5.5 indicates that nearly two thirds of the fatherless families (other than widows' families) not receiving supplementary benefit at the end of 1971 had a gross income of less than £20 a week.   Of these lower income mothers, the majority were found to have a pre-school age child and not to be working full time, whereas the converse was the position in relation to mothers with a gross income of more than £20, who were far more likely to be working and to have their youngest child already at school.

TABLE 5.5

GROSS   WEEKLY   INCOME   OF   FATHERLESS   FAMILIES (OTHER THAN WIDOWS' FAMILIES) NOT ON SUPPLEMENTARY BENEFIT AT THE END OF 1971

Gross weekly income	Full-time employed	Part-time or not employed	All not on supplementary benefit
	Thousands		
Less than £15 ...	13	52	65
£15–£19·99	47	13	60
£20 and over ...	59	15	74
All incomes	119	80	199
	Percentage		
Less than £15 ...	11	65	33
£15–£19·99	39	16	30
£20 and over ...	50	19	37
All incomes	100	100	100

Source: Family Expenditure Survey pooled data, 1969–1971.

5.31   In comparison the following Table in relation to two-parent families shows that about 2 per cent of those with the head in full-time work had a gross weekly income of less than £20 at the end of 1971.

[1] The level of maintenance payments is discussed in Part 4.

TABLE 5.6

GROSS WEEKLY INCOME OF TWO-PARENT FAMILIES WITH HEAD IN FULL-TIME WORK AT THE END OF 1971

Gross weekly income		Full-time employed
		Thousands
Less than £15	...	3
£15–£19·99 ...	...	110
£20–£24·99 ...	...	406
£25 and over	...	5,685
All incomes ...	...	6,204
		Percentage
Less than £15	...	*
£15–£19·99 ...	...	2
£20–£24·99 ...	...	6
£25 and over	...	92
All incomes ...	...	100

* Less than 0·5 per cent.
Source: Family Expenditure Survey pooled data, 1969–1971.

STUDY BY THE OFFICE OF POPULATION CENSUSES AND SURVEYS

5.32 Comparison between the financial position of fatherless families and that of two-parent families is made to considerable effect by the evidence produced by the study of one-parent families undertaken by the Office of Population Censuses and Surveys, *Families and their Needs*.[1] While the study consisted of separate surveys of five different local authority areas, and so does not necessarily provide a representative picture for the country as a whole, a consistent finding in each of the areas was that the average incomes of fatherless families were less than half those of two-parent families. (This supports the contrast between the earning capacity of a two-parent family and that of a one-parent family noted from the Family Expenditure Survey data and brought out in the preceding paragraphs.) In all areas studied at least half the two-parent families had a usual income of at least £20 a week, while the corresponding proportion of fatherless families was nowhere more than 13 per cent.[2] The number of two-parent families with less than £10 a week was negligible, but the proportions of fatherless families below this level ranged from 17 per cent to 41 per cent. The report concluded that, even if the sampling method used had resulted in some over-statement of the proportion of very low-income fatherless families, the financial gap between the majority of fatherless families and the majority of two-parent families was still very great.

[1] Audrey Hunt, Judith Fox and Margaret Morgan: *Families and their Needs*, HMSO, 1973.
[2] The interviewing took place in the summer and autumn of 1970 and the average earnings of full-time manual wage-earners in manufacturing and some of the principal non-manufacturing industries in October 1970 was £28·05 for men and £13·99 for women.

259

5.33   As we have already pointed out in this Section, comparatively few motherless families draw supplementary benefit.   Because of the higher rates of pay available to men, full-time work is generally a much more attractive alternative financially for them than supplementary benefit.   Moreover, it is the policy of the Supplementary Benefits Commission to expect a man in this position normally to rely on earnings rather than on supplementary benefit, and the Commission are prepared to pay benefit without requiring registration for employment only where they are satisfied that the man is needed at home to look after the children.   (We comment on this policy in Section 8.)   Because of the small numbers on supplementary benefit (some 7,200 in November 1972 out of a total of 100,000) detailed analysis of their circumstances is less reliable than for fatherless families and less significant in gaining a general picture of the financial position of one-parent families.   Information from the study of motherless families undertaken by Dr V George and Dr P Wilding of the Department of Applied Social Science at Nottingham University[1] makes it clear, however, that, on the whole, the fathers interviewed who were drawing supplementary benefit were those with larger families.   Other relevant factors in causing them to give up full-time work and claim supplementary benefit appeared to be the presence of children under 5, the long or irregular hours which their normal work involved and the extent to which their normal work required them to stay away from home.   Of the fathers interviewed, who had at some stage since their wife's death or departure received supplementary benefit to stay at home and look after the children, over 55 per cent had received benefit for less than a year and over 35 per cent for less than six months.

5.34   There is no doubt that when the father is in full-time work motherless families tend to be financially better off than fatherless families because of the higher earnings men can command.   From the family income supplements statistics quoted in Table 5.4 above it is evident that supplements are drawn by about 1 per cent of motherless families where the father is in full-time work but by some 30 per cent of fatherless families where the mother is in full-time work.   The average award to motherless families is appreciably lower than that for fatherless families.

5.35   Nevertheless there is clear evidence that motherless families with the father in work, although better-off financially than fatherless families, are considerably worse-off than two-parent families.   George and Wilding[2] found that men considered that their employment prospects were damaged because of their dual role—" the heavy burdens of combining work and the care of children . . . discouraged movement to new and better paid jobs which might turn out to be more demanding."   The same point was made by several organisations and individuals giving evidence to us.   We were also told that men on their own lost earnings through inability to do shift work and overtime, or having to work a shorter working day.   The County Borough of Burnley told us there was evidence that fathers who kept their families together and continued to work could usually accept " only normal day shift work, which

---

[1] V George and P Wilding: *Motherless Families*, Routledge and Kegan Paul, 1972.
[2] *Op cit*.

is usually unskilled and on a low wage". The Women's National Commission said: " Consideration should also be given to the working father on his own with children, who gets no financial assistance from supplementary benefits. He finds it difficult to work overtime, and so cannot accumulate extra money for use in an emergency. Yet there will be weeks when, for instance, one of the children is ill and he will have to stay at home, thus reducing his earnings to a possibly very low level." We also received comments on the difficulty men have in finding part-time work, on their having to move to be near relatives, and on their having to accept jobs beneath their capability.

THE OVERALL PICTURE

5.36 The statistical material and the research studies we have examined overwhelmingly confirmed the general impression of financial hardship amongst one-parent families which had been noted at the time our Committee was set up. It has consistently been shown that, with only a few individual exceptions, fatherless families are considerably worse off financially than two-parent families. They are distinguished particularly by their dependence on one adult alone to provide the family's income, and handicapped by the relatively low level of earnings which mothers with children, particularly young children, can achieve, mainly because of low rates of pay for women's work, but also, to a much lesser extent, because of the restriction they may have to place on the hours for which they can work. The consequence is that a high proportion of fatherless families, particularly those with very young children, rely on supplementary benefit and have little or no other income. It is rarely worth their while to earn more than is disregarded in their supplementary benefit award (currently £2, after allowing for working expenses) unless they can work full time. The standard of living of these families is accordingly that which obtains at, or only a little above, supplementary benefit level, and for a substantial number this remains the position for long periods of time.

5.37 The family of a widow with a widow's benefit are likely to be in a rather better position than most other fatherless families because they are more likely to find that the mother's earnings, although low compared with those of a man or a married couple, supplement the widow's benefit to the extent that they can achieve a level of income well above supplementary benefit levels. In addition they, of all one-parent families, are likeliest to have income from some sort of private provision made by the father, such as life assurance or an occupational pension, and a fully paid-up mortgage on the home.

5.38 In financial terms the lone father, too, will normally be better off than the lone mother. In comparison with the two-parent family his income is likely to be somewhat less as he may have to take a lower paid job or refuse overtime because of the demands which caring for the family make upon him, and there is no wife to supplement the family's income through her own earnings. His earnings are, however, likely to be sufficient to keep his family some way above supplementary benefit levels and, unless he has a large or very young family, he will be unlikely to spend long periods out of work and claiming supplementary benefit.

5.39   A comparative picture of the financial situation of different types of family is given in the diagram below.   This compares the net income levels in April 1973 of families with two children (aged 7 and 4) and assumes a rent of £4 and rates of £1·25 before rebate.   The families used are as follows:

(1) a fatherless family with the mother not working and dependent upon supplementary benefit;

(2) a two-parent family where the father (aged between 35 and 45) has been sick for more than 28 weeks and is receiving invalidity benefit and the mother is not working;

(3) a fatherless family with the mother in full-time work and earning an average wage for manual work of £19·10;

(4) a two-parent family with the father in full-time work, and mother not working, earning an average wage for manual work of £37·40;

(5) a family where the mother is a widow with a widowed mother's allowance and is in full-time work on earnings of £19·10.

Net income is the sum of earnings (after deduction of tax, national insurance contribution and an arbitrary amount of 50p a week for other working expenses), family allowances, appropriate national insurance benefits at the standard rate, supplementary benefit entitlement, family income supplement entitlement, appropriate rate rebate and appropriate rent rebate or allowance.

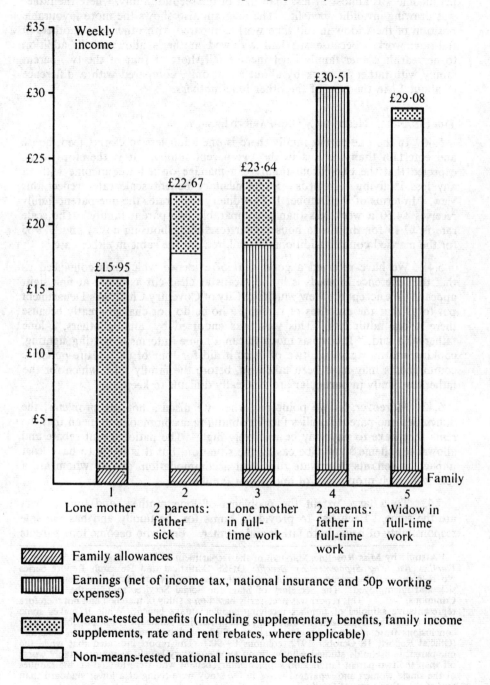

FIGURE 5.11

**COMPARISON OF THE NET INCOME AVAILABLE TO FIVE
TYPES OF FAMILY** (as described in paragraph 5.39)

Weekly
income

£35

£30 — £30·51

£29·08

£25 —

£23·64

£22·67

£20 —

£15 —
£15·95

£10 —

£5 —

Family

| 1 | 2 | 3 | 4 | 5 |

Lone mother | 2 parents: father sick | Lone mother in full-time work | 2 parents: father in full-time work | Widow in full-time work

Family allowances

Earnings (net of income tax, national insurance and 50p working
expenses)

Means-tested benefits (including supplementary benefits, family income
supplements, rate and rent rebates, where applicable)

Non-means-tested national insurance benefits

263

The most striking aspect revealed by the diagram is the great disadvantage of the lone mother whose sole income is supplementary benefit and family allowances, as compared with the four other types of family. Her family's net income was almost £7 less than that of the second family, where the father was drawing invalidity benefit. The diagram also shows the more favourable position of the widow in full-time work compared with other lone mothers in full-time work. Because she had widowed mother's allowance in addition to her earnings, her family's net income fell short of that of the two-parent family with father in work by about £1·50 only, compared with a difference of about £7 in the case of the other lone mothers.

THE FINANCIAL NEEDS OF A ONE-PARENT FAMILY

5.40 In the one-parent family there is one adult less to clothe, feed, house and entertain than there is in the two-parent family. It is therefore to be expected that the one-parent family can manage on a lower income without any loss in living standards. Supplementary benefit scale rates reflect this view. In terms of the October 1973 ordinary scale rates the one-parent family receives £4.50 a week less than a comparable two-parent family. The scale rate is £7·15 for the single householder (excluding housing costs) and £11·65 for the married couple; additions for children are the same in either case.[1]

5.41 We have received a good deal of evidence which has convinced us that the difference in needs is by no means as clear-cut as might at first sight appear. We accept the view which the City of Coventry Children's Department put to us that the expenses of running a home do not change greatly because there is one adult less. This view was endorsed by, among others, a lone father who said, " It costs as much to run a home in terms of heating, lighting, cooking and mortgage for two of us as it did for four of us." Hire-purchase commitments may have been taken on, before the family split, which for the fatherless family in particular are especially difficult to keep up.

5.42 Moreover, as we point out when we discuss housing problems, the difficulties one-parent families face in obtaining accommodation mean that the rents they have to pay may be relatively high. The national rent rebate and allowance scheme should be easing the situation, but it is likely to have least impact on tenants in private furnished accommodation, among whom are a relatively high proportion of one-parent families.

5.43 To a large extent the problems of lone mothers and lone fathers are the same. Each has to provide a home for the family and has the sole responsibility of being both father and mother. Few who become lone parents

---

[1] A study by Miss Rosalind Marshall of the Department of Health and Social Security— *Families Receiving Supplementary Benefit:* DHSS Statistical and Research Report Series No 1—compared the circumstances of some fatherless families and families of the long-term sick and unemployed. The Secretary of State for Social Services said, in the House of Commons, " . . . This report was necessarily based on a study of matched and not therefore representative samples of families receiving supplementary benefit. While it makes some helpful comparisons between the different kinds of families studied it is not possible to draw conclusions from it about the circumstances of one and two-parent families in general." (Official Report, 18 October 1972, columns 89–90.) The report indicated that while the one-parent households studied who were on supplementary benefit were not notably worse off than the two-parent families on supplementary benefit who were looked at, the families of the single women and separated wives in the study were living at a lower standard than any of the other types of family.

seem to be able to carry on the previous life style for their family and each has to make alterations according to individual circumstances. Certain types of problem, however, occur more frequently for fathers, for example, in relation to domestic chores, and others, such as in relation to house maintenance and repair work, occur more frequently for mothers.

5.44 In motherless families " the biggest practical problem is having no woman around the house to cook, sew, repair, and replace personal clothes and bed and table linen etc, washing and ironing—in fact, homemaking—and this could involve the family in a fair amount of expense". This statement by the City of Coventry Children's Department was echoed by others and we accept that it has a great deal of truth in it. One lone father told us how he tackled the problem. He had " an automatic dishwasher, washing machine and dryer. All the sheets are nylon and warmer clothing courtelle, so that there is a minimum of ironing." Organisation of this kind, however, involves the family in expenditure which was not necessary when the mother was present and which is well beyond the means of most one-parent families.

5.45 For the mother on her own, particular problems arise in relation to house decoration and maintenance. The National Council for the Unmarried Mother and her Child[1] mentioned in their evidence[2] that some housing associations find that maintaining accommodation for a fatherless family may cost them as much as £1 a week above the cost for a two-parent family because many household repairs and decorations undertaken by husbands cannot be done by a mother on her own. The mother who is responsible for the maintenance of the home generally has to engage and pay workmen, and this sort of expense makes considerable inroads on any savings from the absence of one adult.

5.46 Fatherless and motherless families both face high expenditure on food because of a need to reduce the time spent on preparing meals. The London Borough of Barnet in their evidence referred to the tendency, where the head of the family is working, to " buy more expensive food for quick meals instead of preparing economical dishes". The families are forced to make use of " convenience " foods, such as frozen or pre-cooked foods, which are expensive and there is little opportunity to economise by home-baking and so on. The working parent also has less time to shop around and take advantage of cut-price offers in the way the mother in the two-parent family often can. Although there is one adult less to feed and clothe, any direct saving is eroded in this way.

5.47 Child-minding may be an additional expense for either fatherless or motherless families. Where there are young children the parent has to make arrangements for them to be adequately cared for at any time when he or she is not able to be with them. This is not a problem solely for those parents who go out to work, although for such parents the problems when a child is sick are particularly severe. There are occasions for all parents, if they are to lead a reasonably normal social life, when they need to be away from the

---

[1] Since 1 November 1973 this organisation has been renamed the National Council for One-Parent Families in recognition of its wider role.

[2] *Forward for the Fatherless*, paragraph 357, published by the National Council for the Unmarried Mother and her child, May 1971.

children for short periods. In the one-parent family there is no second parent to take over and it may well not be possible to enlist help in child-minding unless the parent can afford to pay appropriately.

5.48 These extra expenses are difficult to quantify and the need for them varies from household to household according to circumstances and aptitudes. There are one-parent families which run smoothly and adapt to their circumstances so well that their standard of living does not suffer, even though their income may have fallen. But the evidence convinced us that there are many families where the lone parent is forced into substantial extra expenses of the kind we have mentioned. It is not infrequent for this expenditure to equal or even exceed the saving to the household of not maintaining the other parent.

SECTION 3—THE NEED FOR EXTRA HELP

5.49 The supplementary benefits scheme already provides financial support for lone parents who are not in full-time work and whose own resources are inadequate for their needs. The level to which their incomes are made up, which we shall refer to as the basic level, has been approved by Parliament as the level below which people not in full-time work should not generally be allowed to fall. Unlike many other countries (see paragraph 5.66 below) this country has long accepted that the mother with dependent children should not be expected to support herself by working, and lone mothers who do not work full time can draw supplementary benefit until their youngest child leaves school without being required to register for work. (The requirement to register may also be waived for lone fathers: we discuss this in more detail in Section 8.) In the light of the availability of supplementary benefit some may argue that there is no need for further financial provision for one-parent families. Except where the second parent has died, it may be argued that it is unfair on the rest of the community, who are meeting their responsibilities, for the State to go further in making good any failure of the second parent to provide for his (or less commonly her) own family. Against this we know from the evidence, research studies and statistics available to us, and summarised in the previous Section, what the financial circumstances of one-parent families are like. Generally, they have a considerably lower income than other families; may spend long periods on supplementary benefit with no other significant source of income; and there is a substantial proportion without supplementary benefit and actually living below the supplementary benefit level. Yet, despite this lower income, these families still have many of the expenses of two-parent families, and some additional ones. Three factors seem to us to stand out in considering present financial provision in relation to the needs of one-parent families. These are the lack of any worthwhile financial gain by combining part-time work with supplementary benefit; the low level of income among working one-parent families compared with two-parent families; and the inadequacy and uncertainty of maintenance payments as a source of income. These three factors are examined in the paragraphs which follow.

DETERRENT TO COMBINING SUPPLEMENTARY BENEFIT WITH PART-TIME WORK

5.50 We have noticed earlier (paragraph 5.18) that in November 1972 only 15 per cent of lone mothers receiving supplementary benefit declared any earnings at all, and their earnings averaged only £3·60 a week. We received much evidence that the supplementary benefits scheme discourages the lone parent from doing such work as his or her family responsibilities may leave time and energy to do. Under the supplementary benefits scheme only the first £2 of earnings from part-time employment are disregarded (after deduction of expenses). Earnings above that level are of no advantage to the claimant because the benefit is reduced by the same amount. Thus there is little financial incentive for most lone parents on supplementary benefit to work, although we received a good deal of evidence indicating that some of them were anxious to do so and that the social and psychological advantages to them of doing so could be considerable. The Catholic Housing Aid Society in evidence to us expressed the view that "participation in a working community and the measure of independence that results from a weekly wage, the increase in self-respect and self-help, heal the wounds of marriage breakdown"; and other bodies referred to the mental and physical effects on some lone mothers of being unemployed and on supplementary benefit. The Scottish Health Visitors' Association studied the cases of 380 one-parent families with whom they had had contact and told us that going out to work had improved the morale of many lone mothers who had been depressed and enabled them to think more constructively about the future rather than about what might have been.

5.51 Lone parents have to prepare for their own as well as their children's future, and for the time, after the children have left home, when they are no longer likely to be entitled to any State support. A gradually increasing amount of part-time work may be important in the transition. But the supplementary benefits scheme was not devised for such purposes and is ill-adapted to them. The principles underlying it are not compatible with a programme, which may be best suited to the needs of many one-parent families, by which a parent supports the family partly with a State benefit and partly from earnings. The position of the one-parent family may be contrasted with that of the families of invalidity pensioners, who form another group which may find themselves on State support for long periods. The wife of such a pensioner is able to earn up to £9·59 a week net without producing any effect upon his benefit award. (If the family, however, is receiving supplementary benefit, that benefit is reduced in the normal way to take account of any earnings of the wife over a net amount of £2.) We also noticed that in the overseas countries which we studied, all of which put much greater emphasis on the need for the lone parent to work than we do in this country, much more generous disregards were usual (combined with lower basic rates of social assistance). In Denmark, for instance, only 50 per cent of net earnings are taken into account.

WHERE THE PARENT IS IN FULL-TIME WORK

5.52 Lone parents who are able to work full time (and are not therefore entitled to supplementary benefit) tend nevertheless to be considerably worse off than working two-parent families (see paragraphs 5.27–5.31 above). There are several reasons for this. Chief among them is the low level of women's earnings. We discuss this more fully in dealing with employment problems and demographic matters. Suffice it to say here that the average gross earnings of women manual workers in full-time employment in April 1973 were about half those of men—£19·10 as compared to £37·40. The evidence set out in paragraphs 5.27–5.29 above confirms that women heads of fatherless families earn far less than male heads of families. Because women tend to be employed in predominantly low-wage occupations, the coming of equal pay is not likely to make a dramatic difference to this. The low level of women's earnings means that women who could work, and want to do so, nevertheless live on supplementary benefit because they are financially better off that way. The Women's National Advisory Committee of the National Union of Conservative and Unionist Associations said in evidence to us, "For the unskilled woman there is no encouragement to work, even if she wishes to, for her full-time wage is almost always as low, if not lower, than the amount which she can regularly get from the DHSS, in the form of supplementary benefit and assistance with rent." In none of the overseas countries we studied were women's wages as low in relation to men's as in this country.

5.53 But even if women's wage rates were equal to men's, there would still be problems. As we mention in paragraph 5.35, there is evidence that lone parents suffer some restriction in their ability to earn because they may not be able to work overtime, or they may have to give up work in the school holidays, or take time off when a child is sick. And, of course, most working lone-parent families cannot hope to achieve anything like the standard of living of the two-earner family, which is becoming more general. Thus it is not only the family where the lone parent is not working that is at a disadvantage: the children of the lone parent who is at work are also likely to find themselves considerably worse off than their neighbours in two-parent families.

INADEQUACY AND UNCERTAINTY OF MAINTENANCE PAYMENTS

5.54 The introduction of the family income supplements scheme has helped the working one-parent family, particularly the fatherless family, as paragraph 5.10 shows. This serves to highlight the fact that, for many lone mothers, working full time is financially worthwhile only if there is some other source of income on which they can regularly rely. The working lone mother may be relying on maintenance payments to supplement her income. We discuss in detail elsewhere the present unsatisfactory position in relation to maintenance orders, in particular their uncertainty as a source of income and the inadequacy of arrangements for review, and we make proposals for changes in the system in relation, in particular, to the Supplementary Benefits Commission. It was put to us by several organisations giving evidence that some mothers eventually reluctantly apply for supplementary benefit in order to relieve themselves of the worry and uncertainty of maintenance payments. The National Council for the Unmarried Mother and her Child said in evidence, " The uncertainty of recovering regular maintenance from her child's father is a disincentive to work. . . . When no maintenance is forthcoming she is seriously embarrassed. . . . Many mothers give up the struggle and revert to living on supplementary benefit. . . ."[1] We regard it as most unfortunate that the efforts of women who are trying to support themselves should be frustrated in this way, and think it vital that some way should be found of changing this situation. This can only be by provision outside the supplementary benefits scheme if lone mothers in full-time work are to be helped.

---

[1] *Forward for the Fatherless*, paragraph 141.

CONCLUSION

5.55 In the light of these three factors, combined with the evidence of general and persistent low levels of income, and of needs not very different from those of a two-parent family, we conclude that extra help is needed for one-parent families. There are, of course, other disadvantaged groups; but in terms of families with children, which must be the relevant standard of comparison here, there can be no other group of this size who are as poor as fatherless families, of whom so many lack any State benefit other than supplementary benefit or family allowances, whose financial position is so uncertain, and whose hope of improvement in their situation is relatively so remote.

SECTION 4—WHAT KIND OF HELP?

5.56 In considering what form of State help is needed for one-parent families we have had in mind the problems referred to in paragraphs 5.49–5.55 and the difficulties regarding the inadequacy and uncertainty of maintenance payments which we discuss in detail in Part 4. Ideally we think the help needed should be:

(1) a replacement, so far as the recipient is concerned, for maintenance payments, so that lone mothers should be freed from the worry and distress which the inadequacy and uncertainties of these payments now produce;

(2) large enough to offer the lone parent a genuine choice about whether or not to work;

(3) designed to provide effective help for those with part-time or low full-time earnings;

(4) of universal application; that is, it should be available to all kinds of one-parent families, without discrimination, since all are at a disadvantage;

(5) simple to claim, and avoiding face to face interviews, searching enquiries and constant reporting of changes;

(6) equitable, in the sense that it should not tip the scales too far in favour of one-parent families as compared with low-income two-parent families.

We thought that the implication of the first five of these six principles was that the ideal allowance should be sufficiently large to lift one-parent families off supplementary benefit; for in many respects the advantages sought would not be achieved if many families had to go on receiving supplementary benefit as well as the allowance. The difficulty confronting us was whether such a recommendation would be compatible with the sixth principle—that of equity upon comparison with the condition of disadvantaged two-parent families. We revert to this problem in discussion of the individual schemes which we considered.

WOULD EXISTING SCHEMES DO?

5.57 We looked first at existing schemes to see whether the provision of help of the kind we envisaged could be obtained through development of such schemes. The schemes which at present provide significant income support for lone parents are supplementary benefits, family income supplements and family allowances (or, for the future, child tax credits). It soon became apparent to us that none of these schemes really suited our purpose, though changes in all of them could be made in a way which would be of some benefit to lone parents. In Section 8 we discuss possible improvements to the existing schemes. These are in any case required to operate during the interim period which may need to elapse before a more suitable form of support, following our principal recommendations, is introduced for one-parent families, and also as permanent improvements to schemes which will in some cases continue to be of benefit, even after that period has elapsed, to one-parent families as well as to others. But, for the reasons set out below, we reject the existing schemes as a basis for providing in the future the main source of financial support for one-parent families.

Supplementary benefit

5.58 Supplementary benefit provides a basic level of income for families where the wage-earner is not in full-time work and whose other sources of income, including national insurance benefits, are insufficient for their requirements. It is at present the main means of support of half (200,000 out of 400,000) of all fatherless families, other than widows and their children, and well over half of all families with children on supplementary benefit are one-parent families. Much evidence was addressed to us on the need for improvement in the supplementary benefit rates and disregards as they affected one-parent families; we are in no doubt that there is need for such improvement and our recommendations on this are set out in later paragraphs. But we do not believe that any improvements that could be made would remedy the basic unsuitability of the supplementary benefits scheme as the main source of income for a large proportion of fatherless families. Our principal reasons for this belief are discussed in paragraphs 5.49–5.55. But we also have in mind the very considerable volume of evidence we received about the difficulties families experience in their dealings with the Commission, particularly where they have to ask for discretionary payments for extra needs; and their evident anxiety to be free of the close supervision which these dealings entail. The National Council for the Unmarried Mother and her Child told us in evidence, " There is a widespread belief among our clients that they are regarded with suspicion and disfavour by the officers of the Supplementary Benefits Commission." No doubt the need for Commission officers to make enquiries where cohabitation is suspected is one reason why some lone women react in this way; and unmarried, divorced and separated mothers may often be subject to and sensitive to the feeling that others regard them as at least partly responsible for their own situation. Whatever the cause, the desire of these women to come out of the supplementary benefits system is deeply and almost universally felt, and, as such, constitutes a fact to which we must pay great attention. We were also told that in none of the overseas countries which we studied were anything like half of one-parent families dependent on social assistance. Nowhere did the proportion exceed 20 per cent and in Norway it was only 10 per cent. Improvements in supplementary benefit could not, in any case, provide the whole answer as the system is of no help to the 200,000 one-parent families (nearly half of them motherless families) who work full time, nor to families who are not in full-time work and do not claim supplementary benefit, although apparently entitled to do so.

Family income supplements

5.59 Family income supplements are at present paid only to those in full-time work; at the end of April 1973 37,000 out of the 84,000 recipients were one-parent families (a brief description of the scheme is at Appendix 8). Claims from one-parent families are already determined by reference to the same prescribed amounts as those from two-parent families so that extra support for the one-parent families could only be obtained by raising the prescribed amount for all families or extending the scheme to those in part-time work. We discuss both these possibilities in detail in Section 8 but we do not think that either would have sufficient impact on the generality of one-parent families to provide a significant improvement in the overall level of support. The amount of help that family income supplements can give a family is limited because the award is restricted to half the difference between the family's income and the prescribed amounts; and, since it is payable only to families who already have earnings, many of the one-parent families on supplementary benefit would not be helped at all. There is also a problem regarding take-up of the supplements—it is estimated that about half of those families entitled to a supplement do not claim it, mainly those who would qualify for small awards. Nevertheless, there are some features of the family income supplements scheme which we found attractive (for instance the security given by the long award period, the simplicity for the claimant of the postal procedure for claiming, and the elimination of detailed personal enquiries). We return to these later.

Family allowances and child tax credits

5.60 We received much evidence advocating improvements in the general level of family support, through family allowances, as a method of helping one-parent families. The suggestions for improvements fell into two categories: for some payment to be made for the first child (there are no family allowances for the first child at present—see Appendix 8), and for increases in the general level of family allowances and for regular upratings. Such suggestions have the great advantage that they help one-parent families without the risks of inequity in comparison with other families. The great disadvantage is that this is a very expensive way of improving the lot of the relatively small numbers of one-parent families. The quite separate proposition that there should be a special allowance for the children in one-parent families only is effectively incorporated in the benefit proposals which we consider in paragraphs 5.94–5.111.

5.61. A straightforward increase of family allowances in their present form (that is, taxable and not including the first child) would go to all families except one-child families, and most families would benefit to the extent of 70 per cent of the gross payment. Those on supplementary benefit would gain nothing, because family allowances are taken into account as a resource; families with a national insurance benefit would likewise gain nothing and could, in fact, be worse off if taxable family allowances were to replace an untaxable national insurance benefit. The full benefit would be received by those families who do not pay tax and are not in receipt of supplementary benefit. An increase would be extremely expensive and the gross cost of, for instance, a 50p increase would be around £185 million. About £70 million would be saved in the tax on the benefit and on lower payments of other benefits,

271

such as supplementary benefits. Very little of the net expenditure of some £115 million would go into the pockets of one-parent families.

5.62 To introduce family allowances for the first or only child and pay a taxable £1 a week for each child would cost a gross amount of about £400 million. Tax on the allowances and savings on other benefits would make the net cost about £250 million. This again, considered as a measure to help one-parent families rather than as a general improvement in the family support available to all families, would be extremely expensive.

5.63 We have noted, however, that the Green Paper on tax credits published in October 1972[1] put forward as a general measure of income support for all families, a scheme that would enable unused tax allowances to be paid positively as benefit; and subsequently the Government agreed with the recommendation of the Select Committee on Tax-Credit that child credits should be a cash payment on a universal basis through the Post Office.[2] This scheme will therefore offer both provision for the first child and benefit for children who do not now benefit from tax allowances.[3] (A brief description of the tax-credit scheme is included in Appendix 8.) We are in no doubt that the introduction of child credits will be of very considerable benefit to lone parents; and we are also glad to note that for those who are within the tax-credit scheme there will be additional benefit in the form of the higher credit for a lone parent. If the tax-credit scheme becomes law it will replace family allowances; if, in the event, it should not be enacted into law, we recommend in Section 8 that a similar amount of family support should be made available through family allowances. But neither alternative will provide the complete answer to the needs we have described and lone parents still needing supplementary benefits would receive no advantage from such improvement except that a little more of their income would come from a non-means-tested source. To increase the level of child credits or family allowances by several pounds to a point where they did make a financial difference would be an extremely expensive way of helping lone parents, as can be judged from the costs quoted in paragraphs 5.61 and 5.62. Moreover, increased family support makes no impact on the problem faced by so many lone parents of the irregular receipt of maintenance payments.

THE EXPERIENCE OF OTHER COUNTRIES

5.64 We next looked at what the research into the policy and practice of other countries, which we had commissioned from the International Social Security Association, could show us. The countries studied in depth were Sweden, Denmark, Norway, the Netherlands and the Federal Republic of Germany. An analysis of the findings is made in Appendix 3:[4] we select here some of the main features of financial provision, to which the research was particularly directed. We found that we needed to use the experience of these countries with a good deal of caution: although they were carefully

---

[1] *Proposals for a Tax-Credit System:* Cmnd 5116.

[2] *Select Committee on Tax-Credit: Report and Proceedings of the Committee,* paragraph 60.

[3] In addition the tax-credit scheme will normally avoid the present problems suffered by some lone mothers in claiming refunds of tax overpaid in respect of maintenance payments—see Section 8.

[4] Detailed reports on the individual countries are available on request from the Department of Health and Social Security.

selected as being countries where conditions were not so dissimilar from our own as to invalidate comparisons or to rule out the practical possibility of borrowing from their procedures, the dominant feature which emerged from the research was the way in which the measures adopted in each individual country reflect its own national characteristics and attitudes, and have developed in the context of its own social and economic history.

5.65 We found there were four main planks to income support for one-parent families in the countries studied: first, social assistance, second, family allowances, third, maintenance guarantees and fourth, widows' pensions. The last is discussed in Appendix 3: we do not propose to examine it further here since provision for widows in this country, by comparison with provision for other one-parent families, is already good. The other three are taken in turn in the paragraphs which follow. All of them provided us with some useful insight into financial provision for one-parent families, but none seemed to us to offer the right solution for one-parent families in this country.

5.66 In all the countries social assistance (the nearest counterpart to supplementary benefit) plays an essential role in maintaining the income of non-working lone mothers, apart from widows. In none of them, however, is there a scheme of social assistance as universal and flexible as the supplementary benefits scheme. Usually social assistance schemes are administered locally by individual authorities who make their own policies, a practice which leads to inconsistencies. These schemes are not intended to be, nor are they adequate as, long-term benefits. Mothers are expected to begin to support themselves by working as soon as they are able, and certainly by the time the youngest child has reached school age. This approach is in strong contrast to the acceptance in the supplementary benefits scheme of the principle that lone mothers may be supported by the taxpayer as long as they have a child at school.

5.67 Family allowances are a major source of income support in all the countries studied. Like family allowances in this country they are paid without regard to income (except in West Germany where only allowances for the third and subsequent children are free of a means test). Of particular interest to us were those countries which made special provision in the family allowances system for one-parent families. In Norway, for example, one-parent families get an allowance for one child more than the actual number of children under 16 in the family. Denmark provides several different forms of additions to family allowances for one-parent families, and all children in one-parent families get a special rate of allowance nearly 50 per cent higher than the ordinary rate; family allowances there can add over 40 per cent to the gross earnings of a working lone mother with two children on the average wage.

5.68 The present family allowances system in this country makes a much less significant contribution to family income than do the systems in the Scandinavian countries, but the advent of the tax-credit scheme will change the situation radically. This is partly because it will provide a child credit at a much higher level than existing family allowances[1] and also because it will enable a positive payment to be made to those within the scheme who would not, under

[1] The Green Paper puts the child credit at £2 a week for each child.

a tax system such as the present one, make full use of their tax allowances. The lone parent is to have the higher rate of credit available to a married couple, and in the Green Paper this is put at £6 a week. The result is that a woman with two children and an average wage of £19·10 a week would have an income, after tax and tax-credits, of £23·37—over £4 a week higher than her gross earnings. We consider that the tax-credit scheme will compare well with the measures adopted by the other countries studied for universal support of this kind. But, even at the suggested level of £2 a child, and taking account of the parent's higher rate of credit, an allowance of this kind cannot be a family's major source of income. Its usefulness arises as a supplement to other income and as extra support for the family in work. (It is for this reason that family allowances are particularly appropriate to those countries which expect lone mothers to work.) Nor can such an allowance alone solve the problem of giving the lone parent a real choice between working and staying at home to care for the children.

5.69 The third plank of income support in the Scandinavian countries is the " maintenance advances " system. These maintenance advances seek to provide a guaranteed monthly maintenance level, in addition to family allowances and regardless of paternal willingness or ability to pay. The benefit is considered to be the child's and thus continues notwithstanding the mother's cohabitation with a man other than the child's father; as a corollary, the State makes every effort to trace the father and to make him pay. To make the pursuit of the father as thorough as possible there is, typically, a formal requirement that the administrative authorities be notified of pregnancy or a birth outside marriage.

5.70 A great deal of effort goes into determining paternity and into fixing and enforcing private maintenance. In Sweden, for example, any search for a missing father is likely to encompass access to census registrations to locate the man's whereabouts and to social insurance records to determine both employer and earnings. A high degree of official access to personal information makes the system feasible. Bearing in mind the importance which is attached in this country to the confidentiality of official records, such as census records or those obtained for tax or national insurance purposes, we do not believe that the Scandinavian approach would be acceptable here. Such procedures would be likely to arouse a good deal of resentment, and, moreover, it is not clear that they would achieve more than is at present recovered under existing, less onerous, procedures. In Sweden in 1970, for example, of 23 million kr paid to mothers by way of maintenance advances, only 8·5 million kr was repaid by fathers. We demonstrate in Part 4 that most fathers who have acquired a second family are unable to give much support to their first, and that a more rigorous and intrusive system of recovery is unlikely to increase the rate of recovery in this country. We have also noted that even in the Scandinavian countries the level of maintenance advances is not such as to permit a one-parent family to manage on maintenance advances and family allowances alone; substantial payments of social assistance are still necessary for the lone parent who is not working.

STATE RESPONSIBILITY FOR MAINTENANCE ORDERS

5.71 Perhaps partly influenced by the Scandinavian " maintenance advances " system, one proposal which has been widely canvassed by some of those concerned with the problems of one-parent families is that the State should take over responsibility for all maintenance awards ordered by the courts. We discuss the inadequacies of the present system of awarding and enforcing in Part 4. Many of those who gave evidence to us were concerned about the hardships and the real sense of grievance women suffer, when maintenance to which a court has decided they are entitled, is not forthcoming. Having undergone the mental and emotional strain of taking their claim to court they are often faced with a wearing and frequently vain struggle to enforce their right. Mr J Clark, Chairman of the Greenlow Society which assists fatherless families, put it particularly forcefully in saying, " The difficulties and miseries experienced by many mothers in obtaining monies to which they are morally and legally entitled is nothing short of a national scandal . . . . An immediate reform whereby these sums are payable say through a Post Office allowance book and guaranteed by the DHSS, is called for ." The Mechanics of Payment of Aliment Bill, introduced into the House of Commons during the 1972–1973 Session by Mr Tam Dalyell, had a similar aim, and the proposal has also received support from members of the legal profession. Mr A Samuels, Reader in Law at the University of Southampton, expressed the view that " immediately the court makes a maintenance order the DHSS should assume responsibility for paying it weekly through the Post Office and recouping the money from the father ".

5.72 At present a lone mother who claims supplementary benefit and is likely to require regular payments, and who obtains a maintenance order, or has one already, can apply to the court for payments on the order to be diverted to the Department of Health and Social Security. The advantage of this arrangement is that she can draw an assured weekly allowance from the Supplementary Benefits Commission and so avoid anxiety or hardship if the father fails to pay the order. There is, therefore, already a system whereby the State ensures that one group of lone mothers receives a secure income irrespective of the way the absent fathers meet their liability.

5.73 Moreover the supplementary benefits scheme goes further in that benefit under the scheme may be claimed by lone mothers even when they have no court order against the father, and in appropriate cases the Supplementary Benefits Commission will consider taking the initiative to obtain reimbursement from the father. For women receiving supplementary benefit, therefore, much of the misery associated with obtaining maintenance from an absent father is avoided. We put forward elsewhere in this Report proposals for restructuring the arrangements for the collections of maintenance for women on supplementary benefit, which should take most of the responsibility off the claimant.

5.74 These arrangements cannot, however, be of help to the woman who is in full-time work or who, because of her income, is ineligible for supplementary benefit. We would find it quite unacceptable that the State should guarantee the full amount of maintenance orders for large sums made against wealthy husbands and fathers.

5.75 But these are relatively rare. It is the very fact of the low level of maintenance orders which seems to us to be fatal to the usefulness of the " guaranteed maintenance " proposal as providing any significant measure of relief. The low levels at which orders are set,[1] usually because of the man's

---

[1] This subject is examined in detail in Part 4 and Appendix 7.

limited ability to pay, mean that the guarantee would scarcely ever relieve a family with no other income from having to claim supplementary benefit. Most of the 200,000 or so fatherless families now on supplementary benefit would gain nothing financially out of " guaranteed maintenance " in the sense of an underwriting of maintenance orders.

5.76　Moreover, while there is inadequate evidence on which to estimate this reliably, it is unlikely that more than two thirds of separated, divorced and unmarried mothers have maintenance orders at present. Consequently, unless the other mothers were willing to go through the courts they could not benefit from the proposal. An extension of the guarantee to registered voluntary agreements, which would offer difficult problems of control, would probably be impracticable. In some cases the father would not in any event be traced.

5.77　Nor would the proposal do anything for lone fathers except in the infinitesimal number of cases in which the man is entitled to maintenance against the woman. Nevertheless the evidence has convinced us that, although their situation and problems are in some ways different from those of lone mothers, and their financial difficulties generally less, motherless, as well as fatherless, families are in need of a degree of extra help.

5.78　While it would, therefore, confer limited advantages upon a proportion of one-parent families, a scheme for State guarantees of maintenance orders is entirely inadequate to relieve the financial problems of one-parent families in general. Our attention consequently turned to the possibility of devising a special social security benefit for one-parent families.

SECTION 5—A SPECIAL BENEFIT FOR ONE-PARENT FAMILIES

5.79　We looked for a benefit for one-parent families as such, which could be tailored to their needs and which might meet as many as possible of the " ideal " requirements listed in paragraph 5.56. A number of proposals were put to us on the form that a special one-parent family benefit might take. The two main ones were the proposal put forward by the National Council for the Unmarried Mother and her Child (NCUMC)[1] for a child and child-care allowance (CHAID) and the proposal put forward by Mrs Margaret Wynn for a fatherless family allowance (FFA). We discuss these two proposals in turn in the paragraphs which follow.

CHAID

5.80　The NCUMC have already published their proposal for CHAID, together with the other evidence they gave us, in *Forward for the Fatherless*. In he course of oral evidence they amplified these proposals in some respects. We give here only a brief description of CHAID, together with the conclusions we reached on it.

5.81　The CHAID scheme consists of two parts: a national insurance benefit and a discretionary scheme. In their evidence the NCUMC said, " Under the national insurance part of our scheme, we recommend the introduction of a Children's Aid Allowance, made up of two elements—Child's

---

[1] See footnote to paragraph 5.45.

276

Allowance and a Child Care Allowance .... The benefits we propose should be payable in respect of all children residing in a family with only one parent,[1] with the exception of children living with widowed mothers who obtain more generous benefits under the existing provisions for widows."[2] The allowance would be set at the same level as short-term national insurance benefits. In terms of the rates current in October 1973, this would be £2·30 for the first child, £1·40 for the second child and £1·30 for the third and subsequent children, with a child care allowance of £7·35.[3] These allowances would be taxable.

5.82 The NCUMC place great stress on the importance of an insurance-based benefit: "We have attached the CHAID allowances to the insurance principle, because we believe they must be available as of right; this means there must be some contribution element."[4] Their recommendation is that national insurance provision should be extended to ensure the maintenance of all children in one-parent families. "This does not mean the 'insurance' of a marriage or coverage for mothers. The benefits that we recommend would be wholly *for* the child and for the child's care. It is possible to extend the insurance principle to the child because the child cannot contribute to his status as the child of a one-parent family. It is desirable to extend the insurance principle to this group because the number of children concerned is now quite significant. In the early twentieth century the death of one or other parent was a major cause of child deprivation and was recognised as an insurable risk; now it is the separation or divorce of his parents which puts the child at risk and a refusal to recognise this fact in the social security provisions is to deny the social changes which have occurred in marriage and the status of women."[5] The contribution conditions under which CHAID would be paid could be satisfied on the contribution record of either the mother or the father, or, if necessary, both. The qualifying period of payment of contributions should be as short as possible, and contributions paid by a woman before marriage should count even after a lapse of years.

5.83 Like widowed mother's allowance, national insurance CHAID would be free of any earnings rule: the NCUMC see as one of the most important factors in CHAID that it would supplement the earnings of lone mothers and thus enable those who wished to work and support themselves without recourse to supplementary benefit to do so. CHAID would also follow widowed mother's allowance in that it would cease on remarriage or cohabitation.

5.84 The NCUMC recognise that a benefit awarded on the basis of contributions as set out in paragraph 5.82 above would not be available for all one-parent families: there would be bound to be some, and in particular the very young, who could not satisfy contribution conditions, however limited these might be. They therefore propose that, in addition to the national insurance CHAID, a CHAID allowance should be introduced and administered by the

---

[1] It is subsequently made clear (*Forward for the Fatherless*, paragraph 652) that lone fathers are to receive the child allowance only.

[2] *Ibid*, paragraphs 642 and 644.

[3] In terms of rates current before October 1973, for ease of comparison with other rates used in this Report, the figures would be £2·10, £1·20 and £1·10 for the children and £6·75 for the mother.

[4] *Op cit*, paragraph 659.

[5] *Op cit*, paragraphs 633 and 634.

Supplementary Benefits Commission for children of lone mothers on the following grounds:

(1) in the case of unmarried mothers, that the mother was less than 17 years and 9 months of age when the child was born; or

(2) that a mother who had not qualified for the national insurance CHAID should be able to transfer from present supplementary benefit payments to supplementary benefit CHAID if she wished to enter regular employment and the wage which she could earn in such employment was less than the national average wage.

A mother who paid the necessary national insurance contributions by taking up employment after being awarded supplementary benefit CHAID would have the right to transfer to national insurance CHAID. The amount of allowance paid would be the same but one would be of right whereas the other would have a discretionary element.[1]

5.85 The NCUMC state as a cardinal principle that " the position of the family within our society should not be undermined and fathers should continue to be responsible for maintaining their wives and children."[2] They describe the basis on which contributions from fathers should be assessed as follows: " These contributions should be intended to cover about 80 per cent of the cash payments made for the child's maintenance. . . .[3] His contributions should, however, be on a scale approved by Parliament, which would take fully into account his income and other family responsibilities. The family with which the father is living should receive priority. This would mean that relatively few fathers would be paying the full amount. . . ."[4] The contributions would be collected by the State and the NCUMC suggest that it might be possible to collect them through the PAYE system[5] by taking away child allowances and earned income relief from the father. They estimate that some 30 per cent of the total cost of the scheme might be recovered from fathers.

5.86 Mothers would retain their present rights to go to court and sue for maintenance, but courts would have regard to the national scheme in deciding on any extra financial provision needed. The NCUMC estimate that men with incomes up to one and one third times national average earnings would have their maintenance payments covered by the CHAID scheme. Only men with higher incomes than this would be likely to have orders for additional payments made against them by courts.[6]

5.87 The NCUMC suggest that the cost of the CHAID scheme would be covered in part by the contribution of fathers (which might provide 30 per cent of the cost—see paragraph 5.85) and in part by a small extra national insurance

---

[1] See paragraphs 660–663 of *Forward for the Fatherless*.

[2] *Ibid*, paragraph 631 (*d*).

[3] This refers to the adult's child-care allowance. The NCUMC propose that the assessment against the father could cover the full cost of any allowance for children.

[4] *Ibid*, paragraph 649.

[5] This proposal was submitted before the publication of the Green Paper, *Proposals for a Tax-Credit System*, *op cit*. The tax-credit proposals would necessitate some re-examination of the NCUMC's original scheme.

[6] *Ibid*, paragraphs 640 and 641.

contribution which might cover up to about 20 per cent of the cost. The second 50 per cent would have to met from public funds.[1]

5.88 The scheme, as described, would go some way towards meeting the six conditions set out in paragraph 5.56. It would provide all one-parent families with a stable, certain income, sufficiently large to supplement part-time or low earnings, and it would be simple and trouble-free to claim. We are less confident, however, that it would be large enough to offer the lone parent a genuine choice whether or not to work, or that the proposal would be equitable as regards other groups and as between one-parent families themselves; and we have grave doubts whether the system suggested for recovering payments from fathers would be viable. We discuss these points in turn in the paragraphs which follow.

Freedom for mothers to choose whether or not to work

5.89 The NCUMC intend their benefit to help primarily mothers wanting to work. They told us in evidence that the lone mother " should be in the position of being able to decide whether it is in the best interests of her children and herself for her to go to work or to stay at home. She will have to weigh up her wish to be with her child and her child's need for her care against the depression and apathy and frustration from which many unsupported mothers suffer because of isolation and loneliness."[2] We fully endorse this view; we have mentioned earlier the difficulties lone mothers face in relation to supplementary benefit if they wish to take up part-time work, and the disincentive for them to do so, and we accept that CHAID would go a good way towards solving the problem of combining some work with adequate care for the child. But we regard it as most important that mothers, particularly when they have very young children, should not feel under any pressure to take paid employment. (This question is discussed in Part 8.) CHAID, while benefiting the woman who worked, would leave the woman who did not want to work on supplementary benefit; she would be unlikely to have any other resources than CHAID (since maintenance would only be paid additionally in a few cases——see paragraph 5.86) and even taking account of tax credits the income of a substantial number of fatherless families would be likely to be less than their supplementary benefit level. We have explained earlier (paragraph 5.58) the disadvantages we see in supplementary benefit as the source of support for fatherless families for long periods of time. We consider that if the special benefit were to take a form such as CHAID a lone mother would feel herself under considerable pressure to improve her family's financial lot by going out to work.

Equity

5.90 National insurance CHAID would be paid without any regard to the income or earnings of the recipients and thus would go to some families who were well off. The justification for the expenditure on the well off arises from making CHAID an insurance benefit. But despite their contributory basis most insurance benefits have earnings rules of some sort attached—widows' benefits, including the widowed mother's allowance, are almost alone in not being subject to any earnings rule. Further, in CHAID the contributory principle would be bound to be weak, since, given the circumstances of many

---

[1] *Ibid*, paragraphs 648 and 649 and Appendix J.
[2] *Ibid*, paragraph 137.

recipients, it would be possible, as the NCUMC themselves recognise, to qualify them only by offering very liberal contribution conditions. We consider that the insurance principle is here being stretched so thin as to become somewhat artificial. It would be more appropriate and much simpler to recognise CHAID as a non-contributory benefit. In either form we have grave doubts whether it would be a defensible use of resources, either as among one-parent families themselves or in relation to other families.

5.91 The CHAID proposals were made before the plans for a tax-credit scheme became known. It is intended that the child tax credit will replace increases of short-term national insurance benefits for children dependent upon the beneficiary. We do not know whether the NCUMC, who adopted the short-term benefit rates for CHAID, would wish the proposed child element in CHAID to disappear similarly with the introduction of child tax credits. If so this would mean that the expenditure on CHAID would be limited to the cost of the child-care element, which the NCUMC would make available to mothers only. There would be no CHAID for motherless families.

5.92 We estimate that in terms of 1972–1973 benefit rates (which we use for ease of comparison with figures later in this Report) the gross cost of the child-care element in CHAID would be about £137 million. If parents receiving CHAID were thereby brought into the tax-credit scheme (see paragraph 5.107) the provision of tax credits for them at the rate of £6 for each adult would add about £75 million to the gross cost. To offset against this there would be savings of some £79 million on supplementary benefits,[1] and, if CHAID were taxable, about £46 million would be recovered in tax. The net cost would therefore, we estimate, be in the region of £85 million to £90 million. Nearly £60 million of this additional money would go to families not on supplementary benefit, the vast majority of whom already constitute the better off among one-parent families, and some of whom may well be better off than two-parent families who receive no special State support. The State would be able to recover some of the expenditure through maintenance contributions, but because of the taxation arguments to which we refer in the next paragraph we doubt whether much could be recovered in the way the NCUMC suggest.

Recovery of CHAID from liable fathers

5.93 The NCUMC propose that fathers whose children are receiving CHAID should lose their child tax allowances and, up to a certain level, their earned income relief. They suggest that this gain in tax revenue should go towards financing CHAID and could provide up to 30 per cent of the total cost. There are several reasons why this seems to us to be an over-optimistic view. First, it is often the case now that the father is not receiving the child tax allowance in full, if at all: in general, where the allowance is undivided, it goes to the mother if she has sufficient income to use it, particularly where the maintenance payments made are pursuant to a court order.[2] In many

---

[1] This estimate assumes that the improvements in the supplementary benefits scheme which we recommend in Section 8 have been introduced.

[2] Where payments of maintenance are made under a court order, or are otherwise legally enforceable, the person making the payment is entitled to deduct the amount from his or her income for tax purposes. He (or she) is thus relieved of tax on that amount of income. Such payments do not, however, count in establishing that person's contribution towards the maintenance of a child where there is more than one claimant for the tax allowance for the child.

cases the allowance does not go wholly to one parent or to the other but is divided between them according to their agreed wish. It would therefore be very much a matter of chance how much, if anything, could be recovered in this way from each father. Secondly, the proposed introduction of child tax credits, payable normally to the mother, in place of the present child tax allowances would mean that there was no extra saving at all to be had in this field. Thirdly, under the recently introduced unified tax system, earned income relief as such has disappeared and income tax is payable in the normal way at the basic rate of 30 per cent. Compelling reasons would be needed for eroding the simplicity of this system by introducing differential rates of tax for employers to operate.

FATHERLESS FAMILY ALLOWANCE

5.94 Mrs Margaret Wynn's proposal for a fatherless family allowance (FFA) has been published with the evidence of the Catholic Housing Aid Society and is set out in full in the appendix to that document.[1]

5.95 The proposals for FFA are in many respects similar to CHAID:

(1) the benefit would consist of a child allowance and an adult allowance;

(2) it would be payable as of right, at a flat rate, and without any test of income or earnings rule;

(3) it would be part of total income for the purpose of income tax;

(4) recovery of part of the cost would be made from the father, some of it by tax changes—he would lose all allowances for wife and child and have to pay maintenance out of taxed income.

5.96 There are however a number of important differences:

(1) FFA would not be an insurance benefit—it would be paid as a non-contributory benefit without a means test;

(2) it would be at a higher rate than CHAID, the child allowance being at the higher rate paid to widowed mothers under the national insurance scheme rather than the short-term benefit rate. The adult rate, which would not be available to lone fathers,[2] would be £7·75 from October 1973 (£6·75 before then) and the child rate (including family allowances) £3·80 (£3·30 before October 1973);

(3) it would be payable only on a determination by a court that a one-parent family existed;

(4) the method of effecting recovery from the father would be different—maintenance would be assessed and collected by the court and paid to the administering department.

5.97 Like CHAID, FFA would go some way to meeting our six principles, but again it would do so largely for the benefit of the woman who worked. Although the higher rate of benefit FFA offers is more likely to lift one-parent

---

[1] *Evidence to the Finer Committee on One-Parent Families:* Catholic Housing Aid Society, 189a Old Brompton Road, London SW5 OAR.

[2] The proposal for FFA was originally restricted entirely to fatherless families, but in oral evidence to the Committee Mrs Wynn suggested that where a man is left as head of a one-parent family the child's portion should be payable.

families off supplementary benefit, many women would still be faced with the choice between paid employment and supplementary benefit and much of the improvement would go to working families who are already better off. While, we would strongly support the provision of a benefit which would give mothers a choice whether or not to work, we do not favour giving clear encouragement to mothers to work. As we have already said, we think the choice whether or not to work should be a free one and subject to as little pressure as possible.

5.98 Further, FFA is payable only on a determination of separation by a court. This would run counter to our view that lone mothers should be relieved of court proceedings as far as possible. It would also restrict the numbers of families likely to claim the allowance. Nor would FFA be available to widows, even when they had no widowed mother's allowance, and the adult portion would not be paid to lone fathers.

5.99 Mrs Wynn's method of obtaining payment from the father via the court would not be subject to the difficulties of the NCUMC tax proposals; but we have doubts, as with CHAID, about the amount that would be recovered from the proposed taxation changes and about the extra amount to be gained by taxing the wages of women who return to work. Referring to the assumptions on which her estimates are based, Mrs Wynn says, "The element of doubt in this conclusion (amount of recovery) is mainly in the degree of acceptance of the deliberate policy of recovering the amount of money from fathers and acceptance of the deliberate policy of encouraging mothers to earn more money supported by better child care services. . . . The element of doubt may be substantial . . . ." The gross cost of FFA would depend on how many families could claim it: if all one-parent families could do so the cost of the adult benefit would be slightly higher than for CHAID. If only those who at present are divorced or have separation or maintenance orders claimed the benefit the gross cost would probably be reduced by between one third and one half.

5.100 Taking the child part of FFA into account, and adjusting the amount because of the provisions of child tax credits, the gross cost of FFA for all lone mothers would probably be about £180 million, with a further £11 million for the children of lone fathers. To offset against this and the £75 million or so which would be the gross cost to the tax-credit scheme of extra tax credits if parents receiving FFA were brought into that scheme (see paragraph 5.107), there would be savings on supplementary benefit of about £86 million[1] and about £63 million would be recovered in tax. The net cost would thus be in the region of £115 million to £120 million. FFA would be much more effective than CHAID in helping families now on supplementary benefit and, coupled with tax credits, would probably enable about 160,000 fatherless families to cease claiming supplementary benefit.[1]

A BENEFIT LIKE WIDOWED MOTHER'S ALLOWANCE

5.101 One feature of FFA which held considerable attraction for us was that both adult and child portions would be paid at the same rates as national insurance widowed mother's allowance, and thus it would give all fatherless

---

[1] As for CHAID, this estimate is based on the assumption that the improvements in the supplementary benefits scheme, which we recommend in Section 8, have been introduced.

families a similar basic income. We therefore considered whether it would be possible and acceptable simply to make a benefit equivalent to widowed mother's allowance available to all one-parent families, motherless as well as fatherless, and whatever the cause for the absence of the other parent. We soon concluded that it would not be possible to provide completely uniform treatment because widowed mother's allowance is a national insurance benefit, and we were most reluctant to restrict any one-parent family benefit to those families able to satisfy contribution conditions (see paragraph 5.90 above, where we consider the insurance principle in relation to CHAID). The proposition we considered was, therefore, that of a benefit paid at the same rate as widowed mother's allowance and subject as far as possible to the same conditions, but payable, without contribution conditions, as of right to all families who could establish their status as one-parent families. (How status is to be established is a problem common to all proposals for a one-parent family benefit and is considered in detail in Section 6.) Such a benefit could be paid, like FFA and CHAID, as a substitute, in the hands of the recipient, for maintenance, and the proposals we put forward later for the assessment and collection of maintenance payments could apply. Like national insurance widowed mother's allowance, the benefit would be payable without any earnings rule and would cease on remarriage or cohabitation.

5.102 We gave much thought to the possibilities of a benefit of this kind, but we eventually rejected it for reasons which, fundamentally, are very similar to those which caused us misgivings in relation to FFA and CHAID. As we have rehearsed these in some detail earlier we shall only summarise here; and in paragraph 5.108 we draw comparisons between this type of benefit and our own proposal. Briefly, the main points which influenced us in deciding against a benefit of this kind are as follows:

(1) we doubt the equity of an arrangement which involves paying the same benefit to all one-parent families, regardless of other income. Widows and other one-parent families should not necessarily be treated alike in this respect. Universal widowhood provision recognises the inescapable fact that the husband is no longer able to make any current provision for his family. Other unsupported mothers are in a different position because of the father's obligation to maintain his children and sometimes their mother. This may or may not be complied with, and the State's concern is, we believe, to provide a level of income on which the parent would be able to bring up the children, on a basis which is equitable in relation to other families. If the family is by its own efforts achieving a reasonable income level, the taxpayer could rightly object if his commitments were not reduced;

(2) the equity point becomes particularly acute in relation to motherless families. We are anxious that the lone father should have the same choice as the lone mother between going to work and staying at home to look after the children, and to exclude them from the benefit, or to pay them only the child benefit, would deny them this. But the great majority of lone fathers do in fact work and would probably continue to do so, and to pay the benefit to all of them would involve supplementing earnings already well above those of lone mothers

283

with very little offsetting savings from supplementary benefit and none from maintenance payments. The result would be that a quite disproportionate amount of the net cost of the benefit—nearly £30 million out of a total net cost, before taking maintenance contributions into account, of nearly £150 million—would go to lone fathers;

(3) a benefit at the widowed mother's allowance level, even taking account of the addition of tax credits, would still leave a substantial number of lone parents dependent on supplementary benefit. For these lone parents the new benefit would have brought no real advantage at all, and we fear that this, coupled with the fact that they could retain the whole of the benefit if they went out to work, might make some parents feel that they ought to work and thus deprive them of the real choice which is one of the main reasons for having a special benefit for lone parents;

(4) the initial attraction of the idea of treating all lone parents like widows is considerable reduced once a simple extension of national insurance widowed mother's allowance has been rejected. The new benefit would have to be quite separate and might have to be separately administered. It would not be payable on the basis of contributions and could probably not carry with it the same rights, for example, to credits of national insurance contributions. Most important, it would not carry with it the widow's right to a continuing pension for the rest of her life, if she is over 40 by the time her youngest child leaves home or reaches age 19.

A FLAT-RATE BENEFIT CLAWED BACK THROUGH TAXATION

5.103 We considered whether our objection on the ground of equity to the various benefits we have referred to could be met by introducing a flat-rate benefit and limiting the extent of help it gave to one-parent families on higher incomes by recovering it through the tax system. A lone parent receiving the benefit could be required to pay a higher rate of tax on earnings and other income than the basic rate which would be normally applicable. We saw great difficulties in this arrangement, the major one being how to operate the system fairly. Under the tax-credit scheme employers will normally deduct tax at the basic rate on all earnings unless they have received specific instructions to the contrary, so that it would be necessary to ensure that the employer of each lone parent receiving benefit was aware of the need to deduct a higher rate of tax. This would mean complications for employers, and the onus would have to be on the parent to make sure the right deductions were being made. Where there was any difficulty or delay in employers' making the right deduction—and there are a number of ways in which problems could occur—arrears of unpaid tax would quickly build up. The practical and technical problems involved are formidable, and it is sufficient to say, without here engaging in detailed discussion, that we could see no way round them at the present time.

A SPECIAL ONE-PARENT FAMILY ALLOWANCE

5.104 While we were much attracted by some of the features of CHAID, FFA and the two variants of FFA which we have mentioned, and we are greatly indebted to those who put these proposals forward for the invaluable stimulus and help they have given us, we do not feel that any one of them provides a satisfactory answer to the problems of the parent who wishes to look after his or her children at home, to the question of recovery of maintenance without distress, delay and frustration for the mother, or to the problem of allocation of resources between the better and worse off one-parent families. We have therefore attempted to construct a benefit which avoids these defects and comes more nearly—indeed, we consider as near as is practicable—towards meeting the fundamental problems of the one-parent family. We devote the next Section of this Report to a discussion of this benefit, which we call the guaranteed maintenance allowance (GMA), but we list below the ten main features which we have in mind:

(1) the allowance would normally, in the hands of the lone parent, be a substitute for maintenance payments; maintenance payments would be assessed and collected by the authority administering the allowance; they would be offset against the allowance paid and any excess paid to the mother; the need for lone mothers to go to court to sue for maintenance awards would be largely eliminated;

(2) the level of the benefit would be fixed in relation to supplementary benefit payments, and, like them, would be reviewed regularly, so that, taken in conjunction with whatever family support was generally available (family allowances or tax credits) it would normally be sufficient to bring one-parent families off supplementary benefit even if they had no earnings;

(3) all one-parent families would be eligible for the benefit, including motherless families;

(4) the benefit would be non-contributory;

(5) the benefit would consist of a child-care allowance for the adult and a separate allowance for each child;

(6) the benefit would not be adjusted to the particular needs of individual families, except in so far as it would reflect the size of the family;

(7) for lone parents who are working or have other income the benefit would be tapered, after an initial disregard, so that it fell by considerably less than the amount by which income increased;

(8) the adult benefit would be extinguished by the time income reached about the level of average male earnings, but the child benefit would continue to be payable to all lone parents, whatever their income;

(9) once awarded, benefit would be fixed at that level for three months at a time, without in the normal way being affected by changes in circumstances. There would thus normally be no need for changes, including the beginning of a cohabitation, to be reported, until a fresh claim to benefit was made. Taken in conjunction with subparagraph (6) above this should much reduce the need for detailed enquiries;

(10) the benefit would be administered by post, on the lines of the family income supplements scheme.

5.105 We have attempted, in arriving at these principles, to strike a balance between the need to improve the lot of the parent who wants to stay at home with the children and the need to enable those who want to work to do so to some advantage to themselves. We have treated men and women alike, though many fathers who work would probably be earning sufficient to cause the adult allowance to be much reduced. GMA would need to be kept at a level higher than either FFA or CHAID if it is to be more effective in lifting one-parent families off supplementary benefit (even taking account of the extra income which tax credits would bring to one-parent families). We could not recommend that an allowance of this size, designed for the non-working family, should be paid to all one-parent families, however large their income; to do so would be to put working one-parent families well ahead of the widowed mother's present position and ahead of many two-parent families, besides being an expensive way of channelling help to the most needy. We therefore see no alternative to taking income into account in the award of GMA although, as explained in the previous paragraph, we would do so in a way that would cause least trouble and difficulty to the recipient. We envisage that the authority administering GMA would also be responsible for the assessment and collection of maintenance payments. The authority would already be in possession of information about the woman's financial position and would continue to deal with maintenance questions as long as she received GMA for the child, that is, so long as she remained the head of a one-parent family, irrespective of her income. Only one-parent families with exceptionally high expenses would qualify for some supplementary benefit in addition for any length of time; and the proposals for the collection of maintenance payments should virtually eliminate the role of the Supplementary Benefits Commission in relation to liable relatives.

5.106 There is room for manoeuvre in the exact level at which GMA should be pitched, the steepness of the income taper and the level of income at which the adult allowance should be extinguished entirely. Within a given global sum the money could be differently distributed, according to the ends it was desired to achieve. At one extreme there are solutions which approach the universalism of the proposals outlined earlier in this Section—a relatively low allowance with a very gradual taper not extinguished until high levels of income. At the opposite extreme, if an allowance were desired which would actively discourage lone parents from working, one would have a relatively high allowance with a very steep taper against other income, approaching the pound for pound level. What we propose is something in between—an allowance linked to the supplementary benefit level; and the taper (discussed in more detail below) would be 50 per cent on net income after a disregard, tapering the adult allowance out at about the level of an average full-time wage for a man. The child allowance would, we suggest, remain unaffected. The particular structure outlined here, and explored in greater depth in later paragraphs, is the one which we consider most appropriate to our aim of guaranteeing to lone parents a sufficient level of maintenance to offer them a real choice between working and staying at home to look after the children, without inequity to low-income two-parent families. We recognise that a number of other variations would not be inconsistent with this aim, and we do not advance our chosen solution as being the only possible one within the structure for GMA. Nevertheless, we regard it as essential that GMA should in general be above the supplementary benefit level for those with the lowest incomes, while its expenditure on families who are relatively well off should be limited.

Tax-credit scheme

5.107 Although it is intended that child credits should be paid universally, entry into the tax-credit scheme as such will depend either on normally having earnings above a certain level or on being in receipt of some other qualifying source of income, such as one of the principal national insurance benefits. We regard it as being of the utmost importance that all one-parent families should be included in the tax-credit scheme, where they would get the advantage of receiving the same higher rate of credit as a married couple. An allowance of the kind we have described should be treated as a qualifying source of income enabling one-parent families to be so included. All one-parent families would therefore be entitled to tax credits of at least £8–£6 for the adult and £2 for each child. (The rates quoted are those used in the Green Paper.)[1] This would reduce the extra amount which would have to be paid by way of a special one-parent family allowance to take one-parent families off supplementary benefit and keep a better balance between general family support and special support for one-parent families. We recommend in Section 8 that if, in the event, the tax-credit scheme does not become law comparable improvements in family support should be made, which would, in this respect, have a similar effect for the purposes of our proposals as the tax-credit scheme. If the government of the day were to decide not to improve the lot of families generally in any way, it would be necessary to choose between a lower level of one-parent family allowance, so that many families would qualify for supplementary benefit in addition (a situation our proposals have been designed to avoid), and, on the other hand, paying the full allowance and facing the consequences of the differential between one-parent families and other disadvantaged groups. For the purpose of this Report, however, we present GMA in terms of the tax-credit scheme because it was necessary to make one firm set of assumptions in order to demonstrate the scheme in detail. But our proposals would still be valid, though at different levels because of the different incidence of tax, if there were some other form of family support corresponding in amount to tax credits, or if there were a lower level of family support, provided corresponding adjustments were made in the level of benefit.

Cost and impact of GMA

5.108 GMA would offer extra support to all groups of one-parent families —even some widowed mothers would be likely to gain from GMA and so would motherless families. We are concerned that GMA should in general lift one-parent families off supplementary benefit, and, as we explain in Section 6, we calculate that in 1972–1973 terms this means a minimum rate of £9·50 for the parent and £1 for the child. At this level, and with a 50 per cent taper on other income, it would be a more expensive proposal than either CHAID or FFA, but those two latter proposals would not extend in full to motherless families. Its cost would be much the same as that for a widowed mother's allowance type of benefit which did extend to motherless families. What is important, however, is that the expenditure would be better directed than

---

[1] *Proposals for a Tax-Credit System: op cit.*

CHAID, FFA or a widowed mother's allowance to help the less well off one-parent families: GMA would in general do more than these benefits would for those families whose incomes are now not more than a few pounds above supplementary benefit levels, but less for those families who were better off. Compared, for example, with a net expenditure of about £30 million annually on motherless families under a widowed mother's allowance, the net expenditure under GMA would be about £9 million because few families would receive the full rate. (A benefit at the GMA rate of £9·50 for the adult which was not adjusted to take account of earnings or other income would add as much as £55 million to the net annual cost.) The following Table shows that, on 1972–1973 benefit rates,[1] the one-child family with gross earnings of up to £15 a week would receive more from GMA than from a widowed mother's allowance. The balance would swing as income rose above that level. For larger families the cross-over point would be slightly lower.

TABLE 5.7

COMPARISON OF GMA AND WIDOWED MOTHER'S ALLOWANCE FOR A ONE-PARENT FAMILY WITH ONE CHILD

Gross earnings	GMA		Widowed mother's allowance	
	Benefit	Net income*	Benefit	Net income*
£	£	£	£	£
Nil	10·50	15·35	8·05	13·64**
5	10·50	18·35	8·05	16·64**
10	9·59	20·53	8·05	19·47
15	8·01	22·60	8·05	22·63
20	6·43	24·65	8·05	25·79
25	4·85	26·71	8·05	28·96
30	3·27	28·76	8·05	32·12
35	1·68	30·82	8·05	35·28
40	1·00	33·50	8·05	38·44

* Net income means gross earnings, after tax at 30 per cent, national insurance contributions at 6·75 per cent (on earnings of £8 or more) and working expenses of 50p, plus benefit, adjusted in the case of GMA by 50 per cent of net earnings, and tax credits after tax on benefit at 30 per cent.

** In addition there could be entitlement to some supplementary benefit.

5.109 We estimate that GMA would remove all but a few one-parent families from supplementary benefit: over 90 per cent of all one-parent families who now draw supplementary benefit for three months or more would no longer need it, and even taking account of the short-term cases, who would not be eligible for GMA (see paragraph 5.149), about 80 per cent of all one-parent families would be removed from supplementary benefit.[2] The extra money

[1] We have estimated the level and cost of GMA in terms of supplementary benefit rates current in October 1972, since these are the only rates for which we can get a valid comparison with the tax-credit rates published in the Green Paper and thus attribute the correct amount to likely general improvement in family support.

[2] As for CHAID and FFA, these estimates are based on the assumption that the improvements in the supplementary benefits scheme, which we recommend in Section 8, have been introduced.

going into the pockets of those families now receiving supplementary benefit would be about £35 million and some one-parent families would have their income raised to several pounds above the supplementary benefit level.

5.110   We estimate the annual gross cost of GMA, in terms of 1972–1973 benefit rates, at £224 million.   About £23 million of this would go to widows already getting a widowed mother's allowance, and to motherless families. In addition, the adult tax credits at the married rate (£6) to which one-parent families would become entitled as a result of receiving GMA would amount to £75 million. (This does not include the cost of child credits, which are to be paid universally, or the cost of the adult credit where the family would be getting it anyway, as, for example, where the parent is working full time.)   To set against this would be the tax paid on the benefit and other income which would not otherwise have been taxable—£73 million—and savings in supplementary benefit—£89 million.[1]   These deductions reduce the cost of GMA to between £135 million and £140 million.   Slightly under £15 million of this cost would be the net cost of providing tax credits for those one-parent families who would not otherwise be in the tax-credit scheme.[2]   The GMA cost alone would therefore be between about £120 million and £125 million.   Part of this cost would be recovered from maintenance payments—we describe our proposals for doing this in Section 7.   On the basis of an estimate of the amount of maintenance now paid in respect of one-parent families we think that it might be possible to recover about £50 million in this way, reducing the net cost of GMA to between £70 million and £75 million.   The costings of GMA may be set out as follows:

	£m	£m
Gross cost of GMA	224	
Gross cost of additional adult tax credits	75	
Total gross cost		299
Increased taxation revenue	73	
Savings on supplementary benefit	89	
Total savings		162
Net cost of the total proposal		137
Net cost of tax credits only		15
Estimated maintenance recovery		50
Net cost of GMA		£72

SECTION 6—GUARANTEED MAINTENANCE ALLOWANCE

5.111   In paragraph 5.104 we set out the principles upon which we propose that GMA should be based.   In this Section we describe the allowance in greater detail, and in Section 7 we outline the arrangements we propose for the assessment and collection of maintenance payments from liable relatives, which are an integral part of our conception of GMA.

---

[1] As for CHAID and FFA this estimate is based on the assumption that the improvements in the supplementary benefits scheme, which we recommend in Section 8, have been introduced.
[2] *Select Committee on Tax-Credit: Report and Proceedings of the Committee*, paragraph 101.

5.112   Our aim (paragraphs 5.104 and 5.106) is to set GMA at a level which, taken in conjunction with family allowances or tax credits, would make most one-parent families rather better off than they would be on supplementary benefit.   We consider that this aim could best be achieved by fixing the level of GMA by reference to supplementary benefit payments.   But the level to which supplementary benefit makes up a family's income varies depending on their needs—on the rent, on special needs, on the ages of the children, on whether the parent is a householder or not.   We do not intend that GMA should vary in this way because we want to avoid detailed enquiries into a family's circumstances.   We have therefore to strike a single figure for an adult, including an addition for housing costs and special needs, and one for a child, which would relate to the supplementary benefit figure but would in the normal way give a clear advantage over supplementary benefit for one-parent families with no other income.

5.113   We propose that these figures might be calculated as follows.   The level of adult GMA should be fixed by reference to the supplementary benefit scale rate for long-term dependence on supplementary benefit, including the special additional sum which we recommend later (Section 8) for all one-parent families on supplementary benefit, plus an addition to the scale rate to cover, at an average figure, the variable items allowed for under the supplementary benefits scheme, such as housing costs, and exceptional needs.   The child allowance, which, for the sake of simplicity, we think should be at a single rate, not varying with the age of the child, would be fixed by reference to the average of children's supplementary benefit scale rates, including the scale rate for a young person of 18.   Calculations on this basis would make GMA rather better than the average amount of supplementary benefit paid to one-parent families.   Not all families get the long-term rate, which is not at present paid until a person has been on supplementary benefit for two years, and the child rate would be higher than the average child rate for one-parent families on supplementary benefit because one-parent families on supplementary benefit tend to have young children for whom the scale rate is lower.   These factors, together with the way in which we propose that other income should affect the allowance (which is discussed in paragraphs 5.126–5.140), should mean that almost all one-parent families would be able to manage without more than temporary help from supplementary benefits.

5.114   The evidence we received and the enquires we made left us in no doubt, as Section 2 indicates, that one-parent families are financially a hard-pressed group.   Had resources been unlimited and had one-parent families been the only disadvantaged group in the community we might have favoured setting GMA at a higher level.   But our terms of reference required us to have regard to " the need to maintain equity as between one-parent families and other families " and to " practical and economic limitations ".   The rates of payment under the supplementary benefits scheme and the basic level of income which the scheme provides for beneficiaries have been approved by Parliament, and we do not consider that it would be right for the community to provide a non-contributory benefit, such as GMA, at a level totally out of line with the payments available under the supplementary benefits scheme.   We have, therefore, in GMA sought to provide an allowance the rate of which, while generally more favourable, is linked quite closely to supplementary benefit payments, but the operation and administration of which is devised to meet specific problems in the one-parent family situation.

5.115 To pitch the level of GMA much above supplementary benefit levels would also lead to problems when the family's title to GMA came to an end. For example, the parent who was not able to work full time after the family had grown up, and who had to rely on supplementary benefit, could suffer a significant drop in income. More particularly, it would be difficult to justify a reduction in a family's income when a deserting husband returned home, the GMA ceased and the family claimed supplementary benefit. While GMA calculated in the way we propose does not entirely avoid these problems, we think the likelihood of their occurring is sufficiently small to be tolerable.

Tax credits

5.116 Tax credits (or family allowances) would be taken into account as income for supplementary benefit purposes. Our intention is that GMA should be a qualifying source of income for membership of the tax-credit scheme, and therefore the recipient of the allowance would benefit from the adult credit (at the married rate). In calculating the appropriate level for GMA, therefore, the relevant tax credits would need to be taken into account. This would mean that the amount of the GMA, after tax had been deducted,[1] plus the family's tax credits should together be approximately equivalent to the family's supplementary benefit level calculated as we suggest in paragraphs 5.112 and 5.113. Using the £6 tax-credit rate quoted in the Green Paper,[2] the adult allowance in GMA would be at a rate which, after tax, was £6 less than the supplementary benefit long-term scale rate for the head of a one-parent family with the addition of a specified amount for housing costs and other variable items. The GMA for each child, taking the tax credit as £2, would be at a rate which, again after tax, was £2 less than an average amount for a child under the supplementary benefits scheme. We demonstrate how these calculations are made in paragraphs 5.122–5.124.

Allowance for variable items

5.117 As it is an essential part of our proposals that there should be no need for detailed enquiries into circumstances, the addition for items which are provided for at the discretion of the Supplementary Benefits Commission can only be based on a rough and ready estimate of the average amount to which a one-parent family would be entitled. By far the largest of the variable items is housing costs. The average housing costs of one-parent families in receipt of supplementary benefits in November 1972 were approximately £3·50. Other discretionary payments are very much smaller, and on this basis a total addition of about £4 to the appropriate supplementary benefit scale rate (in 1972 terms) would provide a level of GMA in accordance with our objectives.

5.118 We have, however, found it particularly difficult to assess just how much should be allowed in the make-up of GMA for housing costs. The full

---

[1] We have been advised that for GMA to be a qualifying source of income for membership of the tax-credit scheme it should itself be taxable.
[2] *Op cit.*

impact of the Housing Finance Act 1972[1] is not yet clear: we are faced at present with rising rents on the one hand and, on the other, substantial rebates and rent allowances available to low-income tenants who claim them. With rent levels as they are at the moment, families with incomes at about the supplementary benefit level will be paying very low rents indeed, but whether that situation will hold in future years must depend on the movement of rents and of the needs allowances used in calculating title to rent rebates and allowances. Moreover, for tenants in furnished accommodation the rebate does not relate to the whole of their rent,[2] and the scheme does not affect owner-occupiers at all.

5.119 The situation is further complicated by the fact that people on supplementary benefit at present have their rent rebates or allowances calculated in a different way from those not on supplementary benefit, and they may be paying a higher rent (although covered by a rent allowance from the Supplementary Benefits Commission) than they would be if they had the same income from a different source.[3] The figures available to us for the end of 1972 related only to housing costs incurred by one-parent families on supplementary benefit; no reliable information was available to us about rents paid at that time by other low-income one-parent families.

5.120 In view of these uncertainties we considered the best course was to base our illustration of GMA on the situation as it was in November 1972 (at which date the national rent rebate and allowance scheme applied only to local authority rents) and to take the average housing cost of one-parent families on supplementary benefit at that time as being the only firm figure available to us. Any other course, we considered, would involve us in a great deal of speculation. We wish to stress that this rate is only an illustrative one: what the right level should be would depend on circumstances at the time of introducing GMA.

5.121 The principle however is clear: the rent element should be related to the level of rent actually paid by one-parent families with income at about the supplementary benefit level. Account would have to be taken of the rebates and rent allowances available and the extent to which these were taken up;[4] and we think it important also to look at the range of housing costs incurred, since there might be a case for pitching the allowance above the average if significant numbers of families in a particular group—furnished tenants, perhaps, or owner-occupiers—were incurring very high costs. Information is not at present available to draw this kind of comparison, nor would much purpose be served in seeking it given the current uncertainties of the situation, but we hope that before the introduction of GMA steps would be taken to obtain a fuller and more accurate picture than was available to us.

---

[1] For further consideration of the Housing Finance Act 1972 see Part 6.

[2] This is because, if it did do, they would be placed at an advantage over tenants in unfurnished accommodation who have to provide their furniture without any assistance.

[3] As from 1 April 1974 recipients of supplementary benefits will no longer receive rent rebates and rent allowances individually. Instead the supplementary benefit assessment will make full provision for housing costs.

[4] Information about successful claims for rent rebates or rent allowances was given in a Written Answer to Mr Michael Meacher MP on 18 October 1973. Official Report, columns 293–294.

Illustration of GMA levels

5.122 On the basis of the assumptions described in paragraphs 5.112–5.121 the " equivalent " supplementary benefit levels would be calculated as shown in the Table below. (The illustration is in terms of supplementary benefit rates current in 1972–1973.)

TABLE 5.8
CONSTRUCTION OF GMA

	£
Supplementary benefit single householder scale rate	6·55
Long-term addition	60
One-parent family addition (see Section 8)	1·50
Variable items	4·00
" Equivalent " supplementary benefit level (adult)	£12·65
" Equivalent " supplementary benefit level for each child (average of scale rates for persons up to and including age 18)	£ 2·74

5·123 Our intention is (see paragraph 5·116 and footnote) that GMA should be taxable, giving entry to the tax-credit scheme. One-parent families will then be entitled to the £6 married rate of credit (in terms of the tax-credit rates given in the 1972 Green Paper)[1] and what is wanted, therefore, is a GMA adult rate, which, after deduction of tax and addition of a £6 tax credit, would provide £12·65 a week. This rate is £9·50 (which after tax at 30 per cent becomes £6·65). On a similar basis what is required to achieve £2·74 for a child, after deduction of tax and the addition of a £2 child credit, is £1·06. Table 5.9 illustrates how these rates of GMA work out for different sizes of family.

TABLE 5.9
GMA RATES ILLUSTRATED FOR DIFFERENT SIZES OF FAMILY

One-parent families with:	" Equivalent " supplementary benefit level	Tax credits for family	Amount to be provided by GMA (col 2— col 3)	Col. 4 × $\frac{10*}{7}$	Allowance of £1·06 each child	Allowance for adult (col 5— col 6)
1	2	3	4	5	6	7
1 child ...	£15·39	£8	£7·39	£10·55	£1·06	£9·49
2 children ...	£18·13	£10	£8·13	£11·61	£2·12	£9·49
3 children ...	£20·87	£12	£8·87	£12·67	£3·18	£9·49
4 children ...	£23·61	£14	£9·61	£13·73	£4·24	£9·49

* Column 5 is the before-tax equivalent of column 4.

5.124 In the remainder of this Report, therefore, we shall use the illustrative rate of £9·50 for the adult GMA and £1·00 for the child's allowance (we take

[1] *Op cit.*

round figures for convenience). (We stress that these amounts would be subject to tax at 30 per cent and to the addition of tax credits of £6·00 for the adult and £2·00 for each child.) The Table below shows what the after-tax income of one-parent families of various sizes receiving the benefit would be if they had no other income.

TABLE 5.10

INCOME OF FAMILIES ON GMA

One-parent families with:	GMA	GMA after tax	Tax credit	Net income
1 child	£10·50	£7·35	£8·00	£15·35
2 children	£11·50	£8·05	£10·00	£18·05
3 children	£12·50	£8·75	£12·00	£20·75
4 children	£13·50	£9·45	£14·00	£23·45

Reviews of level of GMA

5.125 We think it important that GMA should be included in the annual reviews of social security benefits, and that it should move in line with the rate of supplementary benefit which is its base. Thus the level of GMA should reflect changes in supplementary benefit long-term scale rates, changes in the special addition for one-parent families and changes in children's scale rates. Changes in housing costs should also be taken into account, as indicated in paragraphs 5.118–5.121. A complicating factor in reviews of the level of GMA would be changes in tax credits or in the rate at which tax was levied; the object should be to produce an allowance which after adjustment for tax and credits would provide "equivalent" supplementary benefit levels, as set out in paragraph 5.122. This might on occasions result in increases in the gross amount of GMA larger than those in the "equivalent" supplementary benefit level (because GMA is taxable), and on other occasions the increase could be smaller (if, for example, the tax credit were being increased).

Effect of Other Income

5.126 The full allowance of £9·50 plus £1 for each child would be payable where the family had no other income of its own (except for tax credits), and we have explained in paragraph 5.105 why we think that GMA should be reduced where there is other income. The main sources of income (other than supplementary benefit) for one-parent families are maintenance payments and earnings. Some families may also have investment income, an occupational widow's or children's pension, or income from national insurance and similar benefits. In the following paragraphs we discuss the ways in which other income should affect GMA and our reasons for considering that the treatment should vary according to the type of income.

Maintenance payments

5.127 One of the main objectives of our proposals for GMA is to provide a guarantee of income for all one-parent families so that they no longer suffer

294

from the unreliability or inadequacy of maintenance payments from the absent parent. To the extent that GMA is payable in the individual case, it is, in the hands of the recipient, a substitute for maintenance. Maintenance payments made by or on behalf of the absent spouse must be fully offset against entitlement to GMA, providing some reimbursement to the State of the income guarantee made to the family. Our intention is that the family's title to GMA would be calculated without regard to any maintenance the absent parent may be able to contribute, and the award would be made accordingly; but, as a corollary, any maintenance payments made to the family would have to be passed over to the authority, up to the level of GMA in payment. We discuss in Section 7 the arrangements we propose for assessing the maintenance liability of an absent parent and enforcing that liability, and we suggest that the responsibility for this should rest with the authority. We consider that the absent parent should be required in the normal way to make maintenance payments to the authority, which would retain the money to the extent needed to cover the GMA award. The authority would pay over any excess to the family. In this way there would not normally need to be any contact about maintenance between the family and the absent parent.

Earnings

5.128 The second main objective of our proposals is to provide a supplement to low earnings: where the parent wished to work but could earn only a modest amount, she (or he) would not have to choose between working part time for a minimum financial gain, because of the reduction in supplementary benefit, and giving up the security of a steady, if limited, income from supplementary benefits in order to work full time with, in many cases still only relatively small financial betterment. (This remains a valid and necessary objective even though the family income supplements scheme has given worthwhile help to the lone parent working full time for a low wage.) Our proposal, therefore, is that earnings should reduce the amount of GMA payable, but that this reduction should be much more gradual than is the case with supplementary benefit or with the earnings rules attached to national insurance benefits, such as retirement pension. The rate of reduction which we propose would serve several aims: first, it would make the real return from earnings much greater than it is for supplementary benefit recipients; second, it would help lone parents to enter employment if they wished, thus avoiding the emotional and psychological disadvantages which may come from social isolation, and easing the transition to the time when their children ceased to be dependent and they, being no longer eligible for GMA (see paragraph 5.160 below) might have to support themselves by full-time work; third, it would limit the extent of the help provided for those families where the head was in well-paid work and thus ensure that the bulk of the money went where it was most needed.

Child portion of GMA

5.129 We except the child portion from the general rule that GMA should be adjusted in relation to earnings. The evidence about the financial circumstances of one-parent families (see Section 2) indicates that it is rare for an individual family not to suffer some measure of financial deprivation, even where the head is able to undertake full-time work at a reasonable wage, and we accordingly think that it is proper for the State to make a small contribution towards the family's income above and beyond general family support provisions for all families with children. (Compare the provision in other countries for a special family allowance for one-parent families—see paragraph 5.67.) We would liken this contribution to the preferential rate for dependent children in widowed mother's allowance, guardian's allowance and child's special allowance, and we see it as a contribution by the State to all one-parent families, irrespective of means, to help with the extra cost of caring for a child where one of the parents is not available.

5.130 Moreover, we have been advised that, because of the structure of the tax-credit scheme, it is desirable that there should be a flat-rate allowance, however small, to act as a passport to the scheme. The child allowance would fulfil this role. A flat-rate allowance is desirable to avoid the position, which could in theory arise with a tapered allowance, that at the stage where the allowance finally tapered out membership of the tax-credit scheme would also terminate, and a small increase in earnings could cause not only loss of the last few pence of the allowance but also of the whole of the adult credit. In that case the loss by way of allowance and credit would be out of all proportion to the increase in earnings. In practice, because we intend that the adult part of GMA should not be fully extinguished by the family's other income until that reached roughly the level of average earnings for men, this situation could not arise, given a continuation of the present conditions for membership of the tax-credit scheme and for full benefit from personal tax allowances. By the time GMA had tapered out the parent would have either acquired title to tax credits through earnings or be receiving the full benefit of the equivalent personal tax allowances. Changes in the future, however, either in GMA or in the relationship between the value of tax credits or tax allowances and average earnings, could alter the position and a flat-rate child allowance would ensure that there was permanently available a mode of entry for one-parent families into the tax-credit scheme.

Adult portion of GMA

5.131 We have already said (paragraph 5.106) that the GMA structure is a flexible one and that a number of different arrangements for the treatment of earnings would be generally consistent with our aims. The solution we have adopted is, as we explain in the following paragraphs, to reduce the adult portion of GMA by half of the amount by which the net earnings (that is, after allowing for tax deductions and other expenses of working) exceed a fixed amount of "disregard". We prefer this solution because we think it would hold the right balance between encouraging the parent who worked and supporting the parent who stayed at home, and between one-parent families and two-parent families. It would mean that GMA would improve the position of most of those families with no income of their own without spending a disproportionate amount on those with other income and therefore better off financially. Before arriving at our solution we considered a number of different alternatives. Some of these are set out in Appendix 11 and one of them, which offers a strong contrast to the arrangement we recommend, is commented upon in paragraph 5.137 below.

5.132 In considering how earnings should affect the adult part of GMA we take the view that there should be a complete disregard of small amounts of earnings. This would avoid the need for any adjustment where total

296

earnings were minimal, and if this disregard were fixed at the same level as that for supplementary benefits (we suggest in Section 8 that this level should be raised—we have assumed a rise to a disregard of £4 net earnings a week) it would prevent the situation arising where people with very low earnings would be eligible for small amounts of supplementary benefit on top of GMA simply because of the different treatment of earnings in the two schemes.[1] We do not consider that a higher disregard would be justified as it would mean allocating an increased proportion of the expenditure on GMA to those families who already had the higher incomes.

5.133   Where earnings exceeded the disregard level a proportion of the excess should be deducted from the adult allowance. We consider that the proportion should be fixed so that the adult allowance would not be extinguished until gross earnings reached about the level of average male earnings,[2] or even higher where the lone parent incurred extra expenses in employment, such as for child care—see paragraph 5.134 below. This would, we believe, give an adequate measure of equity with two-parent families.

5.134   We have considered whether the earnings taken into account should be net or gross, that is whether or not necessary expenses of working should be deducted from gross earnings in calculating adjustments to the rate of allowance. Family income supplements are adjusted according to gross earnings; other benefits, such as retirement pension and supplementary benefit, use a net basis (although the bases used may differ). Both systems have attractions: gross for its simplicity and ease of comprehension, net because it is a truer reflection of the return from working.   Among expenses which could be deducted from the gross earnings to arrive at net earnings are statutory deductions, such as the basic rate of tax and national insurance contributions, other working expenses such as trade union subscriptions, the cost of special clothing, tools, travel to work, and child care.   We realise that there are difficulties in checking on expenses claimed (and this would be more difficult if claims were not dealt with locally where reasonable cost of travel and special equipment could more easily be assessed), but we consider that, for some one-parent families, the expenses of working may be so heavy that it would be inequitable to ignore them.

5.135   This is particularly true of expenditure on substitute care for children. We take the view that, provided the level of expense is reasonable in all the circumstances,[3] it is an essential item to set against the gain from working and should therefore be taken into account. We are aware that there might be difficulties in allowing child care as an expense: some lone parents have relatives

---

[1] The possibility of this cannot be entirely eliminated because, under the tax-credit scheme, all earnings of recipients of GMA would be taxable whereas people on supplementary benefit who are not in the tax-credit scheme would not pay tax on low earnings. But by having some initial disregard of earnings for GMA we hope to keep the problem to a minimum.

[2] By this we mean average earnings of male wage earners in manufacturing and some of the principal non-manufacturing industries, as given in the *Department of Employment Gazette*.

[3] In determining what expenditure is reasonable for the care of a lone parent's children, it should not be assumed that this would necessarily bear a direct relationship to the level of the parent's earnings. Some lone parents may quite properly be prepared to devote a very substantial proportion of their earnings to child-care expenses if this enables them to take a job with good prospects, or a high level of interest, or simply for the psychological value to the parent of being out at work.

or friends who care for the children while they are at work and it would not always be easy for confirmation of the amount paid to be obtained. We bear in mind, however, that the effect of taking the expense into account would be that, on our recommendations, no more than 35 per cent of it would be reimbursed through the GMA.[1] In this connection it would be defeating our purposes if the introduction of GMA were to be seen as allowing increases in local authority charges for child-care services made to one-parent families: we believe that GMA is needed now, in the light of the present costs and expenditure of one-parent families.

5.136 The calculations shown in the Table below indicate that if 50 per cent of net earnings (after disregard) were deducted from the allowance the adult portion would disappear (assuming the minimum payment possible were set at 20p, as in the family income supplements scheme) when gross earnings were about £38 a week (average male earnings in April 1973 were about £37 a week). This would be the situation of a woman whose only expenses of working were tax, national insurance payments and 50p for items such as fares and so on. A woman with, say, £5 child-care expenses would retain some adult allowance until her gross earnings were nearly £45. With a taper at this rate, a person receiving GMA would, taking account of increased tax and national insurance payments (which together amount to nearly 37p in every £1) and the reduction in GMA, be 41p better off after every extra £1 earned.

---

[1] This is because we recommend that net earnings should reduce the gross amount of GMA by 50p in the £1. If net earnings decrease by, for example, £1 (because of the expense of child care) the gross amount of GMA will increase by 50p. The effect of taxing the 50p at 30 per cent is to reduce it to 35p, and this is the extra amount put in the pocket of the parent by GMA.

TABLE 5.11
EFFECT OF 50% TAPER ON GMA

| | GMA taper | | | Effect on net income** | | | | | |
| | | | | Adult + 1 child | | | Adult + 3 children | | |
Gross earnings	Expenses: tax, NI, etc*	Gross earnings less expenses less £4 disregard	Adult GMA	Adult GMA + child GMA	GMA after tax plus tax credit (£8)	Net income**	Adult GMA + child GMA	GMA after tax plus tax credit (£12)	Net income**
£	£	£	£	£	£	£	£	£	£
Nil	Nil	Nil	9·50	10·50	15·35	15·35	12·50	20·75	20·75
5	2·00	Nil	9·50	10·50	15·35	18·35	12·50	20·75	23·75
10	4·18	1·82	8·59	9·59	14·71	20·53	11·59	20·11	25·93
15	6·01	4·99	7·01	8·01	13·61	22·60	10·01	19·01	28·00
20	7·85	8·15	5·43	6·43	12·50	24·65	8·43	17·90	30·05
25	9·69	11·31	3·85	4·85	11·40	26·71	6·85	16·80	32·11
30	11·53	14·47	2·27	3·27	10·29	28·76	5·27	15·69	34·16
35	13·36	17·64	0·68	1·68	9·18	30·82	3·68	14·58	36·22
40	15·20	20·80	Nil	1·00	8·70	33·50	3·00	14·10	38·90
45	17·04	23·96	Nil	1·00	8·70	36·66	3·00	14·10	42·06

*Tax at 30 per cent, national insurance contribution at 6·75 per cent and other items, such as fares, at 50p.

**Net income is defined as earnings (less deductions as above) plus GMA after tax, plus tax credits.

5.137   In Appendix 11 tapers at a number of different rates are illustrated, some steeper, tapering out below average male earnings, and some shallower, tapering out well above that level.   We also illustrate one taper on gross earnings and one which treats earnings in a similar way to that used for national insurance retirement pension, that is, a complete disregard of the first £9·50 of net earnings, a 50 per cent taper on the next £4 and a 100 per cent taper thereafter.   This latter method has the attraction of following the practice under an existing benefit, and one which is well understood, but we think it would fail to allow enough room for the gradual increase in earning capacity as family responsibilities decrease, which is an essential feature of our proposals.

National insurance benefits

5.138   We recommend that the GMA should be available to all one-parent families.   This means that widows already drawing a widowed mother's allowance and families drawing other national insurance benefits (this is more likely to occur where the family is headed by a man) would be eligible for GMA.

5.139   Where there was a long-term benefit in payment to a claimant for GMA, for example, widowed mother's allowance, the amount of it should, we consider, be fully deducted from the GMA award and any balance of GMA should be paid on top.   Short-term benefits, such as sickness benefit, unemployment benefit and maternity allowance, are different.   These benefits are essentially a replacement for earnings, normally carrying with them an earnings-related supplement, and are often paid for quite short periods at a time.   We suggest that, where for a few weeks these benefits came into payment during the three-month award period of GMA (see paragraph 5.170), they should be ignored in the same way as changes in the level of other income.   There would, of course, be a variety of situations between the two extremes of a long-term benefit in payment indefinitely and a short-term replacement of earnings for a few weeks, for example, the situation of a long-term benefit coming into payment during the GMA award, or a short-term benefit already in payment when a claim for GMA was made.   It would not have been an appropriate use of our time or resources for us to have considered all the possible solutions to all the variations: we leave these to be considered at the appropriate time, in the light of the principles we have laid down for the two extremes.

Other income

5.140   Our evidence suggests that few one-parent families have any significant income other than maintenance, earnings, national insurance benefits and supplementary benefits.   Nevertheless we think that other income, where it exists, including income from capital in the form of rents, savings and investment, cannot, in fairness, be ignored and should be taken into account in adjusting the rate of adult GMA in the same way as earnings, and subject to inclusion in the same disregard.   We do not think that the circumstances of one-parent families justify a second or separate disregard.

WHO WILL BE ELIGIBLE FOR GMA?

A non-contributory benefit

5.141   In paragraph 5.90 we pointed out the difficulties of an insurance-based benefit with contribution conditions.   No matter how liberal the contribution conditions might be there would always be, as the National Council for the Unmarried Mother and her Child found in devising the CHAID scheme, some one-parent families, notably those with very young mothers, who would fail to qualify. It is our chief concern that all one-parent families should be able to draw GMA on an equal footing, and we do not see that any useful purpose would be served in devising ways in which an insurance benefit could be extended to groups who do not readily fall within any insurable category. We consider that it would be more sensible, in these circumstances, to make the allowance a non-contributory one, as are family allowances and the attendance allowance for disabled people. Title to the allowance would therefore depend only on establishing status as a one-parent family.

Establishing status as a one-parent family

5.142 For the purpose of GMA the rules for eligibility need to be clearly drawn since we are concerned to include in the allowance all who can be satisfactorily identified as constituting a one-parent family. In deciding what rules are needed, we have kept in mind the following principles:

(1) persons entitled to claim should be able easily to recognise their entitlement so that they should not fail to claim because of ignorance or a misunderstanding of their position and so that the number of abortive claims made would be kept as small as possible;

(2) the definition needs to be seen to be fair both by those entitled to claim and by the rest of the community;

(3) the definition must be administratively practicable, not involving excessive investigation at the time of the claim and being capable of proof by the claimant by means which would generally be readily available.

Definition of a one-parent family

5.143 It would be advantageous if eligibility for GMA could be identical with title to the higher tax credit proposed for single-handed responsibility for a child living with the tax creditor,[1] but this is not essential. What is important is that any recipient of the allowance should automatically be entitled to the higher rate of tax credit. We do not propose to extend title to the allowance beyond the natural, legal or adoptive parent. Our concern is for the lone parent with a child and we do not include in the meaning of " parent " an aunt or uncle, grandparent, older brother or sister, or anyone other than a natural, legal or adoptive parent who may have care of a child. We make no financial recommendations affecting persons other than the parent with a child to care for; generally other public provision, such as guardian's allowance or payments to foster parents, is available to such persons. In this important respect, therefore, eligibility for GMA is likely to be within somewhat narrower limits than might be necessary for the higher tax credit, which, like the present additional personal allowance, may be available to anyone qualifying for a child tax credit and having the child living with him (or her), irrespective of his (or her) relationship to the child.

5.144 It is our intention that GMA should be available to a lone parent (whether father or mother) with day-to-day responsibility for a child. Essentially, this means that child and parent should be living together, though

---

[1] See *Proposals for a Tax-Credit System, op cit.*

temporary absence, for example, at school, in hospital or on holiday, would not bar a claim. We do not propose that the allowance should be paid to a parent who, even though making regular payments for the child's upkeep, has surrendered immediate care of the child to someone else and who cannot be regarded as continuing to live with the child. In the case where a family splits and one or more children live with one parent and one or more with the other, we take the view that there would then be two one-parent families, both of whom would be *prima facie* entitled to GMA. We doubt whether this would give rise to a serious danger that families would separate solely for what they could gain financially, especially in view of the " qualifying period " we propose in paragraph 5.149, or that there would be a problem of bogus separations.

Definition of a child

5.145 We propose that the definition of a child should be similar to that which is applied for national insurance purposes and should include, besides any child under minimum school leaving age, a child who is under the age of 19 and still in full-time education, or an apprentice with low earnings. In the absence of evidence to the contrary, sufficient proof of having the care of the child should be a signed declaration to that effect by the claimant and production of the child's birth certificate.

Proof of status

5.146 GMA would be available on proof of status, and not on proof of need as is the case under the supplementary benefits scheme. Different considerations apply to the way in which status would have to be established according to which of the following categories applied to the claimant: widowed, divorced or marriage annulled, formally separated, separated without any formal agreement or order, unmarried.

5.147 For widows and widowers, divorcees and those claimants with a separation order or formal agreement, it should be a fairly simple matter to establish status. In the absence of evidence casting any doubt upon it their situation is a clear-cut one, and all that would be needed would be copies of the documents certifying the marriage and its later break-up or termination. In many cases the information would already be available in national insurance or tax records and, if that is so, it should be possible to have access to those records to avoid the need for the claimant to produce the documents for a second time.[1] While a maintenance order from the court[2] is not necessarily accompanied by a separation order, and does not automatically establish separation, we take the view that a maintenance order or formal agreement, together with a declaration as to separation by the claimant, would be adequate evidence of separation. For claimants in all these categories the one-parent family status should be treated as having arisen immediately upon the relevant event, that is, from the day the marriage ends or a separation or maintenance order is made.[3]

---

[1] The introduction of the tax-credit scheme will necessitate taking a fresh look at the confidentiality aspects of records held by individual government departments as there will need to be an interchange of information between tax and social security records.

[2] Court maintenance orders would be likely to become much less common under the proposals we outline later for assessing and enforcing the absent parent's liability, but they could be useful in establishing eligibility when the allowance was first introduced.

[3] In cases of divorce or annulment the marriage is terminated by the decree absolute, which normally is not granted less than six weeks after the decree nisi; but we consider that production of the decree nisi within that period should be effective for GMA.

5.148 It is by no means so easy to establish a system for administrative determination of the one-parent family status where there is no court order or formal agreement for maintenance or separation. We discussed this problem with many of those who in their evidence advocated special financial provision for one-parent families, and a variety of possible approaches emerged:

(1) title should depend on an order having been applied for in the courts. It might be necessary to make payment automatically for a short initial period to allow time for action to be instituted;

(2) a sworn declaration of separation by the claimant, supported in cases of doubt by a report from the court welfare officer, or alternatively supported by an officer of the local authority social services department. Some of those giving evidence thought the statement should be confirmed by the other parent;

(3) the claimant's statement should be accepted, subject to periodic checks and, possibly, after a waiting period between the date of separation and bringing the allowance into payment. Suggestions as to the length of the waiting period varied from one to six months.

5.149 We do not consider that any system which required the claimant to apply to a court for some kind of order and which would in effect mean that the *de facto* separated were excluded from the special allowance unless they went to law would be compatible with our aim (which we explain in Part 4 of this Report) of relieving lone parents from what may to them be a distasteful and emotionally disturbing step of engaging in matrimonial litigation. But the situation of the *de facto* separated is often a fluid one, particularly in the early weeks of separation. Even where both spouses are apparently equally determined, shortly after the domestic crisis, to effect a permanent separation there is a possibility that they may quickly change their minds. We have to allow for temporary estrangements, and indeed, to minimise the risk that the formal procedures and declarations associated with a claim to GMA might play their part in turning what would have been a temporary estrangement into a permanent one. We consider, therefore, that a short qualifying period would be necessary to allow the situation to clarify itself and to enable adequate enquiry to be made into the circumstances. Supplementary benefit would be available, as now, to help during this qualifying period. The length of the qualifying period would have to be a compromise between the time needed to ensure that the separation was real and the desirability of the family's receiving a settled income in the form of GMA quickly and ensuring that the higher rate of tax credit was being awarded. The longer the period, the clearer the situation would be likely to become, but we consider that a period of six months, as was suggested in some of the evidence, would be too long for a family to have to wait. We conclude that it would be appropriate to fix the qualifying period at three months.

5.150 In calculating the qualifying period of three months which we recommend, we suggest that there should be discretion to ignore short-lived attempts at reconciliation, such as those not lasting more than a month. We consider that it would be unfortunate if the need to fulfil a continuous qualifying period of three months discouraged genuine attempts at reconciliation between the two parents.

5.151 The claim would need to be accompanied by a declaration as to separation by the claimant. Where possible, the authority administering GMA would have to seek confirmation of this statement from the absent spouse, and if this was given and there was no reason to doubt the statements we consider this might be sufficient without further corroborative evidence. It would not, however, enable the claimant to avoid the three months' qualifying period.

5.152 As regards the unmarried, it could be argued that there is in general no rational basis for the imposition of any qualifying period, and that the parent should be able to claim the allowance immediately upon a statement as to marital status which could be compared with national insurance and tax records. But this would place those unmarried claimants who had been cohabiting in a more favourable position than married claimants who were separated, from which it might follow that unmarried claimants in this class ought to be treated in the same way as separated wives and made subject to a qualifying period, as described in the preceding paragraphs.[1]

5.153 On the other hand this solution might involve great difficulties in establishing which of the unmarried claimants had, and which of them had not been cohabiting. It might, therefore, be thought fairer in practice if all unmarried parents were subject to the qualifying period which might run either from the date of birth of the child or from the day an acknowledged cohabitation ended, whichever was the later; and a qualifying period would also give more opportunity for the position to have clarified and for the mother to have reached decisions about whether or not to keep the child and whether or not to marry the father. But in our view none of these three possible solutions is clearly to be preferred, and we make no firm recommendation.

Young parents

5.154 Single parents between the ages of 16 and 18 who have responsibility for a child and who are not at school may claim supplementary benefit in their own right and we recommend in Section 8 that they should receive adult rates. We consider that they should be similarly treated for the purposes of GMA as adults and should be able to claim GMA and qualify for tax credits in their own right.

5.155 As regards single parents between the ages of 16 and 18 who are in full-time education, there is a case for saying that they are still the dependants of their own parents and that the State should not be responsible for their general maintenance. On the other hand, as parents themselves they have acquired responsibilities which, without help, they are normally unable to fulfil, and the ability or willingness of their own parents to help them may be limited. The Supplementary Benefits Commission exercise their discretionary power under section 9 of the Ministry of Social Security Act 1966 to award benefit in these circumstances for the child's requirements, but not for those of the parent. We refer elsewhere[2] to the disadvantages frequently suffered by a young unmarried mother who is unable to continue her education, and which in turn may affect her child. We are concerned that young people should not be forced for financial reasons to end their education prematurely,

---

[1] For cohabitations which begin while GMA is in payment, see paragraphs 5.161–5.164 below.

[2] See Part 8, Section 5.

a matter to which we again refer when dealing with educational maintenance allowances in a later Section. We think that provision of a reasonable income may in many of these difficult cases encourage the young mothers to continue their studies.

5.156 There are special social considerations to bear in mind in relation to the under-sixteens, and we appreciate that it is a moot point whether they should be eligible for an income independent of their parents whose legal responsibility they still are. But their financial needs are similar to those of 16 to 18-year olds, and we see no good reason for making their families bear a financial burden in addition to the other burdens which caring for a school-girl mother undoubtedly put upon them.

5.157 In all the foregoing circumstances, therefore, we propose that there should be no minimum age for GMA and that the under-sixteens should be included in the scheme. The fact that under GMA the young parent would have an income of her own would, of course, affect assessment of, for example, educational maintenance allowances, and any entitlement of the adult responsible for the young parent to dependency benefits. (See also paragraph 5.139.)

Families of long-term prisoners

5.158 The families of long-term prisoners share many of the characteristics and problems of one-parent families: one of the parents is absent for a long period and unable to give support to the family; a high proportion are on supplementary benefit; the parent with the children has a need, like other lone parents, for an allowance which will help her (or, rarely, him) to go out to work and avoid social isolation. These problems are at least as great as for other one-parent families, and prisoners' families may suffer particularly in that the absence of the parent occurs in circumstances which may cast a stigma over the family and make a social life for the children, and especially for the remaining parent, very difficult. On the other hand, there would be a danger that awarding GMA to prisoners' families might discourage wives from taking their husbands back when they came out of prison, because of the drop in the family's income which the withdrawal of GMA might cause. We consider that although there is a strong case for regarding prisoners' families as one-parent families, so that they became eligible for GMA, any such eligibility would have to be confined strictly to the families of long-term prisoners—those, for example, with a sentence of a year or more. Further, we are concerned that a recommendation that GMA should be paid to the families of long-term prisoners might have implications for penal policy which we are not able to assess. We therefore recommend that the possibility of making long-term prisoners' families eligible for GMA should be looked at by the Home Office in the context of treatment of prisoners' wives generally.

Families of long-term hospital patients

5.159 Some of the factors in favour of treating the families of long-term prisoners as eligible for GMA apply also to the families of long-term hospital patients: for them, too, one of the parents is absent for a long period and unable to give support to the family, and in some cases it must be virtually certain that the parent will never return, or at least will never be able to contribute any financial help to the family. On the other hand, the award of a benefit like

305

GMA, which would cease when the sick parent returned home, despite the fact that he or she might then be causing far more problems and expense than when in hospital, does not seem to be the appropriate form of help for these families. Moreover, such families may well already have invalidity benefit, and, if this is not so, this is likely to be because the parent's contribution record is inadequate. Only if it is the housewife, for whose illness the national insurance scheme makes no provision, who is the hospital in-patient, will the family normally have no financial help from the State. We recognise that the introduction of GMA for one-parent families could highlight this gap in social security provision, since comparisons would be made between the case of the family with the mother in hospital and that where she had died or deserted; but it seems to us that a benefit directly related to such a situation may be needed and that stretching GMA would not be appropriate.

WHEN TITLE TO GMA CEASES

Children growing up

5.160 Since we tie entitlement to GMA to the existence in the family of a dependent child under the age of 19, there would come a time when the family would no longer qualify because the last dependent child had grown up. We do not think it appropriate that any payment of GMA should continue once the children can no longer be regarded as dependent upon the parent, and we would not follow the analogy with the older widow who is entitled to help by way of a widow's pension once her family grows up. We have deliberately framed our proposals so that lone parents may receive a better financial return from working than is possible under the supplementary benefits scheme, and to enable them to obtain financial advantage from increasing the amount they earn, if they wish to, as the family's demands on their time decrease. In this way, we suggest, parents would be encouraged to reach the position where, when GMA came to an end, they were established in work and able to maintain themselves by their own efforts in the same way as do other members of the community.

Marriage or cohabitation

5.161 We describe in Part 4 the legal provisions which give rise to the "cohabitation rule", the consequences of which are that, unless there are exceptional circumstances, a woman cannot claim supplementary benefit in her own right if she is cohabiting with a man as his wife. In Section 8 below we consider whether there is a necessity to retain the cohabitation rule in relation to supplementary benefit, and, if there is, whether its administration can be improved. At this juncture, however, we turn our attention to whether there would have to be a corresponding rule regulating entitlement to GMA.

5.162 GMA is by definition a one-parent family benefit. None of the arguments which have arisen over whether it would be possible to avoid having a cohabitation rule in supplementary benefits could apply to GMA, since it would be a logical absurdity to make an award of a one-parent family benefit to a two-parent family.

5.163 This logical point corresponds to the policy requirement. GMA is intended to help the parent who is bringing up children single-handed, and facing all the financial and social difficulties of doing so. It would be inconsistent with this intention if GMA could be awarded to a claimant who was married and living with his or her spouse, or who was living with a man as his wife (or, in the case of a father, living with a woman as her husband). Further, as we show in Part 4, any realistic approach to the way in which ordinary incomes are likely to be distributed must recognise that men give priority to the family in which they find themselves for the time being, whether the children are their own or not. The ability to contribute to the upkeep of a first family must be measured in accordance with the economic and psychological facts. It would, in our view, ignore reality to treat entitlement to GMA as depending on a legal, as distinct from a factual, answer to the question, " Which is the one-parent family? "

5.164 A cohabitation rule in GMA would therefore be unavoidable. But we later make suggestions for the administration of GMA which we hope would minimise the problems associated with a cohabitation rule. In particular, our recommendation in paragraph 5.172 below that the benefit should be awarded for a period of three months, and should not normally be adjusted or withdrawn for any change of circumstances (except marriage) within those three months, would remove from lone parents the need within that period to decide for themselves and report that a particular relationship had reached the stage of "cohabitation". They would not have to take any action whatever, and would be legally entitled to go on receiving the allowance, until, at the end of the three months' period, a renewal claim had to be made. Investigation of casual relationships would thus generally be avoided. The claim form should make it clear that, subject to the point as to change of circumstances within the three months' period, the allowance would not be payable if cohabitation is taking place, and it should include questions designed to bring to light instances where this might be the case. Coupled with the fact that GMA would remove from supplementary benefit the great majority of one-parent families now receiving it, and that it would be administered by a different authority, these proposals should lead upon the introduction of GMA to a considerable reduction of the tensions, prejudices and suspicions which seem to be associated with the cohabitation rule within the supplementary benefits system.

Abuse

5.165 We recognise that a one-parent family benefit is particularly susceptible to abuse and that, with the relatively undemanding conditions we suggest for establishing status, the administering authority's ability to detect fraud would be limited. Concealed cohabitation could well be a problem. We have tried to weigh the need to restrict opportunities for abuse against the desirability of ensuring that the utility, convenience and acceptability of the allowance to the great majority of claimants would not be impaired, and we have noted that the family income supplements scheme appears to operate without undue criticism in this respect, although it offers similar scope for this kind of abuse. We consider that our proposal for a three months' qualifying period for certain claimants should help to reduce abuse in relation to, for example, fictitious desertion; and that our proposal that entitlement should run for three months, with the claimant being required every three months to answer specific questions and to make a clear and careful declaration, should help to avoid unintentional abuse. Claimants who knowingly make incorrect statements would be committing an offence and would be liable to prosecution.

ADMINISTRATION OF GMA

5.166 The allowance which we propose would quite deliberately be less closely geared to the needs of the individual family than is supplementary benefit and we hope that the business of claiming and substantiating entitlement can therefore be made less burdensome both for the claimant and for the administering authority. We are concerned that some lone parents feel themselves to be in a vulnerable position and are discouraged from pursuing rightful claims by complicated requirements, or by a hostile or intrusive attitude which they believe to be demonstrated by officers of the Supplementary Benefits Commission with whom they come into contact. We would accordingly stress the need for administration of GMA to involve as little burden and as little embarrassment as possible for the claimant.

Making a claim

5.167 Claims and enquiries should as far as possible be dealt with by post. Claimants who wanted further explanation or information about their situation could still have personal interviews if they wished, but we want to protect the nervous and hesitant claimant from unnecessary face-to-face interviews. We understand that approval has been expressed by a number of claimants to family income supplements for the method of dealing with claims through the post rather than by the personal interview system which is usual in the supplementary benefits scheme. It is difficult to measure to what extent the postal system disadvantages the claimant, in that there may be ways of helping the family, through advice, or by reference to professional social workers, which are not brought to the claimant's notice. But many of the families who, following upon an informal separation, did not qualify for GMA for the first three months (see paragraph 5.149) would, in fact, during that time see an officer of the Supplementary Benefits Commission so that personal contact would not, at least in those cases, be lost entirely.

The administering authority

5.168 The introduction of an entirely new allowance involves consideration of the administrative machinery required to operate it. We set out elsewhere our proposals for legal reforms, including suggestions for a system of family courts with the necessary facilities and supporting staff to help families with their difficulties. There would clearly need to be close liaison between these courts and the administering authority, which we recommend should be a national one. It is also clear that the Supplementary Benefits Commission would have to deal with many one-parent families at the moment of time when the family splits, and on other occasions of particular financial hardship, and, obviously, it would be valuable to be able to make use in the administration of the new allowance of the skill of those Commission officers with experience in " liable relative " work. It could indeed be argued that GMA should form part of the supplementary benefits administration; but we do not think that the advantages would be sufficient to outweigh the disadvantages of close association with a system which the evidence given to us indicates is regarded with suspicion or hostility by some lone parents. With postal administration it would not be essential for the authority administering the allowance to be served by a network of local offices: when personal interviews were necessary these could be undertaken on the authority's behalf by staff of local social security offices. Alternatives would be for GMA to be administered directly by the Department of Health and Social Security, like the family income supplements scheme, or for a new independent authority to be established. We see considerable attraction in the establishment of a new authority (possibly linked to the family courts) which could both administer GMA and collect payments from absent parents, but we do not feel called upon to recommend a particular solution which would, in effect, purport to decide machinery of government and organisation and methods questions. We think it suffices for us to note as possibilities that the allowance might be administered centrally or locally from social security local offices associated with the family courts we propose, or by a separate agency. We consider that the whole question of the most efficient way of administering GMA should be examined by the Government bearing in mind, in particular, the importance of convenience for the claimant, the availability of suitable staff and accommodation and the need for liaison between the courts, the benefit office and the Supplementary Benefits Commission. Where in this Report we refer to "the authority administering GMA" we do so for convenience, and not so as to prejudice the issue discussed in this paragraph.

Awards and reviews

5.169 Supplementary benefit awards are designed to respond almost immediately to changes in the claimant's circumstances. This kind of system gives maximum flexibility. As we have already said, however, we are concerned that the business of managing their claim shall be as little burdensome to claimants as possible. We therefore consider there are advantages in making awards for a period of weeks or months at a time, normally ignoring any changes during that period. This approach is already to be found in the family income supplements scheme, although there the award period is a long one (one year).

Changes in income

5.170 The circumstances of one-parent families are often uncertain. Such families are particularly liable to fluctuations of income since the parent's hours of work depend not only on her personal health and employment but also on the need for her presence at home. While the family's demands during, for example, school holidays can be anticipated and their effect on the parent's earning power taken into account, unexpected demands, such as a child's illness, or the breakdown of child-care arrangements, cannot be allowed for in advance. We therefore think that a twelve-month award, as with family income supplements, or even a six-month award, is too inflexible for the purposes of an allowance for one-parent families. The balance between the disadvantage of inflexibility and the advantages of greater convenience and the assurance of a stable payment suggests, and we recommend, fixing the period at three months. Families whose circumstances worsened during the currency of an award would still be able to apply for supplementary benefits (provided they were not in full-time work) to top up GMA.

5.171　In determining the amount of GMA payable we consider that regard should be had to what may be thought of as the family's normal income. If, for example, it is normal for the parent to work intermittently, such as during term-time only, the award should take account of this. We do not, however, think it necessary to enquire in all cases into the family's income pattern over a long period. We note that claimants to family income supplements are asked to supply earnings information over the last five weeks (in the case of weekly-paid earners) or two months (in the case of monthly-paid earners). We suggest a similar assessment period for the income of claimants for GMA, coupled with a simple enquiry as to whether the information given is representative.

Changes in title

5.172　Changes in the amount of GMA payable because of changes in income are different in nature from changes which affect basic entitlement, such as a change in the size of the family, or the marriage or cohabitation of the parent so that the family ceases to be a one-parent family. We have considered whether the consequences of such fundamental changes should be reflected immediately or only at the beginning of a new award period. The family income supplements scheme does not take account of the change until the next award, so that it is possible for benefit to be paid, quite lawfully, for nearly twelve months after the last child has left the family. National insurance benefits, such as widow's benefit or retirement pension, usually reflect the change at the next " pay day ", which is not more than a week ahead. Logically, there is a case for saying that GMA should respond immediately, and we recognise the undesirability of having different rules, in particular in the operation of widow's benefit and GMA. Nevertheless we see overriding advantages in ensuring that the conditions and operation of the scheme we propose should be as simple as possible for claimants to understand and obey and that they should provide stability. We consider that there is particular merit in having a long award period to ease problems associated with cohabitation (see paragraph 5.164 above) since this would go a long way towards relieving claimants of the need to make a spontaneous and immediate decision on whether they were cohabiting and to notify the authority accordingly. We set considerable store by these points and recommend that, with an exception in the case of marriage or remarriage (see paragraph 5.173), there should be no adjustment of title within the three months of the award period. This would generally work to the advantage of the claimant since it is more likely that title would decrease (for example, because of a child leaving the family) than that it would increase (for example, because of the addition or return of a child to the family). We do not consider that an overlap of State provision for a period of between one and twelve weeks would be inequitable in relation to the rest of the community. One-parent families are, on the whole, a hard-hit section of society and we would find it quite acceptable if situations arose in which payment was made to them for a short period after their circumstances had improved. On the other hand, given the availability of supplementary benefit in suitable cases, we do not consider that up to twelve weeks' delay in the relatively rare case where a family's entitlement increased would cause undue hardship.

5.173　We were, however, impressed by arguments for making an exception for marriage or remarriage. We would regard such an event as fundamentally different from other possible changes because, not only would it normally represent a radical change and considerable improvement in the family's circumstances, but it would also bring the one-parent family legally to an end. Moreover, it would seem particularly odd in such a situation for widow's benefit to cease immediately while GMA continued in payment. We consider that it is justifiable to treat marriage and cohabitation differently in this respect.

5.174 To terminate GMA awards immediately on marriage or remarriage would also fit in better with the tax-credit scheme. Under that scheme married women living with their husbands may be treated differently from other women in that they may not themselves be eligible to be tax creditors but may retain some form of wife's earned income relief, with their husbands qualifying for the married rate of credit rather than the single rate.[1] If this were the case, and if GMA were not to cease on marriage or remarriage until the end of the award period, either a special exception would have to be made when mothers receiving GMA married, so that their married rate of credit continued until the end of the award (and the husband's position also remained unaltered until then) or else the tax adjustments to their current GMA award would have to be revised. The first course would be anomalous and the second could well be confusing and troublesome for beneficiaries.

Renewal claims

5.175 We envisage, therefore, that awards would usually be made for three months at a time based on the family's circumstances and normal income at the time of claiming. Except in the case of marriage or remarriage, there would be no requirement on the beneficiary to notify any changes during the course of this period. (For the position if maintenance payments were received direct from the absent parent, see paragraph 5.176.) Towards the end of the three-month period the administering authority would invite a renewal claim and the claimant would have to give specific confirmation of all the information necessary to determine eligibility. We do not consider that the requirement to re-apply four times a year would be unduly burdensome and we think that much anxiety for beneficiaries would be saved by relieving them of a continuous responsibility for recognising relevant changes in their circumstances and notifying them to the authority. There would be no question of fraud arising because of a failure to notify changes, apart from marriage, during the course of an award: eligibility would depend on correct information being given in answer to the initial enquiries. This would mean that unsuccessful attempts at reconciliation with the other parent would normally be ignored, as would short periods of cohabitation.

Maintenance payments

5.176 There would be one further important exception to the general rule that the beneficiary had no need to report changes of circumstances. We have explained (paragraph 5.127) that if the State is to pay a certain income to one-parent families as a guarantee up to that level of the maintenance responsibility of the absent parent, it is essential that where the absent parent to any extent fulfils that responsibility the State should be correspondingly reimbursed. We

---

[1] *Proposals for a Tax-Credit System: op cit*, Chapter 4.

therefore suggest that all maintenance payments be channelled through the administering authority, who would pass on to the family the balance, if any, in excess of the payments to the family by way of GMA. The family's GMA entitlement would be determined without regard to the absent parent's maintenance contribution, but that contribution would have to be made over to the administering authority up to the amount needed to pay for the family's GMA. Consequently, any maintenance payments which the family received from the absent parent, if they had not been channelled through the administering authority, would have to be notified and might have to be paid to the authority.

Right of appeal

5.177 Whatever authority should administer GMA, the question would arise of how disputed issues should be resolved in relation to

(1) one-parent family status and termination of title;

(2) adjustment of the allowance in respect of the family's own income;

(3) the existence of the absent parent's maintenance liability, and the assessment of the amount of maintenance payable.

We think it essential that a right of appeal should exist in all these cases, and that both the absent parent and the claimant should have such a right in case 3 above.

5.178 While evidence of one-parent family status may well be provided by an order of court (such as a divorce decree or separation order) we have already expressed the view (paragraph 5.149) that court action should not be essential. The administering authority should be responsible for determining in the first instance whether the claimant is a lone parent, whether there are qualifying dependent children living with the parent, and similar questions of basic eligibility under case 1 above. In the event, however, of the claimant's disagreeing with the authority's decision, there would need to be an independent body to which the dispute could be referred. For these purposes it would be convenient to make use of existing machinery in the shape of the national insurance local tribunals and commissioners who already make decisions about some similar issues, for example, in relation to qualifying children. It might well be more efficient to extend the responsibilities of these tribunals, which have an established and high reputation, and an ability to build up a body of regular case law, than to introduce any new system.

5.179 Questions under case 2 above should also be dealt with primarily by the administering authority. Claimants would be expected to support their statements as to income and working expenses by pay statements (including details of deductions from pay) and receipts, where possible, for major expenses, such as child care. We would expect that any questions in this area would normally be resolved by correspondence or discussion between the claimant and the authority and that it would be rare for any form of outside adjudication to be needed. Where agreement was not possible, however, appeals would be dealt with by independent tribunals, as discussed in the previous paragraph.

5.180 Case 3 above relates to disputes over whether the absent parent is under any liability to pay maintenance at all, and, if he is, what the amount of the payment should be. Disputes as to liability as such would generally arise upon the assertion that a wife or former wife had lost her own right to be maintained by virtue of her behaviour, although other types of case would be entirely possible, such as where a man denied that he had any responsibility towards a particular child, or himself claimed maintenance from a wife or former wife. We envisage that in the practical course of events the administering authority would seek in the first instance to promote agreed settlements of disputes, both as to liability and amount, in terms satisfactory both to the parties and to itself.

5.181 If the attempt at a negotiated solution failed, the ensuing procedure would depend upon whether liability as such was in issue. If the dispute concerned the amount of maintenance only, that would be fixed in the first instance by a ruling of the administrative authority, from which an appeal would lie either by the lone parent, or by the absent parent, whoever was aggrieved. We consider that this appeal should be determined by the same independent tribunals as would deal with appeals on matters arising under cases 1 and 2. We propose later that guidelines should be established so that assessments are made on a similar basis in similar circumstances, and we regard the tribunals as well suited to apply the principles and promote uniformity. On the other hand, it appears to us that disputes over the liability to maintain as such, possibly involving investigation of matrimonial conduct or the paternity of children, would have to be the subject of appeal by either party to the regular courts. We elaborate on these matters in the next Section.

Interaction with means-tested benefits

5.182 In paragraphs 5.138–5.139 we discuss the interaction of national insurance benefits and GMA, concluding that long-term benefits at least should be fully offset. The position regarding mean-tested benefits is less clear, although as a general principle public provision should not be duplicated. We would regard GMA as the leading provision for one-parent families and would expect other benefits which take account of means to be adjusted according to the amount of GMA in payment, rather than the other way round. In relation to supplementary benefit, for example, the first question to be decided would be entitlement to GMA and supplementary benefit would be paid, as a genuine " supplement ", where GMA, together with any other resources of the claimant as assessed for supplementary benefit purposes, was below the benefit level. That is, the GMA would be a resource, taken into account in full for supplementary benefit purposes. We have not considered the interaction in detail in relation to each of the various available benefits, but we are satisfied that there is no insurmountable problem.

5.183 Supplementary benefits act as a " passport " to a number of other means-tested benefits, such as free school meals, so that these benefits can be awarded to supplementary benefit recipients without further enquiry into means. We would not wish that, in moving from supplementary benefit to GMA, one-parent families should be deprived of this convenient arrangement or find that they have been spared one searching enquiry into means only to be faced with several others. We recognise that, as adult GMA would not taper out until the family's other income was nearly £40 a week, it would be hard to justify making the receipt of adult GMA itself a passport to these other benefits, since some other poor families may cease to be eligible for the benefits involved at much lower levels of income. But we do not consider the same objection would arise if the passport were restricted only to recipients of adult GMA at the full rate, as this would, by definition, be linked to the supplementary benefit level, although the link would not be a precise one. Most lone parents transferring from supplementary benefit would qualify for the full rate, since few of them would have income above the disregard level, and they would only lose the benefit of the passport as their circumstances improved.

THE INTRODUCTION OF GMA

5.184 We are anxious that a new allowance along the lines which we propose should be introduced with the minimum of delay, and, while our recommendations are closely linked with our suggestions for legal reform, we do not see any need for the GMA proposals to be held back pending legal reforms, or the other way round. Our own consideration of the problems involved in working out the details of our scheme has made us fully conscious of the mass of yet more detailed work, especially in the establishment of routines and procedures, which would be necessary before it could be introduced. This must inevitably take time, especially when account is taken of the reorganisation of national insurance, which is currently in progress, and the close interaction between the allowance we propose and the tax-credit proposals. In the meantime, however, we hope that the Government will be able to implement the improvements we suggest in Section 8 in other forms of financial provision for one-parent families. Some of these could, we believe, be introduced very quickly so that, pending the advent of the more far-reaching scheme we have set out, some part of the relief for which they have urgent need could be provided for one-parent families.

SECTION 7—THE ABSENT PARENT'S OBLIGATION[1]

INTRODUCTION

5.185 In Part 4, Section 12, we put forward our proposals for a more efficient way of dealing with the maintenance obligation of an absent parent where the lone mother and her children were in receipt of supplementary benefit.[1] Our proposals involve shifting much of the work of assessing and enforcing maintenance from the courts to the Supplementary Benefits Commission, who are already involved in these cases, and whose procedures we regard as better suited in the normal run to discovering the facts regarding the finances and circumstances of each of the parties and making consistent decisions. We wish to eliminate both the confusion and conflict of procedures and practices which operate as between the different branches of the matrimonial jurisdiction, and the further confusion and conflict arising as between the Commission and courts. Our basic proposal in this connection is that, if the lone mother wishes it, the Supplementary Benefits Commission should assume the whole responsibility of recovery from the liable relative by making an administrative order against him by reference to uniform and disclosed principles, and by applying to the courts for enforcement of the order as appropriate.

---

[1] The discussion in this Section is conducted in terms of the relationship between GMA and the legal system in England and Wales, but, as has appeared from Part 4, Section 15, the recommendations that we make in principle extend to Scotland and are capable of being implemented in the context of the Scottish legal system.

5.186 Also in Part 4, Section 12, we touched on the possibilities of the administrative order procedure being extended to cover the liability of persons, such as ex-husbands, who are not " liable relatives " within the meaning of the Ministry of Social Security Act 1966, or to cover liability in excess of the amount of the supplementary benefit in payment. However, we did not explore these possibilities to any great extent, since our proposals for the administrative order procedure are directed to the improvements that can be achieved within the context of the supplementary benefit liable relative provisions as they now stand in relation to lone mothers with children.[1]

5.187 But the introduction of a new benefit for all one-parent families and our proposal that its administration should be in the hands of a new authority enable us to look beyond the restraints within which the administrative order system described in Part 4, Section 12, would operate. We should then be in the situation where the State was, through GMA, providing a special system of financial support for one-parent families, created to meet the particular situation and requirements of lone parents, and where this system was being operated, on a national scale, through a specialised agency whose interest and activities were wholly concentrated on one-parent families. This would create far larger opportunities than are possible within the limitations of the Part 4, Section 12, administrative order system for disposing of the whole range of defects we have noted in the support systems as they are now divided between the courts and the Supplementary Benefits Commission. It would help to achieve a rational relationship between State support for one-parent families and the private obligation to maintain. It would, as appears later, enable administrative determination to be made regarding the extent of the maintenance obligation in any given case, even where this exceeded the amount of the State-provided support. The main objectives may be stated as follows:

(1) to relieve the lone mother to the maximum extent possible of the pressures and anxieties attendant upon court proceedings for the assessment and enforcement of maintenance;

(2) to assure the lone mother of a regular and stable income for the family regardless of the extent to which the absent parent fulfilled his obligation to support them;

(3) to assess the liability of the absent parent with proper regard to his circumstances as well as to those of the one-parent family, and to keep the assessment under regular review;

(4) to assess the absent parent by reference, to the maximum extent possible, to a standard set of clear, certain and publicly disclosed principles which would produce like results in like cases;

(5) effectively to enforce the assessment made on the absent parent.

We believe that the introduction of GMA would enable great strides to be made towards the achievement of all of these objectives.

---

[1] In the present Section, as in Section 12 of Part 4, we refer throughout to the position of a lone mother with children, since the large majority of lone parents with a title to maintenance are women. What we say, however, would apply equally to the rare situation where the lone parent was the father and the mother had a maintenance liability towards him and the children.

5.188   In expanding our proposals for the relationship between GMA and its administration and the obligation of the absent parent to support his family, we shall for the most part of the discussion assume that this obligation would take the traditional form of an obligation to pay maintenance, that is to say, to make periodical payments. This still is the form which the obligation assumes in the majority of cases where there is no property to be settled or capital out of which to pay lump sums; and we can best explain the nature of our proposals by illustrating them from the usual and simple case. The possibility of the lone mother desiring and the absent parent being held liable for other forms of financial provision, such as payment of a lump sum, does raise problems to which we advert towards the end of this Section. Also in what follows, we shall use the term " liable person " to denote the father with a relevant liability in the GMA system.[1]

PRINCIPALS OF LIABILITY

Supplementary benefit awards

5.189   We discuss in Part 4, Section 10, the liability which the Ministry of Social Security Act 1966, sections 22 and 24, places on husbands and wives to maintain one another, and on parents to maintain their legitimate and illegitimate children. After the introduction of GMA there would still be a residual role for supplementary benefit in relation to one-parent families (see paragraph 5.248 below), and for such purposes the " liable relative " would continue to be defined as he or she now is under the Act of 1966, and to be under the same legal responsibilities.

GMA awards

5.190   But with the introduction of GMA, most one-parent families would not receive supplementary benefit. Among those who still required it, only the families who had not completed the three months' qualifying period (see paragraphs 5.148–5.153) would be ineligible for GMA. The questions which therefore arise for first consideration concern the extent of the liability of the liable person where the family had been awarded GMA, and the relationship between orders of the courts and administrative orders.

Separations

5.191   Normally, in the case of the separation of a married couple, whether this takes place de facto or de jure, the husband will be liable to maintain both his wife and his children. We have already recommended (Part 4, Section 14, paragraph 4.379) that misbehaviour on the part of the wife should be permitted to reduce or destroy her legal rights of maintenance only in exceptional cases, and it remains for discussion (see paragraph 5.199 below) how far even this limited application of a conduct rule would find scope in the GMA system. However, in the standard case of separation there is no doubt about liability and questions arise only as to amount. This would not be affected by the

---

[1] We should point out also that the phrases " administrative order ", " administrative order system " and the like may refer either to the scheme discussed in Part 4, Section 12, or to the scheme which is the particular subject of the present Section, under which the authority responsible for GMA would, after its introduction, be responsible also for making administrative orders for maintenance. The text will sufficiently indicate when we are referring back to the Part 4, Section 12, scheme.

316

introduction of GMA, and the liable person who was a separated husband would therefore come fully within the provisions which are later described for assessment and collection by the GMA authority. Basically, these would be that the authority would assess both the GMA entitlement of the lone mother and the maintenance liability of the liable person, irrespective of whether the amount of the latter was the same as, or larger, or smaller than the amount of the former; enforce the liability by collecting from the liable person the whole of the maintenance he had been assessed to pay; retain out of the amount collected from him a sum (if there was that much available) sufficient to reimburse themselves for the GMA paid out; and in the cases (they would be a small minority) where there was a surplus, remit the surplus to the lone mother.

Divorce

5.192 The basic position as between divorcing or divorced couples would be the same as in the case of separated couples. Questions would arise as to the effect of the wife's misbehaviour on the liability of the liable person (paragraph 5.199 below); and there would be some special considerations regarding the timing of the different procedures and orders, and the relationship between the divorce court and the administering authority (paragraph 5.211 below). But the system in essentials would be the same as that described in paragraph 5.191.

The unmarried

5.193 The mother of an illegitimate child has a claim against the father for the maintenance of the child, but has never had a claim against him on her own account. This fundamental feature of the bastardy laws (the history of liability for an illegitimate child is traced in Appendix 5)[1] is reflected in the law of supplementary benefits, in that under the Ministry of Social Security Act 1966 the putative father is liable in respect of benefit paid for the child, but not in respect of benefit paid for the mother.

5.194 The question arises whether this squirearchical approach towards liability to the mother need or should be extended into the GMA system. We think not. GMA would treat all one-parent families alike, and in doing so would reflect a principle which has governed much of our discussion and underlies many of our recommendations. In adopting this attitude of non-discrimination, GMA would recognise that the needs of one-parent families are similar. There is nothing to distinguish between the measure of support needed by a separated wife with children and by the unmarried mother. The common feature of these and all other one-parent families is the presence of a child or children in the care of a lone parent. GMA would be a child-based benefit directed to every situation of this kind. Once such a benefit, payable out of public funds, became available, there would be no more grounds for exempting a putative father than a husband or former husband from a liability in principle to make good the expenditure to the taxpayer. In some cases a putative father, like a husband, may have cohabited with the mother for a considerable period.

---

[1] The position in Scotland is set out in Appendix 6.

5.195 Even under the existing law of maintenance and affiliation, the distinction between the obligation to support the mother and the obligation to support the child is to some extent artificial. The child requires the presence of the mother, and much of the cost of maintaining her, especially in the necessities of rent, heating and the like, may quite reasonably be regarded as part of the cost of maintaining the child. (We have discussed this point in another context in Part 4, Section 7, paragraph 4.107.) The father is a partner in the conception and, especially when the means of preventing it are easily available, ought to share in the real economic costs of the results. These include the value of the services which the mother renders in taking responsibility for caring for the child—a responsibility which, given what we know of the lives of unmarried mothers, changes her life dramatically and, on the evidence we had, almost always for the worse.

5.196 Factors of the kind last mentioned may argue for a reconsideration of the law of affiliation in general, although we are well aware of the existence of strong countervailing arguments against the extension of the private law obligation to maintain to the unmarried mother as such. We have decided not to trespass on this ground. But the recovery of GMA would involve, in our view, very different considerations. In the GMA world it would be an omnipresent fact that the condition of single parenthood attracted a benefit from public funds. Logic and fairness both demand that in such a world the risks of fatherhood, so far as concerns reimbursement of this specialised benefit to the taxpayer, should be the same for all men. We doubt whether this would give rise to any anomaly as between GMA and supplementary benefit on a strict analysis of the different purposes of the two systems; even if it did, we prefer the anomaly to the incorporation of error into the GMA system.

5.197 We accordingly recommend that up to the level of State payment for mother and child, where this exceeded what the putative father would in any case be liable to pay in respect of the child, he should be a liable person, and subject as such to an assessment and recovery by the GMA authority. The assessment arrangements that we are proposing would ensure that the financial call on him would be limited to what he could afford.

5.198 The position is different, however, as regards maintenance beyond the amount of the support provided by the taxpayer. Except in the circumstances discussed in the following paragraph, the separated or divorced husband would be required, if his means permitted, to contribute to the maintenance of the one-parent family in excess of the amount paid out in benefit. To this extent, the authority would be seeking to achieve an equitable distribution of income in the light of the joint resources of the parties. But the putative father would not be required to contribute towards the maintenance of the child's mother (as distinct from the child himself) more than the State was providing for her. In this respect, his liability would be, within the limits of what he could afford, to make good only what the community had spent towards discharging his responsibilities.

Relevance of conduct

5.199 We have discussed at length in Part 4 the different effects of the bad conduct of the wife on her entitlement to maintenance in the summary as

318

distinct from the divorce jurisdiction, and have argued for the assimilation of the rules of the former jurisdiction with those now prevailing in the latter. However, up to the limits in amount mentioned below, it seems to us that conduct should be entirely disregarded in relation to the recovery from the liable person of GMA. The mother in receipt of GMA should be regarded solely in her capacity of caring for her husband's child. Her right to GMA would arise by virtue only of her having care of a child, not by virtue of her status as a wife or an ex-wife. Her conduct towards the father should not, therefore, absolve him from being treated as liable to repay the taxpayer what the taxpayer had spent in supporting the mother to look after the child. On the other hand, subject always to the liability of the liable person, irrespective of the behaviour of his wife or former wife, to reimburse the authority up to the amount of the GMA which they had paid to her, he would (to the limited extent to which conduct was permitted to affect the maintenance liability) still be entitled to ask that his liability to maintain should be reduced by reference to conduct. This would remain a question for the court. In practice it would mean that when the assessment on the liable person would exceed the amount of the GMA payment, but the conduct of his wife or former wife had been so obviously and grossly improper that it would be unjust to make him pay the assessment in full, the court would retain the power to reduce the assessment to, but not below, the level of the GMA payment. But the assessment from which the court would make the deduction for conduct would still be made in the first place by the authority (see paragraphs 5.210–5.212 below).

Involvement of the lone mother

5.200   As soon as an award of GMA was made[1] the liability question would arise along the lines indicated in paragraphs 5.189–5.199 above. All action necessary to establish and enforce the liability would be taken by the administering authority, not by the lone mother. She would be asked to give information initially to enable the authority to identify and communicate with the liable person where there was one. That would be the only part she would normally play; thereafter it would be rare for her to need to take any part in the authority's dealings with the liable person. It would be the duty of the authority to assess the amount of the liability, make an order for payment and ensure that the order was enforced.

Disputes over liability

5.201   In Part 4, Section 12, we discussed in some detail the principles applicable for determining disputes over administrative orders in the sense that we were then discussing them. We there made a clear distinction between disputes over amount, which we regarded as suitable for administrative determination, and disputes over other issues, mainly affecting liability as such, which it is manifest must be reserved for judicial determination. Exactly the same considerations govern in principle the determination of disputes arising on decisions of the administering authority in the GMA world. Questions on amount would in our view be advantageously retained within an appropriate administrative system which was geared to resolving them on a uniform basis

---

[1] We deal in paragraph 5.248 below with the situation, following the introduction of GMA, where an award of supplementary benefit is made in favour of a one-parent family, or where such an award precedes the GMA award.

and drawing upon investigative procedures. Questions such as the paternity of a child or involving any enquiry into matrimonial conduct would have to remain for the court to decide.

Termination of GMA

5.202 GMA would terminate at the end of the award period after the youngest child in the family ceased to be dependent. It would also terminate on the remarriage or cohabitation of the lone mother. The order on the liable person would then lapse, and the authority would notify both parties to that effect—although it would not, we suggest, inform the liable person of the particular reason for the termination of his liability.

5.203 Although the lone mother would, in the circumstances just described, have lost entitlement to GMA, she or one or more of the children might still be entitled to maintenance under the general law. The question arises whether the authority should in cases of this type retain a jurisdiction to assess, order and enforce the maintenance liability, or whether once the GMA entitlement as such had come to an end the authority should withdraw. In the latter event, the mother would have to go to court (failing agreement) for the maintenance, and the authority would inform her of this position and of the action she might take. In Part 4, Section 12 (paragraph 4.262), we raised a similar question as to whether the administrative order procedure might not be extended to separated wives who had no dependent children, and so were not in a one-parent family situation, although they would benefit just as much from the procedure. We do not think that we need make any hard-and-fast approach to these questions. The better course might be if in the early days the authority were restricted to cases where GMA was in payment, and then had its activities extended as it gained experience.

PRINCIPLES OF ASSESSMENT

The responsibility of the administering authority

5.204 Once the liable person had been satisfactorily identified, the amount of his liability would have to be assessed, an order for payment made, and that order enforced. We have both in the opening paragraphs of this Section and in discussing administrative orders for the purposes of Part 4, Section 12, given our reasons for recommending that functions of this kind, subject to reservations which we have also already identified, should so far as possible be discharged administratively. The introduction of GMA, which would cover all one-parent families and re-shape the income support available to one-parent families, would create the opportunity to extend the administrative order principle so that it became a comprehensive remedy for many of the problems to which we drew attention in Part 4. In association with a family court, such a system would, we believe, open a path to the future which at present is blocked by the debris of history.

5.205 In considering the administrative order for the purposes of Part 4, Section 12, we purposely restricted ourselves to working within the framework of the existing systems of supplementary benefits and maintenance. The result was that our principal recommendations were at that stage limited to an administrative order which could be made only against a liable relative as

such a situation as that where the man's position deteriorated appreciably during that period and meeting his liability would mean that his residual income would fall below his supplementary benefit level.

The normal relation between the administering authority and the court

5.210 It follows from what we have said so far that once GMA was introduced, and the new authority was operating, that authority would in the normal case be entirely responsible for assessing the whole of the maintenance liability and ensuring the enforcement of its own order.

5.211 The application of the principle in the case of a separation without court order is simple to understand. But we should explain further how it would apply in the case where parties became involved in divorce proceedings. Both while proceedings for divorce were pending, and after a decree had been granted, the wife would normally have a claim for maintenance for herself and the children who remained in her care. At present, failing agreement, she has to pursue that claim through the courts. The maintenance to which she is entitled before the decree dissolving the marriage is called " maintenance pending suit", and that to which she is entitled upon the dissolution is called " periodical payments". The distinction between the two is based on historical and procedural reasons which have little practical relevance at present, and we do not see any obstacle of principle to prevent the GMA authority making the assessment on a single occasion at whatever stage the divorce proceedings might have happened to reach. The lone mother might have separated from her husband before instituting any proceedings for divorce, in which event the GMA authority would probably, before the proceedings commenced, already have made the GMA award and the maintenance assessment as in the case mentioned in paragraph 5.191. In that event, the commencement of the divorce proceedings and the subsequent pronouncement of a divorce would in the normal case, where the wife's conduct did not affect her entitlement, have no bearing on the decisions which the authority had already made. These would simply continue to be implemented. If, on the other hand, the GMA and maintenance assessments had not been made by the authority before the commencement of the divorce proceedings, they would be made as soon as possible after that time. If the wife, for example, claimed maintenance in the proceedings, and had not already applied for GMA, she would be referred by the court to the authority for the assessment of the maintenance, although the court would, of course, retain control over other aspects of the litigation. Being so referred, the wife would then also have her GMA entitlement investigated, and thus the maintenance and any GMA claim and the husband's liability to reimburse the authority would all be determined then and there. There would be other possible combinations of circumstances relating to the timing of the different decisions. All this would call for close liaison between the court and the authority, and the making of provision whereby information could be exchanged and cases be remitted from one to the other. This would involve detailed administrative innovation, but the problems are those of machinery, not principle, and could, we have no doubt, be satisfactorily solved.

5.212 In the case of proceedings taken for a formal separation order rather than a divorce precisely similar considerations to those discussed in the last paragraph would apply. In both cases, that is to say whether the proceedings were for a divorce or for a separation, if an issue that might affect quantum arose which was not open to determination by the authority (for example, if the absent parent claimed that his wife's conduct was such as to disentitle her to any maintenance, or reduce the amount she should be awarded) the court would still refer to the authority for the standard assessment (if not already available) to be made. The court would then determine the effect (if any) its findings on conduct were to have upon the amount as assessed.

5.213 If our proposals in Part 4, Section 12, come into effect in the interim period before the introduction of GMA and the system we describe in this Section, many existing maintenance orders made by the courts would have been reviewed and converted into administrative orders of the Supplementary Benefits Commission (see paragraphs 4.258–4.261). But the proposals we are now at this stage making would enable not some, but all, maintenance orders in favour of one-parent families to be converted into administrative orders; and it follows from the whole of the discussion that we consider that this should be done. The conversion process should not, in our view, be made an occasion for altering the amount of orders made by a court within the preceding twelve months merely because the application of the formula in use by the administering authority would produce a different amount. Subject to this, the authority should be entitled in converting court orders to review them. It might be a question of some nicety to determine which of these two principles applied, and rules would no doubt need to be devised for that purpose. We are content here to draw attention to the problem.

COLLECTION

Amounts in excess of the benefit in payment

5.214 We have already stressed that we think it important that the authority should assess and collect the full amount of the liable person's payment, irrespective of whether it exceeded the amount of GMA or supplementary benefit in payment to the family. Where the payments made to the authority exceeded the amount of the benefit in payment, the surplus would be remitted by the authority to the family at intervals. In making the assessment in the first instance, the authority would regard the family as a single unit and make an order for one sum, not dividing it between the various members of the family. Payments received would be regarded as available to the authority to retain against either the adult or the child allowance of the GMA, or both. This means that where there was a grant of GMA, receipts from the liable person could always be set off against the total of the grant, and could not be paid by him under an ostensible allocation to the child alone. This is justified by the fact that the adult allowance in GMA would arise directly from the presence of the child.

Voluntary maintenance agreements

5.215 We anticipate that with all one-parent families able to claim GMA and to rely on the administrative authority to assess and enforce the maintenance liability, the number of voluntary agreements might be considerably reduced. The scope for them would be limited mainly to cases where the liable person was prepared to be more generous to his family than the authority required him to be. Where, however, voluntary agreements were entered into, arrangements would be necessary to ensure that if the lone mother claimed GMA or supplementary benefit the father met his obligation to the authority. The simplest way would be for the payments under the agreement to be channelled through the authority, or for the authority, notwithstanding the agreement, to make an order on the father as a liable person in the normal way, and enforce it. Alternatively, the amount paid on the GMA award could be reduced to take full account of the payment made under the agreement, in so far as this did not exceed the amount which would otherwise have been ordered.

ENFORCEMENT

5.216   The order made on the liable person by the administering authority would, subject to appeal, be legally binding on him, and on his failure to comply it would be for the authority to take enforcement action.   The authority should be able to apply to the court for enforcement of the order as a civil debt; we anticipate that the principal remedy would be attachment of earnings.[1]

ASSESSMENT IN PRACTICE

5.217   We have already in this Section, and elsewhere, argued the case for the administrative determination of maintenance in accordance with a rule which, while leaving discretion to vary for special circumstances, would in most instances enable a calculation to be made on a clearly defined and publicly disclosed basis.

5.218   The Supplementary Benefits Commission at present have frequently to assess the amount which it is reasonable to expect a liable relative to provide towards the benefit being paid for his family.   Their policy is to seek to obtain an amount, up to the amount of the benefit being disbursed by the State, which, broadly, would not reduce the man's resources below a calculated level.   This is an amount corresponding to what he might receive by way of supplementary benefit for himself and any dependants living with him (taking account of scale rates and housing costs) if he were not in full-time work, plus an additional sum, related to his earnings.   The result, in general, is to leave him at a level of resources several pounds above his supplementary benefit level.   The formula is subject to an over-riding discretion where there are special circumstances.[2]

5.219   This procedure seems to us an eminently fair one in the context of supplementary benefits alone, and our proposals in Part 4, Section 12, follow it closely.   But there are two main reasons why the same system would not be appropriate as it stands once GMA had been introduced.   First, we are proposing (paragraph 5.205) that the administering authority should make an order against the absent parent which covered the full extent of his liability towards the lone mother and her family.   The authority would not simply be concerned, as the Supplementary Benefits Commission are, to obtain reimbursement of State payments.   Our intention is that the authority should assess the full liability, even if it exceeded the amount of GMA or supplementary benefit in payment.

[1] See our comparable proposal in Part 4, Section 12, paragraph 4.251, where we discuss the administrative order system in the context of the supplementary benefits scheme.

[2] We discuss this formula in Part 4, Section 10, paragraphs 4.184–4,190.

5.220 Secondly, in contrast to the supplementary benefit family whose resources are necessarily very limited, the GMA family could have significant resources. The adult allowance of GMA would be payable, in part at least, until the family's income reached roughly the level of men's average earnings, and the child allowance would be payable whatever the family's income. A method of assessing the absent parent's liability which allowed his resources, no matter how large, to be reduced to a stated margin above supplementary benefit levels could mean that he, and any dependants he had, would be living at a lower level, perhaps substantially lower, than the family towards whom he was assessed as having a maintenance liability. Such a situation is regarded as impractical and unacceptable in the current policy of the law, and it should not be permitted to arise after the introduction of GMA.

5.221 Accordingly, a more flexible approach would be needed. A formula such as the Commission use could fix the floor below which the absent parent's resources would not be allowed to fall, but this would be inadequate for a fair assessment of liability where the one-parent family had income of its own beyond the GMA provided by the State. It would be necessary to adopt a system of calculation which would take account of the resources and commitments of both parties.

5.222 GMA would formally recognise the part which the State has to play in helping to maintain one-parent families. It is primarily because the absent parent can so infrequently afford to give adequate support to the family from whom he is parted that GMA would come in to make good the deficiency, and, at the same time, to help establish the absent parent's liability within levels which are in line with what he might normally be expected to meet. To some extent, this function is already discharged through supplementary benefit, but GMA in being available to all one-parent families as such would broaden the function and make the role of the State in supporting such families more explicit. It follows that, in assessing the resources of each of the parties, GMA and any supplementary benefit payable to the lone mother should be regarded as income in her hands.

A formula

5.223 For reasons that we have previously elaborated, we intend that the absent parent's maintenance obligation should be administratively assessed by a clearly defined test. This means that a standard formula would need to be devised which could be applied—subject to a discretion to allow for exceptional circumstances—in all cases, and which could be made public. Such a formula would need to take account of resources and commitments on both sides. Where the absent parent was comparatively well off it should enable the lone mother and the children to share in his affluence, while ensuring that he retained a reasonable share of his higher income for himself. It should also be such as would not cause the absent parent's financial position to be worse in relation to his commitment than that of the lone mother in relation to hers.

5.224 While we have not thought it necessary for us to go so far as to draw up and make positive recommendations for a precise formula to carry these principles into effect, we think it worthwhile, in order to show more clearly what we have in mind, to indicate how such a formula might be framed. We do not wish this outline to be regarded in any way as a blueprint. but rather that it might form the starting point for fuller consideration.

5.225 It would be necessary first to ascertain the income of the lone mother and her family (including the GMA) and the income of the absent parent. Aggregated, this would establish the amount of money available to support the two parts of the family. It would also be necessary to know whether the father had any other children to support, or, perhaps, a wife or mistress. A weighting would then have to be given to each adult and each child dependent on each of the parents to enable the balance of commitments between the two family units to be calculated. On this basis the aggregate resources could be divided to show whether, and if so to what extent, the absent parent should contribute towards the maintenance of the lone mother and her family.

5.226 For this division a formula would be needed which would reflect the relative needs of the two families. Unless a more scientific basis came to hand, the supplementary benefit scale rates could provide a starting point. In 1972–1973 they stood as follows:

	£
married (or cohabitating) couple	10·65
single householder	6·55
non-householder aged 18 or over[1]	5·20
young person aged 16 and less than 18	4·05
child aged 13 and less than 16	3·40
child aged 11 and less than 13	2·75
child aged 5 and less than 11	2·25
child under 5	1·90

In addition we are recommending (in Section 8) an additional £1·50 for each lone parent. These amounts can be related to each other roughly as follows:

	Units	Units
married (or cohabiting) couple	1·6	
single householder	1·0 with a child 1·2	
non-householder aged 18 or over	0·8 with a child[1] 1·0	
young person aged 16 and less than 18	0·6	
child aged 13 and less than 16 ... ..: ...	0·5	
child aged 11 and less than 13	0·4	
child aged 5 and less than 11	0·3	
child under 5	0·3	

It would be possible to total the number of " units " to be provided for out of the aggregate income available to support the two parts of the family and calculate the division of the aggregate income accordingly. This might conclude the calculation and the extent to which the lone mother and her family fell short of their prescribed share (if at all) would be the amount of the order which would be made against the father.

---

[1] On the basis of our recommendation in Section 8, the personal scale rate of a non-householder under 18 with a child would be the same as that of a non-householder aged 18 or over.

327

5.227   We fear, however, that to stop there might unfairly penalise the absent parent. To meet this we would follow the precedent of the Supplementary Benefits Commission's formula, and totally exclude a proportion of his earnings from the calculation. The appropriate amount would not be taken into account in making the aggregation. What this amount should be would depend on circumstances at the time, including taxation levels.

5.228   Consideration would also have to be given to the treatment of any income of the father's second family, to the extent that it was not his own income. We suggest that it should be excluded from the aggregate income of the two parties; the persons to whom it belonged should also be excluded in totalling the number of units, unless this meant that they were less well provided for, in which case a proportionate allowance would have to be made for them. It would, we have no doubt, be wrong for independent income of the second family to be fully available in calculating the father's maintenance liability, but equally it would be wrong not to offset against it some part of the cost of providing for them.

Housing costs

5.229   A formula such as we have outlined, using supplementary benefit scale rates alone as the basis for the relative needs of the two families would, we realise, fail to make any allowance for what the families would have to spend on housing by way of rent, rates or mortgage payments. The present availability of rate rebates, rent rebates and allowances, and tax relief on mortgage interest repayments, all help to ensure that housing costs are brought within tolerable proportions. Although an individual or a family may choose to incur high expenditure on accommodation, the chances of being forced into accommodation more costly than they can afford have been much reduced.

5.230   The fact, therefore, that either the mother or the father or both might have substantial housing costs which, if a court maintenance order were being considered, they would claim should be taken into account, would not necessarily mean that some allowance for housing costs should be incorporated in the formula.   In the context of our proposals in Part 4, Section 12, we have explained that allowing specifically for housing costs in calculating the formula for the administrative order could lead into a circular situation.   This is because of the means-testing involved in calculating entitlement to a rebate or allowance and the means-testing involved in determining the amount of an administrative order: the amount of each would respond to a change in the other.

5.231   It might well be possible to devise a system of weighting the formula according to the standard of housing which the family occupied, which would break the circle to which we have referred. However, our own inclination would be to regard this as unnecessary. We are anxious that the formula should not become unduly complicated and in the vast majority of cases we think that to ignore the housing costs of both parties would give rise to no injustice. In the occasional case where there were convincing arguments for special treatment, the overall discretion to adjust the formula (which we recommend) would be available.

Alternative formulae

5.232 Some complexity in the formula is unavoidable, because of the complexity of family situations. We think it important, however, that the formula should be as simple as possible and there should be a discretion to dispense with its application where this might produce injustice.

5.233 Subject to that condition, there is obviously a wide range of formulae which might be adopted. Something quite simple, such as a formula on the lines we have suggested but allocating a single unit to each adult and half a unit to each child, would be possible; or a more refined costing might be employed which made allowance for different patterns of family income and expenditure. We do not wish to suggest that the formula we have chosen as an illustration is the only one we think would achieve the results we seek. We have no doubt that others could be devised to give effect to the principles we have enunciated.

GMA AND FINANCIAL RELIEF OTHERWISE THAN BY WAY OF MAINTENANCE

5.234 So far in this Section we have been assuming that the legal obligation of the absent parent to the lone mother would be to pay in respect of her and the children maintenance in the standard sense of the word, that is to say, periodical cash payments which she would receive as income. The amount of these payments would be determined by the GMA authority. They could be less than or equal to or (except in the case of a putative father) more than the amount of the GMA in payment to the lone mother. If they were more than the GMA, the authority would account to the mother for the difference. Otherwise, the authority would retain the maintenance in discharge of the liability of the absent parent, in his capacity as a liable person, to make good to the authority, up to the amount in question, the GMA paid by the authority to the lone mother.

5.235 This would be a relatively simple system which, given that the maintenance was to be assessed by the administering authority, could be operated without the intervention of the court at any stage. The accountancy would create no problems, because it would essentially involve no more than setting off items of the same description one against the other—periodical cash payments by way of maintenance against periodical cash payments in the form of GMA. The system would be adequate to cover a very large proportion of all cases, seeing that the typical form of order for financial relief is that the husband, or former husband, or putative father should pay so much a week or a year, just as it is the typical form of agreement when parties settle the matter for themselves. Indeed, this is at present the only kind of financial order that can be made in the summary jurisdiction. Although, therefore, it is not possible to quantify, there is no doubt that, after the introduction of GMA, the administering authority would find that in the bulk of cases the claim of the lone mother against the absent parent would not be for relief in any form other than periodical cash payments, and the system of administration so far discussed would apply.

5.236 However, the courts possess a range of powers in granting matrimonial relief which go well beyond the power to order periodical payments. In the divorce jurisdiction, the court may, when ordering periodical payments, order

329

also that they should be secured. It may order a lump sum in cash to be provided. It may also make provision by way of property adjustment orders for one party to transfer to or settle upon or for the benefit of the other, or any child of the family, specified property, or may vary ante-nuptial or post-nuptial settlements, or extinguish or reduce interests thereunder.[1]

5.237 These powers allow of a considerable degree of flexibility in adjusting the available resources of the family upon its breakdown. Whatever form those resources take, be it income or capital in the shape of cash, the matrimonial home, shares, or other property, the court can organise and distribute them to suit the circumstances and justice of the particular case. Clearly, it would be a retrograde step to permit the introduction of GMA to result in any constriction of these powers. We have, in fact, already argued elsewhere[2] for the extension of some of these powers to the first tier jurisdiction in the family court, and have noted[3] that the Law Commission are suggesting that the magistrates' jurisdiction in its present form should have the power to order lump sum payments.

5.238 But the existence of these wider forms of financial arrangements after the advent of GMA would raise problems that could not be solved by the system of setting off one form of periodical cash payment—maintenance— against another form of periodical cash payment—GMA. It is obvious, as a matter of first principle, that the parties would have to be allowed to continue to make whatever form of voluntary financial arrangements they pleased as between themselves whatever the effect of that might be on the liability of the absent parent, as a liable person, to the GMA authority. If, for example, he and the lone mother agreed with each other that he would pay her £2,000 in full and final settlement of all of her claims against him for financial provision, it would be impossible to suggest that such an agreement could be treated as any less valid as between the two of them after the advent of GMA than it is at present. It is just as obvious that if the parties could not agree on financial arrangements they would have to be permitted to take that dispute to some authority for adjudication. We have already recommended that where such a dispute concerned only the amount of periodical payments it should be resolved by the GMA authority by methods which we have indicated. But if the dispute concerned whether, and in what form and to what extent, some other remedy should be granted, either on its own, or in addition to periodical payments, it should not be resolved by the GMA authority. A dispute of this kind could not properly be dealt with by the application of a formula, and it would often involve an investigation into the family circumstances other than of a strictly financial nature, and the determination of facts in controversy which demanded oral evidence, cross-examination and, in general, a judicial as distinct from an administrative proceeding. Disputes of this kind would, therefore, have to be the subject of the court process.

5.239 Given the propositions made in the last paragraph, a number of difficulties then present themselves. We may illustrate them by reverting to the example of the parties coming to an agreement, or the court making an

---

[1] These powers have previously been mentioned in Part 4, Section 4, paragraphs 4.54–4.55 and 4.102, and they are now contained in the Matrimonial Causes Act 1973, sections 23 and 24.

[2] Part 4, Section 14, paragraph 4.379.

[3] *Ibid*, paragraph 4.377.

order, that the absent parent would pay the lone mother the lump sum of £2,000 in full discharge of all his financial obligations, present or future, to his family. The lone mother however would, as the head of a one-parent family, be entitled to GMA, and when the authority paid out GMA to or, they, in their turn, would under the normal GMA rules then approach the absent parent to assess him as the person liable to pay maintenance, out of which the authority would so far as possible reimburse itself for the GMA. It is easy to see that in the exemplified circumstances the man in question would have to be allowed to rely on the agreement or order as protecting him from having to make any further payment for the benefit of the family. But it would not at all follow that he should automatically and for all time be excused from making any reimbursement to the authority for the GMA. If, for instance, the lone mother continued to draw GMA for a period of ten years, this might result in a payment out by the authority of a sum which was in total far greater than the value of the £2,000 lump sum payment; and it is not at all obvious that the liable person should then, irrespective of his means, be excused from making good or contributing towards the excess.

5.240 Progress could be made towards solving a problem of this kind along the following lines. The authority would continue in all cases to assess the absent parent's maintenance liability, exactly as we have earlier recommended, so as to produce the periodic sum which he ought to pay to the lone mother. The authority would also have to convert the lump sum payment which had in fact been agreed upon, or ordered by the court, into its notional value as income. This notional value would then be set against the liability as assessed. An illustration of the result may be given in terms of arbitrarily selected figures. If the GMA were £10 and the assessment on the liable person £5, the lone mother would have £10, and the liable person and the GMA authority each be £5 out of pocket. Suppose, now, that the income equivalent of the lump sum payment was £3. The liable person would pay £5 – £3 = £2 to the authority, which, together with the £3 notional income he had paid the lone mother through the lump sum, would bring up his total liability to £5; the authority would pay GMA at the rate of £10 – £3 = £7, and would be £5 out of pocket after allowing for the £2 received from the liable person; and the lone mother would receive £7 (GMA) + £3 (value of the lump sum) = £10.

5.241 We think that it would be possible to adopt a scheme in the nature of the foregoing when dealing with agreements or orders for lump sums, or for outright transfers of an interest in property—for example, the value of a house or the husband's share in a house—which could be given a cash value. The problem would be to fix on the right formula for turning the capital sum in question into notional income, particularly as regards the number of years over which the capital was to be spread.

5.242 The valuation problem, however, would become more intractable when arising in connection with agreements or orders other than for a lump sum or outright transfer of property. The parties might agree, or the court might order, that the lone mother should stay in possession of the matrimonial home with the children until the youngest of them left school, the parties sharing, or one or other of them paying, the outgoings in the meantime, and that upon the expiration of this period the house should be sold and the proceeds divided in certain proportions. An order of this kind is no great rarity upon

331

a divorce, but it would not readily lend itself to a valuation, in particular to a valuation in terms of notional periodic payments. If a rental value basis were adopted this might be considerably more than the lone mother could afford: the house might be larger than she and the children strictly needed for their accommodation, yet the order might be made because it was important to keep the children at the same school. Such considerations would not readily lend themselves to valuation, but they illustrate the importance of width and flexibility in the process of financial and property adjustment on breakdown.

5.243 We therefore need to re-approach the problem to discover whether its basic terms could yield a different kind of solution. These terms are that it would be essential to remain flexible in the range of financial and property arrangements which parties could agree or which the court could order when the need arose; that the absent parent should not be mulcted twice over; but that, on the other hand, the authority should not, if it paid GMA, be deprived of a proper measure of reimbursement. These objectives might be reconciled by making it the law, first, that either by agreement or by order of the court, as one term of an order for matrimonial relief, entitlement to the GMA benefit could be waived or disallowed, in whole or subject to appropriate qualifications; and, secondly, that such an agreement or order, on being registered with the GMA authority, would be implemented by them. In such circumstances, the objectives postulated would be substantially achieved through the process of free bargaining between the parties or through the decision of the court after it had taken into account the respective contentions on each side.

5.244 To elaborate on this concept: leaving out of account the simple case where there was nothing to dispute other than the amount of periodical payments which the absent parent should make, there would be, in any given situation, a determinate number of factors which the parties, if they were seeking agreement, or the court, if they could not agree, would be taking into account. These might include the matrimonial home, the motor car, cash in the bank, or whatever else might be. They might also include less tangible considerations such as the need for the absent parent to live near his work, or for the children to live near to their school or to a grandmother. The proposal we are now considering amounts, in essence, to adding the GMA entitlement of the lone mother to the bundle of considerations which the parties or the court would take into account. Thus, taking the illustration of a lump sum payment, the absent parent, when such a payment was in negotiation, would know that the lone mother, having received it, would still be entitled to GMA with consequent repercussions upon himself when the authority asked to be reimbursed. He might, therefore, as part of the bargain involving payment of a lump sum, require the lone mother to forgo all or part of her GMA claim. Precisely the same factors would be taken into account by the court if it had to rule on the dispute. This is a simple illustration, but reflection will show that in any set of circumstances, however complicated, the injection of the GMA itself as one of the factors in the bargain struck between the parties or imposed by the court would come as near as possible to producing a just result from the point of view of the GMA authority as well as of the mother and father themselves.

5.245 The point can be made rather differently in terms of the respective economic strengths of the parties in cases where there was property for division on breakdown. Nearly always in such cases it would be the woman who was economically the weaker of the two parties. The introduction of GMA would have the effect of increasing her bargaining power by giving her an assured income for which she was not dependent on the man, but in respect of which he could personally be liable to the authority. The parties in such circumstances could do the best for themselves and the family by being permitted to re-distribute the available assets, including GMA, or, if they could not agree, have them re-distributed by the court.

5.246 In considering the advantages and disadvantages of the two methods we have discussed for resolving the more complicated type of case it is important not to overlook that the standard situation is, and so far as we can see ahead will remain, one in which the need would be only for an offset of GMA against maintenance. If one has regard for the supplementary benefit cases alone, there were in November 1972 220,000 fatherless one-parent families (not counting 26,000 where the lone mother was a widow, and another 6,000 where she was a prisoner's wife) in receipt of supplementary benefit.[1] There would not be many of these 220,000 cases where the absent parent had property to bargain against GMA. Similarly, although owner-occupation may be expected to increase, in most cases of breakdown where a mother sought to remain in occupation of the matrimonial home at the stage where the children were still of school age, there would be a mortgage outstanding; and the principal question would be how were the instalments to be paid, rather than whether the husband should transfer his share of what might be a very small equity.

5.247 We conclude, therefore, that there would be two possible ways of dealing with cases which involved a potential liability on the absent parent going beyond the payment of maintenance. One way would be to absorb these cases wholly into the administrative order system by putting a value on the asset or benefit conferred on the lone mother so as to produce a set-off against the GMA, just as in the standard case of maintenance. This could be more readily done where the asset consisted of a lump sum payment or a transfer of property outright from absent parent to lone mother. The other way would be to let the parties sort matters out for themselves, or have them sorted out by the court, by treating the GMA entitlement as a right which could be traded against other benefits or advantages given by the absent parent to the lone mother. We think that this would be the more flexible method and would avoid some difficult problems which the other would present as regards the formula to be employed for turning the relevant benefit into a notional income payment. We have expressed a preference for the second type of solution for reasons which will have emerged from the discussion. We think that both would be workable, although we do not underestimate the amount of further detailed consideration that either of them would still require.

THE RESIDUAL ROLE OF THE SUPPLEMENTARY BENEFITS COMMISSION

5.248 While we have spoken in the preceding paragraphs of the administering authority taking over most of the Supplementary Benefits Commission's responsibility in relation to the liable relatives of one-parent families on supplementary benefit, a residual role would remain with the Commission. This would occur mainly at the first stages of separation, when a lone mother

---

[1] See Appendix 9, Table 1.

applied for supplementary benefit before qualifying for GMA. We think it important that efforts should be made to trace the liable relative and obtain maintenance payments from him as soon as the woman became dependent on public funds, and if her first contact were with the Supplementary Benefits Commission then it would be sensible for their officers to make the necessary initial enquiries. But since the main bulk of maintenance work would be done by the authority, we think that the information obtained should be passed to the authority, and all consequent action should be taken by them. The difference between this kind of case and a case where GMA was in payment would be that for three months maintenance collected would be offset only against supplementary benefit. If, after the first three months, a lone mother required supplementary benefit in addition to her GMA, this amount as well as the amount of GMA in payment would have to be set against the payment received from the absent parent before deciding whether, exceptionally, there was any excess available to pass on to her (see paragraph 5.209). Thus, although close liaison between the Supplementary Benefits Commission and the authority in respect of a lone mother who received both benefits either in sequence or together would be important, as far as the mother herself was concerned her only dealings with the Supplementary Benefits Commission on the liable relative aspect would be on first application, and the liable relative should not need to have dealings with the Supplementary Benefits Commission at all.

CONCLUSION

5.249   In the preceding paragraphs we have set out the framework for radical revision of the present system for assessing maintenance obligations. First, we propose that, at least where children were involved and the one-parent family claimed GMA or supplementary benefit, maintenance should be assessed by reference to a formula which, subject to room for manoeuvre where exceptional circumstances arose, would enable consistency to be achieved and doubt and uncertainty about rights and obligations largely to be eradicated. Secondly, we propose that assessments should be reviewed at least every twelve months. Thirdly, our proposals would involve the bulk of the work of assessment being entirely taken away from the courts and handled by an administrative authority, subject to appeal to administrative tribunals. The administrative authority would also have the job of collecting the maintenance payments ordered. Finally, for the cases where the situation could not be satisfactorily met by treating the liability of the absent parent as one that involved only the payment by him of maintenance in the form of periodical sums in cash, we have proposed a choice of alternative procedures which should result still in the satisfactory integration of GMA with other forms of financial provision which the parties might agree or the court might order. Far from restricting the rights of citizens by taking maintenance assessment out of the arena of the courts, we are convinced that the system we propose would be much more sensitive to individual circumstances, resulting in practice in greater fairness as between the parties involved.

SECTION 8—OTHER FINANCIAL PROPOSALS

5.250   In the following paragraphs we examine the various forms of financial help at present available to one-parent families. Although our proposals for GMA would significantly reduce the dependence of one-parent families on

334

some of these benefits, especially supplementary benefit, and the tax-credit scheme may eventually replace family allowances, child tax allowances and, for families in the scheme, family income supplements, we thought it wise to deal with these current forms of financial provision in some detail for two reasons: first because it may be possible, while the fine print for GMA is being worked out, and before the tax-credit scheme is introduced, to make some improvements in existing financial provision quickly so as to bring immediate help to, at any rate, some one-parent families; and secondly to provide some fall-back if the GMA proposals were not implemented. Other recommendations, for example, about maternity grant, are unaffected by either the GMA proposals or the tax-credit scheme.

Supplementary Benefit

5.251 The large number of one-parent families drawing supplementary benefits is evidence of the present importance of the supplementary benefits scheme for them. In the long term we hope that our proposals for GMA will avoid lengthy periods of dependence on supplementary benefit, but we anticipate that within the foreseeable future the scheme will continue to have a place in the provision for one-parent families, both during the three months' waiting period in the informal separation cases before GMA would be payable and, in some few cases, in supplementing the allowance.

Scale rates

5.252 The needs of a lone parent who is a householder (that is, one who is responsible for rent and other household outgoings) are assessed at the " single householder " rate (from October 1973 £7·15 a week or £8·15 in the case of long-term dependence on benefit). The amount for children's needs increases with the age of the child. In addition, an allowance is made which usually covers the rent or other household outgoings, such as rates and mortgage interest, in full. The needs of the non-householder are assessed at £5·70 if aged 18 or over (£6·60 in the case of long-term dependence), or £4·40 if aged 16–17, plus a rent allowance of 80p. Where there is a non-householder under age 18 with a child to provide for, the Commission have discretion to make an adjustment for " exceptional circumstances " so that requirements are assessed at the adult non-householder scale rate.

5.253 Many who have given evidence have referred to the inadequacy of the supplementary benefit scale rates in various respects. Some recommended an increased scale rate for the lone parent, or a special addition for one-parent families. It was also suggested that non-householder parents under 18 should get the adult rate of benefit.

An addition to the scale rate for one-parent families

5.254 We were impressed by the arguments put to us on the need for the lone parent to be assessed on the footing of having higher needs than a single person without dependants. We refer earlier (paragraphs 5.40–5.48) to the evidence we were given about the special costs which fall on the lone parent, over and above the ordinary costs of maintaining a home and a family; in our view these offset to some extent the savings which the present construction of the scale rates assumes a family makes when there is one less adult to support.

335

We also note from our research in schemes overseas that in parts of the Netherlands a special supplement is added to the single person's rate of social assistance where there is a family to support. In the Federal Republic of Germany, too, one-parent families are among the groups who are given a supplement to the basic social assistance. The evidence on the balance of savings and expenses is not sufficient to enable us to judge whether a total levelling up of the lone parent's scale rate with that of a married couple would be justified—in any case this would mean that nothing further would be available if the absent parent returned—but we consider that the difference in 1972–1973 of £4·50 between the two scale rates is too wide. We therefore recommend that there should be a special addition to both the long-term and short-term scales rates for lone parents of, in terms of 1972–1973 benefit rates, at least £1·50 a week. We would expect this differential to be increased from time to time in line with rises in the cost of living. The cost of such a change is estimated at about £18 million a year, reducing considerably once GMA could be brought into payment.

Non-householders under 18

5.255   In relation to lone parents under 18 who have left school and who are not householders, we understand that the Supplementary Benefits Commission already make extensive use of their discretion to pay benefit equal to the adult non-householder rate. We consider all such lone parents with the care of dependent children should receive the adult benefit and we therefore recommend that a single parent who is not a householder and who is entitled to supplementary benefit in her own right should automatically be assessed on the basis of the adult non-householder scale rate (£5·70, or £6·60 for long-term dependence, from October 1973). The cost of this change would be quite small and is estimated at £¼ million annually.

Long-term addition

5.256   The long-term addition was introduced in 1966 with a view to reducing the need for individual extra payments by way of exceptional circumstances additions. From October 1973 the addition, which had been 60p weekly, was incorporated into new long-term scale rates, which, for a single householder, are £1 higher than the ordinary rate.

5.257   Families with children have to draw supplementary benefit continuously for two years before qualifying for the addition.[1] Retirement pensioners, on the other hand, receive the long-term rate from the outset of their claim. The reasoning behind this difference is that pensioners who claim supplementary benefit are unlikely ever to be able to lift their resources appreciably and tend, therefore, to be dependent on the income from the benefit for long periods of time. The same does not apply to younger claimants, and, while there is a singificant number of one-parent families who remain on supplementary benefit for long periods of time (see paragraph 5.21), there is also a high turnover of short-term cases. We do not, therefore, think that payment of the long-term scale rate from the outset of a claim by a lone parent could be justified.

---

[1] Claimants who are required to register for employment are not eligible for the addition.

5.258   On the other hand we think that a family with children is less able to manage on such a modest level of expenditure over a long period of time than is an adult without children.   The evidence we have received bears out this view.   The Women's National Commission told us, " The principal source of income on which a deserted wife can rely is the supplementary benefit, based on a means test.   This level of supplementary benefit, while it may suffice in the short term, is inadequate to maintain a home environment for children for a substantial period of time which meets the accepted standards of present-day society.   This inadequacy of the long-term allowance is probably true of the whole country, but more especially in London where rents,[1] fares, food and other necessities are more expensive than elsewhere." Children make unexpected demands on a family's resources in various ways, and we consider that possible deprivation could be reduced by shortening the qualifying period for the long-term addition.   We think a significant reduction is needed and regard it as necessary for families with children, whether with one parent or two parents. We accordingly recommend that the qualifying period be reduced to one year for families with children.   The estimated annual cost of this recommendation is between £2¾ million and £3 million for one-parent families alone and about £3 million for all eligible families with children.   It is estimated that some 53,000 one-parent families would benefit.

5.259   On the question of the differential between the long-term and the short-term scale rate, we see no justification for preferential treatment for one-parent families, especially bearing in mind the addition to the scale rate we have already recommended (paragraph 5.254).

Disregards

5.260   In calculating the amount of supplementary benefit payable to claim-ants certain resources are not taken into account and others are taken into account in part only.   The main disregard of income in the supplementary benefits scheme which affects the one-parent family is that for part-time earnings. This has stood at £2 (net of working expenses) since 1966.   This disregard helps parents who can do the occasional or small job while spending most of their time looking after their family, and who may thereby obtain some personal satisfaction and increased social contacts as well as a little extra income.   But many of those giving evidence to us commented on the £2 disregard as being too severe a penalty on the person who is willing and able to do a little paid work but is unable for one reason or another to contribute materially to his or her own maintenance.   The disregard on charitable payments has likewise stood unchanged since 1966, and we received evidence that charities which might provide worthwhile help for one-parent families are discouraged from doing so because of the smallness of the charitable payments which may be disregarded.

5.261   It would be incompatible with a scheme designed to meet basic need for the disregards to be set very high, as this would mean channelling more resources to those who do not have the greatest need.   But we can see no justification for allowing the real value of the disregards to fall as seriously as it has during the last seven to eight years.   We support the now widely-held

---

[1] It is normal for the full amount of rent paid to be allowed for in a supplementary benefit assessment, so that a family living in a high rent area is not at a disadvantage.

337

view that there should be an increase in the disregards so that, at least, they keep pace with increases in the cost of living,[1] and we note that on 22 June 1973, Mr Paul Dean, Under-Secretary of State at the Department of Health and Social Security, accepted that there is a case for improvement.[2]

Lone fathers

5.262 Normally anyone of working age who claims supplementary benefit and is fit to work is required to register for work and to take any available job which is suitable; an exception to this requirement is made for a woman who has dependent children living with her. The Supplementary Benefits Commission accept in her case that the decision whether the family will benefit more from her presence at home or from the earnings she could get from full-time work should be her own. There is however no corresponding general exclusion from the requirement to register for men who have single-handed responsibility for their children, though it is waived in individual cases if the Commission are satisfied that there is no reasonable alternative to the father's staying at home to look after his children himself.

5.263 We have been assured that in deciding whether a father should be required to register for work the Commission's officers recognise that the size of his family is a material factor, and that a large family will need substantial help if the father is to be able to work. We understand also that, under the current instructions to local offices, Headquarters approval is needed before a man who does not agree with the local officials' view that it is practicable and reasonable for him to work is required to register for employment.[3]

5.264 This policy is based partly on the view, which the Commission believe still to be generally held, that it is usually better for children to look to a father who conforms to the normal role of breadwinner. They also think that if a man becomes accustomed to staying at home over a long period he will have increasing difficulty in readapting to working life, as he must do when his children are older. Usually, too, unless the family is large, they will be better off financially if he is working.

5.265 While we accept that most men probably want to work, and that it may be better for them, financially and psychologically, to do so, these factors may well apply to lone women also. We find it hard to understand why the lone father cannot be given the same freedom of choice as the lone mother: most will decide to work, but there seems no good reason why those who decide to stay at home to look after the children, having weighed all the possibilities, should not be allowed to do so. The lone mother, just as much as the lone father, will have to support herself and provide for her retirement once the children have grown up. In devising the new one-parent family benefit we have treated lone mothers and lone fathers on a footing of complete equality and

[1] See, for example, the debates in the House of Commons on the National Insurance and Supplementary Benefit Bill 1973, Official Report, 30 April 1973, columns 832 and 844 and 22 June 1973, columns 1060–1061.

[2] Official Report, 22 June 1973, columns 1065 and 1068.

[3] There is, moreover, a right of appeal to an independent appeal tribunal against a requirement to register for employment as a condition of receipt of benefit.

we should like to see the Supplementary Benefits Commission do the same. We accordingly recommend that the Supplementary Benefits Commission should waive the requirement to register for work for lone fathers as they do for lone mothers.

Cohabitation rule

5.266 There are few subjects in the field of social security law and administration which give rise to more heat and criticism than the cohabitation rule in supplementary benefits.[1] We have been made conscious of this not only by the literature which abounds and the evidence we have received but also by the frank statement of the Supplementary Benefits Commission of "this basic difficulty—the mere fact of investigation in this emotionally charged field arouses distress and resentment among claimants, social workers and others, perhaps beyond that aroused in any other area of the Commission's administration."[2]

5.267 We quote further from a document in which the Commission have put better than anyone else the vexations and embarrassments of administering a cohabitation rule:

> However humanely the rules may be administered, the inescapable fact is that, in their application to individual cases, questions have to be asked on matters which, to most of us, are essentially private. Whatever the motive for asking these questions, and however sympathetically they may be framed, there is bound to be suspicion that they are sometimes prompted rather by moral prejudice than by a desire for help in making an unbiased judgment of the facts.

> The Commission are constantly seeking, by such means as intensive training and the improvement of communication with their officers on their policies, to reduce the risk of failure in ascertaining the facts and to ensure that judgment is not distorted by prejudice. But it must be apparent that mistakes and errors of judgment sometimes occur, in a service totalling some 18,000 staff, many of them reflecting the values of the local community in which they live, and all of them subject to the tensions inherent in the changing society of which they are a representative cross-section.[3]

> It is unfortunate that, in the process (of investigation), some people innocent of any desire to deceive the Commission will suffer the indignity of having their statements checked; but it is quite unavoidable. It is also unfortunate but equally unavoidable that, in attempting to detect concealment and dishonesty, special investigators have to cross check the accuracy of what they have been told by claimants. They may for example be prompted by an anonymous letter which may be spiteful and unfounded and they may have to make local enquiries without the knowledge of the claimant or to watch a house to see who lives there. This is distasteful work . . . .[4]

5.268 It is obvious that a jurisdiction of this kind must expose the Commission to attacks which are unfounded or exaggerated, but which it is hard for them, especially having regard to the obligation of confidence, to refute. Nevertheless, the testimony of the Commission confirms the evidence from other sources, that however much effort is given to improve its administration, and to inform the endeavours in the field with the care and refinement

[1] We discuss this rule and its operation in Part 4.

[2] *Cohabitation*, Report by the Supplementary Benefits Commission to the Secretary of State for Social Services, HMSO, 1971, paragraph 18.

[3] *Ibid*, paragraphs 16 and 17.

[4] *Ibid*, paragraph 22.

which characterises the thinking at the centre, the cohabitation rule may involve indignities, and sometimes hardship or injustice, for people who fall under its shadow.

5.269 For this reason we had the strong disposition to recommend the abolition of the rule, which potentially affects all claimants who find themselves in the one-parent family situation; and we would have been glad to make such a recommendation had we been able to discover a reasonable and viable basis for doing so. We spent much time in this endeavour, but failed. It is proper to concentrate on the weaknesses in the rule and the hardships it can sometimes produce, so long as this is not permitted to hide or confuse the overwhelming argument in its favour. This is that it cannot be right to treat unmarried women who have the support of a partner both as if they had no such support[1] and better than if they were married. Other arguments are advanced in support of the cohabitation rule which we think are unsound, or which at least lend themselves to dispute. But the principle we have stated is, in our view, both of central importance and beyond refutation; and, it should always be remembered, it applies without any hardship or injustice in the great majority of the cases for which it was intended. In these circumstances we do not think it would serve a useful purpose to debate the whole range of considerations which affect the principle of the cohabitation rule as such, and to traverse a ground which is covered by several recent and authoritative publications.[2] We note, in particular, that the author of *As Man and Wife?*, published by the Child Poverty Action Group in 1973, takes up a hostile position towards the rule but still stops short of suggesting that it can be entirely abolished.[3]

5.270 Granted the necessity for the rule, the task must be to improve its administration so as to minimise the dangers to which everyone agrees it gives rise. We are more than satisfied that the Commission are alive to these dangers and use their best endeavours, although not always with the success they would wish, to eliminate them. The report, *Cohabitation*, from which we have quoted, published in 1971, gives proof of these endeavours. In addition, the *Report of the Committee on Abuse of Social Security Benefits* (the Fisher Report)[4] has even more recently made a number of suggestions with which we would in

---

[1] If there were no cohabitation rule account would have to be taken in determining the amount of benefit payable of the extent to which the other adult in the household supports the family financially. This, however, would in our view require enquiry just as stringent and intensive as the enquiries necessary to investigate alleged cases of cohabitation. (See *Cohabitation, op cit*, paragraph 8.)

[2] The most useful sources are *Cohabitation, op cit*; the *Supplementary Benefits Handbook*, Supplementary Benefits Administration Papers 2, HMSO, revised November 1972, paragraphs 14–23; *Report of the Committee on Abuse of Social Security Benefits* (Chairman, Sir Henry Fisher) Cmnd 5228, 1973, paragraphs 321–347 and 493; Ruth Lister: *As Man and Wife?* published by the Child Poverty Action Group, Poverty research series 2, 1973; Olive Stevenson: *Claimant or Client?*, Allen and Unwin, 1973, pages 142–152.

[3] *As Man and Wife? op cit*, pages 40–42, suggests first that the rule should be abolished " save in cases of an open common-law marriage", failing which, and as an alternative, the definition of cohabitation should be revised. The essence of the first alternative is that the rule should apply only to " a stable and *admitted* relationship which the couple themselves wish to be regarded as that of man and wife." This is tantamount to saying that if a man and a woman who are in fact living as man and wife simply deny it (or both deny and conceal it?) that makes the family eligible for supplementary benefit, but if they admit it (or both admit and assert it?) they are worse off. This seems to substitute for the possibility of injustice in the administration of the current rule the certainty of injustice in the one to take its place.

[4] *Op cit.*

general associate ourselves. In particular, we agree with the recommendation that there is no reason why the relevant statutes should refer to a cohabitation situation in different ways. The test should be the same, and this would apply equally to the test for cohabitation in the GMA system. We would also endorse the recommendations intended to introduce further[1] safeguards into the investigative process.

5.271 There are, however, respects in which we consider that the administration of the cohabitation rule could be improved beyond the recommendations of the Fisher Report. We have given special thought to the problems of the mother who has her benefit summarily withdrawn on the ground of cohabitation and who contests the facts, or who, despite the cohabitation, is unable to secure support for her children by a former union from her cohabitee. Stronger measures of protection are needed in both these cases.

5.272 It has been widely suggested that, in the case where the claimant contests its withdrawal on the ground of cohabitation and gives notice of appeal, supplementary benefit should continue in payment until the appeal is determined. This position was taken in evidence that we received from, for example, the National Executive Committee of the Labour Party and from the working party convened by the Oxfordshire County Council. At their annual meeting in 1973 the British Association of Social Workers passed a resolution to similar effect. The Fisher Report rejects such a change on the ground that it would create opportunity for abuse. It observes, " cohabiting couples might make regular claims, and live on the benefit constantly being provided for the period between claim and Tribunal hearing."[2] For this reason, the Fisher Report proposes instead that where a woman disputes the correctness of the decision to withdraw the benefit, the Commission, under their powers to exercise a discretion in exceptional circumstances, should make urgent needs grants more widely than they now do.[3]

5.273 We have carefully considered the argument for making payments in all disputed cohabitation cases pending appeals but find that such a blanket proposal would create more anomalies than it would solve. It is necessary to draw a distinction between refusing benefit to a woman who makes a new or repeated claim and withdrawing benefit which has been in regular payment. It is the sudden removal of the main source of income that is socially damaging and which gives rise to feelings of insecurity and a sense of injustice. There can be no justification for making automatic payments to a new claimant pending appeal in cases where the Commission are satisfied that cohabitation exists; to do so would create opportunities for abuse as feared by the Fisher Committee. Nor can we envisage a situation in which a woman who admits the facts of her situation but denies that they amount to cohabitation has her benefit continued

---

[1] The Commission's own report, *Cohabitation, op cit*, in 1971 made important proposals intended to discourage junior officers in local offices from initiating, in an excess of zeal, enquiries into cohabitation without sufficient reason for doing so, and to improve the level of decision-taking on whether enquiries should be pursued and on whether cohabitation has been established. These proposals became the subject of instructions in 1972. It is fair to bear this in mind when considering evidence of complaints which relate to earlier incidents.

[2] *Op cit*, paragraph 345.

[3] *Ibid*.

pending appeal; to permit such an arrangement would mean that in virtually all cohabitation cases the claimant would continue to draw benefit for several further weeks before the appeal machinery could be invoked to terminate it.

5.274 In view of all these difficulties we have limited our proposal to those situations in which a claimant who has been regularly in receipt of benefit disputes the alleged facts. In all such cases, before withdrawing benefit, an appropriate officer of the Commission should be required to give the claimant a written statement of the facts on the basis of which cohabitation was alleged, and she should be asked whether she admitted or denied any of those facts. If she admitted all of them, the benefit could be withdrawn, subject to the claimant's ordinary right of appeal. This would apply to the case where all of the facts were admitted, but it was denied that they amounted to cohabitation, or where for any other reason the claimant, while admitting the facts, disputed the withdrawal of the benefit. But if the claimant denied any of the facts in the statement, the Commission themselves would refer the case to the tribunal, and pending the determination of that reference the benefit would continue in payment. Once the case was before the tribunal it would decide not only the issue of disputed fact but also any question of entitlement on the facts as found.

5.275 The advantages of this procedure would be that it would safeguard the income of the genuine claimant entitled to the benefit as of right. It should be noted that appeals arising from the discontinuance of benefit on the ground of alleged cohabitation succeed in about 13 per cent of the cases although in all these cases the woman has been denied benefit in the intervening period.[1] No possibility arises of abuse of the referral system through a chain of claims and appeals. If the Commission were upheld on the reference the benefit would from that time forward be withheld. Should the claimant then make a further application for benefit which was refused she would have a right to appeal but this would not carry entitlement in the intervening period. We would add that in all cases of dispute which were appealed as distinct from being referred no payment of benefit would be made pending the appeal; but the Fisher Committee's recommendation that urgent needs grants should be made more widely in these circumstances would apply.

5.276 The other situation which has given us particular concern is where benefit is withdrawn on the grounds of cohabitation, but the cohabitee is not supporting dependent children of the claimant of whom he is not the father. Currently, the Commission are prepared to deal with such cases by making an exceptional needs payment in the nature of " an adjusting allowance to meet those children's requirements (taking into account their share of family allowance and any maintenance payments made by their father) for a period of four weeks. The purpose of these payments is to cushion the family against the abrupt reduction in their income, give the couple time to claim any family income supplement to which they may be entitled, and time to adapt to a situation in which the whole family must in most cases rely upon the man's income for their support."[2] We regard this period of four weeks as insufficient. Proper as the decision to withdraw the benefit may be, its sudden loss creates in many of the cohabitation cases a crisis within the household of the first order.

---

[1] Although, if she succeeds in the appeal, arrears would be paid back to the date of the decision appealed against or to the beginning of the period covered by that decision.

[2] *Supplementary Benefits Handbook, op cit*, paragraph 21.

Social workers are familiar with this situation: the man who has not been giving support to the dependent children of the woman with whom he is cohabiting is often temperamentally unstable, with limited earning capacity; the loss of income from the benefit may result in the total disruption of what may already be a parlous household economy; rent may fall into arrears, other debts may accumulate and gas and electricity meters become tempting targets. As the Fisher Committee observed, " The Commission . . . recognise that the rarity of payments to meet urgent need in cohabitation cases may well conceal a fair amount of genuine need that is not being met . . . ."[1] We recommend that the four-week period to which we have above made reference should be extended to three months.

FAMILY INCOME SUPPLEMENTS

5.277 Family income supplements were introduced in August 1971 specifically to deal with the problem of families in full-time work but with low wages. The scheme gives the same supplements to a one-parent family as to a two-parent family with similar income and it is proving to be particularly helpful to lone mothers in full-time work. As indicated in paragraph 5.29, well over one third of recipients are lone parents—at the end of April 1973 there were 36,000 fatherless families with average supplements of £2·90 a week, 1,000 motherless families with average supplements of £2·23 a week, and 47,000 two-parent families with average supplements of £2·38 a week.

5.278 The introduction of the tax-credit scheme would mean that the family income supplements scheme would be abolished for families in the tax-credit scheme. As we mention in paragraph 5.250, however, we have considered whether any change is desirable during the interim period.

The full-time work condition

5.279 Many lone parents are unable to work full time (which is defined for the purpose of the family income supplements scheme as thirty hours a week) because of the demands of their family. We have therefore considered whether any change in the full-time work rule would help a significant number of one parent families and would be justified. We have looked at the alternatives of total abolition of the rule (either for one-parent families or for all claimants) and of widening the definition to, for example, twenty-five or twenty hours (again either for one-parent families alone or for all claimants). We have borne in mind that the families who would be helped by such changes would normally be eligible to claim supplementary benefit and would, therefore, be affected by the improvements we are recommending in the supplementary benefits scheme.

5.280 The advantages of abolishing the full-time work rule would be:
  (1) low-income families may prefer to claim family income supplements (which would remain subject to a maximum) rather than possibly larger sums by way of supplementary benefit, with its attendant burden of more detailed checks and conditions;
  (2) the net cost would probably be small because of offsets against supplementary benefit;

---

[1] *Op cit*, paragraph 344.

(3) to the extent that families changed from supplementary benefit to family income supplements there would be administrative economies.

There would, however, be unwelcome complications. It is possible to operate the family income supplements scheme fairly simply because the claimant's main source of income is earnings from a full-time job and reliable evidence of this (such as a pay slip) is available. This would not apply if the full-time work rule were abolished, and it would be less easy for claimants to substantiate their statements of income and much easier for important sources of income to be concealed. Closer checks might be needed.

5.281 This argument would have less force if the abolition of the rule were to apply to one-parent families only. There might be more public sympathy for the change because of the generally low level of income of one-parent families, and there would be smaller numbers to check. If additional checks were thought necessary, however, they could not fail to reduce the attractions, both administratively and for claimants, of the family income supplements scheme.

5.282 As to an extension of the definition of full-time work, this would be difficult to justify for men in ordinary circumstances—for the majority of men full-time work means something over forty hours a week. It can be argued, however, that a woman with a young family (or a lone parent) has much less time available for employment, and certain jobs are on offer where hours are deliberately arranged to recognise a family's demands on the mother. A special definition of full-time work for fatherless families (or all one-parent families) might not, therefore, be regarded as inappropriate, although it would be difficult to represent anything less than twenty hours as full-time.

5.283 Disadvantages of widening the definition for a particular group include the resultant complication to the scheme's entitlement conditions, whose present simplicity is one of its virtues, and greater scope for abuse.

5.284 The family income supplements scheme cease will for one-parent families and others in the tax-credit scheme if the tax-credit proposals come in and GMA is introduced. Changes involving much complexity might therefore become irrelevant in a fairly short space of time. In view of this, and bearing in mind that the supplementary benefits recommendations we are making will help some of those one-parent families who might be assisted by a change in the full-time work rule, we consider that no case is established for such a change in family income supplements at present. But if the tax-credit scheme did not, in the event, become law, and the family income supplements scheme were to continue in being, and if, further, GMA were not introduced or introduced only after much delay, we would see an easement in the full-time work rule for one-parent families as offering a measure of useful help.

The prescribed amounts

5.285 One-parent families already have their entitlement to family income supplements assessed by reference to the same prescribed amounts[1] as for two-parent families. It would not be reasonable to increase the prescribed amounts

---

[1] The way the scheme works and awards are calculated is explained in Appendix 8.

344

for one-parent families above those for two-parent families, and any increase must therefore relate to all low-earning families with the head in full-time work. Since the family income supplements scheme was introduced in August 1971 the levels of the prescribed amounts have been continuously kept under review and they have been increased on a number of occasions, including two occasions in 1973. Their October 1973 level is shown in Appendix 8.

5.286 We have looked at the possibility of recommending increased prescribed amounts with the following condiserations in mind:

(1) the level of increases recently made;

(2) the fact that awards rise by only 50 per cent of any increase in prescribed amounts;[1]

(3) the prescribed amounts are higher already for some families, particularly one-parent families, than the income level at which they start to pay tax; and therefore increasing the prescribed amounts would mean that it would more frequently arise that a family, when the next award of family income supplements was made, would find that as the result of increasing their gross income by £1 they were only 20p better off;[2]

(4) while over 37,000 one-parent families in full-time work were receiving awards in April 1973, and this number would increase if the prescribed amounts were raised, this is only a very small proportion of the 350,000 or so one-parent families not on supplementary benefit; and it excludes the worst off group among them. (See paragraph 5.24 where we refer to estimates that the one-parent families living below supplementary benefit levels are those where the parent is not in full-time work.)

These considerations have led us to believe that there is no strong justification for our recommending an increase in prescribed amounts. The extent to which such a recommendation would help one-parent families is very limited and we take the view that the other recommendations we have to make in the area of financial support are much more significant. Should, however, family income supplements become a more important form of support for one-parent families in the circumstances envisaged in paragraph 5.284, it would be necessary for the adequacy of the prescribed amounts to be reconsidered.

FAMILY ALLOWANCES

5.287 Much of the evidence which has been presented to us has asked for improvements in family allowances to keep pace with rises in the cost of living and has pointed to the gap in provision for a first or only child. This gap is particularly important for one-parent families, which are likely to have fewer children than two-parent families. The Women's National Commission

---

[1] See the explanation of family income supplements in Appendix 8.

[2] Gross income is taken into account in calculating family income supplements and each extra £1 of gross income reduces the amount of the supplement by 50p. If the £1 is subject to tax it will already have been reduced to 70p in the family's hands. The deduction of 50p from the family income supplements means that the family are only 20p better off. This applies to any income above the level at which tax becomes payable and below the prescribed amount in the family income supplements scheme. Where the prescribed amount is already higher than the tax threshold, raising it extends the area of income over which this situation occurs.

said to us in evidence, " It is the first child who is most expensive to keep and requires a large capital outlay, who grows bigger first and needs the new clothes. The mother who is deserted, or the unmarried mother with her own child is prevented from going out to earn her living just as much by having one child as by having two or even three. Accomodation is hard to find, and rents are high whether there is a mother occupying a bedsitter with one child or with two." This omission in the family allowances scheme seems to us to be particularly relevant to one-parent families. The Beveridge Report expressed the view[1] that earnings should normally be sufficient to support a family with one child without extra State payment. All the evidence shows that this norm is particularly unlikely to be achieved in fatherless families.

5.288 Proposals to extend and improve family allowances have now been subsumed by the proposals for a tax-credit scheme. We welcome the decision, following the *Report of the Select Committee on Tax-Credit*,[2] that child credits should be awarded on a universal basis. The introduction of the tax-credit scheme clearly carries important budgetary and administrative implications. It is, we appreciate, a major task to provide machinery for regular payment of child credits to some 7 million first children, 3 million of whom are in families not at present receiving family allowances for other children. Nevertheless we urge that the utmost priority be given to the introduction of child credits, which, since they are to be universal, need not, we understand, depend on the introduction of the tax-credit scheme as a whole. Should the tax-credit scheme not pass into law, we would urge that provision be made, with the same degree of priority, for tax-free family allowances, at rates comparable to those envisaged for child credits.

MATERNITY BENEFITS

5.289 National insurance maternity benefits are maternity grant (a lump sum of £25) and maternity allowance, a weekly allowance for a period, in the normal course, of up to eighteen weeks of £7·35 from October 1973. Both are subject to the satisfaction of certain contribution conditions.

Maternity grant

5.290 Most births qualify for maternity grants—there were 881,000 registered births in 1971 and 832,000 grants were paid in that year. The contribution conditions are not difficult to satisfy—26 contributions paid by husband or wife since entry into insurance and 26 contributions paid or credited in the particular contribution year. Women who satisfy the conditions for maternity allowance qualify for the grant regardless of these tests.[3] Among the mothers who do not qualify for maternity grant are likely to be very young mothers. In 1971 in Great Britain there were 3,248 legitimate and 4,802 illegitimate births to mothers aged 16 or under at the time of the birth. Some of the legitimate births no doubt attracted a maternity grant on the husband's insurance. Others not qualifying include wives of students, wives of polygamous marriages, common law wives, wives of long-stay prisoners and women who have recently

---

[1] *Social Insurance and Allied Services:* Report by Sir William Beveridge, Cmd 6404, 1942, paragraph 417.

[2] HMSO, 1973.

[3] Broadly similar conditions will apply under the Social Security Act 1973 when fully earnings-related contributions start.

arrived from abroad. A family receiving supplementary benefit who do not qualify for the national insurance grant may qualify for an exceptional needs payment.

5.291 If the aim is to help groups, like young unmarried mothers, who may have no contribution record, there is no half-way house between the present contribution conditions and no contribution conditions at all. The real issue is whether maternity grant ought to be provided on a universal basis, like family allowances which do not depend on satisfaction of any contribution condition. This was advocated by a number of those who gave written evidence to the Committee, including the National Executive Committee of the Labour Party and the National Council for the Unmarried Mother and her Child. Their views are well summed up in the following passage from the evidence presented by a working party set up by Oxfordshire County Council:

> The birth of a child—especially a first child—inevitably gives rise to consider-able expense. Clothing, nappies, a cot, pram *etc*, have to be obtained. Most families are assisted in meeting this expenditure by the maternity grant payable under the National Insurance Act, 1965. This was the only aspect of national insurance in relation to which we received reports of difficulties. As an insurance benefit, the grant is payable only if the contribution conditions are satisfied, either by the mother or by her husband. Unmarried mothers qualify for a maternity grant only if they have themselves paid (or had credited to them) the appropriate number of flat-rate contributions. Young mothers, in particular, often fail the contribution test. Thus it happens that those most in need of help in meeting the costs of maternity may be denied the help which most mothers receive as a right.

> Mothers who do not qualify for maternity grant can usually apply to the Supplementary Benefits Commission for a lump-sum grant to meet specific expenses connected with their confinement. Grants of this kind, however, are discretionary and generally smaller than the National Insurance maternity grant. Moreover, they involve detailed investigation of the mother's needs, usually carried out in the last stages of pregnancy, which means that she has little oppor-tunity of planning her purchases and may suffer considerable anxiety from not knowing in advance that she will be able to afford the essential equipment needed for her baby.

> The last Government, at the time of its defeat, was proposing (in the National Superannuation and Social Insurance Bill) to relax the contribution conditions for maternity grants, and it is regrettable that, while parts of the Bill were taken over by the present Government, this was not one of them. We would prefer, however, that the maternity grant should become a non-contributory benefit (just as family allowances are), since there are no grounds for thinking that the need for such a grant is greater among mothers who are married or have paid a given number of contributions to the National Insurance Fund than among those who do not fulfil these conditions.

5.292 The question was also raised in both Houses of Parliament during the passage of the Social Security Bill 1973. An amendment was put down in the House of Lords that maternity grant should be " payable without regard to contributions " but was defeated.[1] The main argument against the proposal was that to remove contribution conditions from a national insurance benefit would weaken the contributory principle in the national insurance scheme.

5.293 We note that in both Denmark and Sweden maternity grants are paid in respect of all births, without any insurance condition. The additional

[1] House of Lords Official Report, 12 June 1973, columns 574–582.

cost of doing the same here and paying a maternity grant of £25 on all births in this country to women resident here would probably be about £1 million a year. (There should, of course, be some small saving of supplementary benefit.) Most of this, as indicated in paragraph 5.290 would go to mothers in needy groups, many of them lone parents. Since maternity grants are now payable in respect of all but a few births, and the benefit represents only a minor part of the national insurance scheme, we do not think that the abandonment of the contributory principle in relation to this benefit could properly be seen as an assault on the national insurance scheme. We therefore consider that universal payment of the grant is justified and we accordingly recommend that the contribution conditions for its award should be abolished.

Maternity allowance

5.294   Maternity allowance is payable only on the mother's own insurance record. It is intended to encourage women who are employed or self-employed to give up work for a reasonable length of time in order to have their baby. The allowance is normally paid for the eighteen week period beginning eleven weeks before the expected week of the child's birth. The standard rate of benefit is the same as for other short-term national insurance benefits and to qualify for that rate the mother must have at least 50 contributions paid or credited (of which at least 26 must be actually paid) in the fifty-two week period immediately preceding the thirteenth week before the expected week of confinement. Reduced rates of benefit are payable if 26 (but less than 50) contributions are paid or credited, of which at least 26 must be contributions actually paid. The rate of benefit varies according to the total number of contributions paid and credited.[1]

5.295   At present an earnings-related supplement is payable with maternity allowance for the period of six weeks before the expected week of confinement until two weeks after the day that the child is born, provided that the mother is over 18 and satisfies the normal contribution conditions for the payment of sickness benefit and had earnings in the relevant income tax year of at least £450 which were subject to " pay-as-you-earn " deductions. The amount of the earnings-related supplement payable with the maternity allowance is the difference between the maternity allowance and the total of sickness benefit and what would have been payable by way of earnings-related supplement to that benefit.

5.296   Under the Social Security Act 1973 maternity allowance will carry entitlement to an earnings-related supplement for the whole of the period for which maternity allowance is paid in the same way as sickness benefit. We welcome this improvement which will help many lone mothers, and we see no justification for proposing any other changes for the particular benefit of one-parent families.

NATIONAL INSURANCE WIDOWS' BENEFITS

5.297   It has been suggested to us in evidence that payment of national insurance widows' benefits should not be subject to contribution conditions

---

[1] Broadly similar conditions will apply under the Social Security Act 1973 except that there will be no special maternity allowance test period. The contribution conditions will be the same as those for sickness benefit, and, like the sickness benefit conditions, they will have to be satisfied in the relevant income tax year.

as these bear harshly on women whose husbands die young, before they have acquired an adequate insurance record. A number of such women have young children to care for. A rough estimate of widows with children whose claims to widow's benefit fail on the contribution conditions is between 100 and 200 annually.

5.298 Under the current provisions two contribution tests have to be satisfied before any widow's benefit is payable under the national insurance scheme. The first is that the late husband must have paid at least 156 contributions, and the second is that he must have had an average of 13 contributions paid or credited for each complete year of insurance. Where the average is at least 50 the full rate of benefit is paid; a reduced rate is paid where the average is at least 13 and less than 50.

5.299 The contribution conditions are to be changed under the Social Security Act 1973. For the national insurance widow's allowance, which is payable for the first six months of widowhood, the only test will be that the husband should have paid contributions in any one tax year on earnings not less than 25 times the lower earnings limit attracting a contribution liability in that year. (In current terms this means contributions on earnings of at least 25 times £8, or £200, in any one tax year.) There will be no second test and no reduced rates of widow's allowance; the standard rate will be paid wherever that one test is satisfied.

5.300 For the long-term widows' benefits, such as widowed mother's allowance, there are still to be two tests. The first will be that the late husband must have paid contributions in any one tax year on earnings of at least 50 times the lower earnings limit attracting a contribution liability in that year; and the second will be that, for full-rate benefit, he must have paid contributions, or had them credited, on earnings of at least 50 times the lower earnings limit in each of not less than 90 per cent of the tax years throughout working life (which is normally from age 16). Reduced rates of benefit will be payable where the second test is not fully satisfied, but a minimum standard has been reached. The changes should, we think, almost invariably make entitlement easier and therefore reduce the chances of a widow's being unable to qualify for national insurance widow's benefit, or receiving benefit at less than the full rate.

5.301 Our proposals for GMA and improvements in supplementary benefits would help those few widows with children who are not eligible for the full national insurance benefit. To make a major benefit, such as national insurance widow's benefit, non-contributory would weaken the contributory basis of the whole national insurance scheme. We can see no scope for further liberalising the contribution conditions.

An extension to widowers

5.302 Several of those giving evidence to us put forward the case for an allowance for widowed fathers by analogy with the provision for widowed mothers under the national insurance scheme. We believe that there is a case for the introduction of a widowed father's allowance: there is a need for financial compensation whether a family suffer the loss of a father or a mother. But given the generally higher earnings of men, we do not see this proposal as one which should have high priority. Under our proposals widowers would be able to qualify for GMA, and, for those who do not work, this would provide a higher income than the national insurance benefit at the current rate. Better provision of home helps and child care would be particularly helpful to motherless families, and we make recommendations in this area in Part 8.

PENSION PROVISION

Retirement pension

5.303 In our proposals for GMA we have sought to combine a choice for the lone parent wishing to work with adequate provision for the parent wishing to remain at home to care for the family. But under present arrangements the decision not to go out to work may well affect the lone parent's retirement pension entitlement in the basic scheme. The married woman who separates from her husband retains full widowhood cover under the State scheme and also remains entitled to claim a retirement pension on her husband's insurance in the same way as if she were still living with him. A divorced woman, however, loses some of these rights, although she is able to make use of her husband's contribution record for the period until the date of divorce in the calculation of her retirement pension. The man or unmarried woman has no cover at all, except by virtue of his or her own contributions. We should have liked the retirement pension of recipients of GMA to be safeguarded under an arrangement whereby, when the lone parent was not working, entitlement to GMA would carry with it entitlement to credits of national insurance contributions which would count for retirement pension. We appreciate, however, that such an arrangement, which would involve awarding credits on the basis of entitlement to a non-contributory benefit, would be contrary to the principles on which the national insurance scheme is based, and we are unable to suggest any strong argument consistent with equity on which an exception for one-parent families could be made.

Occupational and reserve scheme pensions

5.304 We are conscious that one of the consequences of divorce can be that the woman loses her prospective right to a widow's pension under an occupational scheme in the event of her ex-husband's death. We understand that practice among occupational schemes varies, and that where widows' benefits are paid at the discretion of the trustees, some payment might be made to an ex-wife who was being maintained by her husband. The problem was examined by the Law Commission before the Divorce Reform Act 1969 became law.[1] They were unable to find any overall solution, but their proposals for increased and more flexible powers to order lump sum payments and property adjustments, which they considered would alleviate the problem and reduce the extent of hardship, were given effect by the Matrimonial Proceedings and Property Act 1970. We note that it has not been possible to make any further improvement, either through the conditions imposed on occupational schemes in order to secure recognition in the Social Security Act 1973, or in the reserve scheme. We have been unable to devote sufficient time to this intricate problem to make any fresh contribution. We are, however, anxious that the Government should not lose sight of it.

[1] *Report on Financial Provision in Matrimonial Proceedings:* Law Com No 25, HMSO, 1969, paragraphs 112–114.

5.305 There are other matters concerning widows' rights in occupational and reserve schemes and the special position of women as members of these schemes arising from their interrupted employment pattern, lower earnings and earlier retirement age, and the special conditions (for example, as to age of entry) which some schemes impose upon them. Pension rights are of significance to lone mothers, both when they are widows and as sole breadwinners, but the issues extend so far beyond the one-parent family, and have been so recently and exhaustively discussed during the passage of the Social Security Act 1973, that we feel obliged to avoid entering further into this area.

TAXATION

Additional personal allowance

5.306 The personal allowances of particular concern to one-parent families are child tax allowances and the additional personal allowance of £130, available where there is title to a child tax allowance (or part of one) and single-handed responsibility for a child living with the taxpayer.

5.307 The additional personal allowance, which is available on top of the adult's personal allowance and the child allowance, recognises that the one-parent family has special problems. It brings such a family's tax allowances close to those for a two-parent family. We refer earlier to the evidence we received on the difficulties experienced by the lone parent who wishes to work, and the additional expenses involved in going out to work and in bringing up a family single-handed; we consider that there is a good case for treating the one-parent family in the same way as a two-parent family for tax purposes. This principle is already part of the tax-credit proposals,[1] as set out in the Green Paper published in October 1972 and endorsed by the Select Committee on Tax-Credit in their report:[2] the credit for the head of a one-parent family is to be the same as that for a married man, and the intention is expressed of setting the level of personal tax allowances for those outside the tax-credit scheme to correspond in value with the tax credits. We welcome this proposal and think that some useful immediate help could be given to one-parent families by anticipating the improvement and increasing the additional personal allowance from £130 to £180 forthwith. This would give a lone parent the same tax allowance (personal and additional combined) as a married man and bring a relief from tax of up to £15 a year for someone paying tax at the basic rate.

5.308 Because the additional personal allowance is of value only to the better off families (many of them will be families headed by a man) we recognise that the number of families who would benefit from such a change would be small, and far less than the number who would benefit under the tax-credit proposals. But we are in no doubt as to the desirability of putting the lone parent on a footing in this way with the married man, and we think the change worth making as an interim measure and a step towards the tax-credit scheme. The cost of the increased allowance is estimated at about £3 million annually.

---

[1] A similar principle also applies for family income supplements and rent rebates, where the lone parent has the same needs allowance as a married couple.

[2] *Report of the Select Committee on Tax-Credit*, June 1973, Volume 1, paragraphs 99 and 100.

Child tax allowance

5.309   A number of representations were made to us about the award of child tax allowances and, in particular, that a parent may claim part or all of a child tax allowance while taking no interest, financial or otherwise, in the child.   This arises because the allowance is available for a taxpayer's legitimate child (including a legitimated child or step-child) without any condition as to residence or maintenance.   If the child is living with the mother, but her income is not high enough for her to pay tax, there is no point in her claiming the allowance and it is of use only to the father, who may therefore have the benefit of the tax allowance for a legitimate child of his living with the mother, even though he in no way helps to support it.   We can understand the sense of injustice which this situation may arouse.   However, in view of the likelihood that the present tax system has a limited life, and of the fact that to attach more stringent conditions to the award of the child tax allowance where the child is not living with the taxpayer would not help the one-parent family too poor to use the child tax allowance, we do not make a recommendation in this field.   We do, however, hope that arrangements for the payment of credits for children in the tax-credit scheme will, from the outset, be such as to prevent this situation arising.

Maintenance payments

5.310   We are unable to agree with suggestions made to us that maintenance payments should not be treated as taxable income in the hands of the recipient. We see no justification for a section of the population being excluded from the tax system.   Representations have been made to us, however, about delays in obtaining repayment of tax overpaid on maintenance payments, and we recommend that refund claims from lone parents should be dealt with promptly in view of the difficult financial situation which many lone parents experience. We note that this particular problem should diminish with the introduction of the proposed tax-credit scheme as the basic rate of tax will normally be payable by everyone in the scheme on all income.

Delays and lack of information

5.311   We have been particularly concerned about the volume of evidence presented to us which has spoken of loss, hardship and inconvenience experienced by lone parents not only because of delays in dealing with refund claims (to which we referred in the last paragraph) but because of the delays that sometimes arise in dealing with tax business and because of inadequate information.   Delays in replacing emergency coding by personal coding for lone parents starting work, or in adjusting coding where maintenance payments fall below expectation, and lack of information about the tax position in individual cases, were the subject of repeated complaints.   The Federation of Soroptimist Clubs of Great Britain and Ireland told us that all their clubs had made representations about the long delays in getting problems sorted out by the Inland Revenue, and one of the London boroughs referred specifically to the problem of delays in coding.   They said, " The system of taxing on an emergency basis those who return to work after a longish period of unemployment may be administratively convenient, but it is a positive disincentive to the lone mother returning to work, often at a wage little higher than State benefits, but having to meet the full costs of the family upkeep as well as fares, meals, child-minding, *etc.* The delay before the tax code is fixed can be up to five weeks in our experience and this seems excessive even in view of the delays inherent in a centralised system." The National Council for the Unmarried Mother and her Child referred, like several other organisations, to the problems where maintenance payments were irregular or not forthcoming and said, " As her tax liabilities are assessed to include the maintenance money, a mother may be asked to pay tax on money not actually received from the father. This can be coded back to her but only on her application and with information from the court. Mothers do not always know of this procedure. A mother is normally living on such a small margin that to pay tax on what she is not receiving will be a real hardship to her at the time. A simple leaflet about the tax position should be issued to mothers who are granted maintenance and affiliation orders, urging those who are working to go to their tax office to get their code adjusted."[1]

5.312 Some of the representations made to us, even by otherwise well-informed persons, about title to child tax allowances, the additional personal allowance and the housekeeper allowance, about " claw-back " of family allowances and about the different methods of collecting tax on maintenance payments revealed what we can only describe as a frightening amount of ignorance and misunderstanding. It is hardly surprising that many lone parents are confused when persons and organisations with a particular interest in helping them demonstrate so many misconceptions. The system is highly complex and we recognise that there are many problems for the Inland Revenue in presenting information simply. We understand that they are looking into ways of improving and expanding the information available to lone parents. In our view the present situation is most unsatisfactory and steps should be quickly taken to improve it.

EDUCATIONAL MAINTENANCE ALLOWANCES

5.313 A number of organisations giving evidence expressed concern about the numbers of children of lone parents who could benefit from continued education but who leave school at the minimum leaving age in order to reduce the parent's financial burden. The consequences, in terms of failure to develop the child's full potential, can be serious.[2] Educational maintenance allowances are available to low-income families where children stay on at school beyond age 16. They are not intended as a substitute for earnings but to prevent low-income parents from being faced with so much expense in keeping the child at school that they are forced to withdraw him. We believe that a satisfactory system of allowances is essential if the children of such families are to be encouraged to continue their schooling, to the advantage of the individual and the community at large.

5.314 Information about the number and value of allowances granted in England and Wales is not collected regularly, but the Department of Education

---

[1] *Forward for the Fatherless, op cit*, paragraph 226.
[2] We discuss in Part 8 the particular need to encourage girls to acquire skills which would help them to find worthwhile employment in later life as their own family grows up.

and Science have made available to us the results of a special enquiry of local education authorities which was made in 1970. The general picture which emerged from that enquiry was one of wide variations in local authority practice—in the maximum rates of allowance payable, in the levels of parental income which qualify families for the maximum amounts, and in the scales governing reduction of the allowances as parental incomes rise above the minimum levels. In the spring term of 1970 allowances were in payment in England and Wales for just over 20,000 children, representing 3·7 per cent of all pupils staying on at school beyond the minimum leaving age (which was then still 15) at an annual cost of £1½ million. The maximum allowances for pupils aged 15 ranged from £40 to £130, and for those aged 18 from £65 to £180 a year. The average level for an allowance was £73 a year. The majority of local education authorities appeared to apply a common test of means to one-parent and two-parent families but a number were treating one-parent families less generously on the ground that the family's needs were reduced by the absence of one adult. In 1970 the levels of net parental income qualifying for the full maximum allowance varied between £247 and £770 a year.

5.315 In Scotland the system under which the corresponding allowances, higher school bursaries, are provided differs in one important respect. Under section 49 of the Education (Scotland) Act 1962 the local education authorities have, like those in England and Wales, a discretionary power to award bursaries to school pupils over minimum leaving age, but the amounts payable are prescribed by statutory regulations made by the Secretary of State for Scotland and are standard throughout the country. In 1972 the maximum award was £150 a year, and the level of parental income qualifying for the full amount £700 a year. (One-parent families are assessed in the same way as two-parent families.) In the 1970–1971 school year bursaries averaging £72 a year were paid for 7,727 children, 17·6 per cent of those at school beyond the age of 15. (Four education authorities in Scotland provided figures showing that of 3,046 higher school bursaries awarded in 1970–1971 1,248 were for children in one-parent families.)

5.316 There are, of course, factors other than the amounts of the allowance and the parental income levels at which they are payable which significantly affect the pattern of local authority spending on these allowances in different areas. The number of children who stay on at school is closely linked to the type of secondary school they have been attending. In areas with a high proportion of grammar or comprehensive schools the number of children staying on at school is higher than in those areas where such schools are few. It is affected also by the availability of technical college and other alternative courses of education for older children. We recognise that the incidence of low-income families is not uniform from one area to another. But we think it inequitable that such families, wherever they live, should not have access to equal provision for their children who stay on at school beyond the age of 16. In this respect we believe the Scottish system to be superior.

5.317 It has been represented to us that the system in England and Wales has the advantage that the scales for the award of allowances and the method of administration are in the hands of the authorities who are best placed to assess the needs of the particular area and to devise the most appropriate schemes of assistance. This view was expressed by the Government during the course of a debate in the House of Commons in February 1972.[1] We do not accept, however, that access to cash benefits such as educational maintenance allowances should depend not only on the income of the individual family but also on where they happen to be living. For the families involved, these allowances are of vital importance in enabling their children to develop their potential and improve their future prospects.

5.318 We therefore recommend that educational maintenance allowance schemes should be rationalised on a national basis, with standard scales of allowances and qualifying parental income. We think that, as is already the case in Scotland, the same parental income scales should apply irrespective of whether the family has one or two parents. Everything should be done to ensure that pupils and their parents are fully informed about the availability of allowances and how to apply for them.

SECTION 9—SUMMARY OF OVERALL COST OF FINANCIAL RECOMMENDATIONS

5.319 Our main proposal for help for one-parent families is the GMA described in detail in Section 6. This would be a major change and the allowance would be available to all one-parent families within the field we have described in paragraphs 5.141–5.159. The cost is estimated in paragraphs 5.108–5.110 as between £135 million and £140 million (for GMA and tax credits paid as a result of entitlement to GMA) after deduction of tax and savings in supplementary benefit. (This calculation has been made on the assumption that the improvements we recommend in supplementary benefits would have been introduced.) We also estimate that maintenance payments amounting to about £50 million would be collected to offset against the cost of GMA, leaving a net cost of around £85 million, of which about £15 million would represent the provision of tax credits.

5.320 The Green Paper estimates that the cost of the tax-credit scheme will be in the region of £1,300 million a year.[2] People with no earnings, or with earnings below the level which would enable them to qualify for membership of the scheme, will not however benefit from this expenditure, except in so far as there is an intention to pay child tax credits on behalf of all children. A substantial part of the expenditure on GMA would go to members of the population who would, on the basis of the Green Paper proposals, otherwise be outside the tax-credit scheme and who have low incomes. The cost of providing GMA, therefore, needs to be looked at bearing in mind the expenditure of some £1,300 million for the tax-credit scheme.

5.321 Until GMA could be introduced supplementary benefit would continue to play a mjor role in supporting one-parent families. Our proposals

[1] House of Commons Official Report, 23 February 1972, column 1462.
[2] *Proposals for a Tax-Credit System, op cit*, paragraph 117.

for supplementary benefit improvement, and the annual cost,[1] are as follows:

	One-parent families only £	Other supplementary benefit recipients £
Addition to scale rate of £1·50 weekly (for one-parent families) ...	18m	—
Adult rate for non-householders under age 18 (heads of one-parent families) ...	½m	—
Earlier award of long-term scale rate (families with children)	2¾m	½m
Total	£21m	£¼m

We also support the view that the disregards for earnings and " other income " should be improved. If these were double their present level, the cost[1] would be about £14m, less than £2m of which would go to help one-parent families. Nearly all the extra expenditure on supplementary benefits, insofar as one-parent families are concerned, would cease with the introduction of GMA.

5.322 These are our main financial recommendations. The other recommendations we make are for maternity grant to be non-contributory, which would cost about £1 million, and for an increase in the additional personal tax allowance from £130 a year to £180 a year, which would cost about £3 million. We have not been able to cost our proposal for rationalising educational maintenance allowances, but any increase which might result in the £1½ million spent in England and Wales on these allowances would be unlikely to add significantly to the total cost of our proposals.

5.323 The great bulk of the total expenditure would go to one-parent families. Our own studies and research bore out the evidence we received from individuals and interested bodies of the extent to which one-parent families are living on low incomes. Our recommendations for improved financial provision are the least we consider necessary to make a worthwhile attack on the disadvantages suffered by so many such families and to relieve the hardships experienced by something like a million children. In some respects we should have liked to have gone further, but we were conscious of the problem of equity with low-income two-parent families and that there are many other calls on the resources which the community are willing to make available for social security provision. There are about 620,000 one-parent families; about a third of them are receiving supplementary benefit and some 43,000 more are probably eligible to receive it but not doing so. Taking all these matters into account we are sure that substantial expenditure is needed to make the situation of one-parent families at least tolerable in our present-day society.

---

[1] The costs quoted are estimated on the basis of current supplementary benefit recipients. Improving the scheme in these ways would undoubtedly mean that more people would become eligible to claim, but we have not been able to make a reliable estimate of the extent to which that would increase the costs.

PART 6—HOUSING

SECTION 1—INTRODUCTION

6.1 A good and secure home is essential to successful family life. There is an important sense in which this holds particularly true for one-parent families, in that the presence or absence of adequate housing conditions may well tip the balance on whether such families surmount or succumb to the financial and social handicaps from which they are apt to suffer. One-parent families share this vulnerability with other disadvantaged groups, and in some respects the discussion and recommendations which follow have an overlap with or application to such groups which it would take us outside our terms of reference to pursue. In general, it would be our view that where there is an equality of disadvantage in housing between one-parent and two-parent families neither should have priority of remedy over the other. But the evidence we have received puts it beyond doubt that housing problems closely rival money problems as a cause of hardship and stress to one-parent families, and we attach the greatest importance to measures directed to improve their situation in this respect.

6.2 In the next Section we describe the housing circumstances of one-parent families as they appear from the evidence and research findings available to us; and in the remainder of this Part we identify the principal housing problems of one-parent families, and suggest ways of ameliorating them.

SECTION 2—THE HOUSING CIRCUMSTANCES OF ONE-PARENT FAMILIES

6.3 Our information on the housing circumstances of one-parent families came from a variety of sources. We were, in the first instance, supplied with a mass of evidence on the subject (exceeded in volume only by the evidence on financial circumstances), much of it concerned with hardships suffered by individual families. Some of this evidence came from the parents themselves, and some of it from voluntary organisations and local authorities, being drawn from their experience in helping families to find and keep a home.[1] Some of our information is first-hand, derived from visits to families who were living in accommodation far below the standard needed for a stable and contented family life.

6.4 Our principal sources of information on the housing circumstances of one-parent families generally were the study by the Office of Population Censuses and Surveys, *Families and their Needs*,[2] and the analyses of Family Expenditure Survey data (Appendix 10) and of supplementary benefit statistics (Appendix 9) by the Department of Health and Social Security. We have also examined information collected for the Committee on the Rent Acts (the Francis Committee)[3] and an unpublished analysis by Elsa Ferri of material from the National Child Development Study.[4]

---

[1] Particularly cogent evidence was supplied by the Catholic Housing Aid Society, later published by the Society in *Evidence to the Finer Committee on One-Parent Families*, and from the National Council for the Unmarried Mother and her Child, later published by the Council with their other evidence to us in *Forward for the Fatherless*.

[2] Audrey Hunt, Judith Fox and Margaret Morgan: *Families and their Needs*, HMSO, 1973. A note about this survey is included in Appendix 2.

[3] *Report of the Committee on the Rent Acts*, Cmnd 4609, 1971.

[4] A note on the material is in Appendix 2.

357

6.5 None of these sources by itself provides comprehensive information on the housing situations of all the different kinds of one-parent families. Moreover generalisations on a national basis necessarily obscure the marked differences in housing patterns and cost between one locality and another. Nevertheless the available information sufficiently and plainly establishes that there are a number of ways in which the housing circumstances of one-parent families differ from those of two-parent families, some of them to the grave disadvantage of the former. These are reviewed in the paragraphs which follow.

FAMILIES SHARING HOMES

6.6 The biggest single difference between the housing circumstances of one-parent and two-parent families is the very high proportion of one-parent families who share a home, usually with close relatives. In the study *Families and their Needs*,[1] whereas in all five areas studied there were hardly any two-parent families living in shared accommodation, significant proportions of one-parent families did so, ranging from 15 per cent of fatherless families in Haringey to 35 per cent in Glamorgan. Motherless families were also more likely to share accommodation than two-parent families. Family Expenditure Survey data also show a high proportion of lone mothers in shared accommodation—30 per cent were non-householders and about half of those who were householders had some other adult in their home; and 26 per cent of fatherless families on supplementary benefit in November 1972 were non-householders. *Families and their Needs* showed that those lone parents who shared accommodation usually did so with a close relative and that they tended to be the younger mothers with smaller families. Unmarried mothers were particularly likely to be living in someone else's household—the proportions varied widely from 85 per cent in Dundee to 26 per cent in Haringey, but were always higher for unmarried mothers than for other groups. Widowed mothers were the least likely to be sharing a home. The separated and divorced came in between. The supplementary benefit data confirmed this general picture. In November 1972 50 per cent of unmarried mothers, 20 per cent of the separated wives, 11 per cent of the divorced and 3 per cent of widows receiving benefit were non-householders.

6.7 Sharing is not necessarily disadvantageous in all respects for one-parent families; for the unmarried mother, who has never had a home of her own, it will reduce the isolation which so often threatens her. But in our view these high figures for home-sharing demonstrate both the acute financial difficulties of many one-parent families and the problems they face in obtaining and retaining suitable accommodation of their own. In this connection, we note that the study *Families and their Needs* indicated that the mothers with lower incomes were more likely to share a home.

TENURE OF ACCOMMODATION

Owner-occupiers

6.8 Where one-parent families do have their own households the information available to us establishes that lone mothers (and, to a lesser extent, lone

[1] *Op cit.*

358

fathers) are much less likely to be owner-occupiers than are two-parent families. The position in the five areas surveyed in *Families and their Needs* was as follows:

TABLE 6.1

PERCENTAGE OF HOUSEHOLDERS WHO WERE OWNER-OCCUPIERS: 1970

Status of head of family	Dorset %	Dundee %	Glamorgan %	Halifax %	Haringey %
Lone mother	26·2	9·7	22·2	19·7	12·7
Two-parent	50·9	52·2*	82·0*	54·3	45·1

* The samples of two-parent families in the survey were, in effect, heavily clustered random samples, consisting of all such families in a few enumeration districts in each area. Comparison with data from the 1966 sample census indicates that this procedure may have resulted in an overstatement of the percentages of owner-occupiers in Dundee and Glamorgan. The 1971 census data confirm this; in Dundee almost 60 per cent of households were in public authority housing, and in Glamorgan only about 55·7 per cent of householders were owner-occupiers.

Source: *Families and their Needs*, All Areas Summary, paragraph 9.4.3.

There were, of course, wide variations between the five areas, but the lone mothers everywhere were less likely to be owner-occupiers than were two-parent families. A similar picture emerges from other studies. Of the estimated 280,000 lone mothers (other than widows) in the Family Expenditure Survey only 49,000 (17 per cent) were owner-occupiers. The national figure for all families is about 50 per cent (see Table 6.4). The National Child Development Study also found a lower incidence of home ownership among fatherless than among two-parent families, both at the first and second follow-up. (At the first follow-up 23 per cent were found as against 43 per cent among two-parent families; at the second follow-up 25 per cent were found compared with 50 per cent among two-parent families.)[1]

6.9 The study *Families and their Needs* indicated that the small proportion of one-parent families owning their own homes was likely to be related to their low incomes. Home ownership increases with income in all types of family, and according to the General Household Survey[2] 52 per cent of all owner-occupiers (in 1971) were professional workers, employers and managers, and intermediate and junior non-manual workers, while only 15 per cent were semi-skilled and unskilled workers. Median incomes of owner-occupiers paying off a mortgage were higher than the median incomes of the general population and of all other tenure groups. The supplementary benefit statistics show that of unmarried mothers, who would not normally have acquired ownership of a house before the birth of their first child, only 3 per cent were owner-occupiers.

[1] The follow-up studies on the children, born in 1958, were done at age 7 in 1965 and again at age 11 in 1969. See Appendix 2.
[2] Office of Population Censuses and Surveys, Social Survey Division: *The General Household Survey—Introductory Report*, HMSO, 1973.

359

Private tenants

6.10   An even more significant aspect of the housing of one-parent families is the high number and proportion who are private tenants.   The situation in the five areas studied in *Families and their Needs* was as follows:

TABLE 6.2

PERCENTAGE OF HOUSEHOLDERS IN ACCOMMODATION RENTED OTHERWISE THAN FROM A LOCAL AUTHORITY: 1970

Status of head of family	Dorset %	Dundee %	Glamorgan %	Halifax %	Haringey %
Lone mother	24·6	23·9	18·8	16·7	47·8
Two-parent	7·2	10·3	8·1	8·1	38·4

Source: *Families and their Needs*, All Areas Summary, paragraph 9.4.3.

6.11   From the Family Expenditure Survey data, it was estimated that as many as 26 per cent of the fatherless families (72,000) at the end of 1971 were in privately rented accommodation.   In the National Child Development Study 22 per cent of fatherless children as against 12 per cent of two-parent family children were in privately rented accommodation at the first follow-up, and 17 per cent as against 7 per cent at the second.

Local authority tenants

6.12   Largely as a corollary of their under-representation in the owner-occupied sector, lone parents who are householders are more likely than two-parent families to be local authority tenants.   In the areas studied in *Families and their Needs* the position was as follows:

TABLE 6.3

PERCENTAGE OF HOUSEHOLDERS WHO WERE LOCAL AUTHORITY TENANTS: 1970

Status of household	Dorset %	Dundee %	Glamorgan %	Halifax %	Haringey %
Lone mother	40·8	64·9	54·5	58·5	34·8
Two-parent	34·4	35·5*	3·6*	35·9	13·3

* See footnote to Table 6.1.
Source: *Families and their Needs*, All Areas Summary, paragraph 9.4.3.

But the proportion of all one-parent families (as opposed to the proportion of householder families amongst them) who are in local authority accommodation is much lower than this because of the large numbers who are non-householders sharing accommodation with other adults (such as their own parents).

One-parent families in a changing housing market

6.13   This pattern of housing tenure, with one-parent families disproportionately reliant on privately rented accommodation and under-represented in the owner-occupied sector, is one measure of the extent to which they are at a disadvantage compared with other groups.   It is, moreover, a pattern which runs counter to the major housing trend of recent years.

6.14   The last fifty years, and more especially the period since the second world war, have seen fundamental changes in housing tenure patterns.   Before the first world war the majority of new housing was built for private rental. The introduction of rent controls on privately rented property during the first world war stopped this trend.   Since as long ago as 1915 there have been various forms of rent control which have made the building of houses for letting an increasingly unfavourable investment, except at the luxury end of the market. During the inter-war period governments increasingly subsidised council building.

6.15   In the years since the second world war the pace of change in the housing tenure patterns has quickened.   There has been an increasing move towards owner-occupation under the spur of the increasing difficulty in obtaining privately rented accommodation.   Slum clearance programmes have destroyed large areas of privately rented housing which has been replaced by local authority dwellings.   The overall result has been a dramatic decrease in the amount of private housing available to rent, coupled with substantial increases in owner-occupation and in local authority housing.   This is shown in Table 6.4 below:

TABLE 6.4

TENURE OF HOUSING—CHANGES 1950-1971

Tenure	England and Wales			Scotland			Great Britain			
	1961	1966*	1971	1961	1966*	1971	1950	1961	1966*	1971
	%	%	%	%	%	%	%	%	%	%
Owner-occupied	42·3	46·7	51·6	25·2	28·0	27·3	29·5	40·6	44·9	49·2
Rented from local authority/ New Town	23·7	25·7	27·9	42·0	46·8	57·6	18·0	25·5	27·6	30·9
Rented privately, unfurnished ...	23·8	19·1	12·5	22·0	16·5	6·3 }	44·6	23·7	18·9	11·8
Rented privately, furnished ...	4·0	3·4	2·8	2·5	1·7	1·4 }		3·8	3·3	2·7
Others (including service tenancies and housing association lettings)	6·2	5·1	5·2	8·2	6·9	7·4	7·9	6·4	5·3	5·4

* 10 per cent sample.

Sources: Comparisons of data from the 1961 census, the 1966 census, and the General Household Survey for 1971. Table extracted from the *General Household Survey Introductory Report*, HMSO, 1973, Table 5.8. Comparative proportions for 1950 in Great Britain are census based and taken from *Social Trends*, 1971, Table 90.

6.16 In the contraction of the privately rented sector since the last war, both slum clearance and government efforts to preserve and modernise the housing stock have played a major part. Between the end of the war and the end of 1971 nearly one million houses had been demolished in England and Wales and about a further 300,000 in Scotland. The great majority of these houses were in the privately rented sector and their disappearance has meant that previously low rented, densely populated property has been replaced by lower density municipal property. Improvement grants have led to a substantial loss of housing units in inner city areas as previously multi-occupied houses have been modernised into fewer self-contained units. All this has improved the quality of the nation's housing stock; but it has also meant that those who could not obtain local authority housing for whatever reason, and could not afford to buy their own homes, have been forced to compete for accommodation from a shrinking pool of privately rented housing.

6.17 A particularly disturbing feature of this situation is the concentration of one-parent families in furnished accommodation in the conurbations in England and Wales.[1] The tenants' survey which was conducted during 1970 for the Francis Committee[2] found, for example, that in London fatherless families accounted for 31 per cent of furnished tenants with children in the stress areas and 21 per cent in the conurbation as a whole, compared with 11 per cent and 8 per cent respectively of those in unfurnished privately rented accommodation. Table 6.5 below shows that nearly half of the fatherless families in furnished tenancies in the stress areas were unmarried.

TABLE 6.5

FAMILIES WITH CHILDREN AND HAVING ONE PARENT ABSENT: GREATER LONDON, 1970

Percentage of all families with children

	Furnished		Unfurnished	
	Conurba-tion	Stress areas	Conurba-tion	Stress areas
Father absent	21	31	8	11
Mother absent	—	1	1	—
Reasons for father's absence				
Unmarried mothers ...	7	15	3	3
Parents separated or divorced	10	10	4	7
Other	3	3	3	2

Source: *Report of the Committee on the Rent Acts, op cit*, Table 40, page 298.

---

[1] In Scotland, however, this problem hardly exists because the privately rented furnished sector is much smaller. The Francis Committee study found only 6 furnished tenancies (2 per cent) out of a total sample size of 262 in the "stress area" studied in the central Clydeside conurbation and no furnished tenancies at all in the "non-stress" area. See paragraphs 6.24–6.25 for further discussion of the Scottish housing situation.

[2] *Op cit*.

In their report the committee commented on the situation in Greater London as follows:

> It seems that there are two separate groups of furnished tenants. The first comprises those households, often single persons, usually without children, who wish to remain mobile and independent. They usually earn quite well and include a substantial proportion of people in the higher social grades. The second group largely consists of families (including lone parent families) with children, who are too poor to buy a house, cannot find unfurnished accommodation to rent within their means and cannot obtain a council house. The cheapest accommodation available to them is furnished rooms in a run-down area. It is from this involuntary group (who perhaps number some 30 per cent of all furnished tenants in the conurbation and nearly half of those in the stress areas) that applications to the Rent Tribunals must frequently seem to come.[1]

FREQUENCY OF MOVING HOUSE

6.18 Much of the evidence we received suggested that fatherless families were compelled to move home more often that others, and this was supported by the study *Families and their Needs*[2] which found that in four out of five areas considerably higher proportions of fatherless than of two-parent families had moved at least once in the last five years. (In the fifth area—Dorset—the proportions were similar.) In all areas more fatherless than other families had moved more than once.

6.19 The National Child Development Study[3] also found that by the age of 11 more of the fatherless children had moved frequently, and fewer of them had moved once only than had children in other families. Those in privately rented accommodation had moved most often; 37 per cent of them had moved four or more times including a particularly high proportion (59 per cent) of those in furnished accommodation. This survey also found that widows' families had not only moved less often than the families of separated, divorced or unmarried parents, but also less frequently than two-parent families.

6.20 The high mobility among furnished tenants may be associated with poor quality accommodation, which makes a move to conditions which are even marginally better seem worthwhile. One of the results of frequent moves is that a family may go from one local authority to another and lose or fail to establish a place on a local authority housing list, so diminishing the chances of re-housing. Frequent moves are likely to be unsettling for children, especially where a change of school is involved, and may also damage the one-parent family's chances of establishing itself and making social contacts in the community.

HOUSING CONDITIONS AND COSTS

6.21 All the information we have leads to the conclusion that the conditions and amenities in the homes of one-parent families are less adequate than in those of two-parent families, more especially in the privately rented sector. The study *Families and their Needs* showed that in the measurable indices of rooms occupied, rooms and beds shared, and the level of household amenities and equipment, standards were lower in each area for one-parent

---

[1] *Ibid*, page 135.

[2] *Op cit*, paragraph 9.2.

[3] See Appendix 2.

families than for two-parent families.[1] The National Child Development Study[2] similarly concluded that children in fatherless families experienced inferior standards Unsatisfactory housing conditions were frequently cited in other evidence. It is clear that one-parent families tend, through low income, insecurity and factors promoting excessive mobility, to be channelled into inferior types of accommodation.

6.22 These unsatisfactory housing conditions are especially disturbing in view of the relatively high housing costs these families have to bear. The Francis Committee said:

> ... the general picture regarding rent is one where the furnished sector pays higher rents for inferior accommodation (as measured by gross annual value), particularly in the stress areas . . . . The Tenants' Survey shows that the typical rent of a furnished tenancy in Greater London was approximately £290 pa, representing as much as 33 per cent of the relatively low typical take home pay of a furnished tenant (£870).[3]

6.23 The effect of higher rents combined with lower incomes (see Part 5, Section 2) is that housing costs account for a higher proportion of the one-parent family's budget than is the case for other families. We refer later (in Section 7) to the effect of the new schemes of rent rebates and allowances under the Housing Finance Act 1972 and the Housing (Financial Provisions) (Scotland) Act 1972.

SCOTLAND

6.24 We are conscious that the housing situation in Scotland is in some respects radically different from that in parts of England and Wales, particularly the Greater London area. The tenure distribution of housing stock differs considerably from that in England. In particular the public authority sector is much larger and the owner-occupied sector correspondingly smaller. It is now widely recognised that there is no longer in Scotland a crude and acute housing shortage.[4] It has been estimated that, in 1971, there were approximately 1,720,000 potentially separate households in Scotland;[5] the estimated total housing stock at December 1971 was 1,815,000.[6]

6.25 Although local housing shortages do still exist the problems are now seen to be qualitative, rather than quantitative, and to be associated mainly with differences in the standard of the housing stock controlled by local authorities. In particular there are many inter-war housing schemes built under legislation of the 1930s for rehousing residents from slum clearance and over-crowded areas which now cause particular concern. Many of these schemes today form sites of severe social problems and environmental deterioration. There are indications that one-parent families, particularly fatherless families, are likely to be disproportionately represented in these areas. A recent study[7]

---

[1] *Op cit*, All Areas Summary, paragraphs 9.5–9.10.

[2] See Appendix 2.

[3] *Op cit*, Chapter 20, page 131.

[4] See Scottish Housing Advisory Committee: *Planning for Housing Needs; pointers towards a comprehensive approach*, HMSO, 1972.

[5] Estimate made by Housing Research Unit, Scottish Development Department.

[6] Department of Environment, Scottish Development Department and Welsh Office: *Housing and Construction Statistics*, No 1, HMSO, 1972.

[7] Housing Research Unit, Scottish Development Department: *Feasibility Study of Improvement Potential* (unpublished).

of one such housing scheme in a small burgh in central Scotland found that 25 per cent of all the households in the area were one-parent households. Overall it was estimated that at least a third of the one-parent households from the burgh lived in the scheme-area although it contained only 10 per cent of the total households in the burgh. All the one-parent households were fatherless.

SUMMARY

6.26   In summary, not all one-parent families suffer from a housing problem, nor are the problems of those who do common to all. There is, however, an unmistakeable and pronounced incidence of hardship and disadvantage in housing to be found in the group as a whole. Its members are more than normally likely to be sharing accommodation with others. They are much less likely to be owner-occupiers, and much more likely to be living in privately rented accommodation, especially in the furnished sector, and particularly in areas of housing stress, where lone parents and their children live in low grade condition at high rents.

SECTION 3—THE ROLE OF LOCAL AUTHORITIES

6.27   Local authorities have wide responsibilities in meeting the housing needs of their areas by providing rented accommodation, and in England and Wales they are increasingly being encouraged to provide reasonably priced houses for sale.[1] With the rapid shrinkage of the privately rented housing sector the alternatives to a local council house or flat for those who cannot afford to buy in the private sector are becoming progressively limited, and we have no doubt that the main burden of housing one-parent families, especially those who at present can only obtain furnished rooms, must fall increasingly on local housing authorities.

6.28   Both the Seebohm Committee on Local Authority and Allied Personal Social Services in 1968[2] and the Cullingworth Committee on Council Housing Purposes, Procedures and Priorities[3] in 1969 emphasised the need for local authorities to take a comprehensive view of their responsibilities to meet the housing needs of their areas. This was also the view of the Working Party of the Scottish Housing Advisory Committee, whose report, *Planning for Housing Needs*,[4] has been brought to the notice of Scottish local authorities by the Scottish Development Department. In the words of the Seebohm Committee:

> All housing authorities should, we consider, take a comprehensive and extended view of their responsibilities to meet the housing needs of their areas. In particular, they should be generally concerned with assisting a family to obtain and keep adequate accommodation whether it be in the council house sector or not.[5]

We believe that an approach of this kind is vital if the housing problems of existing one-parent families are to be eased and the break-up of other families through housing problems is to be avoided. We welcome acceptance of it in the

---

[1] Department of the Environment: *Widening the Choice: The Next Steps in Housing*, Cmnd 5280, 1973, paragraph 50.

[2] *Report of the Committee on Local Authority and Allied Personal Social Services*, Cmnd 3703, 1968.

[3] *Ninth Report of the Housing Management Sub-Committee of the Central Housing Advisory Committee*, HMSO, 1969.

[4] HMSO, 1972.

[5] *Op cit*, paragraph 390.

Housing White Paper of April 1973,[1] and as informing the philosophy of the recent circular on homelessness[2] to which we make extended reference in Section 5 below.

6.29 In considering the housing needs of their areas it is important that local authorities (and indeed those responsible for housing policy in central Government) should have regard to the important changes in the demographic characteristics of the population and their implications which we have discussed in Part 3. These changes include:

(1) earlier age at marriage;

(2) a higher rate of marriage breakdown among couples who marry young;

(3) a higher incidence of pregnancy at the time of marriage and of children being born in the very early years of marriage;

(4) fewer young families without children, fewer very large families, but a substantial increase in the number of families with two or three children.

These factors will not only influence the nature and size of the housing stock needed in the foreseeable future but will also require a change in allocation and management policies. For example, the higher risk of family breakdown makes it more important than ever that young married couples should not have to live after marriage in the parental home, and, of equal urgency, that the restrictive policies presently adopted by many local authorities on the re-allocation of the tenancy when a marriage fails should be reviewed, as we propose in Section 6 below.

THE POWERS OF LOCAL AUTHORITIES

6.30 Local housing authorities have a statutory obligation under section 91 of the Housing Act 1957 and section 137 of the Housing (Scotland) Act 1966 " to consider housing conditions in their district and the needs of the district with respect to the provision of further housing accommodation ". Under sections 92 and 138 respectively of those Acts they may provide housing accommodation in a variety of ways—by new building, by conversion, by acquiring property, and by altering, repairing or improving it. The general management and allocation of dwellings provided by local authorities are vested in them, subject to the obligations under section 113 (2) of the 1957 Act and section 151 (2) of the 1966 Act, to give reasonable preference to people who " are occupying insanitary or overcrowded houses, have large families, or are living under unsatisfactory housing conditions ". For many years successive governments have chosen not to intervene in the day-to-day management and allocation of council housing, but have instead issued general advice through circulars and reports of the Housing Management Sub-Committee of the Central Housing Advisory Committee, and sub-committees of the Scottish Housing Advisory Committee.

[1] *Widening the Choice: The Next Steps in Housing, op cit;* Scottish Office: *Homes for People, Scottish Housing Policy in the 1970s,* Cmnd 5272, 1973.

[2] Department of the Environment (18/74), Department of Health and Social Security (4/74), and Welsh Office (34/74): *Homelessness,* February 1974.

6.31   Until 1949 local authorities were statutorily restricted to providing houses " for the working classes ".   By then it was generally agreed that council housing, like the social services, should not be restricted to particular classes of persons or income groups, and this limitation was removed.

6.32   The changing pattern of housing tenure, the complexity of urban planning and redevelopment programmes, and the development and reorganisation of related services (more especially the personal social services) have in the last few years focused attention on the wide range of functions and needs which housing authorities now have to cover.   They have led to recognition of the need for housing authorities to be up-to-date on housing needs of their areas and to " take a wider view of their responsibilities and be specifically and directly concerned, not only with building houses and managing those they own, but also with the whole range of housing problems of the area in question."[1]

6.33   We, too, are convinced by our investigations that it is essential for housing authorities to be directly concerned not only with the building, management and allocation of housing stock but equally with the needs of the families who are seeking to live in their areas, whether in the private or public sector. Effectiveness in meeting the housing needs of the area and of individuals depends on adequate knowledge of resources and requirements, good co-ordination with other local services, and a flexible administration responsive to local needs.   Especially is it vital that housing authorities and social services departments should work closely together in tackling the problems of individual families, and nowhere more closely than in preventing and remedying homelessness and eviction (on which see Section 5).

6.34   In this connection we wish to draw attention to the fact that under the two-tier system of local government in England and Wales, in operation from April 1974, responsibility for housing and social services functions outside the six new metropolitan areas will rest with different authorities.[2]   The county authorities will administer the social services whilst housing will be the responsibility of district authorities (as it will be in Scotland from May 1975).   We recognise that the social services need to have a broad population base and that housing, being an essentially local service, needs to be carried out as close to the individual as possible. . But such division of functions increases the need for effective arrangements for co-ordination of policies and action.   We recommend that this aspect of local government reorganisation should be kept under review to ensure that satisfactory links between social services and housing departments are established and maintained.

6.35   We are informed that in Scotland a committee has already been set up to study the relationship between housing and social work services after the local government reorganisation in 1975.[3]

---

[1] *Seebohm Report, op cit*, paragraph 14.   See also paragraph 391 relating to housing aid centres, to which we refer in Section 5.

[2] In Greater London, which is not involved in the reorganisation, both housing and social services functions have been carried out by the London boroughs since the London Government Act 1963 came into operation.

[3] Committee on Links between Housing and Social Work, Chairman: Mrs J D O Morris, MBE.

SECTION 4—THE HOME AFTER THE BREAKDOWN OF MARRIAGE: THE LEGAL SITUATION[1]

6.36 Some of the most severe of the housing problems of one-parent families arise from the breakdown of marriage.[2] Breakdown usually creates a need for two homes where previously the parties and their children have lived together in a single home. It may lead to disputes over the ownership of the existing home, or competition for its possession. It may raise questions as to who in the future is to discharge the burden of mortgage payments, rent, outgoings and arrears. These matters, if they are not settled by agreement, will involve determining the strict rights of property as between the spouses, or invoking the power of the court, when it grants a formal separation or divorce, to adjust those rights as all the circumstances of the case, including the interests of the children, may require. Yet another set of legal considerations may arise when considering rights and obligations concerning the matrimonial home not as between the husband and wife themselves, but as between each of them and third parties, such as the landlord, the building society, or the purchaser of the premises. Yet again, the local authority, either in the capacity of landlord if the parties have been living in a council house or flat, or as bearing the wider responsibilities referred to in Sections 3 and 5, may be called upon to intervene to cope with the housing crisis caused by the breakdown of a marriage.

6.37 All of these elements make up a legal structure of great complexity. We do not propose to examine and comment upon this structure in all its detail; and this for two reasons. First, the Law Commission has the reform of matrimonial property law well in hand. Secondly, our own major concern in this Section is with the practical means of relieving one-parent families of as much as possible of the particular hardships and disadvantages which they suffer in the effort to secure and retain adequate accommodation for themselves; and we consider that for this purpose reform of the law, while relevant and important, comes secondary in effect to what may be accomplished by progress and adaptations in the practice and policy of central and local government in discharging their housing functions.

6.38 However, it is necessary for us to examine some aspects of the law concerning rights in the matrimonial home, with a view to enlarging the perspective of our consideration of housing matters, and setting the context for some of the points on practice and policy to be examined in later Sections.

---

[1] In Scotland the law on the rights of ownership and occupation of the matrimonial home is different from that in England and Wales. In this Section we have not attempted to deal with any technical considerations which may arise in seeking to apply the principles we advocate to Scotland: nevertheless we should like to see the same results achieved there and we note that in Appendix 6 the Scottish Law Commission indicate that in the course of reviewing Scottish family law they will need to examine the law relating to financial provision on divorce, and this will include matters connected with home ownership and local authority practice in allocating tenancies during and after divorce proceedings, particularly where questions of custody of children arise.

[2] The problems may be the same when the breakdown occurs between unmarried parents, but the strictly legal consequences regarding ownership and occupation of the home will be different in such a case, because they arise as between people who are in law strangers to each other. Unless she is a tenant, or has some other distinct title of her own, there is nothing to stop a man turning his mistress out of his house whenever he pleases.

6.39   With the wider spread of owner-occupation to which we have referred in Section 2 and the increase in the breakdown of marriage, rights of ownership are now of great importance to many families involved in marital disputes. So far as concerns ownership of the matrimonial home, there is at present a notable distinction between the approach of the law and the powers of the court when questions arise during the marriage and when they arise upon divorce. As we have mentioned elsewhere,[1] in regulating property rights upon divorce under the powers conferred by the Matrimonial Proceedings Act 1970 the court takes as its starting point a principle of partnership in the home which pays little regard to who provided the money:

> Parliament recognised that the wife who looks after the home and family contributes as much to family assets as the wife who goes out to work. The one contributes in kind. The other in money or money's worth. If the court comes to the conclusion that the home has been acquired and maintained by the joint efforts of both, then, when the marriage breaks down, it should be regarded as the joint property of both of them, no matter in whose name it stands. Just as the wife who makes substantial money contributions usually gets a share, so should the wife who looks after the home and cares for the family.[2]

Thus, when a marriage comes to an end, the court has power to adjust and reform property rights between the spouses, and will tend in the exercise of this jurisdiction to start with the notion of the home as property owned in common.

6.40   On the other hand if the court has to determine a dispute between husband and wife over the ownership of the home during the marriage, it has no power to impose the notion of community, but must settle the dispute by applying itself to discover the strict rights of property.   As in the case of any other dispute over property, it has to look to the name in which the property was purchased, the source of the purchase money, and the actual agreements and intentions of the persons connected with the transactions.   In the case of husband and wife special difficulties may arise because, on the one hand, they often pool their finances and, on the other, rarely record their agreements. But these are difficulties relating to proof rather than principle, and do not affect what has been called the "commercialism" with which English law approaches the determination of property rights within marriage.

The principle of co-ownership

6.41   Yet if the wife's contribution in managing the home and caring for the family, through which she has freed the husband for his economic activities, is to be reflected in the distribution of property when the marriage is dissolved, it should be reflected also in the rights to property while the marriage remains on foot.   Further, it has been factually established[3] that the vast majority of married men and women believe that the home should be jointly owned, irrespective of who paid for it.   These considerations have recently led the Law Commission to recommend[4] that the present rules for determining the

---

[1] Part 4, Section 4.

[2] *Wachtel v Wachtel* (1973) Fam 72, *per* Lord Denning MR at 93.

[3] J E Todd and L M Jones: *Matrimonial Property*, HMSO, 1972. This expounds the results of a national survey carried out on behalf of the Law Commission by the Social Survey Division of the Office of Population Censuses and Surveys.

[4] The Law Commission: *Family Law, First Report on Family Property: A New Approach*, Law Com No 52, 1973, paragraph 30.

interests of a husband and wife in the matrimonial home are in need of reform through the introduction of a principle of co-ownership under which, in the absence of an agreement to the contrary, a matrimonial home would be shared equally between husband and wife.

6.42 We support the principle of co-ownership of the matrimonial home, and believe that, if implemented, it would often help to reduce stress in the breakdown situation, and enable the parent left in care and control of the children to retain the home or acquire a new one. It needs to be emphasised, however, that co-ownership during the marriage will not, any more than transfer of ownership upon dissolution of the marriage, by itself solve the financial problems that will continue to confront many wives who have to continue to house themselves and their children. In the best case, from the point of view of such a wife, she will already own half the house and will have the husband's half transferred to her by the court. If there is no mortgage loan outstanding, she will then have full and unencumbered title to the house. But unless the parties are wealthy, or there are other exceptional circumstances present, the problem will remain of compensating the husband for his transferred share. There will be no capital available from which compensation can be paid, and the alternative will be to make the necessary adjustment in the husband's favour by reducing the amount of maintenance that might otherwise be payable. If, however, there is a loan outstanding on the property—or, as might well happen, the wife has to raise such a loan in order to compensate the husband—the resources must still be found to continue the repayments, or otherwise to cope with the rights of the lender. Thus, even if co-ownership of the matrimonial home were to become the general rule of law, it would not by itself guarantee that upon the breakdown of marriage the retention of the home would follow responsibility for the children. We revert to these problems in Section 8.

RIGHTS OF OCCUPATION

6.43 Disputes concerning the occupation, as distinct from the ownership, of the matrimonial home may arise between the spouses themselves or between either of them and a third party, such as the landlord. They may concern the right to occupy during the continuation of the marriage, or upon its termination by a decree of the court, or through the death of one of the spouses. The regulation of the diverse problems which may arise is the subject of an amalgam of common law, statutory provision and discretionary powers of the court constituting a branch of the law which has attained a very high (and, in our view most undesirable) level of technical intricacy. Fortunately, the Law Commission in its Working Paper on Family Property Law[1] has dealt succinctly

---

[1] *Family Law, Family Property Law*, Working Paper No 42, 1971, paragraphs 1.3–1.26. In an extensive academic literature, reference may also be made to O M Stone: 'The Matrimonial Homes Act 1967', 31 *Modern Law Review*, 1968, pages 304–309; O Kahn-Freund: 'Recent Legislation on Matrimonial Property', 33 *Modern Law Review*, 1970, pages 601–631 especially 609–615; D A Nevitt and J Levin: 'Social Policy and the Matrimonial Home', 36 *Modern Law Review*, 1973, pages 345–369. Two useful short articles are R Burnfield: 'Exclusion from the Matrimonial Home', *New Law Journal*, 1972, pages 729–731, and N Kesselman: 'Injunction for the Battered Wife', *Bulletin of the Legal Action Group*, 1973, pages 174–176 and 203. See also P A Bromley: *Family Law* (4th edition), Butterworths, pages 386–400; and John Eekelaar: *Family Security and Family Breakdown*, Penguin Books, 1971, Chapter 2, especially pages 76–87.

with many of the aspects of rights of occupation which are of concern to us, and has made recommendations for the improvement of the law which closely follow the conclusions to which we are drawn by our own consideration of the law in relation to the evidence submitted to us.[1]

Reforms of the law protecting occupation

6.44   In these circumstances we feel it sufficient to deal with the law concerning right of occupation of the matrimonial home by making reference to the points to which we attach special importance.[2]   These are as follows:

(1) by and large, the Matrimonial Homes Act 1967 enables the court to take appropriate action, during the currency of the marriage, to safeguard and regulate as between the parties themselves the occupation of the matrimonial home in all those cases where one spouse has but the other has not a legal title to occupy as proprietor. Typically (although it would equally cover the converse case) the Act covers the situation where the husband is sole owner or tenant of the matrimonial home and the wife, who has no proprietary interest in it, claims to be protected in her occupation.   The court is then empowered to make such order concerning the occupation of the home as it thinks just and reasonable, having regard to the conduct of the spouses, their respective needs and resources, the needs of any children, and all the circumstances of the case.   Wide though these powers are, it has been held that they stop short of permitting the court to order the owner out of the house altogether, either temporarily or permanently.[3]   Thus, if the husband is the sole tenant, the court may order him to confine himself to one part of the house, but not to leave it.   This gap in the legislation ought, in our view, to be closed;

(2) the court exercising matrimonial jurisdiction has an inherent power, not derived from the Act of 1967, and not subject to the particular limitations attaching to the jurisdiction conferred by the Act, to protect a spouse (nearly always, but not inevitably, it will be the wife) and the children in the occupation of the matrimonial home by injunction.   Thus, the inherent jurisdiction can be exercised in favour of a wife who jointly owns the matrimonial home, and in a proper case so as totally to exclude the husband, even though he is also a joint owner, from occupying any part of it.   This inherent jurisdiction, however, seems to be subject to a limitation of its own, namely, to the general rule that the court grants injunctions only as ancillary to some other and principal relief.   For example, the court can protect the wife and children in their occupation of the matrimonial home while the former is petitioning for divorce, or even after she has been granted a divorce, but it is extremely doubtful whether the court is entitled under the inherent jurisdiction to evict a husband from the

---

[1] The recommendations in the Working Paper are summarised in that Paper at paragraphs 1.119–1.121 and 1.125.

[2] The Working Paper was published before the decision of the House of Lords in *Tarr v Tarr* (1972) 2 All ER, 295, to which our point 1 refers.   Our point 2 is not discussed in the Working Paper, which also proceeds on the assumption that, contrary to the proposal we make in our point 6, local authority tenants will continue to be denied security of tenure. The other points we make are all referred to in the Working Paper.

[3] *Tarr v Tarr, ibid.*

matrimonial home when that is the sole relief which the wife claims. This seems to us to be a gap in the law; and it would become much wider if co-ownership became the rule, thus minimising the number of cases in which the court could deal with disputes entirely confined to occupation under the Act of 1967. We draw attention to this matter, the remedy for which might lie in the willingness and ability of the court to push the inherent jurisdiction a little beyond what has hitherto been considered its boundaries;

(3) under the Act of 1967 the spouse (we assume it, as before, to be the wife) without the proprietary title is assisted to protect the rights of occupation which the Act confers on her by a provision which entitles her to pay the rent, mortgage repayments and other outgoings. The payment shall " be as good "[1] as if made by the owner or tenant husband. The plain object of this provision is to put a deserted wife who remains in occupation of the house which belongs to the husband in his shoes so far as the landlord and the building society are concerned. The decision in *Penn v Dunn*[2] shows how this object may be frustrated. The husband was a statutory tenant who left his wife in occupation, and who, after paying the rent for a time, ceased to do so. The landlord obtained a possession order against the husband. The husband had the right (which he did not exercise) under the Rent Act 1968 to apply to the court to suspend the execution of the order and to restore his tenancy on such terms as to payment as to rent or otherwise as the court saw fit. The wife herself made such an application, but it was held that once the possession order had gone against the husband she herself ceased to be entitled to any rights against the landlord either under the Matrimonial Homes Act 1967 or the Rent Act 1968. We follow the Law Commission in recommending that the Rent Act 1968 be amended to give a right to apply to the court to a statutory tenant's spouse who is in occupation;

(4) the case of *Hastings and Thanet Building Society v Goddard*[3] illustrates how the Act of 1967 may be less efficient than was intended to protect the deserted wife against her husband's building society. It is convenient to postpone discussion of this point to Section 8;

(5) orders of the court regulating the occupation of the home can be made under the Matrimonial Homes Act 1967 only during the currency of the marriage. The injunction procedure discussed in sub-paragraph (2) above is available after dissolution of the marriage but is intrinsically unsuitable to deal long-term with occupation of the former matrimonial home as an element in the re-organisation of the affairs of the family. Yet the powers of the court under the Matrimonial Proceedings and Property Act 1970[4] which are intended for the comprehensive re-ordering and disposition of property and finances upon the dissolution of marriage contain no provision enabling the court to deal directly with occupation. The result is that

---

[1] Matrimonial Homes Act 1967, section 1(5).
[2] 1970, 2 QB 686.
[3] 1970, 1 WLR 1544.
[4] See Part 4, Section 4.

the court has to make an indirect approach, as by way, for example, of reducing the husband's maintenance payments on condition that he undertakes to allow the wife to remain in occupation. The court's powers to order financial provision under the Act of 1970 should include power to deal specifically and directly with rights of occupation in a former matrimonial home;

(6) local authority lettings are not subject to the Rent Acts with the result that local authority tenants do not enjoy the legal rights of security of tenure conferred on occupiers of privately rented accommodation within the Acts. We see no good reason for this distinction, and recommend that rights of security of tenure should be extended to lettings of premises in the public sector falling within the Rent Acts limits of rateable value. It will be more appropriate to elaborate this matter in Section 6;

(7) in granting a decree of divorce, the court may order that a tenancy which is subject to the Rent Acts should be transferred from one spouse to the other.[1] But since local authority lettings are not, as has just been mentioned, at present subject to the Rent Acts, this power of the court does not extend to such lettings. If our recommendation in sub-paragraph (6) above were adopted, this gap in the court's powers would be automatically filled. But we are of the view that even if local authority letting remains outside provisions for security of tenure, it would still be valuable in many cases for the court to be entitled to order the transfer of such a letting from one spouse to the other when terminating their marriage. This, too, is a matter which we take up in more detail in Section 6;

(8) if the husband held a Rent Act tenancy, then on his death the widow would become a statutory tenant by succession, but only if she was residing with her husband at his death. This may put the widow who had been deserted but not divorced in a worse position than if she had been both deserted and divorced, in that the court's power, mentioned in sub-paragraph (7) above, to transfer a Rent Act tenancy would apply to the latter, but not the former. We agree with the proposal of the Law Commission that a wife who has remained in occupation after her husband's departure should have the benefit of the transmission provisions under Schedule 1 of the Rent Act 1968;

(9) we support, also, the recommendation of the Law Commission that a widower should be given the same right to succeed to a statutory tenancy under Schedule 1 to the Rent Act 1968 as a widow.

JOINT TENANCIES

6.45 It was suggested to us in evidence (as it was to the Cullingworth Committee who said there was need for further consideration of the issue)[2] that some problems attendant on family breakdown would be reduced by the more general use of joint tenancies for husband and wife. The Women's

[1] Matrimonial Homes Act 1967, section 7.
[2] *Op cit*, pages 68–69, paragraphs 207–209.

National Advisory Committee of the National Union of Conservative and Unionist Associations saw several advantages:

> One local authority encourages husband and wife to have a joint tenancy, especially for higher rent property where there are three year agreements. This is advantageous for example, in the case of a widow with children, who has security of tenure, and there is no necessity to re-negotiate the agreement. In the case of a lower rent property also, there are advantages. In an unstable home where the father deserts for a period, and then returns for a bit, and goes off again, the wife's security of tenure remains, and especially if she is a reliable person in the eyes of the local authority, they will deal with her for the rent. When there is no alternative income, the Supplementary Benefits will pay the rent for her.

The National Executive Committee of the Labour Party also favoured joint tenancies to ensure that both partners have rights if a marriage breaks down.

6.46 We find that the advantages of the joint tenancy may easily be exaggerated, and that the arguments for and against are somewhat evenly balanced.[1] It may be said that if we are moving in principle towards a law of partnership, irrespective of direct financial contribution, in the ownership of the matrimonial home, so equally must the partnership concept hold good when the home is held only upon a tenancy. Further, the adoption of the joint tenancy as the standard form of rented accommodation for married couples would, it has been suggested, produce a simplification in the law. In particular, it would side-step all that complex machinery which, as we have earlier noted, it has been necessary to provide through the Matrimonial Homes Act 1967 to protect in her occupation a wife who has no legal interest in the home. Chiefly, perhaps, it is argued that there would be a highly beneficial psychological effect as the knowledge grew that under the normal form of tenure wives had equal entitlement with their husbands in the tenancy of the home. In the survey conducted for the Law Commission[2] it was discovered that only 14 per cent of the tenants interviewed had joint tenancies, most of which had been created at the suggestion of the landlord. In 82 per cent of the cases the husband was sole tenant, and the wife was the sole tenant in only 3 per cent. In 90 per cent of the cases where the tenancy was in one name only, the spouses had never discussed having it in joint names, and 64 per cent of them did not know that such a thing was possible. Correction of these imbalances through the joint tenancy arrangement would, it is said, give women a greater sense of security, and lessen the chances that in the breakdown situation they could be pressured or frightened into leaving the home.

6.47 As against these powerful considerations, it is to be remembered that the parallel between joint ownership and joint tenancy is more formal than it is real. The former relates to an asset of marketable value. For most people who own their houses, whether outright or on mortgage, the interest in the house represents their major or only capital asset. The acquisition of this asset has been made possible by the efforts in their respective spheres of both the husband and wife, and it is just that they should share in it. The protection which the wife and children may require when the family live in rented accommodation is protection in occupancy, which may be achieved irrespective of rights of ownership.

---

[1] The case in favour is best argued in D A Nevitt and J Levin: ' Social Policy and the Matrimonial Home', *op cit*, pages 345–369.

[2] J E Todd and L J Jones: *op cit*.

6.48 Next, if the husband and wife have been living in rented accommodation held on joint tenancy, and the wife and children are to have security of tenure after a matrimonial breakdown, it will still (unless she can obtain the co-operation of the husband) in most cases be necessary for the wife to exclude him from occupation, and, sooner or later, to get a sole tenancy for herself. The joint tenancy is a drawback in relation to the first object, and of little practical advantage in the achievement of the second.

6.49 To make joint tenancies the automatic or normal incident of a letting by a private landlord to a married couple, or of a letting to a previously single tenant when he marries, would require legislation. Such legislation would introduce as many complexities as might be eliminated. Nor would a joint tenancy do anything to ease the financial problems affecting a deserted or divorced wife left in occupation of privately rented accommodation; pressure for arrears of rent will probably be applied to her in any case, and it can only worsen her position to be legally liable for them as joint tenant.

6.50 On balance, therefore, we incline to the view that it is both impracticable and of dubious advantage to make joint tenancy the rule in private lettings to married couples, and that the various measures we recommend later in Sections 6 and 7 are more likely to achieve the ends it is sought to further when the landlord is the local authority.

THE IMPORTANCE OF GOOD LEGAL ADVICE

6.51 The reference we have made to some of the legal problems associated with the ownership and occupation of the home when a marriage breaks down is, even though limited, more than sufficient to indicate how intricate these problems can be. The people who need guidance and advice on these matters are ordinary citizens, often enough in a condition of great distress and confusion, and subject to emotional, and, all too frequently in the case of the women, physical pressures. The question of the home is likely to be one of their major preoccupations, dominating the future of themselves and the children. In this situation, when urgent, sympathetic and, above all, expert advice is a necessity, three obstacles stand in the way of its being given. First there may be a lack of consciousness that the law has any part to play in the solution of the problem, or that useful help can be obtained from expert advisers. Next, even when that realisation is present, many of the people concerned feel inadequate or even helpless about how to obtain the assistance they need. Finally, even when they do succeed in getting it, there is a good chance that it will be considerably less well-informed than it should be.

6.52 Social services departments, housing advice centres, citizens' advice bureaux and other welfare organisations should recognise that when they are asked to advise on housing, or about rights in the home, they are being asked to discharge an expert's function. For this purpose responsible staff are required, who ought to be specifically and adequately trained. But it should not be thought that the lack to which we are drawing attention is to be found exclusively among the lay advisers. There are many lawyers whose experience and knowledge do not equip them to give speedy and sound advice in these areas—both attributes being important in a situation of domestic crisis. We consider that far more attention should be given in the training of both branches of the legal profession to ensuring that they have an adequate working knowledge of this branch of the law which will affect so many of their clients.

6.53 We note with appreciation the recent growth of a variety of local legal centres through which lawyers, mostly young in their profession, are concentrating much energy to give legal assistance to the surrounding community, and who in the process of doing so are acquiring an altogether new level of competence in dealing with the legal problems, not least in housing, of the poor. The *Legal Action Group Bulletin*[1] has, since it started publication in 1972, provided a service in educating lawyers and social workers in the law affecting the lives of ordinary citizens; its articles on housing, in particular, demonstrate how much can be done to make the theory and practice of a complex branch of the law available for the benefit of those who have need of its protection. An important feature of the movement which these enterprises represent is that they are bringing together lawyers whose interests lie in the civil as much as or more than the criminal law with social workers and administrators attracted to the same field.

6.54 We here touch upon a subject which, while of great relevance to housing, is of broader application. In commenting on the future of the legal profession one of our number has elsewhere said:

> If the professional ideal is to demonstrate its capacity to stretch to the modern condition, the most important proof of it will be the ability of lawyers to minimise the number of (social) casualties who still go short of legal assistance. The lawyers must positively reach out to all those sections of the population whose way of life has not taught them the self-preserving instinct of calling on the family solicitor when they anticipate or encounter trouble. There are thousands of people who, when threatened with eviction, or denied a pension, or accused of shoplifting, or involved in any other of the crisis-laden situations which life is apt to inflict on them, still do not know what to do, or where or to whom to turn. The welfare state has given them rights; it is the responsibility of the legal profession to do all in its power to ensure that the individual shall have the opportunity to exercise those rights. The legal profession must actively search for the means to achieve this purpose, and must be strong in the determination not to be obstructed by ingrained customs derived from the past.[2]

SECTION 5—HOMELESS FAMILIES

6.55 It is abundantly clear from our evidence, from the findings of research and the conclusions of other committees in recent years that one-parent families are at special risk of becoming homeless. They include families in need not only of help in finding somewhere to live at a price they can afford, but often of skilled social work support and help in managing their financial affairs.

6.56 The problems of the homeless families have recently been investigated in depth by two studies of homelessness in London[3] and in South Wales and the

---

[1] The Bulletin is the publication of the Legal Action Group, an organisation sponsored by the Nuffield Foundation, which describes itself as " a group of lawyers and others who are concerned to improve legal services to the community, particularly to those living in deprived areas."

[2] Morris Finer: ' The Legal Profession', in Michael Zander (ed): *What's Wrong with the Law?* British Broadcasting Corporation, 1970.

[3] John Greve, Dilys Page and Stella Greve: *Homelessness in London*, Scottish Academic Press, 1971.

West of England.[1] The London study found that of families admitted to temporary accommodation in eight London boroughs between 1966 and 1969, 41 per cent were lone mothers with children.[2] Glastonbury's study in South Wales showed that of the families in the sample 30 per cent had one parent only; marital breakdown was the primary cause of temporary homelessness in 36 per cent of the study sample and domestic violence in another 13 per cent.[3]

6.57 Following these studies joint working parties[4] were set up to examine their findings and recommendations on provision of temporary and permanent accommodation, on social rehabilitation of the homeless and on action to prevent homelessness. The first report of the joint working party on homelessness in London concentrated on problems of families with dependent children, including one-parent families, because " it is this group which has most difficulty in finding and keeping accommodation and it is here that most damage can be done in terms of family breakdown, with long term consequences, if effective action is not taken."[5]

CIRCULAR ON HOMELESSNESS[6]

6.58 We found ourselves to be so much in agreement with the recommendations contained in the report of the joint working party which, although directly relating only to the Greater London area, were in many respects also of wide general application, that we had intended to suggest that the report be brought to the attention of all of the new county and district councils. At a very late stage in our deliberations, however, we learned of the intention of the Department of Health and Social Security, the Department of the Environment and the Welsh Office to issue, following upon consultation with the local authority associations, a circular on homelessness. This circular embodies policies which pay regard to all of the various studies of homelessness in recent years, including the report of the working party and the experience of those local authorities who are doing most for the homeless. We regard the circular as a key document not only on the subject of homelessness in general but also in respect of our particular concern, within that subject, for the condition and needs of one-parent families.

THE NATURE OF THE PROBLEM

6.59 For some families homelessness is a temporary misfortune resulting from some isolated event that will not recur or will soon be remedied, such as a loss or change of employment, or a financial crisis arising from entirely

---

[1] B Glastonbury: *Homeless near a thousand homes*, Allen and Unwin, 1971.

[2] *Op cit*, page 90.

[3] *Op cit*, Table II, page 48, Table IX, page 70.

[4] Membership consisted of officials of the Department of Health and Social Security and of the Department of the Environment and the representatives of local authority associations.

[5] Department of Health and Social Security: *First Report of Joint Working Party on Homelessness in London*, May 1971, paragraph 6.

[6] Department of the Environment (18/74), Department of Health and Social Security (4/74), and Welsh Office (34/74): *Homelessness*, February 1974. No comparable circular has been issued to local authorities in Scotland. They have, however, recently been given guidance on measures which they might adopt to avoid the necessity of eviction for rent arrears. A study of homelessness in Scotland, the results of which will be made available to the Morris Committee on Links between Housing and Social Work (see paragraph 6.35), is currently being undertaken by the Central Planning Research Unit of the Scottish Development Department.

exceptional circumstances. For most of those, however, who are compelled to seek temporary local authority accommodation, homelessness is the consequence of a deeper social or personal misfortune, very often connected with family breakdown, and such that the application to the local authority represents, as it were, a final defeat in a long struggle by a lone parent to find secure accommodation. If, on the other hand, the family is still intact when it is rendered homeless, irretrievable damage may be done if arrangements are not made for it to survive as a unit while in temporary accommodation. To provide for mother and children only, leaving the father to fend for himself, is to fail in making proper provision and to court the creation of a one-parent family. Nor should children ever be separated from their parents unless there are, exceptionally, compelling reasons other than the homelessness of the family as such for placing them elsewhere. We warmly welcome the advice in the circular on homelessness that accommodation from which the husband is excluded, or the separation of children from their families, is not acceptable.[1]

RESPONSIBILITY FOR TEMPORARY ACCOMMODATION

6.60 The need for coherent and concerted action makes it essential that the function of providing temporary accommodation for homeless families should be a housing authority function. This was one of the central recommendations in the reports above mentioned, and it has now been accepted and endorsed by the Department of the Environment, the Welsh Office and the Department of Health and Social Security in the circular on homelessness:

> It has been the normal practice hitherto for social services authorities . . . to provide temporary accommodation for homeless people pending the provision of permanant accommodation. Increasingly, this has led to the provision of dwellings by social services authorities, frequently by the allocation of houses to them for this purpose by the housing authority; . . . this practice is undesirable in principle, and should, except where there are short term compelling considerations to the contrary, be brought to an end as soon as possible.[2]

> In the view of the Secretaries of State, the provision (directly or indirectly) of adequate and suitable accommodation for the homeless should in future be undertaken as an integral part of the statutory responsibility of housing authorities for considering and taking into account the housing needs arising in their areas, in accordance with Part V of the Housing Act 1957.[3]

6.61 We welcome also the advice in the circular that above all for the priority groups, which include all families with children:

> It is the authority of the area where the need exists on whom the responsibility falls for helping to meet it. Once the authority are satisfied that people are homeless, they should accept responsibility for dealing with the case. The reason for homelessness whether eviction or housing stress, or any other reason—even lack of foresight—should not be a factor in deciding whether to accept responsibility. An authority should not decline to help those whose last proper home was not in their area, or who have moved away from the area and then returned to it.[4]

6.62 The circular goes on to say that, " In some cases, and particularly in areas of housing stress, however, it may well be appropriate to help people return to where they had been living previously, provided it has been established with

---

[1] *Ibid*, paragraph 12.
[2] *Ibid*, paragraph 25.
[3] *Ibid*, paragraph 26.
[4] *Ibid*, paragraph 37.

the local authority that there will be accommodation for them. "[1]   We agree that sometimes, in the interest of a particular family, the best course may well be to encourage and help them to return to their home areas.   But we strongly endorse the circular's proviso that this should never be done without specific arrangements with the authority in that area to ensure that suitable accommodation is available for them and that they are not turned away a second time. Above all, help for the family should never be lacking because of disagreement as to which authority is responsible.

PREVENTION OF HOMELESSNESS

6.63   It is far better to prevent homelessness than to have to cure it and we welcome the recognition the circular on homelessness gives to this policy.   It is difficult to over-emphasise the importance of preventive action to rescue families from the threat of homelessness before it happens.   The need of one-parent families for this kind of help is self-evident; but we attach equal importance to preventive measures to help two-parent families, as an important contribution to reducing the incidence of family breakdown.   We believe that this involves a general obligation on local authorities to avoid action which itself will create a problem of homelessness—as by evicting a family for which other accommodation then has to be found; and to be alert in seeking advance warning of prospective homelessness so as to be able to take whatever action is practicable to avoid it.

6.64   We believe that the comprehensive schemes for rent rebates and allowances under the Housing Finance Act 1972 and the Housing (Financial Provisions) (Scotland) Act 1972 should materially reduce the number of families with children who get behind with their rent, both in the public and private sectors.   But families who have difficulty over rent may well have difficulty over other debts, for heating or for hire purchase.   Wherever there is a problem of multiple debt it is important for the appropriate social services and housing authorities to be alerted to it as quickly as possible, so as to maximise the chance of effective action.[2]

6.65   Most housing authorities go to considerable lengths to avoid evicting their tenants for failure to pay rent regularly; but there are exceptions to the rule.   The circular indicates that " . . . most applicants for temporary accommodation . . . claim that their homelessness is due to eviction by local authorities for rent arrears. "[3]   The advice given in the circular, is that " . . . rent arrears, should (not) be treated simply as a financial problem attracting as routine penalties the issue of an eviction notice with the possible execution of any subsequent possession order.   To create homelessness with which the local authority itself will have to deal, can only make matters worse both for the tenant and his family and for the local authority. "[4]   We regret however that the circular did not go farther and give firm guidance to local authorities that

---

[1] *Ibid*, paragraph 37.

[2] Cash help through the social services department to families in difficulties is considered in Part 8, Section 3.   Rent arrears are considered specifically in Section 7 below.

[3] *Op cit*, Appendix, paragraph 2.   In fairness the circular also indicates (Appendix, paragraph 2) that the returns on which this statement is based are " . . . less than comprehensive," and " . . . that some people who claim to have been evicted by a local authority have left their homes on receipt of a notice to quit but before a possession order has been obtained or executed."

[4] *Op cit*, Appendix, paragraph 3.

eviction simply for rent arrears is no longer tolerable, and we recommend that such guidance should be issued forthwith. We should also like to see early consultation between housing and social services departments becoming the common practice everywhere; in particular, social workers should give maximum assistance to those families in arrears with their rent when it appears from such consultation that there is a risk of family breakdown. We deal elsewhere with other measures, such as the extended use of rent guarantees and of direct payments of rent by the Supplementary Benefits Commission to the housing authority, which would help to eliminate the risk of eviction for rent arrears.[1]

6.66 As regards families in the private sector, obtaining early warning of impending homelessness is far more difficult; for example, a private landlord might be using rent arrears as an excuse to seek to evict a tenant. It is likely to be harder to make effective arrangements with private landlords similar to those recommended for the public sector for early consultation with social services departments, the extended use of rent guarantees and of direct payment of rent by the Supplementary Benefits Commission. But where landlords are co-operative we see no reason why these opportunities should not be taken to prevent eviction. Steps should also be taken to encourage the family itself to seek advice and help. The housing aid centres proposed in the Seebohm Report,[2] which are already operating in some local authority areas, should have a useful part to play here; one of the functions of these centres is to provide greater assistance to individuals by examining in depth their housing needs and ways to meet them[3] and we are pleased that the Department of the Environment are encouraging authorities to provide them on a wider scale. We have noted the attention which is being given to the possibility of notification by the courts of cases where eviction is likely, and of similar arrangements by rent tribunals:[4] and we endorse the advice given in the circular on homelessness that local authorities " . . . should examine their arrangements for liaison with the Court so as to receive early warning of cases to be considered there and of any final possession order. "[5]

SECTION 6—LOCAL AUTHORITY TENANCIES[6]

ALLOCATION OF LOCAL AUTHORITY TENANCIES

6.67 Much of the evidence we received on the subject of local authority housing was concerned with discrimination in the allocation of council tenancies, either against one-parent families in general, or against unmarried mothers. Points systems and residential qualifications were both said to be particularly disadvantageous to one-parent families, who do not always score

---

[1] Section 7 below.

[2] Op cit, paragraph 391.

[3] The other functions of housing aid centres are to discover more information on individual and district housing requirements through consultation with people with different needs, thereby allowing housing policies to be of maximum benefit to the community; and to bring about a more rational use of both public and private housing resources.

[4] See the First Report of the Joint Working Party on Homelessness in London, op cit, pages 13–14, paragraphs 29–30.

[5] Op cit, Appendix, paragraph 5.

[6] In this Section the problems discussed concern tenancies only; questions concerning rents, in local authority and private housing, are discussed in Section 7.

the missing parent's points and who often have to move across local authority boundaries in search of accommodation (see Section 2 above). We take each of these aspects in turn below.

Discrimination

6.68 Our evidence suggested that unmarried mothers suffer particular discrimination from local authorities in some areas. In their written evidence to us, the National Council for the Unmarried Mother and Her Child said:

> Some housing authorities impose on unmarried mothers special conditions that they would not impose on ordinary families. A member of our Committee of Management was present when an unmarried mother was offered accommodation in an outer London borough. The mother was warned that she must " behave herself or be evicted ".[1]

In their oral evidence, the National Council for the Unmarried Mother and her Child said that there had been a slight change in the attitude of housing authorities, but in their view the tendency was still to regard unmarried mothers as suitable only to occupy poor housing stock.

6.69 A representative of the Association of Directors of Social Work in Scotland told us that in his area, when an unmarried mother applied for accommodation, the social work department might be asked for background information, and perhaps a rent guarantee. The Institute of Housing Managers confirmed the existence of discrimination against one-parent families, and expressed disapproval of it. They said:

> The Institute of Housing Managers are aware of the restrictions that some housing authorities place on the admission of one-parent families, especially unmarried mothers, to their housing lists and they can see no justification for this and recommend that all restrictions should be lifted that militate against families who are not only in housing need, but also have social and economic problems which make life difficult.

More recently, the Scottish Development Department have urged Scottish housing authorities to abolish all rules restricting access to the housing list.[2]

6.70 In recent years there has been increasing recognition of the principle that local authority housing should be available to all families on a basis of needs and not according to someone's notion of who constitute the " deserving." This has been stressed in particular by the Seebohm[3] and Cullingworth Committees. We think it useful to quote from the Cullingworth Report:

> We were surprised to find some housing authorities who took up a moralistic attitude towards applicants: the underlying philosophy seemed to be that council tenancies were to be given only to those who " deserved " them and that the " most deserving " should get the best houses. Thus unmarried mothers, cohabitees, " dirty " families and " transients " tended to be grouped together as " undesirable ". Moral rectitude, social conformity, clean living and a " clean " rent book on occasion seemed to be essential qualifications for eligibility—at least for new houses. Some attitudes may reflect public opinion . . . but this is a case where local authorities must lead public opinion.

---

[1] *Op cit*, paragraph 326.

[2] Scottish Development Department Circular 104/1972.

[3] *Op cit*, paragraph 396.

Whatever justification such attitudes may have had when council housing was on a small scale (which is by no means self-evident), they cannot be upheld in a situation where council housing forms a large and ever increasing proportion of the available rented accommodation. The simple fact is that it is becoming increasingly difficult for those excluded from publicly provided housing (on whatever grounds) to find satisfactory alternatives. . . . . Certainly ," respectable " families whose names have been on a housing list for many years feel aggrieved if they see " less deserving " families being rehoused. Nevertheless, these are the families who have the greatest difficulty in obtaining good accommodation elsewhere and they should . . . be given special priority for council housing.[1]

Our evidence does not enable us to assess the full extent of discrimination against lone parents, but we are in no doubt that some discrimination exists and that it should cease. We note with interest the contrast of attitude demonstrated in Norway and Sweden where it emerges from our investigations that private developers who buy land from local authorities are required to make some of their property available to one-parent families.

Points systems

6.71 Several individuals and organisations who gave evidence to us criticised the points systems used by some local authorities in allocating tenancies. Among these were the Women's National Commission, who thought it was necessary to evolve a system that was fair but did not act as an incentive to marriage breakdown. They said:

There are difficulties in giving priority in housing to families because of marriage breakdown; wrong incentives would be created if the disappearance of the father produced extra housing " points ". Single parent families are, however, often in special need. We believe that the single parent family should receive points as if the other parent were present in the home. Thus there would be no incentive for the father to " desert " but no loss of housing points on death or desertion of a parent.

The National Council for the Unmarried Mother and her Child, speaking generally of the situation in England and Wales, told us in oral evidence that they believed one-parent families were discriminated against because adults received more housing points than children.

6.72 Other evidence given to us suggested, however, that the points systems of many authorities did afford equal treatment to one-parent and two-parent families. The Association of Directors of Social Work in Scotland told us that, in general, they believed one-parent families were treated as having the same housing needs as two-parent families, although they added that they were sometimes housed in poorer accommodation and in areas predisposed to delinquency. We also heard from the Scottish Housing Managers that points systems in Scotland did not usually discriminate against one-parent families.

6.73 We are satisfied, however, that many points schemes, and in particular those which give points for overcrowding or bedroom deficiency, may be disadvantageous to the family which lacks a second adult member. Given the same number and ages of boys and girls in the family, the presence of another parent will make little or no difference to the accommodation required. We consider that a case is established, not for positive discrimination in favour of, but for equality of treatment for one-parent families in points systems.

[1] *Op cit*, paragraphs 96–97.

We recommend that where points systems are used in the allocation of housing, a lone parent should qualify for the same number of points as a married couple with a comparable family.[1]

Residential qualifications

6.74 We are particularly concerned about residential qualifications as a basis for the allocation of council tenancies because their imposition tends to create, and can indeed be so managed as deliberately to create, special difficulties and hardship for one-parent families. We have already referred in Section 2 to the fact that one-parent families move house more often than other families. The National Council for the Unmarried Mother and her Child told us in oral evidence that unmarried mothers often moved frequently in search of suitable accommodation, and that in many cases the first two years of a child's life were spent waiting for his mother to qualify for inclusion on a housing list. Separated families who go to another area meaning to stay temporarily with relatives and friends may find that they lose a place or a claim to a place on one housing list without being able to claim a place on another until they have served another qualifying period. We therefore welcome the fact that residential qualifications of all kinds are increasingly coming to be regarded as undesirable in the allocation of council tenancies.[2]

6.75 There are two different kinds of qualification which need be to distinguished and considered separately. First, there are qualifications for admission to the housing list. The Cullingworth Committee[3] have recommended (as have other committees) that there should be no residential qualification for admission to a housing list, and that no-one should be precluded from applying or being considered for a council tenancy on any ground whatever. Pointing out that only if all applications are admitted is it possible to assess needs, the committee urge that the right of admission to the list should become a statutory obligation.

6.76 This is already the situation in London, where residential qualifications for acceptance on a housing list have been abolished by the London Government Act 1963. Under section 22 of the Act, anyone living in a London borough may apply for housing accommodation as soon as he comes to live there and must be taken on that borough's housing list. If this can be done in London we see no reason why it should not become the rule throughout the country, and we recommend accordingly.

6.77 We were interested in another London practice which we think could be applied with advantage elsewhere. Applications from families living outside the Greater London area who wish to move into the area—for example, a serviceman and his family after his discharge—are made to the Greater London Council, which may itself then select a borough. The borough selected must add the application to its list. We recommend that discussions should be held

---

[1] Our overseas research showed that some of the other countries regard fatherless families as a priority group for public housing. In Denmark they are given the same consideration as married couples with the same number of children.

[2] See, for example, Scottish Office: *Homes for People, Scottish Housing Policy in the 1970s*, *op cit*, which says (paragraph 6):
   " Local policies requiring residential qualifications for admission to waiting lists are gradually, if too slowly, being replaced by more humane and realistic arrangements."

[3] *Op cit*, paragraph 169.

between the Department of the Environment and the new local authority associations to see whether a practice could be devised to enable either the Department of the Environment's regional officers or the new county authorities to act as arbitrators in similar situations arising outside Greater London.

6.78   But admission to a housing list, even if it is as of right, will not lead to the applicant obtaining accommodation if his selection from the list is unduly delayed or prevented by artificial barriers, such as a heavily weighted allocation of points for length of residence in the area or length of time for which the applicant has been registered on the list.   We call these barriers artificial because they have no necessary connection with housing need.   We recognise, however, that in areas of the most acute housing shortage, especially in Greater London, the local authorities may have no alternative to imposing residential qualifications of this kind.   As the standing Working Party on London Housing stated to the Cullingworth Committee in evidence:

> . . . where so many families have lived for years in overcrowded and insanitary conditions, it is not an easy decision to allow newcomers to the area (who on arrival have to accept perhaps even worse conditions) to be given priority for the little accommodation which the local authority can make available for families on the Waiting List.   For this reason, it is not felt at the present time the London Boroughs will reduce the common residential qualification.[1]

The Cullingworth Committee concluded:

> We are reluctantly forced to accept that in areas of extreme housing pressure some residential qualifications (*for rehousing as distinct from acceptance on the list*) may be unavoidable.[1]

Except in areas of acute housing shortage, however, we urge that the right policy as regards all families with children, whether thay are one-parent or two-parent families, is that after their admission to the housing list their claims be considered solely by reference to an assessment of need, with over-riding emphasis on the avoidance of separations between parents and children.

TRANSFER OF LOCAL AUTHORITY TENANCIES

6.79   When a family living in council accommodation separates, and where there are children of school age or below, the housing authority should speedily take action either to enable the parent who is caring for the children to stay in the family home, or, where strained relationships prevent such a course, to provide alternative housing elsewhere.   The parent continuing in charge of the family and needing this assistance will usually be the mother, although the case of the mother who deserts her husband and children is by no means infrequent.   We received evidence that the practices of some local authorities in these circumstances add to the stress and uncertainty of what is already an extremely disturbed family situation.   Our attention was drawn particularly to conditional transfers and rent arrears.   We deal with the question of conditional transfers in the following paragraphs but have recorded our views on this particular aspect of rent arrears in Section 7 where we look at the wider influence which rent arrears have on the lives of one-parent families.

---

[1] *Ibid*, paragraph 154.

Conditional transfers

6.80 We had evidence that it was the general practice of most authorities to refuse to transfer a tenancy to a separated wife before a separation order or divorce had been obtained. The Catholic Housing Aid Society have had a good deal of experience with this problem. In their evidence they included the following letter from a solicitor showing how a local authority may distinguish, for this purpose, between a maintenance order and a non-cohabitation order:

> . . . she obtained a Maintenance Order against her husband for the benefit of herself and her children as the result of her husband's cruelty to her being proved. But the Bench did not make a separation order.
>
> Nevertheless, Mrs A has left her husband and has taken the four children with her. She has also applied to the Greater London Council, her husband's landlord, to be allotted the former matrimonial home as tenant of the council in place of her husband. The Council has refused to comply with Mrs A's request on the grounds that (a) no Separation Order was made, and (b) that she now proposes to take divorce proceedings against her husband. It is the policy of the council not to make any change in tenancy in such a case before the matrimonial proceedings have been brought to finality. It seems that such a change did take place some years ago, as a result of which the council was strongly criticised by the court. Representations have been made, we believe by others besides ourselves on Mrs A's behalf, but the council finds itself unable to change its attitude.
>
> The result is that Mrs A and her four children remain inadequately housed.[1]

The Catholic Housing Aid Society were later informed that the mother and children would be " rehoused after the divorce in about a year's time."[2] The Society also quoted from a letter from the Greater London Council setting out their policy on the transfer of tenancies:

> It is, generally speaking, true to say that in cases where divorce is pending between a tenant and his wife, the council is reluctant to intervene in the matter of the tenancy of a dwelling unless the husband is prepared voluntarily to relinquish his tenancy in favour of his wife. This, we know, is not the case with Mr K, and in view of the unhappy features of this family's affairs over the past years, the council feels unable to take action in advance of the hearing of the divorce action. With regard to your suggestion . . . to provide temporary accommodation. In the event of Mrs K winning her divorce case, and getting care, custody and control of the children, the council would undertake to provide her and the children with accommodation suitable for their needs. It is unlikely that (the present flat) would be available.[3]

6.81 Family disputes undoubtedly tend to put housing authorities in a difficult situation. They have a proper reluctance to intervene precipitately or in a way which may appear to prejudge an issue within the jurisdiction of the courts. We consider, however, that the strict application of a rule of thumb which prohibits the transfer of a tenancy until after a separation order or divorce decree has been granted produces delays and injustice which sometimes can be avoided; there are many cases in which a more active policy could produce a prompt and fair result without exposing the authority to the criticism of being interventionist.

---

[1] Catholic Housing Aid Society: *Evidence to the Finer Committee*, page 68.

[2] It should be added that there is no need for a divorce to take a year. Most of the delays in the divorce jurisdiction are caused by the parties or their advisers failing to press the suit forward. In particular it should be known that no matter concerned with children, including appeals from magistrates, need be delayed for more than a very short time in the High Court, and will be heard immediately if there are circumstances of special urgency. It is the litigant's not the law's delays which are the cause of obstruction in the Family Division.

[3] *Ibid*, page 71.

6.82   In the first place there are many cases in which the parties would agree that the breakdown is irretrievable and that it is inevitable that the wife and children must remain in the matrimonial home. In such cases, the local authority might well be justified, after making the necessary enquiries, in transferring the husband's tenancy with his consent long before the court has formalised the separation, or even if the court never formalises it.

6.83   The chances of an agreement of this kind being reached between the spouses would very often be improved if the local authority in their new comprehensive role saw it as their responsibility to find alternative accommodation for the husband, whenever this was possible. Both sides often recognise that the sensible course is for the wife and children to stay put, and for the husband to go elsewhere; but the difficulty is for the husband to find somewhere else to live, especially if his work, or the proximity of his own friends and relations restrict the area to which it is possible for him to go. Many housing authorities make no provision, or only reluctant provision to help a " single " man in such circumstances. We regret that this should be so. Once it is clear that a real breakdown has occurred, the authority could play a valuable role in helping the man who asks for it to find accommodation elsewhere (not necessarily in the public sector)—thus easing the burden of the breakdown on the family as a whole, giving a measure of tranquility to the wife and children, and promoting the ability and inclination of the husband to maintain them.

6.84   Then again, if, as seems to us to be fundamental, the local authority adopt the general principle that the tenancy should follow the children, there are very many cases in which that principle could be applied before the court makes a final order in the matrimonial dispute. For example, a husband respondent in a divorce suit may be vigorously defending the suit and disputing his liability to maintain his wife without traversing the wife's prayer in her petition for divorce for custody of the children. In many such cases the authority would be justified in transferring the tenancy to the wife without the consent or against the will of the husband, and before the hearing of the suit.

Power for the court to order transfer of local authority tenancies

6.85   As we have previously mentioned[1] the Matrimonial Homes Act 1967, section 7, contains a valuable power for the court to order the transfer from one spouse to another of the benefit of tenancies to which the Rent Acts apply. The power arises at the time when the court is terminating the marriage. The section further provides that when the court so deals with a tenancy it may:

> direct that both spouses shall be jointly and severally liable to discharge or perform any of all of the liabilities and obligations in respect of the dwelling house . . . which have at the date of the order fallen due to be discharged or performed by one only of the spouses.[2]

The section makes provision also for the landlord to be given an opportunity of being heard before the court makes any order.[3]

---

[1] Section 4 above.

[2] Matrimonial Homes Act 1967, section 7(4). This provision well illustrates how, in the absence of some other rule, there are no legal grounds for seeking to recover from a wife arrears of rent due from her husband. This is discussed in Section 7 below.

[3] The Matrimonial Homes Act does not apply to Scotland and there is no comparable legislation (see footnote to the heading of Section 4).

6.86 Since the Rent Acts do not at present apply to local authority tenancies, it follows that the power of the court to order a transfer under the Act of 1967 does not extend to such tenancies.[1] We can see no good reason why it should not apply to premises of a rateable value that would bring them within the Acts when privately let, if let by the local authority.[2] The result would be that upon divorcing a husband who holds a tenancy from the council of the matrimonial home, the wife could request the court to transfer that tenancy to herself. The court would, as under section 7 of the Act of 1967, have power, in transferring the tenancy, to make an order making the wife liable together with the husband for all or part of any rent arrears whenever the circumstances made that seem proper; and the local authority would be entitled to be heard on the wife's application. If the court transferred the tenancy to the wife, she would, as a council tenant, enjoy no greater degree of future security against the council as landlord than her husband had done previously; but she would, of course, be treated as responsibly as any other tenant of a public authority. We believe that this extension of the power of the court would, by its very existence, as well as its exercise, do much to ensure that in difficult and disputed cases local authority tenancies would indeed follow the children.

SECURITY OF TENURE FOR LOCAL AUTHORITY TENANTS

6.87 Nearly all council tenants are granted weekly tenancies. They then become entitled in law to not less than four weeks' notice to quit, but to no further security of tenure such as the Rent Acts provide for the tenant of a private landlord to whom a letting is made of premises within the specified rateable values. The Rent Act 1968 in fact excludes from its protection lettings from the Crown, government departments, local authorities, the Commission for the New Towns, the Housing Corporation, a development corporation, a charitable housing trust, or, in some circumstances, a housing association.[3]

6.88 The reasons for the exclusion of council tenancies from the statutory protection appear to be that the landlord in these cases is a democratically elected public body which can be trusted to behave reasonably in dealing with its tenants, and which also may find itself in a position where its duty to the tenant conflicts with some other public duty, to resolve which it has to retain a free hand.[4] As the court said in one of the leading cases, local authorities " may be trusted . . . to exercise their powers in a public-spirited and fair way in the general public interest ".[5]

6.89 Whatever former validity it may have had, we do not find this reasoning to be nowadays convincing. We have seen[6] that approaching one third of the

---

[1] The question of the application of the Rent Acts in general to local authority tenancies is discussed in paragraphs 6.87–6.90 below.

[2] This would be an automatic result of carrying out our wider recommendation in paragraph 6.90. But the section 7 power of transfer can and ought to be extended as we have suggested even if the larger recommendation is not implemented.

[3] There is a legal argument that the protection of the Rent Acts is denied to a local authority tenant only when the authority want possession for the purpose of exercising their *housing* function, so that if, for example, they want possession in order to widen the road the tenant can rely on the Rent Acts. The argument is deployed by D A Nevitt and J Levin in ' Social Policy and the Matrimonial Home', *op cit*, but has not been tested in court.

[4] For a further explanation see the report of the debate in the House of Commons on 1 March 1972, Official Report, Volume 832, columns 702–714.

[5] *LCC v Shelley* (1947) 2 All ER 720, at 722.

[6] Section 2 above.

housing stock in England and Wales and well over half in Scotland is rented from local or New Town authorities. A single local authority may now own thousands of dwellings in one area. This may involve a degree of monopolisation which makes if difficult to find low-rented accommodation of any other kind. The scale of the public housing enterprise is such as to make special concern for the problems of individual tenants no easier for the authority to keep in the forefront of its policy than it may be for a private landlord. And we note later[1] that there is no reason for supposing that pressure upon deserted or divorced wives to pay arrears of rent owed by their husbands is any less in the public than it is in the private sector. Threat of eviction for rent arrears is of particular concern to us, because accumulation of arrears (given, especially the relatively low rents in council property) is almost a barometer of marital disharmony. When all is well, the husbands bring their wages home, and wives pay the rent with regularity. When things go wrong, the expenditure patterns of the household are disrupted, and rent is an early casualty. By the time the breakdown results in separation, the arrears may be considerable.

6.90 In all these circumstances, we can see no continuing good reason for depriving local authority or New Town tenants[2] of the basic protection in security of tenure which the Rent Acts give to the tenants of private landlords. It may be that the extension of this protection to tenants in the public sector would need to be accompanied by some extension of the grounds upon which the court can order possession against a Rent Act tenant in the case of a private letting. These grounds include arrears of rent, causing a nuisance, neglecting the property, unlawfully sub-letting it, and other grounds which would be equally applicable in the case of a local authority or New Town letting, and would enable the authority to get rid of an undesirable tenant. But it might be appropriate to give additional grounds for possession to a public authority, for example, that the premises are under-occupied and they have offered smaller accommodation suitable to the tenant's needs. These are matters of detail. Our recommendation in principle is that security of tenure similar to the Rent Acts protection be extended to tenancies in the public sector. It should be noted that one effect would be always to interpose the court between an authority wanting possession and a tenant unwilling to go—a safeguard that we think would be of special value when the dispute with the authority was connected with or happened to coincide with some breakdown of marital relations within the home.

SECTION 7—RENTS

THE HOUSING FINANCE ACT 1972 AND THE HOUSING (FINANCIAL PROVISIONS) (SCOTLAND) ACT 1972

6.91 A number of studies, as well as the evidence we received, have demonstrated that fatherless families tend to pay higher rents[3] than two-parent families, and because of their generally lower incomes to be spending a higher

---

[1] Section 7.

[2] In a detailed consideration of the recommendation we make in this paragraph it would be necessary to consider how far it was necessary or desirable to continue to deprive tenants of security of tenure against some of the other types of landlord in the privileged list, for example, housing associations.

[3] In paragraphs 6.91–6.95 rents are net of rates and other costs.

389

proportion of their income on rent. (See Section 2.) But an important new factor in this situation is the Housing Finance Act 1972 and the Housing (Financial Provisions) (Scotland) Act 1972 and the comprehensive schemes of rent rebates and allowances which have now come into operation under them.[1] It is still too early for the full effect of these schemes to be assessed, but provided tenants take up the rebates and allowances to which they are entitled they should considerably ease the rent burden on many one-parent families.

6.92 Under the Acts of 1972 the amount of a family's rent rebate or allowance depends on the excess or deficit of their weekly income in relation to their needs. The Acts prescribe a " needs allowance " which varies with the size of the family. The English bill, when it first came before Parliament, provided a lower needs allowance for a lone parent than for a married couple with the same number of children, with the result that a one-parent family would have been entitled to a substantially lower rebate or allowance than a two-parent family at the same income level. This was out of line with the provisions of schemes such as family income supplements, which from the outset has treated one-parent and two-parent families alike. By this time we had ourselves come to the conclusion, discussed elsewhere in this Report,[2] that although there are some savings, such as for food and clothing, when one partner is absent from the home, these may be offset to some extent against the additional expenditure one-parent families face for items like child care and in paying for work normally done by the missing parent, while housing costs are often greater. We represented to the Secretary of State for the Environment that the lower needs allowance for the one-parent family in the rent rebate and allowance schemes was an anomaly which was inconsistent with the central policy of the scheme—to relieve need. The bill was later amended so that, when it became law, the needs allowances for one-parent and two-parent families were the same.

6.93 The essence of the scheme is that it provides a basic needs allowance for a family with one child of £23·75 (from 1 October 1973). Under the Acts a family with income at this level is required to pay only the minimum rent (this is £1·00 or 40 per cent of the rent, whichever is the greater). For every £1 by which a family's income is below the needs allowance, the rent is further reduced by 25p. Where income exceeds the needs allowance an additional 17p rent is payable for each £1 of additional income.

6.94 The rent allowances now payable by local authorities to tenants in furnished accommodation will assist many one-parent families, particularly the high proportion of lone mothers who, as we have shown (in Section 2), live in furnished flats or rooms. But it should be noted that the proportion of the rent of furnished accommodation eligible to be met by an allowance is the local authority's estimate of the fair rent for the accommodation if it were let unfurnished and provided only with the services which qualify to be met by a rent allowance, plus 25 per cent. Therefore, although extension of rent

---

[1] Under the Housing Finance Act 1972, sections 18 and 19, and the Housing (Financial Provisions) (Scotland) Act 1972, sections 15 and 16, local authorities were required to introduce rent rebate schemes for housing authority tenants by 1 October 1972 and rent allowance schemes for private tenants in unfurnished accommodation by 1 January 1973. For furnished tenancies the Furnished Lettings (Rent Allowances) Act 1973 required schemes to operate by 29 April 1973 in England and Wales and by not later than 1 October 1973 in Scotland.

[2] Part, 5, Section 2.

allowances to furnished tenancies was a welcome improvement it will by no means eliminate the problem of high rent for families obliged to live in furnished accommodation. We make a recommendation later in this Section about the treatment of furnished rents by the Supplementary Benefits Commission; and the improvements in supplementary benefits and the new social security benefit we recommend in Part 5 will, of course, improve the position of many one-parent families. But the real solution is for families to be assisted to leave the furnished sector for more suitable accommodation. This view has been one of the factors underlying a number of our other recommendations, such as those for a wider approach to their housing responsibilities by local authorities (Section 3) and on allocation of council tenancies (Section 6).

6.95 We were interested to see that most of the other countries into which we enquired had schemes of rent allowances for which one-parent families were eligible, and some of them gave special recognition to one-parent families. But none of the schemes which were studied appears to us to make better provision for helping one-parent families with their rents than do the Housing Finance Act 1972 and the corresponding Scottish legislation. In Sweden means-tested housing allowances are available to families with children and can amount from 43 per cent to 61 per cent of the cost of unfurnished housing of a reasonable standard. In West Germany lone parents earning up to the level of male average wages are usually entitled to a rent allowance. Denmark uses a rent allowance formula weighted in favour of one-parent families and a lone parent with two children may be eligible for an allowance amounting to as much as 70 per cent of the rent, 5 per cent more than a couple with two children. In the Netherlands families with average incomes and below do not pay more than one seventh to one sixth of their income in rent.

Variation of fair rents in local authority housing

6.96 There is one respect of particular concern to one-parent families in which we should like to see the Housing Finance Act 1972 amended. Section 66 of the Act,[1] dealing with the variation of fair rents for housing authority dwellings, provides that certain changes of circumstance shall not be accompanied by increases in rent. These circumstances include the cases where:

(1) on the death of a tenant, a member of that tenant's family who was then residing with him is granted a new tenancy; and

(2) there is a change of tenant, or a new tenancy, and the tenant is the wife or husband of the previous tenant, and is treated by the authority as deserted by the other.

These provisions are, in our view, too narrow. We can see no good reason for permitting the authority to increase the rent to a widow to whom they grant a tenancy of the home she occupies when the former tenant, her husband, dies, even though they were not at that time living together. Further (and in particular in the light of our recommendation in paragraph 6.86) we can see no good reason why the second restriction on the power to raise the rent should be limited to cases which the authority treats as involving a desertion. If, say, a tenancy is granted or transferred to the wife after she has been divorced

[1] There is no comparable provision in the Housing (Financial Provisions) (Scotland) Act 1972.

391

from her husband, who was the former tenant, or after they have separated without any desertion, as when they part consensually, she should be equally protected from the authority's treating the occasion as one which affords them the opportunity to increase the rent.

THE SUPPLEMENTARY BENEFITS COMMISSION AND HIGH RENTS[1]

6.97 In the great majority of cases (over 99 per cent of those in which a regular weekly benefit was in payment in November 1972) the amount of supplementary benefit paid to a claimant who is a householder includes an amount to cover his housing costs in full, as well as the appropriate scale rate and any discretionary additions. But there are some cases where housing costs are not fully allowed for. The statutory authority under which the Commission may decide to meet less than the actual housing cost is contained in paragraph 13 of Schedule 2 to the Ministry of Social Security Act 1966 (as amended by paragraphs 5 and 6 of Schedule 9 to the Housing Finance Act 1972 and paragraphs 5 and 6 of Schedule 9 to the Housing (Financial Provisions) (Scotland) Act 1972). This provides for the assessment of supplementary benefit requirements to include the net rent payable (as defined) or " such part of that amount as is reasonable in the circumstances ".

6.98 The Commission have explained their policy on high rents in considerable detail in the Supplementary Benefits Handbook.[2] Paragraphs 44–46 state:

44. In deciding whether a rent is reasonable or not local officers ask themselves:
    (1) whether the rent is reasonable for the accommodation provided;
    (2) whether the accommodation is reasonable for the claimant.

45. The rent is regarded as reasonable for private accommodation where it has been fixed by the Rent Officer, Rent Assessment Committee or Rent Tribunal or is in line with rents fixed for comparable accommodation in the district. Rents charged by a local authority are generally regarded as reasonable for the accommodation though not necessarily for the claimant.

46. In considering whether or not the accommodation is reasonable for the claimant the following principles are observed:
    (1) a claimant is not expected to lower his standard of accommodation unless that standard is clearly higher than is provided, say, in average Local Authority accommodation in the neighbourhood;
    (2) if the accommodation is expensive and unnecessarily large, it would be contrary to the public interest if supplementary benefit were paid to enable him to remain there indefinitely;
    (3) it would similarly be against the public interest if the Commission met a very high rent, eg for a luxury flat in an expensive neighbourhood.

With these considerations in mind, it is the Commission's policy where rent is regarded as unreasonably high to suggest removal to cheaper accommodation, or, where practicable, reduction of the claimant's outgoings, for example, by larger contributions to rent from non-dependants in the household. The Commission may pay the full rent for a short period while alternative arrangements are pending, but thereafter the rent allowance is reduced to the level they regard as reasonable.

---

[1] In paragraphs 6.97–6.102 " rents " or " housing costs " means rent plus rates.

[2] Department of Health and Social Security, Supplementary Benefits Commission: *Supplementary Benefits Handbook*, Supplementary Benefits Administration Papers 2, HMSO, revised November 1972.

6.99   Many submissions of evidence drew our attention to the hardship which could be caused to lone parents who are supplementary benefit claimants by the restriction of the amount allowed by the Commission for rent.   The Association of Directors of Social Services told us that there seemed to be local rules for deciding the maximum rent allowance which would be regarded as reasonable.   Their representatives said it was ridiculous in their view to suggest that families should move to cheaper accommodation when often such accommodation simply did not exist.   They suggested that the Commission's officials should consult local social workers before reaching a decision to restrict the amount allowed for rent.   The Circle Trust also told us that they thought the Commission's attitude toward high rents for private accommodation was unreasonable; it was unrealistic to urge women to seek cheaper accommodation.   Oxfordshire County Council Working Party commented:

> From the point of view of a private landlord, a single person with children is unlikely to be regarded as a desirable tenant . . . .   This fact has two consequences: it limits the range of accommodation to which single parent families would have access, even if they could afford the rents demanded, and it leads to higher rents being demanded of them than of other families for similar accommodation.   Our impression is that the Supplementary Benefits Commission makes little allowance for the weak bargaining position of the single parent family in applying the " reasonable rent " rule.   As a result, while the great majority of claimants have their full rent taken into account in assessing their requirements, many single parent families in privately rented accommodation do not.

6.100   We believe that there has been a considerable improvement in the situation since evidence on this subject was submitted to us.   The publication of the Supplementary Benefits Handbook explains policy both for claimants and officials.[1]   There have also been changes in consequence of the introduction of rent rebates and allowances.   In practice the rents of all supplementary benefit claimants who are local authority tenants are now met in full by way of a rent rebate (generally of 60 per cent) and inclusion in the supplementary benefit assessment of the minimum rent (that is, the remaining 40 per cent).   The same applies to the majority of claimants in private unfurnished accommodation where rents will generally be met in full up to the fair rent level by way of supplementary benefit provision and the payment of a rent allowance by the local authority.[2]

6.101   These new arrangements reflect the fact that the Housing Finance Act 1972 requires local authorities to assess a " fair rent " for their own dwellings (in Scotland to fix rents at a level sufficient to balance housing revenue accounts).   They are also required in calculating rent allowances for tenants in private dwellings to consider whether the dwelling is larger than the tenant reasonably requires and whether the rent is exceptionally high in relation to other comparable tenancies in the area.   In the latter case they may recognise

---

[1] See paragraph 6.98 above.

[2] From 1 April 1974 housing authorities will no longer determine and grant individual rent rebates and rent allowances to continuing recipients of supplementary benefit (other than those who could benefit from them because they are " wage-stopped ").   Instead, they will meet their responsibility under the Housing Finance Act by making a bulk payment to the Department of Health and Social Security whose payment of supplementary benefit will have regard to the whole of the tenant's rent.   This is a purely administrative change which will not affect the total amount of help with rent available to tenants.

less than the full rent as qualifying for a rent allowance.[1] We have been assured by the Supplementary Benefits Commission that a tenant in receipt of supplementary benefit whose rent they had been meeting in full before a local authority rent allowance was awarded to him would not be reassessed on the basis of any lower amount accepted as reasonable by the local authority; in other cases the Commission would follow the local authority's decision on a fair rent for the accommodation.

6.102 The significant problem which remains is that of tenants in furnished accommodation. The Housing Finance Act 1972 does not apply to such tenants while they are receiving supplementary benefit.[2] In their case the Commission are not bound to add as much for rent as the local authority would have recognised as qualifying for a rent allowance. We are assured by the Commission, however, that they would always regard as reasonable whatever amount the local authority would recognise for rent allowance purposes and that they would always welcome any advice local authorities can give on this point. However, as explained in paragraph 6.94 local authorities' calculations based on their estimate of a fair rent if the accommodation were unfurnished may well fall short of the rent actually being charged, so that even where the amount that would be recognised for rent allowance is known the full rent might not be met. We understand that the number of families affected is not large. Probably something of the order of 1,000 one-parent families and about the same number of two-parent families in furnished accommodation were not having their rents met in full in November 1972.[3] This would represent less than 1 per cent of all one-parent and of all two-parent families respectively receiving supplementary benefit. These are the families who, we believe, have the greatest difficulty in finding accommodation at a reasonable rent. The great majority of them are only in furnished accommodation because they can find nothing else. We urge on the Commission the need to give full weight to these difficulties in deciding whether to accept the rent as reasonable.

THE SUPPLEMENTARY BENEFITS COMMISSION AND DIRECT PAYMENT OF RENT

6.103 The Commission's general policy is to pay the benefit due, including the amount for rent, to the claimant and to leave him to pay his rent in the same was as he would have to do if he were not receiving benefit. But the Commission have discretion to pay benefit, in whole or in part, to a third party " where it appears to the Commission that it is necessary for protecting the interests of the claimant or of his dependants . . . or where the claimant so requests."[4,5]

---

1 Housing Finance Act 1972, Schedule 3, paragraph 17(2), and Housing (Financial Provisions) (Scotland) Act 1972, Schedule 2, paragraph 17(2).

2 The Rent Allowances (Qualified Persons) Regulations 1973, SI 1973/676, and the Rent Allowances (Qualified Persons) (Scotland) Regulations 1973, SI 1973/788.

3 Previously published figures on numbers of unmet rents are now believed to have been over-stated and the Commission are in the process of obtaining more reliable information.

4 Ministry of Social Security Act 1966, section 17(3).

5 Circular on Homelessness, op cit, Appendix, paragraph 2, draws attention to the direct payment of the rent element in supplementary benefits in suitable cases as one of the measures which can be taken to prevent the accumulation of rent arrears which may lead to eviction.

6.104 The Commission explained in evidence to us their policy in relation to making payments direct to landlords as follows:

> On the one hand a claimant who is entitled to supplementary benefit should have the right to lay out his weekly income just like any other member of the community. On the other, there is the need to avoid additional expenditure of public funds resulting from misapplication of payments of supplementary benefit made for rent and rates. The Commission attempt to achieve a balance as between these considerations.
>
> It will be seen that the beneficiary's consent is not necessary and this is not sought where direct payment is judged to be appropriate. As the great majority of claimants pay their rent regularly, direct payment of the rent to the landlord in all cases would seem to be unjustified as a general policy as well as being contrary to the terms of the Act. Where, however, it is evident that the welfare of the tenant or his dependants can only be safeguarded by direct payment of rent this is done. The Commission take the view, however, that it would be unwise to be too ready to pay rent direct when a claimant is in arrears with his rent, especially when he is only temporarily out of work, as he might thereby lose the habit of regular rent budgeting with unsatisfactory results both for the landlord and the tenant when the claimant returns to work. Supervision and control are therefore often preferred to direct payment as a means of ensuring that rent payments are not misapplied. Often a warning to the claimant is sufficient remedy. In other cases, it is sometimes decided to withhold the rent portion of the benefit and to pay it weekly at the local office on production of evidence by the claimant that the rent has been paid from the remainder of his income. If these methods are unsuccessful, or seem likely to be unsuccessful, the local office would consider whether to use the special powers in Section 17(3). In 1969 direct payments of rent were being made in more than 7,000 cases, the sum involved being about £1 million a year. Rates were being paid direct in about 1,300 cases, but the amount involved is not known.

6.105 Evidence we received suggested that:

(1) the Commission should be more ready to pay rent direct, especially to private landlords;

(2) the readiness of local offices to pay rent direct varied considerably;

(3) the practice occasionally adopted of paying rent direct quarterly in arrears made difficulties for private landlords and for the tenants.

Some of our witnesses took the view that the Commission's reluctance to apportion money made it more difficult for women to budget. They thought the payment of rent direct was a valid way to help families in difficulties. The Catholic Housing Aid Society, an organisation with considerable experience of rehousing one-parent families, said in oral evidence that if only the mother could have the rent paid direct for a short period she could learn the limits of her income, and the extent to which the non-rent part of her supplementary allowance would stretch. The Scottish Council for the Unmarried Mother and her Child told us in oral evidence that while the payment of rent direct to the landlord was a helpful way of ensuring rent was paid, they did not support it as a general rule; it would be a dangerous restriction of personal choice if it was arranged otherwise than at the beneficiary's own request.

6.106 We do not think there is any easy answer to this problem. We accept that the Commission should retain discretion in this matter. We think, however, that it is important that in looking at each family's problems the Commission should work closely with social services departments and, in the case of public housing, with the housing authority, and should look to them for advice on the best way of tackling the rent problems of particular families. We are also concerned at the apparent discrepancy of practice between different social security offices and we consider that further efforts should be made to bring about consistency in this respect in all local offices administering the supplementary benefits scheme. In particular we consider that:

(1) where the tenant, with the support of the social services department, or the housing authority or an appropriate voluntary organisation, requests the Commission to pay the rent direct, the application should (other than in exceptional circumstances) be granted as a matter of course;

(2) where the social services department and landlord, in the long-term interests of the tenant, ask for the rent to be paid direct there should be greater willingness on the part of the Commission to do so;

(3) any decision to refuse to pay rent direct to the landlord should be taken at a senior level in the Commission so as to improve the consistency of decisions;

(4) even where the Commission's normal procedure is to pay rent quarterly in arrears they should be ready to make payments at shorter intervals at the landlord's request.

LOCAL AUTHORITIES AND RENT ARREARS

6.107 The existence of rent arrears is sometimes used by housing departments as a reason for not accepting families in homeless families' accommodation for permanent rehousing. There are also occasions on which transfers and exchanges are forbidden until rent arrears are cleared,[1] and it is common for tenants moving into local authority housing to be asked to produce a clean rent book. There may be good housing management reasons for these practices but there are many occasions when their application is not in the best interest of the family, or in the long term, of the housing authority itself. We consider that housing authorities should always be flexible and careful in applying such practices, which should be considered in the light of our earlier recommendation that local authorities should no longer evict families simply for rent arrears.[2]

6.108 Where there is an immediate risk of homelessness, financial assistance may be given under section 1 of the Children and Young Persons Act 1963 to clear rent arrears, but only where such assistance is required to diminish the need to receive children into or to keep them in care. But there is some doubt whether section 1 can be used to clear rent arrears where a family is not at immediate risk of homelessness, even though no other source of financial aid may be available to prevent eviction or to secure rehousing. Similar doubt about the operation of section 1 arises in relation to cash payments generally and we recommend later that either by guidance clarifying the section, or if necessary by legislation, it should be made clear that there does not have to be an immediate and pressing prospect of the child being received into care before a cash payment is made.[3]

---

[1] A particular instance of this of special interest to one-parent families is discussed in paragraphs 6.111–6.112 below.
[2] See Section 5.
[3] See Part 8, Section 3.

6.109   But obviously there are limits to the extent to which tenants can be assisted with rent arrears. It is important therefore that every effort should be made to ensure that families are not allowed to build up arrears beyond their capacity to pay. Housing management has a major part to play in bringing to notice families who have difficulty in meeting rent while there is still time for effective help (which may not necessarily be financial) to be given to them.

Rent guarantees

6.110   In particular we should like to see social services departments take wider advantage of section 1 of the Children and Young Persons Act 1963 by providing rent guarantees.[1] There can be no doubt that this could help both in the short term to avert crises caused by the threat of eviction and in the longer term to keep families united who may by their unassisted efforts be unable to keep a roof over their heads. There should be close contact between social welfare and housing authorities in reaching agreed policies on rent guarantees and field staffs should be clear on these policies and their purpose. The restricted use which has until now been made of rent guarantees seems to be due to an over-cautious interpretation of section 1 of the Act of 1963. It is reassuring, in this connection, that the circular on homelessness underlines the need to make rent guarantees available, when appropriate, in both public and private sectors.[2]

Clearance of rent arrears as condition of transfer of tenancy

6.111   We had evidence, oral and written, that it is usual for local authorities to insist on the discharge of any rent arrears incurred by the husband, and frequently to make this a condition of transferring the tenancy to the wife. One lone mother who wrote to tell us of her experiences on marriage breakdown said:

> I had a written undertaking from . . . Housing Committee that as my matrimonial order gave me custody of the 11 year old child and contained a non-cohabitation clause, they would give me the tenancy of our Council house, *providing* arrears of rent, deliberately incurred by my husband, before leaving, were cleared. At the same time as I received written word of this from the Housing Committee, I received notice to quit and had a most unpleasant, and at the start, bullying interview with the Rent Inspector about how easy it would be to have me and the child evicted if the arrears were not paid forthwith . . . . Anyway, I was able to get the arrears paid, solely to ensure I was granted a fresh tenancy, by SSAFA and I was given a new rent book clear of all arrears.

The representative of the Scottish Housing Managers told us that, in general, housing departments take the view that, if a wife and family remain in the family home, there is an obligation on the wife to make good the arrears. The representative said that in the normal course of events it is the duty of housing managers to seek payment of rent arrears. They said that they believed that wives had almost invariably set money aside to pay them. In their own areas it was normal practice to get settlement of rent arrears before the tenancy was transferred. This approach was, we were told, in keeping with the Scottish tradition that wives managed the family budget, and with the view that the rent was a family responsibility.

---

[1] See Part 8, Section 3, where the need for wider use of these powers is considered more generally.

[2] Paragraph 4 iv and paragraph 5 of the Appendix to the circular (*op cit*).

6.112 In law arrears of rent incurred by the husband as sole tenant are not the wife's responsibility. Where a local authority does find it necessary to recover arrears on transfer of the tenancy, it is the former tenant, usually the husband, upon whom they should apply pressure and not the wife if she is not legally liable for the debt. We recommend that guidance to this effect should be given by central government to local authorities.

The retention of family allowances order books to secure payment of rent arrears

6.113 When taking evidence in Scotland, we were surprised and disturbed to light upon a widespread practice among social work and housing departments of holding family allowances order books as a means of ensuring the payment of outstanding debts. We were particularly concerned to discover that the order book may be held in order to force a woman to pay off arrears of rent accumulated by her husband as the tenant before the marriage breakdown—a debt which as we have said is not her responsibility. In July 1969 the Department of Health and Social Security issued a circular to local authorities in Scotland[1] explaining the circumstances in which they might hold order books and the procedure they should operate to ensure the legality of the arrangements:

> It is known that family allowance and other benefit order books are frequently held by Local Authority Officers and Welfare Officers and Children's Officers for beneficiaries who are in arrears with rent, have other debts, need guidance in administrating their income or whose children are in care or are boarded out with foster parents, relatives, *etc*.
>
> The Department has had regard to these factors in considering the application of Section 32 to local authorities holding books.[2] In general, and as at present advised, the Department understands that the key factor in determining whether or not an offence is being committed is the nature of the arrangement with the *payee*. If the arrangement is a purely voluntary one, entered into by the payee (usually a woman, but sometimes a man) of her own free will to enable her to pay off debts or budget satisfactorily, and if she can terminate the arrangements at any time and have her order book returned to her straight away on request without the imposition of any conditions, then it may be regarded as falling outside the terms of Section 32(1). In these circumstances the Secretary of State for Social Services would agree to the continuation of the arrangement and thus it would fall outside Section 32(2) also. If, on the other hand, there is some element of compulsion and enforcement, ie the holding of the book is designed to *ensure* that debts are cleared, and the continued possession of the order book is asserted in derogation of the rights of the beneficiary to take back and hold the book herself, then this would constitute an offence within the meaning of Section 32.

1 Circular Sc 1560/1/17: *Holding of order books issued by Department of Health and Social Security, Section 32 of the Ministry of Social Security Act 1966.*

2 Section 32 of the Ministry of Social Security Act 1966 says:

" (1) Any person who—
 (a) as a pledge or a security for a debt, or
 (b) with a view to obtaining payment from the person entitled thereto of a debt due either to himself or to any other person, receives, detains or has in his possession any document issued by or on behalf of the Secretary of State for Social Services in connection with any benefit, pension or allowance, whether payable under this Act or otherwise, shall be guilty of an offence.

(2) Any person who has such a document in his possession without lawful authority or excuse (the proof whereof shall lie on him) shall be guilty of an offence.

(3) A person guilty of an offence under this section shall be liable on summary conviction to imprisonment for a term not exceeding three months or to a fine not exceeding one hundred pounds or to both."

6.114   The fact that it was thought necessary to issue this circular to local authorities in Scotland presumably is related to the prevalence there of the practice we discovered.   We can see no reason why such a practice should be particularly countenanced in Scotland.   There may be exceptional cases when it is in a family's best interests to deposit allowance books voluntarily to help clear rent arrears, but to generalise the practice runs counter to the policy of the Act, and, we have no doubt, frequently involves the commission of an illegality.   Arrears of rent incurred by a husband as sole tenant are not in any case the wife's responsibility: to hold the family allowances books as a pledge for the payment of such arrears is thus doubly unjustifiable.   It adds, moreover, to the burdens and insecurity of the one-parent family at the precise moment when the mother is struggling to adjust to that status.   We urge that the practice, in Scotland and anywhere else it may prevail, should cease.

SECTION 8—SPECIAL PROBLEMS OF OWNER-OCCUPIERS

6.115   We now consider the problems which may arise when the family which splits up owns the home, commonly upon a mortgage loan.   The house may be in the husband's name only, in joint ownership or, infrequently, in the wife's name.   As we have mentioned in Section 4, the rights of a spouse who, not being an owner or co-owner, has no legal title to occupation are protected by the Matrimonial Homes Act 1967.   The right to occupy the house, however, is only part of the problem.   Unless the mortgage payments on it can be kept up the family will face the risk of foreclosure.

THE RISK OF FORECLOSURE

6.116   Some of the evidence we received indicated that foreclosure, (sometimes contributed to by the Supplementary Benefits Commission's inability to allow for capital repayments–paragraph 6.125 below) was the cause of serious hardship to one-parent families.   We sought further information from those who gave evidence, but received very little definite detail.

6.117   We also made enquiries from the Building Societies' Association and a number of building societies.   Statistics provided by one source showed that the numbers of foreclosures were small.   In the nine months January–September 1971 this society had foreclosed 148 mortgages, 37 of these involving marital breakdown, whereas they had a total of 263,510 current mortgage accounts in June of that year.[1]   The replies we received suggested that generally most societies try to be helpful to families in difficulties by agreeing to accept payments of interest only for a period of six to twelve months.   The General Secretary of the Building Societies' Association wrote, " It seems most unlikely to me that a building society would push for possession if the wife kept interest payments running on the outstanding debt with the help of the SBC."   One society told us that they tried to provide as long a period as possible to allow wives to reassess their future and, if necessary, find alternative accommodation with fewer outgoings.   They said, " We are genuinely concerned to see that the woman gets herself as soon as she reasonably can into a situation which is viable and sustainable out of the resources which are available to her."   Another said that in the great majority of cases where the wife was unable

[1] Building society statistics do not measure the numbers of women who may have left their homes because of pressure before formal proceedings were taken.

to maintain any payments without assistance from supplementary benefits, they were willing to agree to payments of interest only, and to continue this concession for a protracted period if necessary. We consider this to be a desirable practice. Where the Supplementary Benefits Commission are meeting the interest payments we can see no reason why in the small number of cases involved, building societies, or local authorities where they are mortgagees, should not accept interest only for many years if necessary, without hardship to their borrowers or investors.

6.118 Features may exist, however, which make it difficult for a building society to allow the mortgage to run on. One society pointed out that, however sympathetic they might feel, there was a limit to the extent to which they could help, bearing in mind that they also had a duty to their investing members. One category of case which they regarded as requiring stricter treatment than others is where the wife and family are deserted by the husband, who is the sole mortgagor, and both parties thereafter refuse to make any further payments. The motive of the husband in defaulting may be, it is suggested, to induce the society to take possession proceedings so that he may thus realise any surplus equity, whereas the wife's motive, often on the advice of her solicitors, may be to avoid making payments which she may not be able to recover in any subsequent divorce proceedings. In these cases, where the society felt they were being used as a weapon, as it were, in the conflict between the parties, they tended to take action to realise their security at a fairly early stage, after warning both parties of their intention to do so.

6.119 We are unable to reconcile the amount of very generalised complaint made to us of hardship caused to one-parent families by foreclosure with the results of our enquiries of the societies. It may be that a more rigorous investigation of the facts would be useful. In any case, we do not believe that the building societies should be deprived of the power to foreclose or be subject to special limitations of this power when dealing with a one-parent family.

6.120 However, the case of *Hastings and Thanet Building Society v Goddard*[1] to which we earlier made an interim reference[2] does demonstrate a gap in the law which peculiarly affects the wives of defaulting mortgagors and which in our view ought to be closed. In that case, the husband mortgagor deserted his wife and ceased to make repayments on the mortgage. The building society foreclosed against the husband. The first that the wife knew of the husband's default in paying the mortgage instalments or of the foreclosure proceedings taken against him was one year after the desertion, when the sheriff informed her that he had a warrant for possession. Throughout the year, the husband had not been supporting his wife, who had lived entirely on supplementary benefits. The society had made no approach to the wife herself over the whole of this period. The Court of Appeal held that the society had no obligation to inform the mortgagor's wife that the mortgage was in arrears (even though she had immediately before the desertion registered her right of occupation under the Matrimonial Homes Act 1967 as a land charge in the Land Charges Register) and no obligation to serve her, even though she was

---

1 (1970) 1 WLR 1544. The facts of the case provide some hard evidence for the complaints made to ourselves.
2. Section 4.

in occupation, with notice of the foreclosure proceedings against the husband. The law in this respect appears to be lamentable and we support the proposals for its reform which have been canvassed by the Law Commission.[1] These are to the effect that a wife in Mrs Goddard's position should be given notice of the proceedings and a right to apply to the court. We would, however, go further. The Law Commission's recommendations concerning the obligation to notify the wife would bind the building society only where she had registered her right of occupation as a land charge. We consider that the duty to notify the wife should arise whenever the wife is living in the home, whether she has registered her right of occupation as a land charge or not. We agree with the comment that in this type of case the courts have seemed to be more concerned with reducing the administrative burdens of building societies than with safeguarding families in their homes, and that it is no great hardship on a building society to check when a mortgagor falls into arrears whether he has a wife living in the house, and if he has, to inform her that her husband is in arrears with the mortgage payments and of the society's intention to take foreclosure proceedings.[2] These reforms are the more important in the light of the recommendations we proceed to make in succeeding paragraphs, for the local authority can hardly be in a position to assist a woman like the wife in the case we have quoted if the building society do not disclose the impending foreclosure to her.

The role of local authorities

6.121 Local authorities have wide general powers, under section 43 of the Housing (Financial Provisions) Act 1958 and section 49 of the Housing (Financial Provisions) (Scotland) Act 1968, to advance money to help house purchasers.[3] They also have powers, under sections 45 and 50 respectively of the same Acts, to guarantee repayment of advances made by building societies to individuals. These powers would enable local authorities to help families under the threat of foreclosure, but they are little used in this way at present. Section 1 of the Children and Young Persons Act 1963 or section 12 of the Social Work (Scotland) Act 1968, which are already used to guarantee rents, could also be used to guarantee mortgage payments.

6.122 We believe that housing authorities in their new comprehensive role should be ready in appropriate cases to use these powers to help families under threat of foreclosure to retain their homes. In doing so they will obviously want to look at the cost to the local authority of the available alternatives: making satisfactory mortgage arrangements, rehousing in council property, or buying the family home and renting it back to the lone parent; but we emphasise the importance also of considering the social cost or advantage to the family of the various alternatives, including the effect of moving home on the parents' employment and earning capacity, on the children's education, on the family's sense of security, and on the continuity of their contact with relatives and friends. A local authority should be ready where necessary to offer a guarantee to a building society which is prepared to grant

---

[1] Law Commission: *Family Law, Family Property Law*, Working Paper No 42, 1971, paragraphs 1.12–1.14.

[2] D A Nevitt and J Levin: ' Social Policy and the Matrimonial Home ', *op cit*, page 350.

[3] Both these Acts empower local authorities to advance the full value of houses.

or transfer a mortgage, or itself to buy the house and offer either a new mortgage or a letting of the house to the occupier.

6.123 It is particularly important that local authorities should become aware of threatened foreclosures in time for the alternatives to be properly considered. Apart from the changes in the law[1] which have a close bearing on this matter, proper administrative arrangements should be considered to ensure early warning. This might, for example, involve agreeing with the building societies that (with the consent of the borrower) they would notify housing and social services departments of possible foreclosures, particularly when they are aware that dependent children are involved.

AVAILABILITY OF MORTGAGES TO WOMEN

6.124 We received both evidence which suggested that building societies were reluctant to offer mortgages or to transfer existing mortgages to women, and, from the societies, a refutation of this suggestion. One society told us, " This is not the case as far as we are concerned, as we are prepared to consider applications for loans from either sex on an equal basis, always subject to their being able to meet the outgoings, (*ie* mortgage repayment, rates, etc) and maintain the property." We were not able to make any satisfactory estimate of the extent to which discrimination exists. We consider, however, that women who find it difficult to get a mortgage would be helped by the wider availability of advice to would-be borrowers through housing aid centres[2] and by a greater readiness on the part of housing authorities to offer guarantees of repayment of building society loans.

THE SUPPLEMENTARY BENEFITS COMMISSION AND MORTGAGE REPAYMENTS

6.125 The Ministry of Social Security Act 1966 requires the Supplementary Benefits Commission, in calculating a person's weekly requirements, to make separate provision for rent. For claimants who are owner-occupiers the Act lays down that " rent " shall include " . . . in particular, rates, a reasonable allowance towards any necessary expenditure on repairs or insurance, and *such proportion as is for the time being attributable to interest* of any sum payable in respect of a mortgage debt or heritable security charged on the house. . . . "[3]

6.126 This provision follows the earlier and similar provision in the National Assistance Act 1948. It reflects the difference between rent, which is money spent, and repayment of the capital element of money raised by mortgage, which is money saved in the form of a capital asset. Successive governments have held that to provide for mortgage capital repayments in supplementary benefit assessments would be not merely to provide for the beneficiary's current housing cost but at the same time to acquire for him—and eventually his heirs and legatees—a capital asset at public expense. The official view has been that, providing the claimant's accommodation is safeguarded, the principle underlying the present law is sound, and that public funds ought not to be used to increase the capital assets of claimants.

---

[1] See paragraph 6.120 above.
[2] See Section 5.
[3] Ministry of Social Security Act 1966, Schedule 2, paragraph 13(3) (italics added).

6.127   We have been struck by the fact that for those families on supplementary benefit who rent their homes, the whole of their housing costs—rent,
rates, insurance and provisions for repairs—is recognised in the calculation of
their requirements.   The owner-occupier who endeavours to keep up with
the whole of his normal outgoings on housing while on benefit can do
so only at the expense of reducing the amount he has available for his
other weekly needs.   At the same time, he may receive by way of " rent
addition " a sum below the cost of equivalent rented accommodation in
the area.   What we have been able to learn about building societies' poiicy
suggests that they may often be willing to accept interest payments only
for a period, if there is a reasonable chance that the mortgagor's circumstances
will improve and he will be able to resume normal payments, and we have
recommended that they should be ready to accept interest only for long periods
in appropriate cases (paragraph 6.117).   However, it is not clear that mortgagors
themselves are always aware of this possibility, and even where they are they may
well be reluctant to put it to the test.   We recommend that the Supplementary
Benefits Commission should take the initiative in advising claimants with
mortgage liabilities of the possibility that the building society may be willing
to accept interest payments only.   We consider also that the Commission
should ask to be informed if this facility is refused, so that they may take
account of the possibility that hardship will consequently arise.

6.128   The more fundamental issue of the extent to which supplementary
benefit should include provision for capital repayments, is one which concerns
many claimants besides one-parent families, and we have concluded that it
would not be appropriate for us to make recommendations about it. Suggestions
were made to us in evidence that the Commission should meet capital repayments
for a limited period, or should have a discretionary power to meet them,
depending on local circumstances.   We hope that these and other possibilities
will be explored.

Mortgage Repayments and Life Assurance

6.129   Several organisations submitting evidence to us have drawn attention
to the plight of young mothers who are unable to continue mortgage repayments
on the premature death of their husbands.   Some witnesses advocated a
system of compulsory life assurance, either by way of endowment insurance or a
mortgage protection policy, as a means of overcoming this problem.   From
enquiries we have made it is apparent that for some borrowers who obtain a
mortgage at an early age a loan linked with life assurance cover may be obtainable at no extra cost; for certain other groups the extra cost of a mortgage
protection policy may be quite small.   We recognise, however, that some
borrowers might find the additional expense a source of hardship.   It might,
moreover, be thought unnecessary, or even unjust, to compel all borrowers,
including single men and women with no dependants, to assure their lives.
People considered to be bad health risks would have difficulty in securing
cover at rates they could afford to pay.   Nevertheless, the advantages which
flow from adequate insurance are very considerable to those parents who are
widowed and we believe that further consideration should be given to ways of
safeguarding families with dependent children.   Such consideration should, in
our view, include not only the feasibility of compulsory insurance but also

403

the wider use by housing authorities and other bodies who operate home loan schemes of group mortgage protection schemes which reduce the cost of insurance cover. Full information about existing mortgage protection schemes and their advantages should be made available to all new borrowers.

SECTION 9—HOUSING ASSOCIATIONS

6.130 A number of organisations drew attention to the valuable contribution housing associations can make in providing homes for one-parent families, and particularly for those who have difficulty in getting on to a local authority's housing list.

6.131 Whilst we believe that local authorities' rules should be sufficiently flexible to enable all lone parents to be included in these lists,[1] we also see a need in the current housing situation, and for the foreseeable future, for all the additional homes that housing associations can and do provide. Housing associations may, for example, in converting property be able to provide some small units especially suitable for a mother with one child, or may buy houses to convert into flats to house a small number of families together. Purpose-built housing blocks can also be designed to meet the needs of special groups.

6.132 Housing associations can also provide and administer short-stay schemes for young and inexperienced mothers who may benefit from contact with each other and from the supportive services that such schemes make possible.

6.133 We were, however, pleased to find that those housing associations whose work was described to us[2] recognised the dangers of segregation of one-parent families and tried to minimise these by housing them, where possible, among other families. They were also healthily conscious of their own limitations. The financial position and social work resources of the associations often do not enable them to assist the families in the greatest need—those who are socially inadequate, poor rent-payers or difficult neighbours, for whom, as we already said, we believe public provision must be made.

6.134 Nevertheless we do also consider that there is scope for extension of the work of the associations and we would welcome all moves to strengthen and expand the voluntary housing movement and, particularly, to increase the provision of rented dwellings by housing associations.[3] One aspect of this policy which is specially important for our purposes is the proposal to help the associations to make a greater contribution towards solving the problems of unsatisfactory older housing in stress areas.[4]

SECTION 10—FURNISHING THE HOME

6.135 Any family moving into a new home faces special expenses—not only for removal costs, but also for curtains, floor coverings and necessary

---

[1] See Section 6, above.

[2] See Catholic Housing Aid Society evidence, *op cit*, and the evidence from the National Council for the Unmarried Mother and her Child, *op cit*.

[3] See *Widening the Choice: The Next Steps in Housing, op cit*, paragraphs 37–39; *Homes for People, Scottish Housing Policy in the 1970s, op cit*, paragraph 30.

[4] Department of the Environment and Welsh Office: *Better Homes: The Next Priorities*, Cmnd 5339, 1973, paragraph 37; Scottish Development Department: *Towards Better Homes: Proposals for dealing with Scotland's Older Housing*, Cmnd 5338, 1973, paragraph 24.

changes of furniture. The burden on the lone parent tends to be more than average. Mothers who have previously had no home of their own, who have been living in furnished accommodation, or who have left the matrimonial home, may have few possessions to take with them and no money to buy what they need. We think it important that such families should be assisted to equip their homes to a reasonable standard, especially to avoid the risk of their incurring a millstone of debt through private hire purchase agreements.

6.136 There are a variety of ways in which help can already be given to such families. Under section 94 of the Housing Act 1957 local authorities have the power to supply and sell furniture to their tenants, either outright or by hire purchase. Housing association tenants can be assisted similarly;[1] social services departments can make grants or provide furniture under section 1 of the Children and Young Persons Act 1963. Local authorities frequently maintain stores of furniture for these purposes, as do the Women's Royal Voluntary Services.

6.137 People who are receiving supplementary benefit can also be helped to obtain essential items by an exceptional needs payment. The Supplementary Benefits Handbook[2] says on this:

89. Where the Commission decides to meet a need, it usually does so by a cash payment of the amount which is essential in the particular case. Sometimes, however, where for example the need is for essential items of furniture, arrangements will be made for the articles to be supplied from a furniture store of a local authority department or a voluntary welfare organisation which is willing to help. These bodies can also sometimes help to meet needs which the supplementary benefits scheme is not designed to deal with, and in such cases a claimant is advised where appropriate that a voluntary body may be able to assist him. In certain exceptional types of cases the Commission may find it possible to meet the need in full or in part, when the approach to the charitable body has been unsuccessful and there is no other way of preventing hardship.

93. The items normally regarded as essential are sheets, blankets and pillows, curtains and floor coverings (normally linoleum); tables and chairs; beds and mattresses; household appliances such as cookers and gas fires where appropriate. This list is regarded as the normal minimum standard but is not exhaustive. For example, cupboards, wardrobes and kitchen cabinets may be provided if there is no adequate storage space.

94. Where the need is for sheets, blankets, pillows, curtains or floor covering, the payment is sufficient to cover the cost of new items. Where it is for furniture, local authorities or voluntary bodies will normally be approached in the first instance (see paragraph 89). If the need cannot suitably be met in this way, the payment will normally cover the cost of a secondhand item from a shop. Where a household appliance is needed and a safety factor is involved, as with an electric cooker, the item obtained is normally a reconditioned one. The cost of necessary repair, fitting or re-siting of essential household appliances may also be met, as may the reasonable costs of delivery of essential items, including those provided by voluntary organisations.

6.138 We received evidence which suggested that recipients of supplementary benefit experience difficulty in making their applications for these needs to supplementary benefit local offices, and in discovering what it is reasonable for them to ask for. We were told that the Commission do not

---

[1] Section 122 of the Housing Act 1957; section 156 of the Housing (Scotland) Act 1966.
[2] *Op cit.*

provide sufficiently large grants to cover essential furniture. The following comment was made by the Oxfordshire County Council Working Party:

> DHSS confirmed that the aim is to make payments for furniture (where appropriate) in time to enable at least the most important items to be obtained by the time the house is occupied, if this is practicable. Our impression is, however, that the normal practice adopted by the local offices in the area covered by our enquiry is not in accordance with this professed aim . . . . Difficulties arise also from the very narrow definition of essential furnishings adopted by the Supplementary Benefits Commission . . . in our view a family moving into a new home might reasonably regard as essential such items as easy chairs for the adults in the family, a carpet for the living room and enough chairs of some kind to enable the family to eat together round a table. Yet cases occur in which items such as these are excluded from the grants made by the Commission.

When they gave oral evidence to us the Association of Directors of Social Services said one of the main failings was that the Commission's officials do not seem to carry out headquarter's instructions in this whole area of discretion.

6.139   Since we were given this evidence the Commission have published a report showing how they exercise their discretion.[1]   In it they say that proportionately more exceptional needs payments go to women with dependent children than to other recipients of supplementary benefit.   We endorse the statement of policy as set out in the Commission's publications, but think the application of this policy at local office level often falls short.   It is important that officials administering the scheme should recognise the special difficulties faced by one-parent families in furnishing a home.

6.140   There is, in our view, an area of confusion as well as an overlap of responsibilities between the Commission, social services departments and housing departments in the provision of furniture and other household necessities.   We feel that this leads to less effective allocation of resources and a very real possibility that some families may fail to receive adequate help at a time of great need.   The Commission cannot assist families whose head is in full-time work.   Housing authorities have power, as we have explained, to sell or lease furniture and other household equipment to local authority tenants only.   Social services departments have power, under section 1 of the Children and Young Persons Act 1963, to provide assistance which will diminish the need to receive children into or keep them in care. We recommend that consultations should take place between the Department of Health and Social Security, the Department of the Environment, the Scottish Development Department, the Welsh Office and the appropriate local authority organisations with a view to avoiding overlap of responsibilities for this function and to ending the present situation in which families may fall between different authorities and as a result fail to receive help when it is urgently needed.

6.141   In the course of our enquiries we found that a needy family could be allocated a local authority house and yet not be provided with the basic necessities to make that house into a home.   Whilst the housing authority has power to sell or lease furniture and other household equipment there is little point in its doing so where the family have no means and where this would simply add yet another debt to an already overwhelming amount.   We

[1] Department of Health and Social Security, Supplementary Benefits Commission: *Exceptional Needs Payments*, Supplementary Benefits Administration Papers 4, HMSO, 1973.

understand that housing authorities would like to extend help by providing equipment free of charge in such cases. There seems to be some doubt, however, whether they have the legal power to do so. The Housing Act 1957, section 94, provides:

> A local authority may fit out furnish and supply any house erected, converted or acquired by them . . . with all requisite furniture, fittings and conveniences and may sell, or supply under a hire purchase agreement, furniture to the occupants of houses provided by the local authority, and for that purpose, may buy furniture.

This provision is widely construed by local authorities as entitling them to provide under the first head furniture in the sense only of fittings and fixtures to the house, and requiring them under the second head, if they provide furniture in the more usual sense, to sell it, either outright or on hire purchase. This ambiguity could and should be cleared up by a simple amendment to section 94 of the Housing Act 1957 and its Scottish equivalent, to enable housing authorities " to provide " furniture as well as to sell it or lease it under hire purchase arrangements. We should also like to see social services departments take a wider view of and make more use of their powers under section 1 of the Children and Young Persons Act 1963. We recommend the change in housing legislation and the more extensive use of social services departments' powers pending any more general redistribution of functions which may result from the consultations we have suggested in paragraph 6.140.

PART 7—EMPLOYMENT

SECTION 1—THE PROBLEM

7.1 We have said earlier that we hope that our financial recommendations will create a situation in which many more one-parent families are able to support themselves without recourse to supplementary benefit. It is a corollary of this that lone parents should not be disadvantaged in their working lives and in this Part we consider their special difficulties in relation to employment.

7.2 Many of those who gave evidence to us were concerend with the difficulties faced by lone parents who are in employment, or who would prefer to be working and earning if this were practicable. Our study of the evidence and of the general patterns of employment and earnings of men and women in our society has led us to conclude that lone parents in employment suffer from a number of distinct disadvantages in comparison with two-parent families, which we summarise as follows:

(1) the lone parent is the family's sole wage-earner, whereas increasingly the two-parent family is also the two-earner family;

(2) where the lone parent is a woman, her earning capacity is further restricted by the generally lower levels of women's pay and working skills;

(3) because there is only one parent, arrangements for care of the children during working hours are more difficult than where there are two parents to share the family responsibilities.

We discuss the wider question of arrangements for care of children when their parents are unable to look after them in Part 8. In this Part we examine the first two problems.

7.3 Because of their generally lower earning capacity[1] the problems of lone mothers in relation to employment are more acute than those of lone fathers, and for this reason most of this Part is written in terms of the lone working mother. Child-care problems are common to lone fathers and mothers, and there is evidence that his family responsibilities do sometimes impose constraints on a lone father's earning capacity also (see Part 5, section 2). The relative extent of their difficulties, however, is demonstrated by the fact that in April 1971 only about 25 per cent of all lone mothers were working full time and 20 per cent part time, whereas among lone fathers at least 90 per cent were estimated to be in work, virtually all of them full time. Table 7.1 below shows the numbers of lone mothers and the proportions working full time and part time.

---

[1] See Section 3 below: women's earnings are about 60% of those of men.

408

TABLE 7.1

PROPORTION OF LONE MOTHERS IN FULL-TIME AND PART-TIME EMPLOYMENT IN APRIL 1971

Status	Total of lone mothers	Percentage in full-time work	Percentage in part-time work
Single	90,000	27	12
Married	190,000	23	18
Divorced	120,000	30	20
Widows	120,000	24	29
Total	520,000	25	20

Source: Based on an analysis of 1971 Census. Because of differences between the populations these figures differ from, but are not inconsistent with, the Family Expenditure Survey figures used in Part 5.

7.4 Many of the disadvantages from which working lone mothers suffer are part of the larger problem of the position of women workers as a whole. It follows that the benefit to them from the improvements in the pay and conditions of women which are now slowly being achieved will be especially significant. It is for this reason that much of what is said later in this Part of our Report is concerned with the general problems of women workers. But within this framework we are conscious throughout of the special needs of lone mothers. These were summarised for us by the National Council for the Unmarried Mother and Her Child in the following apt words:

> They are dependent upon one wage in a society in which it is becoming more and more common for both parents to work. Where the lone parent is a woman the situation is particularly difficult because of the low level of women's wages and the lack of opportunity for women to participate in skilled and remunerative employment. The position in the labour market of widows, or divorced and separated wives may have deteriorated because of some years of absence from paid employment. Unmarried mothers tend to be younger than other lone mothers and may not even have completed their training or education.

SECTION 2—THE CHANGING PATTERN OF FAMILY SUPPORT

7.5 We have described in Part 3 the demographic changes which have fundamentally altered the shape and quality of women's lives since Victorian times and the consequential changes in the pattern of their working lives.

7.6 A hundred years ago a young woman marrying in her early twenties could expect to have a large family and, if she survived, would be in her mid-fifties before the youngest reached working age. She was unlikely to work after marriage unless forced by widowhood or desertion to earn a living. Today the average young woman expects to work on leaving full-time education. Although she is likely to marry within a relatively few years, she will usually intend to continue working until she has her first child. Unless the wife and mother has strong reasons to continue with a particularly interesting and remunerative career, which can be combined with her family commitments, she will follow the normal pattern and withdraw from the labour market until her children are at school. But once that stage is reached, many mothers return to either part-time or full-time work which they combine with their family and home responsibilities. Increasingly, therefore, the two-parent family, especially where there is no child below school age, is also a two-income family, with a standard of living which is beyond the powers of most one-parent families to achieve.

THE CHOICE FOR MOTHERS IN TWO-PARENT FAMILIES—TO WORK OR NOT?

7.7 Choice can only be freely exercised where there is no compelling financial necessity to earn. Given this condition, whether the mother in a two-parent family is able to work depends on the availability of employment of the kind she can combine with her family responsibilities, on her own health and ability to work, and on her family's acceptance of her doing so. But most of all she needs to be able to ensure that her children are properly cared for when she is not at home.

7.8 Studies of women at work, and particularly the *Survey of Women's Employment* by Mrs Audrey Hunt,[1] have shown that the predominant reason given for returning to work is to increase the family's income as the children grow older and are more expensive to provide for. Given that work is available and that it is practicable for her to take it, the two-parent family mother looks for earnings which are attractive enough to allow her to make a positive contribution to the family budget after allowing for the costs of her employment, such as fares, meals, clothes, income tax and national insurance. Mrs Hunt's survey also showed that financial reasons are reinforced by the desire to achieve independence, to meet and mix with other people, and to gain relief from being absorbed solely with domestic cares. Such considerations may well be sufficient to counteract the additional expenses at home which may result from the time the mother spends at work: less time for cooking, or sewing and mending, for example, means greater reliance on more expensive ready-prepared or ready-made items.

7.9 There are considerable regional variations in availability of work and in attitudes towards mothers working. In 1971 female economic activity rates were highest in the South East (56·3 per cent for women aged 15–59) and lowest in Wales (42·1 per cent).[2] At the time of Mrs Hunt's survey (1965) economic activity among women was highest in the London conurbation at 61·2 per cent, and lowest in Northern England and Wales, where the figures were 42·8 per cent and 41·9 per cent respectively.[3] Regional differences in husbands' attitudes to wives' working outside the home were fairly marked; approval was most common in regions where wives were most likely to be working and where their mothers were most likely to have worked.[4] Nor is it by any means universally accepted by women themselves that married women with children ought to be free to take paid employment. Nine out of every ten women interviewed for the survey thought it right for married women without children to work, but less than two fifths considered that those with children of school age

1 Audrey Hunt: *A Survey of Women's Employment*, HMSO, 1968, pages 19 and 181.
2 *British Labour Statistics Year Book 1971*, HMSO, 1973.
3 *A Survey of Women's Employment*, op cit, page 23 and Tables A7a, A7b and A8.
4 *Ibid*, page 188.

should do so, and less than one in twenty thought it right for those with children under school age. This climate of opinion is reinforced by the effort involved in combining outside work with running the home, and by the often acute difficulties in finding reliable day care for children outside school hours and in school holidays. It is hardly surprising therefore, that when two-parent family mothers do work, it is usually after their children have started school and even then many in the first place prefer part-time work to work which, despite being better paid, seems to demand more time and effort than they feel able to devote to it.[1] Table 7.2 below illustrates the economic activity rates of married women. Nearly two thirds of employed married women are employed for 30 hours a week ar less, nearly 45 per cent for 21 hours a week or less.

TABLE 7.2
PERCENTAGES OF MARRIED COUPLES WITH WIFE ECONOMICALLY ACTIVE AT APRIL 1971

Number of dependent children	Age of mother						
	20–59	20–24	25–29	30–34	35–39	40–44	45–59
0	62·6	84·2	81·3	78·2	76·2	71·0	54·4
1	43·9	19·1	26·6	41·9	56·7	60·1	51·9
2	38·6	12·8	23·3	39·8	51·0	50·8	46·1
3	35·2	9·0	20·9	33·0	42·5	46·8	43·9
4	30·8	6·3	14·7	29·6	38·1	35·5	36·2
5 and over	27·1	6·3	13·9	26·1	31·2	26·5	34·3
All with children ...	39·2	14·2	22·0	34·9	44·6	47·4	49·3
With child 0–10 ...	32·9	15·9	23·3	35·5	42·8	43·0	40·4
With child 0–4 ...	19·9	15·2	18·2	22·1	24·0	24·9	30·9

Source: 1% Census analysis.

THE CHOICE FOR LONE PARENTS

7.10 If the present employment situation is difficult enough for women as a whole, and mothers feel particular restraints and encounter difficulties in seeking suitable employment, then clearly the lone mother is even more handicapped, although her right to work may be more readily acknowledged. Greater need to earn to support her family is not matched by any greater earning capacity than other women, and greater need for help with care of her children while she works usually co-exists with a smaller circle of relatives and friends upon whom she can call and a lesser ability to pay for it.

7.11 We have drawn attention elsewhere[2] to the way in which these factors combine with the treatment of earnings under the supplementary benefits scheme to produce a large proportion of fatherless families depending for their main support on supplementary benefit and having little or no other income.

[1] See Part 3.
[2] Part 5, Section 2.

In contrast with all other able-bodied people of working age, women on their own with dependent children can receive supplementary benefit without being required to register for employment. This reflects the principle that a woman should not be obliged by financial pressures to go out to work when she feels it is in the best interests of her children for her to be at home. We strongly support this principle, which our proposals for guaranteed maintenance allowance are designed to reinforce. We think it should apply equally to lone fathers and lone mothers.[1] But we also consider that freedom to stay at home should be matched, so far as can in practice be achieved, by a similar freedom to work outside the home wherever the parent feels that this is in the best interests of herself (or himself) and the children. In other words, a lone parent should be able to decide whether to stay at home or to work part time or full time without undue hardship or difficulty resulting from the decision.

7.12 It was evident from the studies made for us in other countries that, in marked contrast to the position obtaining under our supplementary benefits scheme, none of the countries studied gives unsupported mothers an unequivocal right to receive social assistance without registering for work so long as they have dependent children under school leaving age.[2] There are frequent examples of measures designed to encourage mothers to work, and mothers of quite young children are both expected to work and themselves expect to do so. For example, in West Germany there is a general requirement in the social assistance law that applicants must seek work and be given the opportunity of working subject to the proviso that the proper upbringing of their children is not thereby endangered.

7.13 Many lone mothers who at present remain on supplementary benefit are anxious to work, and we have no doubt that, financial considerations apart, many of them would benefit psychologically and socially as well. They would gain not only in the opportunities of wider and more varied social contact through their workmates, but also in confidence of their ability to support themselves once their children were no longer dependent on them. But unless they are equipped for a well-paid occupation and can obtain employment in it, they cannot generally hope, if they have to rely on their earnings alone, to approach the income level of a two-parent family even where only the father is earning. A major advantage of the guaranteed maintenance allowance we propose would be that it would provide greater help for those lone parents whose earning capacity was low and a steadier graduation from dependence on State support to independence and self-support.[3]

7.14 Even more than the mother in a two-parent family, the working lone parent needs to be equipped for and to be able to obtain work which will give her a reasonable financial return, and which offers hours and conditions consistent with her family commitments. In the paragraphs which follow we consider these problems under three heads: first, the pay and skills of women workers (paragraphs 7.15–7.20), second, working conditions (paragraphs 7.21–7.26) and third, the need to widen employment opportunities (paragraphs 7.27–7.39).

---

[1] We make a recommendation to this effect in Part 5, Section 8.
[2] See Appendix 3.
[3] Part 5, Section 6, discusses the proposal in detail.

SECTION 3—PAY AND SKILLS OF WOMEN WORKERS

7.15 The change in the pattern of working women's lives has revolutionised the country's labour force in post-war years. But the implications are still not sufficiently understood or taken into consideration by women themselves, by parents and teachers, or by employers. Young women all too frequently fail to be given or fail to take advantage of training and jobs which would fit them not only to contribute more to the family budget but enable them to have a greater degree of independence; and those who may later become lone parents are likely to find that their ability to support their families is seriously reduced. Nor has the greatly increased proportion of their adult lives which many women spend at work—some 25–30 years even with a gap for child rearing—been generally matched by advances in the kind of work they do or the pay they get for it.

7.16 Most women in most industries, whether the labour force is predominantly male or female, are in jobs which are low paid, with little training and few prospects. Many are employed in industries and occupations where comparatively few men are employed and where the work is often part-time or seasonal—for example in retail distribution, laundries, hotels and catering, and clothing. The figures speak for themselves: while in April 1973 47 per cent of women full-time workers earned less than £20 a week, only 3·5 per cent of men earned less than this;[1] and the average gross earnings of women workers at £22·6 were little more than 60 per cent of the men's average of £37·5. It is true that this is partly attributable to the shorter hours normally worked by women, and the lower numbers of women receiving extra payments for shift work. But the average hourly earnings (excluding overtime) of women at 60·3p were only about 64 per cent of the men's average of 93·7p[2] and this again demonstrates the known concentration of women in lower-paid jobs.[3] As against the 1972 Trades Union Congress definition of low-paid work—work irrespective of sex with a basic wage for 40 hours below £20, that is, less than 50p an hour—there were still many women in April 1973 with hourly earnings of less than 40p.[4] Our overseas research showed that women in Britain were proportionately lower paid than those in a number of other European countries. In West Germany, for example, women's earnings in 1971 were about 70 per cent of those of men,[5] compared with 60 per cent in this country in 1973.

7.17 The pattern of awards of family income supplements provides yet another illustration of the low status and pay of working lone mothers. Out of the total of 84,000 families receiving family income supplements in April

---

[1] ' New Earnings Survey ', Table 11, in the *Department of Employment Gazette*, October 1973. Earnings of full-time workers with pay not affected by absence and excluding overtime; women aged 18 and over, men aged 21 and over.

[2] *Ibid*, Table 5.

[3] At the same time the average gross earnings of women manual workers were 49·1p an hour compared with 79·2p for male manual workers; non-manual women workers earned 66·1p an hour compared with 121·7p for non-manual men. Thus women in manual jobs had gross hourly earnings about 62% of those of men, while those in non-manual jobs received only 54% of men's hourly earnings. *Ibid*, Table 5. Pay not affected by absence and excluding overtime.

[4] *Ibid*, Table 13.

[5] Individual country reports prepared by the International Social Security Association are available from the Department of Health and Social Security: see Appendix 2.

1973,[1] 36,000 (43 per cent) were lone mothers, representing nearly 40 per cent of all lone mothers, excluding widows, normally in full-time work; whereas the number of two-parent families with family income supplements (47,000 in April 1973) probably represented less than 1 per cent of all two-parent families with the head normally in full-time work.

7.18   The overall low earning capacity and low status of women in employment has to be tackled if women are to achieve the economic equality and independence which will help to lift the lone parent out of poverty.   A start has been made by the passing of the Equal Pay Act 1970 which comes into force on 29 December 1975.   Its object is to eliminate discrimination between men and women in regard to pay and other terms and conditions of employment.   This is to be achieved by establishing the right of the individual woman to equal treatment where she is employed on work of the same or a broadly similar nature to that of men or in a job which, though different from those of men, has been given an equal value to men's jobs under a job evaluation exercise, and by providing machinery for the elimination from collective agreements and pay structures of discrimination between men and women in rates of pay and conditions of employment.   While, when the Act is fully implemented, it will bring about an overall increase in rates paid to women, it does nothing to tackle the discriminatory practices in education, training and employment opportunities which serve to keep women on the bottom rung of the employment ladder and of the earnings scales.

7.19   The problems which the Equal Pay Act 1970 will leave unaffected are well described in the following extract from the recent *Report on the Employment of Women* by the House of Commons Expenditure Committee:

> Several witnesses referred to the implementation of the Equal Pay Act and argued that " while we may achieve equal pay, we are going to find a great deal of waffling on the part of certain groups of employers with regard to dividing work into women's work and men's work."   One industry was intending to merge the present three rates for women and seven for men into " ten numbered scales, three of which would continue to belong to the men at the top.   That would be one way of continuing to keep women on what in the past had been the women's rate."   This view was echoed by the National Joint Committee of Working Women's Organisations who felt that " very good progress " was being made towards the abolition of the women's rates but that the problem was " one of women's jobs, the categorisation of jobs which in fact only women do where it is not possible, without having a positive battle on the subject, to get rates which are comparable with men's rates doing similar work . . . .   To get women's jobs classified as being of as high a grade . . . is where the problem begins." ...   The ... USDAW (Union of Shop Distributive and Allied Workers) . . . argued that " one of the problems of job evaluating schemes is that in giving weight to certain factors, responsibility, skill and so on, the skills or the abilities that particularly mark women are often weighted and graded much lower, so that dexterity, speed, nimbleness, and perhaps the ability to accept boring jobs, get a very low weighting while so-called responsibility or skill are given a very much higher one."   While we regard the provision of equal pay as very important, we also consider that it is vital to prevent women's jobs being classified in such a way that women are once again relegated to the lowest end of the wage scale.[2]

During the 1972–1973 Session private members' bills, intended to prevent discrimination against women in jobs and education on grounds of sex, were

[1] These figures are provisional.
[2] *Sixth Report from the Expenditure Committee*, Session 1972–1973, HC 182, HMSO, 1973, paragraph 16, page xv.

introduced in both Houses of Parliament, and were considered by Select Committees of both Houses.[1] On 14 May 1973 the Government announced their intention to introduce legislation designed to assist in the removal of unfair discrimination on grounds of sex and to improve opportunities open to women, and in September 1973 issued a consultative document.[2] We hold that anti-discrimination legislation is essential if the Equal Pay Act is to be fully effective, and we welcome the consultative document as indicating the growing acceptability of this point of view.

7.20 While legislation can assist in removing obvious discrimination, probably the most helpful contribution it can make to what is primarily a social issue is to underpin and promote progressive attitudes and policies. In any case legislation can only function effectively if it is understood and used by those it is designed to help. For example, the report of the Office of Manpower Economics on the implementation of the Equal Pay Act[3] showed that two years after legislation had been enacted more than half a million women were in jobs with a differential of more than 20 per cent between their pay and that of men. This experience demonstrates that legislation must be accompanied by a change of attitude on the part of women themselves who must be prepared to take a more active role in their own interests.

SECTION 4—WORKING CONDITIONS
THE NEED FOR FLEXIBILITY

7.21 Official estimates[4] indicate that between 1971 and 1986 the women's work force is expected to increase by about one million and that by 1986 there will be about ten million women and over $16\frac{1}{2}$ million men at work or seeking work. Thus in 1986 women are expected to constitute about 38 per cent of the work force. It is also estimated that by 1986 about 71 per cent of economically active women will be married compared with 50 per cent[5] in 1961 and about 63 per cent[6] in 1971. Increasing dependence on women workers and their increasing importance to the national economy make it more and more essential if they are to make their full contribution to the country's economic and social advance for their working conditions to take account of the combined workload of family, home and job. Employers should recognise and take account of the fact that many women who can give them good and stable service over a long period of years will need to be helped by facilities for part-time or broken service when their family responsibilities are heaviest. Increased flexibility of working hours and arrangements for leave of absence to cope with unexpected domestic crises, for example, while valuable to all working mothers, are especially needed for those who are single-handed. Equally they are needed for men who have single-handed responsibility for children and employers ought to give the same consideration to men in this respect as they give to lone mothers.

---

[1] House of Lords, *Second Special Report from the Select Committee on Anti-Discrimination Bill (HL)*, HMSO, April 1973; *Special Report from the Select Committee on the Anti-Discrimination (No 2) Bill*, HMSO, June 1973.

[2] Department of Employment, Department of Education and Science, and Home Office: *Equal Opportunities for Men and Women*, HMSO, 1973.

[3] Office of Manpower Economics: *Equal Pay—First Report on the Implementation of the Equal Pay Act 1970*, HMSO, 1972.

[4] *Department of Employment Gazette*, August 1971, page 721.

[5] *1961 Census of Population, Occupation Tables*, HMSO, 1966.

[6] 1971 Census.

7.22 Generally we should like to see a wider spread of good employer practice on lines which are now being introduced for civil servants following the acceptance of recommendations made in the *Report on the Employment of Women in the Civil Service*[1] published in 1971. This Report made many constructive proposals, which the Government have commended to other employers, in the hope that they will follow suit. Those which we consider to be of particular value to lone parents are as follows:

(1) wider use of discretion to grant paid and unpaid special leave for urgent domestic affairs;

(2) flexibility in arranging the hours of attendance of women with family responsibilities;

(3) sympathetic consideration of applications from women with children at school for some unpaid leave during school holidays;

(4) provision, where it can appropriately be organised, of part-time work for women who are unable to work full time because they have children, but who wish to continue or resume work;

(5) advising women who wish to prepare to return to work on appropriate ways of re-training;

(6) explanations in recruitment literature of what arrangements there are to assist women to combine a career with bringing up a family.

PART-TIME WORK

7.23 A number of those who gave evidence to us made a plea for more and better opportunities for part-time work. For many mothers part-time work offers the satisfaction of earning and mixing with other people without imposing more demands on their time and energies than they can meet. But part-time work (except for some professional women) tends to be low in status and badly paid. In September 1972 an estimated 18·4 per cent of women employed in manufacturing industries were working part time (defined as ordinarily involving not more than 30 hours a week).[2] The latest available information on the type of work attracting women on a part-time basis shows a concentration in the service industries. Table 7.3 below relates to occupations in which more than 25 per cent of women employed work part time. Of all women at work, 33·4 per cent were working part time in April 1966.

---

[1] Civil Service Department Management Studies 3, HMSO, 1971.
[2] *Department of Employment Gazette*, November 1972, page 1027.

TABLE 7.3

OCCUPATION OF PART-TIME WOMEN WORKERS AT APRIL 1966

Occupation	Percentage of all part-time women workers	Number of women in each occupation who were working part-time as a percentage of all women employed in the occupation
Cleaners	14·0	82·7
Service, sport and recreation workers*	27·8	50·5
Sales workers	14·8	41·6
Food, drink and tobacco workers	1·3	30·5
Clothing workers ...	3·8	29·7
Nurses	3·3	25·8
Textile workers	2·1	25·1

* Excluding cleaners.

Source: *1966 Census of Population, Economic Activity Tables, Part 1*, HMSO, 1968, Tables 10 and 11.

7.24 While there is a need for a general improvement in the level of jobs available to part-time workers, over-emphasis on part-time working is not free from risks in low rates of pay and loss of advantages in working conditions and status achieved for full-time workers through collective bargaining. Part-time workers are, moreover, often ineligible for, or less favourably treated in relation to, not only promotion, but also such features of full-time employment as paid holidays, paid sick leave and pension schemes. Part-time jobs are also likely to be the most vulnerable to redundancy (and may be outside the scope of the redundancy payments scheme). We are concerned that, where work is for less than twenty-one hours a week, an employee has no statutory right under the Contracts of Employment Act 1972 to a minimum period of notice, no statutory right to a remedy under the Industrial Relations Act 1971 for unfair dismissal, and no right to a redundancy payment under the Redundancy Payments Act 1965. We think that the limit of twenty-one hours is too high bearing in mind the importance of part-time work for lone parents, and some reduction should be considered. We recommend that cover under the relevant legislation should be extended and that, as a minimum, all employees working for eighteen hours a week should be included.[1]

7.25 There are many examples of employers who need the skills of women workers who are not available for full-time work and who have been able to organise in such a way that they can offer women workers hours compatible with their home commitments under proper conditions of employment. We urge employers to review opportunities for part-time work, while at the same time safe-guarding conditions of employment, and believe a wider spread of

[1] The Civil Service uses eighteen hours as its lower limit; all employees working eighteen hours or more are entitled to the same benefits, for example, on redundancy, as full-timers, on a proportionate basis.

417

best practices in this field would considerably help one-parent families. We regard it as essential that trade unions and employers should be alert to the disadvantageous aspects of part-time work, so as to protect the conditions of work of this group of employees.

MATERNITY LEAVE AND PAY

7.26　There are few formal agreements for maternity leave outside the public sector. In their memorandum of evidence to the House of Commons Expenditure Committee on the Employment of Women[1] the National Council for the Unmarried Mother and her Child described the situation as follows:

> The general lack of provision by industry and commerce for maternity leave and pay and the fact that employers have no legal duty to hold jobs open for working mothers naturally works to the disadvantage of lone parents. Mothers who do not want to leave their jobs or their pension or increments or their entitlement to promotion may be tempted to return to work too soon after the confinement for the welfare of the baby.
>
> In a survey conducted by the Institute of Personnel Management, some companies in the UK were asked if maternity leave was paid.[2] Only 8 had a definite policy. "The majority of the participating companies said that no leave of absence was granted and employment was normally terminated 13 weeks before the anticipated date of confinement when the maternity allowance became available.[3] Employees could re-apply for a position when they were ready to resume work."
>
> The Civil Service and the Post Office are examples of good, forward-looking employers where single mothers are concerned. Such mothers are in no way penalised and are encouraged to return to work if they wish. They are eligible for maternity leave and pay on the same basis as married women and the staff welfare officers are particularly concerned for their welfare.
>
> Local authorities have similar schemes. Teachers, nurses, social workers and other professionals are now usually allowed to return to their work. Some authorities, like ILEA, are particularly helpful. Some require a teacher to transfer to another school.

Maternity leave and the right to return to her previous job after her baby is born are important aspects of job security for all women and of particular importance to the unmarried mother. We were pleased to note that the recommendation in the *Report on the Employment of Women in the Civil Service*[4] has been adopted that in the civil service three months' paid maternity leave should be granted with an additional entitlement of three months' unpaid leave. We regard this as the minimum standard and recommend that unions and employers negotiate agreements designed to achieve at least this level.

SECTION 5—WIDENING EMPLOYMENT OPPORTUNITIES

7.27　Schools, careers officers, women's organisations, and all with an interest in helping girls starting their careers and older women returning to work, need to know the facts of the employment situation. Employers also need to have knowledge of current trends and best practice in the employment of women, and particularly women with children. Some statistical information

---

[1] *Op cit*, page 151.

[2] *Special Leave Allowances:* IPM Information Report 9, November 1971.

[3] National insurance maternity allowance normally starts in the eleventh week before the expected week of confinement.

[4] *Op cit*, paragraph 31.

418

is contained in a number of official publications, such as the *Department of Employment Gazette* and the *New Earnings Survey*, but the basic information needed for rational and responsible action is all too often not available. We endorse views given in evidence to the Expenditure Committee by the National Joint Council of Working Women's Organisations that the statistical data on women's training and employment are insufficient, that what is available is dispersed and not easily accessible, and that there is a lack of analysis directed to assessing the requirements of women with family responsibilities.[1] We recognise that there are problems in obtaining full data where women are in part-time or casual work, but we think a conveniently available source of statistical information will be essential upon the introduction of anti-discrimination legislation, if its effectiveness is to be monitored. We should like to see statistics on all aspects of women's employment regularly available in one publication.

7.28 Many mothers need advice and help as to the right course to take when they are considering returning to work or training for it. A number of those who gave evidence to us were critical of the difficulty of obtaining such assistance. The new " jobcentres," now being opened by the Department of Employment in shopping centres, are intended to offer both self-service facilities and specialised help and guidance for women seeking work. We think it is important that they should include in their staff officers with specialised knowledge of the needs and problems of women who have to combine care of their children with their employment, and that their liaison with local authority social services departments should be strengthened.

7.29 In evidence to the Expenditure Committee the National Council for the Unmarried Mother and Her Child drew attention to the fact that much could be achieved by special efforts, saying:

> " Family First " in Nottingham and the local Department of Employment office have developed a very close co-operation as a result of which a number of mothers have taken full advantage of opportunities that already existed in Nottingham under the vocational training scheme. Special efforts are made to see that where possible suitable courses can be timed to fit a mother's personal circumstances and if training progress were hampered by her family responsibilities the Department undertook to explore the possibility of extending the normal training period.[2]

7.30 In paragraph 7.12 above we have referred to the evidence in the other countries we studied that mothers are encouraged to work even when they have quite young children. One might have expected, with so many more lone mothers working, to find a wider spectrum of available jobs and more highly developed and better used facilities for guiding them into the most suitable jobs. In most of the countries, measures to assist lone mothers to find or train for employment are an aspect of the general provision for women workers. In Denmark special machinery exists in the " mothers' aid centres " to ensure co-ordination of training and employment, as well as accommodation and child care, to assist mothers to get training. But even with so specialised a scheme only about one in every six unmarried mothers contacting the centres in fact

---

[1] *Op cit*, evidence of the National Joint Committee of Working Women's Organisations, pages 59 and 69.

[2] *Op cit*, page 147.

receives training.[1]   The general picture which emerges is one of disappointment with the extent to which lone mothers in fact succeed in taking advantage of training facilities.   It is not that they are consciously discriminated against, but rather they that are unable to take advantage of the opportunities available— for example they may lack the necessary basic skill, or the courses available may concentrate on predominantly male occupations, or the necessary support- ing child-care facilities may be lacking.

7.31   We believe that there is need for special efforts to help unsupported mothers to overcome these handicaps, and in particular appropriate training and re-training facilities are important for them.   The problem also requires, however, to be tackled at a much earlier stage, so that girls leaving school see the jobs they go to as more than stop-gaps to fill the time before they marry, and are encouraged to look ahead beyond the immediate future.

CURRICULAR AND CAREERS GUIDANCE

7.32   The Department of Education and Science have recently carried out a survey of careers education in secondary schools, by sending question- naires to schools in the sample, and by visiting some of them.   The report suggests that between the ages of 13 and 17, and sometimes later, " young people pass through a zone of critical decision, a period when they must learn to know themselves, to come to terms with their strengths and weaknesses, to make choices, reach decisions and accept the implications of these decisions".[2] The report says that it is during this period that consultations and guidance should take place.   Of the 87 schools visited, 10 were implementing a policy for careers education in its broadest sense, involving all pupils.   There was no evidence of such practice in 47 schools visited.   Overall, it is estimated from the survey, 37 per cent of secondary schools allow time for general careers education courses; while a further 33 per cent provide only special courses for school- leavers; and 30 per cent provide no time for careers education.[3]   82 per cent of secondary modern schools declare that all or some pupils receive careers education during the fourth year at school, as do 79 per cent of comprehensive schools.   Only 32 per cent of grammar and technical schools can claim this.[4] Curricular and career guidance services are important to girls because of the need to overcome not only the traditional view that the years between leaving school and marriage are of small account but also as a stimulus to girls them- selves, many of whom seem to lack ideas of entering anything but traditional women's occupations.   Table 7.4 below illustrates the type of employment entered by girl school-leavers.

---

[1] See Appendix 3.

[2] Department of Education and Science: *Careers Education in Secondary Schools*, Education Survey 18, HMSO, 1973, paragraph 2.

[3] *Ibid*, Table 2, paragraph 17.

[4] *Ibid*, Table 3, paragraph 20.

TABLE 7.4

REGIONAL ANALYSIS OF TYPE OF EMPLOYMENT ENTERED BY GIRL SCHOOL-LEAVERS IN 1972

Percentage

	Apprenticed to skilled craft*	Leading to recognised professional qualification	Clerical jobs	With other training	Other employment
	%	%	%	%	%
London and South Eastern ...	8·5	0·8	48·6	15·0	27·2
Eastern and Southern ...	9·3	1·1	38·0	14·6	37·0
South Western	7·8	2·2	30·9	19·4	39·9
Midlands	7·0	1·6	31·5	22·1	37·7
Yorkshire and Humberside ...	7·3	2·9	30·4	19·2	40·2
North Western	9·2	2·0	33·1	18·4	37·3
Northern	6·2	2·6	27·3	19·3	44·8
Wales	5·9	1·6	30·0	9·5	57·1
Scotland	7·9	1·8	29·9	18·3	42·2
Great Britain	7·9	1·7	34·3	17·7	38·4

* The great majority of apprenticeships are in hairdressing.

Source: *Department of Employment Gazette*, May 1973, based on Table 5, page 456.

7.33   We believe that radical changes are required in the sphere of curricular and career guidance for girls in secondary schools. We note the current proposal for a study to be undertaken of the extent to which curricular differences and customs contribute to unequal opportunities for boys and girls.[1] Certainly the majority of girls still study subjects other than science, and the majority of boys still take at least some science and mathematics subjects. Broadening the curricula in girls' schools is essential if informed careers teachers are to be able to play a part in encouraging girls to qualify for careers which have not traditionally been followed by women.

7.34   To assist careers education staff in schools we welcome the provisions in the Employment and Training Act 1973 under which education authorities throughout Britain will be responsible for a careers service providing vocational guidance for people attending educational institutions and an employment service for those leaving them. This development of the youth employment service, now provided in some areas by the education authority and in others by the Department of Employment, seems likely to be of particular benefit to children and young people with only one parent at home to help them in making crucial decisions about further study and work and in providing career guidance throughout secondary, further and higher education from one source. But unless employers can be persuaded to provide career opportunities and training in jobs which have traditionally been available only to boys, and

[1] *Equal Opportunities for Men and Women, op cit*, paragraphs 3.5 and 3.6.

421

unless girls can be encouraged to take up such opportunities, good counselling of itself will not improve women's training and career opportunities.

INDUSTRIAL AND COMMERCIAL TRAINING

7.35   In modern industry there is a continuing process of change and modernisation for which training and retraining are necessary from the employer's point of view as well as that of the men and women in their labour force.   Much attention has been focused on this problem in recent years.   The Royal Commission on Trade Unions and Employers' Associations, which reported in 1968,[1] considered it essential that in the development of training over the next few years all those with responsibility in the field—education authorities, the youth employment service, industrial training boards, the Department of Employment, employers and trade unions—should grasp the opportunity to bring about a revolution in attitudes and in practical performance so far as the training of women is concerned.   They doubted whether the urgency of the problem—in economic terms—had been appreciated, and called for a sustained attack on outworn ideas and groundless preconceptions at all levels.   That much remains to be done is amply demonstrated by the extensive evidence which was given to the House of Lords Select Committee on the Anti-Discrimination Bill[2] on discriminatory practices and attitudes throughout the fields of education and employment, particularly in apprenticeship opportunities and day-release facilities.

---

[1] *Report of the Royal Commission on Trade Unions and Employers' Associations* (Donovan Commission), Cmnd 3623, 1968.

[2] House of Lords Anti-Discrimination Bill (HL), *Minutes of Evidence*, Sessions 1971–72, 1972–73.

7.36 We were particularly concerned to find that day-release opportunities for girls are fewer than for boys, and Table 7.5 below illustrates this fact:

TABLE 7.5

PERCENTAGE OF YOUNG WORKERS UNDER 18 YEARS OF AGE* GIVEN DAY RELEASE FOR FURTHER EDUCATION AT GRANT AIDED ESTABLISHMENTS: NOVEMBER 1971

England and Wales

Industry of employer	Young men	Young women	Total
Agriculture, forestry and fishing	39·0	9·0	33·6
Mining and quarrying	52·8	23·9	51·4
Manufacturing industries:			
Food, drink and tobacco	15·8	5·2	9·9
Coal and petroleum products	75·2	17·0	54·6
Chemicals and allied industries	52·3	15·0	30·3
Metal manufacture	69·4	39·3	62·0
Mechanical engineering	74·9	22·3	62·8
Instrument engineering	33·3	7·8	23·0
Electrical engineering	82·9	7·0	43·3
Shipbuilding and marine engineering	69·6	22·1	66·1
Vehicles	59·8	18·3	51·0
Metal goods not elsewhere specified	18·5	9·1	15·6
Textiles	9·1	3·6	5·8
Leather, leather goods and fur	3·5	4·3	3·8
Clothing and footwear	10·4	2·0	3·5
Bricks, pottery, glass, cement, etc	16·9	9·9	14·6
Timber, furniture, etc	22·5	3·9	18·9
Paper, printing and publishing	38·3	4·1	19·8
Other manufacturing industries	21·8	6·0	13·3
Construction	47·9	8·2	44·0
Gas, electricity and water	96·0	34·8	75·7
Transport and communication	46·4	17·5	36·0
Distributive trades	5·5	1·9	3·1
Insurance, banking and finance business services	8·5	2·0	3·3
Professional and scientific services	37·0	26·0	29·0
Miscellaneous services	35·5	23·7	29·8
Public administration and defence	106·5	74·2	90·0
Total	35·9	9·6	22·4

* Students aged under 18 years at 31 December, shown as a percentage of the estimated number aged under 18 years and insured under the National Insurance Acts at June (for example, in public administration and defence there were 9,639 young men insured in June 1971, and by November 1971 there were 10,289 enrolled in day-release courses.)

Source: Department of Education and Science; *Statistics of Education 1971*, Volume 3, *Further Education*, Table 40, HMSO, 1973.

Since the primary purpose of day-release schemes is to continue the general education of those young people who leave school at the minimum leaving age and to enable them to overcome some of the consequential disadvantages and handicaps, we deplore the fact that young women are denied equal opportunities. We recommend that employers should be encouraged to extend day release to all their young employees, and particularly that young girl workers should be offered the same day-release facilities as boys.

7.37 Since 1964, the Industrial Training Act has provided the general framework for industrial training, and it was hoped that the industrial training boards would provide incentives for employers to train more women. The boards do not publish separate figures of men and women receiving training, but the numbers of women trained under their arrangements are known to be small. We think it essential that the boards should ensure that employers, in their examination of their training needs, do not fail to identify those of their women employees, and that they make adequate arrangements for their training.

7.38 The Employment and Training Act 1973 has introduced changes in the system for financing and supervising the industrial training boards. The boards will now be under the general supervision of the Manpower Services Commission, which has been empowered to make selective grants to stimulate "key training activities" and itself to promote training where necessary in sectors of employment not covered by training boards. Arrangements made by the Commission may include arrangements for encouraging increases in the opportunities available to women and girls for employment and training. We consider that the Commission should exercise its training functions so as to encourage increased training opportunities for women and girls and the making of arrangements that are sufficiently flexible not to exclude those with family responsibilities.

7.39 Until recently, the main emphasis of government sponsored vocational training has been towards craft level courses in government training centres. In consequence, most of the trainees have been men. Under the new training opportunities scheme (TOPS) full-time courses in a variety of subjects have become more widely available in colleges of further education and employers' establishments. A broad range of training needs is now covered by such diverse courses as sewing machining, hotel and catering, clerical, commercial and management studies. These are attracting an increasing proportion of women who now form about one quarter of all TOPS trainees. In October 1973 about 7,000 women were on TOPS training courses, most of them in colleges of further education on commercial and clerical courses.[1] For people with domestic responsibilities which prevent them from undertaking full-time courses, such as mothers with young children, TOPS is experimenting in some areas with part-time training in clerical and commercial subjects. We welcome the efforts that are being made to encourage more women to take training courses under the scheme, and the diversification of courses to offer them a wider choice of employment. We consider that the scheme should be given wide publicity.

TRAINING ALLOWANCES

7.40 Our attention was drawn to the fact that the training allowances paid under the Training Opportunities Scheme are higher for men than for women. For example the adult rate for single women at £11·65 is currently 70p lower than that for single men. We are glad to note however that to keep in step with the policy on the implementation of equal pay, set out in the Equal Pay Act 1970, the differential will be eliminated by 29 December 1975.

---

[1] House of Commons Official Report, 2 November 1973, column 481.

SECTION 6—CONCLUSION

7.41 In this, as in other Parts of the Report, our terms of reference have compelled us to examine how a major national problem impinges upon the lives of fatherless families. Since the early days of industrialisation, women have constituted both a significant proportion of the country's labour force and a main source of cheap labour. An inescapable conclusion from the many recent studies of women's experience in trying to reconcile the claims of marriage, motherhood and work is the existence of a traditional and firmly rooted double standard of occupational morality. As a society we pay lip service to the ideal of equality for women whilst practising discrimination in the very area where it hurts most. The substantial study of *Sex, Career and Family* by a Political and Economic Planning group observes that women:

> tend not to be offered the same chances of training for skilled work or promotion as men nor to be motivated by their education or work environment to take them; that they tend to be segregated into " women's work ", devalued by unequal pay, treated as lacking in commitment to their work and as unsuitable to be in authority over men, and trained and encouraged not merely to accept these conditions but to think them right; and that husbands, the community . . . and employers have only half-heartedly adapted to the change in the women's labour market due to the increased share taken in it by married women.[1]

Women form the hard core of low-paid workers compressed into a narrow range of predominantly women's occupations, and we have shown how these general disadvantages bear particularly upon lone mothers. We recognise that our recommendations in this Part of our Report are short-term palliatives for a condition which stems as much from the low status of women in the labour market as from the collapse of families. For the future we can do no more than point to the importance to one-parent families of attacking the occupational discrimination between men and women which has characterised the economic history of industrialism.

---

[1] Michael P Fogarty and Rhona and Robert Rapoport: *Sex, Career and Family*, Allen and Unwin, 1971, page 25.

PART 8—PARENTS AND CHILDREN

SECTION 1—THE SOCIAL AND PERSONAL LIFE OF ONE-PARENT FAMILIES

8.1 We feel conscious that the mass of factual and statistical information that is assembled in the preceding pages, and the detailed exposition of the position of the one-parent family within those areas of life which are the subject of organisation by the State and the community—courts, law, financial support, housing—still do not convey the entire truth concerning such families. There is a missing element. This has to do with what it is like in terms of immediate human experience, in the process of living from day to day, rearing children, and coping with the repetitive small problems as well as the pervasive great ones, to be and have the responsibilities of a lone parent.

8.2 It is both a difficult and essential task for us to complete our picture of the one-parent family by adding this missing element. The difficulty arises partly because we have to deal with factors which, to a large extent, operate within the consciousness of individuals and so do not lend themselves to objective measurement; and partly that there is a danger of over emotional presentation.

8.3 It is particularly important to avoid, in the interests of one-parent families themselves, any stereotyping of their condition. One-parent families do not share a common affliction in the sense that this might be said of all who suffer from a physical disablement of a certain kind. Many of the parents and children in such families are successful in their own relationships, form rewarding relationships with others, attain a measure of personal and social competence and success, and enjoy a level of happiness which in no way differentiates them from other families or groupings of families in the community. In all these matters they vary, like all other families, among themselves. In some, the condition of being a one-parent family may even create a process of challenge and response which lifts them to achievements they would not otherwise have attained. For some again, the withdrawal of a violent husband and father or a neglectful wife and mother may create better, even if still unsatisfactory, conditions in the home than existed previously. It would be untrue of one-parent families and do an injustice to them if an account of the disadvantages from which they suffer were to categorise them as a section of our society united in inadequacy, whether self-made or imposed.

8.4 That said, the essential part of the task remains to describe those features of one-parent family life which, because they leave their deepest trace on the minds of individuals, or even because they are so commonplace and recurrent, tend to escape the more formal sort of analysis.

8.5 The source of the material on which we draw for this purpose is the almost overwhelming volume of evidence that was submitted to us and research studies which we examined dealing directly with the experience of lone mothers and lone fathers. Some of this evidence came from individuals recounting their own problems and in the form of individual case studies prepared by organisations in the field and transmitted for our consideration. Our rule in considering this evidence has been to avoid any form of generalisation from a few instances. The material, however, offers no such temptations. The same themes repeat themselves so frequently and so cogently that it is impossible to doubt that they represent part of the stuff of life for their narrators.

8.6 These themes involve or affect both parent and child, and in separating them for the purposes of exposition we are dividing phenomena which in many cases need to be understood in their interaction upon each other.

8.7 It is, in the first instance, to be remembered that bereavement, the break-up of a marriage or a stable association, or an illegitimate birth—all of them events which may create a one-parent family—may involve suffering and a sense of loss which may be long-lasting in their effects. How the parent will be affected will vary with the circumstances. To take one example: unmarried parenthood may be the result of a considered act by a mother, who can afford to look after her child, which brings her fulfilment; or it may be unplanned, bitterly resented, and the starting point of a rupture with her family and economic deprivation.

8.8 But what is of general application to the one-parent situation, irrespective of its origin, is the compulsion in some degree to cope alone with all those circumstances which it is of the essence of the institution of the family to cope with in partnership.

8.9 We have been struck by the evidence of how universally the division of labour is taken for granted by which mothers and fathers in the two-parent family seek to enrich the upbringing of their children by extending their range of activities—especially in their educational and leisure activities. The handicaps of the one-parent family in this respect have been continuously emphasised. Even at the level of disposing of the everyday chores, and despite the degree of merger between the traditional roles of male and female which has taken place in the last decade, many household tasks still tend to be allocated sexually. Men mend fuses and women do the ironing. The necessity for the lone parent to take on both roles may arise suddenly, leaves no alternative, and often is not satisfactorily achieved.

8.10 One of the main personal problems in one-parent families is the parents' social isolation. They suffer from loneliness—not only of surroundings, but also of unshared difficulties. They are lonely in their responsibility for the physical care of the children—a responsibility which often robs them of sleep and makes demands on them beyond their physical stamina. They carry the entire burden of responsibility for the social, emotional and moral upbringing of the children, and for that part of their education which has to take place outside school. They suffer all the strains of being compelled, as one parent, to play the part of two, in order to create within the home a microcosm of the society in which children will become adults.

8.11 On top of these stresses often comes the frustration of foregoing sexual relations or conducting them clandestinely so as to avoid the notice of the children or the neighbours or arousing the suspicions of the officers of the Supplementary Benefits Commission. Then there is the demand for physical omnipresence which young children impose upon a parent who has no standby. However devoted the lone parent may be to his or her child, the unrelieved company of children may become debilitating, both mentally and emotionally. The lone mother in particular—men seem to find it a little easier to draw upon the goodwill of friends and relations—may find herself virtually caged in the home, with little in the way of amusement or relaxation, and no time or opportunity to establish new relationships that might offer a chance for remarriage or the formation of a new stable partnership. More than that, the disruption caused by the breakdown of a marriage or the birth of an illegitimate child tends by a ripple effect to upset the circle of established relationships which grew out of the previous situation. Daughters may have to return to their own parents in circumstances which attract the latter's moral disapproval, create a role-conflict, especially between mother and grandmother, in dealing with the children, and impose the tensions which arise from over-crowding and demand on washing, cooking and toilet facilities which may already be limited or strained. The divorced or deserted wife may feel an outsider in the circle of married couples among whom she and her husband moved when they lived together, and sense herself to be the subject of tittle-tattle or disapproval. If, on the other hand, she moves to a new district, more likely than not to poor accommodation to which she may hesitate to invite new acquaintances, she loses contact with supportive friends. All these factors add up to a social isolation which on the evidence submitted to us emerges as one of the main personal problems of one-parent families.

8.12   We have so far examined these personal burdens and disadvantages from the point of view of the parent in the one-parent family, and in so doing have continued, as in the earlier Parts of this Report, to look at the scene mainly through adult eyes. It has, however, at this point to be emphasised that there are more children than parents in one-parent families, that the number of such children—1,080,000 of them—is very large indeed, and that all of them are at least at risk of suffering the reciprocal effects of those same burdens and disadvantages. These are the two sides of the same coin. Just as the parent may have to cope with the special adversities we have described, so may the child have to cope with a mother who is constantly worried with the effort of making the money go round, who has nothing to spare for extras which most other children take for granted, and who is lonely and depressed. Such a child may have to fend for himself because his parent is working,[1] carry a share of domestic responsibilities beyond his years and capacity, and so be compelled to frequent absence from school.[2]

8.13   These material disadvantages may be imposed upon a child who is already emotionally deprived through the lack of a second parent, or the loss of a father or mother he has known. Some children suffer lasting depression on the death of a parent, and many suffer from bitterness or divided loyalties when their parents have parted. Such children may feel different from the others at school, or in the community at large. They may be made, through the behaviour of their peers or of adults, to feel ashamed of their situation. However it has arisen, disturbed feelings in the child are likely to be part of his response to the loss of a parent.

8.14   We show later[3] how, during the post-war period, a growing awareness has developed among social workers and educationalists of the importance of

---

[1] See for example, the survey by the Office of Population Censuses and Surveys, *Families and their Needs, op cit*, paragraphs 5.4.6 and 5.7.1–5.7.4.

[2] Several of the organisations giving evidence demonstrated that poor attendance, especially among girls, was a feature of school life of children in one-parent families.

[3] Section 2.

environment to the child's development, behaviour and attainments. This view has been expressed in the Newsom,[1] Plowden[2] and Seebohm[3] Reports. A child suffering from personal or environmental difficulties may express a reaction in a number of different ways—for example, through disturbed or anti-social behaviour or by doing badly at school. It would hardly be surprising in view of the multiple disadvantages from which some children in one-parent families suffer to find that they tend to show more signs of stress than children from two-parent families. Some evidence which supports such a conclusion is considered in Appendix 12, which has been prepared by one of our members. The Appendix suggests that among children in one-parent families there may be proportionately more who show signs of disturbed or delinquent behaviour than among children in two-parent families, and that these are less likely to do well at school, which they tend to leave earlier, from which they play truant more often, and at which they tend to achieve a lower level of attainment than children from two-parent families.

8.15　The studies discussed in Appendix 12 suggest that the effects on children of being in a one-parent family are very complex and not well understood. We consider it to be most important that further research into this subject should be undertaken. We welcome particularly the initiative of the last Secretary of State for Social Services in promoting large scale studies to investigate the possibility that there is a cycle of transmitted deprivation.[4] If, as does seem at least possible, the existence of such a cycle can be demonstrated, we consider it likely that one of the most certain triggers of the cycle will be the one-parent family situation. This risk provides, in our view, one of the strongest reasons for offering special help to one-parent families, both in the form of cash to raise their general standard of living, as we have proposed earlier in this Report, and in the form of services to help parent and child cope more adequately with the demands of day-to-day life. We agree with the view of the Seebohm Committee that " expenditure of time, effort, talent and money on children in need of social care is, above all, an investment in the future. It makes no sense to us, either on humanitarian grounds or in terms of sheer economics, to allow young children to be neglected physically, emotionally or intellectually. By doing so, we not only mortgage the happiness of thousands of children, and the children they in turn will have, but also pile up future problems and expense for society into the bargain."[5]

8.16　The emphasis, therefore, in this concluding Part of our Report is that our recommendations for legal reform, financial support, and improvement in the conditions of housing and employment are not the entire answer to the difficulties of one-parent families. There are more intangible consequences of their situation which material benefits and efficient and sympathetic administration can alleviate but not cure. Some of these intangibles are part of the common lot of mankind—ills inseparable from the human condition. But

[1] *Half our Future:* A report of the Central Advisory Council for Education (England), HMSO, 1963.

[2] *Children and their Primary Schools:* A report of the Central Advisory Council for Education (England) volumes 1 and 2, HMSO, 1967.

[3] *Report of the Committee on Local Authority and Allied Personal Social Services,* Cmnd 3703, HMSO, 1968.

[4] Speeches to the Pre-School Playgroup Association on 29 June 1972 and to the Association of Directors of Social Services on 27 March 1973.

[5] *Op cit,* paragraph 191.

we proceed from the notion that social progress depends to a very significant extent upon the expansion of the sphere of what is considered to be remediable. In this process the development of the social and educational services has a principal part to play ; and this is what we go on to consider.

SECTION 2—DEVELOPMENT OF SERVICES FOR PARENTS AND CHILDREN

INTRODUCTION

8.17 In the previous Section we have described how the absence of one of the parents can affect the social and personal lives of the remaining parent and the children. In the rest of this Part of our Report we look at the various services available to help parents and children with some of these difficulties. While the account we give is written almost entirely in terms of England and Wales, any significant difference in the Scottish provision that may be relevant to our remit is mentioned. This section surveys the changing attitudes underlying the development of personal social services, briefly describes the services at present available which are of particular help to one-parent families and makes some general comment on future needs.

8.18 In considering the provision of social services it is important to bear in mind that the effectiveness of services varies enormously throughout the country. In rural areas services may be less accessible than in towns. The level of spending on services varies, depending on local initiative, the availability of resources and even the prejudices and perceptions of local people, including professionals. Similarly, the extent of voluntary initiative is uneven throughout the country. In some areas voluntary organisations are strong and self-reliant, often receiving considerable sums by way of grants from central or local authorities. In other areas, they make little impact on social need, and receive little help from public funds.

CHANGING ATTITUDES TOWARDS PROVISION OF SERVICES

8.19 The major causes of one-parent family situations, death, birth out of wedlock, and family breakdown, are basic to the human condition; but some of the ways in which they affect individuals relate to the social and historical context in which they live. Attitudes to morals, class distinctions and sexual discrimination, rather than considerations of individual needs, have often influenced help offered or refused, and the gradual acceptance of community responsibility for the needs of one-parent families has been a slow and painful process, characterised at times by insensitive reactions to the plight of the people concerned.

8.20 We have described earlier in this Report (Part 4, Section 2 and Appendix 5) how, until quite recent times, the poor law was virtually the only form of public provision for one-parent families who could not maintain themselves, or were not maintained by their relatives. We have shown how harsh was the treatment meted out to the unmarried mother in particular, often involving separation from her child, who would be obliged to spend his or her life in the workhouse until old enough to be sent out to work. We have traced the gradual change in attitudes towards illegitimacy, towards the poor, and towards children in the course of this century and shown how, in 1948, responsibility for services and responsibility for finance were finally separated by the National Assistance Act. This Act made the provision of a basic level of income for families unable to support themselves the responsibility of a national body. We have not so far mentioned, but by no means overlook, the contribution to the beginnings of preventive work with families made by local authority health services, notably through the health visitor's close contact with families with children. Our purpose now is to demonstrate the broad sweep of changes in attitudes during the post-war years towards the treatment of children and families in need, and to one-parent families in particular, as reflected in a series of major reports from committees set up by successive governments. We do so without prejudice to our own views on the direction that services should take, which are set out in the succeeding Sections.

Curtis Committee

8.21 An important area in the development of personal social services for families in the early post-war period was the care of children; and although these services were by no means exclusively used by one-parent families, it is likely that such families formed a significant proportion of clients.[1] The quality of care provided became the subject of a public enquiry towards the end of the second world war, when the Curtis Committee[2] was appointed. Their terms of reference included children maintained by local authorities under the Acts and regulations relating to the poor law; children found to be homeless on the winding-up of the government evacuation scheme; children brought before the courts as delinquent or in need of care or protection and required by the courts to live elsewhere than in their own homes; children cared for by voluntary organisations; and children whose fathers had been killed in the war. Children were cared for in workhouses, children's homes, nurseries, barrack-type institutions, grouped cottage homes, scattered homes, receiving homes and foster homes. Some received kindly, warm and child-centred care. Some were so deprived, physically, emotionally and intellectually, that the Committee's descriptions of what they saw shocked public opinion.

8.22 The Curtis Report led to the Children Act 1948,[3] part of the post-war legislation on which current social services have been built. Children's departments which were then set up took the place of previous piecemeal services to care for children deprived of a normal home life. The Act placed upon local authorities a duty to act in the manner of a good parent for all children received into or committed to their care, many of whom each year inevitably were the children of one-parent families.

Post-war reorganisation of services

8.23 In 1948 the local authority public assistance committees were finally broken up. Their financial functions were taken over by the National Assistance Board, and the duties relating to children by the new children's

---

[1] As they do of child-care services today—see paragraph 8.45.

[2] *Report of the Care of Children Committee:* Cmd 6922, 1946. The Scottish equivalent was the Clyde Committee on Homeless Children which also reported in 1946 (Cmd 6911).

[3] This Act covered Scotland as well as England and Wales, but in relation to Scotland it has now been repealed by the Social Work (Scotland) Act 1968.

departments. Their other functions, including those relating to homeless families and the handicapped, were transferred to welfare services which formed separate departments or, in some authorities, became part of public health departments. These services were by no means the only ones which encountered families in distress. Both education and housing services found themselves dealing with families in difficulties and developed specialised welfare provision such as education welfare, child guidance, the school psychological service and housing welfare; and under the National Health Service Act 1946, and the National Health Service (Scotland) Act 1947, local health authorities had extensive powers and responsibilities on such matters as the provision of health visitors to give advice on child care, the provision of domestic help and day-care services, the prevention of illness and the care and after-care of the sick. Often the same families might be the concern of several of these departments, and of voluntary organisations at the same time.

Ingleby Committee

8.24 While services for families in difficulties were developing in this somewhat piecemeal way, a considerable interest was being shown in families with multiple problems who seemed unable to cope with many aspects of their personal and social lives and who were involved with a wide variety of social agencies.[1] Growing emphasis was being laid on the importance of a secure and adequate home life in childhood as the foundation of proper, healthy development in individuals. Lack of it was increasingly seen as one of the major causes of problems such as mental illness, offences by juveniles and general inadequacy as parent, spouse or worker. The Ingleby Committee, reporting in 1960, said:

> those families which have themselves failed to achieve a stable and satisfactory family life will be the most vulnerable, and . . . the children brought up in them will be those most likely to succumb to whate . . adverse influences there may be in the outside world.[2]

A similar view was to be taken by the Kilbrandon Committee which reported four years later.[3]

8.25 In addition, the concept of preventive services to forestall suffering, family breakdown and the need for more drastic measures, began to emerge, and to engage the thought and energy of social services personnel.[4] The Ingleby Committee was able to say in 1960, " In the child care service, as in other social services, the problem of preventing neglect of children in their own homes has received much attention in recent years, with growing emphasis on the need to treat the family as a unit and to help parents to remedy the conditions that lead to neglect or to avoidable separation of children from their parents."[5] They urged that doctors, clergy, social workers and others should

---

[1] See. for example, Barbara Wootton: *Social Science and Pathology*, Allen and Unwin, 1959, pages 54–62.

[2] *Report of the Committee on Children and Young Persons*, Cmnd 1191, 1960, paragraph 11.

[3] See paragraph 8.30 below.

[4] See, for example, Ministry of Health Circular 27/54 which encouraged local health authorities to use their powers under section 28 of the National Health Service Act 1946 to tackle the " vicious circle " by which " problem families . . . tend to reproduce themselves in the next generation."

[5] *Op cit*, paragraph 19.

learn how to " recognise the danger signals . . . both the obviously inadequate or sub-standard family, and the much less obvious family in which there is maladjustment of personal relationships; "

> In the former, the standard of behaviour and morals will sometimes be as deplorable as the material conditions, but personal relationships may remain good and helpful to the children. In the latter, on the other hand, though outwardly all seems as it should be, the disturbances of family relationships may be a real danger to them.[1]

8.26 The legislation which followed the Ingleby Report, the Children and Young Persons Act 1963, gave specific powers and duties under section 1 of the Act to local authorities to provide a service of advice, guidance and assistance to families where there was a child already in care who might with help return home, or a child who might, without help to the family, have to be separated from them by being received into care, or might appear before a juvenile court.[2]

Seebohm Committee

8.27 Under the stimulus of the powers provided by the 1963 Act, awareness of needs among children and families continued to grow, and the personal social services expanded in an endeavour to meet the need revealed. As they became more involved with preventive work for families, social workers became increasingly aware of the interaction between housing, income, child-care and marital and family problems, and of the corresponding interaction between the various local authority services themselves and between them and the national income support services (provided first by the National Assistance Board, and later by the Supplementary Benefits Commission). Then, in 1965, the Committee on Local Authority and Allied Personal Social Services (the Seebohm Committee) was appointed " to review the organisation and responsibilities of the local authority personal social services in England and Wales, and consider what changes are desirable to ensure an effective family service".[3] The approach the Committee took demonstrated how far things had moved since the " less eligibility " outlook typified by public assistance in pre-war social services.

8.28 The principal recommendation of the Committee, which has since been implemented, was that there should be a new local authority department to provide a community-based and family-orientated service available to all:

> This new department will, we believe, reach far beyond the discovery and rescue of social casualties; it will enable the greatest possible number of individuals to act reciprocally, giving and receiving service for the well-being of the whole community.[4]

The Seebohm Committee had formed the opinion that the "structure of the personal social services ignores the nature of much social distress "[5] and that " we can and should encourage those who need help to seek it ".[6] Looking

---

[1] *Ibid*, paragraph 14.

[2] Children and Young Persons Act 1963, section 1. Section 1 also applied to Scotland until replaced by the wider provisions of section 12 of the Social Work (Scotland) Act 1968.

[3] *Report of Committee on Local Authority and Allied Personal Social Services*, Cmnd 3703, 1968, paragraph 1.

[4] *Ibid*, paragraph 2.

[5] *Ibid*, paragraph 142.

[6] *Ibid*, paragraph 146.

specifically at social services for children, they took the view that there was a need " for a much wider acceptance of the idea of shared responsibility and a greater development of mutual co-operation between parents and those social services with special responsibilities for helping parents with the up-bringing of their children."[1]

> A clear and inescapable responsibility for the social care of all children who require it must be placed upon a particular local authority committee. We recognise that adequate social care is a difficult concept which in any case is liable to change. It includes the care of children at present provided by children's departments for those in its care; preventive work with the families of children at risk; domestic or day nursery assistance to families which are unduly burdened or have insufficient personal resources, and more general provisions, such as play facilities, which we regard as an essential prerequisite for the adequate social development of children . . . . Thus, social care implies various combinations of shared responsibility in order to support and assist parents (including men and women who are having to carry the responsibility without the help of wife or husband) in carrying out their part to the best of their ability.[2]

Reorganisation of social services in 1971

8.29 The Local Authority Social Services Act 1970, which came into operation in 1971, carried out the main recommendation of the Seebohm Committee for the integration of the administration of the personal social services by requiring each authority to set up a social services committee and appoint a director of social services. Along with many other services work with children and with families with children (apart from education welfare, child guidance, hospital social work and the functions of the probation and after-care service)[3] were now the responsibility of one department and administered by one committee.

Development of social services in Scotland after 1963

8.30 The application of section 1 of the Children and Young Persons Act 1963 to Scotland had followed the McBoyle Report of that year on Prevention of Neglect of Children (Cmnd 1966), and in 1964 the report of the Kilbrandon Committee on Children and Young Persons (Scotland) was published.[4] The first conclusion of Lord Kilbrandon and his colleagues was that, among children appearing before the courts, "The distinguishing factor is their common need for special measures of education and training, the normal upbringing processes for whatever reasons having failed or fallen short."[5] They recommended, among other things, the reorganisation of the existing statutory services primarily concerned with children in a comprehensive local department to be known as the " social education department " and to be under the director of education, and that a system of children's panels should replace existing juvenile courts. In 1965 proposals for the reorganisation of social work services in Scotland were published in the White Paper on Social Work

---

1 *Ibid*, paragraph 186.

2 *Ibid*, paragraph 187.

3 Under the National Health Service Reorganisation Act 1973 hospital social work comes under the social services departments. The future of the child guidance service, which is the concern of three separate authorities—local education authorities, social services departments and regional hospital boards—is under consideration. In some areas social services departments have assumed responsibility for education welfare.

4 *Report of the Committee on Children and Young Persons (Scotland)*, Cmnd 2306, 1964.

5 *Ibid*, paragraph 252(1).

in the Community (Cmnd. 3065). The policies proposed in the White Paper were implemented by the Social Work (Scotland) Act 1968 and in November1969 the former child-care, welfare and mental health departments of the local authorities together with the probation and after-care services were merged in comprehensive social work departments.[1] In April 1971 a system of children's hearings on the lines recommended by the Kilbrandon Committee was established under the 1968 Act.

8.31 In regard to children and their families generally, the White Paper of 1965 saw the new social work departments as providing " a range of services which children and their families can be offered on an entirely voluntary basis ", and as working with and ensuring effective support for children and the families of children for whom voluntary help had not been sufficient. All this is now done within the social work departments in Scotland. In particular, they have responsibilities under the 1968 Act in regard to children requiring to be taken into care or who are otherwise deprived which are comparable with those still applicable in England and Wales under the Children Act 1948 and section 1 of the Children and Young Persons Act 1963, as well as the new responsibilities for children who are found by children's hearings, established under the 1968 Act, to require compulsory measures of care.

Developments in the education field

8.32 The emergence in the field of social services of the conviction that the family must be seen as a unit, and that the child should not be treated in isolation, was paralleled by thinking in the education field. The Newsom Committee's remit required them to study the content of the curricula (including extra-curricular activities) for secondary school pupils (age 13-16) of average or less than average ability, but their studies showed them that there was urgent need to strengthen all existing links between home and school and in difficult areas to create new ones, and generally to consider the social life of pupils as well as the education provided. In their report made in 1963[2] the Newsom Committee suggested that there was urgent need for research into the problems of environmental and linguistic handicaps.

8.33 When the Plowden Committee reported on primary education[3] they too drew attention to the need for significant links between educational services and the social world of young pupils, and to the interaction between social factors of children's family lives and learning capacity. Among the important consequences of the Plowden Report are its impact on the development of services for under-fives and recent demonstrations of the practicability of their suggested application to socially deprived areas of the principle of positive discrimination. Such discrimination was later applied to five selected areas in order that the results of intensive educational intervention in the care and educational progress of children in areas of social deprivation might be assessed.

---

[1] Hospital social work is to be included in the social work departments some time after local government reorganisation in 1975. In almost all areas the school welfare services remained with the education department of the local authority in 1969. The child-guidance service continues as an education department responsibility.

[2] *Half our Future:* A report of the Central Advisory Council for Education (England), HMSO, 1963.

[3] *Children and their Primary Schools:* A report of the Central Advisory Council for Education (England), HMSO, 1967.

In the report edited by A H Halsey, *EPA Problems and Policies*,[1] as found in four of the selected areas, it was concluded that the educational priority area was a socially and administratively viable unit through which to apply the principle of positive discrimination.

8.34 The Kilbrandon Committee's views in the social education field were broadly similar to those of the Plowden Committee, and the subsequent integration of many of the social services into social services departments in England and Wales and social work departments in Scotland has made liaison between teachers and social workers easier.

SERVICES AVAILABLE TO ONE-PARENT FAMILIES

8.35 Our purpose here is to give a brief picture of the broad spectrum of services on which one-parent families can call. We deal in more detail in later Sections with those services of particular importance to one-parent families: social work support services (paragraph 8.36 below) are dealt with in Section 3, care of children (paragraphs 8.37 to 8.43 below) in Section 4, family planning services in Section 6 and mother and baby homes in Section 7.

Social work support services

8.36 These are provided under the powers already referred to in section 1 of the Children and Young Persons Act 1963;[2] and local authorities also have a power (though not a duty) under section 1 to provide assistance in kind or, exceptionally, in cash. In Scotland a similar but rather wider power is provided under section 12 of the Social Work (Scotland) Act 1968. Under these powers local authorities provide social work support to families and a survey undertaken for us in a four-week period at the end of 1970 by the Association of Children's Officers showed that about one quarter of all referrals under section 1 were one-parent families.[3]

Help in the home

8.37 Local authorities have a duty under section 13(1) of the Health Services and Public Health Act 1968 to provide home help for households " where such help is required owing to the presence of a person who is suffering from illness, lying-in, an expectant mother, aged, handicapped as a result of having suffered from illness or by congenital deformity or a child who has not attained the age which, for the purposes of the Education Act 1944 is, in his case, the upper limit of the compulsory school age. . . ." The great majority of home helps are employed in the homes of the elderly or chronic sick. Only 8 per cent of clients fall outside these groups including maternity cases which form 2 per cent. Home helps normally undertake domestic work but increasingly local authorities are widening their duties with the intention of expanding the service to families to provide planned support in many different situations and in particular with the aim of preventing children from being

---

[1] A H Halsey (Ed): *EPA Problems and Policies*, Educational Priority, Volume 1, HMSO, 1972.

[2] See paragraph 8.26 above.

[3] See Section 3 for further details of this survey.

436

received into care. A limited amount of help, for example, keeping an eye on the children before school but after the father has gone to work, is also provided for some motherless families.

Day care of under-fives

8.38 Under the National Health Services Act 1946 local authorities have a duty to make arrangements for the care of children under 5 who are not at school. Day-care services are provided for children with only one parent, where that parent has to go out to work, and for other children who need day care for special health or social reasons. Local authorities make day-care provision in a variety of ways: in England and Wales in March 1973, some 24,000 places were provided in day nurseries run by local authorities, but there were also 4,000 children in part-time nursery groups run by local authorities and more than 6,000 placed with registered child-minders, in private day nurseries and in playgroups. More than half the day-nursery places at present go to children from one-parent families.

8.39 In addition to their duty to provide day-care facilities, local authorities are required, under the Nurseries and Child-Minders Regulation Act 1948 (as amended), to register persons looking after a child under 5 to whom they are not related in their own home for payment, and to register any premises (such as private and employers' day nurseries) where children are looked after for more than two hours a day. Local authorities have powers of inspection and lay down standards of care and accommodation. In March 1973 there were over 420,000 registered places but only 82,000 offered full-time care and many of the part-time places were in playgroups.

8.40 Local education authorities provide nursery schools and classes under the 1944 Education Act. At present there are about 45,000 children receiving full-time education in such schools and classes, and 77,000 receiving part-time education.[1] A considerable expansion in the number of classes provided[2] is planned.

Day care of school children

8.41 Under section 53 of the Education Act 1944 a very limited number of facilities are provided by local authorities, often in co-operation with voluntary bodies, for school children out of school hours, mainly in the holidays only— for example, holiday camps for children of low-income families. Some authorities run or sponsor play leadership schemes, and evening play centres; and secondary schools themselves run clubs after school hours. Some authorities provide school meals in the holidays.

Boarding schools

8.42 Local authorities have power under section 8(2) of the Education Act 1944 to provide boarding education and to meet boarding costs for children who need special educational treatment, whose home circumstances are unsatisfactory, or whose parents are liable to move frequently. In 1972 about

---

[1] In addition there are 260,000 children in primary schools who start full-time education there before they are 5.

[2] *Education: A framework for expansion*, Cmnd 5174, 1972.

20,000 school children were assisted in this way. There is a similar power in the Education (Scotland) Act 1962, but there is relatively little boarding education in Scotland and the numbers assisted in this way are small.

Private fostering arrangements

8.43 The Children Act 1958, as amended by the Children and Young Persons Act 1969, lays certain statutory duties in relation to privately fostered children[1] on local authorities and on the parents and foster parents. Foster parents are required to notify the local authority in advance of their intention to receive a child, and if the child is removed to another foster home. Certain types of people are disqualified under the Act from taking private foster children and the local authority may also prohibit placements where they consider that the premises are not suitable. Local authorities have a duty to visit private foster children from time to time " to satisfy themselves as to the child's wellbeing and to give such advice as to their care and maintenance as may appear to be needed." If they consider that a child is being kept by a person " unfit to have his care " or in premises detrimental to him the authority may apply to a juvenile court for an order to remove him to a place of safety and a child so removed may be received into the care of the local authority. About 10,000 children are known to be placed privately with foster parents. In his recently published study, Robert Holman found that lone parents formed a third of all parents placing children.[2]

Children in care

8.44 Under section 1 of the Children Act 1948 local authorities have a duty to receive into care any child who has no parents, or has been abandoned, or whose parents cannot provide for his proper accommodation, maintenance or upbringing. Children may also be committed to the care of a local authority by the juvenile court under sections 1 or 7 of the Children and Young Persons Act 1969. A local authority may accommodate a child in their care in such manner as they think fit. Children in care are generally boarded out with foster parents or placed in a community home, which is a residential establishment managed by a local authority, or a voluntary organisation either on its own or in partnership with a local authority. The Act of 1969 replaced the former powers of the juvenile court to commit a child to an approved school or a remand home with a power to commit to the care of a local authority. Regionally-based systems of community homes, planned by local authorities through children's regional planning committees appointed by them under Part II of the Act, accordingly integrate the previously separate systems of approved schools, remand homes, children's homes, and hostels.

8.45 There were nearly 90,000 children in the care of local authorities in England and Wales on 31 March 1973.[3] There is a high turnover of children

[1] Privately fostered children are defined in section 2 of the Children Act 1958, as amended by section 52 of the Children and Young Persons Act 1969, as children who are " below the upper limit of the compulsory school age whose care and maintenance are undertaken by a person who is not a relative or guardian." The definition excludes children cared for for very short periods (for not more than six days, where the person is a regular foster parent and not more than twenty-seven days where she is not).

[2] Robert Holman: *Trading in children: a study of private fostering*, Routledge and Kegan Paul, 1973.

[3] These and the other figures relating to children in care in this paragraph are provisional figures supplied by the Department of Health and Social Security.

coming in for short periods (these form the bulk of all admissions) often because of the temporary illness or confinement of the mother. But the great majority of children in care at any one time are in long-term care. During the twelve months ended 31 March 1973, over 9,000 of the 50,000 children received into care, 18 per cent of the total, came specifically for " one-parent family " reasons —for example, because the mother had died or deserted and the father could not cope (over half fell into this category) or because the mother could not provide for an illegitimate child. But it is likely that a considerably higher proportion than this came from one-parent families—some of the children coming into care because of evictions, for instance, or because home conditions were unsatisfactory would be likely to be one-parent family children, as would some of the 19,500 coming into care because of the illness or confinement of a parent. Some indication of what the figure might be came from a survey done in 1970 and submitted in evidence by the Association of Children's Officers[1] which found that in 1970 over half of the long-stay cases in the care of 84 local authorities came from one-parent families, and over 60 per cent of short-stay cases.

Services provided by voluntary organisations

8.46 In some areas voluntary organisations play an important part in the provision of services, and a considerable amount of work is done by them, both independently and under the auspices of and with financial help from local authorities. The organisations involved range from large national organisations, employing professional staff and spending many thousands of pounds annually, to small locally based groups of people who come together for mutual support and assistance. Organisations such as the National Children's Home, Dr Barnardo's, Citizens' Advice Bureaux and others provide services which benefit many different groups of people, while the National Council for One Parent Families (formerly the National Council for the Unmarried Mother and her Child) and its Scottish counterpart are geared more specifically to helping the lone parent. Diocesan Councils for Moral Welfare, which formerly provided specially for single women, now offer family services.

8.47 There are two areas of particular relevance to one-parent families in which voluntary organisations play a big role. The first is in providing help for unmarried mothers;[2] traditionally this has often been in the form of mother and baby homes, but there are indications that a more flexible and varied approach may be needed in future (see Section 6). The second is work with neglected or ill-treated children. The pressures to which one-parent families are subject described in Section 1 sometimes result in complete failure to cope adequately with the children, and as a result they form quite a high proportion of families dealt with by the National Society for the Prevention of Cruelty to Children—25 per cent of their caseload in 1972.[3]

---

[1] Information obtained during the survey about the extent to which one-parent families turned or were referred to local authority social workers is given in Section 3.

[2] The former National Council for the Unmarried Mother and her Child and its Scottish counterpart have now decided to extend their interest to other types of lone parent, a decision which we welcome as being in accord with our belief that help to one-parent families should be given in relation to their needs, not in relation to the " type " of family.

[3] *The Child's Guardian*, 2/73. The experience of the Royal Scottish Society for the Prevention of Cruelty to Children has been similar.

8.48   Voluntary organisations also play a useful role as channels of referral to the numerous national and local government services, and as centres for advice and guidance.   Consequently they deal with quite large numbers of cases, many of them one-parent families.   For example, we were told in evidence that in 1969 the seven voluntary organisations making up the Inter-Diocesan Committee for the Greater London Area helped 3,950 unmarried mothers; the Family Welfare Association, in April 1970, had a caseload of 997 of which 283 were one-parent families; and in a six-month period in 1969, the National Council for the Unmarried Mother and her Child dealt with 1,200 requests for help in finding accommodation and employment.

Self-help groups

8.49   A number of groups have been formed by lone parents themselves to provide mutual support—for example, Cruse clubs for widows, Mothers in Action, clubs for the separated and divorced, and Gingerbread.   Some small informal groups of lone mothers meet at regular intervals to provide a social occasion and to offer mutual support.   These groups are sometimes sponsored by established voluntary organisations such as local churches, and some assistance is given by local authorities.   They may provide not only mutual support but practical help in the form, for example, of mutual baby-sitting services and help in the home or with the children in times of family crisis.

Family planning services

8.50   Under the National Health Service Reorganisation Act 1973, the provision of a family planning service will become the responsibility of the national health service.   The service will be provided through clinics, hospitals, domiciliary services, and, if the current negotiations with general practitioners are successful, through family doctors.   The service will be available to all who require it irrespective of age, marital status or sex.   Advice, examination and treatment will be free and supplies will be available at the prescription charge rate, and the normal exemptions will apply.   Similar provisions are being made in Scotland under the National Health Service (Scotland) Act 1972.

THE WAY FORWARD

8.51   We deal in the following Sections with particular proposals for improvements in services, but we make here two points of general application, the first concerning the level of provision of services and the second concerning the need of those using the services for information and advice.

Level of provision

8.52   We have shown how in the period since 1945 more progress has been made in the recognition of need for services than in any previous period of our history, and post-war services have in fact, as many hoped they would, illumined need in an unprecedented way.   Unlike the past, a characteristic of statutory services now is that although many are restricted by legal definition to certain groups, overall they are designed to assist not merely the disadvantaged and those in material or emotional need, but the population as a whole.   This is seen most clearly in educational and health services where there is almost universal provision by the public sector. Such services are available as of right to persons in defined categories, be they rich or poor. Since the demise of the poor law, other services have been increasingly seen by a discerning public as rights, not privileges, and a vocal press and public opinion have been demanding better services of all kinds, including domiciliary services, day-care provision and residential care.

8.53 Social services are not seen, and should not be seen, merely as intervening in crises to forestall breakdown, or picking up the pieces afterwards, but as having a positive role in improving the quality of life and preventing waste and suffering among those who have social problems. This is particularly true of services for children and young people because severe deprivation at an early age may appear in succeeding generations.[1] The provision of good quality social services is one of society's ways of breaking into this social malaise, but to perform this task they must be based on a philosophy which not only changes with the times but of itself encourages change. Such an approach requires a programme on a broad front and a co-ordinated effort from several local authority departments and voluntary organisations; it is also likely to require a substantially higher level of resources, in terms both of money and manpower, than has been committed to the personal social services hitherto.

8.54 We believe that as the inherent difficulties of large-scale organisational change diminish, local authority social services departments will increasingly provide better services to individuals and the community than the former fragmented services set up in 1948, but it is a corollary of this development that, except in the voluntary sector, no services have been designed with the single purpose of assisting one-parent families. The lone parent is one of a wide group of individuals making use of social welfare services, and we welcome this as it means that they are not stigmatised as a group in special need of attention. But the wide-ranging approach also means that to some extent one-parent families will be competing for scarce resources with other needy groups and this at a time when, as indicated in the preceding paragraphs, the personal social services as a whole are moving into an era in which they are likely to have to serve a wider public in a more positive way than hitherto. It is vital, if this sort of approach is to succeed, that resources are made available on a sufficient scale to ensure that needy groups like one-parent families are not neglected in the general march forward.

Need for information and advice[2]

8.55 In spite of the recent organisational changes, the range of statutory and voluntary organisations, their functions, their procedures and interconnections present a bewildering picture even to people who are familiar with the social services. To the family in need they present a confused pattern based on different administrative offices, covering different geographical areas,

---

[1] Discussed, for example, by Sir Keith Joseph, when Secretary of State for Social Services, in his speeches to the Pre-School Playgroups' Association on 29 June 1972 and to the Association of Directors of Social Services on 27 March 1973.

[2] At several other points in this Report we stress the need for improved information and advisory services—for example, in connection with taxation in Part 5, Section 8, in connection with the legal aspects of housing in Part 6, Section 4, and in connection with training for employment in Part 7.

and sometimes giving conflicting advice and information. Even the recent and current reforms do not and will not obviate many of the weaknesses inherent in a system which seeks to provide personalised service at a local level to a wide range of persons. Although families can now go to one department in one authority for personal social services, and the new area health authorities will in the main coincide with local authority boundaries, families are still faced with a confusion of different authorities and boundaries. Housing, for example, is to be dealt with by the same authority as social services and education in metropolitan areas, but by a different authority in the counties; income support is on a different network altogether, being administered from local offices of the Department of Health and Social Security, while employment services are on yet another network run by the Department of Employment.

8.56 The delivery of services is also affected by the variation in level of provision between one authority and another, to which we referred at the beginning of this Section, and by the presence of voluntary enterprise. Services which in one area are provided by the local authority may be provided in an adjoining area by a voluntary organisation. Additionally, different authorities may arrange their services differently so that education welfare may be the responsibility of the director of education in one area, whilst in another it is provided through the director of social services.

8.57 One of the fundamental problems faced by organised social services is how to be available to people who require them at the right time and at the right place. It is still difficult for the family with a problem to know where to turn for advice. We have already shown how many turn to voluntary organisations for guidance. The National Citizens' Advice Bureaux Council is perhaps the organisation with the widest remit to provide information about services of all kinds but social services departments and health visitors also have considerable knowledge. However, detailed information about benefits and how to claim them, and even the names and addresses of local organisations, are notoriously difficult to keep up-to-date as benefits change and secretaries and chairmen are replaced. So much so that, although they may have received extensive training, neither social workers nor health visitors, much less many other professional workers, are able to provide the detailed advice and help which many people need to find their way through the benefits network.

8.58 We received a considerable amount of evidence about the difficulties of securing information about services. It was suggested to us that more publicity was needed so that one-parent families and others in need of assistance could more readily seek help. A number of organisations felt that some kind of register of one-parent families should be compiled by local authorities so that appropriate services could be offered; and some favoured the idea that those responsible for administering national insurance and supplementary benefits should notify social services and local education departments of the names of those whom they learned through benefit claims were widowed or otherwise on their own.

8.59 We have given careful consideration to these proposals but we are wholly opposed to the introduction of a system by which the names of lone parents and their children are automatically passed from one public office to another, or from a public office to a voluntary organisation, without the knowledge and consent of the persons concerned. Furthermore, unless the ground is carefully prepared beforehand, a visit by a social worker may be seen by the parent concerned as an intrusion into personal affairs.

8.60 There are, however, a number of ways in which lone parents could be better helped to make contact with the services they need. A good deal could be done by organisations in touch with lone parents keeping information about other possible sources of help. We see value, for example, in officers of the Supplementary Benefits Commission, registrars of births and deaths, local authority social workers and others having up-to-date information available about services for lone parents so that they can give advice where appropriate. Some already stock leaflets issued by other authorities and make their own available in other public offices: for example, the Department of Health and Social Security issue to local authorities a guide designed for social workers and others who come into personal contact with those who may be eligible for grants and pensions. A few local authorities have prepared leaflets setting out services generally available, but it would be helpful if they were to produce one aimed at lone parents in particular, setting out all the major statutory and voluntary services available and showing how they can be obtained. We consider that this service would be of particular value to lone parents, because of the bewilderment and confusion which many experience at the point of break-up and because lone women may have difficulty in finding their way about if they have relied on their husbands to cope with any previous contact with official bodies.

8.61 We believe it would also be of help to lone parents if some more rational system in the provision of advice prevailed. We have already referred to the number of different agencies which may be involved in helping them, and over recent years, in an attempt to provide a better service, numbers of different offices providing advice of various kinds have been set up—on consumer problems, for example, legal problems, housing problems—working alongside older foundations such as the Citizens' Advice Bureau. Some local authorities also provide information services and their social services departments offer a range of information and advice. We recommend that local authorities should review existing advice services in their areas, both statutory and voluntary, to prevent overlapping and to make it easy for people to know where to apply and convenient for them to do so.

8.62 One of the advantages claimed for automatic notification was that social services departments would be enabled not only to offer advice but also to provide counselling to the lone parent at the point of crisis. Bereavement, desertion, separation and divorce all give rise to anxiety, grief and depression which, without adequate help, can impair the lone parent's ability to face the future and care for his or her children. Social services departments are already committed to providing a wide range of services, though with a shortage of trained personnel and the current effects of major organisational changes it is not surprising that counselling services for the lone parent do not receive priority at present. Medical social workers offer counselling to the bereaved and moral welfare organisations in many parts of the country provide personal counselling for unmarried mothers. In recent years self-help groups, to which we have already referred, have endeavoured to establish similar services; notable among these are the Cruse clubs, with their panel of counsellors to help widows with emotional problems. There is scope here for considerable experiment and development and we recommend that the Department of Health and Social Security, the Social Work Services Group of the Scottish Education Department and local authorities should encourage the provision of such services.

SECTION 3—SOCIAL WORK SUPPORT SERVICES

LEGISLATIVE FRAMEWORK AND GROWTH OF THE SERVICES

8.63 In this Section we follow the summary of available services in Section 2 with a more detailed examination of the main social work support services available to one-parent families.

8.64 As explained in Section 2, the social work support services used by one-parent families are in the main provided under the Children and Young Persons Act 1963. We quote section 1(1) of that Act in full, as the exact wording is of significance in the proposals we make later:

> It shall be the duty of every local authority to make available such advice, guidance and assistance as may promote the welfare of children by diminishing the need to receive children into or keep them in care under the Children Act 1948, the principal Act or the principal Scottish Act or to bring children before a juvenile court; and any provisions made by a local authority under this subsection may, if the local authority think fit, include provision for giving assistance in kind or, in exceptional circumstances, in cash.

This Act, and the Scottish Act referred to in the next paragraph, also empower local authorities to make arrangements whereby voluntary organisations or other persons may assist them in the discharge of their duties.

8.65 The comparable provision in Scotland is section 12 of the Social Work (Scotland) Act 1968. This places a general duty on local authorities to promote social welfare in their area and enables assistance to be given in defined circumstances of need to adults as well as families with children. We quote section 12 in full:

> (1) It shall be the duty of every local authority to promote social welfare by making available advice, guidance and assistance on such a scale as may be appropriate for their area, and in that behalf, to make arrangements and to provide or secure the provision of such facilities (including the provision or arranging for the provision of residential and other establishments) as they may consider suitable and adequate, and such assistance may be given to, or in respect of, the persons specified in the next following subsection in kind or in cash, subject to subsections (3) and (4) of this section.
>
> (2) The persons specified for the purposes of the foregoing subsection are—
>
> > (a) a person, being a child under the age of eighteen, requiring assistance in kind, or in exceptional circumstances in cash, where such assistance appears to the local authority likely to diminish the need—
> >
> > > (i) to receive him into, or to keep him in, care under this Part of this Act, or
> > >
> > > (ii) of his being referred to a children's hearing under Part III of this Act,

444

(*b*) a person in need requiring assistance in kind or, in exceptional circumstances constituting an emergency, in cash, where the giving of assistance in either form would avoid the local authority being caused greater expense in the giving of assistance in another form, or where probable aggravation of the person's need would cause greater expense to the local authority on a later occasion.

(3) Before giving assistance to, or in respect of, a person in cash under sub-section (1) of this section a local authority shall have regard to his eligibility for receiving assistance from any other statutory body and, if he is so eligible, to the availability to him of that assistance in his time of need.

(4) Assistance given in kind or cash to, or in respect of, persons under this section may be given unconditionally or subject to such conditions as to the repayment of the assistance, or of its value, whether in whole or in part, as the local authority may consider reasonable having regard to the means of the person receiving the assistance and to the eligibility of the person for assistance from any other statutory body.

8.66 " Persons in need " as referred to in subsection (2)(*b*) of section 12 are defined in the Act as persons who:

(*a*) are in need of care and attention arising out of infirmity, youth or age; or

(*b*) suffer from illness or mental disorder or are substantially handicapped by any deformity or disability; or

(*c*) have been rendered homeless and are in need of temporary accommodation; or

(*d*) being persons prescribed by the Secretary of State who have asked for assistance, are, in the opinion of a local authority, persons to whom the authority may appropriately make available the services and facilities provided by them under this Act.[1]

8.67 These two Acts are the statutory basis on which most preventive services now used for one-parent families are provided by local authorities, but supportive work with families in need goes back much further. Child-care officers and children's departments undertook a good deal of casework with families prior to the 1963 Act, particularly following the Children and Young Persons (Amendment) Act 1952 which conferred a duty on children's depart-ments to investigate, or cause to be investigated, cases in which they received information suggesting that a child might be in need of care, protection or control. Mental health social workers, homeless family social workers, health visitors and probation officers all undertook work of a preventive nature with families and local health authorities have for many years been aware of the need to use their domiciliary services to help keep families intact.[2] The 1963 Act placed this work within a statutory framework of child-care services.[3]

8.68 The powers embodied in the 1963 Act led to a greatly increased volume of work being undertaken by local authorities, particularly in relation to advice services. Some authorities established offices for the provision of advice to families in difficulty. A study of these " family advice centres " in 1966[4] showed that they were already established in a variety of forms. Some were

---

[1] Section 94 (1) of Social Work (Scotland) Act 1968. A prescription under (*d*) has never in fact been made.

[2] See, for example, Ministry of Health Circular 27/54, which referred to help in the home which could be provided under sections 28 and 29 of the National Health Service Act 1946.

[3] It also extended it by permitting assistance in kind or in cash—see paragraphs 8.80–8.88 below.

[4] Aryeh Leissner: *Family Advice Services*, Longmans, 1967.

internal parts of a children's department's central or area offices; some were separate units serving several local or statutory agencies or both; some were organised under the auspices of a voluntary agency, financed and partly supervised by the children's department and others were working at detached centres or " outposts " serving a specific sub-area neighbourhood or community. The sorts of problems with which these centres dealt predominantly concerned child-rearing, marital conflict, debts and inadequate housing.

8.69 Work of this kind has continued to develop and the centres described, and many others, were taken over by the social services departments on their creation in April 1971, and in some cases became the basis for district offices providing a wide range of social work services. The reorganisation of services following the Local Authority Social Services Act 1970 made it easier for social workers undertaking preventive work with families to make full use of supportive services such as home helps and day nurseries.

8.70 The extent and quality of social work services to families are largely dependent on the number and the training of social work staff. Until 1971 this work was primarily undertaken by child-care officers employed in children's departments. Statistics relating to the numbers of child-care officers during that period illustrate the steady development of these services. Since April 1971 the work has been merged with other social work activities and staffing figures are not a reliable guide to the development of preventive work with families. In 1971, in England and Wales there were on average 25 social workers, trainees and assistants for each 100,000 members of the population, although this average covered a wide variation between different authorities. In a recent circular to local authorities[1] the Department of Health and Social Security suggested a national guideline which would imply an increase of 3 for each 100,000 during each year for the next decade.

WORK WITH ONE-PARENT FAMILIES

8.71 Social services departments assist with many different family problems, including help with tenancy problems and rent arrears in order to prevent homelessness or the reception of children into care, and support and guidance to keep the one-parent family intact after divorce, desertion, death or the illness of a parent or child neglect.[2] Additionally, local authority social workers supervise children on behalf of courts of various kinds and arrange adoptions.

---

[1] Department of Health and Social Security Circular 35/72.
[2] Illustrative of the severity of the problems some one-parent families present to social workers are the following examples summarised from details given to us by a county borough children's officer:
    A mother, said to be educationally sub-normal, an orphan herself and having been in an approved school, has an educationally subnormal child.
    A widow with two children of the marriage, expecting a third, and three by a previous common law marriage. Her 16-year old daughter was received into local authority care because of behaviour problems.
    A separated father retained two children by the marriage; the mother had four by cohabitation which ended in desertion; a seventh child was born from a casual relationship, rejected and received into care.
    A mother aged 28 had four children (one educationally sub-normal), the first was illegitimate, two resulted from a marriage ending in divorce, the fourth was a child of a casual relationship.
    A father, separated for four years, with seven children, two sub-normal.
    A mother aged 23 had four children. The father of the first returned to his own country; the mother then lived with another man and had the second, third and fourth children. The relationship was volatile and finally terminated.

8.72   Evidence we received from the Association of Children's Officers,[1] based on questionnaires completed by their members, demonstrated the extent to which one-parent families of all types turn to or are referred to local authority social workers for assistance.   Over a period of four weeks (1–28 November 1970) about a quarter of the new referrals to 84 authorities came from one-parent families—this amounted to 1,756 referrals involving 3,902 children.   The replies to the association's questionnaire also indicated that 36 per cent of all long-term supportive casework undertaken by the 84 children's departments was with one-parent families, of whom one fifth were motherless.

8.73   Of the 1,756 one-parent families referred, continuing casework support was expected to be necessary in 617, or nearly one third, of the cases.   In other cases the children's departments were being called on to help in a crisis: of the 3,902 children, 1,728 were dealt with by action of a non-recurring kind, and of the 521 children taken into care, 373, about 70 per cent, stayed less than six months.   Informally separated parents, both men and women, and unmarried mothers constituted 68 per cent of one-parent family referrals, and the association deduced from this, and the relatively low numbers of the legally separated and divorced, that the children's departments were functioning primarily as a crisis referral service.   In all, of the 1,756 families, 414 (24 per cent) were the families of unmarried mothers, 725 (41 per cent) the families of separated wives (163 of them legally separated), 174 (10 per cent) the families of divorced women and 93 (5 per cent) the families of widows; of the 350 motherless families, 251 (72 per cent) were the families of separated men (31 legally), 32 (9 per cent) were the families of divorced men and 67 (19 per cent) were the families of widowers.

CRITICISMS OF SERVICES

8.74   A number of criticisms were made in evidence to us about the adequacy of social work assistance provided by local authorities.   Some of the evidence was compiled before the creation of social services departments in April 1971, and later evidence was submitted while the new departments were still in the early stages of development.   We recognise that some of these criticisms will have been overtaken by the reorganisation and expansion which has taken place since much of our evidence was submitted, and we therefore confine ourselves to fairly brief statements on the main points of criticism.   We should emphasise, however, that there was a good deal of criticism of the failure of social services departments to offer assistance,[2] both in times of family crisis and for long-term support, and the level and standard of service was said to vary enormously between different authorities.   Several organisations stressed the value of trained volunteers in supplementing scarce public resources.

---

[1] During the period in which we were taking evidence this association ceased to exist because of the creation of the new social services departments. The association had already submitted written evidence to us, but oral evidence was given later on their behalf by the Association of Directors of Social Services.

[2] For example George and Wilding, in their study of 588 motherless families in the East Midlands, found that 20% of the total number of fathers in the sample applied for and were refused help. (Victor George and Paul Wilding: *Motherless Families*, Routledge and Kegan Paul, 1972, page 151.)

Fragmentation of services

8.75 Several submissions called for a greater co-ordination of social welfare services, and pointed out that some families were referred to a number of different agencies for help. One voluntary body drew attention to the fact that an unsupported mother may be required to meet a number of officials, and " it is quite possible that no single social worker or officer has an interest in or finds time to devote to the mother's total situation ". Other evidence suggested that each social services department should have a specific section to deal with the problems presented by one-parent families.

8.76 While recognising the need for improvements in the provision of social work services, we would not regard it as in the interests of one-parent families if each social services department were required to establish a special service to cater for their needs. Such an arrangement would tend to isolate one-parent families from other families with social problems, and a certain amount of stigma might come to attach to the new service. Moreover the establishment of a special service for one-parent families might defeat its own purpose, since other groups might be thought to require similar treatment and fragmentation of the social services departments would result. We consider that a better course would be to make advice and guidance on using the services more readily available to one-parent families, as we have suggested in Section 2.

Reluctance to come for help

8.77 Also in evidence we received comments about the reluctance of some lone parents to seek assistance, of their fear of being criticised, of their sense of guilt, and of their uncertainty as to what would be provided and what they could reasonably expect. It was said that when they did come forward, some people were deterred from further encounters by the reception they received. One council for social services expressed the view that the social work system was " ingrained within a patronising complacency that the individual is psychologically inadequate—not the system ". A voluntary worker from a religious body told us that the lone parent finds " that the encounter with official-dom is usually traumatic ".

8.78 These examples may not reflect in any general way experience of contact with public services—satisfactory services are more likely to be taken for granted and attract little comment—but some unmarried and separated parents do seem to be discouraged from seeking help by the fear that public attitudes may be critical. This problem can be overcome to some extent by more effective publicity, setting out what services are available, as we have suggested in Section 2, and by the growth of mutual-aid groups which offer support and encouragement to lone parents and disseminate information about services. Much needs to be done however by local authorities to ensure that the anxieties of lone parents and others are understood by staff coming into contact with them and that reception and interview facilities are of an adequate standard. A thoughtless interviewer or a long wait in an overcrowded waiting room can easily convince a parent seeking help that he or she is regarded as a nuisance. We believe that it is important that public services should maintain a consistently sympathetic and approachable attitude to those who need them.

Convenience of services

8.79 It was pointed out to us that the lone parent who is working may be unable to make use of those services which are available only during usual office hours. We recognise that extending services beyond this would have an effect on staffing and staffing costs, but we regard such development as important if services are to be made available to people in need. We therefore recommend that every effort should be made to make services available more extensively, for example, in the evenings and on Saturdays. Further, we endorse the view of the Seebohm Committee, who, in considering the reorganisation of the personal social services, were concerned that they should be made readily accessible to those who need them and within a structure, including area boundaries, which made sense administratively and to users.[1]

OPERATION OF CASH PROVISION IN SECTION 1

8.80 We referred earlier to the fact that section 1(1) of the 1963 Act extended the powers of local authorities by permitting them to give families assistance in kind, or, exceptionally, in cash. The provision is quoted in full in paragraph 8.64, and the corresponding Scottish provision in paragraphs 8.65 and 8.66.

8.81 Up to 1969 local authorities were required to make returns showing the amounts of money spent under the power to provide cash assistance, and over the four years figures were kept the amount increased year by year rapidly and steadily; in England and Wales, spending increased from £88,000 in 1965–66 to £261,000 in 1968–69. In Scotland, where regular returns are still kept, expenditure has increased from £25,000 in 1965–1966 to £196,500 in 1971. Within these levels, expenditure has varied widely from authority to authority, although this variation is in part a reflection of different accounting procedures and of the use of other powers to give similar sorts of assistance. A large proportion of the expenditure has gone on rent guarantees, rent arrears, debts to public utilities, and the provision of temporary care and accommodation for homeless families.

8.82 A study of the workings of section 1 of the 1963 Act was undertaken between 1966 and 1970 because there was " a good deal of concern and confusion in children's departments about the giving of financial aid".[2] Home Office guidance to local authorities stated that section 1 " does not give power to intervene in family difficulties or domestic problems unless there is some reason to suppose that these may create the risk of children having to be received into or committed to the care of a local authority. Nor does it give power in any circumstances to impose guidance on parents who are not willing to receive it."[3] Both the Act itself and the guidance to local authorities made it clear that the use of cash was intended to be exceptional rather than something of a routine nature. Financial or material help, however, was clearly to be part of the casework plan in which parents would co-operate to prevent their children having to be received into the care of the local authority or committed to their

---

[1] *Op cit*, paragraph 111.
[2] Jean S Heywood and Barbara K Allen: *Financial Help in Social Work*, Manchester University Press, 1971, page 70.
[3] Home Office Circular 204/1963, paragraph 8.

care by a juvenile court. It was inevitably a discretionary power which the social worker used. The study referred to above found that " the absence of precise eligibility rules, the apparent arbitrariness of decisions, the responsible nature of public accountability, the stigma imposed by society upon their particular clients, the history of charity as opposed to rights, and additional feelings about giving or withholding money . . . made the problem . . . acute for the (social) workers."[1]

8.83 We consider that there must always be a discretionary element in the provision of this kind of assistance and we see no way of converting eligibility into a right to help. We are convinced, however, that the powers contained in section 1 are a necessary and important adjunct to the local authority social services for one-parent families; in our view the ability of social workers to step in with a cash grant adds significantly to the flexibility and efficacy of the help they can give. We have already drawn attention to the considerable variation in the use of the powers between local authorities and we are concerned that some authorities place such strict limitations on what they are prepared to do under section 1. In Part 6 we give some instances of the operation of these powers in the housing field, where some local authorities use them to give rent guarantees, to clear rent arrears and to provide furniture; and we point to the need for local authorities to be more ready to help families in these ways.[2] Another example of a limited interpretation was given to us by the National Council for the Unmarried Mother and her Child who said:

> The fact that local authorities themselves have often asked our Grants Committee for financial help indicates the restricted use that some of them make of this Section of the Act. In some areas, even mothers under 17 years of age do not seem to be covered for fees for mother and baby homes unless their families can afford to pay and requests have been made to us by the children's departments for this purpose.[3]

8.84 One of the reasons why some authorities make little use of section 1 is their doubt about the extent of the powers it confers; and the fact that the English and Scottish Acts are differently drawn adds to the general confusion and misunderstanding which seem to surround this piece of legislation. But some authorities are operating successfully on a broad interpretation of the powers, and this seems to imply that others are taking too narrow a view; and the reference in the circular on homelessness to the use of rent guarantees by social services departments supports the wider approach.[4] A situation in which local authorities are left in doubt about the extent of their powers is not conducive to the full use of this piece of legislation. We should like to see a situation in which it was quite clear that it was not necessary for there to be a pressing or immediate prospect of the child's being received into care for cash payments to be made; action should be possible long before matters have come to this point if social services departments are to act as a preventive service rather than continuing to cope with successive crises. We consider it important that the position should be clarified, either by more explicit guidance to local authorities on payments which are permissible, or if necessary by amending legislation.

---

[1] *Op cit*, page 71.
[2] See Part 6, Sections 7 and 10.
[3] *Forward for the Fatherless*, paragraph 200.
[4] See paragraph 6.110.

Overlap with supplementary benefits

8.85   It was never intended that the 1963 Act or its Scottish counterpart in 1968 should duplicate in any way entitlement to supplementary benefits under social security legislation.[1]   But there is an awkward area of possible overlap in the making of lump sum grants: the Supplementary Benefits Commission can give help with lump sum payments for exceptional needs under section 7 of the Ministry of Social Security Act 1966 to people receiving regular weekly payments of supplementary benefit and in certain circumstances to others whose income is at or about the supplementary benefit level but who are not in full-time work.   The creation of two sets of statutory powers in this area has led to difficulties which have not entirely been overcome.

8.86   The Association of Children's Officers instituted a survey among 76 children's departments in 1970 into areas of difficulty which existed in the relationship between social workers of children's departments and officers of the Supplementary Benefits Commission.   In their unpublished report the association drew attention to difficulties being encountered because of the shared responsibilities for financial assistance and the tendency for both sides to negotiate about payments.   It was suggested to us by the association that in some cases local authority staff were able to approve emergency payments more rapidly than Supplementary Benefits Commission officers, and that local authority services were more often available outside normal office hours. We understand that the Department of Health and Social Security are reviewing the general question of payment out of normal office hours.

8.87   In recognition of their common interest in meeting the needs and promoting the welfare of people who require their services, and in particular of the overlap of powers in the Ministry of Social Security Act and the 1963 Act (the 1968 Act in Scotland), the Supplementary Benefits Commission and local authorities have jointly produced memoranda entitled *Assistance in Cash*, for England and Wales (in 1971) and for Scotland (in 1969).   These memoranda were issued to the Commission's local offices and to local authorities; they examine the main areas of related responsibilities where the provision of cash is concerned, and they set out agreed general guidelines for handling individual cases falling within them.   The Supplementary Benefits Commission have also prepared, in agreement with the local authorities and the fuel authorities, a memorandum of guidance on the handling of fuel debts, recommending close local liaison between the various statutory authorities and practical working arrangements for dealing with individual cases.   A corresponding memorandum for Scotland has been issued by the Social Work Services Group of the Scottish Education Department.

8.88   The case can be argued for straightening out the situation by arranging for all exceptional needs payments for families with children to be made by social services departments, leaving only weekly subsistence allowances to be paid by the Supplementary Benefits Commission.   This would create other anomalies, and raise matters of principle, the implications of which, discussed at length by Olive Stevenson in *Claimant or Client?*,[2] extend well beyond our terms

---

[1] Indeed section 12 (3) of the Scottish Act specifically requires the local authority to have regard to eligibility for assistance from any other statutory body before making a payment.

[2] Olive Stevenson: *Claimant or Client?*, Allen and Unwin, 1973, pages 53–59.

of reference. We understand that since the issue of the memoranda referred to in the previous paragraph standing arrangements have been introduced for consultation between local authorities and the Commission (in Scotland between local authorities, the Commission and the Social Work Services Group) but we believe that, in the light of the current wider use of section 1 powers, which we hope to see go still further in the future, the time has come for a more fundamental review of the whole situation.

CHARITABLE GRANTS FOR THE RELIEF OF POVERTY

8.89 A problem of overlap somewhat similar to that discussed above in relation to the respective cash grant powers of the Supplementary Benefits Commission and local authorities arises in relation to charitable grants and the statutory services, both central and local. Charities sometimes feel that their funds are being used inappropriately to subsidise State funds, and it can be difficult for a charity to help a needy family as much as they would wish because of the current rules of interaction with State-financed income support services.[1] The Charity Commissioners have said that charitable funds should not be used in such a way as directly to relieve public funds. The advice given to charities by the Commissioners is as follows:

> Charities for relief in need operate in the same field as statutory services; trustees who administer such charities should be careful to avoid repeating or abating those services. Charity trustees should accordingly acquaint themselves with the system of social benefits, the effect upon them of grants from charitable sources and the gaps left by them which can be filled by charitable services or facilities to relieve those in need.[2]

8.90 The Supplementary Benefits Commission told us that their policy in meeting exceptional needs was to give help with items which they considered to be essential and that generally a claimant was advised to approach a voluntary or charitable organisation only when the need was one which, in principle, the supplementary benefits scheme was not designed to meet: there was no question of trying to transfer to voluntary organisations responsibilities which the Commission had the duty to meet within their statutory or discretionary powers.[3] Where an applicant to charitable funds has a clear entitlement to statutory financial assistance few difficulties arise: the charity can ask the Supplementary Benefits Commission to consider the circumstances of the applicant and the need will be met. Sometimes a small sum is required urgently or the applicant refuses to consider seeking help from the Supplementary Benefits Commission, in which case the charity may make the necessary payment. Such assistance may not conflict with the principle outlined by the Charity Commissioners since, unless the applicant is able and willing to claim from the Supplementary Benefits Commission, the payment is not one which can be met from statutory sources. However, sometimes there is difficulty where the Supplementary Benefits Commission have a discretionary power to assist the family; the lines are then much less clear-cut and in some instances brought to

---

[1] An example is the restriction of payment made by some voluntary organisations to lone mothers to £1 a week because above that sum supplementary benefit would be commensurately reduced—see Appendix 8.

[2] *Report of the Charity Commissioners for England and Wales* 1967, HMSO, 1968, page 39.

[3] For a description of the way in which the Supplementary Benefits Commission exercise the power to give help with lump sum payments, see *Exceptional Needs Payments*, Supplementary Benefits Administration Papers 4, HMSO, 1973.

452

our notice the Commission have sought to negotiate with the charity that each makes a contribution towards meeting a particular need. Instances were also quoted to us where, when the charity had refused to assist, or had offered a smaller amount than that requested, the Supplementary Benefits Commission reviewed the situation and made a higher offer; in other cases charities made payments where the Supplementary Benefits Commission refused to exercise discretion to help, although they were firmly convinced that in doing so they were shouldering burdens which should have been met from public funds.

8.91 Problems also arise between charities and local authorities, since different authorities use their powers to give cash grants under section 1 of the Children and Young Persons Act in different ways. The situation is particularly awkward where the grant is required in order to clear a debt to the local authority itself—rent arrears, to prevent an eviction or to enable a family to be rehoused, for example, or, less frequently, arrears of rates. We hope that a wider use of section 1 powers and the recommendations we make about evictions and rehousing in Part 6, Sections 5, 6 and 7, will alleviate the situation, but it seems inevitable that some conflict will remain.

8.92 The problems posed here are wider than this Committee's terms of reference. We are not suggesting that there is a constant battle between charities on the one hand and the Supplementary Benefits Commission and local authorities on the other. Mostly relationships are good. Nevertheless, this is clearly an area in which friction can arise; the stronger and more independent the charity the more it is likely to question the policies of statutory services. We were told that smaller charities, who rely on local authorities for guidance, are sometimes regularly giving assistance which relieves public funds. The situation is one which we believe calls for continuing consultation and co-operation at a national level between local authorities, the Supplementary Benefits Commission, and the charitable organisations. We note that the National Council of Social Service have convened a number of meetings between statutory and voluntary bodies which led recently to the production of a memorandum along similar lines to that of the Supplementary Benefits Commission paper on fuel debts associating the voluntary sector with the liaison arrangements established between the statutory bodies.

SECTION 4—CARE OF CHILDREN IN ONE-PARENT FAMILIES

INTRODUCTION

8.93 Parents with single-handed responsibility for children face special difficulties in caring for them adequately. When the responsibility is unshared or unrelieved, all of the burdens and the risks are likely to be magnified. The most obvious way in which this shows itself is in the lone parent's task of making arrangements for the care of the children when he or she has to be—or wants to be—absent from home. This, however, is only one facet of the range of disadvantages from which the lone parent tends to suffer in providing a satisfactory environment for the child's personal and social development. Much evidence has been given to us on this subject. It has emphasised the strain which the demand for continuous physical presence makes on the energies and emotional resources of the lone parent, the worry and disappointments suffered in the search for reliable help, and the risk that a failure to cope may lead to the removal of the child from his own family and his reception into the care of a local authority or voluntary organisation.

8.94 The evidence given to us was heavily concentrated on the working, or would-be working, lone mother of young children, taking her plight as the central argument in favour of a policy for the substantial increase of day-care facilities for one-parent families. It should be stressed, however, that one-parent families in which the mother (or, it may be, the father) does not go out to work also have a particular need for help of this kind. Generally, we see the provision of adequate day care, in appropriate forms, as vital to the needs of all one-parent families, across the board, as a practical means of supporting parent and children in their everyday existence, as enhancing the quality of their lives, and as lessening, or overcoming, the social disadvantages from which many of them suffer. In this Section we shall be considering day care, first in respect of children under 5, then in respect of schoolchildren, particularly where their mothers are at work, and finally in terms of help that can be given in the home.

CHILDREN UNDER FIVE

8.95 We shall see later that although more than half of the places in day nurseries provided by local authorities are taken up by children of one-parent families, these children with day-nursery places form a very small proportion of the total number of one-parent family children under school age. It is in this context that we have to consider the evidence—we had more than sixty submissions to the same effect—demonstrating an overwhelming desire among many lone parents and the organisations representing their interests for the expansion of day-nursery provision by local authorities. Most of this evidence was centred on the problems experienced by working parents in making satisfactory arrangements for their children to be looked after while they are at work. Criticism was made that the hours of day nurseries are frequently inconvenient for working mothers, particularly those on shift work or working at weekends; of the difficulty in securing a place in a day nursery within easy reach both of the home and the place of employment; and of the lack of day-care facilities in general for mothers who wish to work part time—some authorities providing only for full-time care.

8.96 Although this evidence did reflect an appreciation of the value of good quality day care for the under-fives as a means of helping parents and children, it focused on the subject almost entirely from the adult's point of view. Virtually no consideration was given to the needs of the child as such in his experience of day care. Moreover, all proposals for expansion in this field raise acute economic problems which require decisions on the most efficient form of investing the human and material resources which are likely to become available. This in turn demands consideration of the balance to be established between different forms of day care, or the evolution of new forms. Elsewhere in this Report we have laid emphasis on the principle of maximising the freedom of choice of lone mothers whether to go out to work or not. There is another principle, written into much of our legislation, that in matters concerning children their welfare shall be regarded as paramount. Both principles are of first rate importance, but neither of them can be given proper effect if they are treated in isolation from each other. They must be taken together. The task is complicated by the fact that the principle of paramountcy for the welfare of the child may lead to no certain conclusion as to what course in any given case does best serve his interests. Certainly, the contentment of the mother is likely to be a strong factor, which in turn may involve helping her, particularly if she is a lone parent, to find some occupation outside her own four walls. But our predictive capacities are limited, and, especially when dealing with the disadvantaged and the children of broken homes, the search for the best interests of the child would often be better described as a search for the least detrimental of the available alternatives.

8.97 In all of this, our purpose is to show that the problem of adequate provision of day care for children under 5 is not to be solved by simple prescription. Our own approach requires that we look first at the way in which the public day-care service, and the other forms of child care which are in some sense alternative to it, have developed, and at their existing state. We then go on to consider future needs and the way in which we think those needs might best be met.

The development of day-care services

8.98 Many local authority day nurseries were set up during the second world war primarily for children of working mothers as a means of helping to meet the wartime needs of industry for women workers. At their peak in 1944 they were providing places for nearly 72,000 children. Once the war was over, however, with the return of men from the forces to civilian life, and the change to a peace-time economy, a different view was taken of the extent to which public policy and the public services should facilitate employment of mothers with young children. Post-war policy discouraged the provision of day-nursery places except for the children in greatest need of them. The priority groups for whom local authorities were encouraged to continue to provide fell into three main categories—" children whose mothers are constrained by individual circumstances to go out to work, or whose home conditions are in themselves unsatisfactory from the health point of view or whose mothers are incapable for some good reason of undertaking the full care of their children."[1] The effect of this policy, and of post-war financial and economic difficulties and cuts in public expenditure, was a severe and long-lasting contraction of the service.

8.99 However, contrary to expectation, there was no corresponding decline in demand, and in the absence of sufficient public day-nursery places, even for priority groups, parents have had to turn to other arrangements, and new facilities have appeared. These facilities fall into two groups. The private nurseries and child minders aim primarily to provide services that cover the whole or a large part of a normal working day; whereas the voluntary playgroups, nursery classes and nursery schools provide part-time facilities. The characteristic of these part-time facilities is that they focus on the child. The voluntary playgroup movement caters for the social and educational needs of the children, and of parents in relation to their children. Nursery education is now the subject of an expansion programme that constitutes a major advance in making public

---

[1] Ministry of Health Circular 221/45 (see also paragraph 8.105).

provision for the educational needs of 3 to 5-year-old children. But the division in the nature of the facilities has no necessary correspondence with the categories of children's needs. The child who is in full-time day care has as much need as any other child of attention to his social, emotional and educational development. The two groups of facilities grew up divided by reference to the adult's needs, so that although neither of them constitutes an exclusive province, the former group is for the most part used by mothers who go out to work, and the second group by the other mothers.

8.100 Ever since the second world war it has been implicit in the policy of the public provision of day nurseries that a lone mother without adequate support from the absent parent may have to go out to work, and that day care should be provided to help her to do so. This policy has not been affected by the availability to lone mothers of financial support from public funds. Neither the replacement of local schemes of public assistance by national assistance in 1948, nor the introduction in 1966 of the supplementary benefits scheme (with its increased emphasis on " benefit as of right ") led to any change in the view that priority in day-nursery provision should be given to the children of a lone working parent, even though if such a parent did not go out to work a basic income would still be provided for the needs of the family. In Part 5, Section 2, we draw attention to the dramatic increase in the numbers of lone parents who rely on supplementary benefit and do not go out to work. One of the principal advantages that would flow from our proposal for a guaranteed maintenance allowance is that it would both make better provision for the lone mother who stays home, and provide more extensive and flexible opportunities for those who wished to combine part-time or full-time work with responsibility for the care of children. The guaranteed maintenance allowance thus serves the philosophy of maximising freedom of choice, and its introduction, so far from weakening, will reinforce the continuity of the policy of providing day-care facilities to help those mothers who decide to go out to work. Against this background, we go on to consider the present state of the various day-care services for the under-fives.

The existing services

8.101 A striking feature of the existing services for the day care of under-fives is their wide variety and different standards. The public services include nursery schools and classes within the responsibility of local education authorities, and day nurseries for which the local social services departments are responsible. Officially recognised private facilities include day nurseries, playgroups, child minders and nursery schools, all of which the local authority has a duty to register. Increasing numbers of children attend voluntary playgroups and we know that many parents make their own informal arrangements to leave their children with relatives or neighbours while they work.[1] A minority of local authorities are also able to provide home helps or resident houseparents for crisis situations such as the parent's illness, and some are experimenting with alternative day-fostering arrangements. Even after the unification of the former health and children's services within the social services

---

[1] Some information about this emerged from the study by the Office of Population Censuses and Surveys published as *Families and their Needs*, HMSO, 1973, and is discussed in paragraph 8.112 below.

departments of local authorities, however, there is still a recognisable division of responsibility between education departments, whose concern is nursery schools and classes, and the social services departments, who are concerned with child care, including full-day or part-day care, and playgroups. And there is also believed to be a significant amount of unregistered, and therefore illegal, child minding (see paragraph 8.113).

Nursery education

8.102 We received a good deal of evidence asking for an increase in places in nursery schools. Since then, an important development in educational provision for 3 to 5-year-olds has taken place through the announcement in the White Papers of December 1972[1] of the intention to expand nursery education over a ten-year period. For England and Wales these proposals entail provision of education on a part-time basis for 35 per cent of 3-year-olds and 75 per cent of 4-year-olds and full-time education for 15 per cent of 3 and 4-year-olds. Altogether there will be provision for 90 per cent of the 4-year-old and 50 per cent of the 3-year-old children; this will require up to 250,000 additional full-time equivalent places by 1982. The objective is to make nursery education available for children whose parents want it from the beginning of the term after the child's third birthday, and it is assumed that the demand for places for 3-year-olds will be much smaller than for 4-year-olds.

8.103 Following the recommendations of the Plowden Report[2] the White Paper accepted the view that part-time school attendance is preferable to full-time attendance for the majority of children aged 3 and 4. As the Plowden Report recognised, however, there are a number of children aged 3 and 4 for whom full-time provision may be desirable for both educational and social reasons. In making plans for nursery education, local education authorities have been asked to consult social services departments and relevant voluntary organisations, and wherever possible to give priority to meeting the needs of disadvantaged children. Thus, the projected expansion should make a considerable impact on the lives of many children in one-parent families by enriching their experiences educationally and emotionally, and removing some of the pressing burden on the lone parent. It should be noted, however, that nursery education does not commence until after the child's third birthday, that the majority of places will be part-time and that the school day and the school year do not coincide with adults' normal working hours. Nursery education is an important part of the educational system; it is only incidentally that it will help parents who are working.

Day nurseries[3]

8.104 By 1969 the number of local authority day nurseries in England and Wales had fallen from the wartime peak (see paragraph 8.98 above) to 444,

---

[1] *Education: A Framework for Expansion*, Cmnd 5174, 1972 and *Education in Scotland: a statement of policy*, Cmnd 5175, 1972.

[2] *Children and their Primary Schools*. A report of the Central Advisory Council for Education (England), HMSO, 1967.

[3] These are different from nursery schools, because their function is to provide (normally for a full day) for children from early infancy until they start school, whereas nursery schools will provide education, normally part time, for 3 and 4-year-olds. Day nurseries are part of the social services and not part of the educational system.

providing 21,000 places. More recently, partly under the stimulus of the urban programme, the number has increased to 493 (at 31 March 1973) with 24,000 places. This, however, is still only one third of the peak figure of nearly thirty years ago.

8.105 The present policy in respect of day nurseries stems from a Ministry of Health circular issued in 1945 (221/45) which included the following statement:

> The Ministers concerned accept the view of medical and other authority that, in the interests of the health and development of the child no less than for the benefit of the mother, the proper place for a child under two is at home with his mother. They are also of the opinion that, under normal peacetime conditions, the right policy to pursue would be positively to discourage mothers of children under two from going out to work; to make provision for children between two and five by way of nursery schools and nursery classes; and to regard day nurseries and daily guardians as supplements to meet the special needs (where these exist and cannot be met within the hours, age, range and organisation of nursery schools and nursery classes) of children whose mothers are constrained by individual circumstances to go out to work or whose home conditions are in themselves unsatisfactory from the health point of view, or whose mothers are incapable for some good reason of undertaking the full care of their children.

These views were the subject of much debate and criticism at that time and since. A circular issued in 1968, following a review of day-nursery policy by the Minister of Health,[1] re-affirmed the advice that local authorities should concentrate on providing day care for children in special need:

> Since the issue of Circular 221/45 much attention has been focused on the needs of children and on social situations that can endanger family stability. Day care is one way in which help can be given, but it must be looked at in relation to the view of medical and other authority that early and prolonged separation from the mother is detrimental to the child, that wherever possible the younger pre-school child should be at home with his mother, and that the needs of older pre-school children should be met by part-time attendance at nursery schools or classes. Accordingly the Minister considers that the responsibility of local health authorities should continue to be limited to arranging for the day care of children who, from a health point of view or because of deprived or inadequate backgrounds, have special needs that cannot otherwise be met.

> The need for day care may arise from one or more of a variety of circumstances in which the child or family need help. Priority will normally need to be given to children with only one parent (eg the unsupported mother living with her child) who has no option but to go out to work and who cannot arrange for the child to be looked after satisfactorily. Other children who may need day care, some for the whole day, others part-time, will include those:—

> (a) who need temporary day care on account of the mother's illness;

> (b) whose mothers are unable to look after them adequately because they are incapable of giving young children the care they need;

> (c) for whom day care might prevent the breakdown of the mother or the break-up of the family;

> (d) whose home conditions (eg because of gross overcrowding) constitute a hazard to their health and welfare; and

> (e) whose health and welfare are seriously affected by a lack of opportunity for playing with others.

> The above list is not intended as any indication of the order in which various types of need should be met; the question of priority can only be determined according to the circumstances of the individual child or the family.

---

1 Ministry of Health Circular 37/68.

8.106 The national average of day-nursery places is 5·4 for every 1,000 children under the age of 5, but there are considerable variations between different local authorities. For example, 50 local authorities have no day-nursery provision, while 2 have more than 30 places for each 1,000 children in this age group.

8.107 The method of assessing priority and the proportion of day-nursery places occupied by children from one-parent families also show considerable variations. The latest available information suggests that an average of 55 per cent of all available day-nursery places are taken up by children of one-parent families,[1] but the proportion in different areas varies from 12 per cent to 85 per cent. On this basis, some 13,200 out of the total of about a quarter of a million one-parent family children under 5 attend day nurseries.

8.108 The current demand for day-nursery places far outstrips the supply. Long waiting lists are common and in some areas the number of children on the waiting lists exceeds the total number of places provided. Local authorities in preparing ten-year plans for the period 1973–1983 have been asked to set a target of eight day-nursery places for each 1,000 children under 5. That would give a national total approaching 34,000, that is, a rise of 50 per cent between 1972 and 1983. Assuming that the proportion of places available for one-parent family children were to remain at 55 per cent (and there were no change in the number of such children under 5) this total would cater for 18,700 such children—about 7 per cent of the relevant age group.

8.109 Despite the high demand for places in day nurseries, it is by no means obvious that this form of care best meets the child's needs. We refer later to the importance to the very young child, who is to be cared for by someone other than his mother, of having a regular substitute whom he knows well (paragraph 8.125 below). This may not be possible in a day nursery because of staff shortages and frequent changes in staff, arising from high staff turnover and students having to be moved round to different jobs within the nursery for training purposes. Moreover, in the past, some matrons of day nurseries have been trained in the care of sick children, and have naturally been more aware of the health aspects of child care than of children's total requirements. Staff have been motivated towards working with children alone, and may have felt insecure in contacts with parents. These factors have sometimes created situations in which children have been totally isolated from their parents for the greater part of their waking day, in somewhat clinical surroundings and segregated into narrow age groups. Their emotional and intellectual needs have not always been understood or provided for.

Private arrangements for care for children of working mothers

8.110 The continual decline in public day-nursery provision in the fifties and sixties stimulated a big expansion in private and voluntary services—including registered private nurseries and child minders caring for children in their own homes. By 1973, in England and Wales there were about 950 registered private and voluntary nurseries (including those provided by employers) with full-time places for 25,000 children. There were also some 25,000 registered child minders providing full-day care for over 57,000 children.

---

[1] Department of Health and Social Security: unpublished evidence.

8.111   Local authorities have been encouraged (in Circular 37/68 issued by the Ministry of Health) to consider providing places for larger numbers of priority children by placing them with private and voluntary nurseries and with selected child minders.   Under section 22 of the National Health Service Act 1946, local authorities can meet the cost of such placings, but location, suitability and availability of places often limit the extent to which local authorities can make use of these facilities to supplement their own day nurseries.

8.112   Relatives, friends and neighbours play a significant part in the provision of day care for children of one-parent families.   This can be ideal during short-term emergencies and family crises, but may not be so for extended periods.   Such heavy reliance on these arrangements as was found in the study by the Office of Population Censuses and Surveys, *Families and their Needs*,[1] reflects the shortage of formal day-care places and also the additional cost which day nurseries and paid daily minders can entail.   It may be assumed that, in general, arrangements with relatives, friends or neighbours can provide an element of individual and loving care which other forms of child minding probably do not, but this is not likely to be an expanding form of provision, since the modern trend towards two-generation nuclear families, and the employment of women generally, are likely to curtail the numbers of those available to care for other people's children on an informal basis.

8.113   The full extent of unregistered child minding is unknown.   One estimate in a recent article[2] by Brian Jackson, director of the Childminding Research Unit, suggested that at least 60,000 and possibly as many as 100,000 children were spending their days with an unregistered minder.   The descriptions which he and other writers have given of the conditions in which some of the children are kept, even if they are representative of only a small minority of cases, show how bad "caretaker" conditions for children can be; and some standards in this area are lower than society should tolerate.   Moreover, even where standards are satisfactory, private arrangements of this kind lack the security of public provision and can well produce harrowing problems for the lone parent who has to rely on them.   In oral evidence from Mothers in Action we received a graphic account of the procedure used by some mothers for securing the services of the daily minder.   An unmarried mother told us that after obtaining addresses from shop-window advertisements she took her child from door to door, asking whether there were any vacancies; the minder would look the mother and child up and down before answering, and if the answer was "Yes", the fee would then have to be discussed.   Nor are the problems solved once the child has been placed.   If, for example, she has illness in her own family the minder may, without notice, discontinue the service; on the other hand, if the mother is late collecting her child or through illness misses a day, she may find that the minder refuses to accept the child any longer.[3]

1 *Op cit*. In the three urban areas of Dundee, Halifax and Haringey the proportions of children of working lone mothers cared for during the day by relatives and (unpaid) neighbours were 36 per cent, 55 per cent and 33 per cent respectively.   In the rural areas of Dorset and Glamorgan, where there were no day nurseries, the proportions appeared to be much higher but the sample was too small to be statistically reliable.

2 Brian Jackson: ' The childminders ', *New Society*, 29 November 1973, pages 521–524.

3 See paragraph 8·135 for recommendations on child minding.

Employers' day nurseries[1]

8.114   We are aware of differing views on provision of day nurseries by employers.   There are those who see it as the responsibility of central and local government to make adequate provision and do not think it right that employers should be called upon to relieve them of this task.   Normally employers, in the public as well as the private sector, only provide child-care facilities for key personnel or in a situation of acute labour shortage, and this provision may be seen by employees as tying them to jobs or to pay and conditions which they would not otherwise accept.   And while there are material advantages for mother and child if the nursery is near her place of work, charges may be heavy.   But in the present scarcity of public provision we have no doubt that employers' nurseries do help some mothers to work who are anxious to work and would not otherwise be able to do so.

Playgroups[2]

8.115   A new development in the provision of facilities for pre-school children in the last ten years has been the growth of the voluntary playgroup movement. Starting as a self-help movement by middle-class mothers seeking to make good the absence of nursery-school provision for their children, it has been promoted by organisations like the Pre-School Playgroups Association, the Save the Children Fund, and the Women's Royal Voluntary Services.   It is estimated that there are now a quarter of a million children attending playgroups, and with assistance from central government, local authorities and grants from urban programme funds, it is beginning to be a thriving movement in many deprived areas.   Some local authorities also run their own play groups and some have appointed advisers to help the voluntary movement.   As with other services, provision throughout the country is patchy, depending on the availability and enthusiasm of volunteers, the financial resources provided, and the availability of suitable premises.   Playgroups offer a valuable service for 3 and 4-year-olds, especially so for those who are under-privileged or deprived. They assist in the process of socialising young children and provide opportunities for constructive play.   The Education White Paper of December 1972[3] which announced the new policy of expanding educational provision for the under-fives also advised local authorities to consider carefully the role of playgroups and how they could fit in with the new programme.

8.116   Playgroups have helped mothers as well as children.   They have enabled many mothers to escape from the loneliness and inertia they may experience at home into the activity and companionship they may enjoy at work.   In planning together and working for their children's needs mothers are able to gain in skill, self-esteem and confidence in themselves as parents. This aspect is of particular significance to lone parents who can so easily become detached from the community.   In the comradeship of united effort for their children, groups of isolated and lonely parents can grow into a " caring community " which may go far in providing a substitute for the wider family group and circle of friends which many of them lack, both for the parent and the child.   In this kind of atmosphere, arrangements can be made for baby-sitting and for positive help in times of trouble, for example, if a mother

---

[1] See also paragraph 8.138.
[2] See also paragraph 8.139.
[3] *Op cit.*

suddenly goes into hospital. In many areas also, mother and toddler groups for children under 3 are emerging and these are particularly valuable in helping parents to a fuller understanding of child development and play needs, and in strengthening relationships between parents and children, at the time when the children's need for mental stimulation is at its greatest.

The general picture

8.117 Although day-care services for young children have been provided or supervised by a single local authority department since 1948—formerly the health, now the social services department—they are generally run in a fragmentary and unco-ordinated way. For the lone parent seeking day care for a young child there is a large element of chance as to the kind of care he or she can obtain. The availability of public day-nursery places varies considerably according to the area in which the family live. Standards of physical care in day nurseries are usually good, but by no means all provide the environment which the young child needs for his social, emotional and intellectual development. Staff are often inexperienced or too over-burdened to provide more than physical care for the children; the children suffer from the frequent changes among the staff. Daily minding in registered nurseries or by minders caring for a few children in their own homes is variable in quality. Little attempt has as yet been made to offer advice or training to daily minders to increase their skills and sense of commitment to the children; at worst young children may be inadequately or badly cared for during prolonged periods by unsuitable minders, or a succession of minders, with risk of further handicap to an already disadvantaged group.

Future needs

8.118 We have no doubt whatever that there is urgent need for a considerable expansion in day-care services for children under 5 provided or supported by public authorities. The demand already greatly exceeds the amount of available provision, and it is one which we believe will not only persist, but will grow as parents, whether working or not, become increasingly concerned to obtain the kind of day care that will best serve their children's needs. There is, on any view of the matter, a severe shortage in the facilities that are available to meet plain cases of social need, such as arise upon a mother's illness, or to help deprived children considered wholly in their own right, as when a child's home conditions are such that an appropriate form of day care may make the difference between his remaining at home and being received into care by the local authority. Indeed, the high proportion of one-parent family children in the care of local authorities, and the heavy incidence of child neglect and cruelty among these families (as shown by cases coming to the attention of the National Society for the Prevention of Cruelty to Children)[1] make a forceful argument in themselves for additional day-care facilities (and, where necessary, help in the family home). We are deeply concerned, also, at the extent and the standards of unregistered child minding and private fostering. We have already referred to a recent estimate of unregistered child minding by day; and in addition about 10,000 children are known to be living with foster parents with whom they have been placed privately. Robert Holman's recent study of private fostering[2]

---

1 See paragraphs 8.45 and 8.47 above.

2 Robert Holman: *Trading in Children: a study of private fostering*, Routledge and Kegan Paul, 1973.

showed that the parents, many of whom were unmarried mothers or deserted fathers, had often resorted to private fostering because of their inability to find a source of day care sufficient to cover their working hours.

8.119 In addition to the pressures for additional facilities originating in social need and the existence of abuses—which, therefore, have the highest claim to be satisfied—there is the mass of general demand which, as we have previously explained, reflected itself in the evidence in the form of the proposal for an increase of public day-care facilities to ease the burdens of the working lone parent. There are no grounds for supposing that this demand will decrease. The guaranteed maintenance allowance we have recommended would broaden the true scope of choice for the lone mother between staying home and going out to work, but it is impossible to forecast what the effect of this might be. We suspect that it might significantly increase the numbers wishing to work part time rather than full time while their children are small. It must be remembered that only a minority of mothers of very young children are likely to want employment outside the home, but experience shows that this desire tends to find an outlet in unsuitable arrangements for the child if suitable ones are not available. As a general proposition, we are in no doubt that there has to be a much larger provision, through public or publicly assisted means, of adequate and suitable arrangements for the children of working lone parents.

8.120 It by no means follows that the resources can or should be allocated to make this provision available on demand or that extra provision should take the form of a vast expansion of the local authority day-nursery service. Three matters have to be considered: the resources likely to be available; the effects of day care on the child as well as its convenience for the parent; and the suitability of the form of day care to the needs of the family as a whole.

Resources

8.121 Three major resource problems restrict the expansion of the local authority day-nursery service. Firstly, large scale development cannot take place without an extension of training facilities and realistic salaries to attract staff. Compared even with other social services staff carrying commensurate responsibilities, day-nursery matrons are poorly paid. Without better pay and better career prospects the service will not attract the recruits it needs. Secondly, in the central areas of large cities suitable building sites are difficult to find and often there is competition for a site from different social service interests. Thirdly, finance is a resource always in short supply; rocketing site values and escalating building costs are continuously increasing the cost of day-nursery provision and social services departments must allocate limited resources between a number of different services. Each local authority day-nursery place now costs some £1,300 to provide and some £350 each year to run. As some indication of the sums of money involved, if places were provided for only half of all one-parent family children under 5 the additional capital cost would be of the order of £150 million and the additional running costs would approach £40 million a year.[1] For all these reasons there is unlikely in the near future to be more than a modest rate of expansion of the day-nursery service.

[1] Charges contribute little towards offsetting these high running costs because they are related to parents' income.

The needs of the children and parents

8.122 A great deal is now known about the intellectual, social and emotional needs of young children and we believe that national policies should reflect a recognition of the significance of experience in the early years on the development of healthy and mature adults fully able to play their part in the community as citizens, spouses and parents. The child who is insecure in his emotional life or deprived in his environment is likely to be inhibited in his social and intellectual development. In recent years the findings of longitudinal studies of groups of children (of which those carried out by Dr Douglas,[1] and the National Children's Bureau[2] are major examples) have greatly illumined the study of human growth and development, which they have shown to be at their most rapid in the early years of life. It is in this period of rapid growth that the child's total environment is most important. Deprivation of opportunity at this period can lead to lifelong disadvantage.

8.123 Many modern studies have demonstrated the importance to the young child of attachment to his mother, or to a mother substitute, as the foundation for his social and emotional development and the forming of relationships with others. Given this stable background, the child as he grows will become increasingly able to feel secure in his mother's absence with someone else who has become familiar to him. He also needs the opportunity to have new experiences, to play and experiment, to develop manual skills, speech, reasoning, and creativity, to gain a sense of achievement, worth and personal identity, and to relate to other children and adults.

8.124 By about the age of 3 most children are becoming increasingly able to feel secure away from their mothers with known relatives or substitutes like nursery teachers, and can accept and profit from limited periods of separation. The Plowden Committee, in their findings on nursery education, concluded that:

> . . . . it should be part-time rather than whole time because young children should not be separated for long from their mothers. Attendance need not be for a whole half-day session and in the earlier stages only one, two or three days a week will often be desirable. In the words of Susan Isaacs " the nursery school is not a substitute for a good home: its prime function . . . is to supplement the normal services which the home renders to its children and to make a link between the natural and indispensable fostering of the child in the home and social life of the world at large . . ."[3]

To face this situation with confidence the child needs to know where his mother is and to be able to rely on her returning to fetch him at the end of the session.

8.125 If longer periods of separation from his mother are to be faced without adverse effect, the child needs mothering from a skilled and familiar substitute who knows his mother's child-care practices well. Younger children's needs for skilled and familiar substitute care are even greater. Summarising resent research, Dr Sula Wolff writes:

> In summary we can say that between six months and three years of life, the baby depends for his future emotional and intellectual development on stimulation

---

[1] J W B Douglas: *The Home and the School*, MacGibbon and Kee, 1964, and (with J M Ross and H K Simpson): *All our Future*, Peter Davies, 1968. This study is discussed briefly in Appendix 12.

[2] R Davie, N Butler and H Goldstein: *From Birth to Seven*, the Second Report of the National Child Development Study (1958 Cohort), Longman, 1972. This, too, is referred to in Appendix 12.

[3] *Op cit*, paragraph 309.

and affectionate care from people he knows well and who know him as an individual. Whether such needs can be met in the absence of a continuous mother figure is not yet known. What is known is that loss of the mother, especially if followed by care in an impersonal institution, is likely to have long-lasting and perhaps permanent, adverse effects.[1]

It is our view that, wherever possible, children under the age of 3 should not be parted from their mothers for long periods, and that services for them should be so framed as to involve the parent as well as the child. When absences are unavoidable special care should be taken to ensure that the child is being looked after by a person with whom he has already become familiar before his mother leaves him.

8.126 For some mothers, the freedom to work will be as valuable, and as necessary, both for themselves and the children, as the freedom to stay at home. The unmarried mother, for example, who is isolated, lonely, and lacking in family or other adult relationships may be better able to cope if she has the stimulus and mental refreshment of a job and a place of work with colleagues and workmates, and contact with the world outside the home. More money, where this is the net result of working, may provide a better material standard, and a greater enjoyment of life for the family. Against this, the lone mother or father who works in the child's early years may be left with insufficient time to devote to the child, and damage may result to their relationship with each other. If there is no grandmother or other parent-substitute living near, the family's whole childhood experience may be significantly restricted. One opinion of what this may in some cases involve was indicated by Yudkin and Holme[2] who described the possible effects as:

> . . . not that the children may not be adequately cared for, nor even that their emotional needs may not be met by the substitute parent but that the mothers themselves have no opportunity to develop the sensitive and loving relationship with their children which they can enjoy and which is so necessary for the children as they grow up into their own family.

8.127 A number of committees have considered this problem before us. The Seebohm Committee in their report described the attitude of society towards working mothers as ambivalent. They said:

> It is widely accepted that it is detrimental to the child to be separated from its mother for long periods during early childhood, . . . On the other hand, it is also a fact that many mothers do and will continue to work.[3]

The Plowden Committee also, after examining certain research studies, concluded that:

> Such research as we have been able to examine does not prove that children with mothers at work are necessarily worse off. Prolonged and early separation from mothers is known to be disadvantageous, but a short absence during the day does not harm the child who is ready for it . . . . In quoting this research we are not saying that it is better or unharmful for mothers with children under five to work. Our conclusions are that many mothers will work, and that their children will, as a result, need places in nurseries.[4]

[1] Sula Wolff: *Children under Stress*, Allen Lane, The Penguin Press, 1969, pages 19 and 20.

[2] Simon Yudkin and Althea Holme: *Working Mothers and Their Children*, Michael Joseph, 1963, pages 130–131.

[3] *Op cit*, paragraph 195.

[4] *Children and their Primary Schools:* A report of the Central Advisory Council for Education (England), Volume 1, HMSO, 1967, paragraph 305.

8.128   Our own consideration of the needs of children and parents has led us to the following general conclusions:

(1) that generally the very young child needs to be looked after by his mother or, if this is not possible, by a regular substitute whom he knows;

(2) for most young children, as has been recognised in the current educational policy for 3 to 5-year-olds, their social and emotional needs are best met if the periods they spend away from their mothers are short rather than long.   Ideally therefore for the child, half-day rather than full-day nursery schooling is to be preferred.   Similarly, for children not yet ready for nursery schooling or not having access to it, part-time day care or playgroup is more suitable than full-time day care;

(3) this, however, pre-supposes a satisfactory home situation, in which the mother is able and willing to look after the child adequately for the rest of the day.   The hours she works or any of a number of adverse social conditions, such as poor housing, social isolation, a large family or her illness or incapacity, or sometimes a combination of these circumstances, may prevent her from doing this, and make it necessary for the child to be given full-day care;

(4) some lone mothers will want and will take employment outside their homes.   This is a feature of modern life for one-parent (and indeed for two-parent) families which cannot be disregarded.   If satisfactory arrangements for care of their children do not exist these mothers will feel compelled to find others which are not satisfactory.   The facts of this situation should be recognised and help given to ensure that the best practicable arrangements are available to serve the interests of both mother and child.

The pattern for development

8.129   It follows that the much-needed expansion of day-care services ought not to be channelled primarily into the development of public day-nursery facilities.   The reconciliation of the diversity of principles and needs we have tried to expound in this Section can be achieved only through a pattern of services through which balanced expression may be given to a range of values. We need a variety of services which take account of the child's needs for stable and consistent care in an atmosphere which is socially and emotionally, as well as educationally, satisfactory and which take account also of the needs of parents, whether working away from home or not.   A flexible range of day-care and nursery-education services can provide valuable opportunities for the involvement of parents, offering them advisory service and parental education, and enabling them to gain a greater understanding of their children's needs.

8.130   This challenging objective can, we believe, be achieved, but only through full co-ordination of the various policies and services for the under-fives, at central and local government levels, and embracing both day care and nursery education.   We note that plans for the expansion of nursery education[1] have important implications for the other services for the under-fives, and thus in themselves already mark the beginnings of the broader policy:

In preparing for the expansion of nursery education, local authorities will need to take account of other facilities for under fives, existing or planned, so as

---

[1] *Education: A Framework for Expansion, op cit*, paragraph 23.

to prepare a scheme for their areas in which nursery classes and schools, voluntary playgroups, day nurseries and other forms of day care all play their part. The Government attach importance to a full assessment of local resources and needs, and will welcome diversity in provision so long as it is efficient and there is no sacrifice of standards in the education and care of the children. The main burden of this responsibility must rest on education departments, but other departments of local authorities will need to share in it, and consultation with voluntary bodies will also be necessary in many areas.

8.131 We proceed to outline, in the light of the whole of the preceding discussion, developments which we should like to see take place in the various services provided. We have already indicated that it would not be desirable for expansion to be channelled primarily through day nurseries, and to ensure that day-care services are adequate it will in our view be necessary for there to be a considerable increase in non-institutional services. We believe that for the children of working mothers, and particularly where the mother works full time, local authorities should be encouraged to develop comprehensive day fostering,[1] or family day-care services. We also consider it important that proper supervision should be maintained over private arrangements made by parents for the care of their children so as to ensure that the child does not suffer and we make some recommendations to this end.

8.132 *Nursery centres* Within the public sector experiments are already taking place in a number of local authority areas, with the joint participation of social services and education departments, in the provision of nursery centres where day-nursery facilities and a nursery class or playgroup are on the same site, or of combined residential and day nurseries. A nursery centre linking all forms of pre-school provision may meet a wide range of needs for both parents and children, and we believe there is scope for further research and experiment on these lines.

8.133 *Day fostering* Day-fostering schemes should be developed by local authorities as a branch of their child-care services. Some authorities and voluntary organisations are already operating schemes of this kind, which offer a number of advantages over the registered child-minder service we have described earlier. A major difference is that the local authority itself recruits and pays women to look after children by the day or part of the day. Parents may be expected to make a contribution towards the cost of care, as they are for a day-nursery place, but do not have a direct financial arrangement with the day foster parent.

8.134 This kind of home-based service can offer the child the care which is nearest to that which parents normally provide, while at the same time enabling him to attend nursery school or a playgroup in the same way as other children in the neighbourhood. It offers scope for extension to cover, for example, continued day fostering of children over 5 before and after school hours and in the holidays or, if there is room in the day foster mother's house, for occasional overnight care if the mother is ill. It provides opportunities, too, for in-service training and provision of equipment by local authorities in ways which will enable day foster parents to develop their understanding of the social needs of the children in their care.

---

[1] Day fostering is a child-minding service in which minders are employed by local authorities and paid by them.

8.135 *Child minding* Arrangements such as those now existing for the registration of private child minders, not employed by the local authority and paid by the parents, will continue to be required alongside the day-fostering service. We have already referred (paragraph 8.113 above) to some of the deficiencies of these arrangements and to the large amount of unregistered child minding which is believed to exist. We consider that in carrying out their responsibilities under the law for the registration and inspection of child minders local authorities, by adopting an understanding and helpful approach where appropriate, should work towards encouraging minders to improve their standards and comply with the registration requirements. However, we recognise that it may not always be possible to take such a constructive approach and that local authorities may have to take other steps to reduce the amount of unregistered child minding. But any reduction in a facility which is in short supply must be accompanied by the increase in other child-care facilities we recommend, and, in particular, by the development of the day-fostering service. We consider, however, that local authorities, who have very wide discretion, could make the process of registration as a child minder rather less laborious and more appropriate if they were to administer the regulations governing child minding with more emphasis on the suitability of the child minder herself for the task as opposed to the present emphasis on the suitability of her premises; and positive efforts to improve the quality of child minding might be supported by training courses for minders and the provision of toys and equipment on loan. Meanwhile, we welcome the decision of the Social Science Research Council to support research into illegal child minding[1] so that a better attempt can be made both to estimate the size of the problem and to get a broader view of the conditions in which the children live.

8.136 *Private fostering* We refer earlier (paragraph 8.118) to the fact that lone parents sometimes resort to private fostering because they cannot find adequate day-care facilities. We hope that as day-care facilities expand they will not have to use this expedient, but in the meantime we should like to see the legislation governing private fostering (described in Section 2) tightened up. Robert Holman's recent study[2] showed that some of the foster parents were evidently not providing satisfactory care; one in eight had previously been rejected by the local authority as foster parents for children in care. Most of the children were under 5. More than half had experienced more than one foster home, and over a third had had three or more. The situation revealed by this study is one with which social workers have long been familiar.

8.137 We consider that the present legislation governing private fostering is inadequate to achieve acceptable standards of care for these children. There are two particular respects in which we recommend the legislation should be changed. We consider it most important that proper notice should be given to the local authority of the intention to place a child with the foster mother under a private arrangement, and to achieve this we believe that there should be an obligation on the natural parent as well as the foster parent to give notice of the placement. We also consider that the standard of supervision of placements that applies to local authority fosterings should apply to private fosterings also, and there should be a statutory requirement laid on local authorities to this effect.

---

1 The Childminding Research Unit, director Brian Jackson—see paragraph 8.113.
2 *Op cit.*

8.138 *Employers' day nurseries*[1] In our discussion of employment problems in Part 7 we emphasise the desirability of a flexible and constructive approach by employers to the needs of workers with family responsibilities; we therefore welcome the contribution they make in the day-care field, and we hope that central and local government will encourage additional provision. Now that new development often takes place on industrial estates, we consider that thought might be given to joint day-nursery provision by local authorities and employers, with financial participation by industry, perhaps on a *per capita* basis. This would reduce the dependence of working mothers on a particular employer and the need to exclude a child from the nursery as the result of his mother's giving up a particular job. The managers of some factories show concern and understanding of the problems faced by young parents, and, given encouragement, might well experiment in providing services which not only allow a mother to develop her skills and earn a salary, but also provide positively for the children by creating a suitable environment for them during the day.

8.139 *Playgroups* We have referred earlier in this Section to the benefits which mothers and children can derive from involvement in playgroups, and to the recent trend towards the promotion by central and local governments of playgroups in deprived areas. We welcome the latter and should like to see this develop on an increasing scale.

Charges for day care

8.140 Local authorities have discretion in the charges they make for day care, and generally we understand that day-nursery charges are related to the parent's means with the result that the charge to the lone parent is usually small. We do not think any change in this general approach is called for in the context of our proposals in Part 5 for improved financial support for one-parent families, but we see advantage in rationalising the system, with a standard method of assessment of parents for payment of day-care charges, such as applies, for example, in the case of school meals. By equalising standards in different parts of the country, it may be possible to include day-care charges in the general " passport " arrangements for claiming and determining title to means-tested benefits which are already developing.[2] The standard system should cover both day nurseries and day fostering.

CHILDREN OVER FIVE

Day care

8.141 It is increasingly common in two-parent families for mothers to work once their children have reached school age. We discuss in Part 7 the particular problems and handicaps affecting lone parents in relation to employment. However, without day-care facilities for times when their children are not at school some one-parent families will remain seriously disadvantaged.

8.142 Many submissions of evidence which we received pointed to the need to improve day-care services for the school child so that the parent could seek and retain employment. We recognise the value to the family of the lone parent's being able to work outside the home as the child grows older

1 See also paragraph 8.114.
2 See Part 5, Section 6.

and becomes less dependent on the parent for care throughout the day. Indeed, in some cases this may be essential if the parent is to retain his or her skills in the labour market and be ready for financial independence when the children are grown up. However, school hours are not related to the normal hours of adult employment; caring for children outside school hours and accompanying young children to and from school may both be difficult for the working parent. Even minor changes arising from such circumstances as a mid-term day's holiday, use of the school as a polling station, or a sudden emergency such as loss of heating, can lead to problems for the school and parents. Further, since the length of the school term is primarily governed by the educational interests of the child, the intervals between terms—and particularly the long summer holidays—leave wide gaps in which no adequate care for the child is offered to the lone parent in employment. For the most part lone parents resolve these difficulties in the same way as working mothers in two-parent families, by making their own provision with friends, relatives and neighbours, or by recourse to paid child minders or simply by leaving their children to look after themselves.[1]

8.143 We have described in Section 2 such very limited facilities as are made available under section 53 of the Education Act 1944; most of these are for holiday times—holiday camps, play leadership schemes and the like—and very few authorities assume regular responsibility for the gaps between school hours and those of a parent's employment. The two main difficulties arising for them are the problems of legal responsibility for minors and the cost and availability of staff. Out-of-school activities, such as school journeys, school holidays and after-school activities are socially and educationally valuable, but are not capable of being organised on anything like the comprehensive scale required for the child whose parent works full time. A small number of local education authorities have organised after-school care of children and care during school holidays on a considerable scale. In many areas, however, even the school playgrounds remain locked before and after normal school hours.

8.144 Local authorities have generally entered the field of day care for school children with some diffidence. One of the difficulties is that it is only the educational system, and to a lesser extent the youth service, which receives considerable financial support from local education authorities, which has resources of premises and equipment which are under-used during the period that day-care services are required. On the other hand social services departments have wide powers to develop services which will prevent the need to receive children into care or to bring them before a juvenile court; and it is they who provide the service and largely meet the cost when reception into care is necessary or a juvenile court appearance takes place. In the division of responsibilities within the local authority services they have the caring function as distinct from the educational and healing functions of the education and health services. We consider, therefore, that responsibility for the provision of day care for school children lies logically with social services departments; but in this area, as in others where more than one local authority service may be involved, if the needs of individuals are to be met effectively the resources of the different services should be deployed as a whole to serve the interests of the

---

[1] See *Families and their Needs, op cit*, paragraphs 5.4.1 to 5.7.4, and Tables 14 and 15.

whole community. It is in this spirit that we believe that education departments should co-operate with social services departments, so that educational facilities can be utilised with social services financial support to promote more effective day-care services for school children than now exist.

Boarding education

8.145 We have referred in Section 2 to local authorities' power to provide boarding education for children who need it, under which some 20,000 children benefit. Children from one-parent families represent, of course, only one category who may be in special need of boarding education, but information made available to us by the Dartington Research Unit into the Sociology of Education indicates that, in two local authority schools they had studied, over 20 per cent of boys in the sixth form came from one-parent families. The Unit also gave us evidence on the relevance of boarding education for one-parent family children, which has been of great assistance to us in formulating the views put forward in these paragraphs.

8.146 Boarding education can help a child from a one-parent family by providing him with an education which offers companionship and activity which his family may not be able to provide, and which may also assist his parent in solving some of the practical problems of care and supervision particularly during the period of adolescence. As a method of providing accommodation, care and education, boarding education for some older children in particular may be more acceptable to both parent and child than residential care or fostering would be.

8.147 It is important, however, that in providing boarding education, the child's needs as a whole, and not just educationally, should be taken into account. Some styles of boarding education, particularly if the child is placed at a long distance from home, may cut him off from his family ties through long absences and infrequent parental visiting. Similarly insufficient suitable staff to provide care during out of classroom hours may produce an institutional life which gives him the worst of both worlds. This may be particularly damaging in single-sex schools and may lead to repression of everyday emotional expression, thus weakening close affective ties with a remaining parent.

8.148 The most suitable style of boarding education for one-parent family children is likely to be that in which the school is within reasonably easy distance of home, children are allowed frequent contact with home and community and parents are encouraged to participate in the life of the school and decisions concerning their children. It would also offer adequate adult support and care while at school and provide co-education of a socially integrated kind.

8.149 To summarise, boarding education can be a useful aid for some one-parent family children, and we recommend that local education authorities should look sympathetically at the needs of these children. We also recommend that careful thought should be given to the choice of schools, bearing in mind the special emotional needs of one-parent family children, and that wherever possible education and social services departments should jointly consider which children can be assisted in this way and how best to make the assistance most effective.

Home helps

8.150   The local authority home-help service had its statutory origins in the Maternity and Child Welfare Act 1918 which permitted local authorities to provide domestic help during confinements.   During the second world war provision was extended to include the sick and infirm and families with children, and subsequently emphasis was increasingly laid on the importance of the service as a preventive measure in keeping families together and the children out of care.[1]   Under section 13 of the Health Services and Public Health Act 1968, which came into force in April 1971, the power to provide a home-help service became a duty.[2]

8.151   The extent to which local authorities have used the home-help service to assist one-parent families has generally been small.   The large majority of home helps work in the homes of the elderly or chronic sick, who together accounted for 92 per cent of those assisted in 1972.   Of the remaining 8 per cent which included one-parent families, maternity cases accounted for 2 per cent.[3] As with other local authority social services, the size and scope of the home-help service vary in different areas.   Local authorities have discretion as to the number of home helps they employ and the types of family to be regarded as eligible for help.   Where the person helped has the means to pay, the vast majority of local authorities make a charge for the service.   Householders with an income which does not exceed the general level of supplementary benefit can normally expect to receive help free of charge.

8.152   The abilities and skills of home helps and the training they receive also vary very considerably, but a review of the service by the Department of Health and Social Security in 1972 indicated that increasing attention was being given to the extension of the service to families with children and to providing help in the home in a variety of situations with the aim particularly of preventing the need to receive children into care.   The need for home helps to be used in this way to support one-parent families was emphasised by a number of those giving evidence to us.

8.153   Our attention was also drawn to the particular contribution the home-help service can make to easing the problems of motherless families.   Worries about looking after the children seem to bulk larger in motherless than in fatherless families: the father is unlikely to be accustomed to taking the main responsibility for the children's welfare and he may face unfamiliar tasks and problems in seeing to them as well as in running the house.[4]   In these circumstances any help with either house or children is likely considerably to lighten his load: George and Wilding found, in their study of motherless families in

---

1 See, for example, Ministry of Health Circular 27/54.

2 The section also extended the scope to include the younger physically handicapped, and the provision of laundry facilities for those receiving or eligible for home help.

3 Department of Health and Social Security Annual Report 1972.

4 In this connection we note the findings of the Motherless Families Project run by the Bristol Council of Social Service, where worries about care of the children were the most frequently reported.   In 29 cases studied, the worries mentioned most often were how to find a housekeeper (12 cases), and worries about getting help with the children during the working day were mentioned in 9 cases. Mervyn Murch: ' Motherless Families Project ', *British Journal of Social Work*, Volume 3, Number 3.

the East Midlands, that lone fathers saw the home-help service as the social service most in need of improvement.[1]   We consider that it would be particularly valuable if help could be provided in the mornings, to get the children off to school, and in the late afternoons, to span the gap between the end of the school day and the father's return from work.   This may make it possible for him to keep his job and his family together, thus avoiding the need for the children to be received into care.

8.154   This latter consideration is particularly important where the mother is in hospital, and the children may have to go into care on several occasions because their father cannot cope.[2]   During the twelve months ended 31 March 1973, in England and Wales, the numbers of children received into care because of the illness of a parent was about 16,000—15,000 for under six months, and nearly 1,000 for over six months; and over 3,500 because of the mother's confinement.[3]   We are concerned about the effects on the children of being received into care, particularly when they have to go in and out several times, in circumstances where the family are already under strain because of the parent's illness; and we consider that local authorites should do their utmost to keep families together in these circumstances.

8.155   We are conscious of the difficulties to be overcome in extending the home-help service in this way.   Many women who are able to work in the middle of the day are occupied in the morning and evening with their own families: an important task for the organisers is to match the resources of the service with the needs of the clients.   Some authorities nevertheless have already begun to develop the family-care side of the service.   In Nottingham, for example, there is a special scheme, financed under the urban programme, for assisting one-parent families.   In Lindsey there is a scheme supervised by a social worker for providing regular home helps for members of a mother and baby group.   We welcome these developments and we consider that local authorities should be given every encouragement to provide help in the home for one-parent families, and especially for those that are motherless.

Relief mothering

8.156   A home help cannot ordinarily act as a substitute mother and usually does not work in the evenings or at weekends.   Some local authorities however have been able to recruit " relief mothers" who are available in times of family crisis to move in as a member of the household and provide a twenty-four hour child-care service.   A service of this kind undoubtedly avoids the necessity of receiving children into care when the mother is absent or ill.   We should like to see it used to help a father over the immediate emergency when his wife has died or left him, during which he may, if not quickly helped, despair of keeping his family together;[4] and it would be invaluable to many lone parents who, being alone and often having only one extended family to call on in an emergency, are particularly vulnerable in this respect.   We know there are considerable

---

[1] Victor George and Paul Wilding: *Motherless Families*, Routledge and Kegan Paul, 1972, page 157.

[2] Other comments on the families of hospital patients are made in Section 7 below.

[3] Provisional figures supplied by the Department of Health and Social Security.

[4] The Motherless Families Project referred to in the footnote to paragraph 8.153 mentioned the temporary state of shock experienced by many fathers immediately after separation.

practicable problems; people with the appropriate ability, training and domestic circumstances for this work are likely to be scarce and may be discouraged by lack of financial and career incentives; and the standard of accommodation, equipment and furnishings available in any particular household may be inadequate. Nevertheless "relief mothering" would be of so much help to some one-parent families that we think it important that local authorities should be encouraged to press ahead with the development of such a service. We should also like to see considerably more resources put into the service; for example by the provision of mobile homes, cars and equipment, so that it might become possible to help a wider range of domestic situations.

SECTION 5—SOCIAL ASPECTS OF EDUCATION

INTRODUCTION

8.157 We believe that education is of particular concern to children in one-parent families because of its significance in relation to general personality development, social maturation, and eventual employment and earning capacity. Accordingly, we consider in this Section of our Report whether any special help need and can be given them within the education system, how education can be used to prepare children to cope more effectively with domestic and personal life and so lessen the risk of a new one-parent family emerging, and the situation of schoolgirls who become pregnant.

8.158 We refer in Section 1 to indications in reports on relevant research that some children of one-parent families are at risk of being retarded in their educational development. Some others of these children may demonstrate their insecurity or unhappiness in other ways or those other ways may be combined with educational difficulties. In illustration of the ways in which the development of such children may be disturbed by their familial experiences, one of our members has written an account, reproduced as Appendix 12, of indications in evidence and in reports of research of how some of those children demonstrate the stress they experience in their school work or through disturbed behaviour. Although there has been more relevant research into delinquent behaviour than into other forms of response to stress, and hence more space devoted to it in the Appendix, it is likely that the strains and stresses of an insecure or unbalanced home life result much more frequently in a lack of concentration at school, or in maladaptive behaviour that does not result in demonstrable under-achievement at school, or bring the child into open revolt against authority, than in behaviour seen by the community as possibly requiring punishment or control, and therefore, as delinquent. Where, for instance, a child seeks relief from his fears through inattention at school and retreat into himself, or in physical habit disorder such as enuresis, or in the behaviour field, through truancy or petty stealing, the inattention and withdrawal are least likely to be seen to need appropriate support and treatment or to be recorded in any study of children.

8.159 There is considerable research and evidence to show the impact of environmental factors on the development of abilities. Hebb, the Canadian psychologist and physiologist, wrote in 1949 of "two determinants of intellectual growth; a completely necessary innate potential and completely necessary

474

stimulating environment".[1] The absence of this stimulating environment has been the subject of many important researches, for example, by Douglas,[2] by Halsey and colleagues[3] and research done for the Plowden Committee;[4] and our account in Section 1 of the social and personal lives of one-parent families makes it clear that for many such children this environment must be lacking. The immediate effect of the absence of such stimulation may be for the child to appear to those concerned in school as much less able than he in fact is.

ESTABLISHING RELATIONSHIPS BETWEEN HOME AND SCHOOL

8.160 We believe that it is important, if schools are to be able to offer constructive help to children from one-parent families, that good relations between home and school should always be established when the child first starts school and continued throughout his school career. There should then be an opportunity to discuss any existing problems and to make parents feel they have joined a partnership with the teachers to promote their child's development and welfare. If this is done successfully, a parent may well turn to the school for help and understanding with any problems which may arise subsequently, often finding great comfort in talking to the teacher whose name is a household word. The knowledge that a child is the subject of care and concern at school can also help to lighten the lone parent's burden of responsibility; and it may be possible for the parent to be drawn into the life of the school on an informal basis. For parents who cannot visit during the normal school day, opportunities for making contact should be created through, for example, occasional evening appointment sessions.

8.161 Within the primary school, serving as it does a fairly small catchment area, a great deal of background information about a child's family is acquired naturally over the years. Where it is felt that a child will need continuing help in the secondary school, in appropriate cases acceptable means must be found for passing on this information, so that the problems which may affect him whatever stage of education he has reached can be looked at as a whole.

USE OF WELFARE PROVISIONS

8.162 These early contacts should also help to ensure that the parents know of the existence of welfare provisions obtainable through the school, for example, free school meals and help with clothing, and give them confidence that if they approach the school for help they will be sympathetically received. In relation to health problems, contact with families through the family doctor and health visitor will have been established long before school days begin, and there should be adequate machinery for communication and co-operation with the school health authorities[5] which should enable significant health problems to be dealt with quickly. Schools should also have close liaison with social service

[1] D O Hebb: *Organisation of Behavior*, Wiley, 1949, page 302.

[2] J W B Douglas: *The Home and the School*, MacGibbon and Kee, 1964, and (with J M Ross and H K Simpson): *All our Future*, Peter Davies, 1968.

[3] A H Halsey (ed.): *EPA Problems and Policies; Educational Priority*, Volume 1, HMSO, 1972.

[4] *Children and their Primary Schools*, HMSO, 1967 (Volume 1: Report, chapters 2 and 3; Volume 2: Statistics, Appendix 10).

[5] From April 1974 school health services form part of the community medical service.

475

agencies, both statutory and voluntary, so that, with the parent's consent, they can be called upon for help when necessary. Information about the range of school welfare benefits should be regularly brought to parents' notice.

8.163 While it is important to ensure that every child in need secures the maximum benefit from the help that is available, it is also important to ensure that help is given in ways which do not cause embarrassment to the recipient. We are aware that lone parents tend to be more numerous in those stress areas which have become eligible for positive discriminatory assistance and where the receipt of free meals and other benefits may well be the norm. But bereavement and family breakdown are no respecters of class and even in schools where problems of deprivation are rare a family's suddenly changed financial circumstances may make reliance on school welfare important. In all circumstances great care should be taken to see that the manner in which the benefit is distributed does not cause a child to feel personally diminished or socially "different" at a time of family distress.

EDUCATION WELFARE SERVICE

8.164 Education welfare officers carry out a wide variety of tasks in relation to the "non-educational" needs of schoolchildren, and, although their main job is school attendance work, they are also involved in arranging for provision of free school meals and clothing, acting as liaison officers between home, school and other social agencies helping and advising parents of delinquent children. There has been considerable debate in recent years about the future role of the service, and whether it should remain school-based or whether it would be better integrated with other social services as the Seebohm Committee recommended.[1] We understand that these problems are under consideration in the departments concerned—Education and Science and Health and Social Security. We do not regard it as part of our task to consider this organisational problem, but we would stress the importance, whatever solution is adopted, of dealing with the child in all aspects of his life—family, friends, neighbourhood—and not just at school.

GUIDANCE

8.165 Where adolescents from one-parent families are disturbed by personal and family problems, further support from outside the family may be crucial for the well-being of that family. A marked and important change in education in the last decade has been the development of pastoral guidance in secondary education. The three main aspects of pupil guidance are curricular, vocational or career, and personal, and in all three fields pupils with only one parent at home may be helped significantly. Because the first two are so closely related to employment possibilities we have considered them with other aspects of employment in Part 7; here we deal with personal guidance only.[2]

---

[1] *Report of the Committee on Local Authority and Allied Personal Social Services*, Cmnd 3703, July 1968, paragraph 226.

[2] We understand that in an education context the term guidance may embrace a variety of practice and a number of jobs in schools. However, we could not find a word as appropriate to describe what we are discussing in this and the following paragraphs; but to avoid any confusion it should be understood that where the word "guidance", or the terms "personal guidance" or "pastoral guidance" are used, we are referring to help and advice with the pupil's personal and social life and not, for example, with curricular choice, vocational or career education and planning.

8.166 While teachers with responsibility for pastoral guidance are available to protect and promote the personal development of all children, they are especially well placed to give extra support to the pupil who has less support from within his family than most pupils. The concern of guidance staff with the normal child is in effect an extension of the function of the teacher into areas of life and growth normally dealt with by good parents. We believe that for lone parents support of their children by the guidance staff must be valuable, even for the family who are managing well on the whole, and we should like to see such support more generally given.

8.167 The guidance staff will be concerned where there are indications that any pupil may require special help, and they will indicate to the parent the available avenues of assistance that seem to be needed for the child. Occasionally, the sudden death of a parent, or the break-up of a marriage, may seem likely to be so damaging to the progress of the child, if he is at a crucial stage of his education, that the local education authority or school will wish to consider, among possible ways of helping him, whether the provision of a place in an appropriate boarding school would enable him to complete the course of education planned for him before his home was broken, without diminishing his relationship with his remaining parent.[1]

8.168 Personal guidance may require confidential co-operation with the pupil and sometimes also with his parent over a number of years. Where the problems of a pupil suggest that skilled outside help is needed for him, and perhaps also for some of his family, the parent who has been helped to understand the " caring " intention of the personal guidance given to the child in school is more likely to co-operate readily with any specialist helper suggested by the guidance teacher. Frequently, that helper will be a social worker from the social services department of the local authority who may be associated with the school, but increasingly home/school liaison teachers are being appointed with this type of work as their special responsibility. Teachers work closely, too, with the school welfare or attendance officer, who may have been in touch over the years with lone parents known to have problems and who may sometimes act as an excellent liaison officer in relation to the families.

SOCIAL EDUCATION

8.169 We believe that adolescents in particular may be helped to overcome difficulties that the absence of one-parent may put in their way by increased emphasis on the social aspects of the education they receive at school. We think this if of particular importance where the family suffers from multiple deprivation, as so many one-parent families do: it is help given to the child which is likely to be most effective in preventing the same difficulties recurring when he himself becomes a parent. Children need to see in broader settings than those of their own experience how lives may be patterned and personal relationships enhanced, and to be aware of the importance of foresight and of understanding the needs of others. Such a wider view and sensitive understanding may enable those who are taking decisions for themselves to appreciate that what they are doing may affect those for whom they are or hope to become responsible. Many young people from deprived homes feel that they count for nothing, and latent capacity may be encouraged when youngsters are enabled

[1] See also Section 4, paragraphs 8.145–8.149.

477

to see that they too can become significant members of their local community. Where school is involved in activities for and within the surrounding community the children may come to take for granted that they and their family have responsibilities to the community and those in it.

8.170 Social education is implicit in education in general. The study of the personal and social implications of literature, modern studies, science, economics and religion is necessary in developing the awareness of a pupil and his understanding of how people live in conditions different from his own. Emphasis on this aspect is now seen to be much more important and teaching material is becoming available. Specific courses in social education which supplement the personal and social context of courses such as literature and science may do even more to arouse the pupil to the need to prepare for making decisions in his own adult life, and to assess the probable consequences of a course of action that he has in mind. It is particularly significant for one-parent families that increasingly social education is accepted as an important element in a child's education and is covering national, community and personal aspects of life in a wide variety of ways. Thus it may be possible for a teacher to consider personal relationships and questions of personal responsibility as well as physical development and health generally; all of which could be seen as parts of a broadly based course that sought to cover the various personal, emotional and social problems of the developing adolescent. The new courses in health education and home economics are particularly valuable in this context.

8.171 Adolescents who did not have a stable family life as young children, and particularly those who have only one parent as a model, may have difficulties in these respects that can be eased, if not resolved, by the kind of courses in social education that we have in mind. Some pupils may afterwards feel able to discuss with a responsible adult many matters that previously had been pondered alone. Such relief of tension in a young adolescent may help a lone parent who has possibly been very worried by feelings of inadequacy in attempting to cope with what she or he knew as a major crisis in the development of her son or his daughter. Many young people seem to have difficulty in appreciating all the implications of sexual development and personal relationships. The parent and concerned teachers will have to take opportunities for repeated discussion of the questions that concern the youngsters. For older adolescents with a lone parent, many social and personal problems may still be unresolved or just emerging. To meet their needs we should like to see expansion of courses of social education in institutions such as colleges of further education.[1]

8.172 Schools may have another contribution to make to the social education of children from one-parent families in that they may provide wider contacts with adults of both sexes than the children experience in their sometimes socially isolated lives at home. We particularly welcome the fact that increased numbers of men teachers are now serving in junior schools, for this can be of help to a fatherless child. Infant and nursery schools and day nurseries remain female preserves and we believe that the recruitment of more male staff in these establishments could serve the same purpose for smaller children.

---

[1] The importance of social education in bringing home to young people the need to control both the number and timing of the birth of their children is referred to in Section 8 below.

Home Economics

8.173 It was suggested to us in evidence that a not uncommon cause of marital discord, leading to break-up, particularly in very young marriages, was difficulty over budgeting. As single people, particularly if they had been living with their parents, both husband and wife may have had quite a large proportion of their earnings for personal spending; setting up a home may involve a substantial increase in their commitments, while their income is likely to fall if the wife stops working when the first child is born. Most marriages face this hurdle; but if the wife is without domestic skills, and the couple do not attempt to plan a domestic budget together, their marriage is likely to have a bad start. Should the marriage break down in such circumstances the difficulties facing the parent with whom the children remain will be particularly depressing, and the strain of running a home single-handed and also working elsewhere, whether whole time or part time, could be insuperable. We consider that in secondary schools many subjects should be used to increase pupils' awareness of the realities of family life, and their knowledge of all the practical skills required in a home. It is important that both boys and girls should have instruction in such matters as the purchasing and preparation of food, house maintenance, budgeting, hire-purchase schemes, house tenure and house purchase.

Schoolgirl Pregnancies

8.174 As we show in Section 8, the number of births among schoolgirls in Britain is still very small: only 1,624 births occurred to girls under 16 in 1971, out of a total of nearly 900,000 legitimate and illegitimate births, and the number of abortions was less than 2,500. But the birth of a child in such circumstances is likely to be particularly damaging and we hope that the increasing emphasis on social education which we have recommended and the direction of family planning services towards the young, which we recommend in Section 8, will help to prevent such pregnancies in future, and that abortion will continue to be available in the appropriate case. If a girl does become pregnant, however, it is important for her future and the child's, if she is to keep it, that she should not rush headlong into a decision to discontinue her education as soon as possible.

8.175 It is essential, in our view, that those in schools who have educational responsibility for a girl who is to become an unmarried mother should act in close liaison with her parents and others concerned, including any social worker, in making or assisting in the making of the best possible arrangements for the continuation and resumption of her education or training, provided that this does not involve the imposition of decisions on the girl whose own wishes are of the utmost importance.[1] No girl who wants to complete a planned course or to sit examinations for which she has been working should be prevented, except on health grounds, from doing so. Many girls whose first reaction to pregnancy is a determination to leave school may be persuaded to resume their studies. Some older schoolgirls who remain determined not to return to their school may be persuaded to take a further education course

---

[1] We have been told that on occasion pressure is brought upon girls in this position, for example, in hospital, to keep their babies; we deplore any such pressure, especially at a time when the girl is particularly vulnerable.

which they can see as likely to lead to work enabling provision of a good home for the child. Where a schoolgirl is in the process of having her baby adopted, it may be most desirable that she should not discontinue her schooling until she has had time to recover a little and to plan her own future.

8.176 Special arrangements for minimising the disruption of a girl's schooling may be necessary during part of her pregnancy, and the provision of special teachers for her and tuition at home[1] when appropriate should reduce considerably the emotional stresses of that period and make it less difficult for her to return to school after the baby is born.

SECTION 6—MOTHER AND BABY HOMES

8.177 Mother and baby homes have their origins in the penitentiaries and reformatories, residential charitable institutions established in the eighteenth and nineteenth centuries. Their name reflects a moral atittude: the aim was to reform. Unmarried mothers were admitted for periods of one to three years, parted from their babies and required to expiate their sins in a regime of austerity, religious guidance and unremitting hard work. Modern mother and baby homes have moved far away from these grim beginnings. Some homes now exist—mainly those run by local authorities—which see their function solely in terms of the provision of accommodation and care; other homes may still have a reforming purpose, but pursue this end far less obtrusively than in the past. Although there are still restrictions, rules in the majority of homes are not as stringent as they were, and most homes are now prepared to allow a resident to stay for as short or as long a time as necessary.[2]

8.178 In 1966, about one sixth of all unmarried mothers in England and Wales (one tenth in Scotland) were accommodated in mother and baby homes. In that year, there were 172 homes in England and Wales, 148 provided by voluntary (mainly religious) organisations and 24 by local authorities. In Scotland there were 11 homes, all run by voluntary organisations. The number of homes is falling: the National Council for the Unmarried Mother and her Child have told us that currently there are 65 homes in England and Wales of which 10 are maternity homes and 55 provide care before and after the confinement. The main reason for the decline in numbers seems to be lack of demand,[3] although there were also difficulties over staffing the homes. More mothers seem to prefer to remain in the community before and after confinement; the stigma attaching to illegitimacy appears to be less than it once was, and parents may be more willing now to allow their daughters to stay at home with their babies. In addition, mothers who intend to have their babies adopted are more likely to have them placed with a foster mother or prospective adopters before they go to their adopted families than previously.

8.179 In 1964 the Ministry of Health in co-operation with the Gulbenkian Foundation sponsored a research project undertaken by the National Council for the Unmarried Mother and her Child to examine the policies and practice

[1] The local education authority has power under section 56 of the Education Act 1944 to provide home tuition in certain circumstances.

[2] National Council for the Unmarried Mother and Her Child: unpublished evidence.

[3] This would seem attributable to changes in attitude rather than to the reduction in the number of illegitimate births. There has been such a reduction since the peak in 1967, but numbers are currently still much higher than in the 1950s and early 1960s—see Part 3.

of mother and baby homes in the light of preesnt-day needs. The report by Mrs Nicholson,[1] from which some of the figures quoted in the previous paragraph are drawn, showed that there was considerable confusion about the purpose and function of the homes among the persons running them, among the mothers themselves, and even among social workers. Mrs Nicholson also found that standards were generally below what would be tolerated in other forms of residential accommodation and that residents were faced with more rules, restrictions and invasions of privacy than would be found in, say, a hostel or boarding house. This may well be connected with the " reforming " purpose of some homes: Mrs Nicholson found that " the two Homes where rules were most numerous and restrictive were also those in which an evangelical approach was most evident."[2]

8.180   We believe that the problem of mother and baby homes must be tackled at two levels. That there is a need for special accommodation for some unmarried mothers before and after the baby is born, we do not doubt. Mrs Nicholson thought that mother and baby homes were needed to provide accommodation, to provide care, and in some cases treatment.[3] The national Council for the Unmarried Mother and her Child said, " There is, however, still a place for Mother and Baby Homes. Mothers who need them will be mainly those who have very special difficulties in addition to the pregnancy. They will include mothers who are very young, or who have no families, or who have grave emotional problems, as well as mothers who are disabled or have histories of psychiatric or physical illness or delinquency."[4] We consider that further investigtaion is needed into the future likely demand for residential accommodation for unmarried mothers, and into the type of accommodation that should be provided. In the meantime, local authorities should squarely face the responsibilities that they already have, under section 1 of the Children and Young Persons Act 1963 and section 22 of the National Health Service Act 1946, to ensure that there are adequate facilities for unmarried mothers who need them. What is required is a concerted plan with voluntary organisations; and we believe it to be particularly important that in tackling this local authorities should make efforts to see that non-sectarian accommodation is available for those mothers who prefer it.

8.181   Next, the standard of provision must be raised. There is no statutory requirement for mother and baby homes to register as places providing residential accommodation; and local authorities do not customarily register them as maternity homes (although they probably could do so under the Public Health Act 1936), except where deliveries take place on the premises, presumably because they are reluctant to impose the staffing and other requirements consequential on such registration. In England and Wales, mother and baby homes are thus one of the few forms of residential provision for which no arrangements have been made for registration or inspection.[5] Registration and inspection are,

---

[1] Jill Nicholson: *Mother and Baby Homes*, Allen and Unwin, 1968.

[2] *Ibid*, page 86.

[3] *Ibid*, page 142.

[4] *Forward for the Fatherless, op cit*, paragraph 281.

[5] In Scotland, mother and baby homes were until 1969 registered as voluntary children's homes under section 29 of the Children Act 1948; since November 1969 they have been registered as residential establishments under section 59 of the Social Work (Scotland) Act 1968 and are subject to the arrangements for inspection provided under that Act.

of course, far from being a universal panacea.   Mrs Nicholson found that " one of the worst voluntary Homes had been inspected regularly for years."[1] Nevertheless, a requirement on local authorities to lay down standards and a determined effort to see that they were respected would be a significant move in the right direction.

SECTION 7—SPECIAL GROUPS

8.182   In this Section we refer briefly to a number of relatively small groups of one-parent families of whose special needs we became aware during our deliberations without having either the information or the expertise to consider their problems fully.   The groups concerned are the children of women prisoners,[2] the families of long-term hospital patients and immigrant families. In each case we consider that further study of the size of the problem and the difficulties experienced by these groups is called for, so that some body more expert in these fields than ourselves can make a proper assessment of what needs to be done.   In the meantime we mention here the main problems as as they appeared to us.

CHILDREN OF WOMEN PRISONERS

8.183   We are particularly concerned at the consequences for a family of the imprisonment of the mother.   The numbers involved are not large, but in a high proportion of cases the family background has already been disturbed: in a survey of women in prison in 1967 it was found that over one quarter of those with dependent children were single, and one third divorced, separated or widowed.[3]   The situation involving the birth of a child to a mother serving a term of imprisonment, where the mother's sentence extends beyond the child's early infancy, is also of concern to us.   We understand that a child born during the mother's period of imprisonment may remain with her until he is two years of age; and that it is accepted as a matter of principle that a woman may bring her child with her into prison[4] if he is under two years of age and that he may remain with her until he reaches that age.   This does not, however, mean that all mothers who want to take their young children into prison with them are allowed to do so: accommodation is limited and even where it is available there are circumstances (for example where there is a background of cruelty or the child has developed strong links with other members of the family) when it may be judged better for the child to be with relatives or received into care.   The Home Office have told us that a considerable expansion in the accommodation for mothers with small children is planned, and that they hope eventually that a mother will be able to bring more than one child with her, and for children to remain until they are 5; their aim is to avoid having to refuse a place solely on the grounds that accommodation was not available. We welcome this recognition that the present state of affairs is unsatisfactory, and we should like to see the proposed expansion implemented as soon as possible so that at least the very youngest children never have to be separated

---

[1] *Op cit*, page 149.

[2] We refer to the families of long-term prisoners generally in Part 2 and in Part 5, Section 6.

[3] Carole Gibbs: *The Effect of the Imprisonment of Women upon their Children*, Stevens and Son Ltd, 1971.

[4] This includes women remanded or committed in custody to await trial or sentence as well as those sentenced to imprisonment or Borstal training.

from their mothers for lack of accommodation. We are especially concerned where mothers are remanded in custody and are not subsequently sentenced to imprisonment,[1] and we recommend that the Home Office should look particularly at their situation to see if unnecessary disruption of relationships between mother and child can be avoided.

FAMILIES OF LONG-TERM HOSPITAL PATIENTS

8.184 Although we conclude (Part 5, Section 6) that it would not be appropriate to extend guaranteed maintenance allowance to the families of long-term hospital patients, we are conscious that these families face special problems particularly when, as is commonly the case, the absent parent is suffering from mental illness.[2] Illness of the mother in particular sometimes results in the children's being received into care because the father cannot cope;[3] and where a mentally ill mother comes in and out of hospital the children may be received into care several times. We believe that this shuttlecock situation might be avoided if more help were given to the fathers to enable them to keep the children at home, and we refer to this need in Section 4. We also consider that close co-operation is needed between hospitals and social services departments to ensure that the arrangements made are those best for the family as a whole; and in this connection we welcome the recent decision that social workers in hospitals should form part of the local authority social services department.

8.185 Although the foregoing paragraph is written in terms of the family of the long-term hospital patient, a good deal of what is said there applies also to the situation of the ordinary one-parent family where the lone parent has to go into hospital for a short time, for example, because of confinement. In these cases, as we have mentioned in Section 4, the extension of " relief mothering " services, so that the children could remain at home while the parent was in hospital instead of having to be taken into care, would be of particular value.

IMMIGRANT FAMILIES

8.186 Several organisations giving evidence to us pointed to the special difficulties of one-parent families who are also immigrants, particularly coloured immigrants who tend to live in overcrowded areas and are already disadvantaged in many other ways. The British Association of Social Workers said, " The immigrant one parent family has, as it were, a double handicap—that of its colour and situation in a strange land, and all the problems associated with one parent families." In addition, different patterns of culture and family

---

[1] During 1972 only 659 of the 3,406 women remanded in custody before trial or before sentence subsequently received custodial sentences. (The result of the trial was unknown in 111 cases.) *Report of the Work of the Prison Department 1972*, Statistical Tables, Cmnd 5489, Table D22.

[2] In 1971, for example, there were only about 500 people who had been in general hospitals for a year or more who were between the ages of 15 and 46, and only a proportion of these would be married with dependants. In mental illness hospitals, at the end of 1971, on the other hand, there were 2,485 married patients between the ages of 15 and 54 (1,018 men and 1,467 women) who had been in for a year or more, although again we do not know how many had children. (Department of Health and Social Security—unpublished statistics.)

[3] In the year ending 31 March 1973 15,000 children were received into care because of the short-term illness of a parent, 1,000 because of long-term illness and 3,500 because of the mother's confinement. (Provisional figures supplied by the Department of Health and Social Security.)

life may lead to different attitudes towards marriage and illegitimacy from those commonly accepted in this country. The British Association of Social Workers again: "We would point out the varying significance that illegitimacy has in different cultures. In Pakistani communities, a girl who has an illegitimate child may be cast out from her family, whereas for many West Indian girls it is the normal pattern to have one or more children before marriage, and a husband who may stay with her for only a short time. Whereas in the West Indies, however, the girl will have the support of her extended family, in Great Britain this is probably lacking, and instead she may have to turn to the Social Services for help." Other associated problems also arise which fall beyond our remit—for example the difficulties facing the child who has been left in the home country when his parents emigrated and only rejoins them as an adolescent. We do not feel we are competent to deal with the particular problems associated with immigrant communities. We see however a need for further study in this area and we recommend that joint discussions of their problems between social services and education services should be held both at local and national level.

SECTION 8—MEASURES TO PREVENT THE CREATION OF ONE-PARENT FAMILIES

8.187 Our terms of reference require us to look at the problems confronting the one-parent family, not at the causes—marriage breakdown and illegitimacy—of the family being in this plight. Little is known about the social, psychological and environmental influences which lead to the formation of one-parent families and we have not attempted to enter this field. But it would be wrong to complete this Report without some reference to the most immediate means of limiting the number of new one-parent families—birth prevention. We comment only briefly because of the number of other bodies and investigators active in this field: the Committee on the Working of the Abortion Act have now reported[1] and the Department of Health and Social Security are engaged in discussing how the family planning services may be operated and developed in hospitals and in general and community practice during the early years of the reorganised national health service.[2]

8.188 Table 8.1. brings together information about the timing of pregnancies and the incidence of illegitimate and legitimate births and abortions among single and married women in different age groups.

---

[1] The report had not been published at the time we wrote this Section.

[2] The Scottish Home and Health Department are conducting similar discussions in Scotland.

484

TABLE 8.1

NUMBER OF ILLEGITIMATE AND LEGITIMATE LIVE BIRTHS AND ABORTIONS ON SINGLE AND MARRIED WOMEN RESIDENT IN GREAT BRITAIN: 1971

Age	Illegitimate births[1]	Abortions on single women[2]	Legitimate births[1]	Abortions on married women[3]
11	1	3		
12	4	16		
13	32	80		
14	247	551	1	
15	1,338	1,785	1	
Under 16	1,622	2,435	2	
16	3,180	3,647	3,246	
17	5,763	4,580	11,368	
Under 18	10,565	10,662	14,616	
18	6,610	5,268	22,145	
19	6,524	4,915	31,377	
Under 20	23,699	20,845	68,138	643
20–24	24,592	17,759	292,591	6,062
25–29	12,712	5,086	260,542	10,522
30–34	6,922	1,446	115,548	11,718
35–39	3,511	587	47,296	9,880
40–44	1,171	154	12,212	4,667
Over 45	78	13	804	421
Total	72,707[4]	46,698[5]	797,176[6]	44,807[7]

[1] *Registrar General's Statistical Review of England and Wales for the Year 1971, Part II, Tables, Population*, Table AA(a); the *Annual Report of the Registrar General for Scotland, 1971, Part II, Population and Vital Statistics*, Table 52.5.

[2] England and Wales: *Registrar General's Statistical Review of England and Wales for the Year 1971, Supplement on Abortion*, Table 7C; Scotland: *Scottish Home and Health Department Bulletin*, Volume XXXI, No 1, January 1973, and Scottish Home and Health Department unpublished figures.

[3] England and Wales: *Registrar General's Statistical Review of England and Wales for the Year 1971, Supplement on Abortion*, Table 8; Scotland: *Scottish Home and Health Department Bulletin*, Volume XXXI, No 1, January 1973.

[4] Includes 22 illegitimate maternities in Scotland where the mother's age was not stated.

[5] Includes 808 women whose age was not stated.

[6] Includes 45 legitimate maternities in Scotland where the mother's age was not stated; the 1,932 similar instances in England have been distributed among the age groups by the Registrar General.

[7] Includes 894 women whose age was not stated.

485

8.189   The Table shows that 69 per cent of legitimate births in Great Britain in 1971 occurred to women in the age group 20–29.   By contrast, only 9 per cent of legitimate births occurred to women under the age of 18 and over the age of 35; yet this age group experienced 21 per cent of all the illegitimate births, one quarter of the abortions on single women and one third of the abortions performed on married women.   Even more striking is the experience of the women under 20 and over 35 years of age.   These women carried no more than 16 per cent of legitimate births but 39 per cent of all illegitimate births; and they experienced 46 per cent of the abortions performed on single women and 35 per cent of those on married women.   Many induced abortions represent unwanted pregnancies and hence reflect the inadequacy of family planning services.   The truth of this statement is beyond dispute and independent of the fact that some women will carelessly risk pregnancy however good and easily accessible family planning advice and services may be.   Abortions are experienced disproportionately by women in the earlier and later phases of their reproductive period when the risk of adverse medical and social effects is probably highest.   Moreover, there is a considerable body of evidence that the biologically most advantageous years for childbearing are the early twenties for the first birth and the later twenties and early thirties for the second and third births.   Special risks often attach to later births.   For example, Down's syndrome comprises about 30 per cent of all severely retarded children in the United States and Western Europe, and mothers aged 35 years and over are likely to contribute 35 per cent of the cases.[1]   But there is much greater knowledge of the medical than of the psychological and social implications of a mother's age.   In the extreme and very rare case of a birth to a girl under the age of 16, the result will probably be a ruined life.   Nor are the prospects much brighter for the larger number of unmarried mothers—they constitute 15 per cent of the total—under the age of 18.   These young women will have no period of independence between reliance on their parents and responsibility for their own children, and they will face restricted opportunities for education and employment.   Mr Bernard Berelson, President of the Population Council in the United States, comments that:

> in all probability a good deal of reproduction at the young and old ages is not really wanted—is the product of indifference, fatalism, tradition, ignorance, inaccessibility of means.   To the extent that is the case, an effective alternative in behaviour is needed . . . .   Today a new ethic toward childbearing is needed . . . .   The idea of concentrating human reproduction in the " best years " for child-bearing may have much to recommend it.   If no children were voluntarily born to women below 18 or 20 or above 35, the benefits to mankind, and especially to womankind, would appear to be considerable.   The idea promises an ameliora-tion of both individual and societal concerns at minimal costs in personal freedom. It is certainly good for mother and child on medical grounds and it is probably good for both of them on psychological grounds as well.   It would tend to reduce the number of large families, with their attendant disabilities to the children. It would contribute to the broad goals of economic development and women's status.   It would be based on an informed guide to reproductive behaviour in place of tradition and sometimes ignorance.[2]

We urge that the concept of " the best years for childbearing " be examined by those responsible for family planning services with reference to the desirability

---

[1] Zena Stein, Mervyn Susser and Andrea V Cuterman: ' Screening Programme for Prevention of Down's Syndrome ', in *The Lancet*, 10 February 1973, paragraphs 305–310.

[2] *Annual Report of the Population Council (1971)*, New York, excerpts from pages 22–27.

on medical, psychological, social and economic grounds of incorporating specific advice about the timing of pregnancy into courses in health and social education directed to the young. Control over fertility is now universal in Britain; we hope that it will become an objective of family planning policies to enable people to choose not only how many babies to have but when best to have them.

8.190 Part 3 of our Report sets out some of the main demographic changes which have occurred among recent generations. We have there commented on the achievement of the small consciously planned family, on the universality of birth control and on the resulting separation of sex from pregnancy for many women in the childbearing ages. We show how the welcoming official attitudes and political enthusiasm for extensions of family planning services in the last few years are the tardy product, not the explanation, of the spread of birth control. We welcome the extension of these services now proposed.[1] But we are concerned about the large number of pregnancies, most of which we assume to be unwanted, occurring among very young women. It is inevitable that a society which is only just beginning to establish provision for birth control services within the national health service will be ignorant of the attitudes and practices of young people. Effective policies for preventing unwanted births must be grounded in knowledge and we are glad to learn that the Department of Health and Social Security have commissioned, from the Institute for Social Studies in Medical Care, a study under the direction of Dr Ann Cartwright of the extent and sources of contraceptive knowledge among 16 to 19-year-olds, and among newly qualified doctors. Only from such studies will it be possible to learn where to direct educational efforts. The only national study of the sexual behaviour of teenagers in England[2] was conducted in the early 1960s and demonstrated a deplorable lack of sexual instruction at home and in school. Two thirds of the boys and one quarter of the girls had learnt nothing about sex from their parents:[3]

> Half the boys and 14 per cent of the girls did not receive any sex education at school. In all types of state schools, including grammar schools, as often as not there was no sex education for the boys. It was the working class boys who were least likely to learn about sex from their parents and were least likely to receive sex education at school.
> In view of all the discussion about sex education in recent years, it was surprising to find so many teenagers who said they were never taught about sex at school. A possible explanation is that the teachers think they are giving sex education but the adolescents do not recognise it as such.[4]

There was no question of an unwillingness among teenagers to be instructed. Dr Schofield reported that there is:

> plenty of evidence from this research that teenagers are anxious to be informed about sex and want sex education providing it is given with an assurance which is backed by knowledge and with a proper understanding of their particular problems.[5]

---

[1] Referred to by Sir Keith Joseph, when Secretary of State for Social Services, in the House of Commons in December 1972, and March 1973. Official Report. 12 December 1972, columns 234–240 and 26 March 1973, columns 934–939. A brief description of the new service proposed is given in Section 2.

[2] It was undertaken on behalf of the Central Council for Health Education by Michael Schofield and published as *The Sexual Behaviour of Young People*, Longmans, 1965.

[3] *Ibid*, Penguin Books, 1968, page 225.

[4] *Ibid*, page 226.

[5] *Ibid*.

8.191 What Edward Lyttelton, a headmaster of Eton, described in a pioneering book of 1900 as the necessity of *Training of the Young in the Laws of Sex*[1] has advanced but little since Dr Schofield's survey of the early 1960s. In this area of education, a plenitude of good intentions has still to yield extensive achievements. We note with satisfaction that active study is now being given to some of the groups which are our special concern, and we quote in full the short account of a private conference on pregnancy among adolescent girls, organised in 1972 by the Rainer foundation, at which senior representatives of public and private agencies and the Church, sociologists, doctors and lawyers discussed the question of teenage pregnancies and the use of oral contraceptives:

> Sir Richard Doll, Regius Professor of Medicine at Oxford, described the medical aspects of oral contraception and clarified the controversial question of harmful side effects. He put the total risk of death rate from the pill at 1 or 2 *per* 100,000 a year—comparable to the effect of smoking one cigarette a day and rather less than that of a girl being killed by a motor car.
>
> Professor T C N Gibbens, of the Institute of Psychiatry, London University, drew upon his long experience of the attitudes and behaviour of promiscuous maladjusted girls and the social effects of unwanted pregnancies. Even if they wanted to keep their babies most girls were completely ignorant of what motherhood entailed. The main arguments for the use of contraception in such cases were that the children of single maladjusted girls were frequently disadvantaged and themselves maladjusted, and that attempts to reduce promiscuity by confinement and control led to greater hysteria, agitation and maladjustment; a more stable life could perhaps be attained if girls had some degree of freedom to establish relationships, protected from pregnancy. He felt that parents were often left out of the picture and should be consulted, and that the general practitioner should prescribe rather than the psychiatrist. In the discussion which followed participants expressed the view that social casework, often jeopardized by pregnancy, could be carried out more effectively if oral contraception were available for girls at risk and that this situation should be acknowledged by parents, society and the law. More fundamental was the question of education for responsible parenthood and sexual behaviour as an antidote to ignorance and misuse of sex. They felt that an informal approach, free of stigma, to information about sex, personal relationships and child rearing was required, for boys as well as for girls—a need which extended to young people as a whole and not only those in a casework relationship. The churches and the media could play a part in making this type of " sex education " socially acceptable.[2]

8.192 We hope that other bodies, public as well as voluntary, will take an active part in this work of understanding and education. In particular, we think it desirable that the Department of Health and Social Security should put itself in a position, by promoting research and experiment, to give empirically based guidance relating to facilities for the young in the family planning service within the reorganised national health service.

8.193 Detailed information about the need for advice on birth control is contained in the enquiry carried out by Margaret Bone, on behalf of the Department of Health and Social Security, into *Family Planning Services in England and Wales*.[3] The survey distinguishes three groups of women more prone than others to have unwanted pregnancies; they are women who marry under the age of 20; those who conceived prenuptially; and the wives of the

---

[1] The Reverend the Honourable Edward Lyttelton: *Training of the Young in the Laws of Sex*, Longmans, 1900.
[2] The Rainer Foundation: *Annual Report, 1973*, page 10.
[3] HMSO, 1973.

least skilled workers.[1]   We have shown in Part 3 the extent to which the first two of these three categories of mothers both overlap and experience significantly higher rates of marriage breakdown than those affecting the generality of married women.   Of course, the likelihood that such women will be married to unskilled workers is also high.   We are satisfied that the situation in Scotland is similar.   On the basis of longitudinal studies of married primigravidae resident in Aberdeen, Dr Thompson and Professor Illsley concluded that:

> large, unplanned families are drawn primarily from three major overlapping categories of women—those who marry before the age of 20, those who conceive prenuptially, and those who marry a semi-skilled or unskilled manual worker. This finding reflects the great influence of premarital education and cultural values on post-marital behaviour.   Thus, modern techology may produce new contraceptive methods . . . but their adoption depends on social values and attitudes built up during childhood and adolescent experience . . . .[2]

8.194   Special measures will be required to reach some of these groups: domiciliary services in particular may be useful for those reluctant to attend clinics or to consult their general practitioners, and the provision of transport to clinics or to doctors' surgeries and child-minding facilities there would help women who already have children.   We do not think that we can usefully attempt a more detailed commentary upon the measures which are available to prevent an increase in, and possibly to reduce the numbers of, one-parent families; but we recommend that those responsible for designing birth control and family planning policies[3] should give special attention to the groups in the population statistically most likely to produce illegitimate children and high rates of marriage breakdown.

---

[1] Ibid, page 51.

[2] Barbara Thompson and Raymond Illsley: ' Family Growth in Aberdeen ', Journal of Biosocial Science, Volume 1, Number 1, page 37.

[3] We refer to birth control as well as to family planning policies and services because the phrase family planning does not adequately describe measures which may be necessary for the young or the single.

PART 9—SUMMARY

9.1   In this final Part of our Report we bring together in summary form the main themes and conclusions of the earlier Parts so that, as far as is possible in so wide-ranging an investigation, the reader may be provided with an overall view of its results.   We give a brief narrative description of each Part, followed by a list of the recommendations which emerge from it, numbered consecutively for ease of reference.   We have restricted these lists to recommendations for positive and specific action on particular points; more general expressions of views or hopes for the future are, where of major importance, included in the narrative.   Not all the recommendations listed apply to Scotland because in some respects the law there is different.   It would have been too cumbersome to deal with specific differences in this summary and the reader is referred for the Scottish position to the relevant sections in the main body of the Report.

THE MAKING OF ONE-PARENT FAMILIES (PART 3)

9.2   This Part of the Report deals with the demographic characteristics of one-parent families: it is purely descriptive and contains no recommendations.

9.3   We estimate that there were, in April 1971, 620,000 one-parent families with over 1 million children.   Of these families 100,000 were motherless and the other 520,000 fatherless.   Of the fatherless families 190,000 were separated, 120,000 divorced, 120,000 widowed and 90,000 single.   One-parent families formed about one tenth of all families with children; there are no figures available of the extent to which families move in and out of the one-parent category, but movement must be considerable, and a significantly higher proportion must spend some time as one-parent families.

9.4   Today a higher proportion of the population marry than ever before, they marry younger and, with much reduced mortality rates, their marriages last longer than in previous generations.   They also have smaller and consciously-planned families, so that a woman's childbearing years are compressed into a relatively short period.   The result has been a transformation of women's working lives: instead of work being undertaken between school and motherhood, motherhood is taking place in the interval between school and work.

9.5   It is against this background, of virtually universal marriage and a dramatic change in women's working role, that the evidence about marriage breakdown must be viewed.   There is, in fact, very little information which would enable us to trace changes in the pattern of marriage breakdown as such: we can trace only those changes which are formally recorded–deaths, divorces, maintenance proceedings.   We know that death rates have fallen sharply over the last forty years and are now so low, in the relevant age groups, that no foreseeable change is likely to have much effect on the number of one-parent families.   We know that the number of divorces has increased rapidly since the late 1950s and that a higher proportion of marriages now terminate in divorce; we do not know whether this means that more marriages are breaking down or whether more breakdowns are coming to court.   Marriages between young people are particularly likely to end in divorce and, with the age of marriage falling, this in itself may have contributed to a higher breakdown rate; on the other hand there are grounds for believing that, with the spread of legal aid, the greater social acceptability of divorce and the improvements in the status and earning capacity of women, divorce is being resorted to more readily.

490

9.6   Although unmarried mothers are often thought of as " typical " one-parent families, they form less than 15 per cent of the total, and an even smaller proportion of children in one-parent families—about 11 per cent—belong to this group.   Statistics here are particularly difficult to interpret because there may be no close connection between the number of unmarried mothers bringing up their own children and the total number of illegitimate births.   The proportion of illegitimate births has undoubtedly risen—from 5·1 per cent of total births in England and Wales in 1950 to 8·6 per cent in 1972.   (In absolute numbers a peak was reached in 1967.)   But many of these children—perhaps as many as one in three—are born to married women or women living in stable unions; others become members of two-parent families when their mothers marry; and yet others are adopted.

FAMILY LAW, SOCIAL SECURITY AND ONE-PARENT FAMILIES (PART 4)

9.7   In this Part of our Report we examine the law and legal procedures relevant to family breakdown.   We show how one-parent families are the subject not of a single system of family law, but, in effect, of three systems, administered respectively by the divorce courts, the magistrates' courts and the supplementary benefit authorities.   This fragmentation of the law and the agencies through which it is administered is the result entirely of historical causes deriving from a society in which there was one family law for the rich, a second for the destitute, and a third for people in-between.   The triple system in its modern form still bears the marks of its discriminatory origins.   Its persistence is irrational and productive of much inefficiency and personal hardship.   It needs thorough reform.

9.8   Since 1969, the sole ground for divorce has been that the marriage has irretrievably broken down.   It is not essential to establish matrimonial fault, nor will the commission of a matrimonial offence prevent—other than in wholly exceptional circumstances—the divorce courts from making financial orders in favour of a " guilty " wife.   In the magistrates' courts, on the other hand, neither an order for maintenance nor a separation order can be obtained without establishing a matrimonial offence; and a wife who commits such an offence forfeits her right to be maintained.   The divorce law gives effect to the public policy that dead marriages should be decently interred.   The summary matrimonial jurisdiction of the magistrates encourages the status of permanent breakdown within the marriage tie, the formation of illicit unions, and, through them, the birth of illegitimate children.

9.9   Even within its own sphere of operation, the matrimonial jurisdiction of the magistrates suffers from grave and unacceptable defects.   Its association with the administration of the criminal law constitutes an affront to the people who bring their family troubles to the magistrates.   Its procedures for assessing, collecting and distributing maintenance leave much to be desired.   The magisterial jurisdiction is used almost exclusively by the poorer sections of society.   The men against whom maintenance orders are made often have insufficient money to maintain both themselves and their family in separate households.   If they acquire a second family, they usually cannot maintain the first at a level which even approaches subsistence.   The orders fall into arrears, and fail to respond to changes in personal circumstances or in the cost of living.   But the chief problem is that even if the maintenance orders made by the magistrates were honoured regularly and in full, hardly any would suffice to support the family without other income. The root of the hardship is not the unwillingness, but the inability, of men to support their first families.

9.10 The result is that very large numbers of lone mothers have to apply to the Supplementary Benefits Commission. The Commission are entitled to recover the cost of the benefit from any person liable under the law of supplementary benefits to maintain the beneficiary. A husband is a liable relative in respect of benefit paid to his wife (but not to his former wife); and a father in respect of benefit paid for the children. The Commission may therefore approach the liable relative for his agreement to repay the amount of the benefit, or so much of it as they think he ought to repay. Failing agreement, the Commission will encourage the woman to take maintenance proceedings before the magistrates, so that there will be an enforceable court order. But since the amount she receives from the Commission is likely to exceed the amount of the maintenance order, this procedure is often not of the slightest direct or immediate benefit to her.

9.11 It is not possible, in summary, to convey more than a hint of the complexity and ill-effects of this tangled web of law and administration. Our recommendations have two main objectives. First, we wish to see a reform of the law concerned with family breakdown and the method of its administration, principally so as to eliminate the anachronisms and disamenities which characterise the summary matrimonial jurisdiction of the magistrates: to which end we make detailed proposals for the establishment of a unified institution, the family court, which will apply a single and uniform system of family law. Secondly, given that the community already bears much of the cost of sustaining the casualties of broken homes and of unmarried parenthood, and cannot avoid continuing to do so, we wish to rationalise the methods through which it discharges these responsibilities, primarily in the interests of the lone mother and her child, but also with the view of achieving a more satisfactory recovery from the liable relative where that is possible. We recommend, in this connection, that the Supplementary Benefits Commission should themselves be able to assess and collect maintenance by means of an administrative order against the liable relative, and that a woman who has in any case to come to the State for financial aid should be relieved of the necessity to pursue the man through legal processes which may confer much distress but little or no advantage upon her. It may be noted that there is a strong nexus between these recommendations for an administrative order and the recommendations we make in Part 5 regarding the power of the authority to be responsible for administering the new one-parent family benefit (GMA) to make administrative orders for maintenance: see recommendations 93–117 below.

RECOMMENDATIONS ON LAW

1 The obsolete procedure of distress upon goods, as a remedy for the recovery of maintenance, should be abolished (paragraph 4.135).

2 Imprisonment of maintenance defaulters should be abolished (paragraph 4.163).

3 The criminal offence under section 30 of the Ministry of Social Security Act 1966 of failure to maintain a person for whom there was a liability should be abolished (paragraph 4.211).

The machinery of support: a new model

4 The basic proposals are:

(1) the Supplementary Benefits Commission will assess the means of the liable relative and determine what it is proper for him to pay to the Commission in or towards satisfaction of the money they have paid out;

(2) the Commission will be entitled to order the liable relative to pay to the Commission the amount so assessed. We call such an order made by the Commission an " administrative order ";

(3) subject to rights of review and appeal, the administrative order will be legally binding on the liable relative and enforceable against him by the Commission through normal court processes;

(4) the amount of the administrative order will in no case exceed the amount of the lone mother's entitlement to supplementary benefit. Within this limit, the amount will be within the Commission's discretion. In exercising this discretion, the Commission will act in accordance with published criteria for assessment, framed so as to produce a fair result in the normal run of cases; but the discretion will always be available to allow for individual circumstances;

(5) the Commission will never be in a position of having to pass judgment on matrimonial conduct (paragraph 4.229).

5 No encouragement should be offered by the Supplementary Benefits Commission to a lone mother to bring legal proceedings of her own against the liable relative: assessment and enforcement of the liable relative's contribution should be regarded as processes which take place entirely between the Commission and the liable relative, and which do not involve the lone mother (paragraph 4.228).

6 A woman who considered she had a claim for maintenance at a rate higher than her supplementary benefit entitlement would as now have to go to court for a maintenance order. If she subsequently had to apply for supplementary benefit the diversion procedure, but not the administrative order, would be available to her (paragraph 4.232).

7 The Commission should have discretion (within the amount of supplementary benefit in payment) as to the amount they require the liable relative to pay; but in the normal case assessment should be by reference to published standards (paragraph 4.233).

8 The standard rules of assessment should be such as to leave the liable relative an amount out of his own income which usually exceeds by a fairly generous margin the amount to which he and any dependants would be entitled if he were on supplementary benefit. The

493

present formula used by the Commission meets this criterion and such a formula (kept up to date), or some version of it suitable to give effect to the same principle, should become the standard assessment (paragraph 4.235).

9 The calculation of income for the purposes of rate rebates and rent rebates and allowances should exclude maintenance payments made by the householder under either an administrative order or a court order. There should be no specific allowance for housing within the formula for arriving at the level to which a liable relative's income could be reduced by an administrative order (paragraphs 4.241–4.242).

10 Any earnings the lone mother may have should not be taken into account separately in the assessment of liability: they will already be reflected, subject to an initial disregard, in the amount of supplementary benefit in payment and hence in the maximum amount that can be recovered from the liable relative (paragraph 4.244).

11 After assessment, the Commission should seek the agreement of the liable relative to the payment; if he does not agree, an administrative order should be made on him. Further consideration should be given to the question whether an administrative order is also necessary even where the liable relative does agree to the payment (paragraph 4.246).

12 Administrative orders might be registered in court; and, if the man consented, an attachment order made at the same time (paragraph 4.246).

13 The administrative order should be binding on the liable relative and enforceable by the Supplementary Benefits Commission against him (paragraph 4.247).

14 If the liable relative will not provide the necessary information on which to make an assessment, the Commission should be entitled to make the best assessment they can, and to make an order (which will be open to appeal) for the amount assessed (paragraph 4.248).

15 The amount payable under an administrative order should be reviewable on the application of the liable relative at any time if there has been a material change of circumstances. In addition the Commission should review orders at fixed intervals (paragraph 4.249).

16 The Commission should maintain an account as between themselves and the liable relative; the method of accounting should be clearly defined and made public (paragraph 4.250).

17 The Commission should be empowered generally to remit any arrears accrued under administrative orders (paragraph 4.250).

18 If the liable relative fails to comply with an administrative order, the Commission should be empowered to apply to the court for the enforcement of the order by any of the means of execution available for the recovery of civil debt (paragraph 4.251).

19 Where the liable relative disputes the amount of the assessment, or the refusal of a review, on grounds which do not involve any reliance on matrimonial conduct, he should have the right of appeal to the supplementary benefits appeal tribunal (paragraph 4.252).

20 The Commission should not deal with any disputed questions involving matrimonial conduct (paragraph 4.254).

21 Where the liable relative raises a point on conduct, the Commission should make a provisional assessment which would be suspended pending the determination of the court on the point of conduct. If the court found that the liable relative's obligation should be reduced, it would be for the court to make the appropriate discount from the assessment (paragraph 4.256).

22 Appeals against any findings of the court with regard to conduct would be determined within the court system (paragraph 4.256).

23 At the point of transition from the present system, the Commission should have the power, with the consent of the beneficiary, to terminate any outstanding maintenance order and substitute an administrative order on the basis of a new means enquiry and a current assessment (paragraph 4.260).

24 The administrative order system, although designed in terms of the separated wife with children, would be applicable also to separated wives without children, separated husbands where they had a claim for maintenance, unmarried mothers, divorced or separated wives with children but no claim for maintenance for themselves, and wives who have begun divorce proceedings. In the third and fourth categories recovery would be limited to that portion of the benefit attributable to the child (paragraphs 4.262–4.263).

25 Consideration should be given to the possibility of extending the administrative order system still further, for example, to enable the Commission to collect payments due to a divorced wife from her former husband, and to make administrative orders for more than the amount of benefit in payment, accounting to the woman for the balance (paragraph 4.271).

The family court: principles

26 In principle the family court should:

    (1) be an impartial judicial institution, regulating the rights of citizens and settling their disputes according to law (paragraphs 4.283 (1) and 4.285);

    (2) be a unified institution in a system of family law which applies a uniform set of legal rules, derived from a single moral standard and applicable to all citizens (paragraphs 4.283 (2) and 4.286–4.287);

    (3) organise its work in such a way as to provide the best possible facilities for conciliation (in the particular sense defined in paragraph 4.288) between parties in matrimonial disputes (paragraphs 4.283 (3) and 4.310–4.314);

(4) have professionally trained staff to assist both the court and the parties appearing before it in all matters requiring social work services and advice (paragraphs 4.283 (4) and 4.335–4.336);

(5) work in close relationship with the social security authorities in the assessment both of need and of liability in cases involving financial provision (paragraphs 4.283 (5) and 4.337);

(6) organise its procedure, sittings and administrative services and arrangements with a view to gaining the confidence and maximising the convenience of the citizens who appear before it (paragraphs 4.283 (6) and 4.338).

The family court in operation

27 The family court must make use of existing manpower—professional judges, lay and stipendiary magistrates, registrars and justices' clerks —and existing buildings, but reorganised into a new structure (paragraph 4.347).

28 In particular, the family court will have a continuing need for the services of the lay magistracy, as an indispensable source of lay experience and outlook (paragraph 4.348).

29 The family court should provide facilities for the local determination of cases as quickly and as cheaply as the nature of the case permits (paragraph 4.349).

30 The Family Division of the High Court should remain in being as the top tier of the family court, and as its link with the rest of the higher judicial system (paragraph 4.350).

31 The local branches of the court, comprising the first tier, should be drawn from the county court judges, stipendiary magistrates and lay magistrates (paragraph 4.351).

32 The structure of the family court should not allow for the options which exist within the present system for litigants to select the court from which to ask for a remedy: there should be no duplication of remedies and no possibility of choosing between tiers otherwise than as may be determined by the rules of the court itself (paragraph 4.353).

33 The focus of the family court at local level should be the county court judge, and the work of the court should, so far as possible, be carried on at the county court building (paragraph 4.355). (See also recommendation 44.)

34 Reliance on stipendiary magistrates should be avoided once there was sufficient manpower to do so, except where they were prepared to specialise in matrimonial work (paragraph 4.355).

35 There might be an intermediate tier between the local tier and the top tier dealing with appeals on questions of fact (paragraph 4.356).

36 In the first tier lay magistrates should sit with county court judges, and advantage should be taken of opportunities offered to associate lay magistrates with a broader and more interesting range of work than tends at present to fall their way (paragraph 4.357).

37 Magistrates serving in the family court should be drawn from a panel of volunteers in much the same way as the rules now provide for a juvenile court panel (paragraph 4.358).

38 Training for magistrates should be extended and adapted to meet the needs of the family court (paragraph 4.358).

39 No proceedings, except possibly care proceedings under the Children and Young Persons Act 1969, which may involve investigation into criminal conduct, should be included in the family court jurisdiction (paragraph 4.363).

40 With the advent of the family court, the whole of the present matrimonial jurisdiction of the magistrates should be abolished (paragraph 4.379 (1)).

41 The family court will continue, in substitution for the abolished jurisdiction, to provide financial relief for spouses and their children otherwise than in connection with the termination of marriage, and also in affiliation proceedings (paragraph 4.379 (2)):

    (1) the grounds for relief in these cases should be failure to maintain, desertion, and behaviour by the respondent such that the applicant cannot reasonably be expected to live with the respondent (paragraph 4.379 (3));

    (2) there should be no absolute bars to relief sought on any of these grounds (paragraph 4.379 (4));

    (3) the court should be entitled to take conduct into account, but only on the same basis as it does in divorce: namely, only in circumstances where the applicant's own behaviour has been so obviously and grossly blameworthy that it would offend justice to ignore it (paragraphs 4.379 (5) and 4.374);

    (4) in making financial provision as between parties who remain married, or for their children, the court should be empowered to order lump sum payments and secured maintenance, as well as unsecured maintenance; the same choice of remedy should be available in affiliation cases (paragraph 4.379 (6));

    (5) the court should be given specific guidance as to the factors to be taken into account when assessing the amount of financial orders (paragraph 4.379 (7)).

42 Two years after a maintenance order or an administrative order in a subsisting marriage has been made, the circumstances of the parties should be examined at a conference to which all interested parties should be invited. The purpose of the conference should be to consider whether, in the case of a court order, it remains appropriate in the light of the current needs and means of the parties, and to encourage the parties to consider their matrimonial future. All the

legal, social and financial information and assistance necessary to help them make rational choices should be provided. Where the parties chose to take no further action, provision should be made for further conferences at regular intervals to ensure that the amounts of court orders were properly examined and varied if necessary (paragraph 4.393).

43 All payers and recipients of maintenance under administrative orders or the orders of the family court should be put on the same footing in respect of their tax liabilities (paragraph 4.396).

44 Where it is not possible to house the family court in the county court buildings, and business has to be conducted in magistrates' courts' buildings, efforts should be made to separate those using the family court from others, particularly the police, and defendants in criminal cases, who are appearing before the summary jurisdiction. This might be made possible by, for instance, designating particular magistrates' courts' buildings for the exclusive use of the family court (paragraph 4.400).

45 Attempts should be made to hold some sittings of the family court out of ordinary hours—for example, on Saturday mornings (paragraph 4.401).

46 Further investigation is necessary before deciding whether greater informality in court proceedings will best satisfy the user's desire for fairness and dignity in the determination of matrimonial cases (paragraph 4.404).

47 The bench of the family court, which will not itself contain experts or assessors as such, should be able to call for any investigation or expert assessment it requires from ancillary services which are attached to or can be called on by the court but whose personnel are not themselves members of the court (paragraph 4.405).

48 Courts should examine their existing procedures to ensure that the statutory provisions relating to the securing of the welfare of children are being fully implemented (paragraph 4.407).

49 The chambers practice operative in the High Court should be extended to all hearings in the family court which the public interest did not decisively demand should be conducted in open court (paragraph 4.408).

50 The family court structure will need officials discharging a combination of duties of the kind now done by the High Court registrar and magistrates' clerk. A proper career structure should be developed for these officials and, if possible, training given in the welfare as well as the strictly legal aspects of court work (paragraph 4.409).

51 Special attention should be paid to keeping full and standardised records of all summary proceedings in the first tier of the family court (paragraph 4.411).

Recommended improvements in the official statistics

52 The practice of publishing information about family proceedings in magistrates' courts in the annual *Criminal Statistics* should cease forthwith (paragraph 4.413).

53 A statistical system should be devised which will provide annual and integrated data about the work both of the local tier and of the top tier of the family court (paragraph 4.415).

54 Scottish civil judicial statistics should also be examined, and the Scottish and English statistics relating to the work of the family court should be standardised to the maximum extent possible (paragraph 4.418).

55 Estimates of the number of one-parent families in Great Britain, showing the different categories of family breakdown, the sex of the lone parent and the number of children, should be published regularly (paragraph 4.420).

56 The Department of Health and Social Security should examine their policy towards the publication of statistical data with the object of providing better and regular series of statistics about the work of the Supplementary Benefits Commission and about the Commission's beneficiaries (paragraph 4.421).

57 Demographic statistics should be provided on a Great Britain basis, with breakdown by country or region where relevant (paragraph 4.422).

58 Consideration should be given by the Central Statistical Office to the production, in one annual publication, of a volume of family statistics containing the main legal, demographic and social data concerning the family. This might take the form of a special section in *Social Trends* (paragraph 4.423).

The system in Scotland

59 The system of administrative orders to be made by an administering authority, both as it applies before (see recommendations 4–25) and after the introduction of guaranteed maintenance allowance (see recommendations 93–117) should be implemented in Scotland as in England (paragraph 4.471).

60 If irretrievable breakdown of marriage becomes the sole ground for dissolution of marriage in Scotland, steps should be taken to ensure that reform of the sheriff court jurisdiction marches in step (paragraph 4.472).

61 The considerations of principle which lead to our conclusion that there should be a family court system in England apply equally to Scotland but the application in detail of these principles in the context of Scots law and procedure should be investigated by the competent authorities (paragraphs 4.473–4.474).

62 The procedures of the sheriff court in dealing with alimentary actions need to be simplified and made cheaper for the litigant and this matter should be pursued by the competent authorities (paragraph 4.475).

63 The considerable differences between the private family law systems of England and Wales and of Scotland should not be permitted to obscure the identity in practical terms of the solutions which are required for the problems of one-parent families in both countries (paragraph 4.477).

9.12   Our examination of the financial circumstances of one-parent families showed that they were, in general, much worse off than two-parent families. Two groups among them are slightly better off than the others, though still worse off than two-parent families generally: widows, who already have a State insurance benefit, and lone fathers, who can command higher earnings than lone mothers.   For the rest, over half are on supplementary benefit; for most of these it is their main source of income, and some live at this level for many years.   Of those not on supplementary benefit, about 15 per cent appear to be living actually below the supplementary benefit level, managing on maintenance payments and part-time earnings.   Those who work full time are better off financially than the others but, because of women's low earnings and the restrictions that having to run a home and a job are likely to put on their earning capacity, they are still much less well off than two-parent families, and far below the level of those where both parents are earning. The main factors in determining whether or not a mother can work full time, and hence achieve the higher level of income which goes with it, are the number of children, the age of the youngest child and whether or not she shares her home: mothers with several children, at least one of them under 5, and living on their own, are least likely to be able to go to work.

9.13   This depressing picture of widespread financial hardship, and the difficulties in modern society of bringing up children alone and in such conditions, led us to look for some means of affording these families some financial relief. We saw little beyond illusion in the idea put forward for State guarantees of maintenance payments: maintenance orders are inadequate as a means of support even if they are paid regularly.   A real improvement in a lone mother's financial circumstances can now mostly be achieved only if she enters into full-time work, something which, if done only because of strong financial pressure, may lead to considerable strain on her and the children.   The income which can be secured by part-time work is generally not sufficient to produce any real improvement in material circumstances, since (but for a small disregard) it serves only to reduce supplementary benefit payments.   Yet part-time work may in other respects be rewarding for many mothers.   Many want to work in order to break out of the social isolation in which they find themselves, and working only part time may enable them to cope with the double burden of home and work without undue strain.   Then, as the children grow older, the mother could gradually increase the amount of work until by the time they left school she could be self-supporting.   But a pattern of this kind is not consistent with the social security benefits at present available.   The supplementary benefits scheme discourages more than a minimal amount of work by its treatment of earnings, and family income supplements are available only to those who work full time.   What is wanted, we believe, is a benefit which is adapted to fit in with the idea of varying the amount of work done according to family circumstances: full-time, part-time, or none.   This implies either a benefit paid at a given rate without regard to income, or one which responds to changes in earnings more gradually than does supplementary benefit.   We have decided in favour of the latter.   We did not regard it as sensible to give a benefit to a woman regardless of her other resources, which could be considerable, and a tapered benefit would enable more to be given to poorer families within a particular global sum.   We believe that an improvement in the circumstances of these families, now living on supplementary benefit, is essential if lone parents are to be given full freedom of choice whether or not to work and how much paid work to do. To give more to the working mothers while leaving all those who cannot or do not want to work on supplementary benefit would, we believe, tip the balance too far in favour of taking paid employment.

9.14 We recommend that one-parent families should be entitled to a new social security benefit which we call guaranteed maintenance allowance (GMA). This benefit would be available to all one-parent families on a non-contributory basis; and for those families receiving it, it would act as a passport into the tax-credit scheme. GMA would consist of an adult allowance, which, in terms of 1972–1973 benefit rates, we recommend should be at £9·50 a week for those without other income, and an allowance of £1 for each child. These rates, in conjunction with tax credits, would be sufficient to lift most lone parents above the supplementary benefit level. (If tax credits were not brought in, and there were no comparable family benefit, the GMA rates would need adjustment.) After an initial disregard of net income of £4, the adult allowance would be tapered so that it fell as other income rose by 50 per cent of the net increase, finally being extinguished when other income had reached about the level of average male earnings. The child allowances would be paid to all one-parent families regardless of income.

9.15 There would be title to GMA regardless of whether or not maintenance was being paid by the absent parent. But, as the name implies, we intend it as a replacement of maintenance for those who receive it, not as an addition: any maintenance payments received directly by the lone mother would have to be declared and deducted from the GMA payable. But generally it should not be necessary for the lone mother to concern herself with maintenance at all, since we propose that arrangements similar to and more far-reaching than those we have put forward in Part 4 for maintenance to be assessed and collected by administrative order by the Supplementary Benefits Commission should be applied by the authority administering GMA.

9.16 Until the new benefit could be introduced, supplementary benefit would continue to be the mainstay of many one-parent families. We recommend a number of improvements in that scheme, and make a number of other recommendations designed to improve the financial situation of one-parent families.

RECOMMENDATIONS ON INCOME

Guaranteed maintenance allowance

64 There should be a special social security benefit for one-parent families (GMA) (paragraph 5.104).

65 GMA should act as a qualifying source of income for the tax-credit scheme: families entitled to GMA would thus get the benefit of the £6 credit for a lone parent as well as the universal child credit of £2 for each child (paragraphs 5.107 and 5.116).

66 GMA should be set at a level linked to supplementary benefit, which, with tax credits (see recommendation 65), or, failing tax credits, other family benefits, would bring income above supplementary benefit level for most one-parent families (paragraphs 5.107 and 5.112).

67 The appropriate level for GMA at the time of introduction would depend on, in addition to levels of tax credits and tax rates, long-term supplementary benefit rates then current for one-parent families, children's scale rates, the level of additions for exceptional circumstances and exceptional needs and the level of rents and other housing costs (paragraph 5.113).

68 The rent element in the equation should be related to the level of rent actually paid by one-parent families with income at about the supplementary benefit level, taking account of rebates and rent allowances available, the extent to which they are taken up and the range of housing costs incurred (paragraph 5.121).

69 In terms of 1972–1973 benefit rates, the appropriate level for GMA would be £9·50 for an adult and £1 for each child. After tax and with tax credits this would give a total of £12·65 for an adult and £2·70 for each child (paragraphs 5.123–5.124).

70 GMA should be included in the annual reviews of social security benefits and be kept in line with supplementary benefit which is its base, taking account of changes in housing costs, tax credits and tax rates (paragraph 5.125).

71 Entitlement to GMA should be assessed without regard to maintenance payments; these would normally be collected and retained up to the level of GMA by the administering authority (paragraph 5.127). (See also recommendations 93–117.)

72 The child portion of GMA should be paid to all one-parent families regardless of income. It should be receipt of the child portion of GMA which acts as a passport to the tax-credit scheme (see recommendation 65 above) (paragraphs 5.129–5.130).

73 For the adult portion of GMA there should be an initial disregard of earnings (net of such items as national insurance, tax, travelling, and child-care expenses) of the same amount as the earnings disregard in the supplementary benefits scheme (which is assumed to be raised to £4—see recommendation 121 below); thereafter the adult element should be reduced by 50 per cent of net earnings, so as to extinguish it entirely by the time earnings reached about the level of average male earnings (paragraphs 5.132–5.136).

74 Long-term national insurance benefits, such as widowed mother's allowance, should be deducted in full from GMA. Short-term benefits paid for short periods within an award period of GMA should be disregarded (paragraph 5.139).

75 Other income, including income from capital, should be treated in the same way as earnings and included in the same disregard (paragraph 5.140).

76 GMA should be a non-contributory benefit (paragraph 5.141).

77 Title to GMA should depend on establishing status as a one-parent family, that is, on there being only one parent (mother or father) with day-to-day responsibility for the child (paragraphs 5.144 and 5.160).

78 The definition of a child should be similar to that used for national insurance purposes (paragraph 5.145).

79 Where the parent has legal evidence of separation—that is the widowed, divorced and legally separated—production of that legal evidence should be sufficient to establish her lone status which should be treated as having arisen on the day the marriage ended or a separation or maintenance order was made (paragraph 5.147).

80 For those with a maintenance order but no separation order production of the order and a declaration of separation by the claimant should be accepted as adequate evidence of separation and as establishing lone status (paragraph 5.147).

81 For those separated without a court order a qualifying period of three months from the time of separation should elapse before GMA became payable. Proof of separation would be a declaration by the claimant, confirmed where possible by the absent spouse (paragraphs 5.149–5.151).

82 There should be no minimum age limit for receipt of GMA (paragraph 5.157).

83 The possibility of making families of long-term prisoners eligible for GMA should be examined by the Home Office (paragraph 5.158).

84 Title to GMA should cease on marriage or cohabitation (in the latter case at the end of the three-month award period—see recommendation 88 below) (paragraphs 5.163–5.164).

85 Claims to GMA should be dealt with as far as possible by post (paragraph 5.167).

86 GMA should not form part of the supplementary benefits administration (paragraph 5.168).

87 Awards of GMA should be made for three months at a time. Changes in income (other than maintenance payments) during that time should not affect the payment (paragraphs 5.170 and 5.176).

88 Changes in title during the three-month period should not affect the award, except in the case of marriage (paragraphs 5.172–5.173).

89 Renewal claims should be invited towards the end of the three-month period, and the claimant would have to give specific confirmation of all the information necessary to determine eligibility (paragraph 5.175).

90 There should be a right of appeal on eligibility for and the amount of GMA to an independent tribunal (the powers of the national insurance tribunals and commissioners might be extended to take on this responsibility). Appeals as to the amount of the absent parent's maintenance liability should also normally go to this tribunal, but where the question concerned liability as such, involving, for example, a determination upon matrimonial conduct or paternity, it should go to the regular courts (paragraphs 5.177-5.181 and 5.188). (See also recommendations 93–117.)

91 Means-tested benefits should be adjusted to take account of GMA, rather than the other way about (paragraph 5.182).

92 Receipt of adult GMA at the full rate should act as a passport to those means-tested benefits for which receipt of supplementary benefit so acts (paragraph 5.183).

The absent parent's obligation

93 In relation to supplementary benefit, the definition of " liable relative " contained in the Ministry of Social Security Act 1966 should continue (paragraph 5.189).

94 The extent of liability where GMA had been awarded should be:

    (1) in the standard case of separation where there was no doubt about liability and questions arose only as to amount, the liable person should come fully within the provisions for assessment and collection by the GMA authority; the amount assessed could be the same, or more or less than, the amount of the GMA entitlement (paragraph 5.191);

    (2) the basic position as between divorcing or divorced couples would be the same as in the case of separated couples (paragraph 5.192);

    (3) the putative father of an illegitimate child should be a liable person subject to assessment and recovery by the GMA authority of an amount up to the level of State payment for mother and child (paragraph 5.197).

95 Conduct of the wife should be entirely disregarded in relation to the recovery from the liable person of an amount up to the level of what the taxpayer had spent in supporting her to look after the child. The question of conduct, where it remained relevant, would be for the court (paragraph 5.199).

96 All action necessary to establish and enforce the liability should be taken by the administering authority, not by the lone mother. She should only be asked to give information initially to enable the authority to identify and communicate with the liable person where there was one (paragraph 5.200).

97 Disputed questions on amount should be retained within the administrative system, geared to resolving them on a uniform basis, and drawing upon investigative procedures. Questions such as the paternity of a child or involving any enquiry into matrimonial conduct would remain for the court to decide (paragraph 5.201).

98 The authority should not be limited to making orders for amounts which are no more than sufficient to reimburse the benefit paid out. Irrespective of any court proceedings that were being or were likely to be taken, as for divorce, or separation, or custody of children, the determination of the total amount of maintenance, whether it happened to be less or more than the GMA entitlement, would (except where judicial issues such as conduct were involved) be a matter for the authority (paragraph 5.205).

99 Appeals on the amount of administrative orders for maintenance should go to the national insurance local tribunals, and, from them, to the national insurance commissioners. Appeals could be made either by the liable person or by the lone mother (paragraph 5.207).

100 The authority should initiate a review of the administrative order every twelve months. There should also be provision for an application for review to be made by either party during the course of the twelve-month period (paragraph 5.209).

101 If the parties became involved in divorce proceedings, and the wife claimed maintenance in the proceedings, she would, if a claim for GMA made earlier had not already resulted in an assessment of maintenance, be referred by the court to the authority for that assessment to be made. Similar considerations would apply in the case of proceedings taken for a formal separation order (paragraphs 5.211–5.212).

102 Where there was an issue of conduct the court would determine the effect of its findings on conduct on the amount of maintenance as assessed in full by the authority (paragraph 5.212).

103 Upon the introduction of GMA, all maintenance orders in favour of one-parent families should be converted into administrative orders. The conversion process should not be made an occasion for altering the amount of orders made by a court within the preceding twelve months merely because the application of the formula in use by the authority would produce a different amount. Subject to this, the authority should be entitled, in converting court orders, to review them (paragraph 5.213).

104 Where payments to the authority exceeded the amount of the benefit in payment, the surplus should be remitted by the authority to the family at intervals (paragraph 5.214).

105 Receipts from the liable person should be set off against either the adult or the child allowance of the GMA, or both (paragraph 5.214).

106 Where voluntary maintenance payments were being made, if the mother claimed GMA, arrangements should be made for the father to meet his obligation to the authority, preferably by the payments being channelled through the authority, or for the authority, notwithstanding the agreement, to make an order on the father as a liable person in the normal way. Alternatively the amount paid on the GMA award should be reduced to take account of the payment (paragraph 5.215).

107 The administrative order would be legally binding and enforceable by the authority as a civil debt (paragraph 5.216).

108 A flexible approach would be needed towards assessing the absent parent's liability. A formula such as the Supplementary Benefits Commission use could fix the floor below which the absent parent's resources should not be allowed to fall, but a system of calculation would be necessary which would take account of the resources and commitments of both parties (paragraph 5.221).

505

109 In assessing the resources of each of the parties GMA and any supplementary benefit payable to the lone mother should be regarded as income in her hands (paragraph 5.222).

110 The absent parent's maintenance obligation should be administratively assessed by a clearly defined test. A standard formula would need to be devised which could be applied—subject to a discretion to allow for exceptional circumstances—in all cases, and which could be made public (paragraph 5.223).

111 Where the absent parent was comparatively well off, the formula should enable the lone mother and the children to share in his affluence, while ensuring that he retained a reasonable share of his higher income for himself. It should also be such as would not cause the absent parent's financial position to be worse in relation to his commitments than that of the lone mother in relation to hers (paragraph 5.223).

112 In framing a suitable formula it would be necessary:

    (1) to aggregate the income of the lone mother and her family (including the GMA) and that of the absent parent, thus establishing the amount of money available to support the two parts of the family (paragraph 5.225);

    (2) to calculate the balance of commitments between the two family units so that the division of resources would reflect the relative needs of the two families (paragraphs 5.225–5.226);

    (3) to exclude a proportion of the absent parent's earnings from the calculation (paragraph 5.227);

    (4) to consider the treatment to be given to any income of the father's second family, to the extent that it was not his own income (paragraph 5.228).

113 The formula should be as simple as possible, and there should be a discretion to dispense with its application where this might produce injustice (paragraph 5.232).

114 Parties would have to be allowed to make whatever form of voluntary financial arrangements they pleased—periodical payments (" maintenance "), cash lump sums, property transfers or any other (paragraphs 5.236–5.238).

115 In the event of a dispute concerning whether, and in what form and to what extent, some financial remedy or provision other than maintenance should be granted, this should be the subject of a court process (paragraph 5.238).

116 There are two possible ways of dealing with cases which involved a potential financial liability on the absent parent going beyond the payment of maintenance. Either they could be absorbed wholly into the administrative order system by valuing the asset or benefit conferred on the lone mother so as to produce a notional amount which could be set off against the GMA; or the parties could be permitted to sort matters out for themselves, or have them sorted out by the court, by treating the GMA entitlement as a right which could be traded against other benefits or advantages given by the absent parent to the lone mother (paragraph 5.247).

117 Efforts should be made to trace the liable relative and obtain maintenance payments from him as soon as the woman became dependent on public funds, and if her first contact were with the Supplementary Benefits Commission, then their officers should make the necessary initial enquiries. The information obtained should be passed to the authority, and all consequent action should be taken by them (paragraph 5.248).

Supplementary benefits

118 Lone parents should be entitled to a special addition of £1·50 in terms of 1972–1973 benefit rates to whichever single person's scale rate (long-term, short-term, householder or non-householder) they would otherwise receive (paragraph 5.254).

119 Lone parents under 18 receiving supplementary benefit in their own right who are not householders should automatically receive the full adult non-householder scale rate (paragraph 5.255).

120 The qualifying period for the long-term addition should be reduced from two years to one for families with children (paragraph 5.258).

121 There should be an increase in the disregards so that, at least, they keep pace with increases in the cost of living (paragraph 5.261).

122 The requirement to register for work should be waived for lone fathers (paragraph 5.265).

123 Before benefit is withdrawn on grounds of cohabitation from a claimant in receipt of weekly payments of supplementary benefit, she should be given a written statement of the alleged facts, and if she denies any of them, the case should go to the appeal tribunal, benefit being continued in the meantime (paragraph 5.274).

124 Where benefit is withdrawn because of cohabitation, but the cohabitee is not supporting dependent children of the claimant of whom he is not the father, the exceptional needs payment for the children which the Commission are now prepared to pay for four weeks should be continued for three months (paragraph 5.276).

Family income supplements

125 In the event that tax credits and GMA are not introduced or are substantially delayed, the full-time work qualification for one-parent families in the family income supplements scheme should be eased (paragraph 5.284).

Family allowances (and child tax credits)

126 The utmost priority should be given to the introduction of child credits; if the tax-credit scheme fails to materialise, provision should be made, with the same degree of priority, for tax-free family allowances at rates comparable to those envisaged for child credits (paragraph 5.286).

Maternity grant

127 Maternity grant should be paid without any contribution conditions (paragraph 5.293).

Taxation

128 The additional personal allowance should be increased from £130 to £180 so as to give the lone parent the same tax allowance (personal and additional combined) as a married man (paragraphs 5.306–5.308).

129 Claims from lone parents for repayment of tax overpaid on maintenance payments should be dealt with promptly (paragraph 5.310).

130 Steps should be taken to improve and expand the information on taxation available to lone parents (paragraph 5.312).

Educational maintenance allowances

131 Educational maintenance allowances should be rationalised on a national basis, with standard scales of allowances and qualifying parental income. The scales should be the same whether there is one parent or two (paragraph 5.318).

HOUSING (PART 6)

9.17 Second only to financial difficulties, and to a considerable extent exacerbated by them, housing is the largest single problem of one-parent families. Large numbers of one-parent families do not even have a home of their own, and have to share, usually with relatives. In November 1972, half the unmarried mothers and one fifth of the separated wives receiving supplementary benefit were not householders. A high proportion, too, are forced into the rapidly shrinking privately rented sector, where they generally have to pay high rents for poor conditions. They tend to move more often than two-parent families, and are more likely to become homeless. Conversely, a much smaller proportion of one-parent than of two-parent families own their own houses: at the extreme, only 3 per cent of unmarried mothers on supplementary benefit are owner-occupiers. The most acute difficulties arise among unmarried mothers, who often have no home of their own to start with; and among other one-parent families particularly at the point of marriage breakdown, when the ownership and occupation of the marital home may come into question.

9.18 Some of the many developments in housing in the last few years are likely to be helpful to one-parent families. For example, we received a good deal of evidence on problems of high rents; but changes in the Supplementary Benefits Commission's policy since then, and the advent of national rent rebate and allowance schemes, have already brought considerable relief to low-income families. We have also seen the acceptance in the Housing White Papers published in April 1973 of the principle that housing authorities should have a comprehensive responsibility for all housing needs in their areas, not restricted to council houses and eligibility for them. We believe that active pursuit of this principle, coupled with active and close co-operation between housing authorities and social services departments, offers the best hope of decent housing to those who, like most one-parent families, are at a serious and double disadvantage in the housing market because they have children and a low income. We also welcome the recently issued circular on homelessness which embodies many of the policies which we ourselves advocate. We were particularly glad to see in the circular acceptance of the recommendation of the Joint Working Party on Homelessness in London that responsibility for securing accommodation for the homeless should be undertaken as a housing responsibility.

RECOMMENDATIONS ON HOUSING

132 Local and central government should have regard to recent changes in the demographic characteristics of the population in considering housing needs (paragraph 6.29).

133 The division of functions between county and district authorities, with social services a county responsibility and housing a district responsibility, should be kept under review to ensure that satisfactory links between the two departments are established and maintained (paragraph 6.34).

The home after the breakdown of marriage: the legal situation

134 The Matrimonial Homes Act 1967 should be amended so that where the husband is sole owner or tenant, and the wife, with no property interest, claims to be protected in her occupation, the court has the power under that Act to order the owner out of the house altogether where the circumstances warrant it (paragraph 6.44 (1)).

135 The court should have an inherent jurisdiction to evict a husband from the matrimonial home even when that is the sole relief the wife claims (paragraph 6.44 (2)).

136 The Rent Act 1968 should be amended so as to give a right to apply to the court for suspension of a possession order and restoration of tenancy to a statutory tenant's spouse in occupation (paragraph 6.44 (3)).

137 The court's powers to order financial provision under the Matrimonial Proceedings and Property Act 1970[1] should be extended to include power to deal specifically and directly with rights of occupation in a former matimonial home (paragraph 6.44 (5)).

138 A wife who remains in occupation after her husband has left should be able to become a statutory tenant by succession after his death (paragraph 6.44 (8)).

139 A widower should be given the same right to succeed to a statutory tenancy under Schedule 1 to the Rent Act 1968 as a widow (paragraph 6.44 (9)).

140 Social services departments, housing advice centres, citizens' advice bureaux and other welfare organisations should ensure that housing advice is given by responsible staff specifically and adequately trained for this purpose (paragraph 6.52).

---

[1] The powers now arise under the Matrimonial Causes Act 1973, but for reasons of convenience we continue both in this Summary and in the earlier Parts of the Report to retain references to the Act of 1970.

141 More attention should be given in the training of both branches of the legal profession to ensuring that they have an adequate working knowledge of the legal problems associated with the ownership and occupation of the home when a marriage breaks down (paragraph 6.52).

Homeless families

142 In temporary accommodation the husband should not be excluded, nor children separated from their families, unless there are, exceptionally, compelling reasons other than the homelessness of the family for placing them elsewhere (paragraph 6.59).

143 Help for a homeless family should never be lacking because of disagreement as to which authority is responsible. Normally this will be the authority in whose area the need exists, and families should never be encouraged to return to their home area unless specific arrangements have been made with that area to ensure that suitable accommodation is available for them (paragraphs 6.61–6.62).

144 Local authorities should be alert in seeking advance warning of prospective homelessness both in the public and private sectors (paragraphs 6.63 and 6.66).

145 Where there is a problem of multiple debt, social services and housing authorities should be alerted to it as quickly as possible (paragraph 6.64).

146 Guidance should be issued to local authorities indicating that eviction simply for rent arrears is no longer tolerable (paragraph 6.65).

147 Early consultation between housing and social services departments should become the common practice everywhere when families are in arrears with their rent. and social workers should give maximum assistance to such families when there appears to be a risk of family breakdown (paragraph 6.65).

Local authority tenancies

148 Discrimination against lone parents in the allocation of council houses on grounds that they are " less deserving " than others should cease (paragraph 6.70).

149 Where points systems are used in the allocation of housing, a lone parent should qualify for the same number of points as a married couple with a comparable family (paragraph 6.73).

150 Anyone should be able to apply for housing accommodation as soon as he comes to live in a particular local authority area and should then be eligible for that local authority's housing list (paragraph 6.76).

151 Discussions should be held between the Department of the Environment and the new local authority associations to see whether a practice could be devised to enable either the Department of the Environment's regional officers or the new county authorities to act as arbitrators in deciding on whose housing list prospective newcomers should go (paragraph 6.77).

152 Except in areas where acute housing shortage makes it impossible to abolish residential qualifications altogether, once families with children have been admitted to the housing list, their claims should be considered solely by reference to an assessment of need with over-riding emphasis on the avoidance of separations between parents and children (paragraph 6.78).

153 In considering transfer of council tenancies after separations, local authorities should take action as soon as it is clear that irrespective of any intervention by the court a breakdown has occurred; in doing so they should ensure that the tenancy follows the partner with care of the children and be ready to make provision, if necessary, for the other partner (paragraphs 6.82–6.84).

154 The power the court has under section 7 of the Matrimonial Homes Act 1967 to transfer from one spouse to another tenancies to which the Rent Acts apply should be extended to local authority tenancies (paragraphs 6.86 and 6.44 (7)).

155 Security of tenure similar to the Rent Acts protection should be extended to tenancies in the public sector (paragraphs 6.90 and 6.44 (6)).

Rents

156 The circumstances in which a local authority rent may not be increased, as set out in section 66 of the Housing Finance Act 1972, should be widened so as to include any change of tenant or new tenancy where the new tenant has been occupying the home and is the widow or widower, wife or husband, or ex-wife or ex-husband of the previous tenant (paragraph 6.96).

157 The Supplementary Benefits Commission should give full weight to the difficulties of one-parent families in finding accommodation when they decide whether to accept the amount of the rent as reasonable (paragraph 6.102).

158 Where a tenant receiving supplementary benefit requests, with the support of the social services department or the housing authority or an appropriate voluntary organisation, the Supplementary Benefits Commission to pay the rent direct the application should normally be granted as a matter of course (paragraph 6.106).

159 Where the social services department and landlord, in the long-term interests of the tenant, ask for the rent to be paid direct there should be greater willingess on the part of the Supplementary Benefits Commission to do so (paragraph 6.106).

160 Any decision to refuse to pay rent direct to the landlord should be taken at a senior level in the Commission so as to improve the consistency of decisions (paragraph 6.106).

161 Even where the Commission's normal procedure is to pay rent direct quarterly in arrears, they should be ready to make payments at shorter intervals at the landlord's request (paragraph 6.106).

162 Where housing authorities require as a general rule the clearance of rent arrears before rehousing, transfers or exchanges, they should

be flexible and careful in applying such practices to the individual case, since there are many occasions when their application would not be in the best interest of the family, or in the long term of the housing authority itself (paragraph 6.107).

163 Rent guarantees should be used more extensively by local authorities (paragraph 6.110).

164 Guidance should be given by central government that local authorities, when finding it necessary to recover rent arrears on transfer of a tenancy, should apply pressure to the former tenant, usually the husband, and not the wife if she is not legally liable for the debt (paragraph 6.112).

165 The practice of holding family allowances books as a pledge for the payment of rent arrears should cease (paragraph 6.114).

Owner-occupiers

166 If the Supplementary Benefits Commission are meeting interest payments, building societies or local authority mortgagees should be prepared to accept the payment of interest only for as long as may be necessary (paragraph 6.117).

167 A wife occupying the marital home should be notified by the mortgagee of impending foreclosure proceedings against her husband and given the right to apply to the court (paragraph 6.120).

168 Local authorities should use their existing powers to help a family under threat of foreclosure. They should be ready to guarantee mortgage repayments to building societies or buy the house and offer either a new mortgage or a letting of the house to the occupier (paragraph 6.122).

169 Arrangements should be made to ensure that local authorities get early warning of threatened foreclosure, for example, by building societies notifying them of possible foreclosure, particularly if children are known to be involved (paragraph 6.123).

170 The Supplementary Benefits Commission should take the initiative in advising claimants with mortgage liabilities of the possibility that the building society may be willing to accept interest payments only; and they should ask to be informed if the facility is refused (paragraph 6.127).

171 The question of the Supplementary Benefits Commission meeting capital repayments should be explored (paragraph 6.128).

172 The question of extending (possibly on a compulsory basis) mortgage protection insurance for families with children should be considered (paragraph 6.129).

173 Full information about existing mortgage protection schemes should be made available to all new borrowers (paragraph 6.129).

Furnishing the home

174 The Supplementary Benefits Commission should ensure that their officers recognise the special difficulties faced by one-parent families in furnishing a home when considering applications for exceptional needs grants (paragraph 6.139).

175 Consultations should be held between the Department of Health and Social Security, the Department of the Environment, the Scottish Development Department, the Welsh Office and local authority organisations with a view to avoiding the present overlap of responsibilities in the provision of furniture (paragraph 6.140).

176 Local authorities should have power to provide furniture free of charge as well as to sell or lease it, and section 94 of the Housing Act 1957 should be amended accordingly (paragraph 6.141).

177 Social services departments should take a wider view and make more use of their power under section 1 of the Children and Young Persons Act 1963 to provide furniture (paragraph 6.141).

EMPLOYMENT (PART 7)

9.19   In formulating our financial recommendations we took a stand on the principle that lone parents, whether mothers or fathers, should not be obliged by financial pressure to go out to work when they feel it is in the best interests of the children that they should stay at home.   But we also believe—and guaranteed maintenance allowance (GMA) has been devised with this in mind—that the lone parent who wants to work should have freedom to do so, and that financial arrangements, employment arrangements and child-care arrangements should be such that this is possible.   Financial arrangements are dealt with in Part 5, and child-care arrangements in Part 8; in this Part we deal with the employment situation which faces one-parent families.

9.20   The fundamental difficulties facing the lone parent who wants to work are that there is only one parent to share the wage-earning and homemaking responsibilities normally carried by both parents, and that most lone parents are women, suffering from disadvantages of low pay, low level of skill and inadequate training common to many women workers.   In order to make it easier for lone parents to cope with their responsibilities, we should like to see employers adopt a far more flexible attitude to working hours and conditions, along the lines of those already accepted for civil servants.[1]   But the fundamental issue is the need to raise the pay and status of working women. A start has been made in the passing of the Equal Pay Act 1970 but we believe that anti-discrimination legislation, proposed in the consultative document, *Equal Opportunities for Men and Women*,[2] is essential if the Act is to be fully effective. We also consider it essential to widen the employment opportunities open to women so that they are no longer concentrated in a relatively narrow range of low-paid jobs; and we make a number of recommendations to this end.   We emphasise, however, that all this must be accompanied by a change of attitude on the part of women themselves, who must be prepared to take a more active role in their own interests.

RECOMMENDATIONS ON EMPLOYMENT

178 Entitlement to a minimum period of notice under the Contracts of Employment Act 1972, to a remedy for unfair dismissal under the Industrial Relations Act 1971 and to a redundancy payment under

---

[1] As set out in the *Report on the Employment of Women in the Civil Service, op cit.*
[2] *Op cit.*

the Redundancy Payments Act 1965 should be extended to employees working less than twenty-one hours a week. As a minimum, employees working eighteen hours a week should be covered (paragraph 7.24).

179 Employers should review opportunities for part-time work to see if they can be expanded, while both they and trade unions should remain alert to the need to protect the conditions of work for part-time workers and encourage the spread of best practices in this field (paragraph 7.25).

180 Unions and employers should negotiate agreements designed to achieve at least the standard of maternity leave recommended by the *Report on the Employment of Women in the Civil Service*—three months' paid and three months' unpaid leave (paragraph 7.26).

181 Statistics on all aspects of women's employment should be regularly available in one publication (paragraph 7.27).

182 Department of Employment " jobcentres " should include on their staff officers with specialised knowledge of the needs and problems of women who have to combine care of their children with employment, and liaison with local authority social services departments should be improved (paragraph 7.28).

183 Radical changes are required in the sphere of curricular and careers guidance for girls in secondary schools (paragraph 7.33).

184 Employers should be encouraged to extend day-release facilities to all their young employees, and in particular young girl workers should be offered the same day-release facilities as boys (paragraph 7.36).

185 Industrial training boards should ensure that employers, in their examination of training needs, do not fail to identify those of their women employees, and that they make adequate arrangements for their training (paragraph 7.37).

186 The Manpower Services Commission should encourage increased training opportunities for women and girls and the making of arrangements that are sufficiently flexible not to exclude those with family responsibilities (paragraph 7.38).

187 The new training opportunities scheme (TOPS) should be given wide publicity (paragraph 7.39).

PARENTS AND CHILDREN (PART 8)

9.21 In this concluding Part of our study of one-parent families, we look at their ordinary day-to-day family and social life and at the services provided to help them. One-parent families vary widely in their circumstances and in their responses to the problems they face, but a number of themes, which we rehearse in Part 8, recurred throughout the evidence we received and the research studies we examined. They concerned the sense of loss and suffering, the social isolation, the burden of coping alone with the emotional and material needs of children and with unfamiliar household tasks; and, for the child, the risk of suffering the reciprocal effect of these same burdens in the shape

514

of a lonely and depressed mother or father, grief at the loss of the other parent and a sense of being different from other children. The result for some children may be poor performance at school or disturbed or delinquent behaviour.

9.22   Not all of these problems are amenable to help from organised services, but we believe that the personal social and education services could play a more significant role than they do now in the lives of one-parent families, and in this Part we suggest ways in which they might do so. For these families, as for other groups with special problems, social services need to move out from their present " crisis " role to play a positive part in improving the quality of life and preventing waste and suffering. We do not believe that any special services are required specifically for one-parent families, but it is vital, if this wider approach is to succeed, that resources are made available on a sufficient scale to ensure that needy groups like one-parent families are not neglected as services expand.

9.23   We make a number of recommendations, set out below, in relation to particular services, but we draw attention here to the view we have taken of day-care services which we believe require considerable expansion. These services have in the past been regarded by those administering them and by lone parents as a means of enabling the lone parent with young children to work. Our recommendation for a guaranteed maintenance allowance (GMA) for lone parents will mean that it can no longer be said that the lone parent is obliged to work (though this has never strictly been true because of the availability of supplementary benefit). But it does not follow that lone parents should lose the priority they at present generally receive in the allocation of day-care places. The advantages to the lone parent of going to work, financial, psychological and social, may be such that we consider it vital to preserve freedom of choice; and for the lone parent with young children who wants to work this means access to satisfactory day care. It does not necessarily follow that the day care has to take the form of a place in a day nursery, or that it has to be full-time provision. Our detailed proposals on these matters are included in the list of recommendations set out below.

RECOMMENDATIONS ON PARENTS AND CHILDREN

188 Further research should be undertaken into the effects on children of living in a one-parent family (paragraph 8.15).

189 Services coming into contact with lone parents, especially at the point of breakdown or death, should keep information about other services available; and local authorities should prepare leaflets aimed specifically at the lone parent giving details of the major statutory and voluntary services (paragraph 8.60).

190 Local authorities should review existing advice services in their areas, both statutory and voluntary, to prevent overlapping and to make it easy for people to know where to apply and convenient for them to do so (paragraph 8.61).

191 The provision of counselling services for lone parents should be encouraged (paragraph 8.62).

Social work services

192 Local authorities should ensure that the anxieties of lone parents are understood by staff coming into contact with them and that reception and interview facilities are of an adequate standard (paragraph 8.78).

193 Every effort should be made to make services available more extensively, for example, in the evenings and on Saturdays (paragraph 8.79).

194 It should be possible for social services departments to make cash payments without there being an immediate and pressing prospect of a child's being received into care; guidance to local authorities should make this clear, and if necessary, the legislation should be amended (paragraph 8.84).

195 The overlap of powers in the provision of lump sum payments between the Supplementary Benefits Commission and local authorities should be reviewed (paragraph 8.88).

196 There should be continuing consultation and co-operation at national level between local authorities, the Supplementary Benefits Commission and charitable organisations over the provision of charitable grants for the relief of poverty (paragraph 8.92).

Care of children under five

197 There should be a considerable expansion in day-care services for children under 5 provided or supported by public authorities, including adequate and suitable arrangements for the children of working lone parents (paragraphs 8.118–8.119).

198 Wherever possible children under 3 should not be parted from their mothers for long periods; services should be framed so as to involve the parent as well as the child; and where the mother's absence is unavoidable the aim should be for the child to be looked after by a skilled and familiar substitute who knows the mother's child-care practices (paragraph 8.125).

199 Part-time day care, nursery schooling or playgroup is more suitable than full-time care, unless social need dictates otherwise (paragraph 8.128).

200 The expansion of day-care services ought not to be channelled primarily into the development of public day-nursery facilities; a variety of services is required which takes account of the needs of both parent and child (paragraph 8.129).

201 There should be full co-ordination of the various policies and services for under-fives at central and local government levels (paragraph 8.130).

202 Further research and experiment is needed in the provision of nursery centres (paragraph 8.132).

203 Day-fostering schemes should be developed by local authorities (paragraph 8.133).

204 Local authorities should work towards encouraging child minders to improve their standards—for example, by training courses and the

516

provision of toys and equipment on loan—and to comply with the registration requirements; they should also administer the latter with more emphasis on the suitability of the minder for the task (paragraph 8.135).

205 Legislation governing private fostering should be amended so that the natural as well as the foster parent has to give notice of a placement; and so that the standard of supervision of private placements has to be the same as for local authority fosterings (paragraph 8.137).

206 Central and local government should encourage the provision of day nurseries by employers, including provision on a joint basis with local authorities (paragraph 8.138).

207 The promotion of playgroups in deprived areas by central and local government should develop on an increasing scale (paragraph 8.139).

208 Charges for day care should be rationalised on a national basis (paragraph 8.140).

Care of children over five

209 Social services departments should have responsibility for providing day-care services for children of school age (paragraph 8.144).

210 Education departments should co-operate with social services departments so that educational facilities can be utilised with social services financial support to provide more effective day-care services for schoolchildren (paragraph 8.144).

211 Local education authorities should look sympathetically at the needs of one-parent family children for boarding education; they should bear in mind the special emotional needs of one-parent family children in selecting a school, and wherever possible decisions about children who should receive boarding education should be made in consultation with social services departments (paragraph 8.149).

Help in the family's own home

212 Local authorities should be encouraged to provide more help in the home for one-parent families, especially those who are motherless. This is important even where the absence of the parent is only temporary, for example, where the mother is in hospital (paragraphs 8.153–8.155).

213 Local authorities should be encouraged to develop " relief mothering " services and more resources, by way of equipment, should be put into the service (paragraph 8.156).

Social aspects of education

214 To enable schools to offer constructive help to children in one-parent families, good relations between home and school should always be established when the child first starts school, and continued throughout his school career; there should be opportunities for parents to visit the school in the evenings; and in appropriate cases acceptable means must be found of passing background information about a child from primary to secondary school (paragraphs 8.160–8.161).

215 Information about the range of school welfare benefits should regularly be brought to the notice of parents; care should be taken to see that the manner in which a benefit is distributed does not make a child feel " different " from others; and there should always be close liaison between schools and both health and social services agencies (paragraphs 8.162–8.163).

216 Support from guidance staff should be more generally available to children from one-parent families (paragraph 8.166).

217 Increased emphasis should be put on the social aspects of education both in the personal and social implications of subjects ordinarily studied and in specific courses of social education; and the latter should be provided more extensively in institutions such as colleges of further education (paragraphs 8.170–8.171).

218 More male staff should be recruited to infant and nursery schools and day nurseries (paragraph 8.172).

219 In secondary schools many subjects should be used to increase pupils' awareness of the realities of family life and both boys and girls should have instruction in practical home economics (paragraph 8.173).

220 Schools should make the best possible arrangements to assist schoolgirls who become pregnant and who want to continue their education, including the provision of special teachers and home tuition where appropriate (paragraphs 8.175–8.176).

Mother and baby homes

221 Further investigation should be made into the future demand for residential accommodation for unmarried mothers and the type of accommodation needed (paragraph 8.180).

222 Local authorities should ensure with voluntary organisations that there are adequate facilities for unmarried mothers who need them and as far as possible non-sectarian accommodation should be available for those who prefer it (paragraph 8.180).

223 Local authorities should be required to lay down standards for mother and baby homes and see that they are respected (paragraph 8.181).

Special groups (children of women prisoners; families of long-term hospital patients; immigrant families)

224 Further study is needed of the difficulties experienced by these groups, and the size of the problem, so that a proper assessment can be made of what needs to be done (paragraph 8.182).

225 The proposed expansion of facilities so that children up to the age of 5 can stay with their mothers in prison should be implemented as soon as possible; and the Home Office should look particularly at the situation of mothers on remand, to see if unnecessary disruption of relationships between mother and child can be avoided (paragraph 8.183).

226 Close co-operation should be maintained between hospitals and social services departments to ensure that the arrangements made for long-term hospital patients are those best for the family as a whole (paragraph 8.184).

227 Joint discussion between social services and education services on the special problems of one-parent immigrant families should be held at local and national level (paragraph 8.186).

Family planning services

228 The concept of " the best years for childbearing " should be examined by those responsible for family planning services to see if specific advice on timing of pregnancy should be incorporated into the health and social education of young people (paragraph 8.189).

229 The Department of Health and Social Security should put itself in a position, by promoting research and experiment, to give empirically based guidance relating to facilities for the young in the family planning service within the reorganised national health service (paragraph 8.192).

230 In designing birth control and family planning policies, special attention should be given to those groups in the population statistically most likely to produce illegitimate children and high rates of marriage breakdown (paragraph 8.194).

(Signed)   Morris Finer (Chairman)
                D C H Abbot
                J M Scott-Batey
                W B Harbert
                Sydney Isaacs
                Barbara J Kahan
                O R McGregor
                Norman Murchison
                Marie Patterson
                Marjorie Proops
                H G Simpson
(Secretary)   M L Meadon

22 March 1974

Printed in England for Her Majesty's Stationery Office by Oyez Press Limited
Dd256112 K16 12/74